SOCIETY, CRIME, AND CRIMINAL CAREERS

SOCIETY, CRIME, AND CRIMINAL CAREERS

second edition

DON C. GIBBONS

Portland State University

An Introduction to Criminology

Prentice-Hall, Inc., *Englewood Cliffs, New Jersey*

Library of Congress Cataloging in Publication Data

GIBBONS, DON C
 Society, crime, and criminal careers.

 Includes bibliographical references.
 1. Crime and criminals. I. Title.
HV6025.G46   1972   364   72-6704
ISBN 0-13-820084-X

SOCIETY, CRIME, AND CRIMINAL CAREERS:
An Introduction to Criminology, *2nd edition, by Don C. Gibbons*

Printed in the United States of America

10 9 8 7 6 5 4 3 2 1

Prentice-Hall International, Inc., London
Prentice-Hall of Australia, Pty. Ltd., Sydney
Prentice-Hall of Canada, Ltd., Toronto
Prentice-Hall of India Private Limited, New Delhi
Prentice-Hall of Japan, Inc., Tokyo

To Carlo Lastrucci,
teacher, critic, and good friend

CONTENTS

PREFACE

The second edition of this book follows the same general format as the first edition. Like the earlier edition, this one is addressed to the crime problem in modern society. It attempts to identify the major outlines of criminality in contemporary America and to specify some of the major etiological forces responsible for lawbreaking. Additionally, the book devotes considerable space to the analysis of social responses to criminals, including the workings of the police, courts, and other parts of the legal machinery.

Society, Crime, and Criminal Careers is a typologically-oriented work. Its basic premise is that progress in explaining and correcting lawbreaking behavior depends on our sorting the heterogeneous assortment of criminal roles into homogeneous patterns for study. The chapters which explore the complexities of criminality, crime causation, and reactions to offenders will continually confront the reader with evidence that lawbreaking is complex and difficult to comprehend. For one thing, the forms of criminality are so extremely varied that no single explanatory formula will make sense of this behavior. Moreover, these various kinds of illegality are so closely woven into the structure of modern society that to unravel crime one must also unravel the fabric of social organization.

This text departs from the format of most criminology books, which contain two general and separate parts—one dealing with etiology and the other with correction. Most of those books imply that causation has little to do with correctional responses directed at lawbreakers, and devote many pages to describing in detail administrative processes in corrections. This book, however, deals early with the activities of police agencies, prosecuting attorneys, judges, juries, and other administrative structures and persons that convert "suspects" into "criminals," unlike other texts which cover those topics only at the end. Also, it attempts to identify some of the ways in which correctional reactions may inadvertently contribute to causal processes: for example, those persons who are sent to penal institutions may encounter liabilities stemming from their status as "ex-cons" that subsequently make it very difficult for them to adopt law-abiding behavior patterns.

The second edition of *Society, Crime, and Criminal Careers* differs in some important respects from the first edition. For one thing, a considerable amount of new material has been added to this revision. More important, some major modifications have been made in the viewpoint of the book. I have been led to revise some of my contentions about criminal role-careers, in the direction of acknowledging that many offenders do not exhibit clear-cut careers in lawbreaking. Many of those persons are involved in transitory episodes of mundane "folk crime." These changes in viewpoint have been made in response to criticisms voiced by my criminological peers, including students, and also as the result of recent research studies which have turned up evidence pointing to the lack of clear-cut criminal careers on the part of many offenders. I hope that the second edition is a better book as a result of these changes, but at any rate, as a criminological statement it is empirically more accurate than its predecessor.

A number of persons provided valuable help in the preparation of the second edition of this book. Professor John P. Clark made many incisive suggestions for improvements in the book, as did Professor Peter G. Garabedian. Many of my students at San Francisco State College and Portland State University have made useful comments about the material. Miss Irene Boschler and Mrs. Roslyn MacDonald cheerfully provided excellent typing help on the revision.

1

INTRODUCTION

The most common image of criminality in the United States centers about "garden-variety" crime such as homicide, aggravated assault, strong-arm robbery, car theft, and other direct acts of stealing. Police departments report such lawbreaking to the Federal Bureau of Investigation, which in turn classifies the acts as "Index Crimes." This sort of crime also forms the basis for FBI contentions that lawlessness is both endemic and increasing at alarming rates in the United States. Finally, most people have this kind of crime in mind when they voice the hue and cry for "law and order" and repression of "crime in the streets."

Citizens often view garden-variety crime within a "good guy–bad guy" framework; they frequently believe that although lawbreaking is on the increase, criminal miscreants are still only a bothersome minority in contrast to the law-abiding, upright citizens. Public conceptions of the crime problem often resemble the common theme of American cowboy movies, in which the citizens of good moral character, particularly the heroes, wear clean white clothing; are clean shaven; refrain from drinking, swearing, kissing women; and ride white horses. The frontier "bad guys," the movie counterpart of criminals, are attired in black, are unshaven, and generally appear as mean and vicious types. Insofar as they think about the causes of crime, laymen are likely to view criminals as the product of defective chromosomal structure, faulty parental control, psychopathic personality, or other similar factors.[1] Such views bear a good deal of similarity to nineteenth century stereotypes of the crime problem, in which many citizens believed that crime was the work of members of "the dangerous classes."[2]

The apprehensiveness of American citizens about crime in the streets has been amply documented. For example, opinion surveys undertaken for the President's Commission on Law Enforcement and Administration of Justice in 1967 noted that most people throughout the United States felt that crime is

[1]Ramsey Clark's *Crime in America* (New York: Simon and Schuster, 1970) deals in a much more sophisticated way with the root causes of crime.

[2]J. J. Tobias, *Crime and Industrial Society in the 19th Century* (London: B. T. Batsford, 1967).

a worsening problem in their communities (although they did not feel unsafe near their homes, even when they live in high crime areas).[3] The majority of them asserted that breakdown of moral standards is responsible for increased crime, rather than deleterious social conditions. Most of them recommended repressive rather than ameliorative steps to curb crime, and many of them claimed that the courts are too lenient with offenders. More recently, a study conducted by the Center for Sociological Research at Portland State University questioned citizens in Portland and San Francisco concerning their views of the crime problem. In both cities, most of the citizens felt that crime is on the upsurge and is a problem of first magnitude in their community.[4]

There is a sense of urgency about the crime problem. Perhaps on a relative scale, contemporary American society is no more criminal-ridden than it was a century ago. But because the absolute number of offenders in present-day America is so large, it is little wonder that laymen express concern about lawbreaking. However, the thesis of this book is that the reduction or solution of the crime problem ultimately rests on the development of a body of objective knowledge about the social roots of crime, in short, on the progress of criminological inquiry.

THE STUDY OF CRIMINALITY

Scientific study of lawbreaking and serious attempts to uncover the causes of criminality have usually taken place within a field of study called criminology, which is concerned with the objective analysis of crime as a social phenomenon. Criminology includes within its scope inquiry into the process of making laws, breaking laws, and reacting to the breaking of laws.

Not everyone uses the terms *criminology* and *criminologist* in a consistent manner. Criminology sometimes serves as a label for the scientific techniques of law enforcement and detection. In this usage, criminologists are persons who work in police laboratories and are involved in the collection and analysis of evidence concerning crimes. Additionally, lay persons who write essays or novels concerning crime are sometimes labeled as criminologists, as are psychiatrists or psychologists who concern themselves with various facets of criminality. But these terms are most commonly used in the study of criminal-

[3]Jennie McIntyre, "Public Attitudes Toward Crime and Law Enforcement," *Annals of the American Academy of Political and Social Science*, 374 (November 1967), 34–46; somewhat different results were obtained in a survey of readers of *Psychology Today*, in that these predominantly middle-class citizens more frequently voiced approval for treatment rather than punishment of offenders. See "Your Thoughts on Crime and Punishment," *Psychology Today* (May 1969), pp. 53–58.

[4]Don C. Gibbons, Joseph F. Jones, and Peter G. Garabedian, "Gauging Public Opinion About the Crime Problem," *Crime and Delinquency*, 18 (April 1972), 134–46. See also John E. Conklin, "Dimensions of Community Response to the Crime Problem," *Social Problems*, 18 (Winter 1971), 373–85; Sarah L. Boggs, "Formal and Informal Crime Control: An Exploratory Study of Urban, Suburban, and Rural Orientations," *Sociological Quarterly*, 12 (Summer 1971), 319–27.

ity as a form of social behavior. Those sociologists who specialize in this substantive topic are called criminologists. This text is a statement of sociological propositions and research evidence about criminality developed, for the most part, by sociologists interested in the study of law violation as social behavior. Most theorizing and research regarding criminality has been the work of sociologists.

Historically, in the United States a relatively small, specialized group of sociologists inquired into criminology. Currently, however, there is lively interest in criminological topics as evidenced in the work of students of *deviance, large-scale organizations,* and *sociology of law.* That is, the social origins of law and societal reactions to it are being studied in a number of areas within sociology. Criminality and responses to it are increasingly being seen as implicated in the phenomena that many different sociologists study. Criminology as a field of specialization within sociology will probably attract fewer recruits in the future, even though interest in facets of criminality will likely continue to grow. In short, criminology as a distinct field of specialization may ultimately disappear.[5]

PROBLEMS OF EXPLANATION

The study of crime and criminals involves so many topics or questions that criminological analysis represents a large and continuing responsibility of sociologists. We can impose some order on the diverse interests of criminologists by sorting these interests into major categories: definition of *crime* and *criminals,* origins of criminal law, epidemiology of crime, the sociology of criminality, social-psychology of criminal careers, and societal reactions to crime. Let us look at what is involved in each of these areas of interest.

Definition of Crime and Criminals

Speaking on the general topic of deviant behavior, of which criminality is one form, Albert Cohen declared: "The most pressing problem in the field of social disorganization and deviant behavior is to define these terms. If we cannot agree on what we are talking about, we cannot agree on what is relevant, much less on what is important."[6] Just as the first step in the analysis of deviance is defining the phenomenon of attention, the first stage in the study of criminality and criminals centers about explicit specification

[5]I have discussed this point and these trends in some detail in Don C. Gibbons, "Goodbye and Good Riddance to Criminology," paper presented at the Pacific Sociological Association annual meeting, April 1970.

[6]Albert K. Cohen, "The Study of Social Disorganization and Deviant Behavior," in *Sociology Today,* eds. Robert K. Merton, Leonard Broom, and Leonard S. Cottrell, Jr. (New York: Basic Books, 1959),

of the scope and meaning of these labels. What do we mean by criminality? What is a criminal or a noncriminal? Who and what should we include or exclude from criminological scrutiny?

Not everyone agrees on the meaning of crime and criminals, for considerable controversy has raged in criminology over questions of this kind. Some authorities have suggested that the proper subject matter encompasses only those persons convicted in a criminal court of criminal violations of law, whereas other criminologists include within the population of criminals persons who have been arrested but not convicted. Still others study "white collar criminals," who have violated criminal laws but have been processed informally or through civil courts. Probably the majority of students of criminality focus on individuals who have violated criminal laws, whether or not they have been apprehended. Finally, a few persons contend that the proper area of inquiry is the study of "norm violations" and "norm violators," of which criminal acts and violators of criminal law constitute only a part.

Clearly, the definitional task is more complicated than first appearances suggest. Moreover, it has priority over other tasks, for all succeeding steps in criminological analysis hinge on clear and valid initial definitions of the phenomena of study. A major part of Chapter Two is concerned with the explication of a criminological frame of reference. The chapter presents various perspectives of criminological inquiry, along with judgments on the proper means of investigation.

Criminologists have traditionally been most concerned with definitional questions of the previously mentioned sort. But we might ask whether particular acts *should* be defined as crimes as well. Sociologists have begun to raise such questions and have joined citizens who are critical of the overreach of criminal law. These comments center about the contention that American society is *overcriminalized;* that is, criminal law reaches too far, covering socially harmless behavior such as marijuana use, homosexuality, gambling, or other "crimes without victims." Chapter Two notes these criticisms of criminal law, which suggest that we should decriminalize some kinds of behavior by removing the acts from the criminal statutes.

The Origins of Criminal Law

In the last analysis, society "creates" crime by singling out acts as "bad" and "criminal." By "society" is meant groups of persons who manage to get some act included within a set of statutes that declare certain behaviors criminal in form. Crime is not inherent in behavior; somebody has to identify acts

---

p. 461; a more recent essay indicating that terminological and definitional confusion persists in the study of deviance is Don C. Gibbons and Joseph F. Jones, "Some Critical Notes on Current Definitions of Deviance," *Pacific Sociological Review*, 14 (January 1971), 20-37.

of one kind or another as criminal. For behavior to become criminal, some-one's conception of an act as criminal must get widespread adoption. Legislatures must pass a law that publicly asserts a defined crime.

The social character in conceptions of crime is evident in the fact that the number of acts regarded as crimes has steadily increased over the past several hundred years as lawmaking bodies have created more and more criminal statutes. Definitions of criminal acts are subject to variations from place to place. Within the United States, marked variations in both the language and the content of criminal codes occur from one state to another so that no uniform set of criminal laws exists in this country. Crime is not an invariant and universal phenomenon, consistently the same in all places and at all times.

The processes of lawmaking constitute social behavior. Particular criminal laws have identifiable antecedents; reasons exist for the emergence of laws at some particular time or in some specific place. Moreover, persons whose actions can and should be made the subject of sociological attention create statutes. But we know relatively little about the development of criminal laws and the variables that account for these origins, for this area of inquiry has been neglected until recently. In Chapter Two, we shall examine a number of theories regarding the genesis of criminal laws, along with several pieces of research evidence on the development of theft laws, vagrancy statutes, and several other kinds of criminal laws.

The Epidemiology of Crime

We usually associate the term *epidemiology* with public health studies of the extent, distribution, and characteristics of various forms of physical illness or disease; hence, the epidemiology of tuberculosis concerns facts about the number of tubercular persons in the population, their social characteristics, and so forth. Criminologists have used the term in reference to the number, location, and social characteristics of criminals. Epidemiological data are nec-essary prior to any attempt to explain criminality. A clear and detailed picture of the phenomenon to be explained is prerequisite to causal inquiry.

If we were to employ a definition of criminality that restricted the scope of the term to persons convicted of criminal offenses in criminal courts, the matter of epidemiology would be relatively simple. We could glean the facts of crime from records of court proceedings. However, if we use a broader definition of crime, in which commission of illegal acts would be required for an individual to be termed a criminal but in which conviction in a court (or police apprehension) is not required, epidemiological problems of some complexity arise to plague the student of criminology.

We shall use the broader conception of criminality in this book. We intend to examine the actions of persons who violate criminal laws, only a fraction of whom are apprehended and subsequently convicted of such offenses. As a result, we must assemble a picture of crime in American society that will clarify the size and characteristics of various components of the offender universe. For example, we need to determine the proportion of all lawbreakers represented by individuals reported to the police. In addition, we want to discover whether some kinds of violators are more likely to be reported to the police than are others. Do variables such as social class backgrounds, racial characteristics, and offender–victim relationships influence police referral policies? Throughout Chapter Five, the grossly inadequate state of the basic statistical data regarding crime in the United States complicates the task of epidemiological presentation. Much more reliable and detailed statistics are maintained for professional baseball behavior than for deviant social behavior.

The Sociology of Criminality

Discovery of the causes of crime (and juvenile delinquency) is the principal task of the criminologist–sociologist. His major aim is to develop a body of generalizations or propositions accounting for criminality. Although this task is many-faceted two main components of the explanatory job exist. These are closely related but analytically separate problems. The first has to do with the development of explanations for the *kinds and degree of criminality* observed in a society; the other centers about discovery of the processes involved in the *acquisition of criminal behavior patterns by specific individuals.* Concerning these two problems of analysis, Donald Cressey says:

> . . . a theory explaining social behavior in general, or any specific kind of social behavior, should have two distinct but consistent aspects. First, there must be a statement that explains the statistical distribution of the behavior in time and space (epidemiology), and from which predictive statements about unknown statistical distributions can be derived. Second, there must be a statement that identifies, at least by implication, the process by which individuals come to exhibit the behavior in question, and from which can be derived predictive statements about the behavior of individuals.[7]

Investigators have not always kept the distinction between these two queries clear. As Cohen has indicated:

> Much that travels under the name of sociology of deviant behavior or of social disorganization is psychology—some of it very good psychology, but psychology. For example, Sutherland's theory of differential association, which is widely regarded as preeminently sociological, is not the less psy-

[7]Donald R. Cressey, "Epidemiology and Individual Conduct: A Case from Criminology," *Pacific Sociological Review,* 3 (Fall 1960), 47.

chological because it makes much of the cultural milieu. It is psychological because it addresses itself to the question: How do people become the kinds of individuals who commit criminal acts? A sociological question would be: What is it about the structure of social systems that determines the kinds of criminal acts that occur in these systems and the way in which such acts are distributed within the systems? In general, a sociological field is concerned with the structure of interactional systems, not with personalities, and the distribution and articulation of events within these systems.[8]

Edwin Sutherland's theory of differential association is an argument we shall examine in some detail in Chapter Nine, for it represents the most sophisticated attempt to date by a sociologist to account for the development of criminality in individuals. In brief, Sutherland's theory argues that persons learn criminal attitudes and behavior through a process of differential association or interaction with carriers of criminal culture.

If Sutherland's theory is not directed to the sociology of crime, what would such a theory be like? Let us examine a hypothetical illustration. Suppose that an epidemiological study of lawbreaking patterns within a particular city shows that certain forms of juvenile gang delinquency and certain kinds of adult property crime are heavily concentrated in slum areas and uncommon elsewhere in the city. The focus of attention here should be on such questions as: "Why are these kinds of crime so common in some areas and virtually nonexistent in others?" or "Does something within a community's social organization, such as different social class patterns, result in these observed patterns of delinquency and crime?" These questions are primarily concerned with the explanation of *rates*. Some particular criminologist might come forward with hypotheses alleging that variations in neighborhood social structure and differences in expectations of material success in American society, which exist between lower- and middle-class citizens, are responsible for the widely divergent rates of deviation. To test such claims, data would be necessary to provide indices of neighborhood social organization, differential social class values, and so on. In turn, these hypotheses would be confirmed or disproved to the degree that correlations or covariations were observed between crime rates and the measures of social organization. Insofar as those areas with high crime rates are also the most disorganized, and to the degree that low crime neighborhoods are the most cohesive, the hypotheses would be verified.

Another illustrative case falling within the sociology of crime is found in comparative figures for the United States and certain European nations, which seem to indicate that American society is the most ridden with criminality. According to a common sociological hypothesis, American society is more "criminalistic" or "criminogenic" than other societies because of the inordinate emphasis on material success and endemic disrespect for law and order in

[8]Cohen, "Social Disorganization and Deviant Behavior," p. 462.

American values and beliefs. Although these claims have not been adequately tested, and such research would be difficult to carry out, the kinds of evidence called for are relatively clear. Crime rates would have to be assembled to rank societies in terms of criminality, whereas indices of cultural values, attitudes toward materialism, law enforcement, and so on would be required to test causal propositions.

Regarding the causation of criminal conduct, Austin Turk argues that criminology should turn away from "the behavior question": "Why do they do it?"[9] Turk contends that more attention should be given to explanation of variations in crime rates, that is, to the processes that apply criminal status to persons in a society. He notes that the population of persons labeled "criminals" is not identical to the population of those engaged in illegal acts. Turk then offers a conflict and power theory to explain crime rates in American society.

In addition, Richard Quinney argues that we have not paid enough criminological attention to processes of law creation and the imposition of criminal status upon persons.[10]

In the following chapters, we shall consider theories and evidence centered about the lawmaking process, differentials in crime rates, and explanations for such variations. However, we shall devote a good deal of attention to the matter of the etiology of criminal conduct as well.

The Social-Psychology of Criminal Careers

Etiological or causal analysis in criminology involves both explanation of differentials in crime rates *and* exploration of the processes by which specific individuals acquire criminal attitudes and behavior patterns. The latter is what Cohen has identified as a psychological issue. Our preference is for the term *social-psychology of criminal careers*, in that social-psychology is that discipline concerned with *socialization*—the processes through which individuals learn to behave in a human fashion. Thus, we speak of socialization of children in reference to those experiences that create humans out of the biological raw material represented by the neonate. We also use the term to direct attention at learning experiences through which mature individuals come to acquire new behavior patterns, such as the socialization of the medical student, the worker, or the homosexual. The roles of physician, automobile worker, homosexual, or criminal are all learned patterns of behavior.

The earlier example of different crime and delinquency rates in a specific city clarifies the difference between social-psychology of criminal careers and the sociology of crime. Suppose we have noticed, in addition to the facts already specified, that juveniles in the high delinquency area have several different patterns of behavior. Some boys have high occupational aspirations,

---

[9]Austin T. Turk, *Criminality and Legal Order* (Chicago: Rand McNally and Co., 1969).
[10]Richard Quinney, *The Social Reality of Crime* (Boston: Little, Brown and Co., 1970).

are highly motivated in school, and are conformist in behavior. Other juveniles are "corner boys," not heavily involved in delinquency but also not intensely meshed in patterns of mobility striving or achievement. They are unmotivated, conformist juveniles whose actions center about short-run hedonism. A third group is heavily caught up in delinquent activities; the major social role is that of "tough kid" and "delinquent." One social-psychological problem in this case is the discovery of factors that led these specific youths into several different behavioral careers. One hypothesis might include the proposition that the delinquent boys may be the ones with more personality problems than conformist working-class boys. Perhaps the delinquents are from more lax or criminalistic family backgrounds than are the nondelinquents; or, additionally, differential association in conformist or delinquent peer groups may be a factor of considerable importance.

We can easily identify other examples of explanatory problems concerned with deviant socialization patterns and the development of criminal role patterns. Some study has been made of the impact of being apprehended and processed as a lawbreaker. Sometimes these events appear to encourage deviation, whereas in other cases the experiences seem to deter the individual from further involvement in deviance. In the same vein, some attention has been given to the developmental processes by which embezzlers manage to rationalize deviant acts in advance of carrying out defalcations. Some work has been carried out on the question of variations in behavior among diffferent juveniles in high delinquency areas. These and other cases are more clearly concerned with social-psychological matters than anything else.

At this point, someone might object to these distinctions on the grounds that truly adequate causal analysis should explain both variations in rates of criminalistic deviance and variations in involvement in criminality or law-abiding behavior on the part of individuals in particular neighborhoods, social classes, or other settings. Many specific instances of criminological theory and/or research are, in fact, jointly concerned with these two problems. Nevertheless, it makes sense to keep these two matters analytically separate.

We can trace much of the ambiguity and confusion in contemporary theorizing and commentary regarding criminality in part to our failure to clearly explain the problem. For example, consider the psychiatric hypotheses which allege that offenders are pathological persons suffering from various psychological impairments. Are such claims intended to account for variations in rates of criminality, as among different social class groups? Do they imply that much larger numbers of working-class individuals, criminals and conformists alike, suffer from personality problems as compared to members of other social classes? Such an inference follows if psychogenic hypotheses are put forth as an explanation of rate variations. On the other hand, psychiatric arguments that account for the development of deviant or nondeviant careers on the part of certain individuals *within* a social class group leave the matter of rate variations an open question. As an explanation of career development, the personality pathology framework is logically compatible, at least, with a socio-logical explanation of rate variations that emphasizes such variables as differences in neighborhood organization. Conceivably, high crime rates based on specific criminal careers might most commonly be found in social areas with community influences conducive to criminality, where, in addition, relatively large numbers of persons with personality problems are located and serve as candidates for criminality. Conversely, in neighborhoods more cohesive in character, individuals with personality aberrations may be prone to behavior of a noncriminal kind.

This discussion merely serves as a hypothetical illustration rather than as an exposition of the version of etiological theory to be introduced later. The empirical accuracy of these notions is not an issue here.

Societal Reactions to Crime

There are myriad forms of reactions to such deviant behavior as criminality in complex societies such as the United States. Some kinds of crime are rarely reported to any social control agency, such as the police. Other instances of deviation are reacted to with police arrest or court action in some cases but not in others, depending on such contingencies as variations in social class backgrounds of the offenders and the amount of incriminating evidence that can be assembled against the lawbreaker. In addition, those violators who are processed in the social control machinery to the point of court trial are subjected to a variety of subsequent experiences. Some are placed on probation, others incarcerated in jails, and still others sentenced to penal institutions of various types. The social events that occur to deviants which constitute societal reactions are the consequence of a number of factors, some of which are only slightly understood at present. In any event, the elaborate pattern of social control devices and experiences that law violators undergo as they are processed through this machinery represent basic topics for the criminologist to study. Indeed, we might argue that primarily the sociologist-criminologist should investigate the workings of social control patterns and structures. In modern societies, control, repression, or alteration of deviants has been formalized and turned over to several special occupational groups. As a result, the sociological analysis of social control machinery ranks in importance with the study of social stratification, family behavior, or certain other "core" institutions of modern society. Elaborate social inventions for the control of deviants represent prominent social oganizations in modern societies.

One major point developed in later chapters is that the societal reactions to offenders at any point in time in a particular society reflect other characteristics of that social organization. Actions taken against law violators in different historical periods have changed over time, in the general direction of treatment or rehabilitative orientation and away from punitive actions. Societal reactions are a part of ongoing social structure; so as social conditions change, reactions to deviants become altered. One task of the criminologist is to develop generalizations to account for the historical trends observed in societal reactions.

The emerging therapeutic or treatment orientation toward offenders in the United States (and elsewhere) is a relatively new development.[11] As a result, the social control devices now used in contemporary America constitute a not entirely harmonious mixture of rehabilitative approaches, punitive devices, and other reactions. Subsequent chapters will examine in detail the matter of contradictory correctional goals, for the present schizoid character of the sum of reactions to deviants poses severe obstacles to efforts to change law-breakers into conforming citizens.

THE ROLE-CAREER PERSPECTIVE

This book argues that criminological attention must turn away from the study of crime and criminals to the examination of various types or role careers in criminality. We aver that the situation of criminology is similar to that of medicine: there is not one form of sickness, there are many. There is not one cause of illness, there are a number of causes, each related to a particular form of sickness. So it is with criminality, for that rubric is a broad one indeed, containing under it a large number of behavioral forms having little in common with one another. If this idea is true, then it is doubtful that a general theory of criminal etiology can be discovered which will explain all of the disparate forms of criminality. Instead, specific theories or subtheories are required to account for different criminal role careers.

This criminology text is not the first to acknowledge the importance of differentiation of offender types or the need to develop propositions specific to the types. Several other recent works have given some recognition to this general point.[12] Indeed, it would be hard to imagine anyone who could ignore the obvious differences among such kinds of criminals as violent rapists, professional thieves, white-collar offenders, and prostitutes. But it is one thing to acknowledge differences among offenders and another to develop a systematic analysis of criminality oriented around the study of criminal role careers. Among other things the sociologist often demonstrates the existence of types by pointing to similarities among offenders that may have gone unnoticed by both the lawbreakers and the citizens concerned about them. The criminol-

[11]For a detailed discussion of treatment theory and the deficiencies of that material, along with the statement of treatment theory based on offender role careers, see Don C. Gibbons, *Changing the Lawbreaker* (Englewood Cliffs, N.J.: Prentice-Hall, 1965).

[12]See Richard R. Korn and Lloyd W. McCorkle, *Criminology and Penology* (New York: Holt, Rinehart and Winston, 1959), pp. 142-56; Paul W. Tappan, *Crime, Justice and Correction* (New York: McGraw-Hill Book Co., 1960), pp. 215-34; Walter C. Reckless, *The Crime Problem*, 4th ed. (New York: Appleton-Century-Crofts, 1967), pp. 185-373; Herbert A Bloch and Gilbert Geis, *Man, Crime, and Society*, 2nd ed. (New York: Random House, 1970), pp. 167-379; Marshall B. Clinard and Richard Quinney, eds., *Criminal Behavior Systems* (New York: Holt, Rinehart and Winston, 1967).

ogist's activities are parallel to those of the policeman, who also sorts offenders into types. The case of burglary serves as an illustration, in that among citizens, burglars and burglaries are viewed as pretty much alike. However, the policeman speaks of "cat burglars" and of "regular burglars." He applies the "cat burglar" label to persons who burglarize dwelling units while the occupants are on the premises. These individuals differ in criminal techniques from "regular burglars," who take special pains to make sure that no one is at home during the time they are engaged in their crimes. In the policeman's view, "cat burglars" are thought to differ in psychological makeup from other burglars. "Cat burglars" or "hot prowlers" are suspected of aberrant motives and are viewed as "weirdos" who get "kicks" from their crimes, unlike the utilitarian, businesslike, run-of-the-mill burglars. Hence, policemen and the rest of us see "cat burglars" in the population of offenders only after we have developed observational concepts that tell us to look for certain recurrent features of behavior on the part of some lawbreakers.

How are law violators to be sorted into types or role careers? How are etiological variables to be organized and brought to bear for the study of role careers? These are the kinds of theoretical and conceptual issues that we must be concerned with if the study of role careers is to bring about improvements in criminological knowledge. Many of the subsequent chapters endeavor to work out these theoretical problems of criminology. Types of offenders can be observed when lawbreakers are examined in terms of a few major variables or dimensions. Two of these have to do with offense behavior, described in ways that differ from criminal statute definitions of offenses, and with the situational context within which criminality occurs. Two other major dimensions, social-psychological in form, are self-concept and attitudinal patterns. In this perspective, an offender type such as the professional "heavy" criminal is comprised of individuals who engage in similar patterns of criminality and exhibit common social-psychological characteristics. Much of the remainder of this text attempts to show that persons who fall into one of the role careers thus defined also exhibit common etiological or causal background experiences.

One caveat concerning classifications of criminality is in order at the outset. Those who have advocated a "typological" approach to crime causation, in which patterns of lawbreaking would be studied, have devoted most of their atttention to professional thieves, Skid Road alcoholics, or other persons who are caught up in a long-term pattern of criminality and who are often members of a deviant subculture. The ingredients of a persistent role career are relatively apparent in these cases. However, other cases of criminal behavior are relatively transitory in form. The persons involved in these cases cannot easily be described as engaged in a role career.[13] We should not lose sight of the fact that many individuals exhibit some fleeting involvement in lawbreaking in

[13]For further discussion of this matter, along with some evidence, see Don C. Gibbons, "Crime in the Hinterland," Criminology, forthcoming.

our society, often in response to situational inducements of one kind or another. Role-career perspectives do not apply with equal force to all criminality. We shall return to this point in more detail in Chapter Ten.

SUMMARY

This introductory chapter has noted that the question of the proper subject matter for study has been a controversial one about which authorities have disagreed. We have seen that attention must be given to the complexities of criminal law. Criminologists also have the task of investigating the origins of criminal statutes so as to throw light on the factors implicated in lawmaking as a form of social behavior. The study of criminal law also requires that the sociologist assess the extent to which particular criminal codes at any particular time are congruent with social sentiments, so as to place the law within the larger system of social order.

This chapter has also enumerated the major questions involved in the explanation of criminality as a form of deviant behavior. The criminologist has the job of unraveling the contributions that various strands of the social fabric make to patterns and rates of criminality. We need to strive to comprehend the variety of social influences that operate in the acquisition of criminal roles by various kinds of lawbreakers. Finally, criminology seeks to reveal the workings of the social control machinery as it attempts to convert offenders into law-abiding citizens.

The thrust of this brief chapter is that criminality is an exceedingly complex matter, which is unlikely to be understood in terms of simple explanations holding that offenders are the product of defective heredity, psychological aberrations, or a few abnormal and atypical features of society. In the same way, the control of crime is not likely to be accomplished through the application of a few simple panaceas. Instead, if we are to make sense of criminality, we must grapple with a host of complicated questions.[14] Chapter Two turns our attention to the first of these questions, nature of laws and definitions of criminality.

[14]Other criminology texts that have endeavored to unravel the complexities of criminality include Korn and McCorkle, *Criminology and Penology*; Tappan, *Crime, Justice and Correction*; Reckless, *The Crime Problem*; Bloch and Geis, *Man, Crime, and Society*; Clinard and Quinney, *Criminal Behavior Systems*; Martin R. Haskell and Lewis Yablonsky, *Crime and Delinquency* (Chicago: Rand McNally and Co., 1970); Quinney, *The Social Reality of Crime*; Richard D. Knudten, *Crime in a Complex Society* (Homewood, Ill.: The Dorsey Press, 1970); Donald R. Cressey and David A. Ward, eds., *Delinquency, Crime, and Social Process* (New York: Harper & Row, Publishers, 1969); Elmer Hubert Johnson, *Crime, Correction, and Society*, rev. ed. (Homewood, Ill.: The Dorsey Press, 1968); Edwin H. Sutherland and Donald R. Cressey, *Criminology*, 8th ed. (Philadelphia: J. B. Lippincott Co., 1970); Robert G. Caldwell, *Criminology*, 2nd ed. (New York: The Ronald Press, 1965); Ruth Shonle Cavan, *Criminology*, 3rd ed. (New York: Thomas Y. Crowell, 1962); Donald R. Taft and Ralph W. England, *Criminology*, 4th ed. (New York: The Macmillan Co., 1964); briefer discussions can be found in Edwin M. Schur, *Our Criminal Society* (Englewood Cliffs, N.J.: Prentice-Hall, 1969); Gresham M. Sykes, *Crime and Society*, 2nd ed. (New York: Random House, 1967).

2

DEFINITION: ORIGIN AND TRENDS IN CRIMINAL LAW

Chapter One identified the definitional task as the first order of business in the study of criminal behavior. Unless criminologists can first agree upon the nature and scope of the phenomena they are to study, little or no progress can be made in the understanding of crime and criminal behavior. Chapter One also noted that consensus on the proper subject matter of criminology does not now exist. Instead, various arguments have been advanced to the effect that the concept of crime should be broadened to include more than that behavior identified by criminal statutes. This matter of definition is addressed in this chapter; several issues centering around definitional problems will be discussed in the following sections.

Whatever final decision the investigator of criminology makes regarding the appropriate subject matter of criminology, his starting point must necessarily be with the criminal laws. These statutes specify the legal entity, "crime"; they identify the constituent elements of action that must occur for an individual to acquire the legal identity of "criminal"; and they specify the attendant penalties invoked against "criminals." If he is to investigate a body of subject matter different from that identified by the criminal laws, the criminologist must be prepared to indicate the points of divergence of his definitions from legal ones and to defend his departure from convention. Conversely, if he is to take a legal stand on the proper scope of inquiry, the criminologist must possess some understanding of the nature of criminal laws.[1] The following section discusses some major features of criminal law as distinct from other social control inventions or bodies of normative proscriptions.

The second part of this chapter is concerned with the sociology of criminal

---

[1] Edwin M. Schur, among others, has pointed out that until recently the sociological study of law and legal institutions has been a neglected area of inquiry in sociology. See Edwin M. Schur, *Law and Society* (New York: Random House, 1968), pp. 5–16. Schur's book is a useful, brief introduction to the sociological study of law. For other indications of the central concerns in the study of law and legal institutions, particularly criminal law and its implementation, as well as samples of sociological inquiry regarding legal processes, see Richard Quinney, ed., *Crime and Justice in Society* (Boston: Little, Brown and Co., 1969); William J. Chambliss, ed., *Crime and the Legal Process* (New York: McGraw-Hill Book Co., 1969); Rita James Simon, ed., *The Sociology of Law* (San Francisco: Chandler Publishing Co., 1968); Richard J. Quinney, *The Social Reality of Crime* (Boston: Little, Brown and Co., 1970).

law, and explores the origins of criminal law in some detail. We shall note a variety of theories that attempt to account for the development of legal norms, along with several investigations of the social sources of certain criminal laws. Another aspect of this matter concerns the extent to which social sentiments support criminal laws; hence, we shall look at several studies that illuminate this question. Finally, the last portion of the chapter grapples with the issue of whether the criminologist should take a legalistic or some other viewpoint regarding crime. Should "antisocial " persons be the focus of attention? Should the criminologist study all norm violations, or should he restrict his attention to violations of criminal laws? In summary, this chapter lays the definitional groundwork for the analysis of crime and criminal behavior.

ELEMENTS OF CRIMINAL LAW

Law and Social Control

Criminal laws may first be said to represent only one of a number of devices intended to accomplish the goal of social control. The term *social control* designates those social arrangements that have been contrived to promote predictability of behavior and social regularity. Social control stands in contrast to *personal control*, which refers to those mechanisms inside the actor that constrain behavior. They consist of internalized or introjected norms, along with such internal or psychological mechanisms of control as feelings of guilt. A major share of the predictability of human behavior is the result of personal control rather than external coercion. In turn, a central task of the socialization process centers about the inculcation of mechanisms of personal control. Personal and social control are not entirely independent phenomena, but social control develops to take care of behavioral instances in which personal control has broken down. In brief, social control is brought into play when the individual fails to be "his own policeman"—when he fails to curtail his deviant impulses.

The forms of social control are varied so that criminal laws comprise only one kind of social control. On this point, Marshall Clinard has observed that all groups and societies contrive ways of dealing with unusual behavior that falls outside of their norms. "Negative sanctions" in the way of penalties are imposed on those who violate norms, whereas "positive sanctions" such as praise or recognition are bestowed on exemplary persons. These positive and negative sanctions are forms of social control. Some types of social control are "formal" or official, whereas others are "informal" or unofficial in character, such as gossip and ridicule. Some official apparatus established for that purpose exercise formal controls. In the case of criminal laws, enforcement and implementation rests with an elaborate machinery of law enforcement, judicial, and correctional structures.[2]

The formalization of bodies of law, including criminal statutes, is a relatively recent development. For many centuries, men restrained themselves and other persons from some actions by various informal procedures and through unwritten, informal norms, often called *folkways* and *mores* by sociologists. Moreover, the accretion of modern law made up of formalized norms and sanctions has been uneven throughout the world. Law has flourished in urbanized, Western nations, although in some contemporary societies laws are still relatively undeveloped and traditional informal controls still dominant.

Karl Llewellyn and E. Adamson Hoebel have identified the distinctive features of law as a form of social control.[3] They note that laws are a part of the normative structure of a society; that is, they constitute one set of definitions of obligatory or forbidden actions. Laws involve sanctions, so they are accompanied by penalties or punishments invoked in instances in which they are disobeyed. A third characteristic of laws is that in cases of conflict with other interests, laws must be followed, even in violation of other norms. Laws must prevail over other injunctions. Finally, laws are part of a larger legal *system*, which includes a relatively explicit underlying rationale or philosophy, a set of procedures for applying and enforcing laws, and a body of recognized officials delegated the responsibility of carrying out legal procedures. Each of these characteristics must be present for a normative system to be considered legal.

Although it exhibits the aforementioned characteristics, *criminal law* is at the same time only one of a number of legal systems. Criminal law possesses distinctive features setting it off from other bodies of law. Let us examine the nature of criminal law more closely.

Ingredients of Criminal Law

Broadly speaking, criminal laws are those rules that prohibit or compel instances of conduct held to be important for the welfare of society or the state. Criminal laws exist in contradistinction to civil laws, which are regarded as a body of legal rules governing the conduct of individual persons in their private lives. The wrongs identified by civil law are considered to be private ones rather than wrongs against the state. A "tort" is a violation of civil law, or an offense against an individual. The injured individual must set the court machinery in operation, and he is the recipient of redress from the offender.

[2]Marshall B. Clinard, *The Sociology of Deviant Behavior*, 3rd ed. (New York: Holt, Rinehart and Winston, 1968), pp. 205–6.

[3]Karl N. Llewellyn and E. Adamson Hoebel, *The Cheyenne Way* (Norman: University of Oklahoma Press, 1941).

But a crime is a violation of criminal law and an offense against the state. The state acts as the plaintiff, initiates the action against the offender, and exacts the punishment assigned the offender.

Edwin Sutherland and Donald Cressey have identified the essential characteristics of criminal law as involving *politicality, specificity, uniformity,* and *penal sanction.*[4] These components are identified in legal theory; in other words, these elements of criminal law would be present in a completely rational, ideal system of criminal statutes. The law in practice can and does depart from these characteristics. Also, the differences between criminal laws and other bodies of conduct regulations are sometimes less clear-cut than these rubrics imply.

Politicality means that the criminal laws originate through the actions of the state rather than some private organization or group. Only those rules promulgated by legislatures of the state and its subdivisions constitute criminal laws so that regulations of labor unions, social fraternities, college faculties, and so on do not qualify as criminal statutes even though they often show some similarity to the rules created by legislative processes.

Specificity as a characteristic of the criminal law means that criminal statutes provide strict definitions of the particular acts that constitute crimes. In turn, those acts not clearly and unmistakably included in descriptions of crimes within the statutes are not to be labeled as crimes. However, in practice, specificity is a matter of degree, for some laws are relatively broad and general in language, such as those defining vagrancy and disorderly conduct, or omnibus clauses in definitions of juvenile delinquency, which list "immorality" and "ungovernability" as forms of delinquent behavior. Societies have sometimes adopted broadly worded statutes that depart markedly from the principle of specificity. Thus, in Nazi Germany, the German Act of 1935 provided that persons could be tried for acts analogous to, but not identical with, those acts proscribed in existing statutes. Similar laws were enacted in the Soviet Union in 1926.[5]

Uniformity as a feature of criminal acts refers to the effort to specify crimes and invoke sanctions against offenders evenhandedly. Criminal laws do not contain exclusionary provision allowing some categories of individuals to be dealt with differently from other groups that have committed similar law violations. Instead, criminal liability is supposed to be uniform for all, irrespective of social background or social status. However, the principle of uniformity breaks down in practice at several points. Law enforcement processes are not always uniformly administered, and judicial decisions are not always free from theoretically extraneous or irrelevant considerations of background variations or social influence.

Penal sanctions as an aspect of criminal law means that penalties are speci-

---

[4]Edwin H. Sutherland and Donald R. Cressey, *Principles of Criminology,* 8th ed. (Philadelphia: J. B. Lippincott Co., 1970) pp. 4-8.

[5]Jerome Hall, *General Principles of Criminal Law* (Indianapolis: Bobbs-Merrill Co., 1947), p. 42.

fied for violation of the statutes. Laws declare that certain acts are forbidden or required and that violators of the law will be punished in some way. The latter half of this book is concerned with the detailed study of penal sanctions in operation.

The foregoing elements of criminal codes are essentially *external* characteristics: they indicate the outward ingredients of the criminal law. Political bodies create criminal statutes, which involve penalties when they are violated. A number of authorities have attempted to identify the *differentiae of crime*, those elements of behavior that must occur for certain actions to be brought within the criminal law.[6] The differentiae of crime are those characteristics of the behavior of an individual that must be present for the behavior to constitute criminal conduct.

// The first requirement of crime is that the behavior constitute a "harm." The act must result in visible, external consequences detrimental to social interests// Insofar as an act is held to result in injuries only to the parties immediately concerned in the act, that behavior does not qualify as a crime. Private injuries are civil offenses, not criminal acts.

// To be identified as a crime, an act must legally be forbidden." In other words, antisocial conduct is not criminal until it has specifically been proscribed in the body of criminal law. In the proceedings against a person, careful attention is usually paid to the question of whether an act has explicitly been forbidden. It is not enough that the behavior in question be reasonably similar to actions proscribed by law. Instead, the instance at hand must clearly fit within an existing category of forbidden conduct. Moreover, an elaborate appeal system has been contrived as a safeguard against misapplication of laws, so detailed scrutiny is often given to alleged acts of unlawful conduct.

In addition to the foregoing, "conduct" must occur for a crime to take place. Intentional behavioral events, resulting in some harmful consequence, must have taken place. For instance, to convict an individual of murder, it must be proven that the person actually pulled the trigger of a gun or behaved in some other way that led directly to the death of the victim. It is not enough to show by a chain of circumstantial reasoning that a particular harmful consequence *probably* ensued from some illegal actions of a suspect. To convict an alleged offender of murder, more would be required than simply a demonstration that the suspect owned the weapon used to kill a person; someone else might have used the gun and committed the murder.

A fourth and critical element in crime is that of *mens rea*, literally "evil mind" or "guilty mind." *Mens rea* refers to *intent* rather than to *motivation*// To demonstrate *mens rea*, it must be shown that an actor intended or calculated to behave in a manner defined as illegal. Thus, for example, an individual is guilty of arson if he deliberately sets a fire in a dwelling, with the result

---

[6]Sutherland and Cressey, *Criminology*, pp. 12–15; Richard R. Korn and Lloyd W. McCorkle, *Criminology and Penology* (New York: Holt, Rinehart and Winston, 1959), pp. 102–6; Hall, *General Principles of Criminal Law*, pp. 19–20.

that the house burns to the ground. If a fire occurs as a result of an accidental action by the actor, the crime of arson has not occurred.

A guilty individual may have engaged in a line of conduct or formed criminal intent out of various reasons or motives, but his reasons or motives are not directly relevant to the question of *mens rea*. For example, a person who, out of feelings of compassion, deliberately kills an invalid spouse suffering from an incurable and painful disease is equally guilty of a crime as is a professional killer who murders someone in "cold blood" and for pay. *Mens rea* would be present in both cases. Of course, the penalty handed out to each of these murderers may be considerably different, and the professional killer might receive a decidedly more punitive sentence than the other murderer. Variations in sentences that are a function of social background differences among offenders, differences in motivation, and so on are commonplace in the workings of the legal machinery. However, the basic point remains that "good" motives are not taken into account in the determination of whether a crime has occurred, at least in legal theory.

The notion of *mens rea* is basic to the plea of insanity as extenuating in criminal court trials. In brief, the claim that an individual was insane at the time that a harmful act took place, if successfully sustained, relieves that person of culpability of a criminal act. The actor is held to be guiltless because of an incapacity to form criminal intent, from the absence of *mens rea*.

A fusion of *mens rea* and conduct or a simultaneous occurrence is also a necessary element of crime. For example, a crime has not taken place in the instance of an intended but abortive attempt by A to murder B, followed by a somewhat later event in which B dies through the unintended negligence of A, who has left a gas stove turned on but unlighted, resulting in B's death from gas poisoning.

A causal relationship between someone's voluntary misconduct and the legally forbidden harm is another requirement. In other words, it must be shown that the harm was a direct consequence of the misconduct rather than an indirect one or a result of some other antecedent events. An obvious illustration of the causal connection would be an instance of homicide in which a drunken driver runs over a pedestrian having the right-of-way in a crosswalk, and the pedestrian dies immediately after being hit by the car. A not-so-clear instance might be the case of an abortion in which the aborted female receives medical care in a hospital, recovers from the infection resulting from the abortion, but then succumbs to another disease contracted while in the hospital. In the latter case, the accused abortionist could plead not guilty of homicide by reason of a lack of causal connection between his illegal acts and the death of the victim. The abortionist would be guilty of abortion, but not of the death of his customer.

The final element of crime is that the forbidden act must carry a legally prescribed punishment. The voluntary conduct of the violator must be punishable by law.

Criminal law in practice shows discrepancies from these criteria of crimes. In particular, the requirement of *mens rea* is not part of the so-called strict liability offenses. That is, with certain kinds of offenses the intent of the actor is not considered so that certain actions and consequences constitute crimes even though the perpetrator did not intend harmful consequences. "Statutory rape" and "contributing to the delinquency of a minor" are cases in point, as are certain automobile violations. In the instance of contributing to the delinquency of a minor, an individual can be held liable for law violation for a number of acts carried on with a minor female (or male) in which no criminal conduct was intended. Similarly, an actor can be convicted and punished for statutory rape if he has sexual intercourse with a minor female, even though he went through elaborate efforts to determine her age and was completely convinced that the girl was above the age of consent. In these cases, it is enough that the actor engaged in some line of conduct; his intentions are legally irrelevant.

CRIMINAL LAW REVISION

As we shall see later in this chapter, criminal law has a history. For example, over the past hundred years, modern property law has been expanded in a number of ways to take account of the needs of changing social conditions. A recent example would be laws relating to credit cards. These statutes were developed in response to the problems created by the rapid diffusion of credit cards as an alternative to retail purchases by means of cash or checks.

Commentary and criticism of the criminal law, calling for statutory revisions of one kind or another, is a constant phenomenon in the United States. One constant complaint has been that the various state criminal and penal codes are varied and inconsistent, with differing statutory definitions of particular crimes and also with criminal penalties that differ markedly from one jurisdiction to another. For instance, the dividing line between petty and grand larceny is specified as $50 in some states, $75 in others, and $100 in still others. Along the same line, statutory definitions of sexual offenses sometimes punishable as misdemeanors are dealt with as felonies in other jurisdictions. Frequently, the same criminal offense calls for quite different maximum prison terms in individual states. In short, "the criminal law" in American society does not exist; rather, a large number of state penal codes bear some loose relationship to one another.

Another criticism of American criminal statutes centers about the allegation that the law is often employed as a means for dealing with behavior that should not be of criminal concern. Currently, a considerable number of critics contend that use of criminal law as a means of controlling "personal vices" such as marijuana use or homosexuality is improper and unwise.

Herbert Packer believes that criminal sanction is too widely employed in

American society. Hence, he offers the following criteria for the use of criminal laws and penalties to control behavior.[7]

1. The conduct is prominent in most people's view of socially threatening behavior and is not condoned by any significant segment of society.
2. Subjecting the conduct to criminal sanction is not inconsistent with the goals of punishment.
3. Suppressing it will not inhibit socially desirable conduct.
4. The conduct may be dealt with through evenhanded and nondiscriminatory enforcement.
5. Controlling the conduct through the criminal process will not expose that process to severe qualitative or quantitative strains.
6. No reasonable alternatives to the criminal sanction for dealing with the conduct exist.

Applying these criteria to current criminal statutes, Packer would have us "decriminalize" a number of forms of behavior such as certain moral offenses, by expunging the relevant laws from the statute books. Edwin Schur has expressed similar views. He argues that existing laws concerning "crimes without victims" represent good candidates for repeal.[8] "Crimes without victims" are those offenses in which both parties to the offense are voluntary participants and in which no clear danger to the public welfare can be perceived in the conduct. Schur discusses drug addiction, homosexuality, and abortion as cases in point, along with certain other victimless crimes.[9]

The most ambitious attempt to impose order upon the chaos of criminal codes in the United States is found in the work of The American Law Institute, culminating in the drafting of the Model Penal Code in 1962.[10] Among the many problems tackled in that model code was the matter of definition of specific crimes, along with the removal of certain offenses from the purview of the criminal law.[11] The model code retains forcible rape and forcible deviate sexual intercourse as criminal offenses, but it expunges consensual homosexual acts from the statutes.

This recommendation was paralleled in England in the proposals of the "Wolfenden Report," named for the jurist, Sir John Wolfenden, who presided over the work of the governmental commission.[12] That report urged that consen-

---

[7]Herbert L. Packer, *The Limits of the Criminal Sanction* (Stanford, Calif.: Stanford University Press, 1968), p. 297.

[8]Edwin M. Schur, *Crimes Without Victims* (Englewood Cliffs, N.J.: Prentice-Hall, 1965).

[9]For a study of public attitudes toward laws relating to victimless crimes, see Elizabeth A. Rooney and Don C. Gibbons, "Social Reactions to 'Crimes Without Victims,'" *Social Problems*, 13 (Spring 1966), 400–410.

[10]The American Law Institute, *Model Penal Code* (Philadelphia: The American Law Institute, 1962).

[11]*Ibid*, pp. 123–241.

[12]Departmental Committee on Homosexual Offenses and Prostitution, *Report* (London: Her Majesty's Stationery Office, 1957).

sual acts of homosexuality between adults be removed from the scope of the criminal law, along with prohibitions against prostitution. The decriminalization of homosexuality was accomplished in Great Britain in 1966.

The Model Penal Code also tackled the thorny issue of criminal responsibility and the insanity defense, which has a long and stormy history.[13] Until recently, the most common standard for determining responsibility for criminal acts has been the M'Naghten rule, formulated in 1843. This rule arose out of an English homicide case, in which M'Naghten killed Drummond, the secretary to Sir Robert Peel. A principle emerged from this trial: for a person to be declared insane and not responsible for a criminal act, it must be shown that "at the time of the committing of the act, the party accused was laboring under such a defect of reason, from disease of the mind, as to not know the nature and quality of the act he was doing; or, if he did know it, that he did not know he was doing what was wrong."[14]

Critics of the M'Naghten standard argue that the rule pays too much attention to intellectual capacity and ignores emotional states. According to this view, a person may "know" in some cognitive sense what he is doing at the same time that he is incapable of controlling his behavior. Then, too, the M'Naghten rule can only be applied to markedly disordered persons so that many psychotic individuals end up being dealt with as criminals rather than mentally ill persons. Psychiatrists have often voiced harsh objections to the M'Naghten ruling on the grounds that it calls upon them to make judgments about a legal state, "insanity," even though their knowledge and expertise centers about a quite different phenomenon, mental illness.

Even though it has suffered a barrage of attacks, the M'Naghten standard has persisted as the most widely used test of criminal responsibility. A few states have added a second rule, the "irresistible impulse" test, in which persons are held not responsible for criminal acts if these acts can be shown to have resulted from the inability of the mind to control the will due to some uncontrollable impulse.

An alternative standard was formulated in *Durham* v. *United States* in the Court of Appeals for the District of Columbia. The ruling in that case was that "an accused is not criminally responsible if his unlawful act was the product of mental disease or defect."[15] However, that standard has not become widely adopted. Critics of the Durham rule have noted that it does not define mental disease or defect and thus opens the door to the possibility that relatively minor or innocuous disorders of personality might be offered as grounds for avoiding criminal responsibility. Then, too, no standard is provided for indicating the degree of causal linkage between the mental state

[13]An excellent summary of this story can be found in Paul W. Tappan, *Crime, Justice and Correction* (New York: McGraw-Hill Book Co., 1960), pp. 401–11; see also Herbert A. Bloch and Gilbert Geis, *Man, Crime, and Society*, 2nd ed. (New York: Random House, 1970), pp. 476–81.

[14]Tappan, *Crime, Justice and Correction*, p. 403.

[15]*Ibid.*, pp. 403–4.

and the lawbreaking conduct, which is required. How directly must the psychological factors be tied to the criminal conduct?

The American Law Institute endeavored to formulate a standard for criminal responsibility more in keeping with modern thought on criminal motivation and psychopathological states—a standard that would at the same time avoid some of the looseness and fuzziness of the Durham standard. The Model Penal Code states: "A person is not responsible for criminal conduct if at the time of such conduct as a result of mental disease or defect he lacks substantial capacity either to appreciate the criminality [wrongfulness] of his conduct or to conform his conduct to the requirements of the law."[16] The model code specifically excludes mental disease or defects that include abnormality manifested only by repeated criminality or by other antisocial conduct.

The Model Penal Code also seeks to bring order into the matter of penalties, sentencing, and corrections. The code identifies three degrees of felonies, each carrying specified minimum and maximum sentences.[17] First degree felonies have minimum prison sentences of not less than one year or more than ten years with a maximum period of life imprisonment. Second degree and third degree felonies have lesser minimum and maximum terms. The model code also provides for "extended terms" of imprisonment for the three grades of felonies when the individuals involved in them meet certain criteria such as chronic recidivism or habitual criminality. For example, a ten to twenty year minimum extended sentence is provided for Class I felonies meeting the criteria.[18] Finally, the model code establishes a large number of procedural rules for due process for offenders in the postconviction stage of corrections. For example, provisions are made for lawyers to represent probationers at probation revocation hearings, ensuring that the rights of the individual will be upheld.

Since 1962, and the appearance of the Model Penal Code, over thirty states have embarked on reform efforts directed at revision of their criminal codes. For example, the new criminal code enacted by the Oregon legislature in 1971 embodies a number of the suggestions of the model code.[19] In the set of statutes, adultery, lewd cohabitation, seduction, and private consensual acts of homosexuality between adults are removed from the codes. The provisions regarding statutory rape allow the individual to offer as a defense that he was reasonably mistaken as to the age of the female. Also, the model code standard for criminal responsibility is incorporated in place of the M'Naghten test. The statutory definitions of assault and murder are also revised in the direction suggested in the model code.

[16]The American Law Institute, *Model Penal Code*, p. 66.

[17]*Ibid.*, pp. 91–100.

[18]The philosophy behind these recommendations concerning sentencing is indicated in Tappan, *Crime, Justice and Correction*, pp. 468–75.

[19]Criminal Law Revision Commission, *Proposed Oregon Criminal Code* (Salem, Ore.: Criminal Law Revision Commission, 1970).

To conclude this discussion of criminal law revision we might note that the processes of statutory modification show no signs of abating. In recent years, much agitation has developed in the area of abortion law reform, with several states including California liberalizing the conditions under which women are now able to obtain legal or therapeutic abortions. Along a related line, it takes no great prescience to suspect that laws prohibiting simple possession of marijuana will come under even more vocal attack as marijuana continues to spread through the general population, making those statutes virtually unenforceable.

THE SOCIAL SOURCES OF CRIMINAL LAW

The Problem

The immediate answer to the question, "Where do criminal laws come from?" is that they are produced by individuals acting as members of state legislatures. But such a brief answer is unsatisfactory. Criminal laws do not encompass all antisocial or harmful acts, and as previously mentioned they include some acts that many would claim are not antisocial or social harms, such as homosexual acts between consenting partners or the use of various narcotic drugs. Moreover, criminal laws have varied from place to place and from one time period to another. Contemporary criminal codes contain many more acts specified as illegal than the criminal laws of a century or two ago. Lawmaking is a continuous process and exists as a response to social influences operating in societies at different points in time. In short, the making of criminal laws represents a fundamental social process that should attract the attention of the sociologist.[20]

Philip Selznick describes the sociological study of law as "an attempt to marshal what we know about the natural elements of social life and to bring that knowledge to bear on a consciously sustained enterprise, governed by special objectives and ideals. Thus understood, legal sociology follows a pattern similar to that of industrial sociology, political sociology, and educational sociology."[21] In this same discussion, Selznick suggests that the sociological study of law has not developed much beyond an earlier stage of relative immaturity and general neglect.[22] In a similar vein, Clarence Jeffery argues that American criminology has been restricted almost entirely to the study of crimi-

---

[20]A recent casebook on criminal law that places issues in contemporary criminal law in their social contexts is Richard C. Donnelly, Joseph Goldstein, and Richard D. Schwartz, *Criminal Law* (New York: The Free Press, 1962).

[21]Philip Selznick, "The Sociology of Law," in *Sociology Today*, eds. Robert K. Merton, Leonard Broom, and Leonard S. Cottrell, Jr. (New York: Basic Books, 1959), p. 116.

[22]*Ibid.*, pp. 115–27.

nal behavior, rather than to "crime."[23] He points out that behavior is not inherently criminal but becomes so through social processes in which it is defined as criminal. Yet the major thrust of sociological attention has centered on the processes by which persons become individuals who act out or behave in ways already defined as illegal rather than on the social processes leading to the creation of criminal laws. On this point, Jeffery is quite right in claiming that we have paid little attention to the social conditions that explain the emergence of criminal codes.

Formalized bodies of criminal law, including mechanisms for the implementation of codes, represent a relatively recent human invention. As we have already noted, personal controls and informal social control devices have regulated behavior for much of human history. But as Western societies have grown in size, complexity, and impersonality, the folkways and mores have become inadequate for the task of maintaining social stability. Consequently, the legal institutions have developed to support the more traditional forms of control. In this sense, lawmaking is the behavior of desperate men trying to reverse the deterioration of informal norms. Joseph Eaton's study of social changes among the Hutterites is a microcosmic illustration of this development. The Hutterites, a contemporary North American religious sect, practiced an Anabaptist faith coupled with a socialistic economy.[24] As this group was drawn into more intense contacts with the surrounding social organization of non-Hutterites, many unwritten customs of the group were challenged. In response to these perceived breakdowns, the elders of the group formalized previously informal norms and created specific punishments for rule violations.

At least in general terms, the development of criminal codes of various sorts and at various points in time is related to conditions of general social structure. Criminal statutes reflect basic interests and values in the societies in which they are found. A large number of criminal laws surrounding property rights with the protection of law characterize Western, capitalistic societies because of their value of private property and emphasis on acquired wealth. In the same way, many other criminal norms in force at some point in time can be taken as a crude index of the core interests large and important segments of the population hold in common. However, the assumption that all criminal laws reflect cultural consensus on values would be erroneous. Some laws grow out of special interests of particular groups in the population, and other segments of the society may well resist and resent these laws.

A number of more specific theories have been advanced regarding the origins of criminal law.[25] In the classical view, criminal norms were seen as

---

[23]Clarence R. Jeffery, "The Structure of American Criminological Thinking," *Journal of Criminal Law, Criminology and Police Science*, 46 (January–February 1956), 658–72; see also Austin T. Turk, *Criminality and Legal Order* (Chicago: Rand McNally and Co., 1969).

[24]Joseph W. Eaton, "Controlled Acculturation: A Survival Technique of the Hutterites," *American Sociological Review*, 17 (June 1952), 331–40.

[25]Sutherland and Cressey, *Criminology*, pp. 8–12.

originating in torts or private wrongs, from which the state eventually came to redefine some private injuries as social ones. However, this theory has several defects, one being that the process by which private harms were converted into public or social ones has largely been left unspecified.

Some authorities have held that criminal laws arise as expressions of rational processes that take place as societies become unified. According to this line of argument, as societies emerge out of earlier states of disunity, in which the area has been divided up into independent fiefs, tendencies toward the development of uniform behavioral codes, including criminal laws, develop. Still another contention, the converse of this one, holds that the enactment of law is a somewhat irrational, emotional response to social problems. Illustrative of this hypothesis is the frequent claim of foreign visitors to the United States that this nation placed undue and somewhat unthinking faith in the power of legislation to eradicate social problems. Thus, Americans are sometimes said to pass laws first and only later to make effective efforts to understand or solve problems against which they have already legislated.

Another theory on the origin of criminal laws asserts that they are an outgrowth or product of the mores. According to this view, statutes represent an attempt to codify the mores and develop a coherent supportive rationale for the body of formalized mores. We have noted a somewhat different contention regarding the relation between custom and law: the latter grows up in response to perceived shortcomings in the mores or their implementation. Finally, some criminal norms are said to be the consequence of conflicts of interest between different power groups so that these norms symbolize the victory of one faction over another. Certain criminal laws represent devices created to serve some special interest group in its effort to dominate another group.

Each of these theories may explain the genesis of some criminal laws but fail to account for other statutes. Moreover, little systematic and detailed evidence exists concerning the social origins of particular criminal laws. Specific studies of particular criminal laws, designed to collect evidence that would confirm and clarify the applicability of one or another of these general theories, are needed in considerable quantity. However, some data are already at hand concerning the rise of particular criminal laws.

Some Studies of Criminal Laws

William Chambliss has examined the origins of vagrancy laws in England and the United States and the shifts in their nature since their creation.[26] He noted that the first vagrancy statute, enacted in England in 1349, made the giving of alms to any unemployed person of sound mind and body a crime. This

---

[26]William J. Chambliss, "A Sociological Analysis of the Law of Vagrancy," *Social Problems*, 12 (Summer 1964), 67–77.

law was the indirect result of the Black Death, which struck England about 1348 and had the effect of decimating the English labor force. Half of the English population is estimated to have died during the plague epidemic. As a result, the supply of cheap labor was severely reduced precisely at a time when serfdom was beginning to break down and peasants began to flee from the manors. Landowners had begun to experience great difficulties in the maintenance of their holdings. According to Chambliss, "It was under these conditions that we find the first vagrancy statutes emerging. There is little question but that these statutes were designed for one express purpose: to force laborers (whether personally free or unfree) to accept employment at a low wage in order to insure the landowner an adequate supply of labor at a price he could afford to pay."[27] In effect, the vagrancy laws attempted to sustain conditions of serfdom after the breakdown of the serf-manor system had already begun.

For most of the period after their enactment in 1349 to the sixteenth century, vagrancy laws remained a dormant statutory device because the conditions that spurred their development had disappeared. However, about 1530 the statutes were revised in language and restored to use. The new phraseology focused attention on criminals rather than on unemployed persons. In effect, these revamped vagrancy codes were intended to provide the control of persons suspected of being robbers or other sorts of criminals but not yet apprehended for some specific violation of law. Chambliss accounts for these changes as a social response to the growth of commerce and industry in England. The large number of foreign merchants abroad in England in the sixteenth century were subject to frequent attacks by robbers. We shall see later, in Jerome Hall's study of the origin of theft laws, that the same concern for the regulation and protection of commerce and merchants in England provided the source of early statutes identifying theft as a crime.

Further elaborations and changes in vagrancy laws have occurred over the past several hundred years. However, the general trend has been to broaden the range of kinds of individuals who come within the definition of "vagrant." A mechanism has been devised that provides police agencies with broad powers to "clear the streets" of various sorts of "suspicious" and "undesirable" persons. Accordingly, vagrancy laws are frequently a means of controlling the denizens of such city areas as Skid Road. As Chambliss notes, the individual states in the United States borrowed the eighteenth century English vagrancy laws substantially in toto so that the laws in both countries are relatively similar.

Chambliss argues that the creation of vagrancy laws, and the subsequent changes in the language of these statutes and their interpretation or implementation, represent one case consistent with the interest group theory regarding the origin of criminal codes. The vagrancy statutes were contrived and later

[27]*Ibid.*, p. 69.

altered to protect the interests of such specific groups as landowners and merchants.

A second, well-known study of the development of law is Jerome Hall's investigation of the growth of modern theft laws.[28] Hall traces the growth of property and theft statutes back to the Carrier's Case of 1473. In this case, a defendant had been charged with a felony because he failed to carry out properly an assignment from a merchant. The carrier had been hired to carry certain bales to Southampton, England, but instead had absconded with them, broken them open, and taken the contents. In the ensuing deliberations, some of the judges argued that no felony had been committed and that the carrier could not steal what he already had in his possession. This line of argument was in accord with decisions previously rendered in the most common kinds of property crimes occurring up to this point, thefts of cattle. There the taking of property meant literally the physical removal of it. No such act had occurred in the Carrier's Case. Nonetheless, the defendant was ultimately found guilty on the grounds that he had broken open and taken the contents of the bales. Although he had possession of the bales, he did not have possession of their contents. Hall asserted that this case laid the foundation for an emerging distinction between *custody* of goods and *possession* of them, which was to become the basis for succeeding elaborations of theft law. In short, Hall's study shows that the judiciary revised existing legal rules to solve a social control problem posed by the carrier and his actions.[29]

According to Hall, the following social conditions gave rise to the creation of new legislative interpretations beginning with the Carrier's Case:

> With the growth of manufacturing in the fifteenth century came marked changes in the manorial system and numerous departures from its mediaeval form. Came also the decay of serfdom and the rise of a new class of tenants whose rights were gradually recognized by the courts. But most important of all is the fact that during this period the older feudal relationships gave way before a rising middle class which owed its influence to the development of a rapidly expanding industry and trade. For example, in the middle of the fourteenth century there were only 169 important merchants, but at the beginning of the sixteenth century there were more than 3,000 merchants engaged in foreign trade alone. . . .
>
> The great forces of an emerging modern world, represented in the above phenomena, necessitated the elimination of a formula which had outgrown its usefulness. A new set of major institutions required a new role. The law, lagging behind the needs of the times, was brought into more harmonious relationship with the other institutions by the decision rendered in the Carrier's Case.[30]

[28]Jerome Hall, *Theft, Law and Society*, 2nd ed. (Indianapolis: Bobbs-Merrill Co., 1952).

[29]*Ibid.*, pp. 4–33.

The remainder of Hall's analysis is concerned with subsequent elaborations of modern theft law up to the present. The major conclusion drawn from the Carrier's Case, which germinated this process, was that new laws governing property rights emerged correlative with the emergence of commerce and industrialization in the Western world. Thus, Hall and Chambliss both show the linkages between certain laws, the Industrial Revolution, and the growth of the marketplace.

Leon Radzinowicz's massive study of changes in English law, police systems, and criminal policy between 1750 and 1833 investigates more recent developments in criminal law.[31] One volume of this study is concerned with historical analysis of the shift in English criminal law from the situation current in 1750, when capital offenses were numerous and executions commonplace even for what we would presently regard as petty offenses, toward a reduction in the number of capital crimes and executions under the law. According to Radzinowicz, many factors impeded the development of a more rational and humane system of correctional control. He declared that

> . . . among the effects of the Industrial Revolution were the emergence of great urban agglomerations and industrial regions, the formation of a large and mobile class of wage earners, the disintegration of some of the ancient orders of society, and the rapid accumulation of wealth by some sections of the community coinciding with the spread of poverty and economic instability, the evils of which were accentuated by the lack of a protective social policy. . . . England was in a state of transition and it is a truism that in such periods of social tension the Legislature becomes overridingly preoccupied with the strengthening of the State against the danger of an anticipated wave of lawlessness, inclined to lay stress on the deterrent function of criminal law and to oppose any attempt to change the established system of criminal justice, particularly if it would entail the relaxation of severity.[32]

Radzinowicz's analysis traces the emergence of a more equitable, humane, and less punitive system of legislation and correctional machinery from the writings of Beccaria and Jeremy Bentham. His study also shows the growth of modern metropolitan police systems during the latter part of the eighteenth century out of an earlier pattern of conflicting, overlapping police systems in which officers were employed parttime.[33] To a marked degree, the legislative, penal, and law enforcement reforms that Radzinowicz studied laid the foundation for contemporary systems of criminal justice.

[31]Leon Radzinowicz, *A History of English Criminal Law and its Administration from 1750,* 3 vols. (New York: The Macmillan Co., 1948–1957).

[32]*Ibid.,* vol. 1, pp. 351–52.

[33]*Ibid.,* vol. 3, "Cross-Currents in the Movement for the Reform of the Police."

We should acknowledge the significance of Radzinowicz's arguments for the contemporary scene. We can draw some striking parallels between the punitive sentiments of eighteenth century England and those insistent demands heard in the United States today for more repressive responses to offenders as a way of turning back the tide of lawlessness. One of the sentiments that citizens called out over the matter of racial turmoil in American cities has been the proposal that the police "get tough" with those involved in racial incidents. In the same way, longer and harsher penalties have been advocated for drug users and several other kinds of criminals. The sense of all these recommendations is that, if the responses to criminality are harsh enough, individuals will be deterred from such behavior. European experience suggests that the application of brutal punishments to large numbers of lawbreakers did little to curtail this behavior. Thus, the chances are not great that these measures will prevent those who have long-standing grievances against society from expressing them in militant and sometimes criminal ways.

A more recent inquiry into the social factors implicated in the development of criminal statutes is found in Edwin Sutherland's work concerning sexual psychopath laws.[34] The first of these originated in Illinois in 1938, followed in rapid succession by sexual psychopath laws in other states. In nearly every case, their enactment followed a few dramatic, well-publicized sexual attacks in the state in question, so these laws represent a legislative reflex action. Sutherland points out that these laws are hopelessly ambiguous, usually defining a sexual psychopath as someone who has demonstrated an inability to control his sexual urges. These statutes are based on a number of faulty or erroneous assumptions, not the least of which is the belief that such a clinical entity as a sexual psychopath exists in identifiable form. This particular legislative device seems to represent an attempt to ameliorate a behavioral problem through legislation, in advance of the requisite knowledge of the basic dimensions of the problem. For all these reasons, sexual psychopath laws are essentially inoperable.

Joseph Gusfield's inquiry into the social background of the Volstead Act bears on the interest group theory regarding origins of criminal laws.[35] That legislation, designed to enforce the Eighteenth Amendment of the United States Constitution, was passed in 1919 and repealed in 1933. The law banned the sale of beverages containing more than one half of one percent alcohol. Organized crime and gangsterism arose to satisfy widespread public clamoring for alcoholic beverages, private citizens often made their own "bathtub gin," and the Volstead Act was disobeyed on a grand scale.

[34]Edwin H. Sutherland, "The Sexual Psychopath Laws," *Journal of Criminal Law and Criminology*, 40 (January–February 1950), 543–54; Sutherland, "The Diffusion of Sexual Psychopath Laws," *American Journal of Sociology*, 56 (September 1950), 142–48.

[35]Joseph R. Gusfield, *Symbolic Crusade* (Urbana: University of Illinois Press, 1963); see also Gusfield, "On Legislating Morals: The Symbolic Process of Designating Deviance," *California Law Review*, 56 (January 1968), pp. 54–73.

What kind of explanation can we offer for legislation as unpopular as the Volstead Act? Gusfield maintains that this law was a symbolic reaffirmation of more basic interests of one segment of the population, native, white, rural, Protestant Americans, who perceived their values as under attack by foreign-born groups within the population. By getting this statute adopted, the group hoped to assert the dominance of their values over these "alien" ones. According to Gusfield:

> Prohibition was an effort to establish the legal norm against drinking in the United States. It was an attempt to succeed in coercive reform. But in what sense can a legal norm, which is probably unenforceable, be the goal of a reform movement? If the drinking behavior which the movement sought to end occurred in communities in which the Temperance advocates were unlikely to live and the laws were not likely to be enforced, what was the rationale for the movement? We have shown that Prohibition had become a symbol of cultural domination or loss. If the Prohibitionists won, it was also a victory of the rural, Protestant American over the secular, urban, and non-Protestant immigrant. It was the triumph of respectability over its opposite. It quieted the fear that the abstainer's culture was not really the criterion by which respectability was judged in the dominant areas of the total society.[36]

Anthony Platt's analysis of the rise of the juvenile court in the United States turned up findings somewhat similar to Gusfield's.[37] Platt notes that the creation in 1899 of the juvenile court was the culmination of a long series of correctional developments in the direction of mitigating the severe handling of youthful offenders. In addition, he observes that the motives of many of those who sponsored the juvenile court movement were less positive and therapeutic than has sometimes been supposed, for many of the advocates of the court saw it as a device through which idle and deviant urban youths could be coerced into adopting life styles of working-class conformity.

Our final piece of evidence regarding the backgrounds of particular laws comes from Howard Becker's study of the development of criminal norms designed to repress the use of marijuana.[38] Becker notes that the Marijuana Tax Act of 1937 had forerunners in earlier criminal statutes designed to suppress the pursuit of vices and ecstatic experiences, such as the Volstead Act (alcohol) and the Harrison Act (opium and derivatives). The Narcotics Bureau of the Treasury Department was unconcerned with marijuana in its earlier years, arguing instead that the regulation of opiates was the real problem. However,

[36]Gusfield, *Symbolic Crusade*, p. 110.

[37]Anthony M. Platt, *The Child Savers* (Chicago: University of Chicago Press, 1969).

[38]Howard S. Becker, *Outsiders* (New York: The Free Press, 1963), pp. 121–46; see also Troy Duster, *The Legislation of Morality* (New York: The Free Press, 1970). Duster points out in some detail how moral outrage directed at drug addicts resulted *from* legislation, rather than providing the original impetus for the lawmaking.

in the several years before 1937, the Narcotics Bureau came to redefine the matter of marijuana use as a serious problem. As a consequence, this agency acted in the role of moral entrepreneur, in which it attempted in several ways to create a new definition of marijuana use as a social danger. For example, the bureau provided information to mass media systems on the dangers of marijuana, including "atrocity stories," which detailed the gruesome features of marijuana smoking. Finally, in 1937, the Marijuana Tax Act was passed, ostensibly as a taxation measure but with the real purpose of preventing persons from smoking marijuana. One revealing sidelight on this legislation is that this bill encountered some strenuous objections from users of hempseed oil and the birdseed industry, which held that hemp seeds constituted a vital ingredient in various birdseed mixtures. These objections stalled the bill temporarily but were finally satisfied through changes in the act which exempted hemp seeds from control. This modification highlights interest group involvement in the passage of criminal laws.

These few studies indicate some of the factors that give rise to various criminal laws. They are all illustrative of the kind of research into the social sources of criminal law needed in greater quantity.

CRIMINAL LAW AND SOCIAL SENTIMENTS

As we have seen, a criminal statute may be born out of widely shared social sentiments, or it may have only a narrow base of public support. Criminal laws that once received general approval may fall into disfavor as they become out of tune with social values. In the same way, court actions are sometimes highly congruent with citizen preferences, while at other times significant discrepancies exist between correctional practices and the attitudes of the citizenry. In this sense, criminal laws and correctional practices mirror social values but sometimes in a distorted manner. In the extreme case, when laws or practices depart too far from public preferences, pressures for revisions or modifications in laws develop. We have not given much attention to this matter of social sentiments toward the law and its implementation. But some studies do illuminate these concerns.

Arnold Rose and Arthur Prell conducted a study of lay attitudes toward forms of lawbreaking and the punishments thought to be appropriate to them, in which thirteen minor felonies in California state law, which provided nearly equal minimum and maximum penalties, were selected for analysis.[39] Students at the University of Minnesota were asked to choose the most serious offenses among these crimes, which included childbeating, assault with a deadly weap-

---

[39]Arnold M. Rose and Arthur E. Prell, "Does the Punishment Fit the Crime? A Study in Social Valuation," *American Journal of Sociology*, 61 (November 1955), 247–59.

on, and issuing fictitious checks. A pronounced rank order of judgments was found, in which childbeating and assault with a deadly weapon were held to be the most serious offenses, whereas unlawful manufacture, sale, or possession of weapons was judged to be least serious. These opinions about crimes seemed unrelated to the sentencing policies of the California courts, in that inmates in a California prison who had been convicted of childbeating received considerably shorter sentences than did those involved in crimes judged as less important.

In a second investigation of this kind, carried on in the San Francisco area, a number of citizens were asked to complete a questionnaire inquiring about the kind of knowledge they had of criminality, correction, and kindred matters.[40] The principle of "out of sight, out of mind" described the responses, for most of the persons knew about a few flamboyant or bizarre cases of criminality, but few had any detailed knowledge of the workings of the law enforcement, judicial, or correctional systems.[41]

Elizabeth Rooney and Don Gibbons conducted an inquiry into citizen views regarding "crimes without victims,"[42] in which a group of San Francisco area residents were questioned about policies they felt should be pursued in cases of abortion, homosexuality, and drug addiction.[43] The respondents agreed generally that the laws regarding the legal grounds for abortions should be liberalized. For example, 79 percent held that women should be allowed to obtain therapeutic (legal) abortions if they have contracted German measles early in their pregnancy, whereas 83.6 percent agreed that a pregnancy resulting from rape or incest should be allowable grounds for an abortion. At the time of the study, the legal fact was that in California, as in over half of the other states, the only condition under which an abortion could legally be carried out was if the pregnancy imperiled the life of the woman. Obviously, current abortion laws have not kept pace with changing social values. Legislators will apparently come under increased pressure to liberalize abortion statutes as this gap between what the law permits and what people are willing to tolerate grows.[44] Indeed, California statutes were modified early in 1967.

The citizens in this research investigation were much less sympathetic to

[40]Don C. Gibbons, "Who Knows What About Correction?" *Crime and Delinquency*, 9 (April 1963), 137–44.

[41]A nationwide sample of citizens expressed similar opinions. Joint Commission on Correctional Manpower and Training, *The Public Looks at Crime and Corrections* (Washington, D.C.: Joint Commission on Correctional Manpower and Training, 1968).

[42]Schur, *Crimes Without Victims.*

[43]Elizabeth A. Rooney and Don C. Gibbons, "Social Reactions to 'Crimes Without Victims,'" *Social Problems*, 13 (Spring 1966), 400–410.

[44]Alice Rossi has reported a National Opinion Research Center study of a national sample of 1,484 persons, in which 71 percent approved of abortions when the mother's health is endangered and about half favored abortions in cases of rape and in instances in which birth defects are probable. Only 20 percent of the respondents approved of abortions for reasons of low income, illegitimate, or unwanted pregnancy. See Alice S. Rossi, "Abortion Laws and Their Victims," *Trans-action*, 3 (September–October 1966), 7–12.

proposed reforms in the laws that would ignore voluntary acts of homosexuality. Instead, they generally opted for a continuation of policies that treat consenting homosexual conduct as criminal. Finally, most respondents were quite antagonistic to any changes in statutes that would result in drug users being dealt with outside the framework of the criminal law.

In another study, closely related to the Rose and Prell investigation, San Francisco citizens indicated the degree of punishment they deemed appropriate for a wide range of crimes.[45] The criminal acts were described in some detail, so as to elicit responses to run-of-the-mill or usual instances of these offenses. The respondents selected the disposition they thought most fitting from among a series of choices ranging from execution to no penalty.

The severest penalties were selected for cases of murder, robbery, rape, and certain other "garden variety" crimes. Also, a good many persons offered some penalty other than the ones included in the questionnaire for certain offenses. Nearly all of those for rape, narcotics use, childmolesting, and exhibitionism centered about psychiatric care for persons involved in that conduct. As a way of summarizing the findings, the penalty choices on the questionnaire were treated as a crude scale, with a score of 8 given to execution, a score of 1 to "other," a score of 0 to no penalty, and scores of from 7 to 2 for intervening choices. Mean scores on offenses for the total sample and for males and females in the sample are shown in Table 1.

The rank order of scores in Table 1 indicates that the harshest penalties were chosen for five offenses included within the FBI classification of index offenses (serious crimes); hence criminal acts that are highly visible and often involve coercive attacks on property are the ones citizens would have punished heavily. These crimes often do result in long prison sentences for the perpetrators. However, these citizens also deemed quite serious several offenses that now tend to receive relatively lenient penalties. Over half elected sentences of a year or more in prison for embezzlers and antitrust violators.

The level of public support is currently unclear for a good many cases of criminal law and practice. The area of "white collar crime" is a case in point, for the character of citizen sentiments regarding business crimes is open to conjecture and speculation. Some light is shed on this question through Donald Newman's investigation concerning violations of the Federal Food, Drug and Cosmetic Act, revised 1938.[46] He asked a sample of about 175 adults to indicate the degree of punishment they thought appropriate for cases of product misbranding and food adulteration selected from the files of a federal district attorney. He then compared these choices with the sentences actually imposed. About 78 percent of the citizens felt that the penalties should be

[45]Don C. Gibbons, "Crime and Punishment: A Study in Social Attitudes," *Social Forces*, 45 (June 1969), 391–97.
[46]Donald J. Newman, "Public Attitudes Toward a Form of White Collar Crime," *Social Problems*, 4 (January 1957), 228–32.

Table 1 MEAN PENALTY SCORES, TOTAL SAMPLE AND BY SEX

Offense	Total Sample	Males	Females
Murder, second degree	6.6	6.6	6.5
Robbery	6.3	6.3	6.5
Manslaughter	6.3	6.2	6.7
Burglary	6.2	6.2	6.2
Rape	6.0	6.0	5.8
Embezzlement	5.3	5.3	5.6
Antitrust	4.6	4.6	4.5
Auto theft	4.2	4.2	4.4
Childmolesting	4.3	4.1	4.5
Check forgery	3.7	3.6	4.1
Narcotics	3.9	3.8	3.9
Assault	3.4	3.4	3.5
Misrepresentation in advertising	3.2	3.4	2.8
Draft evasion	3.0	3.2	2.6
Marijuana	2.8	2.8	2.8
Exhibitionism	2.9	2.9	3.0
Drunk driving	2.9	2.9	2.9
Tax evasion	1.9	2.0	1.7
Statutory rape	2.1	2.2	1.9
Homosexuality	1.9	1.9	1.9

more severe than the actual court decisions. However, nearly all respondents selected punishments currently within the maximum allowable by law. Thus, public disapproval in this instance was centered on the administration of food and drug laws rather than upon the laws themselves. Finally, the penalties the citizens chose were not as severe as those sanctions imposed on such run-of-the-mill offenders as thieves and burglars.

In addition to these studies focusing on adults, some reports are available concerning public perceptions of the juvenile justice system. In one of these, William Lentz surveyed a sample of Wisconsin adults concerning attitudes toward juvenile control.[47] Most citizens favored swift and impartial justice toward juveniles, many felt that punishment should fit the crime, over half advocated publishing the names of juvenile offenders, most favored probation in place of institutional commitment, and many asserted that juvenile offenders are "ill" and in need of expert treatment.

A second study, by Howard Parker, dealt with citizen views of the juvenile court in four Washington state communities.[48] Many of the respondents

[47]William P. Lentz, "Social Status and Attitudes Toward Delinquency Control," *Journal of Research in Crime and Delinquency*, 3 (July 1966), 147–54.

[48]Howard Parker, "Juvenile Court Actions and Public Response," in *Becoming Delinquent*, eds. Peter G. Garabedian and Don C. Gibbons (Chicago: Aldine Publishing Co., 1970), pp. 252–65.

definition: origin and trends in criminal law

claimed that the juvenile court was not tough enough in its dealings with offenders. But, when these same laymen were asked to indicate what they would have done in the way of punishment to actual offenders, their penalty choices were similar or less severe than the ones actually handed out by juvenile courts.

CRIMINOLOGY, CRIME, AND CRIMINALS

Legal Versus "Sociological" Crime

In an earlier section we saw that crime consists of violation of certain conduct norms possessing a specified character. Similarly, a criminal, from a legalistic viewpoint, is an individual who has behaved in ways that diverge from the prohibitions or injunctions in the criminal law.

Now, obviously criminal law in any country has changed over time so that it does not represent a body of stable behavioral norms. Similarly, in a single nation such as the United States, variations exist from one jurisdiction to another in both the content and the language of criminal codes. In short, what is crime in one area may not have been crime at an earlier time or in another place. Because criminal codes are far from entirely capricious in character, much of the criminal law of Western societies is concerned with the regulation or repression of many common forms of behavior. Still, the lack of consistency in statutes has led a number of students of crime to suggest that criminology should abandon legalistic definitions of its field of inquiry in favor of some other universal and unchanging area of study. Jeffery summarizes a number of these "sociological" approaches to crime, which eschew legalistic definitions of the phenomena of study in favor of conduct norms and the violation of them.[49] Similarly, Herbert Bloch and Gilbert Geis comment on approaches to criminology that would substitute the study of such phenomena as moral aberrance, parasitism, or deviancy for the investigation of legally defined crime.[50] The rationale for these definitional innovations is that criminology should be concerned with the study of antisocial conduct, whether or not that activity happens to be included within the criminal law. According to this view, criminology would be directed at the study of a homogeneous body of subject matter rather than at a heterogeneous mixture of behavior haphazardly singled out by criminal laws, which at the same time ignore other forms of sociological crime. Bloch and Geis quite properly criticize these concepts of moral aberrance, parasitism, or deviancy as little more than figures of speech devoid of specific meaning. To substitute these concepts for a legalistic defini-

---

[49]Jeffery, "The Structure of American Criminological Thinking," pp. 660–63.
[50]Bloch and Geis, Man, Crime, and Society, pp. 18–21.

tion of the field of inquiry would mean that criminology would be mired in even more terminological and definitional confusion than would result from use of a legalistic criterion of crime.

Thorsten Sellin's work, concerning "conduct norms," is a well-known attempt to devise a substitute for a legalistic definition of crime.[51] Sellin suggests that criminology should study the violation of such norms and declares: "These facts lead to the inescapable conclusion that the study of conduct norms would afford a sounder basis for the development of scientific categories than a study of crime as defined in the criminal law. Such study would involve the isolation and classification of norms into universal categories, transcending political and other boundaries, a necessity imposed by the logic of science."[52]

At first glance, these recommendations might appear as appealing solutions to the definitional difficulties imposed by legal definitions of crime. However, the study of conduct norms is still only in its infancy; we are a distance away from any sort of inventory of conduct norms, even within the United States. The development of cross-cultural listings of conduct standards is an even more distant goal, however laudable it might be as an end to pursue. Moreover, even if such inventories of conduct definitions were available, they would not accomplish the results Sellin forsees. In their critique of Sellin, Sutherland and Cressey have identified the shortcomings of social norms as the unit of study. They argue: "In this respect crime is like all other social phenomena, and the possibility of a science of criminal behavior is similar to the possibility of a science of any other behavior. Social science has no stable unit, for all social sciences are dealing with phenomena which involve group evaluations."[53] Conduct norms are no more stable, universal, or unchanging than legal norms, and they are a good deal more ephemeral in character. Conduct norms vary over time and from place to place, so that we gain little (and perhaps lose much) by employing them rather than legal norms in the definitions of the boundaries of inquiry.

Furthermore, if we employ the concept of *deviance* current in sociology, in which deviance is considered behavior that departs from some conduct norm and is reacted to by some significant number of other individuals, the field of study becomes heroic in proportion. Deviance is a label for diverse kinds of behavior, ranging from violations of small group norms in work settings and other relatively primary relationships to instances of such societally disapproved forms of conduct as certain types of criminality. We are unlikely to make much progress in the study of deviance as a subject matter. Instead, development of more valid generalizations about deviant behavior is probably contingent on the discovery of confirmatory evidence regarding theories and hypotheses specific to particular, relatively homogeneous forms of deviant

[51]Thorsten Sellin, *Culture Conflict and Crime* (New York: Social Science Research Council, 1938).
[52]*Ibid.,* p. 30.
[53]Sutherland and Cressey, *Criminology,* p. 20.

conduct. The criminologist would do well to carve out the area of legally proscribed behavior as his subject matter and would profit as well from an approach to legally defined crime in which different orders of criminality are made the focus of theoretical and research attention.

A final remark on the matter of variability of criminal codes, and hence of crime, is that this variability presents the investigator with a problem for investigation rather than with an obstacle to be circumvented by redefinition of the field. Criminal laws do vary temporally and from place to place, but, as we previously suggested, the study of social origins and influences in criminal law should be a major subject of sociological attention. As part of this inquiry, the sociologist of law should attempt to pinpoint the factors responsible for particular statutory variations in criminal law.

Who Is the Criminal?

Efforts to articulate a sociologically meaningful conception of the criminal have accompanied the search for extralegal definitions of crime. Indeed, the conduct norm position on crime contains obvious parallel views on criminals so that the latter group is comprised of all violators of social norms. However, the controversy over the proper meaning of criminal has been more complex than simply a quarrel as to whether norm violators are to be considered criminals.

If we take a legalistic standpoint on the meaning of criminal, a criminal becomes some individual who has violated a criminal law. But some people find this definition objectionable. Ernest Burgess has advanced one of these counterpositions. Burgess would focus attention on only a portion of those individuals engaged in violations of criminal law. He declares: "A criminal is a person who regards himself as a criminal and is so regarded by society. He is the product of the criminal-making process."[54] Burgess made these remarks in conjunction with a discussion of Frank Hartung's study of violations of OPA regulations in Detroit during World War II. Burgess claims that, although they may legally constitute criminal conduct, such activities are not "sociologically" classifiable as criminal.

We submit that Burgess's claims are not well thought out. If we followed his recommendations, many prison inmates would be excluded from study on the grounds that they do not define themselves as criminals! Additionally, the notion of societal condemnation of crime implies the dubious presumption that we can discern uniform societal reactions. We agree that criminals are the product of the criminal-making process so that we should identify as

---

[54]Ernest W. Burgess, "Comment" on Frank E. Hartung, "White-Collar Offenses in the Wholesale Meat Industry in Detroit," *American Journal of Sociology*, 56 (July 1950), 32–33; see also Hartung, "White-Collar Offenses," pp. 25–32; "Rejoinder," *loc. cit.*, pp. 33–34; Burgess, "Concluding Comment," *loc. cit.*, p. 34.

criminals only those persons who have violated criminal laws. But the varied self-definitions of offenders and the divergent societal reactions to criminal acts represent phenomena to be studied rather than criteria for assigning boundaries to the field of study. Criminologists should be attentive to variations in self-image on the part of different law violators. Similarly, variations in societal reactions to different kinds of criminality form an important substantive topic for investigation. But to identify these as critical items for inquiry is different from including them as definitional criteria, as does Burgess.

Our position on the question of who is or is not a criminal is close to that of Paul Tappan. In one well-known essay on the question "Who is the Criminal?" Tappan offered some trenchant criticism of views that equate the study of criminals with the study of violators of conduct norms.[55] He also attacks the use of the label "white-collar crime" to cover those myriad instances of antisocial or "sharp" business practices or other occupational behavior not specifically included within some body of criminal statutes. In another place, Tappan offers a definition of crime (and, implicitly, of criminals) with which we agree. He says: "What then is the legal definition of crime as it has been employed in practice not only in our courts of law, but in criminology as well? *Crime is an intentional act or omission in violation of criminal law (statutory and case law), committed without defense or justification, and sanctioned by the state as a felony or misdemeanor*" (emphasis in the original).[56] Tappan does not demand that the terms *crime* or *criminal* be restricted to acts that have resulted in court conviction or to persons adjudicated as criminals by a court. In an earlier essay, he quite properly suggested that the legal tag of criminal be restricted to persons so adjudicated. His intent was apparently to emphasize that the legal status of criminal is different from that of noncriminal, in that the former carries a number of penalties with it, such as loss of civil rights and restrictions upon movement, which are not imposed on nonadjudicated offenders.[57] Acquisition of the legal status of criminal also results in social stigma being attached to the actor in addition to the penalties and deprivations authorized in the criminal law. Thus, to be a criminal is to acquire a negative public identity of more than slight importance.[58]

The demand that we keep clearly in mind the special legal status occupied by individuals who have been adjudged to be criminals has much merit. We should not use the term *criminal* indiscriminately, without distinguishing between those who occupy the legal status as a result of being processed through

[55]Paul W. Tappan, "Who is the Criminal?" *American Sociological Review*, 12 (February (1947), 96–103.

[56]Paul W. Tappan, *Crime, Justice and Correction* (New York: McGraw-Hill Book Co., 1960), p. 10.

[57]Tappan, "Who is the Criminal?" 100–103.

[58]One revealing study of the stigmatizing consequences of being convicted of a criminal offense (and even of being acquitted of crime!) can be found in Richard D. Schwartz and Jerome H. Skolnick, "Two Studies of Legal Stigma," in *The Other Side*, ed. Howard S. Becker (New York: The Free Press, 1964), pp., 103–17.

a court and those who do not, because they have escaped detection or prosecution. At the same time, we should reject the demand, sometimes insistently put forward, that criminologists study only persons legally identified as criminals. Criminology should be concerned with the study of criminalistic *behavior* rather than with the related but separate matter of judicial processing. Differentials in the correctional process do exist: some offenders do not become "known" or reported whereas others are reported to the police; some reported offenders are apprehended and others are not; some are prosecuted whereas others are not; or some receive penalties not handed out to others. Such differentials depend on a number of variables, including differences in the kinds of criminal behavior that occur, differences in police policies from one area to another, and variations in social background among offenders. This eminently sociological phenomenon of differential outcomes of criminal acts at various stages of the societal reaction process has not received the attention it deserves.[59] However, the point is simply that the criminologist takes, as his primary data, lawbreaking behavior, or, in Sutherland's words, "behavior which would raise a reasonable expectancy of conviction if tried in a criminal court or substitute agency."[60] Differential experiences of criminal deviants are important topics for the criminologist's concern, but he should not restrict his attention to deviants who reach the adjudication stage in the correctional process.

Richard Korn and Lloyd McCorkle have advanced a position on the definitional question of the scope of criminology identical to the one in this book. They point out, as did Tappan, the necessity to distinguish *criminals-by-adjudication* from *undetected offenders-in-fact* who have not been processed through the court machinery.[61] They suggest further that criminology be concerned with the broader class of offenders. They identify four categories and a number of subtypes of actual and/or convicted offenders, including persons who have committed offenses but are not known to the police, because the offense was undiscovered or unreported or the offender not identified. A second category consists of those who committed actual offenses and have become known but are unpunished because of the prosecutor's failure to indict them, the court's inability to obtain a conviction, or the failure of the conviction to be sustained on appeal. The third class of law violators consists of persons who have actually engaged in offenses and have been convicted and punished, and the final category involves those who have been convicted and punished for offenses which they did not, in fact, commit.[62]

---

[59]For an attempt to amalgamate a large body of bits and pieces of data on differential correctional reactions to juvenile and adult offenders, see Paul S. Fong, Social and Legal Factors in the Differential Societal Reactions to Offenders (master's thesis, San Francisco State College, 1964).

[60]Edwin H. Sutherland, "White-Collar Criminality," *American Sociological Review*, 5 (February 1940), 6.

[61]Korn and McCorkle, *Criminology and Penology*, p. 45.

[62]*Ibid.* These distinctions are specific cases of Becker's four categories of "deviants." See Becker, *Outsiders*, pp. 19–22.

If we adopt a legalistic conception of crime, we must attend to all instances of behavior fitting that definition. Hence, we need to examine a number of forms of lawbreaking now given scant attention. In particular, H. Laurence Ross draws attention to traffic law violations as a case of "folk crime."[63] These offenses are violations of laws introduced to solve problems arising out of the increased complexity and division of labor in modern societies. Traffic law violations, "chiseling" on unemployment compensation, and violation of regulatory statutes governing business and commerce are instances of folk crime. Most of these offenses provide a low degree of social stigma and involve persons of high social status. They are also dealt with in a variety of administrative ways; for example, traffic violation cases are disposed of through violations bureaus, bail forfeiture, and in other ways outside of courts. As Ross notes, modern societies have given rise to a large number of folk crimes that merit sociological attention. These offenses make up a large proportion of modern-day criminality, so they cannot be ignored or dismissed as "not really crime."

Felonies, Misdemeanors, and the Classification of Offenders

Chapter One briefly stated the orienting framework of this book: that a *role-career* perspective on crime and criminals offers the most promise for progress in the study of crime causation. In other words, we must break from the tradition that studies criminals and delinquents as representatives of homogeneous categories of behavior. Instead, we must develop specific theories related to particular types of criminality.

Chapter Ten considers, at some length, the complex question of how offenders are to be meaningfully classified into types. However, at this point we should take up one aspect of the taxonomic problems of criminological classification: the issue of the extent to which the criminologist should base his classificatory efforts on existing legal categories.

The body of conduct definitions and attendant penalties for their violation contains several systems of classification. One system involves sorting offenses into felonies and misdemeanors. Felonies are crimes thought to be most serious or heinous and carry maximum penalties of death or imprisonment in a state prison. Misdemeanors, on the other hand, are regarded as relatively petty acts of lesser significance. They are punishable by county jail terms of less than a year or by fines. Although criminal codes in all states distinguish between the two categories of offenses, the specific misdemeanor–felony dis-

---

[63]H. Laurence Ross, "Traffic Law Violation: A Folk Crime," *Social Problems*, 8 (Winter 1960–1961), 231–41; see also Clayton A. Hartjen and Don C. Gibbons, "An Empirical Investigation of a Criminal Typology," *Sociology and Social Research*, 54 (October 1969), 56–63; Gibbons, "Crime in the Hinterland," *Criminology*, forthcoming.

tinctions are not uniform from one jurisdiction to another. In one state the felony of grand larceny involves theft of goods valued at over $25.00, whereas in another state grand larceny is defined as any theft involving a loss of more than $50.00. Accordingly, behavior considered a misdemeanor in one area is a felony in another.

As the discussion of specificity as an element of criminal law indicated, and as is relatively apparent to all adult citizens, the criminal code of any jurisdiction consists of a body of specific prohibitions against various forms of conduct. Thus, the body of criminal laws is composed of a set of definitions of acts identified as burglary, arson, murder in the first degree, statutory rape, sodomy, grand larceny, larceny by bailee, and so forth. However, these specific acts, as with felony–misdemeanor distinctions, are subject to jurisdictional variations in definition.

Statistical tabulations on criminal behavior, research studies, and other reports on criminality commonly employ legal felony–misdemeanor distinctions or offense labels to classify offenses or offenders. As a consequence, these materials are of reduced significance, certainly in their use as generalizations regarding causation of criminality. Legal labels are inadequate as a basis for etiological classification of crimes or criminals, for several reasons. They reveal nothing about such important elements of criminal acts as offender–victim relationships or the social context of the deviant act, which are probably of considerable importance in the understanding of different patterns of criminality. To illustrate, criminologists would probably profit from an approach to the analysis of criminality in which cases of burglary involving "cat burglars" or "hot prowlers" (acts of burglary involving only a single burglar and carried on in a dwelling occupied by the tenants at the time of the burglary) are singled out for attention from the general class of all burglary. Similarly, we should study persons involved in the burglary of unoccupied dwellings and who carry out their deviant acts with confederates in a gang as another class of offenders.

Legal offense labels are deficient as the basis for classification in another way, too. Criminal actors classified at one point in time as "assaultists" do not engage only in that single offense. Thus, if he is to study careers in criminality or behavioral types the criminologist will have to contrive schemes for classifying lawbreakers in which a variety of different acts are included within the sociological type.

The foregoing discussion implies that legal labels attached to offenders are accurate, but are deficient for other reasons. Actually, another major problem is that the legal tag attached to an offender at the terminal end of the legal operation, after he has been processed through the office of prosecutor or through a court, is frequently a label different from the one initially assigned the offender at the stage of apprehension. Also, the initial label more commonly comes closer to accurately describing the offender. This discrepancy between behavior and legal label comes about through a process usually termed "pleading guilty for consideration," or, in the argot of offenders and law enforcement workers, "copping out" or "plea copping." That is, the prosecutor often offers the suspect a "deal," taking the form of an agreement to reduce the charge against him in return for a plea of guilty on his part. This is a *quid pro quo* arrangement, profitable to both the prosecutor and the offender. The prosecutor is assured a successful outcome to the case in the form of an automatic conviction, and at the same time the court workload is relieved because a trial is not required in the instance of a "guilty" plea. The offender receives a lesser sentence than he would if his plea of "not guilty" to the more serious offense is not sustained in court.

For these reasons, legal offense labels are eschewed as the basis for etiological classification of crimes and offenders. Instead, as discussed in some detail in Chapter Ten, the criminologist takes as his primary data proscribed acts included within the body of criminal laws, and persons who have engaged in these forbidden activities. But the criminologist should be free to contrive his own classifications of offenders or of crimes, which cut across existing legal labels, combine several specific legally defined offenses into a single category, sort some offenders charged with a specific offense into a category that includes other persons charged with a related but different offense, or define careers in criminality by assembling particular offenses into *patterns* of conduct. The approach we advocate is similar to Cressey's position,[64] and which can be seen in application in some of Julian Roebuck's.[65]

SUMMARY

This chapter has examined a number of facets of criminal law, including the distinguishing characteristics of criminal statutes, the social origins of laws, and the meshing of criminal codes with other social sentiments. Criminal laws define the boundaries of the category of "offenders." This collectivity includes those who breach the law; this population is the primary concern of criminology. However, one segment of this collectivity is made up of criminals, in

[64]Donald R. Cressey, "Criminological Research and the Definition of Crimes," *American Journal of Sociology*, 56 (May 1951), 546–51; Cressey, *Other People's Money* (Belmont, Calif.: Wadsworth Publishing Co., 1971).

[65]Julian B. Roebuck and Mervyn L. Cadwallader, "The Negro Armed Robber as a Criminal Type: The Construction and Application of a Typology," *Pacific Sociological Review*, 4 (Spring 1961), 21–26; Roebuck, "The Negro Drug Addict as an Offender Type," *Journal of Criminal Law, Criminology and Police Science*, 53 (March 1962), 36–43; Roebuck and Ronald Johnson, "The Negro Drinker and Assaulter as a Criminal Type," *Crime and Delinquency*, 8 (January 1962), 21–33; Roebuck and Johnson, "The Jack-of-all-Trades Offender," *Crime and Delinquency*, 8 (April 1962), 172–81; Roebuck, "The Negro Numbers Man as a Criminal Type: The Construction and Application of a Typology," *Journal of Criminal Law, Criminology and Police Science*, 54 (March 1963), 48–60; Roebuck and Johnson, "The 'Short Con' Man," *Crime and Delinquency*, 10 (July 1964), 235–48.

other words, offenders who have been apprehended and processed through the legal machinery. The next three chapters are devoted to the workings of the police; Chapter Four deals with procedures from arrest to trial; and Chapter Five discusses the epidemiological facts resulting from these processes.

BECOMING
A
"CRIMINAL":
THE
POLICE

Where do criminals come from? The citizen, the psychiatrist, and the sociologist have usually given roughly similar answers to this question. Depending on one's theoretical preferences, lawbreakers have been seen as willfully deciding to violate the law, as driven into deviance by urges from deep within the psyche, or as impelled toward criminality by adverse social circumstances.

These views assign police agencies a minor role in crime causation. The police are thought of as reacting *after* crime has broken out but playing no part in the etiology of criminality. Given these presuppositions, no wonder chapters dealing with law enforcement agencies are normally tucked into the back pages of criminology textbooks.

In the view of this text, police organizations deserve much more attention than they have traditionally received, if for no other reason than their omnipresent character in modern life. Formalized police agencies have grown rapidly in size and number from their beginnings in the 1800s. Police agencies were initially restricted to nighttime activity carried on by citizen volunteers but eventually gave way to organized, full-time police systems. The London metropolitan police force was created in 1829, and the first day and night, "professional" police force in the United States originated in New York City in 1844. From this beginning, police agencies in the United States have grown to some 420,000 people working for approximately 40,000 separate agencies that spend more than 2.5 billion dollars per year.[1]

We challenge the notion that the police exercise a minor or insignificant influence on criminality and that their role is restricted to responding to law violation. To begin with, individuals may become involved in actions forbidden in criminal law as a result of a variety of influences. Some individuals become officially designated as criminals, whereas others remain as covert or hidden deviants. In this discussion of the police and throughout this book, we assert emphatically the possibility that the experience of police apprehension may

[1]The President's Commission on Law Enforcement and Administration of Justice, *Task Force Report: The Police* (Washington, D.C.: U.S. Government Printing Office, 1967), p. 1. See this volume, pp. 1–12, for a detailed examination of the current status of American police.

be an important causal one. Briefly stated, this hypothesis contends that offenders who fall into the hands of the police may have difficulty withdrawing from criminal careers. Being singled out publicly as a criminal may operate as a career contingency that cuts the individual off from nondeviant pathways. Indeed, this factor may be more important in criminal recidivism than many of the variables to which criminologists have usually attended. If this notion is plausible, study of the police ought to be elevated to major status in criminological inquiry. We shall have more to say about the etiological effects of social and legal reactions on law violators in Chapters Nine and Ten.

How do some violators fall into the hands of the police while others remain undetected? Complaints of misbehavior against persons originate from a variety of sources, but usually the policeman effects an arrest of a miscreant. The private citizen's authority to arrest individuals is rarely invoked. Still, let us be clear on one point. The urban police are usually engaged in *reactive* rather than *proactive* police work. Somewhere in the neighborhood of 90 percent of police contacts with citizens are in response to calls initiated by citizens, rather than the result of the police drumming up business through detection of offenses. Drawing on data from studies in several American cities, Albert Reiss observes that: "Our observational studies of police activity in high-crime-rate areas of three cities show that 87 percent of all patrol mobilizations were initiated by citizens. Officers initiated (both in the field and on view) only 13 percent. Thus, it becomes apparent that citizens exercise considerable control over police patrol work through their discretionary decisions to call the police."[2]

Law enforcement officials are not apprised of a vast amount of offender behavior occurring in modern societies because this activity is not reported to them. Prostitutes and their clients, addicts and drug peddlers, and kindred souls frequently manage to avoid the scrutiny of the police, for their behavior involves no victim who complains to the police. In addition, much criminality reported to the police fails to result in apprehension of the actors responsible for the lawbreaking, largely due to the obstacles to efficient police work inherent in modern societies. That is, many burglaries, robberies, and so on go unsolved because the criminals are highly mobile in their operations and skilled in the practice of crime. The police have few tools with which to deal with this kind of criminality. Much crime known to the police is handled in informal and discretionary ways as, for example, when the authorities "wink at" gambling or minor traffic offenses. In other cases, law enforcement officials deal out warnings and admonitions instead of arresting offenders. Finally, some individuals known to the police are arrested and started on their way through the legal machinery that tags them as criminals.

[2]Albert J. Reiss, Jr., *The Police and the Public* (New Haven, Conn.: Yale University Press, 1971), p. 11.

We should know a good deal about the activities of police agencies, the contingencies that determine whether offenses become known to the police, and the variables that influence the differential handling of cases of which the police are apprised. But until recently, social scientists have paid little attention to studying police agencies. Several reasons account for this lack of attention, but the major one is the problem of rapport involved in efforts to study law enforcement agencies. Policemen are frequently the targets of public hostility, and they reciprocate these feelings. A sociologist would get an especially cold reception in many police stations, for he would be suspected of having a major interest in exposing the police to further public condemnation.

For such reasons, much of the social scientists' commentary on the police has dealt with relations of police agencies to the "host" society, including such factors as public hostility toward them. Relatively few investigations have studied the internal workings of police systems. However, in recent years Michael Banton,[3] Jerome Skolnick,[4] James Wilson,[5] Arthur Niederhoffer,[6] and others have made some important studies. Banton has provided descriptions of the workings of the police in "Carolina City," a community of 200,000 population, "Georgia City," a city of 500,000 population, and "Felsmere City," a town of 60,000 population in Massachusetts. Skolnick conducted his investigation in Oakland, California. Wilson inquired into six city police departments in New York, one in Illinois, and the Oakland police department; and Niederhoffer has reported a number of facets of police work in New York City.

Much commentary on law enforcement agencies has dealt with municipal police systems primarily because city policemen are responsible for the largest portion of arrests in the United States. However, we should note that a large number of police agencies of different forms characterize American society. The 40,000 separate police organizations in the nation involve 39,750 local agencies, 200 state police contingents, and 50 federal police systems.

One local police organization is the sheriff system found in nearly every county in the United States. County sheriff departments in metropolitan areas are often quite large, for these departments are responsible for law enforcement in all unincorporated parts of the county. The sheriff system is an anomaly in contemporary America: the sheriff is an elected official who usually comes to office without any special training in police work. The job of sheriff involves

[3]Michael Banton, *The Policeman in the Community* (New York: Basic Books, 1964).

[4]Jerome H. Skolnick, *Justice Without Trial* (New York: John Wiley and Sons, 1966).

[5]James Q. Wilson, *Varieties of Police Behavior* (Cambridge, Mass.: Harvard University Press, 1968); see also Reiss, *The Police and the Public*, for data on the operations of a number of police departments, including those in Detroit, Chicago, and Washington, D.C.

[6]Arthur Niederhoffer, *Behind the Shield* (Garden City, N.Y.: Doubleday and Co., 1967). Several useful collections of essays on the police are Niederhoffer and Abraham S. Blumberg, eds., *The Ambivalent Force: Perspectives on The Police* (Waltham, Mass.: Ginn and Co., 1970); David J. Bordua, ed., *The Police: Six Sociological Essays* (New York: John Wiley and Sons, 1967).

rapid turnover of personnel because the incumbent is often defeated when he runs for reelection. In many sheriff's departments, the deputy officers obtain their positions as political favors. For such reasons, sheriff's departments are particularly vulnerable to corrupt practices.[7]

Federal police of several kinds represent another major group of law enforcement personnel in the United States. The most famous federal police agency is, of course, the Federal Bureau of Investigation. However, there are eight national police organizations in all, including the Bureau of Narcotics, the Secret Service, and Post Office inspectors.

Still another collection of law enforcement groups is found at the state level. The best known state policing agency is identified variously as the State Police, or the State Highway Patrol. The latter are sometimes restricted to enforcement of motor vehicle laws, where state police usually have more general law enforcement powers. In addition, most states also have state narcotics bureaus, tax enforcement organizations, wardens, liquor inspectors, and other police groups.

Private police of various kinds represent a final form of police organization. Suburban shopping centers frequently employ police officers paid by the merchants, although the agent has certain law enforcement powers. Store detectives and hotel protective personnel constitute another kind of private police agency.

The following pages have more to say about municipal police systems than about these other organizations. In general, the chapter comments on the relations of police agencies to the "host" society and remarks on the internal workings of police departments. In the plan of the chapter, we shall touch on a number of things not specifically connected with the work of the police in apprehending offenders. That is, the intent of the chapter is to provide a discussion of police structures as social organizations.

The chapter emphasizes throughout the ways the structural features of the society in which the police operate tend to determine the central dimensions of law enforcement practice. Our view differs from the laymen's, which often interprets police activity in terms of assumed stupidity or venality on the part of policemen. We agree with Skolnick, who holds:

> It is rarely recognized that the conduct of police may be related in a fundamental way to the character and goals of the institution itself—the duties police are called upon to perform, associated with the assumptions of the system of legal justices—and that it may not be men who are good or bad, so much as the premises and design of the system in which they find themselves.[8]

[7]One study of the sheriff system is T. C. Esselstyn, "The Social Role of the County Sheriff," *Journal of Criminal Law, Criminology and Police Science*, 44 (July–August 1953), 177–84.
[8]Skolnick, *Justice Without Trial.*, pp. 4–5.

This chapter is not concerned with "police administration." Rather, it deals with the police as they actually operate. Such individuals as the distinguished police administrator, O. W. Wilson,[9] have discussed in great detail operating standards and procedures for efficient, "professional" police work.

THE POLICE AND SOCIETY

Public Hostility Toward the Police

Policemen have probably been the targets of negative responses from citizens from nearly the beginnings of organized law enforcement. In the United States, the idea of individual liberty and freedom from external interference has always been a central theme. Accordingly, in the eyes of many people, the less the police intrude into their affairs, so much the better.

In American history, another source as well has fed antagonistic perspectives on the police. Urban law enforcement agencies have frequently been linked with organized criminals and corrupt city officials in the operation of vice of various kinds.[10] In this arrangement, city police have often operated as regulators of prostitution, gambling, and other forbidden activities and have shared in the division of spoils from these enterprises. Although prostitution and gambling depend for their support on a public that presses for provision of illicit services, this fact has not prevented a good many citizens from venting their indignation on the police, particularly on the occasion of recurrent exposés of police corruption reported in urban newspapers.

A third source of citizen dissatisfaction with law enforcement agencies has grown from police use of various illegal or questionable enforcement procedures. Abundant testimony exists concerning the practice in many police stations of the "third degree," by which officers have physically coerced confessions from suspects. Other instances of gratuitous use of police force can be found in mob control as well as cases of entrapment and "manhunting." These incidents have encouraged the spread of public notions that the police department is a haven for incompetents and sadists. Whether or not they square with the facts, such images have contributed to the low esteem in which policemen are held in this society.

Another aspect of public hostility concerns the antagonism of the police toward the citizenry. American law enforcement agencies have often assumed many characteristics of a "secret society." They have adopted the posture that they are besieged by enemies of all kinds, including most members of the

[9]O. W. Wilson, *Police Administration*, 2nd ed. (New York: McGraw-Hill Book Co., 1963).

[10]For a journalistic account of police corruption, see Albert Deutsch, *The Trouble with Cops* (London: ARCO Publishers, Ltd., 1955); Ralph Lee Smith, *The Tarnished Badge* (New York: Thomas Y. Crowell Co., 1965).

general public. As a consequence, these organizations have closed ranks to prevent disclosure of any information about their internal workings.[11] At the same time, they have gone to great lengths to protect even the most deviant and lawless officer on the force. The tension between the police and the society that employs them is evident in the former's response to efforts to create civilian review boards to "police the police." Such suggestions have frequently been violently opposed by the department in question.

Some evidence is at hand concerning the matter of public hostility toward the police. Research indicates that citizens' views of law enforcement workers are probably more negative in the United States than in many other nations. Yet at the same time, the majority of American citizens continue to voice supportive attitudes toward the police so that public hostility is perhaps not as great as we sometimes assume. For example, James Q. Wilson has discussed some national opinion survey data on this question.[12] These findings indicate that black citizens have less positive views of the police than do whites, whereas higher-income blacks are more critical of the police than are lower-income blacks. At the same time, over three-fourths of the whites and over 60 percent of the black respondents at all social class levels aver that the police are doing a "very good" or "pretty good" job of protecting the people in their neighborhoods. Charles McCaghy, Irving Allen, and J. David Colfax reported similar results in a 1966 study in Hartford, Connecticut.[13] These investigators indicate that two-thirds of the persons surveyed were satisfied with the police, although black citizens were less enthusiastic about the police than were white citizens.

Limitations on Police Powers

We expect law enforcement agents to bring about near total repression of criminality, or at the very least we charge them with the responsibility of apprehending all lawbreakers reported to them. At the same time, the police labor under a variety of restraints in the way of rules of arrest, evidence, and so on, which render this task almost impossible to accomplish. For example, an officer who arrested an individual detained for a misdemeanor by a citizen would be guilty of illegal arrest and could be sued by the person arrested, if the officer did not observe the misdemeanor being committed. Law enforcement agencies are placed in a situation of great strain in that they are given a mandate to

[11]One study of police deviancy and the "secret society" character of police organizations is Ellwyn R. Stoddard, "The Informal 'Code' of Police Deviancy: A Group Approach to 'Blue-Coat Crime,'" *Journal of Criminal Law, Criminology and Police Science*, 59 (June 1968), 201–13. Stoddard notes that the police in a Texas city were "on the take" and involved in other extralegal activities, but police department norms discouraged individual officers from reporting this behavior to their superiors or to outsiders. Also see Reiss, *The Police and the Public*, pp. 121–72.

[12]James Q. Wilson, *Varieties of Police Behavior*, p. 28.

[13]Charles H. McCaghy, Irving L. Allen, and J. David Colfax, "Public Attitudes Toward City Police in a Middle-Sized Northern City," *Criminologica*, 6 (May 1968), 14–22.

promote social order at the same time that they are circumscribed by a variety of restraints on police practice. Modern societies are a far cry from "police states," in which the police have such virtually unlimited powers that technical efficiency is the only limit on their tactics. Skolnick has presented a succinct but incisive discussion of the inherent conflict between the goals of social order and rule of law to be observed by policemen.[14] He has noted:

> The police in democratic society are required to maintain order and to do so under the rule of law. As functionaries charged with maintaining order, they are part of the bureaucracy. The ideology of democratic bureaucracy emphasizes initiative rather than disciplined adherence to rules and regulations. By contrast, the rule of law emphasizes the rights of individual citizens and constraints upon the initiative of legal officials. This tension between the operational consequences of ideas of order, efficiency, and initiative, on the one hand, and legality, on the other, constitutes the principal problem of police as a democratic legal organization (emphasis in the original).[15]

Skolnick has observed that another ingredient in the conflict between social order and rule of law derives from the varied conceptions of order in modern society. Some persons would applaud the police for harassing transients, homosexuals, or some other group, but other individuals would contend that these matters are not the business of the police.[16]

According to Skolnick, the police bitterly resent the legal restrictions imposed on them. They see themselves as craftsmen, skilled in the work of crime detection and law enforcement. They view the world in probabilistic terms and contend that when their observations lead them to suspect someone of wrongdoing, they are nearly always correct in their suspicions. From this perspective, they often regard procedural rules as obstacles that prevent the officer from doing his job to the extent of his capabilities.[17]

The case for police restraints to prevent infringement of civil rights has been stated many times. In 1928, Justice Oliver Wendell Holmes, Jr. declared: "We have to choose, and for my part, I think it is less evil that some criminals should escape than that the government should play an ignoble part."

The citizen in American society enjoys freedom from improper police actions through the guarantees of the Bill of Rights, specifically the first eight amendments, which protect the citizen from illegal searches, from being compelled to testify against himself, and so on. However, throughout United States history, the Supreme Court has been reluctant to extend the provisions of the Bill of Rights beyond instances of federal cases. For decades, the police

[14]Skolnick, *Justice Without Trial*, pp. 1-22.
[15]*Ibid.*, p. 6.
[16]*Ibid.*, pp. 10-12.
[17]*Ibid.*, pp. 182-203.

in various states have not felt themselves to be under any obligation to desist from searches without warrants or the use of other indefensible tactics.

Police work in city police departments has included the third degree, that is, the use of force to coerce confessions from suspects. Policemen have engaged in searches without warrants, interrogated suspects for unduly long periods of time, and employed a variety of other expedient techniques, such as the use of informants, to make arrests. Thus, historically, the police have promoted social order by circumventing or ignoring the procedural rules that supposedly control their activities.[18]

Over the past two decades, the police have come under greater pressure to conform to the rule of law. The Supreme Court, in a series of decisions extending over this period, has moved to sharpen the conflict over social order versus rule of law. Herbert Packer has summarized these Supreme Court changes:

> The choice, basically, is between what I have termed the Crime Control and the Due Process models. The Crime Control model sees the efficient, expeditious and reliable screening and disposition of persons suspected of crime as the central value to be served by the criminal process. The Due Process model sees that function as limited by and subordinate to the maintenance of the dignity and autonomy of the individual. The Crime Control model is administrative and managerial; the Due Process model is adversary and judicial. The Crime Control model may be analogized to an assembly line, the Due Process model to an obstacle course.

> What we have at work today is a situation in which the criminal process as it actually operates in the large majority of cases probably approximates fairly closely the dictates of the Crime Control model. The real-world criminal process tends to be far more administrative and managerial than it does adversary and judicial. Yet, the officially prescribed norms for the criminal process, as laid down primarily by the Supreme Court, are rapidly providing a view that looks more and more like the Due Process model. The development, with which everyone here is intimately familiar, has been in the direction of "judicializing" each stage of the criminal process, of enhancing the capacity of the accused to challenge the operation of the process, and of equalizing the capacity of all persons to avail themselves of the opportunity for challenge so created.[19]

[18]For a discussion of how police employ informants in detective work and of the reciprocity between the police and the informants, see *ibid.*, pp. 122–38. The use of informants is *not* an illegal police procedure. Moreover, most policemen argue that informants are vital to successful law enforcement. For a report on narcotics enforcement patterns and the use of informants, see Skolnick's discussion, *ibid.*, pp. 139–63. He notes that unlike routine narcotics work or "good pinches," "big cases" provide the police with the conditions under which constitutional standards of legality can best be met. For example, officers do not labor under the same time pressures in "big cases" as they do in others.

[19]Herbert L. Packer, "The Courts, The Police, and the Rest of Us," *Journal of Criminal Law, Criminology and Police Science*, 57 (September 1966), 239; see this entire issue for a series of papers presenting

The older "hands-off" policy of the Supreme Court, as concerned with local police abridgment of constitutional guarantees, is illustrated in the *Wolf* decision handed down in 1949. In that case, the court exempted the states from the exclusionary rule disallowing use of evidence obtained through illegal search or seizure. The court voiced reluctance to intrude in that instance into a situation of long standing, in which state courts had been accepting evidence obtained illegally.

One of the first signs of court movement toward what Packer calls the Due Process model came in the 1947 case of *Adamson*. In that appeal, the court debated the question of whether the states must be bound by the provisions of the Fifth Amendment concerning the right of the accused to remain silent and to refuse to testify against himself. Although four of the justices took the affirmative view in this case, the five-man majority ruled that the states would violate due process only by action that "shocks the conscience." Somewhat later, in the case of *Mallory* heard in 1952, the court ruled that a person under arrest in a federal case must be taken "without unnecessary delay" before a federal commissioner to be apprised of his rights to silence and legal counsel. Then in 1961, in the *Mapp* decision, the court ruled that the states must enforce the Fourth Amendment guarantee against unreasonable search and seizure. The exclusionary rule was thus extended to the states, compelling the police to have valid search warrants before seizing evidence.

The *Gideon* decision of 1963 represents another landmark in the rise of the Due Process model, for in that case the court extended the Sixth Amendment guarantee of legal counsel to all serious crimes. This decision has meant that an indigent accused will be said to have been deprived of a fair trial unless he has been provided with adequate legal assistance.

The most controversial actions of the Supreme Court have occurred in the past few years, beginning with the *Escobedo* decision in 1964.[20] In that case, the court voided a murder confession because the accused, Danny Escobedo, had been prevented from seeing his lawyer, who was present in the police station house. Since the *Escobedo* case, decisions in a series of other cases, including *Miranda*, have had the effect of making it mandantory that the police inform any person whom they detain or take into custody of his right to remain silent. As illustrative of the consequences these decisions have had on police practice, the San Francisco Police Department now equips all officers with warning and waiver cards. These cards inform suspects that: "1. You have the right to remain silent. 2. Anything you say can and will be used against you in a court of law. 3. You have the right to talk to a lawyer and have

discrepant views of the correctness and significance of these decisions. Also on the Crime Control model, see Packer, *The Limits of the Criminal Sanction* (Stanford, Calif.: Stanford University Press, 1968), pp. 149–246; Abraham S. Blumberg, "Criminal Justice in America," in *Crime and Justice in American Society*, ed. Jack D. Douglas (Indianapolis: The Bobbs-Merrill Co., 1971), pp. 45–78.

[20]The court decisions are summarized in Niederhoffer, *Behind the Shield*, pp. 161–74.

him present with you while you are being questioned. 4. If you cannot afford to hire a lawyer one will be appointed to represent you before any questioning, if you wish one." This same card contains two questions that ask the suspect if he wishes to waive his right to silence, and it provides space for the accused to sign this waiver of rights.

A great deal of heated controversy and acrimonious comment have surrounded these decisions. Supporters of these court actions argue that all the decisions merely extend protections to accused individuals which have been standard in England for a long time. Moreover, these persons contend that the recent rulings will have the salutary effect of correcting laziness among policemen. These rulings will make it difficult for them to depend solely on confessions to obtain convictions and will force them to work harder at building a strong framework of evidence obtained through diligent detective work to support accusations against suspects. Opponents of these actions contend that these rulings against interrogation will further tie the hands of the police, who have already been rendered relatively impotent by court rulings at the very time that crime is increasing dramatically.

Many angry words have been exchanged in this controversy, but little real evidence has been assembled. Data concerning the effects of these rulings on police practice are needed. However, Theodore Souris has reported one instance that appears to indicate that the post-*Escobedo* period has not been one of law enforcement breakdown.[21] Souris observed that the Detroit police reported that in 1961 they obtained confessions in 60.8 percent of the criminal cases in that city, and they deemed these confessions essential to conviction in 13.1 percent of the cases. In 1965, the Detroit police claimed that they obtained confessions in 58 percent of the offenses, 11 percent of which were critical in leading to conviction.

Another study of the impact of court rulings on police practice was conducted in New Haven, Connecticut.[22] This research dealt with the *Miranda* ruling, which requires the police to inform the suspect in clear and unequivocal terms that he has the right to remain silent and the right to legal counsel, which will be provided him if he cannot afford a lawyer. Observers were stationed at the police station. The results showed that although the student observers were present, the police advised only 25 of 118 suspects of their rights. Interestingly, the detectives obtained a greater percentage of confessions from those who were given thorough warnings. Apparently, the police were being careful to warn fully those individuals accused of serious crimes, after which they questioned them vigorously. In general, the researchers concluded that the *Miranda* ruling had altered police practices in New Haven only slightly.

[21]Theodore Souris, "Stop and Frisk or Arrest and Search—The Use and Misuse of Euphemisms," *Journal of Criminal Law, Criminology and Police Science,* 57 (September 1966), 251-64.

[22]"Interrogation in New Haven," *Yale Law Journal,* 76 (July 1967), 1521-1648.

An inquiry in Washington, D.C., concerning the *Miranda* rule provided related findings.[23] That investigation found that the police in that city often failed to properly advise suspects of their rights. Nonetheless, nearly half of those warned of their rights made incriminating statements anyway. Also, only 1,262 of 15,430 persons arrested for serious crimes during the year of the study requested the volunteer attorneys available to them. In both New Haven and Washington, D.C., the investigators found that *Miranda* warnings were delivered to suspects in a wooden, unsympathetic manner so that many individuals were probably dissuaded from taking advantage of their rights.

Finally, Neal Milner's study, dealing with four Wisconsin communities of under 200,000 population, provides evidence on compliance with the *Miranda* rule.[24] He ranked the police departments in these cities in terms of professionalism and found that police attitudes were most positive toward legal rights of suspects in the most professional department. However, the actual interrogation practices of the police were similar in all four cities.

The general trend of Supreme Court decisions in the past decade has been in the direction of further protection of the rights of individuals in juvenile court proceedings, court sentencing, postconviction handling of offenders, and other areas of the criminal justice machinery. Doubtless controversy will continue regarding these trends and decisions. Whatever the end result of Supreme Court decisions, the police will continue to face the dilemma of contradictory expectations. They will be held responsible for the repression of crime at the same time that they are expected to behave with scrupulous attention to individual rights. The solution of this problem will come only when we recognize that both these goals cannot be realized. If we are to have police agencies that respect individual rights, we shall have to become reconciled to the situation in which a good many persons escape the law enforcement machinery.

The Police and Discretionary Action[25]

Although police chiefs often publicly assert that their departments enforce all laws equally, the fact is that police everywhere go about selective enforcement of criminal laws. This discretionary and selective enforcement is of two kinds. In one case, the police do not attend to certain statutes at all. In many localities, they ignore archaic laws designed for earlier social conditions. In

[23]Richard J. Medalie, Leonard Zeitz, and Paul Alexander, "Custodial Police Interrogation in Our Nation's Capital: The Attempt to Implement Miranda," *Michigan Law Review*, 66 (May 1968), 1347–1422.

[24]Neal Milner, "Comparative Analysis of Patterns of Compliance with Supreme Court Decisions: 'Miranda' and the Police in Four Communities," *Law and Society Review*, 5 (August 1970), 119–34.

[25]For a detailed discussion of arrest procedures used by the police, along with reports on police discretionary behavior, drawn from a study of police in Kansas, Michigan, and Wisconsin, see Wayne LaFave, *Arrest, The Decision to Take a Suspect into Custody* (Boston: Little, Brown and Co., 1965).

other cases, the police do not enforce certain laws, even though the conditions these statutes attempt to regulate do exist in the community. Rules against various forms of gambling represent a case in point, for in many areas the police have evolved tolerance policies that allow such statutes to be violated with impunity. The second general form of discretionary police activity centers about the differential application of laws to different individuals. That is, the police often apprehend some, but not all, persons whom they observe violating some statute, or in the more frequent case, who have been reported to them by some irate citizen.

The usual defense for discretionary actions is based on the claim that total enforcement would almost immediately bring the judicial machinery to a halt, jails and prisons would overflow, and chaos would result. The argument has also been advanced that judicious enforcement of laws is needed to keep petty offenders out of the legal machinery at the same time that intractable or difficult lawbreakers receive intensive attention and handling. According to this view, selective law enforcement, rather than legal intervention applied indiscriminately, best serves the interests of society. However, the problem with this perspective comes when efforts are made to implement basic policies of police discretion. The danger is that what begins as selective enforcement might degenerate into discriminatory law enforcement.

What principles guide the police in exercising discretionary powers? According to Banton, the police are attuned to notions of popular morality. They endeavor to take official action in cases where even the people who suffer from this intervention will be compelled to concede that the police are morally right in their activity. In short, Banton maintains that policemen are much like other citizens in certain ways and are sensitive to many widely held cultural values.[26]

Joseph Goldstein has provided one of the most incisive discussions of the problems inherent in use of police discretion.[27] He maintains that selective enforcement represents low-visibility interaction between individual officers and various citizens. The exercise of discretion is not guided by clear policy directives, nor is it subject to administrative scrutiny. For such reasons, selective enforcement can easily deteriorate into police abuse and discriminatory conduct. In Goldstein's view, an impartial civilian body should scrutinize the decisions as to which laws should be enforced. In that way, discretionary conduct would become more visible and might result in selective law enforcement that would then become a subject for open public dialogue.

Several pieces of information are at hand regarding the exercise of police

---

[26]Banton, The Policeman in the Community, pp. 127–55.

[27]Joseph Goldstein, "Police Discretion Not to Invoke the Criminal Process: Low Visibility Decisions in the Administration of Criminal Justice," Yale Law Journal, 69 (March 1960), 543–94.

discretion dealing with juvenile offenders.[28] One report, concerning a census of cases of known delinquency in Washington, D.C., showed that only a fraction of the delinquency cases known to the police and other public agencies resulted in juvenile court referral.[29] Also, the percentages of juveniles referred to the court carried from one offense to another. Most known thieves ended up in the court, whereas almost none of the truancy cases were handled in that way.

Nathan Goldman conducted another investigation of juvenile arrests in Allegheny County, Pennsylvania, in a small mill town, an industrial center, a trade center, and an upper-class residential area.[30] The data indicate that two-thirds of the juveniles the police apprehended were released without court referral, although 91 percent of the auto thieves they encountered were taken to court and only 11 percent of the mischief cases were reported. A major differential in police reporting practices was that 65 percent of the black offenders were taken to court, in marked contrast to 34 percent of the white juveniles so handled.[31]

Goldman also found that males and females were reported to the court in about the same proportions, but referrals increased with the age of offenders.[32] Somewhat surprisingly, the upper-class residential area had the highest arrest rate of the four communities. But the communities with the lowest arrest rates, "Trade City" and "Steel City," had the highest proportion of arrests for serious offenses. Citizens and police in "Trade City" and "Steel City" generally ignored complaints leading to juvenile arrests in the upper-class area and the mill town. In short, the police in the latter communities apparently found themselves engaged in more serious business than responding to juvenile peccadilloes.[33]

---

[28]Evidence concerning differential law enforcement and juveniles is summarized in Peter G. Garabedian and Don C. Gibbons, eds., *Becoming Delinquent* (Chicago: Aldine Publishing Co., 1970), pp. 74–127; Gibbons, *Delinquent Behavior* (Englewood Cliffs, N.J.: Prentice-Hall, 1970), pp. 35–44.

[29]Edward E. Schwartz, "A Community Experiment in the Measurement of Juvenile Delinquency," *National Probation Association Yearbook, 1945* (New York: National Probation Association, 1945), pp. 157–81.

[30]Nathan Goldman, *The Differential Selection of Juvenile Offenders for Court Appearance* (New York: National Council on Crime and Delinquency, 1963).

[31]*Ibid.*, pp. 35–47. This matter of differentials in handling racial groups is fairly complex in character. Goldman indicates that the referral rate was about the same for white and black youths involved in serious offenses. But Negroes apprehended for minor delinquencies were much more likely to be taken to juvenile court than were their white counterparts. Sidney Axelrad made much the same observation concerning black and white training school wards. The Negro boys were younger and less delinquent and had been placed on probation fewer times than the white youths. Axelrad maintains that these actions are taken against the black youths because of their deprived social backgrounds rather than as a result of prejudicial attitudes on the part of the police and court officials. See Sidney Axelrad, "Negro and White Male Institutionalized Delinquents," *American Journal of Sociology*, 57 (May 1952), 569–74.

[32]Goldman, *Differential Selection of Juvenile Offenders*, pp. 44–47.

[33]*Ibid.*, pp. 48–92.

Goldman gathered some interview material from the police regarding the factors influencing their decisions about juvenile offenders. The officers were attentive to the seriousness of offenses. They were also affected by their views of the juvenile court; those who thought the court had deleterious effects on youths referred few of them. They also gave a good deal of emphasis to the demeanor of the juveniles; they were more likely to refer surly or defiant youths than polite, contrite youngsters.[34]

Irving Piliavin and Scott Briar had findings similar to those of Goldman.[35] These investigators studied the behavior of policemen in a large California city and reported that discretion was widely used in police dealings with juveniles. Most of the youngsters the officers apprehended for serious forms of lawbreaking were subsequently referred to the court. However, the less serious cases were differentially reported; some youngsters were turned loose with admonitions to behave themselves, whereas others were taken to court. Officers made such discretionary decisions in terms of the general demeanor of the youngsters. Those who seemed to be members of gangs, who were Negroes, who dressed like "cats," or who were flippant ended up in juvenile hall.

Theodore Ferdinand and Elmer Luchterhand also found evidence of differential handling of black and white juvenile delinquents in a study carried on in "Easton," an eastern city of 150,000 population, 30 percent of which is black.[36] The black offenders who got into the hands of the police in that community were more likely than the white youths to be referred to the juvenile court. However, Ferdinand and Luchterhand did *not* attribute this higher rate of referral for Negro juveniles to involvement in more serious offenses or to age differences between them and white youths. Instead, they concluded that black juveniles in all offense groupings were more frequently referred to court than white youngsters and, in addition, that black juveniles who were referred to court appeared to be less aggressive and antisocial than the white court referrals. Ferdinand and Luchterhand assert that at least some of the differential reporting of black youths to juvenile court is due to racial prejudice on the part of police officers so that they are motivated to be more harsh with black delinquents than white ones.

James Wilson provides a different focus on discretion in juvenile police work.[37] Wilson looked at two relatively large cities: "Western City" had a "professionalized" police department, whereas "Eastern City" showed a "fra-

[34]*Ibid.*, pp., 93–124.

[35]Irving Piliavin and Scott Briar, "Police Encounters with Juveniles," *American Journal of Sociology*, 70 (September 1964), 206–14. See also George W. Mitchell, Youth Bureau: A Sociological Study (master's thesis, Wayne State University, 1958).

[36]Theodore N. Ferdinand and Elmer G. Luchterhand, "Inner-City Youth, the Police, the Juvenile Court, and Justice," *Social Problems*, 17 (Spring 1970), 510–27.

[37]James Q. Wilson, "The Police and the Delinquent in Two Cities," in *Controlling Delinquents*, ed. Stanton Wheeler (New York: John Wiley and Sons, 1968), pp. 9–30.

ternal" law enforcement agency. The former city selected its recruits impartially, practiced consistent law enforcement, and had a formal, bureaucratic organizational structure. "Eastern City" had a department recruited entirely from among local residents, practiced differential law enforcement, showed considerable graft, and commonly had informal and fraternal relations in its operation.[38]

The juvenile bureaus of the two police departments differed on a number of points. In "Eastern City," the police were moralistic in outlook, holding that faulty personal or family morality produced delinquents. They verbalized restrictive and punitive attitudes toward offenders. In "Western City," the officers were less moralistic and more therapeutic in their opinions.[39] Somewhat surprisingly, in view of these differences, the "Western City" police processed a larger proportion of its city's juvenile population than did the "Eastern City" police. Also, a larger share of those contacted were arrested in "Western City" than in the other community. These results suggest that professionalization of police departments leads to more formal handling of offenders and stricter enforcement of the law.

The previously mentioned studies have to do with discretionary activities concerning juvenile offenders. We could assemble a large amount of impressionistic evidence suggesting that the police commonly engage in selective law enforcement with adults as well. One piece of evidence on this point comes from Skolnick's study.[40] He indicated that the Oakland officers make discretionary decisions in their traffic warrant enforcement operation. Some offenders who have traffic fines outstanding are arrested for nonpayment, and other individuals are allowed to remain at liberty while they arrange to pay these fines. Proportionately more blacks than whites are arrested instead of being dealt with more leniently, but not because of racial factors per se. According to Skolnick, the police are about as biased in their attitudes toward blacks as citizens generally, customarily referring to blacks in uncomplimentary terms and showing other signs of prejudicial attitudes. However, the reason they arrest more blacks is that these persons are more likely to be unemployed, so they have difficulty in satisfactorily settling their affairs with the warrant bureau. Skolnick maintains that the police manage to keep their antiblack sentiments from intruding on their work in warrant bureau operations, even though these prejudices do enter into other aspects of police relations with minority group members.

Some firm evidence has begun to accumulate concerning differential law enforcement and adult offenders. One case in point is John Gardiner's study of the enforcement of moving traffic regulations in four Massachusetts cities.[41]

[38]*Ibid.*, pp. 10–14.
[39]*Ibid.*, pp. 14–19.
[40]Skolnick, *Justice Without Trial*, pp. 71–90.
[41]John A. Gardiner, *Traffic and the Police* (Cambridge, Mass.: Harvard University Press, 1969).

He notes that in the larger communities surrounding Boston, the rates for traffic tickets handed out during 1964 varied from 12 tickets to 158 citations per 1,000 motor vehicles.[42] In the same way, traffic citations were issued in markedly different numbers in the four cities he studied, even though actual traffic offenses seemed to be equally distributed in these communities. Gardiner maintains that these variations in traffic law enforcement result in considerable part from departmental policy, particularly as defined by the police chief or other policy-setting agency. In some cities, traffic enforcement is viewed as a "residual police function," whereas in others it is seen as a major form of police business.

James Wilson's investigation of eight separate police agencies also contains a good deal of information on differential law enforcement.[43] Among other things, he observed that the arrest rates for moving traffic violations ranged from 11.4 to 247.7 per 1,000 population in the cities he studied.[44] Enforcement of laws concerning vice and other criminal matters also varied in the eight communities. Wilson contends that police agencies often exhibit one of several styles of police activity and organization. Those police organizations that pursue the "watchman style" emphasize maintenance of public order and make few arrests. Police agencies structured on the "legalistic style" handle most complaints as matters of law enforcement and produce a high arrest rate; organizations that follow a "service style" intervene frequently into complaints and behavioral episodes that come to their attention but handle relatively few cases formally. [45] Wilson summarizes differential enforcement thus:

> How frequently the police intervene in a situation, and whether they intervene by making an arrest, will depend in part on the number and seriousness of the demands the city places on them. Second, some police behavior will be affected by the tastes, interests, and styles of the police administrator. Finally, the administrator's views of both particular problems and the general level and vigor of enforcement may be influenced, intentionally or unintentionally, by local politics.[46]

The foregoing evidence suggests some major dimensions involved in selective law enforcement. However, more investigation of this activity is in order, particularly on discretionary actions concerning adult offenders. One aspect of this matter that needs further study is the process by which officers learn to practice discretion in law enforcement. The police are not generally empowered to enforce laws selectively so that this feature of law enforcement is not usually articulated in the formal socialization of recruits in police acade-

[42]*Ibid.*, p. 11.
[43]Wilson, *Varieties of Police Behavior.*
[44]*Ibid.*, p. 95.
[45]*Ibid.*, pp. 140–226.
[46]*Ibid.*, p. 83.

mies. Instead, the rookie patrolman probably acquires norms governing discretion through informal socialization in a squad car, in which an older, more experienced officer relates "the facts of life."

We have not directly discussed one facet of selective or differential enforcement—the matter of discriminatory police behavior directed at minorities. What about gratuitous physical force or verbal abuse on the part of the police, directed at black citizens and other minority group members? We tackle this question in a later section of this chapter and also in more detail in Chapter Eight.

New Tasks for the Police

Many citizens likely think of the police in stereotyped images that portray their main business as the pursuit of violent and dangerous criminals. Actually, the police officer's job resembles many other occupations in that much of the work is tedious, routine, and unglamorous. Much of the routine character of police work in American society stems from the delegation of a great many responsibilities as peace officers in addition to tasks of crime detection and repression. That is, American police are held responsible for the maintenance of orderly social life. They spend much of their time patrolling Skid Road to make certain that the vagrants remain out of the vision of other citizens. They give over time to regulating the flow of traffic throughout the city, supervising the movements of pedestrians, and taking care of a host of other regulatory functions that have come to them by default. In many cities, the police are responsible for all licensing functions. They are usually the persons appealed to when a citizen perceives that someone he associates with has begun to act "crazy"; thus, the police routinely process referrals to psychiatric wards of county hospitals. The police handle a myriad other chores of this kind, most of which are relatively distinct from crime repression or prevention.

A study by Elaine Cumming, Ian Cumming, and Laura Edell[47] documents the extent of peace officer activities of the police. In recording police calls coming into the complaint desk of an American city, they found that over half of these calls dealt with appeals for assistance or support on personal or interpersonal problems rather than with criminal matters. Their data suggest that although citizens may not always admire policemen, the police are the first persons who come to mind when members of the general public are casting about for someone to rescue them from the complexities of urban life.

Some further insight into the peace-keeping roles of American policemen comes from a study of law enforcement practices on Skid Road.[48] Egon Bittner

[47]Elaine Cumming, Ian Cumming, and Laura Edell, "Policeman as Philosopher, Guide and Friend," *Social Problems*, 12 (Winter 1965), 276–86.

[48]Egon Bittner, "The Police in Skid-Row: A Study of Peace Keeping," *American Sociological Review*, 32 (October 1967), 699–715.

reports that patrolmen assigned to this section of the city see themselves not as "law officers" but rather as mainly concerned with keeping order. They receive few explicit directives from their superiors as to how they are to keep the peace. Thus, as craftsmen, they contrive their own techniques and procedures.

Skid Road officers seek to accumulate a rich supply of information on area residents and such community operations as flophouses and missions. As they go about their peace keeping, they are relatively unconcerned with strict notions of culpability and evidential standards. Instead, they tend to ignore fine distinctions between "offenders" and "victims," and act toward Skid Road denizens as though all were lawbreakers. Moreover, policemen make arrests informally, even though they could arrest persons for illegal acts. In short, decisions to use force or to refrain from coercion, to arrest or not to arrest, and other choices are made with an eye toward maintenance of order. Their behavior is less a response to lawbreaking than it is to the aim of peace keeping.

Bittner has also provided some data concerning order keeping endeavors of policemen concerned with the mentally ill.[49] Urban law enforcement persons are routinely involved in large numbers of cases contending that someone is mentally ill. The officer in these cases must act the role of quasi-psychiatrist; he must decide whether to make an emergency apprehension of a person to be held for psychiatric examination. Bittner suggests that emergency apprehensions are most common in instances of attempted suicide, extreme agitation, or serious disorientation on the part of the person. On the other hand, informal dispositions of complaints occur most often when the officer can find someone who will take charge of the disturbed individual.

The principal problem in making the police serve as a "jack-of-all-trades" organization is that budgets have often failed to increase at the same rate as additions to responsibilities. As a result, the police in various municipalities frequently engage in chronic appeals to the city government for more funds and personnel. The addition of peace maintenance tasks to the traditional responsibilities of the police further complicates their law enforcement activities. Critics who would have them make large numbers of arrests often fail to take into account both the procedural restrictions and the manpower limitations under which the police function.

Social Structure and Police Efficiency

We would usually not challenge the contention that the Federal Bureau of Investigation is a highly efficient, "professional" police force from which offenders rarely escape as we would the contrasting claim that inefficiency,

---

[49]Egon Bittner, "Police Discretion in Emergency Apprehension of Mentally Ill Persons," *Social Problems*, 14 (Winter 1967), 278–92.

laxness, and poor performance mark city police forces.[50] Nevertheless, some people aver that much of this adulatory picture of the FBI is a carefully constructed myth.[51] But let us assume that the municipal police do solve fewer crimes than do the federal police, even though the disparity in performance may not be as great as we sometimes think. Such an assumption is probably a correct one. How are we to account for this difference? One possible explanation is that the FBI recruits intelligent agents, whereas the city police attract dullards and incompetents. Doubtless some persons favor such an explanation. However, a more likely hypothesis is that the kinds of criminality with which these agencies deal and the circumstances surrounding them play a major determining role in police practice. In short, the municipal police may be faced with offenders who are less "catchable" than those the federal authorities encounter.

Consider the following case as an example of the effects of social circumstances and patterns of criminality on law enforcement.[52] Some years ago, the city newspapers in Vancouver, B.C., Canada, became greatly alarmed about a "crime wave" of robberies of grocery stores, particularly because the criminals had shot several proprietors when they interfered with the offenders. The newspapers alleged that the police were doing less than they might have done to repress these robberies. A check on robberies known to the police in Seattle, a city of size nearly equal to Vancouver's, revealed that many more of these offenses occurred in Vancouver. However, a tabulation of the number of small grocery stores (through the telephone directories of these two communities) also revealed that approximately twice as many such places were in Vancouver as in Seattle. In part, then, the crime wave was simply a function of greater opportunities for robbery in Vancouver. These small stores constituted attractive "marks" or victims, for most of them were manned by a single individual, were without alarm systems, and were widely scattered throughout the city. These stores could speedily be robbed and the offenders disappear into the night before the police could be summoned. We can easily imagine the difficulties the police might encounter in trying to anticipate the scene of future robberies so as to lie in wait for the culprits. A postscript to this incident is that the robbers were eventually captured, but in connection with another crime. While in custody awaiting trial for that offense, they confessed to the grocery store robberies. The solution to the robberies came about more by luck than by dint of detective work!

Arthur Stinchcombe has discussed some structural conditions influencing police practice.[53] He points out that "private places" can be distinguished from

---

[50]This view is seen in Don Whitehead, The FBI Story (New York: Random House, 1965).

[51]Fred J. Cook, The FBI Nobody Knows (New York: The Macmillan Co., 1964).

[52]The facts in this case were gathered by the author.

[53]Arthur L. Stinchcombe, "Institutions of Privacy in the Determination of Police Administrative Practice," American Journal of Sociology, 69 (September 1963), 150–60.

"public" ones. The police do not have access to the former without warrants, although they can freely enter public settings. Some crimes normally occur in private places, whereas others usually take place in public ones. Some crimes involve violence, whereas others are free from violence. Following these distinctions, Stinchcombe identifies a number of different patterns of criminality, along with their law enforcement consequences. For example, coercion in private life, such as wife-beating and similar actions, occur in private places. Although they are usually reported to the police, these cases infrequently result in convictions. The complainants tend to be reluctant to testify against the accused persons. Wives who have been beaten do not wish to have their spouses prosecuted, for fear this action will bring about a permanent rupture in their marriage.

Another form of criminality centers about illegitimate businesses and "dangerous" organizations. Prostitution, gambling, and traffic in drugs are cases in point. Some of these activities occur in public places, whereas others take place in private situations. In either event, these offenses are victimless because they have to do with illicit commodities that are widely desired. The participants are motivated to keep their conduct secret from the police, so there is no one to act as a complainant. As a result, the police must "drum up their own business" by means of undercover agents, informants, and other techniques which they do not employ in other kinds of criminality.

Still another general form of lawbreaking has to do with criminal invasion of private places; for example, burglary. This kind of crime is usually reported to the police, but it infrequently results in apprehension of the responsible parties. These offenses are carried on with stealth; providing few clues for the police, the culprits are highly mobile and exceedingly difficult to intercept. Finally, disorders and nuisances in public places constitute a form of criminality that the police can easily observe and the courts can successfully process.

If we now return to the original question about the performance of federal and municipal police, the foregoing analysis suggests that the large number of crimes unsolved by the city police stems from the difficulty of observing or solving many of these offenses. The federal law enforcement business more commonly involves such criminal actions as tax evasion, in which incriminating evidence against offenders is easily gathered through perusal of tax records or kindred enforcement techniques.

SOCIAL ORGANIZATION OF THE POLICE

In the past several decades, sociological inquiry has concentrated heavily on the study of complex social organizations. Industrial settings, welfare agencies, educational institutions, correctional facilities, and a number of other kinds of organizational structures have been extensively studied. However, police departments represent important organizations that, for the most part, have escaped the attention of sociologists. In the past few years, this gap in the data has begun to be corrected through the accumulation of some studies of police forces as organizations. Let us examine some of this material in the remainder of this chapter.

The Social Role of Policemen

The notion that a man's occupation influences his personality and his social life is familiar to sociologists. They often assert that the varied conditions under which men earn a living in complex societies heavily influence their general perspectives on life and their modes of social participation. On this point, Skolnick has sketched some features of the policeman's "working personality."[54] According to Skolnick, the elements of danger and authority, which are central to police work, lead law enforcement persons to develop certain common personality characteristics. One of these is suspiciousness; another is conservatism. Policemen come to be especially attentive to unusual situations, for the unpredictable is also likely to be dangerous. The police are cast as defenders of the status quo, so they come to prefer stability and lack of rapid social change. The dangerous aspects of their work and their task of compelling others to obey laws, many of which are unpopular with citizens, give rise to police solidarity and social isolation from nonpolicemen. Skolnick presents evidence to show that the police he studied were involved in more off-the-job interaction with one another than most other occupational groups.

The thrust of Skolnick's observations and of Banton's parallel report on American police[55] is that there is indeed a "cop mentality," as claimed by laymen. The difference between the views of Skolnick or Banton and the views of laymen is that the former suggest that the nature of the job produces the personality elements, and the latter imply that certain personalities seek out police work. The first view is clearly favored in this book.

Police Bureaucracies

Metropolitan police organizations are structured along the lines of complex bureaucracies or formal organizations. A variety of specific organizational tables or patterns describe how the police divide up tasks, but in every case a formal and highly complex division of labor characterizes these systems.[56] Most police departments are placed under administrative surveillance of a police commission, which is supposed to "police the police," but the control exercised through this device is often minimal. In most cases, the real power and leadership of the department emanates from the office of the Chief of Police.

[54]Skolnick, Justice Without Trial, pp. 42–70.

[55]Banton, The Policeman in the Community, pp. 110–26.

[56]For a detailed discussion of police organizational patterns, see O. W. Wilson, Police Administration.

Police bureaucracies usually involve a group of deputy chiefs immediately under the control of the chief. These administrative persons are responsible for the major divisions of the departmental organization, patrol supervision, crime prevention, juvenile services, traffic management, detective services, and other major tasks of the police force. These officials are housed in a Hall of Justice or other headquarters facility located in the city center and are held responsible for the citywide supervision of the police force. Also located downtown are police workers who perform such staff functions as planning and research, the detectives whose work takes them throughout the city, crime prevention personnel, and clerical workers. These headquarters personnel are arranged into a vertical hierarchy of ranks so that some are captains, others lieutenants, sergeants, or patrolmen.

City departments are further segmented through the precinct pattern of operation. Most large municipalities are divided into police districts or precincts, with district police stations out of which the patrolmen operate. These police stations are organized in hierarchical fashion, headed by a captain assisted by lieutenants and sergeants.

One feature of police activity about which little is known at present concerns occupational mobility within departments. City police organizations are usually included within a civil service system; entry into the department is by means of standardized recruiting procedures, testing, and other regularized practices. Civil service regulations govern advancement from the rank of patrolman upward, with standard examinations used for selection of sergeants and more advanced ranks. This aspect of occupational mobility in police departments is the familiar one of bureaucratic progression through stages of the occupational system.

Factors operating as determinants of job assignments within the department are much less evident. Nearly all officers start with the department as patrolmen, but some move into coveted police jobs, such as detective assignments. These jobs often put the incumbents in line for advancement into the administrative hierarchy. Other police officers remain in precinct patrol work and never rise beyond the rank of sergeant in the system. Finally, some officers receive distasteful assignments, such as "fixed post" jobs directing traffic at downtown street intersections. Civil service procedures do not govern an officer's assignments. Individual policemen account for assignment practices through a variety of informal processes, which they sum up by such expressions as "clout" and "juice." These terms refer to interpersonal influence resulting in desirable assignments for certain officers. There are several forms of "clout"; in different departments ethnic background, kinship ties to high officials, a record of having made a number of dramatic "big pinches," or other variables contribute to "juice."[57]

---

[57]One study of ethnic factors in police organizations is James Q. Wilson, "Generational and Ethnic Differences Among Career Police Officers," *American Journal of Sociology*, 69 (March 1964), 522–28.

Doubtlessly informal factors are implicated in mobility patterns in police departments, just as these considerations are apparently often found in other bureaucratic organizations. The formal organization in which explicit rules govern all events does not exist, except in the abstract formulations of sociologists. However, the nature of these unwritten norms and influences in police mobility needs further study, for little investigation of this topic has been conducted.

Another general observation about police bureaucracies has to do with ecological peculiarities in these organizations. Many formal organizations are located in one place, such as a college, a prison, or a factory. Visual surveillance makes easier control of individuals. But the police organization is scattered about the community in headquarters and precinct stations. The largest single group of police employees are the patrolmen, most of whom are in patrol cars and not at the station house at all. These conditions make it difficult for police officials to conduct systematic evaluations of job performance of the workers, except through such devices as recording the number of official arrests. The ecological structure of police work also creates difficulties in the way of control over deviant workers. Many deviant acts in which policemen sometimes engage, such as drinking on the job, are extremely difficult for administrators to observe. The spatial peculiarities of police systems probably go some way toward explaining the persistence of corrupt practices in the face of reform efforts occurring on the occasion of police scandals.[58]

Police Violence

We have already noted that one of the chronic complaints against policemen in American cities has dealt with gratuitous use of force. The observation has repeatedly been made that the police have engaged in the use of force to extract confessions from suspects. Additionally, innumerable cases have come to light in which the police have assaulted suspects or physically abused other citizens. In recent years, criticism of the police over illegal use of violence has been most apparent in the areas of civil rights demonstrations, racial disturbances, political demonstrations, and campus unrest. Although some charges may have been exaggerated, with little doubt law enforcement officers have often used force in their dealings with citizens in which the violence clearly exceeded the demands of the situation.

William Westley has made the most detailed study of police use of violence.[59] He argues that the police lean to the view that any technique helpful in making arrests is acceptable so that force is justified on expedient grounds.

---

[58]For a discussion of police control systems, see David J. Bordua and Albert J. Reiss, Jr., "Command, Control, and Charisma: Reflections on Police Bureaucracy," *American Journal of Sociology*, 72 (July 1966), 68–76.

[59]William A. Westley, "Violence and the Police," *American Journal of Sociology*, 59 (July 1953), 34–41.

In particular, police values uphold the use of force if it contributes to the making of "good pinches," that is, arrests in well-publicized and serious criminal cases. Along the same line, many policemen regard violence as particularly useful in handling such cases as sex offenses, where prosecutions are difficult to obtain. They argue that application of a beating to a sex offender operates as a deterrent to future episodes of such conduct on his part.

Westley asked a number of officers in a city department to indicate the circumstances they deemed appropriate for violent techniques. The largest number of responses centered about the use of force to obtain respect from hostile or defiant persons. Over one-third of the officers said that they regarded force as appropriate in these cases.

Westley's research was done some years ago. Accordingly, we might wonder what the current situation is with respect to police abuse of citizens. In 1967, a task force of The President's Commission on Law Enforcement and Administration of Justice reported that its studies indicated that brutality, intimidation, and dishonesty remain as common features in many American police departments. As a consequence, police relations with minority groups are at explosive levels in a number of cities, including Washington, Baltimore, Detroit, Newark, St. Louis, New Orleans, Atlanta, Memphis, Chicago, Cleveland, Philadelphia, and Cincinnati.[60]

What form does police abuse take? The National Advisory Commission on Civil Disorder (Kerner Commission) noted in its 1968 report that many ghetto residents in American cities believe that the police frequently use tactics of violence in their dealings with citizens.[61] At the same time, the President's Commission on Law Enforcement surveys indicate that abusive physical force is much less commonly encountered than is harassment of various forms and verbal abuse of citizens by the police.[62] James Wilson provides this summary:

> Observations of police behavior by researchers hired by the President's Commission also suggest that unnecessary force occurs in but a tiny fraction of police-citizen contacts, that discourtesy is more common, and—most important—that such incidents seem to be provoked more by *class* than racial differences and by unconventional or bizarre behavior on the part of the suspect (emphasis in the original).[63]

In contrast, recent studies such as the one by Paul Chevigny in New York City demonstrate that police abuses, including violence and brutality, continue

---

[60]The President's Commission on Law Enforcement and Administration of Justice, *Task Force Report: The Police*, pp. 144-207.

[61]*Report of the National Advisory Commission on Civil Disorders* (New York: Bantam Books, 1968), pp. 299-322.

[62]These data are summarized in James Q. Wilson, *Varieties of Police Behavior*, pp. 34-38; see also Reiss, *The Police and the Public*, pp. 121-72; Reiss, "Police Brutality—Answers to Key Questions," *Trans-action*, 5 (July-August 1968), 15-16.

[63]*Ibid.*, p. 46.

to be widespread enough as to cause considerable alarm.[64] Then, too, from one standpoint, *any* abuse of citizens by law enforcement agencies should be cause for concern, in that isolated instances of undue force can touch off citizen protests and disorder as well as undermine public confidence in the police.

How are the police to be brought under control so that they refrain from abusive conduct directed at citizens? Chevigny aptly summarizes one major impediment to efforts to "police the police":

> The police themselves are the most formidable obstacle to redress for police abuses. An arrest, together with the necessary testimony, is used to cover almost all street-corner abuses. The testimony is usually effective in covering the abuse for perfectly natural reasons—for example, because there is no one in court to contradict it except another policeman, and he will not do so. The graded structure for advancement in the Police Department, together with its tradition of hostility to outsiders, tends to create almost complete solidarity up the police chain of command. This protects any individual officer from criticism, even by people higher up in the chain, and it reinforces the effectiveness of cover charges and other obstacles to redress, simply because substantially all policemen share similar values and because they are forbidden by their code to betray one another's mistakes.[65]

The Kerner Commission recommended a number of steps to reduce police violence and abusive conduct in the ghetto and to improve citizen perceptions of the police.[66] These include several strategies for getting superior police officers assigned to urban ghettos, along with the creation of a specialized agency, independent of the police, to handle, investigate, and make recommendations on citizen complaints. In short, the commission opted for improved personnel and civilian review boards to "police the police."

Racial Attitudes in Police Departments

Let us take up the matter of racial attitudes in police departments in a bit more detail. One of the most revealing studies on this subject is William Kephart's investigation into the Philadelphia police force.[67] In interviews with patrolmen in that department, Kephart found that 91 percent overestimated the number of blacks on the police force.[68] He presents a good deal of evidence that black officers in that organization were discriminated against, for

[64]Paul Chevigny, *Police Power* (New York: Vintage Books, 1969).

[65]*Ibid.*, pp. 248-49. See also Stoddard, "The Informal 'Code' of Police Deviancy."

[66]*Report of the National Advisory Commission on Civil Disorders*, pp. 299-322.

[67]William M. Kephart, *Racial Factors in Urban Law Enforcement* (Philadelphia: University of Pennsylvania Press, 1957).

[68]*Ibid.*, p. 93.

they received the least desirable assignments.[69] The commanding officers of the department contended that no conflict existed between black and white officers and that, generally, race played no part in the operations of that department.[70] At the same time, nearly 60 percent of the patrolmen Kephart interviewed maintained that they would object to a patrol car assignment in which their partner was a black officer.[71] The commanding officers apparently chose not to believe or acknowledge unpleasant facts about the department.

The patrolmen in this study also exhibited a common set of attitudes toward black citizens. Three-fourths of the officers overestimated the proportion of the arrests in their areas in which blacks were involved.[72] Over one-half of the officers claimed that they had found it necessary to be more strict with black offenders than with white lawbreakers.[73] Finally, the majority of the police felt that black offenders were generally more difficult to deal with than were white criminals.[74]

Black citizens, particularly in slum areas, are probably somewhat more hostile toward policemen than are white groups. In the past decade hardening of racial sentiments in both whites and blacks in the United States has probably heightened the antagonistic views that minority group members hold toward the police. However, antiblack sentiments in the police may have become intensified too, as the police have been subjected to more and more troublesome experiences in slum areas.[75]

Several devices have been created in various parts of the United States as techniques for reducing the friction between minority groups and the police. One such device, the police review board, involves citizens and police officials who jointly consider complaints of improper police behavior. Another effort to control racial antagonisms is community relations bureaus within the police department, which have the responsibility of dealing with minority groups and of improving police–community relations. Finally, race relations has become part of the curriculum of police academies in an effort to create objective attitudes on the part of law enforcement workers.

SUMMARY

This chapter has considered a number of facets of police behavior in the United States, with particular emphasis on the variables that result in persons being

[69]*Ibid.*, pp. 26–56. For a recent study in New York City, reporting similar discrimination against black policemen, see Nicholas Alex, *Black in Blue* (New York: Appleton-Century-Crofts, 1969).

[70]*Ibid.*, pp. 57–74.

[71]*Ibid.*, p. 78.

[72]*Ibid.*, pp. 88–89.

[73]*Ibid.*, p. 81.

[74]*Ibid.*, p. 64.

[75]For a recent report of law enforcement agencies and racial problems, see Paul Jacobs, "The Los Angeles Police," *Atlantic*, 218 (December 1966), 95–101.

apprehended or individuals escaping from police attention. This discussion has centered on how police action might start offenders on their way to becoming criminals. But this is only half the story. We also need to examine the workings of the legal machinery as it takes arrested persons and turns out various products from this human material. This is the topic of Chapter Four, where we shall consider what happens to different individuals apprehended by the police.

4

BECOMING A "CRIMINAL": FROM ARREST TO TRIAL

This chapter traces out what can happen to a person identified as an accused or a suspect. In Chapter Three, we saw that the police dispose informally of a great many cases they learn about, exercising discretion in moving persons into the official legal machinery. What happens to those individuals whom the police start on their way through this processing? What events ensue when citizens take complaints to a district attorney? We shall begin with a brief examination of the major elements of state and federal legal systems. A more detailed look at the workings of various parts of these systems will follow this discussion.

ELEMENTS OF THE LEGAL SYSTEM

State Systems

The chief legal officer in state criminal systems is the county prosecuting attorney (district attorney). This elected official, along with his deputy prosecutors in larger counties, is responsible for representing "the state" in criminal actions against accused individuals. The prosecutor's adversaries, whose task is to represent and defend the accused, are criminal attorneys hired by the accused, lawyers provided the indigent by a legal aid society, or legal counsel supplied through a public defender's office. Other functionaries in the legal system are the personnel who maintain the county jail or lockup in which persons awaiting trial are held. Certain private citizens are systematically involved in the handling of persons caught up in this machinery. The chief group of these is the bail bondsmen who arrange bail for accused individuals.

The state courts, which constitute the central component of the legal operation, are diverse in character throughout the United States.[1] Nonetheless, we can discern a general pattern of court structure indicating two basic forms

[1]Delmar Karlen, The Citizen in Court (New York: Holt, Rinehart and Winston, 1964), pp. 3-7.

of courts—trial courts and appellate courts. Trial courts are, in turn, divided into several levels.

One group of trial courts consists of inferior courts, which are variously termed justice of the peace courts or municipal courts. In urban areas, elected officials who are full-time, qualified judges with legal training preside over these courts. These magistrates hold hearings in municipal courts and other courtlike surroundings. In rural areas, on the other hand, relatively unqualified magistrates are more likely to control the municipal courts. These hearings are frequently conducted in out-of-the-ordinary circumstances. The business of inferior courts centers about the processing of minor civil cases, adjudication of such minor criminal cases as misdemeanor charges, and preliminary hearings regarding serious criminal cases.

The higher trial courts in the various states are usually organized on a county basis. These courts deal with serious felony cases and are variously called circuit courts, superior courts, county courts, or district courts. In some states, these courts have general jurisdiction, hearing criminal, civil, matrimonial, and probate matters. In other states, the courts are fragmented so that each handles only one of these matters.[2]

Appellate courts on the state level are usually called supreme courts. These courts mainly hear appeals, in which they review the proceedings of trial courts to determine whether errors have occurred in the trial of an individual that would require reversal of judgment or a new trial. Appellate courts also have the responsibility of scrutinizing the constitutionality of new legislation.

The Federal System[3]

The legal officers and courts of the federal government have jurisdiction over offenders who commit ordinary crimes on federal reservations or against federal instrumentalities. Thus, although no federal law prohibits murder, homicides occurring on military posts or similar places fall within federal court jurisdiction. However, the largest group of lawbreakers with whom the federal machinery is concerned are persons who violate federal laws.

Although the federal criminal code runs to almost 2,500 sections, federal concern with criminality is considerably narrower than that of the individual states. The federal criminal code grows out of the legislative powers accorded Congress,[4] which is empowered to regulate interstate and foreign commerce, establish post offices, declare war, maintain order, and organize armed forces.

---

[2]The backgrounds and activities of judges in the United States have received relatively little research attention. For two studies of the sort needed, see Shirley D. McCune and Daniel L. Skoler, "Juvenile Court Judges in the United States, Part I: A National Profile," *Crime and Delinquency,* 11 (April 1965), 121–31; Regis H. Walther and Shirley D. McCune, "Juvenile Court Judges in the United States, Part II: Working Styles and Characteristics," *Crime and Delinquency,* 11 (October 1965), 384–93.

[3]Karlen, *The Citizen in Court,* pp. 14–23.

[4]*Ibid.,* pp. 7–8.

Congress also has jurisdiction over counterfeiting and piracy, naturalization procedures, and rules on bankruptcy, patents, and copyrights. Finally, Congress is authorized to make all laws "necessary and proper" to executing its powers. Federal criminal law centers about these matters; for example, the Mann Act deals with interstate traffic in prostitution, and the Dyer Act is directed at transportation of stolen vehicles across state lines.

The federal court system consists of three kinds of courts: district courts, courts of appeals, and the Supreme Court. The 91 district courts are trial courts with control over federal offenses in all or part of a single state. The 11 appellate courts receive appeals from district courts and from federal administrative agencies. Lastly, the Supreme Court takes up questions of constitutionality.

We should not suppose that state and federal courts have an equal share of the criminal workload. Although there are about 400 federal judges, New York State alone has eight times that number of state magistrates. Even when we exclude justices of the peace from this comparison, New York judges are still twice as numerous as their federal counterparts.[5]

PROCESSING THE SUSPECT THROUGH THE LEGAL MACHINERY[6]

Let us examine the flow of business through the state courts, for this pattern is closely paralleled in federal courts. The criminal processing machinery is usually set in motion by the arrest of an individual by the police, who take him into custody. However, in some cases a preliminary investigation by the district attorney or the grand jury leads to a formal accusation against an individual, followed by issuance of a warrant for his arrest. Embezzlement is an offense for which preliminary investigation is commonly carried on prior to arrest. A third means of entry into this system is through citizen complaints to the prosecuting attorney. Common cases of this type are bad checks and other improper business conduct, nonsupport and other domestic quarrels, borderline offenses against the person, such as negligent homicide, and obscene literature and other borderline offenses against morality. Many cases in this latter group are dealt with informally by the prosecutor and are not moved farther along. For example, district attorneys often endeavor to settle bad check complaints without prosecution by sending letters to the offender directing him to settle his financial affairs with the complaining citizen. If the check forger complies, the district attorney then terminates the case.[7]

---

[5]*Ibid.*, pp. 23–35.

[6]*Ibid.*, pp. 38–57; see also The President's Commission on Law Enforcement and Administration of Justice, *Task Force Report: The Courts* (Washington, D.C.: U.S. Government Printing Office, 1967).

[7]Frank W. Miller and Frank J. Remington, "Procedures Before Trial," *Annals of the American Academy of Political and Social Science*, 339 (January 1962), 111–24.

After the police have apprehended an individual he is supposed to be taken almost immediately before a magistrate of an inferior court. In the instance of petty misdemeanor offenses, a police officer or private citizen makes a formal accusation called a *complaint* against the person. These petty cases are normally dealt with quite swiftly, usually through a plea of guilty, which the accused individual enters. In felony charges, appearance before a magistrate is for the purpose of setting bail and arranging for a *preliminary* hearing. This hearing, also before a magistrate, is an inquiry to determine whether there is "probable cause," that is, enough evidence against an individual to warrant holding him for prosecution. Normally, only the prosecutor presents evidence at a preliminary hearing, and then only the minimum necessary to establish "probable cause." If the preliminary hearing results in the judgment that "probable cause" has been demonstrated, a formal accusation is made against the accused. In about half the states, a *grand jury* made up of citizens chosen by judges hears testimony in secret and draws up a formal accusation called an *indictment*; in other states the prosecutor formulates the accusation, called an *information*, without going through grand jury hearings. The general trend in the United States in recent decades has been to bypass the grand jury. For example, in California, less than 10 percent of the felony cases proceed through the grand jury.[8]

When a preliminary hearing has resulted in holding an accused individual for prosecution, the suspect has reached a critical juncture in his travel through the machinery. At this point, the prosecutor may offer him a "deal" so that if the accused agrees to plead guilty, he will be allowed to plead to a reduced charge. In the offender's terminology, he is given an opportunity to "cop out" to a "knocked-down" charge. If the accused agrees to this arrangement, an indictment will be drawn up alleging that he committed a different and less serious offense than the one for which he was originally apprehended. We shall return to this bargaining process later in this chapter.

The next step in the criminal process in felony cases is *arraignment*, which takes place in the court empowered to try the case. At arraignment, the accused is read the indictment, or information, and asked how he pleads to the charge. If he pleads guilty, which occurs in three-fourths or more of the cases, the judge will then sentence him. If he contends that he is not guilty, he will be held for trial before a judge or a *petit jury* (trial jury). The usual outcome of a trial is that the accused is found guilty, eventually receiving a sentence from the judge. The end product ground out by this machinery is a legal entity, "the criminal," who becomes, among other things, a statistic in crime reports. He also becomes a target for correctional activities, which attempt to change him from a "bad guy" into a "good guy."

The criminal justice system goes into operation at the point that crimes

[8]Herbert A. Bloch and Gilbert Geis, *Man, Crime, and Society*, 2nd ed. (New York: Random House, 1970), p. 419.

occur, for these events set the police to work. From that point onward, a large number of subsequent actions and dispositions are made of criminal cases. Figure 1 shows a general view of the parts of the legal machinery in terms of the flow of cases through that apparatus.

Figure 1 outlines the elements of the criminal justice system and of the juvenile system as well. On the whole, the juvenile justice structure follows the form of the criminal system but has tended toward informality and less concern for "due process" than the criminal courts. However, recent thinking has moved in the direction of modifications in juvenile justice designed to restore "due process" to accused juveniles. Thus, in some places, attorneys have been provided to charged juveniles, more attention has been paid to due process for youths, and court proceedings have become more legalistic.

SOME PROBLEMS OF CRIMINAL COURTS

Recent reports of The President's Commission on Law Enforcement and Administration of Justice make it abundantly clear that many American courts fall far short of ideal in operation.[9] Lower or inferior courts in particular turn out to be inferior in a number of ways.[10] According to the commission, many lower courts are nearly swamped with impressively large workloads. They are staffed by ill-trained personnel. Little or no screening or investigation of cases occurs. Assembly-line justice is dispensed to the misdemeanants who appear there. In the case of justice of the peace courts, the commission indicated that in three states the justice still receives payment only when he convicts and collects his fee from the defendant, a practice the United States Supreme Court ruled unconstitutional 40 years ago![11]

Individual Justice Versus Bureaucratic Processing

A rising chorus of opinion holds that in the American criminal justice system the accused rarely receives justice of any kind, getting, instead, processed through the bureaucratic machinery with relatively little concern for his rights. Proponents of this view see the criminal justice machinery as a gigantic operation paying lip service to the ideals of individual justice but dominated in fact by the pressure to meet production workloads in the way of people handled and moved through the system. Those who man this bureaucracy—judges, prosecutors, defense attorneys, bail bondsmen, sheriffs, probation officers, and others—are often involved in tacit bargains and arrangements of one kind or

[9]The President's Commission on Law Enforcement and Administration of Justice, *Task Force Report, passim.*
[10]*Ibid.,* pp. 29–36.
[11]*Ibid.,* p. 34

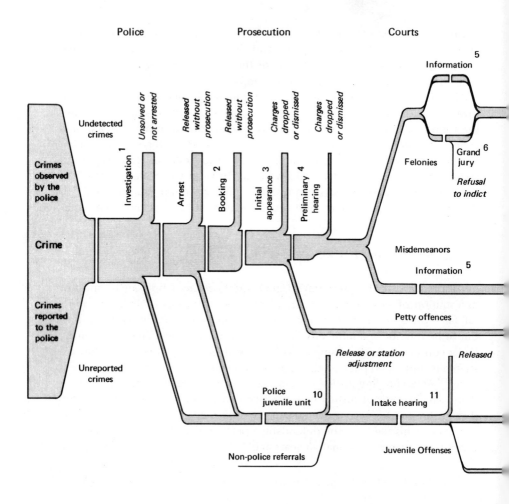

Police   Prosecution   Courts

1 May continue until trial.

2 Administrative record of arrest. First step at which temporary release on bail may be available.

3 Before magistrate, commissioner, or justice of peace. Formal notice of charge, advice of rights. Bail set. Summary trials for petty offenses usually conducted here without further processing.

4 Preliminary testing of evidence against defendant. Charge may be reduced. No separate preliminary hearing for misdemeanors in some systems.

5 Charge filed by prosecutor on basis of information submitted by police or citizens. Alternative to grand jury indictment; often used in felonies, almost always in misdemeanors.

6 Reviews whether Government evidence sufficient to justify trial. Some States have no grand jury system; others seldom use it.

FIGURE 1 A General View of the Criminal Justice System. This chart presents a simple yet comprehensive view of the movement of cases through the criminal justice system. Procedures in individual jurisdictions may vary from the pattern shown here. The differing weights of line, indicating the relative volumes of cases disposed of at various points in the system, is only suggestive because no nationwide data of this sort exist.

Corrections

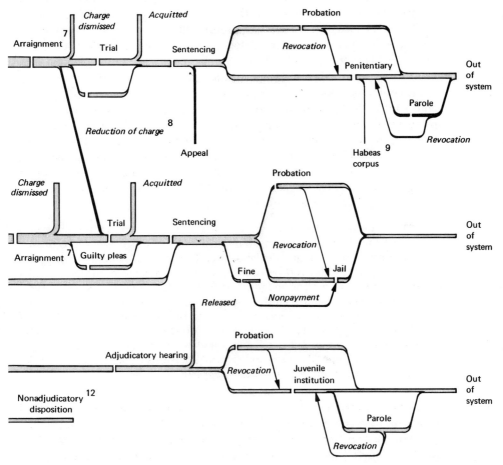

7   Appearance for plea; defendant elects trial by judge or jury (if available); counsel for indigent usually appointed here in felonies. Often not at all in other cases.

8   Charge may be reduced at any time prior to trial in return for plea of guilty or for other reasons.

9   Challenge on constitutional grounds to legality of detention. May be sought at any point in process.

10   Police often hold informal hearings, dismiss or adjust many cases without further processing.

11   Probation officer decides desirability of further court action.

12   Welfare agency, social services, counseling, medical care, etc., for cases where adjudicatory handling not needed.

This chart is taken from pp. 8–9 of The President's Commission on Law Enforcement and Administration of Justice, *The Challenge of Crime in a Free Society* (Washington, D.C.: U.S. Government Printing Office, 1967).

becoming a "criminal": from arrest to trial   83

another, designed to push the accused individual from one stage to another in the operation. Throughout this process, the rights and interests of the alleged offender are secondary to the needs of the machinery.

One of the most incisive commentators of this persuasion is Abraham Blumberg, a criminologist and former defense attorney. He contends that the role of criminal lawyer has a good deal in common with that of the criminal "con man," in that the criminal lawyer is a "double agent" serving the interests of the court more than those of his client.[12] The lawyer, according to Blumberg, enters into "deals" with the prosecutor, agreeing to persuade his client to plead guilty. In turn, the courts often cooperate with criminal lawyers by arranging for continuances so that the attorney can collect his fee from the client. These linkages are not part of the common stereotype of the defense attorney, vigorously endeavoring to gain his client's freedom by whatever trick or stratagem he can devise. On the issue of individual rights and the bureaucratic pressure to get cases dealt with, Blumberg argues:

> To meet production requirements in our criminal courts, a tenuous resolution of the dilemma has emerged: a variety of bureaucratically ordained and controlled shortcuts, deviations, and outright violations of the rules are employed by all court personnel, ranging from lawyers and prosecutors to probation officers and judges. Fearfully anticipating criticism on ethical as well as legal grounds, all the significant participants in the court's structure are bound into an organized system of complicity. The rhetoric of official rules governing the behavior of police, prosecutors, judges, and probation officers is not a reliable guide to their actual behavior, which consists of patterned, covert, and informal evasions of due process in order to meet production requirements.[13]

Blumberg's arguments concerning the lack of individual justice in criminal courts are based on his investigations in New York State. George Cole reports much the same pattern of relationships in the King County (Seattle), Washington Prosecutor's Office.[14] He avers that the various participants in the system are bound together in a pattern of symbiotic relationships:

> The legal system may be viewed as a set of interorganizational exchange relationships analogous to what Long has called a community game. The participants in the legal system (game) share a common territorial field and collaborate for different and particular ends. They interact on a continuing basis as their responsibilities demand contact with other participants in the process. Thus, the need for the cooperation of other participants can have a bearing on the decision to prosecute. A decision not to prosecute a

---

[12]Abraham S. Blumberg, "Criminal Justice in America" in Crime and Justice in America," ed. Jack D. Douglas (Indianapolis: The Bobbs-Merrill Co., 1971), pp. 45–78; Blumberg, Criminal Justice (Chicago: Quadrangle Books, 1967); Blumberg, "Lawyers with Convictions," Trans-action, 4 (July–August 1967), 18–24.

[13]Blumberg, "Criminal Justice in America," p. 51.

[14]George F. Cole, "The Decision to Prosecute," Law and Society Review, 4 (February 1970), 331–43.

narcotics offender may be a move to pressure the United States Attorney's Office to cooperate on another case. It is obvious that bargaining occurs not only between the major actors in a case—the prosecutor and the defense attorney—but also between the clientele groups that are influential in structuring the actions of the prosecuting attorney.[15]

Cole observes that many of the decisions reached within the justice system have little to do with guilt or innocence, individual rights, and the like. The prosecutor may drop some cases where the evidence points strongly to the suspect, and in other instances take to court flimsy cases to quiet public agitation. Then, too, the prosecutor adjusts the flow of cases into court to respond to prison overcrowding and other factors of that kind. Concerning defense attorneys, Cole notes that most of these individuals are not specialists in criminal law but do take some criminal cases along with divorce actions, probate work, and other kinds of legal problems. All of them retain close ties to the prosecutor's office to engage in plea bargaining, which is perhaps the most important single action they perform for their clients.[16]

Clearly, the judicial portion of the criminal justice system falls short of being an organization that dispenses swift and fair justice to persons accused of criminal acts. We shall see in later chapters of this book that the postconviction part of this machinery also leaves much to be desired. Although the purpose of prisons, probation services, and other correctional experiences is to treat and rehabilitate, time serving and punishment remain in most parts of the nation. Let us continue this chapter by examining some of the criminal court system in more detail.

Bail

As we have already observed, one of the concerns in preliminary hearings has to do with the setting of bail. Bail is a sum of money, determined by the judge, which the accused must post to guarantee his appearance in court at a later date. The individual either produces his own money as bail or obtains it from a bail bondsman at a high rate of interest. If he is not allowed bail or cannot obtain bail funds, the person must then remain in jail until his trial. In a good many cases he may languish in a lockup for a number of months before his trial takes place.

The bail practices of American courts have received a great deal of negative commentary.[17] The bail set at preliminary hearings is often considered unrea-

[15]*Ibid.,* p. 332.

[16]*Ibid.,* pp. 338–43. Other studies of criminal lawyers include Jack Ladinsky, "Careers of Lawyers, Law Practice, and Legal Institutions," *American Sociological Review,* 28 (February 1963), 47–54; Jerome E. Carlin, *Lawyers on Their Own* (New Brunswick, N.J.: Rutgers University Press, 1962); Arthur Lewis Wood, *Criminal Lawyer* (New Haven, Conn.: College and University Press, 1967).

[17]Ronald Goldfarb, *Ransom: A Critique of the American Bail System* (New York: Harper & Row, Publishers, 1965); Charles Ares and Herbert Sturz, "Bail and the Indigent Accused," *Crime and Delinquency,* 8 (January 1962), 12–20.

sonably high. An investigation of the accused person's financial status, social stability, or other factors might lead to a low bail figure being set, but such inquiry is rarely held. A second complaint about bail practices is that the ultimate decision on whether an accused awaits trial in jail rather than in the community rests with a private citizen, the bail bondsman, rather than with a court functionary. Finally, bail practices are vulnerable to criticism on the grounds that those persons held in jail unnecessarily suffer severe handicaps as a result. They do not have easy access to lawyers, their entrance into the court in the company of a guard may bias their case with a jury, and, in the event of acquittal, they have undergone incarceration without being guilty of a crime.

Caleb Foote has reported two studies of the operation of the bail process.[18] These investigations took place in Philadelphia in 1953 and in New York City in 1957. Foote's major findings indicate that many defendants were unable to furnish bail even when the amount set was nominal. In the Philadelphia experience, almost one-half of the accused individuals could not post bail and were detained from 50 to 100 days before trial.[19] Furthermore, as the amount of bail increased beyond $1000, decidedly fewer persons managed to secure pretrial release. Foote notes that bail was usually set at such a high figure in serious felony cases that most defendants could not obtain bail. Although some 10 to 20 percent of those defendants confined in jail before trial were not convicted, on the whole, jailed defendants were more likely to be convicted and also received more severe sentences than counterparts freed on bail. Finally, these studies indicate that bail was often used for purposes other than to ensure the defendant's court appearance. For example, persons accused of attacks on policemen either were not offered bail or had an excessive bail figure set in their cases.

One response to these criticisms of bail procedures has taken the form of efforts to have defendants released on their "own recognizance," that is, without posting bail. One of these projects is the Manhattan Bail Project, started in 1961 in New York City.[20] A group of New York University law students interviewed indigent defendants and in many cases were able to secure their release on parole pending trial. The unnecessary character of bail in many cases is apparent in the finding that only three of the 275 persons paroled on the basis of information provided by the bail project failed to appear in court.[21]

A parallel project to that in New York was conducted in a United States district court in Michigan, where about 72 percent of the defendants were

[18]Caleb Foote, "The Bail System and Equal Justice," Federal Probation, 23 (September 1959), 43–48.

[19]Caleb Foote, "Compelling Appearance in Court: Administration of Bail in Philadelphia," University of Pennsylvania Law Review, 102 (June 1954), 1031–79.

[20]Ares and Sturz, "Bail and the Indigent Accused"; see also Frederic Suffet, "Bail Setting: A Study of Courtroom Interaction," Crime and Delinquency, 12 (October 1966), 318–31.

[21]Herbert Sturz, "An Alternative to the Bail System," Federal Probation, 26 (December 1962), 49–53.

released on their "own recognizance." No difference was observed in absconding by bonded and nonbonded persons. Only 12 of 12,400 defendants failed to appear in court.[22] In recent years, a number of other such projects designed to obtain pretrial release for indigent accused persons have been conducted in widely separated parts of the United States.[23]

"PLEA COPPING": PLEADING GUILTY FOR CONSIDERATIONS

Many citizens probably carry around a view of the legal machinery based on movie and television portrayals. This picture characterizes the legal process as usually culminating in a jury trial of the accused person, who has pleaded not guilty. In point of fact, most criminal cases end with guilty pleas by offenders, so trials are the exception rather than the rule. Jerome Skolnick reports that 86 percent of the cases in federal courts between 1960 and 1963 were settled by guilty pleas, whereas such pleas were only slightly less frequent in state courts.[24]

Donald Newman conducted a detailed study of guilty pleas in felony cases in a Wisconsin county and found that over 90 percent of the offenders had been sentenced on a guilty plea, although about a third of them had originally entered pleas of not guilty.[25] In nearly every case, the offense to which an offender pleads guilty is lesser than or different from the original charge or charges.

The incentive to the prosecutor for accepting a guilty plea is readily apparent, for this arrangement allows the state to avoid a costly and lengthy court trial. But what does the accused receive in exchange for a guilty plea? Newman indicates four kinds of bargains offered the offender. Some had reduced charges placed against them. About half the offenders received a "deal" in the form of a reduction in sentence for pleading guilty. A third group got concurrent sentences rather than separate ones for each offense committed. Finally, some suspects had some charges dropped in exchange for a guilty plea.

David Sudnow provides further detail on guilty pleas and allied matters in an investigation carried on in a public defender's office in a metropolitan

---

[24]Jerome H. Skolnick, *Justice Without Trial* (New York: John Wiley & Sons, 1966), pp. 12-15;
[22]Talbot Smith, "A New Approach to the Bail Practice," *Federal Probation*, 21 (March 1965), 3-6.

[23]For a summary of these projects, see Dorothy C. Tompkins, *Bail in the United States, A Bibliography* (Berkeley, Calif.: Institute of Governmental Studies, 1964).

[24]Jerome H. Skolnick, *Justice Without Trial* (New York: John Wiley & Sons, 1966), pp. 12-15; see also the President's Commission on Law Enforcement and Administration of Justice, *Task Force Report*, p. 9. The commission report indicates that negotiated pleas of guilty were responsible for convictions in between 66 and 96 percent of the cases in a sample of different state jurisdictions for which information was available.

[25]Donald J. Newman, "Pleading Guilty tor Considerations: A Study of Bargain Justice," *Journal of Criminal Law, Criminology and Police Science*, 46 (March-April 1956), 780-90.

community in California.[26] The job of the public defender, an employee of the county, is to defend indigent accused persons in criminal trials. The public defender system has grown as a replacement for legal aid societies and as a device to ensure that low-income persons will not be deprived of legal counsel.

Sudnow's discussion includes the distinction between "necessarily-included-lesser-offenses" and "situationally-included-lesser-offenses." Assault is an example of the first category. It must occur prior to battery in that assault refers to menacing gestures, such as verbal threats, and battery consists of carrying out the threats. Similarly, second-degree homicide is necessarily included in first-degree murder because the latter involves premeditation along with all the other ingredients of second-degree homicide. Situationally included offenses are crimes that usually occur with another law violation, even though the one is not incorporated in the other in the criminal statutes. Drunkenness as an accompaniment of vehicular homicides illustrates this category.

At first glance, we might suppose that most reduced charges against offenders would involve necessarily included or situationally included lesser offenses. But this is not the case, at least in the situation that Sudnow observed. Instead, both the prosecutor and the public defender act out their roles with a shared conception of "normal crimes." For example, both perceive that most rapes grow out of flirtations between persons who have been drinking and have engaged in sexual byplay. These generalizations about the way offenses usually occur constitute a classification of "normal crimes."

When they are bargaining about a "normal crime," the prosecutor and public defender cast about for a reduced charge that will meet the ends of justice and provide an incentive to the accused to plead guilty. Quite often the offense they eventually settle on is neither situationally or necessarily included in the crime with which the person was originally charged. Sudnow notes that both the prosecutor and the public defender strive to obtain a guilty plea wherever possible so as to avoid a trial. But each party is concerned that the defendant "receive his due" in the way of a penalty. The reduced charge must be of such a nature that the offender will plead guilty to it, but it must also lead to a sentence the person "deserves."

The day-to-day operations of the public defender system and the prosecutor's office depart markedly from the image of the combative struggle between the state and the counsel for the accused. Sudnow observed that the public defender views his interests as close to those of the prosecutor—to move offenders in an orderly fashion through the legal machinery. The public defender assumes at the outset that the persons he serves are guilty. His interviews with his clients are designed to determine whether the person's offense

---

[26]David Sudnow, "Normal Crimes: Sociological Features of the Penal Code in a Public Defender Office," *Social Problems*, 12 (Winter 1965), 255–76.

is a "normal" one so that they can reach a bargain with the prosecutor. In most "normal" cases, the public defender persuades the accused individuals to plead guilty. However, the prosecutor does not solicit or accept guilty pleas from those lawbreakers who have engaged in crimes that are atypical and not "normal."

TRIAL BY JURY

The Structure of Jury Trials[27]

The right to jury trial is Constitutionally guaranteed in all states in cases of serious crimes and in some states for minor crimes. Although a jury trial can be waived in favor of trial before a judge, relatively few defendants exercise this option.

The trial jury (or *petit jury*) of twelve citizens is drawn from a larger panel or group of potential jurors previously selected for jury duty by a jury commissioner or court clerk. In principle, jury duty is an obligation of all citizens who meet some minimal qualifications, such as citizenship and literacy. Conversely, blacks or other groups of persons are not supposed to be excluded from jury duty, for juries are intended to be representative of the larger community. A specific jury is assembled out of a panel of potential jurors through a selection process in which both the prosecutor and defense attorney participate. Both are allowed to "challenge for cause" prospective jurors thought to be unfit for jury duty. Potential jurors are challenged on such grounds as being related to the defendant or having already formed an opinion of the guilt or innocence of the accused. The presiding judge excuses these persons from jury duty. In addition, potential jurors are the target of *peremptory challenges*. Both the prosecutor and defense attorney have a limited number of these challenges, for which no reason has to be stated.

After the completion of jury selection, the prosecutor makes an opening statement, outlines the evidence he expects to introduce against the accused, and usually the defense presents opening remarks as well. Following these statements, the prosecutor presents the state's evidence, and the defense attorney cross-examines witnesses. When the prosecution has completed its case, the accused may make a motion for acquittal on the grounds of insufficient evidence. If the judge deems the evidence sufficient to proceed, the defense then has its opportunity to present evidence to undermine the state's case. After presenting the case for the accused, the defense may move for a directed verdict of acquittal by the judge.

If the judge does not direct a verdict of acquittal, the trial moves to final arguments to the jury by both sides. The judge gives his instructions to the

[27]Karlen, *The Citizen in Court*, pp. 48–54.

jury, and the jury retires behind closed doors for secret deliberations. If the jury brings in a verdict of not guilty, the case is closed forever. But if the accused is found guilty, his attorney may move for a new trial, arguing that the trial proceedings erred at some point. If the judge does not grant this motion, the defendant is sentenced and becomes the legal entity, a criminal.

Research on Jury Behavior

The jury study conducted by the University of Chicago Law School has enriched the research literature on the workings of various segments of the law enforcement and correctional machinery.[28] The volume that resulted from this investigation is a goldmine of information concerning the behavior of criminal trial juries in the United States. Harry Kalven and Hans Zeisel note that controversy has surrounded the jury system almost from its inception. On the negative side, critics have argued that the process of jury selection works to load juries with ignorant persons incapable of making sound judgments. The spokesmen for the jury system have been equally emphatic in asserting that juries act as a check on judges who might otherwise apply the law in a heavy-handed fashion. However, most of this debate has consisted of opinion rather than hard facts.[29] The Kalven and Zeisel research has gone some distance toward illuminating this quarrel with empirical findings.

How frequent are jury trials? Kalven and Zeisel estimate that there were about 60,000 trials carried through to a verdict in the United States in 1955, with an additional group of 20,000 jury trials begun but not carried to a jury verdict. Although these figures indicate that jury trials are numerous, such trials are nonetheless relatively uncommon occurrences. As previously noted, guilty pleas represent the most usual ending of charges against an individual. Similarly, Kalven and Zeisel note that 75 percent of the cases of major crimes in the United Staves terminate with guilty pleas, whereas 10 percent result in bench trials (trial before a judge) and 15 percent eventuate in jury trials. In addition jury trials are largely an American device, for it appears that over 80 percent of the criminal jury trials in the world take place in this country. However, jury trials do not occur at the same rate in all fifty states. In Connecticut, for example, where jury trials are allowed only in cases of major crimes, the number of jury trials is quite small, whereas in jurisdictions where jury trials are available in a wide variety of offenses such trials occur much more commonly.[30]

Kalven and Zeisel's evidence on jury behavior came from questionnaires completed by a sample of 555 judges from throughout the United States. These judges provided information on 3,576 trials over which they had presided.[31]

[28]Harry Kalven, Jr., and Hans Zeisel, *The American Jury* (Boston: Little, Brown and Co., 1966).
[29]*Ibid.*, pp. 3–11.
[30]*Ibid.*, pp. 12–32.
[31]*Ibid.*, pp. 33–44.

Table 2[32] VERDICT OF JURY AND JUDGE

		Jury Verdict Rendered		
		Acquits	Convicts	Hangs
Judge's Decision	Acquits	13.4%	2.2%	1.1%
	Convicts	16.9%	62.0%	4.4%

The investigators asked a large number of questions concerning the judges' evaluations of the outcomes of these trials. For the most part, these queries had to do with whether the judge was in accord with the decision of the jury; if not, the reasons for his disagreement were sought.

One major finding of this research centered about the convergence of jury decisions with the views of judges. Table 2 indicates the pattern of jury–judge verdicts. The statistics, along with other findings of this research, strongly indicate that juries do usually render sound and reasonable verdicts.

As Table 2 indicates, the judges contended that they would have rendered the same decision as the jury in over 75 percent of the cases. Also, the instances of disagreement are heavily weighted in one direction, with juries acting in a more lenient fashion than judges. In few instances would judges have acquitted persons convicted by juries.

Judges may dispute the decisions of juries in ways additional to the matter of guilt or innocence. Kalven and Zeisel note that the judges in the study sometimes disagreed with the juries on the charge for which a person was convicted or the penalty handed down. These instances of disagreement, when added to discordant views on guilt or innocence, brought the proportion of disagreements between judge and juries to 33.8 percent.[33]

What are the issues over which judges and juries disagree? Kalven and Zeisel discovered a large number of specific reasons for disagreements, which can be grouped into five major categories: sentiments on the law, sentiments on the defendant, issues of evidence, facts only the judge knew, and disparity of counsel. Disagreements revolving about the law had to do with instances of the sort where juries took into account contributory negligence on the part of the victim, even though the law makes no such allowance. For example, in rape cases, the rape victim has often behaved in a manner that provoked the offender into sexual aggressiveness. Similarly, sentiments about defendants concerned characteristics of these persons that influenced judge or jury opinions. Disparity of counsel refers to cases in which the superiority of either the prosecutor or the defense attorney contributed to a trial outcome. Kalven and Zeisel indicate that issues of evidence are at the heart of about half the judge–jury disagreements, whereas 29 percent of them were based on sen-

[32]Ibid., p. 56.
[33]Ibid., pp. 59–62.

timents on the law. Sentiments about defendants, facts known only to the judge, and disparity of counsel entered into only a few of the disagreements.[34]

The phenomenon of judge–jury disagreement on evidential grounds is complicated. According to Kalven and Zeisel, judges and juries disagree infrequently when evidence alone is at issue; rather, they disagree when evidential questions occur accompanied by sentiments. They aver that: "The sentiment gives direction to the resolution of the evidentiary doubt; the evidentiary doubt provides a favorable condition for a response to the sentiment."[35]

Throughout Kalven and Zeisel's detailed report of findings, juries come out remarkably well. When disagreements arise on questions of evidence, the views of juries are reasonable. On the whole, judges rarely characterized juries as gullible.[36] Juries are occasionally willing to entertain greater "reasonable doubt" about cases than are judges, but the magistrates do not view the juries as having excessively loose standards.[37]

Juries bring to bear a variety of sentiments about the legal codes as they go about their decision making. In some instances, they incorporate into their decisions considerations about self-defense not found in the statutes. Thus, they sometimes acquit individuals who have harmed persons who had earlier acted violently toward them, even though the offender's actions were retaliatory rather than in self-defense.[38] Juries also condition their evaluation of evidence when they perceive contributory negligence on the part of the victims, even though the law makes no such allowance.[39] Juries sometimes acquit individuals when the evidence demonstrates their guilt because the jury regarded the offense as too trivial to be punished.[40] For example, in a case involving indecent exposure before an adult female, the jury might find it difficult to perceive real social harm in the misbehavior. Other kinds of jury sentiments that intrude into decision making include unpopular laws, such as game laws, where juries are loath to convict offenders. Juries also occasionally bring in verdicts that do not accord with the evidence when they think that the defendant has already received an adequate measure of punishment of some sort or regard the threatened punishment as out of keeping with the act.[41]

A final matter regarding the Kalven and Zeisel research is the "cross-over phenomenon." This term refers to those infrequent instances in which judges would have acquitted persons whom juries had convicted. These cases appeared to involve such factors as the unattractiveness of the accused person, to which the jury attended but the judge ignored. Cross-overs were sometimes

[34]Ibid., pp. 104–117.
[35]Ibid., p. 165.
[36]Ibid., pp. 168–81.
[37]Ibid., pp. 182–90.
[38]Ibid., pp. 221–41.
[39]Ibid., pp. 242–57.
[40]Ibid., pp. 258–85.
[41]Ibid., pp. 286–312.

attributable to the jury's placing less faith in the credibility of the accused person's testimony than did the judge.[42]

We have not exhausted the material in this jury research volume. The Kalven and Zeisel study is truly an important one in advancing our comprehension of the social workings of the legal apparatus.

Other studies dealing with juries have been conducted, usually using groups of individuals who engage in simulated jury deliberations after having listened to a recording of a jury trial. Fred Strodtbeck, Rita James, and Charles Hawkins indicate that persons of higher social status are often the ones who dominate jury interaction.[43] In addition, Rita James Simon indicates that persons who were presented with psychiatric testimony deferred to the psychiatrists as experts, but they did not reach their decision on the basis of this expert opinion.[44] In only 13 percent of the trials before sixty-eight juries was a verdict of not guilty by reason of insanity reached. Finally, Simon and Linda Mahan conducted some interesting experiments with juries, asking persons to make a probability estimate of the likelihood that a suspect was guilty or not guilty before they came to a final decision.[45] Those jurors who went through this process were less likely to find a person guilty than were those jurors who simply deliberated the guilty–not guilty question.[46]

THE JUVENILE COURT

The largest portion of this book is concerned with adult criminality rather than juvenile delinquency and juvenile delinquents. That is, our analysis centers on the criminal courts and persons processed through them rather than on juvenile courts and juvenile lawbreakers. Juvenile courts and juvenile delinquents are usually the subject of separate books and college courses from those dealing with adult or criminal offenders. But at the same time, we should acknowledge that many of the individuals who get caught up in the criminal justice machinery are youthful violators. As Chapter Five indicates in more detail, over half of the police arrests in the United States in 1970 involved individuals under twenty-five years of age. In many of the following pages, we shall onserve that many criminal offenders began their lawbreaking activities as juveniles, so we shall have occasion to touch on much of the theorizing and research that has dealt with juvenile delinquents.

In any survey of the criminal justice machinery in American society, we

[42]*Ibid.*, pp. 375-94.

[43]Fred L. Strodtbeck, Rita M. James, and Charles Hawkins, "Social Status in Jury Deliberations," *American Sociological Review*, 22 (December 1957), 713-19. See also Rita M. James, "Status and Competence of Jurors," *American Journal of Sociology*, 64 (May 1959), 565-66.

[44]Rita James Simon, "Jurors' Evaluation of Expert Psychiatric Testimony," in *The Sociology of Law*, ed. Simon (San Francisco: Chandler Publishing Co., 1968), pp. 314-28.

[45]Rita James Simon and Linda Mahan, "Quantifying Burdens of Proof: A View from the Bench, the Jury, and the Classroom," *Law and Society Review*, 5 (February 1971), 319-30.

[46]*Ibid.*, pp. 319-24.

cannot arbitrarily separate juvenile offenders from adult ones, and we cannot entirely ignore the juvenile court system. Let us briefly mention the juvenile justice system sketched in Figure 1.

The American juvenile court grew out of a series of developments in the 1800s, designed to mitigate the severity of punishment handed out to juveniles.[47] The first juvenile court was created in Cook County, Illinois, in 1899, and within ten years, twenty states had created juvenile court laws; by 1945, court legislation had been extended to all the states.

The motives of those who sponsored the juvenile court movement were mixed, but generally their intent was to create a structure that would minister to the needs of children, treating them rather than punishing them. Omnibus juvenile delinquency statutes were created in all the states, giving the court jurisdiction over juveniles who were "wayward," "ungovernable," and the like, as well as those who had violated criminal laws.[48] A new language and special procedures for juvenile justice were concocted. A "petition," rather than an "information" or an "indictment," is filed alleging that a juvenile is a delinquent. The youngster is housed in "juvenile hall" rather than in jail, and he is "adjudicated" rather than "convicted." Finally, he is supposed to be treated according to his individual needs rather than punished for his lawbreaking.

Much commentary on juvenile courts in the past has centered on the failure of the states to implement juvenile court philosophy by providing adequate probation personnel, diagnostic and psychiatric services, and other arrangements that would allow the court to carry out its rehabilitative mandate. In short, criticism of the court has centered on "bread and butter" issues, noting that these organizations represent inadequately fabricated social machinery.[49]

Although there has been much dialogue on the juvenile court, studies of the actual operations of these tribunals have been relatively few in number. However, a collection of investigations dealing with the factors in police referral of youths to the court is now available.[50]

Aaron Cicourel has studied the workings of the juvenile court and strongly suggests that the court often inadvertently pressures youthful offenders in the direction of more rather than less deviance.[51] Robert Emerson has provided a research report on a juvenile court in a northern United States metropolitan area.[52] His book provides a relatively dismal view of the court, observing that it is deficient in resources and that it provides assembly-line handling of offenders rather than individualized treatment. Finally, Frank Scarpitti and Richard Stephenson have examined the flow of 1,200 cases within a juvenile court

[47]The origins of the juvenile court are discussed in Don C. Gibbons, Delinquent Behavior (Englewood Cliffs, N.J.: Prentice-Hall, 1970), pp. 5–12; Anthony M. Platt, The Child Savers (Chicago: University of Chicago Press, 1969).

[48]Delinquency laws are discussed in Gibbons, Delinquent Behavior, pp. 5–12.

[49]Juvenile courts in operation are discussed in ibid., pp. 47–58.

[50]See Chapter Three, pp. 60–63; ibid., pp. 33–46.

[51]Aaron V. Cicourel, The Social Organization of Juvenile Justice (New York: John Wiley & Sons, 1968).

[52] Robert M. Emerson, Judging Delinquents (Chicago: Aldine Publishing Co., 1969).

in a large eastern county.[53] Their data indicate that judicial sorting of delinquents into those who receive probation, institutional commitment, or some other disposition is not capricious. Instead, most of these decisions revolve around assessments of delinquency risk so that the most socially disadvantaged, delinquent, and psychologically atypical boys get sent off to training schools.[54]

The pendulum of opinion has begun to swing back from early criticisms of the court for not treating enough juveniles to cautionary injunctions against overuse of the court machinery. A growing number of jurists, sociologists, and others have begun to question whether the court can ever manage to serve in a *parens patriae* role on a grand scale, diverting misbehaving youths into law-abiding pathways.[55] Those who express this kind of cynical realism contend that the juvenile court can never be made into more than a crude piece of social apparatus. On this point, Edwin Lemert remarks:

Neither the Spartan gymnasium, nor the Russian creches, nor the Israeli kibbutz nurseries, nor scientifically run children's homes have been found to successfully duplicate the sociopsychological mystique which nurtures children into stable adults. Explicit recognition of this might very well preface the juvenile court codes and statutes of the land. At the same time it might be well to delete entirely from such laws pious injunctions that "care, custody and discipline of children under the control of the juvenile court shall approximate that which they would receive from their parents" which taken literally becomes meaningless either as ideal or reality. Neither the modern state nor an harassed juvenile court judge is a father; a halfway house is not a home; a reformatory cell is not a teenager's bedroom; a juvenile hall counselor is not a dutch uncle; a cottage matron is not a mother. This does not mean that the people referred to should not be or are not kindly and dedicated, but rather that they are first and foremost members of organizations, enforcers of superimposed rules. Where conflicts arise between the interests of a youth and those of the organization to which these functionaries are bureaucratically responsible there is no pattern of action which can predict that they will observe an order of value satisfaction favorable to the youth's interest.[56]

The critics of the court do not advocate that we abandon it, but they do argue that we should entertain only modest expectations for it. We should not expect the court to rehabilitate all those wards who proceed through it. Then, too, the critics contend that we should discard omnibus provisions in

[53]Frank R. Scarpitti and Richard M. Stephenson, "Juvenile Court Dispositions: Factors in the Decision-Making Process," *Crime and Delinquency*, 17 (April 1971), 142–51.

[54]For a collection of reports on juvenile court operations, including the working styles of judges and probation officers, see Peter G. Garabedian and Don C. Gibbons, eds., *Becoming Delinquent* (Chicago: Aldine Publishing Co., 1970).

[55]Edwin M. Lemert, "The Juvenile Court—Quest and Realities," in the President's Commission on Law Enforcement and Administration of Justice, *Task Force Report: Juvenile Delinquency and Youth Crime* (Washington, D.C.: U.S. Government Printing Office, 1967), pp. 91–105.

[56]*Ibid.*, p. 92

delinquency laws and at the same time make due process standards for court processing more stringent.

These criticisms of the court have not gone unnoticed. Thus, in California in 1961, a number of revisions of juvenile court law were enacted, providing for closer adherence to standards of due process.[57] More recently, the United States Supreme Court has handed down several rulings requiring individual courts to adhere more closely to standards of due process. The 1967 decision in *Kent* v. *United States* centered about the practice of remand of some youths to the criminal court. The *Kent* ruling asserts that when they are being considered for transfer to an adult court, juveniles are entitled to a hearing, assistance of legal counsel, access to records, and statement of the judge's reasons for waiving juvenile court jurisdiction.

Another 1967 Supreme Court decision was *In re Gault*, in which a youth was sent off to a training school as an outgrowth of an extremely informal court hearing. In this case, the court held that due process requires that juveniles be provided with notice of charges, legal counsel, right of confrontation and cross-examination of witnesses, protection against self-incrimination, transcript of the hearing, and right of appeal. These provisions are among the rights enjoyed by adults in criminal courts.

The most recent Supreme Court decision is *In re Winship*, holding that proof beyond a reasonable doubt, which the due process clause requires in criminal trials, is among the essentials of due process and fair treatment required during the adjudicatory stage when a juvenile is charged with an act that would constitute a crime if committed by an adult. This standard replaces the "preponderance of evidence" rule (used in most courts in the past), requiring a quantum of proof similar to that required in civil court actions. As a result of the *Winship* decision, courts cannot easily exercise wardship over juveniles.

We saw in Chapter Three that Supreme Court rulings regarding due process for adults in the hands of the police are sometimes ignored or circumvented in practice. In a similar way, we might wonder about the pace at which these rulings of the court will spread to the individual courts.[58]

Some evidence on this point comes from Lemert's inquiry into the implementation of 1961 changes in California juvenile court procedures.[59] The new law required split hearings, with the court jurisdictional part being conducted separately from the dispositional portion. Four years later in 1965, Lemert discovered that two-thirds of the judges studied were still reading social inves-

---

[57]For a detailed discussion of these developments, see Edwin M. Lemert, *Social Action and Legal Change: Revolution Within the Juvenile Court* (Chicago: Aldine Publishing Co., 1970).

[58]For a general discussion of the implications of court rulings, see Lyell Henry Carver and Paul Anthony White, "Constitutional Safeguards for the Juvenile Offender: Implications of Recent Supreme Court Decisions," *Crime and Delinquency*, 14 (January 1968), 63-72. For an example of the way one court has dealt with the *Gault* ruling, see William H. Ralston, Jr., "Intake; Informal Disposition or Adversary Proceeding?" *Crime and Delinquency*, 17 (April 1971), 160-67.

[59]Lemert, "The Juvenile Court—Quest and Realities."

tigation reports on youths prior to the adjudicatory hearing. The development of bifurcated hearings was designed to eliminate that practice. Then, too, Lemert discovered that the use of legal counsel varied widely from county to county, even though by law juveniles were guaranteed lawyers.

Several studies have been produced on the *Gault* ruling and its implementation. Charles Reasons observed that in Franklin County (Columbus), Ohio, the number of lawyers in court and dismissals of cases increased in the post–*Gault* period, whereas the number of cases reaching adjudication declined.[60] Obviously, the *Gault* ruling had some consequences for court practice in Ohio. On the other hand, Norman Lefstein, Vaughn Stapleton, and Lee Teitelbaum's study, conducted in three large eastern cities, indicates that the extent of full compliance with due process requirements in the courts in these three cities was relatively slight.[61] Court officials often failed to advise juveniles of their rights or did so in an unanimated fashion that tended to dissuade many youths from asserting their rights.

The *Winship* decision is of too recent origin for us to assess the speed with which it will be implemented. However, in Oregon in 1971, legislation was introduced to bring the state standard of proof in line with that in the ruling. The foregoing material indicates that although recent Supreme Court rulings may not be fully implemented overnight, in the long run they promise to bring about drastic reforms in juvenile court procedure.

SUMMARY

This chapter concludes our overview of the workings of the parts of the law enforcement machinery through which individuals come to be tagged as criminals or delinquents. In the next chapter, we turn to the epidemiological facts that this enforcement structure generates, as well as to some data concerning those persons who commit offenses but manage to stay undetected by the police.

[60]Charles E. Reasons, "*Gault*: Procedural Change and Substantive Effect," *Crime and Delinquency*, 16 (April 1970), 163–71.

[61]Norman Lefstein, Vaughn Stapleton, and Lee Teitelbaum, "In Search of Juvenile Justice: *Gault* and its Implementation," *Law and Society Review*, 3 (May 1969), 491–562; see also David Duffee and Larry Siegel, "The Organization Man: Legal Counsel in the Juvenile Court," *Criminal Law Bulletin*, 7 (July–August 1971), 544–53. In a study in a New York county these investigators found that offenders represented by lawyers in a juvenile court received more severe dispositions than those unrepresented by legal counsel. Apparently, the juvenile court in question was careful to obtain lawyers for those offenders that were regarded as in need of incarceration. In these cases, legal counsel shielded the judge from criticisms of the decision to incarcerate.

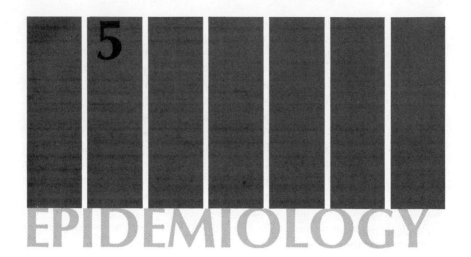

5

EPIDEMIOLOGY

The opening remarks in Chapter One indicated that the study of criminality must address itself to epidemiological questions at an early point. We want to identify the number of offenders in society, the various forms their offenses take, their social characteristics, and other features of lawbreaking and law-breakers. This chapter is concerned with such matters.

We should acknowledge at the outset that epidemiological ventures are inevitably frustrating and unsatisfactory. For one thing, the agencies that process known violators have often been more interested in distorting the epidemiological facts than in reporting them accurately. However, the basic problem confronting persons who amass statistical facts on criminality is that most lawbreakers take pains to keep their violations secret. Estimates of the extent of illegal behavior must be made from data on those offenses known to the authorities. This is a small and perhaps biased sample of total crime, and gauging the relationship between the two is exceedingly difficult.[1]

This chapter centers exclusively on epidemiological observations, but a number of the following chapters are concerned with the facts of crime distribution. In particular, Chapters Thirteen, Fourteen, and Seventeen examine statistics on forms of lawbreaking rarely reported to the police, such as gambling and "white-collar crime."

SOURCES AND PROBLEMS OF CRIMINOLOGICAL DATA

Sources of Information

On a few occasions, criminological investigators have endeavored to discover the extent of criminality in American society through self-reports of citizens. In these studies, which we will make use of later in this chapter, the researchers

---

For other general summaries of crime rates and allied matters see Edwin H. Sutherland and Donald R. Cressey, *Principles of Criminology*, 8th ed. (Philadelphia: J. B. Lippincott Co., 1970), pp. 25–47; The President's Commission on Law Enforcement and Administration of Justice, *The Challenge of Crime in a Free Society* (Washington, D.C.: U.S. Government Printing Office, 1967), pp. 17–53.

have asked citizens to acknowledge the illegal acts they have performed. However, the more common index used to estimate the magnitude of crime in society has been constructed from statistics concerning crimes reported to the police, persons arrested, and other reports of this sort.

Official figures and reports are of several kinds. The Children's Bureau of the United States Department of Health, Education and Welfare gathers national statistics on juvenile delinquents. Since 1955, this bureau has collected data on juveniles reported to juvenile courts from a national sample of such courts. The Federal Bureau of Prisons within the United States Department of Justice compiles figures regarding the number of individuals incarcerated in prisons each year. These data are reported in *National Prisoner Statistics*. Additionally, the National Office of Vital Statistics collects information on homicides through the records of coroners in the United States, reporting this information in *Vital Statistics in the United States*. A number of state agencies gather and publish data on criminality, which criminologists use. The state of California has the best developed social bookkeeping system of this kind, and material from publications of statistical agencies in that state will be used throughout this book.

The Federal Bureau of Investigation gathers the most widely-used data on American criminality, which is reported annually in *Crime in the United States*. Statistics include "crimes known to the police" for seven major offenses, which comprise the bureau's Crime Index. Reports from about 8,000 towns and cities in the United States are collated to provide Crime Index information about nearly 91 percent of the total population. In addition to figures on index crimes known to the police, the FBI also gathers and publishes information regarding arrests for nonindex crime.[2]

Problems of Official Data

Crime statistics are among the most unreliable and questionable social facts, as a number of authorities have pointed out. For example, Edwin Sutherland and Donald Cressey have indicated that crimes known to the police constitute only a fraction of all offenses. Moreover, the ratio of known illegal acts to committed criminal acts varies from offense to offense. Variations in legal codes from one jurisdiction to another reduce the possibility of meaningful statistical comparisons between areas and communities. Sutherland and Cressey also note that police agencies have not always reported statistics honestly. They cite the case of Chicago, in which robberies reported by the police increased from 1,263 in 1928 to 14,544 in 1931, whereas burglaries jumped from

[2]For history and critique of the *Uniform Crime Reports*, see Marvin E. Wolfgang, "Uniform Crime Reports: A Critical Appraisal," *University of Pennsylvania Law Review*, 111 (April 1963), 708–38; see also Paul Ward, " 'Careers in Crime': The F.B.I. Story," *Journal of Research in Crime and Delinquency*, 7 (July 1970), 207–18; Leroy C. Gould, "Crime and Its Impact in an Affluent Society," in *Crime and Justice in American Society*, ed. Jack D. Douglas (Indianapolis: The Bobbs-Merrill Co., 1971), pp. 81–118.

879 to 18,689 within the same period. Clearly, these changes were due more to alterations in reporting practices than anything else.[3]

The report of The President's Commission on Law Enforcement and Administration of Justice provides some more recent evidence on police tampering with statistics. The report discusses an instance in Philadelphia in 1953, in which the police reported 28,560 index crimes, negligent manslaughter offenses, and cases of larceny under fifty dollars. This figure represented an increase of 70 percent over that for 1951, but the sudden jump was a result of modifications in reporting procedures rather than an increase in crime. An even more dramatic case of reporting problems had to do with Chicago, which from 1935 to 1950 reported many more burglaries and robberies than did New York City, even though it had only about one-half the population of New York City.[4]

The President's Commission report discusses in some detail the factors implicated in variations in crime reporting practices. The commission suggests that relatively more offenses are now being subjected to official attention, so they turn up in official statistics more often than was formerly the case. The changing expectations of slum area citizens may have made them less tolerant of lawbreaking and more likely to complain to the police. In turn, the professionalization of police agencies may make them more likely to take official actions against offenders rather than to handle violators informally.[5] Citizens may be quicker to inform the police of thefts than they once were, because of the belief that theft insurance policies require that offenses be reported to law enforcement authorities. On the other hand, the Commission avers that police manipulation of crime statistics continues to create problems in the interpretation of official data. According to the commission report:

The reporting problem arises at least in part from the tendency of some cities, noted in 1931 by the Wickersham Commission, to "use these reports in order to advertise their freedom from crime as compared with other municipalities." This tendency has apparently not yet been fully overcome. It sometimes arises from political pressure outside the police department and sometimes from the desire of the police to appear to be doing a good job of keeping the crime rate down. Defective or inefficient recording

[3]Sutherland and Cressey, *Principles of Criminology*, p. 28.

[4]The President's Commission on Law Enforcement and Administration of Justice, *The Challenge of Crime in a Free Society* pp. 24–27.

[5]Wilson reported precisely this difference for two juvenile operations in separate police departments. In one the juvenile officers were well-trained, and in the other the officers were untrained in juvenile work. In the professionalized department, more juveniles were processed officially than in the less professional force. Wilson asserts that the professional training of the officers made them more likely to be stringent with the offenders than were the untrained officers. Also, in the professionalized department, the juvenile bureau was centered at headquarters rather than dispersed in precincts. The effect of this arrangement was to encourage policemen to take official action. See James Q. Wilson, "The Police and the Delinquent in Two Cities," in *Controlling Delinquents*, ed. Stanton Wheeler (New York: John Wiley & Sons, 1967), pp. 9–30.

practices may also prevent crimes reported by citizens from becoming a part of the record.[6]

Those who would generalize about the total population of offenders on the basis of official statistics have usually taken a pessimistic view toward these data. For example, Sutherland and Cressey advise us:

> Ordinarily, a statistical index, such as a "cost of living index," is a compilation of fluctuations in a sample of items taken from the whole; the relationship to the whole is known, and the index serves as a convenient shortcut to a sufficient approximation of variation in the whole. But in crime statistics the rate as indicated by any set of figures cannot be a sample, for the whole cannot be specified. Both the true rate and the relationship between the true rate and any "index" of this rate are capricious "dark figures" which vary with changes in police policies, court policies, and public opinions. The variations in this "dark figure" in crime statistics makes it almost fookhardy to attempt a comparison of crime rates of various cities, and it is hazardous even to compare national rates or the rates of a given city or state in a given year with the rates of the same jurisdiction in a different year. International comparisons are even more difficult.[7]

Some investigators have argued that we should study official statistics for what they tell us about the processes and procedures of official labeling agencies in the correctional apparatus.[8] In this view, the official statistics are not a defective and biased representation of "true crime" but are accurate indicators of the workings of official agencies, which go about isolating and labeling some individuals as deviants and lawbreakers. In other words, the real deviants and criminals in modern societies are those individuals enforcement and control organizations have identified as such. Similarly, this argument holds that sociologists should concentrate on the activities of these agencies, including the business of how these structures go about identifying and processing their clientele.

Jerome Skolnick provides an illustration of sociological analysis of statistics making. He points out that the clearance rate concerning offenses the police solve is subject to a good deal of manipulation. Of the offenses reported to them, policemen can classify a number as "unfounded," thereby increasing the percentage of offenses cleared. Also, clearance of a case may mean that the police have arrested someone, or it may mean that the officers have persuaded an offender apprehended for another crime to "cop out" to a series of hitherto unsolved cases.[9]

[6]The President's Commission on Law Enforcement and Administration of Justice, *The Challenge of Crime in a Free Society*, p. 27.

[7]Sutherland and Cressey, *Principles of Criminology*, p. 25.

[8]John I. Kitsuse and Aaron V. Cicourel, "A Note on the Uses of Official Statistics," *Social Problems*, 11 (Fall 1963), 131–39.

[9]Jerome H. Skolnick, *Justice Without Trial* (New York: John Wiley & Sons, 1966), pp. 164–81.

The suggestion that the sociologist treat crime and delinquency statistics as primary sociological phenomena for study has considerable merit. However, criminologists will probably also continue to grapple with the problem of gauging the extent of total crime from the data on offenses known to authorities. In short, the study of statistics making should go hand in hand with efforts to assess the magnitude of criminal acts, including those acts known to agencies and those unreported and undetected.

Another problem with crime statistics, even if they are carefully and consistently amassed, is that they are often misused. Most crime statistics are presented in terms of rates for the *total* population rather than computed for the population groups most usually involved in lawbreaking. In a situation where the component group of young individuals is increasing disproportionately in the general population, we expect an increase in total crime, in that young persons are most frequently involved in crime. But in this case, the crime *rates* for young persons might not be increasing; that is, the amount of crime among youthful individuals might simply be increasing at the same pace as the increase in the size of this population group. However, when crime rates are calculated in terms of the total population, a misleading impression could emerge, suggesting that the extent of lawbreaking is outstripping the growth of the population.[10]

Other students of crime data have suggested that we might portray crime patterns more realistically if we relate statistics on offenses to changes in the supply of "victims" of various kinds. For example, Leroy Gould has observed that although rates for auto thefts and bank robberies computed on the basis of population have been increasing in recent decades, the rates of occurrence of these offenses in terms of units of property available to be stolen have decreased.[11] In other words, the number of auto thefts and bank robberies has not increased as markedly as has the number of registered motor vehicles or the amount of cash in banks available to be stolen. Although these kinds of rate computations are unfamiliar ones to laymen, they are, perhaps, more accurate indicators of the seriousness of crime than are conventional rates.

SOME DIMENSIONS OF KNOWN CRIME

The Extent of Known Crime

As indicated earlier, the FBI Crime Index is made up of seven major felonies; the FBI collects information regarding the number of these offenses known to the police. These seven felonies were chosen to comprise the Crime Index

[10]One case in point of this situation is found in Roland Chilton and Adele Spielberger, "Is Delinquency Increasing? Age Structure and the Crime Rate," Social Forces, 17 (March 1971), 487–93. These investigators indicated that most of the increase in juvenile court cases in Florida between 1958 and 1967 was attributable to changes in the age structure of that state.

[11]Gould, "Crime and Its Impact in an Affluent Society"; Gould, "The Changing Structure of Property Crime in an Affluent Society," Social Forces, 48 (September 1969), 50–59.

because they are types of criminality likely to be reported to the police when they occur. Table 3 shows the number for each of these index crimes reported in 1970.

The President's Commission on Law Enforcement and Administration of Justice has provided some further evidence regarding the nature and extent of serious crimes in the United States. The commission's report indicates that a survey of 297 robberies in Washington, D.C. showed that injury was inflicted upon the victims in about one-fourth of the cases. Injuries were caused to victims in large proportions of other cases, too. The commission concluded that the likelihood of serious personal attack of any American in a given year is about 1 in 550. In the view of the commission, the risk of a personal attack is high enough to warrant concern on the part of all Americans.[12]

As previously mentioned, the FBI collects nationwide statistics on arrests, rather than on crimes known to the police, for nonindex crimes. These two kinds of data are difficult to match, in that the ratios between crimes known to the police and arrests vary. About 90 percent of known murders culminate in arrests, whereas only about 20 percent of known larcenies are solved by arrests. The FBI indicates that, in 1970, 86 percent of all known murders were cleared by arrest, whereas the figure for negligent manslaughter was 81 percent. Forcible rapes were cleared in 56 percent of the cases; 65 percent of the aggravated assaults were cleared, as were 29 percent of the robberies, 19 percent of the burglaries, 17 percent of the car thefts, and 18 percent of the larcenies.[13]

FBI statistics on nonindex crimes far outnumber index offenses. Table 4 shows the numbers and rates of arrests for the ten most frequent offenses in the United States in 1970. As we can see, drunkenness arrests and other peace-keeping matters occupy much of the time and attention of the police. Although arrests for drunkenness decreased from 1,280,000 in 1960 to 1,097,260

Table 3 INDEX OF SERIOUS CRIMES, 1970[14]

Offense	Number Known to the Police
Total	5,568,200
Murder	15,810
Forcible rape	37,270
Robbery	348,380
Aggravated assault	329,940
Burglary	2,169,300
Larceny $50 and over	1,746,100
Auto theft	921,400

[12]The President's Commission on Law Enforcement and Administration of Justice, *The Challenge of Crime in a Free Society*, pp. 38–43.

[13]Federal Bureau of Investigation, *Crime in the United States*, p. 32.

[14]Federal Bureau of Investigation, U.S. Department of Justice, *Crime in the United States: Uniform Crime Reports, 1970* (Washington, D.C.: U.S. Government Printing Office, 1971), p. 6.

Table 4 NUMBER OF PERSONS ARRESTED FOR THE TEN MOST FREQUENT OFFENSES, 1970[15]

Offense	Number
Drunkenness	1,097,260
Disorderly conduct	436,862
Larceny (over and under $50)	432,272
Driving while under the influence	281,450
Narcotic drug laws	265,734
Simple assault	208,813
Burglary	200,261
Liquor laws	136,679
Vagrancy	82,311
Gambling	75,325

in 1970, arrests for narcotic drug law violations rose from 31,600 in 1960 to 265,734 in 1970. The largest share of these were for marijuana possession, behavior which in the eyes of many persons should be "decriminalized," that is, removed from the purview of the criminal law.

Another category of criminal acts not discussed in FBI reports concerns federal crimes. According to the President's Commission report, the federal cases filed in court in 1966 included 7 antitrust offenses, 350 food and drug violations, 863 income-tax evasion cases, 2,729 liquor law violations, 2,293 narcotics cases, and 3,188 immigration crimes.[16] These figures suggest that federal crimes are relatively few in number. However, we shall see in Chapter Fourteen that white-collar violations of regulatory statutes are much more frequent than the aforementioned data imply.

The Victims of Crime

The President's Commission report contains considerable information on the topic of victims, a matter that has received little attention in the past.[17] One set of data comes from a survey that the National Opinion Research Center undertook for the commission. That study asked a representative sample of 10,000 American citizens whether they had been the victims of a crime in the previous year. Table 5 shows the rates of victimization, that is, the number of victimized persons per 100,000 citizens, classified by income. Although these rates show a mixed pattern, low-income persons are the most frequent targets of rape, robbery, and burglary. Other observations of the President's Commission note that nonwhites are victimized relatively more often than

[15]*Ibid.*, p. 122.
[16]The President's Commission on Law Enforcement and Administration of Justice, *The Challenge of Crime in a Free Society*, p. 20.
[17]*Ibid.*, pp. 38–43.

Table 5 VICTIMIZATION BY INCOME[18] (rates per 100,000 population)

	Income			
	$0-2999	$3000-5999	$6000-9999	$10,000 and over
Total	2369	2331	1820	2237
Forcible rape	76	49	10	17
Robbery	172	121	48	34
Aggravated assault	229	316	144	252
Burglary	1319	1020	867	790
Larceny ($50 and over)	420	619	549	925
Motor vehicle theft	153	206	202	219

are whites by all index crimes except grand larceny. Men are the victims of crime about three times more frequently than women.[19]

What are the relationships between offenders and victims? The President's Commission report observes that homicides occur most commonly among acquainted offenders and victims. Similarly, findings from a crime commission survey in Washington, D.C., indicate that about two-thirds of the rape victims are assaulted by someone they know at least casually. The same study notes that aggravated assaults usually occur among individuals acquainted with each other. Finally, observations in Chicago reveal that assaultive crimes are usually intraracial rather than extraracial.[20]

The Economic Costs of Crime

The President's Commission report also includes some estimates of the economic costs of crime.[21] According to the commission, crimes against persons cost about $815,000,000 per year through losses of earnings, hospitalization, and so on. Crimes against property cause annual costs to the public of around $3,932,000,000. Index crimes contribute only about $600,000,000 in economic costs to this figure, unreported commercial thefts are thought to cost about $1,400,000,000 annually, and embezzlement results in losses of about $200,000,000 per year. Frauds are estimated to involve economic losses of around $1,350,000,000 yearly, forgeries cost $82,000,000, and arson and vandalism result in losses of about $300,000,000. Clearly, such garden-variety property offenses as larceny and burglary are economically less costly than a variety of "white-collar" and "hidden" crimes.

The President's Commission sets the annual cost of crimes involving illegal

[18]*Ibid.,* p. 38.
[19]*Ibid.,* p. 39.
[20]*Ibid.,* pp. 39-41.
[21]*Ibid.,* pp. 31-35.

goods and services, such as prostitution, gambling, and other forms of organized crime, at $8,075,000,000. The economic cost of law enforcement and criminal justice operations is estimated to be about $4,212,000,000 annually, comprised of $2,792,000,000 in police expenses, $261,000,000 in court costs, $125,000,000 in prosecution and defense counsel expenses, and $1,034,000,000 for the operation of correctional services.

The usual comments by citizens and social critics about the costs of crime emphasized the costs of ordinary crime. However, these figures of The President's Commission make clear that the major economic consequences stem from organized crime and certain forms of "hidden" or unreported criminality. Further, these figures suggest that a dramatically sudden reduction of crime in the United States would have major consequences, some of which would be disruptive. The reduction of crime would alter the economic workings of society and probably produce revenue that could be used for more positive ends. But a major reduction in criminality would also result in employment dislocations, rendering many social control agents idle. In this sense at least, crime is functional in American society in that it produces employment opportunities in some quantity.

Spatial Distribution of Crime

Crime rates vary markedly from one state to another. The rates for index crimes known to the police in 1970 show that Georgia had the highest murder and nonnegligent manslaughter rate, 14.6 per 100,000 population. Alabama, South Carolina, Florida, and Mississippi had high rates, and Wisconsin, Iowa, Vermont, Maine, New Hampshire, and North Dakota had the lowest rates. Aggravated assaults were most frequent in the southern states of North Carolina, Florida, Maryland, Alabama, and Louisiana, whereas the lowest rates were in North Dakota, New Hampshire, Kansas, Hawaii, and Wisconsin. Colorado had the highest rate of forcible rape, followed by California, Missouri, Arizona, and Alaska. Low rates were observed in New Hampshire, Wisconsin, Rhode Island, North Dakota, and West Virginia. New York, Michigan, and Maryland had the highest robbery rates, whereas North Dakota, Vermont, and New Hampshire had the lowest rates. California, Nevada, and Florida led the nation in burglaries, whereas North Dakota, Mississippi, and West Virginia had the lowest rates. California and Colorado showed the highest rates of larceny over $50, and Massachusetts, Rhode Island, and California had the highest automobile theft figures.[22]

Crime rates also vary considerably within the urban areas. Table 6 shows rates for index crimes for the fifteen largest standard metropolitan areas in 1970. San Francisco had the highest rates for two of the seven offenses, but generally the rates are not consistently higher in one community than another.

---

[22]Federal Bureau of Investigation, *Crime in the United States*, pp. 66–71.

Table 6 CRIME RATES, STANDARD METROPOLITAN AREAS, 1970[23] (rates per 100,000 population)

	Murder, Nonnegligent Manslaughter	Forcible Rape	Robbery	Aggravated Assault	Burglary	Larceny over $50	Auto Theft
Baltimore	13.2	34.9	564.4	395.9	1,351.4	1,309.1	701.0
Boston	4.4	14.8	136.2	95.0	1,053.9	809.9	983.9
Chicago	12.9	25.4	362.5	232.7	829.6	617.2	708.4
Cleveland	14.5	18.7	287.9	132.1	826.1	595.2	1,208.1
Detroit	14.7	31.1	648.5	222.5	1,986.3	1,488.2	757.6
Houston	16.9	27.1	335.3	183.2	1,532.1	757.6	740.6
Los Angeles	9.4	50.0	307.3	370.8	1,980.5	1,401.3	944.6
Minneapolis	2.6	16.8	178.6	88.6	1,198.4	1,146.1	614.7
Newark	9.5	20.5	333.1	182.1	1,315.4	952.6	666.8
New York	10.5	19.9	664.8	285.6	1,821.0	1,471.2	947.1
Philadelphia	9.3	15.2	173.3	123.4	754.0	470.0	534.1
Pittsburgh	4.4	14.0	145.1	108.1	695.5	526.1	537.0
St. Louis	14.8	34.4	279.5	202.7	1,458.2	736.2	840.2
San Francisco	8.3	42.9	347.7	226.1	2,163.7	1,583.4	957.0
Washington	11.4	23.0	503.5	232.0	1,432.5	1,141.4	766.8

[23]Ibid., pp. 82–97.

Most apparent from Table 6, crime rates for the index crimes are of quite different magnitudes within the fifteen areas so that, for example, robbery rates range from 136.2 to 664.8 per 100,000 population.

How do crime rates for standard metropolitan statistical areas compare with those for other portions of the United States? Index crime rates are shown in Table 7 for standard metropolitan areas, other cities, and rural parts of the country.

In that the majority of the American population lives in metropolitan areas, we should not be surprised to find that most crimes occur there. But Table 7 also indicates that the *relative* occurrence of crime is less in rural areas; metropolitan areas show high rates of crime, as well as large numbers of offenses. Table 7 also shows that homicide rates are nearly equal in metropolitan and rural areas and that the number of forcible rapes is nearly equal in all areas. The pronounced contrast of rates is for robbery, burglary, larceny, and auto theft. The high rates of property crime in urban areas are probably explained in terms of the loosened social bonds, lack of legitimate opportunities, and other concomitants of urbanization. We shall have more to say about differential social organization in cities and its link to criminality in later chapters.

CHARACTERISTICS OF KNOWN OFFENDERS

Age Variations

In 1970, 23.2 percent of the total population of 203,165,699 Americans were under 25 years of age. Persons 15 to 25 years old made up 8.6 percent of the population. However, the 15- to 25-year-old group was involved in criminality far out of proportion to its numbers in the population. Conventional crime is heavily concentrated within this group, although variations from crime to crime exist in the contribution by young persons. Table 8 shows the arrest figures for 1970 by age.

Table 8 indicates that persons under 25 years of age accounted for 52.4 percent of all arrests. However, these individuals were particularly implicated in those serious property crimes occurring most frequently and causing the most concern to the community. Thus, persons under 25 years of age carried out 77.0 percent of the robberies, 83.1 percent of the burglaries, and 86.3 percent of the auto thefts. Persons over 25 years of age were most frequently involved in fraud, embezzlement, gambling, drunkenness, vagrancy, and offenses against the family.

Sex Variations

One of the most striking features of known crime in the United States is that it is mainly the work of males. In 1970, males were responsible for 90.4 percent of the violent offenses and 81.3 percent of the property crimes among index

Table 7 CRIME RATES, METROPOLITAN AREAS, OTHER CITIES, AND RURAL AREAS, 1970[24] (rates per 100,000 population)

	Total	Murder, Nonnegligent Man-slaughter	Forcible Rape	Robbery	Aggra-vated Assault	Burglary	Larceny $50 and Over	Auto Theft
U.S. total	2,740.5	7.8	18.3	171.5	162.4	1,067.7	859.4	453.5
Standard metro-politan areas	3,396.4	8.7	22.3	238.0	188.1	1,302.1	1,031.3	605.8
Other cities	1,847.6	4.4	8.8	37.8	130.3	725.4	756.4	184.3
Rural areas	927.4	6.4	9.9	14.1	89.6	434.1	302.7	70.7

[24]Ibid., p. 64.

Table 8 TOTAL ARRESTS OF PERSONS UNDER 25 YEARS OF AGE, 1970[25]

Offense Charged	Total	Number of Persons Arrested Under 25	Percentage Under 25
Total	6,570,473	3,445,363	52.4
Criminal homicide			
(a) murder and nonnegligent manslaughter	12,386	5,575	43.4
(b) manslaughter by negligence	3,020	1,332	44.1
Forcible rape	15,411	9,940	64.5
Robbery	87,687	67,510	77.0
Aggravated assault	125,971	58,510	46.4
Burglary—breaking and entering	285,418	237,092	83.1
Larceny—theft	616,099	476,757	77.4
Auto theft	127,341	109,886	86.3
Other assaults	287,027	135,030	47.0
Arson	9,409	7,286	77.4
Forgery and counterfeiting	43,833	23,124	52.8
Fraud	76,861	26,640	34.7
Embezzlement	8,172	2,864	35.0
Stolen property: buying, receiving, etc.	61,517	42,330	68.8
Vandalism	111,671	97,805	87.6
Weapons: carrying, possessing, etc.	102,725	50,958	49.6
Prostitution and commercial vice	49,344	30,284	61.4
Sex offenses (except forcible rape and prostitution)	49,328	25,400	51.5
Narcotic drug laws	346,412	269,069	77.7
Gambling	84,804	12,154	14.3
Offenses against family and children	56,620	18,224	32.2
Driving under the influence	423,522	85,666	20.2
Liquor laws	222,464	184,536	83.0
Drunkenness	1,512,672	216,416	17.3
Disorderly conduct	589,642	317,453	53.8
Vagrancy	101,093	52,500	51.9
All other offenses (except traffic)	804,780	501,684	62.3
Suspicion	70,173	49,717	70.8
Curfew and loitering law violations	105,548	105,548	100.0
Runaways	179,073	179,073	100.0

[25]Ibid., p. 128.

offenses.[26] Males made up 84.6 percent of the arrests for murder and non-negligent homicide, 100.0 percent of those for forcible rape, and 93.9 percent of those for robbery. Aggravated assault arrests involved males in 87.4 percent of the cases, as did 95.3 percent of the burglaries, 72.0 percent of the larcenies, and 94.9 percent of the auto thefts.

Women are not equally involved in all forms of crime. In 1970, females accounted for 79.3 percent of the prostitution arrests, 27.9 percent of the grand larceny arrests, 27.1 percent of those for fraud, 24.6 percent of those for embezzlement, as well as 51.6 percent of those for runaway activity (an offense restricted to juveniles). Reports for individual states contain much the same information. In California in 1965, females were involved in 10.6 percent of all felony arrests. Women were implicated in 21.9 percent of the forgery and checks arrests, 15.9 percent of the homicide arrests, but only 1.7 percent of the "other sex offenses" arrests and 0.1 percent of the rape arrests. Similarly, women were involved in 33.5 percent of the misdemeanor arrests for thefts but only 7.3 percent of the misdemeanor assaults.[27]

What is the explanation for the disproportionate contribution of males to criminality? Perhaps something about the female role in American society deters women from lawbreaking. However, Otto Pollak has advanced another thesis: women are really as criminally involved as men.[28] Pollak's argument is that the sex-role socialization that women experience leads them to act deviously and cunningly. As a result, they commit a variety of "hidden" and unreported crimes. They carry on surreptitious poisonings that result in homicides, they shoplift, and they engage in other unrecognized deviations. Pollak has marshaled some evidence of uneven quality which he believes demonstrates that true rates of female crime equal those for men. Our assessment of this argument and the evidence adduced for it is that it is overstated. Females do engage in some kinds of crime with a low probability of being detected or reported; thus the male and the female rates of crime are probably closer together than revealed by arrest statistics. Yet males are also probably more criminally involved than females because of different social experiences and the greater opportunities they have for lawbreaking.

Racial Variations

The major concern of those curious about racial characteristics of lawbreakers centers about the extent of black involvement in criminality. In 1970 black citizens constituted 11.2 percent of the American population so that they represent the major racial group other than Caucasians in the United States.

Blacks are apparently strongly overrepresented in crime. Table 9 shows the

[26]Ibid., p. 129.

[27]State of California, Crime and Delinquency in California, 1965 (Sacramento: Bureau of Criminal Statistics, 1966), pp. 43–49.

[28]Otto Pollak, The Criminality of Women (Philadelphia: University of Pennsylvania Press, 1950).

Table 9 ARRESTS BY RACE, 1970[29] (arrests of persons 18 years of age and over)

Offense Charged	Total	Black	Black Percentage of Total
Total	4,448,648	1,221,854	27.5
Criminal homicide			
(a) Murder and nonnegligent manslaughter	9,997	5,823	58.2
(b) Manslaughter by negligence	2,513	542	21.6
Forcible rape	10,761	4,893	45.5
Robbery	47,504	28,714	60.4
Aggravated assault	91,840	41,272	44.9
Burglary—breaking and entering	120,841	41.696	34.5
Larceny—theft	274,736	90.861	33.1
Auto theft	49,566	19,906	40.2
Other assaults	212,470	78,682	37.0
Arson	3,206	987	30.8
Forgery and counterfeiting	33,642	10,490	31.2
Fraud	68,841	15,914	23.1
Embezzlement	6,875	1,768	25.7
Stolen property: buying, receiving, etc.	30,268	11,434	37.8
Vandalism	27,375	7,462	27.3
Weapons: carrying, possessing, etc.	74,801	38,802	51.9
Prostitution and commercial vice	38,040	24,270	63.8
Sex offenses (except forcible rape and prostitution)	35,583	7,088	19.9
Narcotic drug laws	212,444	51,054	24.0
Gambling	67,840	44,912	66.2
Offenses against family and children	50,424	14,802	29.4
Driving under the influence	387,152	66,904	17.3
Liquor laws	127,194	18,327	14.4
Drunkenness	421,261	287,974	20.3
Disorderly conduct	442,088	151,878	34.4
Vagrancy	56,199	14,142	25.2
All other offenses (except traffic)	496,283	125,000	25.2
Suspicion	48,904	16,257	33.2
Curfew and loitering law violations	---------	--------	-----
Runaways	---------	--------	-----

[29]Federal Bureau of Investigation, Crime in the United States, p. 133.

distribution of blacks among persons arrested in 1970. Blacks comprised 60.4 percent of the persons arrested for robbery, 58.2 percent of those apprehended for murder and nonnegligent manslaughter, 45.5 percent of those arrested for forcible rape, and 34.5 percent of those involved in burglary. Table 9 also indicates that blacks were much less frequently involved in certain patterns of criminality, including liquor law violations, drunkenness, sex offenses other

epidemiology   113

than forcible rape, fraud, and embezzlement. In general, the high crime pattern for blacks is comprised of incidents of unskilled personal assaults or property crimes.

These arrest statistics suggest two factors that may account for these patterns. First, blacks are overrepresented in criminality in part through differential law enforcement. That is, these arrest figures reflect the policies of the police, who sometimes deal officially with black offenses that would be handled informally or ignored entirely if they had been the work of Caucasians. Gambling and prostitution arrests are striking cases in point, for the police are known to enforce the laws against these activities differentially against blacks. In particular, the police often harass black streetwalkers but allow white prostitutes to conduct their criminal activities.

The criminogenic social experiences to which many Negroes are subjected in American society also explain figures in Table 9. If racial characteristics per se influence criminality, we would expect to find crime rates for different offenses to be relatively uniform. Instead, black and white rates are quite varied. In the chapters ahead we shall examine a number of the criminogenic factors in American social life implicated in black criminality. Chapter Eight contains a fairly detailed consideration of crime-inducing social factors that operate to produce crime among blacks.

TRENDS IN CRIME

In the America of the mid-twentieth century, it is fashionable to assume that lawlessness is at an unparalleled high point. In recent presidential and gubernatorial elections, much has been made of the apparent breakdown of law and order and the consequent increase in lawbreaking.

But hard evidence that conclusively demonstrates this hypothesized upsurge of criminality is hard to come by. Even inadequate statistics of the sort discussed in this chapter have been gathered for only a short time, so long-term trends cannot be identified. However, some evidence suggests that America prior to the twentieth century may have been more lawless than it is now.[30]

Crime trends can be studied for relatively short periods in the immediate past, and these data do suggest that criminality has been growing at an accelerated pace in the past decade or so. Figures 2 and 3, taken from The President's Commission report, show the trends in index crimes known to the police between 1933 and 1965. These two charts indicate that all index crimes increased between 1960 and 1965 at a much more pronounced rate than they grew over the long period since 1933. The rates for property crimes burgeoned most prominently, in that the 1960 to 1965 increase in violent crimes was 25

---

[30]Daniel Bell, "Crime as an American Way of Life," *Antioch Review*, 13 (June 1953), 131-54; The President's Commission on Law Enforcement and Administration of Justice, *The Challenge of Crime in a Free Society*, pp. 22-23.

percent, whereas the increase in property offenses was 36 percent.[31] Nonindex violations also increased prominently during the period from 1960 to 1965.

The trends revealed in Figures 2 and 3 have apparently continued at an accelerated pace since 1965. The crime rate for index property offenses was approximately 1,250 per 100,000 population in 1965, but was 2,380.5 per 100,000 persons in 1970. The comparable figures for offenses involving violence were 180 in 1965 and 360 per 100,000 population in 1970. Figures 4 and 5 show these changes.

In the view of The President's Commission, the 1960–65 statistics reveal a real increase in criminality. Our view of these recent trends is consistent with that of the commission. We would have difficulty arguing that criminality is no less common in the 1970s than it was in earlier decades. The President's Commission attributed the growth in criminality to such factors as the changing age structure of the population, with more persons in the younger, crime-prone age groups; increased urbanization and the criminogenic influences it creates; and the growing affluence of American society, which produces more opportunities for property crimes.[32] In addition, the current sensitivity to the "crime problem" in American society may be implicated in these trends, producing a greater willingness of citizens to report the occurrence of crimes to the police.

"HIDDEN" CRIMINALITY

The crime information we have examined to this point concerned offenses that have been reported to the police or resulted in an arrest. What relation does this known criminality bear to the total volume of lawbreaking? What of deviant behavior that is unreported, unknown by the authorities, and thereby "hidden"? How much of this activity exists? Is known criminality only a small fragment of the body of crime? Is unreported or hidden lawbreaking common among population groups that are underrepresented in the group of known law violators? Are middle-class citizens engaged in acts of illegality, which they keep from the eyes of the police?

Most of the work done on these questions has concerned juvenile delinquency. Many years ago, Sophia Robison observed that the cases of delinquency various public agencies in New York City had observed were much more numerous than those known to the police and juvenile courts.[33] Edward Schwartz conducted a survey of delinquency cases in Washington, D.C., in 1944, which demonstrated that schools, the police, and other social agencies and institutions deal with many cases of juvenile delinquency not referred

[31]The President's Commission on Law Enforcement and Administration of Justice, *The Challenge of Crime in a Free Society*, pp. 23–24.

[32]*Ibid.*, pp. 27–31.

[33]Sophia Robison, *Can Delinquency be Measured?* (New York: Columbia University Press, 1936).

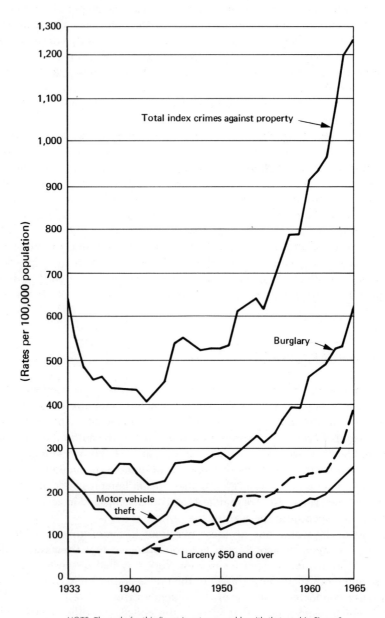

NOTE: The scale for this figure is not comparable with that used in Figure 3.
Source: FBI, Uniform Crime Reports Section, published data.

FIGURE 2 Index Crime Trends, 1933–65; Reported Crimes Against Property

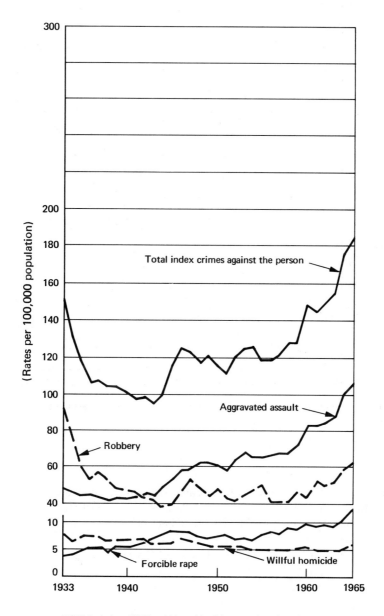

NOTE: Scale for willful homicide and forcible rape enlarged, to show trend.
Source: FBI, Uniform Crime Reports Section, unpublished data.

FIGURE 3 Index Crime Trends, 1933-65; Reported Crimes Against the Person

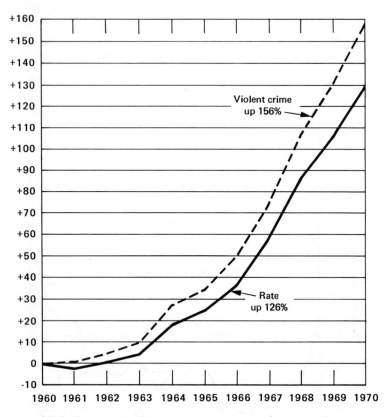

Limited to murder, forcible rape, robbery, and aggravated assault

FIGURE 4[34] Crimes of Violence, 1960-70 (percent change over 1960)

to the juvenile court.[35] A study in Cambridge and Somerville, near Boston, dramatically indicated that acts of delinquency and misbehavior are much more frequent among youths in high delinquency areas than is revealed in police arrests or court statistics. These data suggest that delinquent conduct is truly a way of life or regularized behavior pattern for many youngsters in urban slum areas.[36]

[34]Federal Bureau of Investigation, *Crime in the United States*, p. 3.

[35]Edward E. Schwartz, "A Community Experiment in the Measurement of Juvenile Delinquency," *National Probation Association Yearbook*, 1945), pp. 157-81.

[36]Fred J. Murphy, Mary M. Shirley, and Helen L. Witmer, "The Incidence of Hidden Delinquency," *American Journal of Orthopsychiatry*, 16 (October 1946), 686-96.

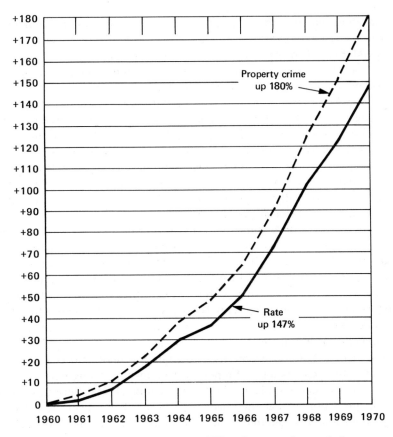

Limited to burglary, larceny $50 and over, and auto theft

FIGURE 5[37] Crimes Against Property, 1960-70 (percent change over 1960)

For some time, delinquency researchers have been interested in the participation of children who live in comfortable, middle-class neighborhoods in
juvenile lawbreaking. Austin Porterfield, a pioneer in the study of these
youths, elicited reports from college students about the misbehavior they had
been involved in prior to entry into college. Porterfield found that nearly
all of them had been active in delinquency, although virtually none had become known to the police or courts.[38] Porterfield's study was quite crude,

---

[37]Ibid., p. 4.
[38]Austin L. Porterfield, "Delinquency and Its Outcome in Court and College," American Journal
of Sociology, 44 (November 1943), 199-208.

so that quite possibly the respondents fabricated some of the confessions. However, a group of investigators, starting with F. Ivan Nye and James Short,[39] improved methods of gaining self-reports about delinquency.

The recent studies of hidden delinquency are quite varied in that they have been conducted in dissimilar communities and with different groups of youngsters. However, they add up to a broad picture of the undetected deviations of youngsters. Most of these children admit that they have been engaged in at least one or another delinquent act, but most misbehavior they report tends to be relatively innocuous. Also, when youngsters from different social class levels have been compared concerning involvement in *relatively petty acts of delinquency*, no relationship between delinquency and social status has been observed; that is, petty juvenile offenders are found in about the same numbers at all social class levels.[40]

On the other hand a plethora of evidence indicates that official delinquents are disproportionately from lower income backgrounds. Some people have taken the findings on petty hidden delinquency and economic status and have jumped to the conclusion that the undetected delinquents are similar to detected ones, only luckier. That is, the argument that juveniles find their way into juvenile court or training schools because the police discriminate against low status persons rather than because they are more delinquent than hidden offenders has been put forth.

However, such a conclusion does not stand up under closer scrutiny. In one early study comparing self-reported delinquency among training school wards and high school students, Short and Nye found that the institutionalized delinquents reported that they had engaged in all the relatively petty acts high school students admitted.[41] But, in addition, the training school subjects

[39]F. Ivan Nye and James F. Short, Jr., "Scaling Delinquent Behavior," *American Sociological Review*, 22 (June 1957), 326–31; Short and Nye, "Extent of Unrecorded Juvenile Delinquency, Tentative Conclusions," *Journal of Criminal Law, Criminology and Police Science*, 49 (November–December 1958), 296–302; Nye, *Family Relationships and Delinquent Behavior* (New York: John Wiley & Sons, 1958); Harwin L. Voss, "Socio-Economic Status and Reported Delinquent Behavior," *Social Problems*, 13 (Winter 1966), 314–24; Ronald L. Akers, "Socio-Economic Status and Delinquent Behavior: A Retest," *Journal of Research in Crime and Delinquency*, 1 (January 1964), 38–46; John P. Clark and Eugene P. Wenninger, "Socio-Economic Class and Area as Correlates of Illegal Behavior Among Juveniles," *American Sociological Review*, 27 (December 1962), 826–34; Robert A. Dentler and Lawrence J. Monroe, "Social Correlates of Early Adolescent Theft," *American Sociological Review*, 26 (October 1961), 733–43; William R. Arnold, "Continuities in Research: Scaling Delinquent Behavior," *Social Problems*, 13 (Summer 1965), 59–66; Nancy Barton Wise, "Juvenile Delinquency Among Middle-Class Girls," in *Middle-Class Juvenile Delinquency*, ed. Edmund W. Vaz (New York: Harper & Row, 1967), pp. 179–88; Nils Christie, Johs. Andanaes, and Sigurd Skirbekk, "A Study of Self-Reported Crime," *Scandinavian Studies in Criminology*, 1 (1965), 86–116. These studies are summarized and discussed in Don C. Gibbons, *Delinquent Behavior* (Englewood Cliffs, N.J.: Prentice-Hall, 1970), pp. 20–30.

[40]Dentler and Monroe, "Social Correlates of Early Adolescent Theft;" Clark and Wenninger, "Socio-Economic Class and Area as Correlates of Illegal Behavior Among Juveniles"; Akers, "Socio-Economic Status and Delinquent Behavior"; Arnold, "Continuities in Research"; Voss, "Socio-Economic Status and Reported Delinquent Behavior."

[41]Short and Nye, "Extent of Unrecorded Juvenile Delinquency."

confessed to more serious and repetitive offenses to which hidden delinquents did not admit.

Further evidence of this sort is contained in Maynard Erickson and LaMar Empey's study involving fifty high school nondelinquent boys, fifty boys who had appeared once in a juvenile court, fifty juvenile repeaters, and fifty incarcerated delinquents.[42] The official records of the delinquents were compared against self-reported delinquency. All the boys admitted acts of lawbreaking, most of which went undetected. However, the officially recognized offenders were implicated in delinquency with greater frequency, and the persistent offenders were involved in the most serious delinquencies. In general, those boys engaged in numerous repetitions of delinquency had also been in court most frequently. Finally, Martin Gold's study of a representative sample of teen-agers in Flint, Michigan, turned up parallel findings.[43] Youths involved in the most serious and repetitive delinquencies tended to come from low status backgrounds. The persistent offenders also were the most likely to have been apprehended by the police and referred to juvenile court.

Claims that appearance in a juvenile court or commitment to a training school are events visited on youths no more delinquent than youngsters from higher social status groups are incorrect. Nonetheless, we should hasten to point out that not all misbehavior of hidden delinquents is minor in form. Fred Shanley, as well as Larry Karacki and Jackson Toby, have discussed groups of juveniles from comfortable economic circumstances implicated in relatively serious kinds of lawbreaking.[44] Nonetheless, much hidden misbehavior appears to be hidden and unreported, in part, because it is relatively petty.

Investigations of unreported adult criminality are few. James Wallerstein and Clement Wyle asked a cross-section of the adult population to report the acts of law violation in which they had engaged.[45] Most respondents admitted one or more deviant acts that had gone unreported. Many of these self-reported incidents appear to be relatively harmless, of little concern to the police. For instance, one woman reported an assault, by which she meant that she had thrown an ashtray at a suitor. Such cases suggest the need for caution lest we draw the conclusion that nearly all citizens are engaged in criminality.

[42]Maynard L. Erickson and LaMar T. Empey, "Court Records, Undetected Delinquency, and Decision-Making," Journal of Criminal Law, Criminology and Police Science, 54 (December 1963), 456–69.

[43]Martin Gold, "Undetected Delinquent Behavior," Journal of Research in Crime and Delinquency, (January 1966), 27–46.

[44]Larry Karacki and Jackson Toby, "The Uncommitted Adolescent: Candidate for Gang Socialization," Sociological Inquiry, 32 (Spring 1962), 203–15; Fred J. Shanley, "Middle-Class Delinquency as a Social Problem," Sociology and Social Research, 51 (January 1967), 185–98; Shanley, D. Welty Lefever, and Roger E. Rice, "The Aggressive Middle-Class Delinquent," Journal of Criminal Law, Criminology and Police Science, 57 (June 1966), 145–57.

[45]James S. Wallerstein and Clement Wyle, "Our Law-Abiding Lawbreakers," Probation, 25 (April 1947), 107–12.

In providing evidence on unreported crime, The President's Commission report discusses a National Opinion Research Center national poll of 10,000 households, along with detailed surveys conducted in Boston, Chicago, and Washington, D.C.[46] The national survey dealt with the extent to which persons had been victims of crimes. The rates of victimization that emerged are compared with FBI rates of crime in Table 10.

Table 10 indicates that crime involves persons in the general population much more frequently than the official figures reflect. The same conclusion emerges from the observations in three precincts in Washington, D.C., where various crimes were three to ten times more frequent than police statistics indicate. Similar findings resulted in the Boston and Chicago surveys. In the NORC investigation, the most frequent reason given by respondents for not reporting crimes to the police was that they believed the police incapable of dealing with them.

Obviously, the group of offenders that comes to the attention of the authorities represents only a segment of a large collection of criminals. We will have occasion to examine some further evidence on selected forms of unreported crime in the following chapters. Thus, we shall see that "white-collar crime," involving violations of business regulations, is widespread in American society.

Table 10 COMPARISON OF SURVEY AND UCR RATES[47] (rates per 100,000 population)

Index Crimes	NORC Survey, 1965-66	UCR Rate for Individuals, 1965	UCR Rate for Individuals and Organizations, 1965
Willful homicide	3.0	5.1	5.1
Forcible rape	42.5	11.6	11.6
Robbery	94.0	61.4	61.4
Aggravated assault	218.3	106.6	106.6
Burglary	949.1	299.6	605.3
Larceny ($50 and over)	606.5	267.4	393.3
Motor vehicle theft	206.2	226.0	251.0
Total violence	357.8	184.7	184.7
Total property	1761.8	793.0	1249.6

[46]The President's Commission on Law Enforcement and Administration of Justice, *The Challenge of Crime in a Free Society*, pp. 21–22.
[47]*Ibid.*, p. 21.

SUMMARY

This chapter has identified some major dimensions of known crime in American society. In addition, we have explored some aspects of hidden criminality. We have seen that criminality is extremely widespread and costly, and we have observed that lawbreaking is patterned in a variety of ways so that it is more common in some areas than others. It is also apparent that some individuals, such as those who are male, young, black, or from low-income backgrounds, are more likely to be apprehended as criminals than are other persons. These materials provide the beginnings to a study of crime causation, to which our attention now turns. Chapter Six initiates the exploration of etiology by taking up a number of those paths earlier students of criminality have explored in their search for the causes of lawbreaking.

CAUSAL ANALYSIS: BACKGROUND AND HISTORY

In Chapter One, dealing with causal analysis, we noted that the study of criminal etiology involves three separate but related problems. The first is the epidemiological question, in which "the facts" are at issue. Once the basic facts of criminality have been drawn together, the explanatory job involves the sociology of criminality, in which attempts are made to account for rates and patterns of crime, as well as the social psychology of criminal careers, in which the analyst endeavors to account for the genesis of criminal role behavior in specific individuals. The preceding chapter was concerned with epidemiology. This chapter is concerned with some of the theoretical answers to causal questions that criminologists of an earlier generation regarded as valid. Chapters Eight through Seventeen focus on a variety of contemporary theories and hypotheses regarding criminality.

Man's attention to lawbreaking and deviant conduct of various kinds goes back to antiquity. Two general kinds of views of criminality have been advanced, the "demonological" and the "naturalistic" frames of reference.[1] Demonological views entertain the belief that "other world" powers of spirits are at the root of criminality, whereas naturalistic theories hold that events and characteristics of the directly observable physical and material world are the active agents producing crime. This book is concerned with naturalistic hypotheses, for only these are linked to contemporary social science perspectives on deviant behavior.

As we have already noted, there are two kinds of causal questions: the sociology of criminality and the social psychology of criminal behavior and criminal careers. In turn, we might classify etiological answers criminologists have offered to these questions in a variety of ways. One common categorization recognizes *biogenic, psychogenic, sociogenic,* and *typological* approaches. Biogenic hypotheses contend that the causation or genesis of criminality lies

[1]George B. Vold, *Theoretical Criminology* (New York: Oxford University Press, 1958), pp. 4–8. Vold provides a succinct summary and critique of a number of these historically important notions about crime. See also Stephen Schafer, *Theories in Criminology* (New York: Random House, 1969).

in biological factors and processes; psychogenic formulations maintain that offenders are responding to various kinds of psychological pressures and personality problems that drive them to lawbreaking. Sociogenic arguments aver that various aspects of social structure produce rates and patterns of criminality or that lawbreakers acquire their criminal motives and behavior patterns through such normal socialization experiences as differential association. Typological views advise us to eschew the pursuit of theories of "crime" and "criminal behavior" and to zero in on particular forms, patterns, syndromes, or role careers in lawbreaking.

Table 11 presents the diversity of explanatory approaches to crime causation and indicates where specific theories of etiology fit within the previously outlined distinctions. Chapter Six is concerned with biogenic theories along with some other early approaches to causation, such as the classical view, cartographic notions, and socialist theories. Chapter Seven takes up a host of psychological theories and research studies. Chapters Eight and Nine deal with sociogenic materials, the first of these chapters centering on social structure and criminality and the second dealing with the socialization processes through which criminal attitudes and behavior are acquired. Chapter Ten turns to typological views, in which specific offender patterns and role careers are singled out for attention. Finally, Chapter Eleven summarizes the current state of causal analysis, drawing the materials from the preceding chapters together into a synthesis of sorts.

The entries in Table 11 are the specific causal arguments we shall examine in the chapters ahead. For example, Chapter Seven deals with psychogenic theories rising out of psychoanalytic thinking, but it also looks at some claims about psychopathy and certain other psychological hypotheses. Similarly, Chapter Eight explores a number of sociogenic arguments about social structure and criminality, including the anomie formulation, social disorganization, and differential social organization.

As we shall see, some of the theoretical assertions examined in this chapter are concerned with rates problems, such as the socialist explanation, whereas others account for the process by which certain persons become criminals. Much of the early work in criminology centers around biogenic propositions, in which biological variables are seen as critical in causation. This chapter deals with historically old and historically recent analyses of criminality. For example, socialist views of crime developed around 1850 and were followed by investigations of lawbreaking and economic trends that have continued up to the present. Similarly, biogenic viewpoints originated with Cesare Lombroso about 1875, but a long line of biological investigations stemmed from Lombroso's work. This chapter is concerned with the various lines of inquiry going on currently and we shall examine the historical roots and the contemporary manifestations of a number of frames of reference.

Table 11 THE STRUCTURE OF CAUSAL ARGUMENTS IN CRIMINOLOGY

Explanatory Problem	Basic Approaches			
	Biogenic	Psychogenic	Sociogenic	Typological
Sociology of criminality ("rates questions")	Biogenic theories have not paid attention to rates questions.	Psychogenic arguments tend not to pay attention to rates questions.	cartographic studies, socialist theories ‐ ‐ ‐ ‐ ‐ ‐ ‐ ‐ multiple-factor views ‐ ‐ ‐ ‐ ‐ ‐ ‐ ‐ social disorganization ‐ ‐ ‐ ‐ ‐ ‐ ‐ ‐ anomie ‐ ‐ ‐ ‐ ‐ ‐ ‐ ‐ value pluralism ‐ ‐ ‐ ‐ ‐ ‐ ‐ ‐ differential social organization ‐ ‐ ‐ ‐ ‐ ‐ ‐ ‐ racism and crime	Specific explanation for each type of criminality
Social psychology of criminal careers (Why do they do it?)	biological types ‐ ‐ ‐ ‐ ‐ ‐ ‐ ‐ feeblemindedness ‐ ‐ ‐ ‐ ‐ ‐ ‐ ‐ hereditary transmission ‐ ‐ ‐ ‐ ‐ ‐ ‐ ‐ XYY chromosome abnormality	psychoanalytic theories ‐ ‐ ‐ ‐ ‐ ‐ ‐ ‐ general emotional disturbances ‐ ‐ ‐ ‐ ‐ ‐ ‐ ‐ psychopathy	deviance theories ‐ ‐ ‐ ‐ ‐ ‐ ‐ ‐ differential association ‐ ‐ ‐ ‐ ‐ ‐ ‐ ‐ home factors ‐ ‐ ‐ ‐ ‐ ‐ ‐ ‐ risk-taking, situational factors	specific explanation for each type of criminal

A HISTORY OF ERRORS

What can we learn from the "pioneers in criminology"?[2] The most accurate, brief answer is: "Not a great deal." Probably the most important lesson that the pioneering figures in criminology have to teach us centers about explored blind alleys. Historical efforts in criminology have all too often been fruitless meanderings into theoretical terrain, which have failed to account adequately for criminality. Clearly, work on criminality starting a century or so ago was not a steady cumulation. Modern views are not the end product of some multiplicative process, building on the contributions of the criminological "giants" of the past. Instead, current sociological and psychological viewpoints are relatively unrelated to earlier theorizing regarding criminality. On this point of discontinuity between the past and contemporary efforts in criminology, George Vold assesses historical searches for evidence that criminals represent a physical type: "Physical type theories turn out to be a more-or-less sophisticated form of shadow-boxing with a much more subtle and difficult to get at problem, namely, that of the constitutional factor in human behavior."[3] Behind Vold's specific evaluation of physical type theories and underlying the more sweeping negative judgment regarding historical endeavors as a whole is the assertion that modern social science puts forward an image of man and society infinitely more complicated than the representation implied in earlier arguments.

Reduced to barest essentials, modern sociological perspectives on criminality aver that discovery of *causal relationships*—some finite or limited number of factors bearing an invariant or constant relationship to criminality—is possible. The social scientist assumes that statements of the form, "If A, B, and C occur, then behavior of form X will occur," are discoverable by the methods of science. Human behavior in all its forms is exceedingly complex, but particularly with regard to lawbreaking because many divergent forms of behavior fall under the terminological umbrella, "crime." Variations in the forms and rates of crime are the product of basic features of social organization. Crime is no more or less "normal" than any other kind of behavior so that modern-day criminologists eschew the "evil causes evil" kind of perspective in which criminality is attributed to bad homes, inadequate parents, or other evils. Instead, the modern sociologist is inclined to scrutinize closely social-structural variables included within such broad categories as value patterns, social stratification influences, differentials in family structure, or interactions with agencies of social control.

---

[2] This term is taken from a series of articles in the *Journal of Criminal Law, Criminology and Police Science* of a few years ago in which the writings of a number of pioneers or early figures in criminology were examined. See, for example, Elio D. Monachesi, "Pioneers in Criminology: IX-Cesare Beccaria (1738–94)," *Journal of Criminal Law, Criminology and Police Science*, 46 (November–December 1955), 439–40.

[3] Vold, *Theoretical Criminology*, p. 74.

Certain kinds of personality dynamics and characteristics could act as predisposing conditions leading certain individuals in the direction of criminal careers. However, the sociologist would argue that most crime is accomplished by actors lacking in personality pathology so that the personality dynamics that interact with social or situational influences are more subtle in character. Also, different personality correlates are probably influential in the varied forms of criminality. Finally, certain specific biologically related conditions, such as brain damage, may play a contributory part in particular instances of deviation, but if so, the relationships involved are complicated ones to uncover. In summary, modern views on the crime problem involve a posture of modesty, growing out of the recognition that human behavior of even a limited and simple kind is rarely the product of some easily identifiable causal process.

This view of human behavior, in which social action is regarded as a mysterious but ultimately known product of manifold variables in subtle interaction, is relatively recent. Particularly recent is the body of behavioral science theory presenting component processes and variables that make up the structure of social action. For most of history, simpler and more straightforward beliefs about man and his behavior have been in vogue. In earlier times, the actions of men were believed to be reducible to relatively simple hedonistic pleasure seeking, activity patterns dictated by the force of biological imperatives or capable of reduction to other simplistic formulas. So it has been with criminological theories too. An examination of the history of criminology turns up many viewpoints, which by modern standards are naive, oversimplified, and in other ways inadequate to deal with the complexity of behavior. Most of the work done on biological hypotheses in criminality seems clearly defective, apart from the inadequate research methodology of these studies. Nearly all the biogenic works proceed on the basis of faulty assumptions, one of which is that "nature" and "nurture" (heredity and environment) can be separated from each other and studied in isolation. Another erroneous presupposition is that criminality is a constant, unchanging kind of behavior. But crime, in fact, varies from place to place and from time to time. Therefore, if biological forces are involved in criminality, hypotheses to discover them will have to be sufficiently sophisticated to determine how such culturally and temporally variable phenomena as crime could be transmitted genetically. No existing biological theory is equipped to handle this problem.[4]

Doubtless, historical efforts in criminology are of considerable value as indicators of theoretical paths that we might bypass in the search for causes of criminality. Certainly, in this sense, these earlier efforts have much significance for contemporary criminology. The person attempting to comprehend

---

[4]For an incisive critique of theories seeking to find the causes of crime in genetically inherited traits, see Richard R. Korn and Lloyd W. McCorkle, *Criminology and Penology* (New York: Holt, Rinehart and Winston, 1959), pp. 199-204.

crime must begin with an examination of the writings of prior generations of criminologists. But our main point has been that a hiatus exists between contemporary theoretical and empirical work and the endeavors of earlier generations of students of criminal conduct. The substantive body of contemporary criminological theory is more directly allied to concepts and insights from the body of modern behavioral science theory than it is to the works of earlier analysts. Thus, we shall see in the pages to follow that many earlier studies of criminality came to abortive conclusions. The generalizations from these works have not stood the test of time to become building blocks for modern criminological theory.

THE CLASSICAL VIEW

The classical school refers to the writings of a number of European scholars in the late 1700s, particularly Cesare Beccaria in Italy (1738-94) and Jeremy Bentham in England (1748-1832).[5] The core concepts of the classical frame of reference are hedonism and free will. Vold notes that all classical theorists accepted as valid, as did most of their lay contemporaries, certain beliefs about human behavior, including the existence of human "will" as a psychological reality. Prevailing opinions of the time agreed that all men, criminals included, act rationally and deliberately to avoid pain and encounter pleasure.[6] Following from these premises, the criminal makes a deliberate, rational, hedonistically oriented decision to engage in lawbreaking. If this is the case, to deter him or others from crime, an amount and kind of punishment of such magnitude as to counterbalance the pleasure from criminal acts must swiftly and surely be administered to miscreants. In the works of some classical scholars, attempts were made to develop highly detailed scales or hedonistic calculi of punishment, in which specific amounts of pain were identified for each type of lawbreaking. In the criminal codes that grew out of classical writings, constant punishments were decreed for particular violations of law, so the effect of these codes was to render judges as simply instruments for the application of the law. Codes were drafted in such a way as to severely circumscribe the discretionary powers of judges in assigning penalties to offenders.

Early criminologists such as Bentham and Beccaria were not involved in the statement of criminological theories out of any fundamental or overriding interest in the explanation of crime. Instead, the classical version of criminological theory represented a by-product of other kinds of interests. Bentham, Beccaria, and others were social critics and reformers, interested in modifying

---

[5]Vold, *Theoretical Criminology*, pp. 14–26; see also Leon Radzinowicz, *A History of English Criminal Law and its Administration from 1750*, vol. 1 (New York: The Macmillan Co., 1948), for a detailed discussion of classical perspectives and the social conditions that gave rise to these notions.

[6]Vold, *Theoretical Criminology*, pp. 16–18.

the social control practices of their native societies. They were concerned about the severe and barbaric punishments commonplace during the late 1700s. Similarly, they were appalled by the existence of tyrannical and capricious judges administering harsh and inequitable punishments to offenders.[7] Out of these conditions, and a concern for their alleviation, the classical perspective developed.

Initial attempts to devise specific, detailed, and strict codes following the themes of classical teachings encountered a number of difficulties in practice. As a result, exceptions to penalities were made, and statutes were redrafted giving judges some latitutde in application of penalties. Such revisions have continued up to the present; and such developments as the juvenile court movement and the separate, theoretically nonpunitive handling of juvenile lawbreakers, the use of probation and parole, and other innovations have altered the strict form of classical theory and procedure. Nonetheless, the classical view of matters has not passed from the scene. As we shall see in later chapters, the major outlines of Anglo-Saxon criminal law and procedure are still essentially consistent with classical arguments. Moreover, lawyers and citizens alike usually resist attempts to deviate from freewill premises and from relatively harsh and uniform penalties with considerable fervor. For example, recent endeavors to widen the exclusionary operation of courts by freeing mentally disordered individuals from responsibility for their illegal acts represent one prominent case in which modern perspectives on behavior have clashed with the surviving elements of the classical tradition. This battle is not yet won, but it does not yet appear that the classical view will be declared the eventual loser. The prosecutor and the judge are not yet in danger of being replaced by the psychiatrist.

THE CARTOGRAPHIC SCHOOL

The cartographic or geographic school of criminology pursued the ecological facts of crime; that is, it examined the distribution of forms and rates of criminality among spatial areas.[8] Two of the best-known persons associated with the development of this orientation were Adolphe Quetelet in Belgium and A. M. Guerry in France. Alfred Lindesmith and Yale Levin listed many factual studies of crime and delinquency following this approach.[9] They argue that the founding of modern criminology is erroneously attributed to Lombroso,

[7]Radzinowicz has enumerated these practices in great detail. See Radzinowicz, *A History of Criminal Law.*

[8]Edwin H. Sutherland and Donald R. Cressey, *Principles of Criminology*, 8th ed. (Philadelphia: J. B. Lippincott Co., 1970), p. 51.

[9]Alfred Lindesmith and Yale Levin, "The Lombrosian Myth in Criminology," *American Journal of Sociology*, 42 (March 1937), 653–71; see also Levin and Lindesmith, "English Ecology and Criminology of the Past Century," *Journal of Criminal Law and Criminology*, 27 (March–April 1937), 801–16.

for the cartographic scholars preceded Lombroso's work by fifty years. Moreover, the works of cartographic students have more in common with contemporary criminological efforts than does Lombroso's work.

The cartographic school arose out of the development of systems of social bookkeeping first established in European countries in the 1500s, such as the systematic recording of births and deaths.[10] Quantitative studies of crime began to appear in England and France around 1800. Guerry's ecological study of crime rates in France appeared in 1833, and Quetelet produced an elaborate analysis of crime and social conditions in France, Belgium, Luxembourg, and Holland in 1836.

These early endeavors were forerunners of a long line of studies that have continued to the present. One of these persistent interests has centered about the relationship, if any, between economic conditions and fluctuations in crime and delinquency. Literally hundreds of studies have appeared on this question.[11] The following section on socialist views, crime, and economic trends discusses some of the major conclusions from this work.

Another interest stemming from cartographic beginnings is in regional variations in crime. Sutherland and Cressey have enumerated a large number of these investigations carried on since the 1800s.[12] For example, a study by Enrico Ferri showed that homicide convictions varied widely from province to province in major European nations, and another study of major crimes known to the police in England observed that variations in crime rates were relatively stable among regions in that country.[13] The commentary in Chapter Five on the epidemiology of crime noted the existence of rural–urban and regional variations in crime rates in the United States. Stuart Lottier and Lyle Shannon's studies of these patterns represent relatively modern instances of cartographic investigations.[14]

Studies of ecological variations in crime and delinquency rates in individual cities provide another modern version of cartographic interests.[15] The work of Calvin Schmid is notably representative of such activity.[16] In a recent inves-

[10]For a summary of these developments, see Vold, *Theoretical Criminology*, pp. 162–65.

[11]Many of these are summarized in *ibid.*, pp. 165–82.

[12]Sutherland and Cressey, *Principles of Criminology*, pp. 173–76.

[13]*Ibid.*, pp. 183–84.

[14]Stuart Lottier, "Distribution of Criminal Offenses in Metropolitan Regions," *Journal of Criminal Law and Criminology*, 29 (May–June 1938), 37–50; Lottier, "Distribution of Criminal Offenses in Sectional Regions," *Journal of Criminal Law and Criminology*, 29 (September–October 1938), 329–44; Lyle W. Shannon, "The Spatial Distribution of Criminal Offenses by States," *Journal of Criminal Law, Criminology and Police Science*, 45 (September–October 1954), 264–73.

[15]See, as one example, Lyle W. Shannon, "Types and Patterns of Delinquency in a Middle-Sized City," *Journal of Research in Crime and Delinquency*, 1 (January 1964), 53–66.

[16]Calvin F. Schmid, "A Study of Homicides in Seattle," *Social Forces*, 4 (June 1926), 745–56; Schmid, "Urban Crime Areas: Part 1," *American Sociological Review*, 25 (August 1960), 527–42; Schmid, "Urban Crime Areas: Part II," *American Sociological Review*, 25 (October 1960), 655–78. See also Don C. Gibbons, *Delinquent Behavior* (Englewood Cliffs, N.J.: Prentice-Hall, 1970), pp. 103–13, for a review and discussion of a series of ecological studies of delinquency.

tigation in Seattle, some 35,000 cases of "offenses known to the police" and 30,000 "arrests" were examined from an ecological perspective. Elaborate correlational analyses were undertaken of a number of types of criminal activities and social characteristics of census tracts in Seattle. This research showed that certain forms of criminal acts are heavily concentrated in the central business district of the city, whereas others are more common in other parts of the city. Similarly, a variety of concentrations of specific kinds of criminal persons is found in different areas in the city. In general, illegal activities and criminal actors are most common in areas of low social cohesion, weak family life, low economic status, physical deterioration of property, high population mobility, and various forms of personal demoralization.

The difficulty with these investigations based on official data is that it is not clear whether they reveal the ecological distribution of criminality, the spatial patterning of police and judicial practices, or some blend of both. We suspect that these studies tell us more about law enforcement policies and record keeping than they do about total crime.

Schmid's presentation indicates another characteristic of studies of the cartographic form—the facts do not speak for themselves. At one time in the development of the behavioral sciences, a widely held view was that the job of social science was principally to accumulate a mountain of factual data from which scientific generalizations would automatically emerge. However, we have come to learn that the investigator must speak for the facts; he must interpret empirical observations. The last section of Schmid's research report is devoted to a *post factum* examination of a number of theories that might account for the results reported. Although such studies are important for an understanding of criminality, they do not stand as an equivalent to theory construction and testing. We draw attention to this point as a limitation to ecological fact-gathering research endeavors rather than as an indication of a basic flaw in them.

SOCIALIST VIEWS, CRIME, AND ECONOMIC TRENDS

Socialist explanations of crime grew as an expansion of Karl Marx's theory, first published in 1867.[17] According to socialistic arguments, exploitation of workers in capitalistic societies leads to endemic poverty and misery. In turn, these conditions produce a variety of criminalistic responses, including alcoholism, prostitution, and larceny. The systems of criminal justice prevailing in capitalistic societies protect the exploitive interests of the owner class.[18] Thus,

---

[17]Karl Marx and Friedrich Engels, *Das Kapital* (New York: Random House, 1906).

[18]For a socialist interpretation of fluctuations in penal policies, see Georg Rusche and Otto Kirchheimer, *Punishment and Social Structure* (New York: Columbia University Press, 1939).

prevention of criminality demands reorganization of the economic order along socialist lines.

The most eminent contributor to socialist theories was Dutch sociologist William A. Bonger (1876-1940), who argued that the very nature of the capitalistic economic system encourages *egoism*, that is, the relatively unrestrained pursuit of self-interest.[19] He summarizes his perspective thus:

> In recapitulating now the egoistic tendencies of the present economic system and of its consequences, we see clearly that they are very strong. Because of these tendencies the social instinct of man is not greatly developed; they have weakened the moral force in man which combats the inclination towards egostic acts, and hence towards the crimes which are one form of these acts. To mention only the most important things, in a society in which, as in ours, the economic interests of all are in eternal conflict among themselves, compassion for the misfortunes of others inevitably becomes blunted, and a great part of morality consequently disappears. The slight value that is attached to the opinion of others is also a consequence of the strife of economic interests, for we can be responsive to that opinion only when we do not see adversaries in our fellows.[20]

Much of Bonger's work should have a familiar ring to the modern sociology student. Bonger anticipated a host of later sociological analyses of criminality in capitalistic societies, in which a variety of social and economic conditions are held to be involved in the genesis of criminality.[21] Bonger's writings bear more than a slight similarity to such recent thinking represented by the delinquency theory of Richard Cloward and Lloyd Ohlin.[22]

Studies of economic influences on criminality have been numerous since Bonger's early works. In their summary of the principal findings of such inquiries, Sutherland and Cressey note that one frequent conclusion is that lower economic class groups have much higher crime rates than upper class groups.[23] A plethora of investigations has been conducted of samples of arrested, convicted, or committed adult or juvenile offenders, all of which show that working class groups are heavily overrepresented in the population of detected lawbreakers. For example, in Glueck's study of 1000 juvenile delinquents in

---

[19]William A. Bonger, *Criminality and Economic Conditions* (Boston: Little, Brown and Co., 1916); see also William A. Bonger, "The Criminal—A Product of the Capitalistic System," (edited excerpts) in *Criminology*, ed. Clyde B. Vedder, Samuel Koenig, and Robert E. Clark (New York: Dryden Press, 1953), pp. 158-65.

[20]Bonger, "The Criminal—A Product of the Capitalistic System," in Vedder, Koenig, and Clark, *Criminology*, p. 164.

[21]See, for example, Donald R. Taft and Ralph W. England, Jr., *Criminology*, 4th ed. (New York: The Macmillan Co., 1964), pp. 275-79; Robert K. Merton, *Social Theory and Social Structure*, rev. and enl. ed. (New York: The Free Press, 1957), chaps. 4 and 5.

[22]Richard A. Cloward and Lloyd E. Ohlin, *Delinquency and Opportunity* (New York: The Free Press, 1960).

[23]Sutherland and Cressey, *Principles of Criminology*, pp. 234-42.

the 1930s, over 70 percent were found to be from families of marginal or dependent economic status.[24] Ecological studies of the distribution of crime and delinquency rates in cities have repeatedly pointed to the concentration of criminality in lower class neighborhoods.[25] However, Sutherland and Cressey question the validity of the argument that lawbreaking is peculiarly lower class in distribution, on the same grounds as we have earlier challenged this conclusion in Chapter Five. Although certain juvenile and adult forms of crime, such as gang delinquency, do appear to be disproportionately the activity of working class individuals,[26] the same is not true of "total crime." If statistics were available on white-collar offenses and a variety of other kinds of underreported or unreported criminality, the socioeconomic picture of illegal conduct might well be quite different.

Studies of fluctuations in crime rates and the business cycle have also been numerous since the days of Bonger.[27] A variety of theoretical and methodological inadequacies have flawed these investigations, but taken as a whole the studies appear to show that serious crimes increase during times of depression, whereas the general or total crime rate tends not to increase during periods of economic decline. These studies also suggest that property offenses accompanied by violence increase during depressions, whereas nonviolent property crimes do not. Drunkenness and crimes against persons do not show any consistent relationship to economic fluctuations, but rates of juvenile delinquency seem to increase during depression periods.

Vold has raised a series of important questions. He notes that different assumptions regarding the time interval between the onset of economic changes and alterations in rates of criminality lead to drastically different conclusions from the same basic data.[28] He shows that in a study by Dorothy Thomas of crime rates and economic variations in England and Wales for the period 1857–1913, the correlation coefficient between economic conditions and criminality was –.25 when the crime rates and economic measures for the same years were correlated.[29] However, the correlation between economic conditions for particular years and the crime rates observed *two years later* was +.18. As Vold argues, we should assume that some time lag is required before economic and business changes have repercussions on the volume of lawbreaking.

The most sensible conclusion on this issue is equivocal. At best, the influ-

---

[24]*Ibid.*, p. 236.

[25]*Ibid.*, p. 239.

[26]Albert K. Cohen, *Delinquent Boys* (New York: The Free Press, 1955).

[27]Many of these have been summarized in Thorsten Sellin, *Research Memorandum on Crime in the Depression* (New York: Social Science Research Council, 1937); see also Vold, *Theoretical Criminology*, pp. 162–81; Sutherland and Cressey, *Principles of Criminology*, pp. 225–26.

[28]Vold, *Theoretical Ciminology*, pp. 177–81.

[29]Dorothy Swaine Thomas, *Social Aspects of the Business Cycle* (London: Routledge and Kegan Paul, 1925).

ence of economic changes and business trends on crime appears to be relatively slight. The total of criminal behavior is compounded out of many discrete forms of behavior, some of which economic variations may influence and others of which may be insensitive to such fluctuations. The causative factors in criminality are doubtless too many and too complex for the kinds of indices of economic fluctuations that are at hand to easily reflect or measure.

A study of crime trends and economic factors by Daniel Glaser and Kent Rice[30] supports these interpretations. They found some support for the hypothesis that rates of juvenile delinquency are inversely correlated with unemployment so that juvenile misconduct is most prominent during times of prosperity. On the other hand, criminality among adults between 18 and 35 years of age seems to be most frequent during periods of widespread unemployment. Glaser and Rice interpret these findings in terms of sociological theories that stress the demoralizing influences of unemployment on adults.

THE SEARCH FOR BIOLOGICAL TYPES

The central theme of biogenic views is familiar to layman and criminologist alike. The belief that biological factors determine human behavior generally, and criminal behavior specifically, is of ancient origins. It has been phrased in a variety of ways and persists in the minds of many citizens today. Vold has identified the core propositions of biological theories as follows: "Back of all physical type theories is the general idea of biological differences in behavior. All biological explanations rest on the basic logic that *structure determines function*. Individuals behave differently owing to the fundamental fact that they are somehow structurally different" (emphasis in the original).[31]

In this section, we shall examine a number of variants on this common theme. We shall begin with the writings of Lombroso, and follow the elaborations on biogenic theory and research to the contemporary efforts of William Sheldon, directed at the search for temperament and physical type patterns related to criminality. Given the benefit of hindsight, we might judge some of these endeavors to be preposterous in form. Modern behavioral science foundations contradict most of Lombroso's theories, such as the concept of *atavism* and the hypothesized criminal nature of prehistoric man. But at the time that Lombroso wrote, close on the heels of the appearance of Darwin's evolutionary teachings in *Descent of Man* (1871), claims that criminals constitute evolutionary throwbacks seemed much more plausible. There is a sociolo-

---

[30]Daniel Glaser and Kent Rice, "Crime, Age, and Employment," *American Sociological Review*, 24 (October 1959), 679–86.

[31]Vold, *Theoretical Criminology*, p. 43.

gy of knowledge, in which particular ideas that develop grow out of social conditions in some era. So it is with criminological views, for they have been the rather natural product of social conditions in different historical periods.

Lombroso and Positivist Viewpoints

Lombroso (1835–1909) stands as a giant of criminology, although, as Vold has pointed out, he has often been a misunderstood pioneering figure. Lombroso has often been described as the originator of the theory of atavism and of the criminal as a biological type, without his later, modified views being mentioned or without recognition of the key role he played in development of the positivist approach to criminality.[32] Positivism emphasizes crime as a natural phenomenon, produced by a variety of factors (multiple causation), some of which are biological, others environmental. Lombroso was the original spokesman for this viewpoint, which, in broad outlines, is the prevailing criminological opinion of today.

Lombroso's famous claims center about the notion that the criminal is of different physical type than the noncriminal. According to a frequently told tale, Lombroso, as a physician, was once asked to perform an autopsy on a famous Italian brigand. In the course of this autopsy, he discovered a number of physical abnormalities in the brain of the criminal. He was struck by these observations, out of which he formulated the view that criminals are *atavists*, or genetic throwbacks to an earlier kind of human species, *homo delinquens*. Lombroso supposed that modern man, *homo sapiens*, evolved out of this earlier lower type of human. He assumed the earlier species to have various kinds of asocial behavior. Accordingly, a contemporary criminal is simply a biological reversion to this primitive form of man. These views were published in *The Criminal Man*, which went through five separate editions. In this book, Lombroso maintained that the degenerate and atavistic criminal type could be identified by a number of characteristics or stigmata, including facial asymmetry, eye defects and peculiarities, ears of unusual size, excessively long arms, and other physical peculiarities.[33]

In addition to these notions, Lombroso held that although some offenders were throwbacks, others were not. In the revisions of his book, the manuscript grew in size from several hundred pages to nearly 2,000 in length. In the later editions, a host of causal factors were enumerated, in addition to reversion to an earlier biological type. In the native version of his thinking Lombroso asserted that there are three major kinds of criminals: *born* criminals, *insane* criminals, and *criminaloids*, who are individuals of normal physical and psy-

---

[32]*Ibid.*, pp. 29–32. See Vold's entire discussion of Lombroso, for a detailed and balanced evaluation of Lombroso's place in criminology, pp. 28–32, 50–54.

[33]*Ibid.*, pp. 50–51.

chological makeup who commit crimes in unusual circumstances. Less than half of the total population of offenders were asserted to be of the first type.

In the early 1900s, Charles Goring mounted a mortal assault on Lombroso's theories of the offender as a physical type.[34] Along with a number of collaborators he undertook a series of careful measurements of approximately 3,000 English convicts and large numbers of noncriminals. Almost without exception, Lombroso's hypothetical physical anomalies were no more common among the prisoners than the nondeviants. In Goring's words, "Our inevitable conclusion must be that *there is no such thing as a physical criminal type*" (emphasis in the original).[35]

The two most famous followers of Lombroso were Enrico Ferri (1856–1928) and Raffaele Garofalo (1852–1934).[36] Ferri, a student under Lombroso, expanded on the ideas of his teacher, claiming that social, economic, and political factors are involved in crime, as well as Lombroso's suggested biological causes. Ferri is also recognized for his fourfold classification ot offenders as insane, born, occasional, and criminals by passion. These notions are not too different in general form from claims often put forward in contemporary works on criminality.

Garofalo was the third major Italian positivist. Among his other interests, he attempted to formulate a universal definition of "natural" crime, in which he held that the sociological conception of crime refers to offenses that violate the sentiments of probity and pity. In this sense, Garofalo anticipated some of the later concern with such cross-cultural definitions of crime as those of Sellin, which we examined in Chapter Two.

Over the years in which positivist perspectives developed, attention veered away from biological hypotheses toward emphasis on a variety of psychological and sociological dimensions in crime causation. Nonetheless, curiosity regarding biogenic variables continued in a number of forms. This interest was revived most dramatically in the work of Harvard physical anthropologist Earnest A. Hooton.

Hooton's Research

Arguments on constitutional or physical type waned in influence for some time following Goring's work. However, these claims were dramatically resurrected in Hooton's work, published in 1939.[37] This book was the result of

---

[34]Charles Goring, *The English Convict: A Statistical Study* (London: His Majesty's Stationery Office, 1913). See also Vold, *Theoretical Criminology*, pp. 52–55.

[35]Goring, *The English Convict*, p. 173. Although Goring's conclusion stood almost unchallenged, other investigations in the late 1800s and early 1900s did turn up some apparent physical variations between offenders and nonoffenders. See Vold, *Theoretical Criminology*, pp. 55–58.

[36]For a resumé of the works of Ferri and Garofalo, see Vold, *Theoretical Criminology*, pp. 32–39.

[37]Earnest A. Hooton, *Crime and the Man* (Cambridge, Mass.: Harvard University Press, 1939).

a twelve-year study of over 13,000 prisoners in ten states, compared with a smaller number of civilian nonoffenders, on some hundred anthropometric measurements. Hooton's observations led him to conclude that "the primary cause of crime is biological inferiority."[38] Moreover, he averred that biological inferiority was inherited so that eugenic programs of sterilization represent the most efficacious solution to criminality. According to Hooton:

> ... inherently inferior organisms are, for the most part, those which succumb to the adversities or temptations of their social environment and fall into antisocial behavior ... it is impossible to improve and correct environment to a point at which these flawed and degenerate human beings will be able to succeed in honest social competition.[39]

Despite the impressive number of subjects in this research, sociologists, criminologists, and anthropologists greeted Hoooton's work with hostility and criticism.[40] The major deficiencies in his research are clear.[41] His control groups of nonoffenders were small in size and markedly unrepresentative of noncriminal citizens as a whole. The control group of 1,976 persons included 146 municipal firemen from Nashville, Tennessee, along with an odd assortment of militiamen, bathhouse patrons, and outpatients from Boston. Some of the subgroups within the control sample differed more from one another than they did from the prisoners. A second defect of his work was that many of the subsamples on which he based ethnic comparisons between convicts and civilians were extremely small. A third counterargument to his conclusions is that, even if we assumed that the research techniques in this investigation were adequate, prisoners do not constitute a representative sample of criminals. There are good reasons for supposing that those offenders who fall into the hands of the police, and later into prison, might be in poorer physical shape than those who escape detection. Finally, one of the most devastating criticisms of his work is that he had no explicit criterion of "biological inferiority." As Vold notes:

> His method of translating physical deviations into evidence of inferiority is nowhere made clear. Unless there is independent evidence of the inferi-

---

[38]*Ibid.*, p. 130.

[39]*Ibid.*, p. 388.

[40]Some of these evaluations of Hooton's work are Robert K. Merton and M. F. Ashley Montague, "Crime and the Anthropologist," *American Anthropologist*, 42 (July–September 1941), 384–408; James S. Wallerstein and Clement J. Wyle, "Biological Inferiority as a Cause for Delinquency," *Nervous Child*, 6 (October 1947), 467–72; N. S. Timasheff, "The Revival of Criminal Anthropology," *University of Kansas Law Review*, 9 (February 1941), 91–100; William B. Tucker, "Is There Evidence of a Physical Basis for Criminal Behavior?" *Journal of Criminal Law and Criminology*, 31 (November–December 1940), 427–37.

[41]Sutherland and Cressey, *Principles of Criminology*, pp. 118–19; Korn and McCorkle, *Criminology and Penology*, pp. 216–19, Vold, *Theoretical Criminology*, pp. 59–64.

ority of certain kinds of physical characteristics, conclusions regarding inferiority must be drawn from the association with criminality—a nice illustration of circular reasoning: use the criminality to discover the inferiority, then turn around and use the inferiority to explain or account for the criminality.[42]

Some Other Lines of Activity

The preceding commentary has centered on some of the more prominent and influential inquiries into biological factors in criminality. However, other interests have been popular at different stages in criminological history. For example, the now discredited phrenological arguments of Franz Joseph Gall (1758-1828) and John Gaspar Spurzheim (1776-1832) were at one time thought to represent powerful explanations of behavior generally and criminality specifically.[43] Persons of phrenological persuasion argued that conformations of the skull reveal "faculties" or propensities to behavior which are the product of biological inheritance. Criminals were held to be deficient in some of the normal faculties influencing behavior.

A related line of analysis, prominent in the past, centered on the hypothesis that tendencies toward criminality are inherited.[44] In this view, "like father, like son," so criminal parents pass on to their offspring genetic tendencies toward lawbreaking. One kind of evidence brought forth to demonstrate the hereditary transmission of deviant tendencies concerns studies of identical (one egg) and fraternal (two egg) twins.[45] The logic is that environmental influences are controlled or constant for twins, so if hereditary influences are of importance in behavior, the one-egg twins should show concordance or similar behavior. If one is a criminal, the other should also be a deviant. However, the two-egg twins should show more discordant behavior, for they do not share the same hereditary backgrounds. Those investigations which have made such comparisons have turned up evidence of greater concordance of behavior among one-egg than two-egg twins, hence these analyses seem to constitute proof of hereditary transmission. Yet the assessment of most biologists is that such a conclusion is not valid, in view of some serious defects in these studies. All of them are based on small samples. Identification of identical twins is fraught with possibilities of error because it rests on observation of external physical characteristics. Insofar as mistakes are made, they tend to be in the direction of misidentification of fraternal twins as identical

[42]Vold, *Theoretical Criminology*, p. 64.

[43]*Ibid.*, pp. 44-49.

[44]These arguments are summarized in Sutherland and Cressey, *Principles of Criminology*, pp. 113-18.

[45]A number of these studies are summarized and criticized in M. F. Ashley Montague, "The Biologist Looks at Crime," *Annals of the American Academy of Political and Social Science*, 217 (September 1941), 46-57; a good discussion of these studies can be found in Korn and McCorkle, *Criminology and Penology*, pp. 198-204.

so that observations are biased in favor of the hereditary hypothesis. Also, environmental influences are not controlled in these comparisons, for identical twins may receive more comparable parental treatment than do two-egg twins. Consequently, whatever concordance of behavior might be observed could be attributable to environmental influences.

Fundamental difficulties plague all attempts to discover hereditary influences on behavior, criminality included. Korn and McCorkle have identified some of the theoretical issues that we must untangle if we are to identify hereditary influences.[46] For one thing, hereditary and environmental influences interact almost from the point of conception of the human organism. As a consequence, separation of the unique contribution heredity makes to behavior of any kind is almost impossible.

An additional complication is that modern genetic theory indicates that inherited traits are specific in nature so that a person inherits blue eyes, hair color, and so on. But criminal behavior is not specific in that it covers a wide gamut of activities. Moreover, many criminals engage in an assortment of criminal acts. How can genetic endowment account for this variability? Perhaps offenders inherit general tendencies to break laws. This is a flawed argument, for it runs counter to genetic theory. Also, most criminals obey most laws. Their behavior does not square with any hypothesis of inherited general "badness."

Korn and McCorkle summarize the hereditary transmission theory thus: "The enormous labor expended in the search for hereditary causes of crime illustrates the extent to which research may be diverted into blind alleys by careless definition of terms and by a failure to examine the implications of an underlying point of view."[47]

Following the arguments of Louis Berman and others in the 1920s on the relationships of glandular processes and personality, several persons attempted to devise theories showing that criminality is a result of endocrine malfunctioning.[48] The writings of Max Schlapp and Edward Smith represent the best known of such extreme and speculative claims, asserting that the explanation of criminality is in glandular malfunctioning.[49] However, in general, careful research has failed to support these claims. The general position of most endocrinologists at present is that we do not know nearly enough about endocrine functioning to be able to identify accurately personality consequences of endocrine patterns or connections of endocrine malfunction to criminality.[50]

---

[46]Korn and McCorkle, Criminology and Penology, pp. 202–4.

[47]Ibid., p. 204

[48]Louis Berman, The Glands Regulating Personality (New York: The Macmillan Co., 1921); Berman, New Creations in Human Beings (New York: Doubleday & Company, 1938).

[49]Max G. Schlapp and Edward H. Smith, The New Criminology (New York: Boni and Liveright, 1928).

[50]R. G. Hoskins, Endocrinology (New York: W. W. Norton Co., 1941).

Body Type, Temperament, and Criminality

When one of Shakespeare's characters uttered the injunction, "Beware yon Cassius for he hath a lean and hungry look; such men are dangerous, they think too much," he was expressing the ancient and widely popular thesis that man's physical structure explains his behavior. Hence, fat men are also jolly men because corpulence produces a jovial temperament, and slim persons are destined to be introverted. Such ideas have been extended to the area of criminality, with the supposition that deviance is a function of physical structure. Two contemporary versions of this thesis are found in the works of Ernst Kretschmer and of William Sheldon.[51] Kretschmer is a German scholar who produced a book in the 1920s arguing that certain patterns of physical structure lead to particular temperament types and that, in turn, specific kinds of mental disorder and criminality are related to these somatic and personality structures. Kretschmer and others have reported research findings that suggest a relationship between body type and patterns of criminality, but they fail to demonstrate the hypothesized temperament linkages to these patterns.[52]

The most recent version of the body type and temperament argument is found in the work of Sheldon and associates.[53] Sheldon asserts that somatic structure can be classified in terms of the degree to which *endomorphic, mesomorphic,* or *ectomorphic* physical characteristics are most apparent in different individuals. He argues that *viscerotonic, somotonic,* or *cerebrotonic* temperament patterns tend to accompany certain of the body types. He has developed scales for measuring these dimensions, in which individuals are scored on each component on a range from 1 to 7, with the largest score denoting predominance of that particular somatic pattern. Vold summarizes the characteristics of the somatic and personality patterns:[54]

Sheldon's Basic Types:

Physique	Temperament
1. *Endomorphic:* relatively great development of digestive vis-	1. *Viscerotonic:* general relaxation of body; a comfortable

[51]For summaries of Sheldon and Kretschmer's work, see Vold, *Theoretical Criminology*, pp. 66–74; Korn and McCorkle, *Criminology and Penology*, pp. 219–23; Sutherland and Cressey, *Principles of Criminology*, pp. 119–20.

[52]For a description of Kretschmer's work, see Vold, *Theoretical Criminology*, pp. 68–69; American research following Kretschmer's notions is found in George J. Mohr and Ralph H. Gundlach, "The Relation Between Physique and Performance," *Journal of Experimental Psychology*, 10 (April 1927), 117–57; Mohr and Gundlach, "A Further Study of the Relations Between Physique and Performance in Criminals," *Journal of Abnormal and Social Psychology*, 24 (April-June 1929), 91–103.

[53]William H. Sheldon, S. S. Stevens, and W. B. Tucker, *Varieties of Human Physique* (New York: Harper & Row, Publishers, 1940); Sheldon and Stevens, *Varieties of Temperament* (New York: Harper & Row, Publishers, 1942); Sheldon, Emil M. Hartl, and Eugene McDermott, *Varieties of Delinquent Youth* (New York: Harper & Row, Publishers, 1949).

[54]Vold, *Theoretical Criminology*, p. 71.

cera; tendency to put on fat; soft roundness through various regions of the body; short tapering limbs; small bones; soft, smooth, velvety skin.

person; loves soft luxury; a "softie" but still essentially an extrovert.

2. *Mesomorphic:* relative predominance of muscles, bone, and the motor-organs of the body; large trunk; heavy chest, large wrists and hands; if "lean" a hard rectangularity of outline; if "not lean" they fill out heavily.

2. *Somotonic:* active, dynamic person; walks, talks, gestures assertively; behaves aggressively.

3. *Ectomorphic:* relative predominance of skin and its appendages which includes the nervous system; lean, fragile, delicate body; small, delicate bones; droopy shoulders; small face, sharp nose, fine hair; relatively little body mass and relatively great surface areas.

3. *Cerebrotonic:* an introvert; full of functional complaints, allergies, skin troubles, chronic fatigue, insomnia; sensitive to noise and distractions; shrinks from crowds.

Although variations in individual physique do exist, we can hardly accept the hypothesized temperament relationships to body structure as correct. Sheldon's research has so far failed to demonstrate convincingly the accuracy of that hypothesis. Several attempts have been made to extend the somatotype argument to the area of deviant behavior. In one study of several hundred residents of the Hayden Goodwill Inn in Boston, a specialized rehabilitation home for boys, Sheldon claims to have demonstrated linkages between delinquency and certain body types.[55] However, critics have not been kind to Sheldon, pointing out that he employed a loose and atypical definition of delinquency, centering around a notion of "disappointingness" rather than on involvement in illegal behavior. Because his methodological procedures were deficient in other ways, too, he failed to provide a convincing case for these hypotheses.[56] Sheldon and Eleanor Glueck, who carried on another study of this kind, indicate that delinquent boys in their sample were somewhat more mesomorphic or athletic in body structure than were the nondelinquents

[55]Sheldon, Hartl, and McDermott, *Varieties of Delinquent Youth.*

[56]Edwin H. Sutherland, "Critique of Sheldon's Varieties of Delinquent Youth," *American Sociological Review,* 16 (February 1951), 10–13; S. L. Washburn, "Review of W. H. Sheldon's *Varieties of Delinquent Youth,*" *American Anthropologist,* 53 (October–November 1951), 561–63.

in this investigation.[57] But such a discovery is not particularly surprising for we could argue that delinquent subcultures recruit new members selectively, placing a premium on agile, muscular boys because these characteristics make for a successful career in delinquent role behavior. Excessively fat or overly thin and sickly youngsters make poor candidates for rough delinquent behavior, so they are excluded from delinquent peer groups. If so, this is a social process, not a biologically determined pattern of behavior.

FEEBLEMINDEDNESS AND CRIME

The most popular single theory of crime causation adhered to by laymen, and by many serious investigators as well, is that offenders are defective in some psychological fashion. In this view, the causes of crime and delinquency are "inside the person." An early version of this theme sought for the mainsprings of deviance in feeblemindedness, whereas later ideas centered on the search for mental abnormality in the form of psychotic symptoms in offenders. The modern variant of this orientation is concerned with the possibility that law-breakers are responding to a variety of subtle kinds of emotional problems.[58] This chapter is concerned with the first of these hypotheses, and Chapter Seven is devoted to a detailed examination of current psychogenic perspectives on criminality.

In this section and in Chapter Seven, our view is that many psychological claims of one kind or another are clearly erroneous and that other claims represent gross overstatements. Although some lawbreakers may be respond-ing to emotional tensions, many of them are not. In all probability, the majority of offenders are no more or less "normal" than are nonoffenders. We agree with Cohen, who has argued: "A major task before us is to get rid of the notion, so pervasive in sociological thinking, that the deviant, the abnormal, the pathological, and, in general, the deplorable always come wrapped in a single package."[59]

At one time in the history of criminology, the thesis that criminality is the product of low mentality was exceedingly popular. This theory averred that general hereditary degeneracy, including feeblemindedness, leads to criminal-ity because the physically and intellectually degenerate individual cannot cope with life circumstances in a normal and satisfactory way.

---

[57]Sheldon and Eleanor Glueck, *Physique and Delinquency* (New York: Harper & Row, Publishers, 1956).

[58]For general discussions of the feeblemindedness investigations, see Vold, *Theoretical Criminol-ogy*, pp. 75–89, and Korn and McCorkle, *Criminology and Penology*, pp. 259–67. For a useful review of this entire body of inquiry, see Lawson G. Lowrey, "Delinquent and Criminal Personalities," in *Personal-ity and the Behavior Disorders*, vol. 2, ed. J. McV. Hunt (New York: The Ronald Press, 1944), pp. 794-821.

[59]Albert K. Cohen, "Social Disorganization and Deviant Behavior," in *Sociology Today*, ed. Robert K. Merton, Leonard Broom, and Leonard S. Cottrell, Jr. (New York: Basic Books, 1959), p. 463.

This argument grew out of a series of studies of families, disguised by such fictitious names as the Jukes, Kallikaks, and Nams,[60] which came to light in the late 1800s and early 1900s. In each of these studies, presumably feeble-minded ancestors produced a long family line of social misfits. The conclusion from these observations was that feeblemindedness is inherited and leads to social inadequacy, deviation, and criminality. Subsequent inquiry on the question of low mentality has, of course, indicated that the simple hereditary transmission view of feeblemindedness is erroneous. The involvement of successive generations of individuals in deviant behavior is probably the result of *social transmission*.

In the early 1900s, the development of intelligence tests led to the application of these measures to samples of offenders. Initial results seemed to confirm the picture of lawbreakers as uncommonly characterized by mental impairment. Thus, Henry Goddard reported results of different studies showing that a high percentage of the criminals investigated were feebleminded.[61] Goddard concluded from these data: "It can no longer be denied that the greatest single cause of delinquency and crime is low-grade mentality, much of it within the limits of feeble-mindedness."[62]

All these early studies of the intelligence of criminal persons were carried on without control group comparisons and without knowledge of the average mental age of law-abiding citizens. Instead, the average citizen was assumed to have attained a mental age of 16; that is, if tested, he would presumably respond correctly to all the questions asked of 16-year-old individuals. Measured against this standard, criminals seemed to be markedly deficient in intelligence. The error of these studies came to light with the publication of intelligence test results from the World War I draft experience. The average mental age of adult draftees, presumably a representative sample of law-abiding citizens, turned out to be 13.08, not 16![63] In short, citizens proved to be less intelligent than had been supposed. When criminal samples were compared to the standard from the army testing, the offenders appeared to be no more defective than the draftees. Thus, Sutherland discovered that the average proportion of criminals diagnosed as feebleminded in some 350 studies surveyed was about 50 percent for the period 1910–14 but only about 20 percent for the period 1925–28.[64] Carl Murchison and Simon Tulchin each carried out systematic comparisons of prisoners and draftees showing negligi-

[60]Richard L. Dugdale, *The Jukes* (New York: G. P. Putnam, 1877); Henry H. Goddard, *The Kallikak Family* (New York: The Macmillan Co., 1912); A. H. Estabrook, *The Jukes in 1915* (Washington, D.C.: Carnegie Institute, 1916); A. H. Estabrook and C. B. Davenport, *The Nam Family* (Lancaster, Pa.: New Era Publishing Co., 1912).

[61]Henry H. Goddard, *Feeblemindedness: Its Causes and Consequences* (New York: The Macmillan Co., 1914).

[62]Henry H. Goddard, *Juvenile Delinquency* (New York: Dodd, Mead and Co., 1921), p. 22.

[63]For a summary of the results of World War I testing, see Vold, *Theoretical Criminology*, pp. 82–83.

[64]Edwin H. Sutherland, "Mental Deficiency and Crime," in *Social Attitudes*, ed. Kimball Young (New York: Holt, Rinehart and Winston, 1931), pp. 357–75.

ble differences in intelligence between the two groups.[65] In summary, it is now evident that low mentality is not a significant cause of criminality. There are intelligent and stupid criminals just as there are intelligent and stupid nonoffenders, but the proportions of high and low mentality citizens and lawbreakers are approximately equal.

If it were at hand, the evidence would quite possibly show one relationship of intelligence variations to criminality. Prison inmates are likely to show intelligence test scores lower on the average than those of nonincarcerated offenders. Quite possibly one of the contingencies influencing the probability of apprehension, conviction, and incarceration is intelligence. Probably, prisons are collection places for the less able among the criminal population, in the same way that unskilled jobs tend to be the occupational niche to which many of the dullards in the general population are allocated.

In addition, individuals who vary in mentality are likely to occupy different criminal role patterns. Intelligence probably helps to determine which offenders become recruits to skilled professional forms of criminality. Similarly, we might expect to find that certain kinds of criminals, such as embezzlers, abortionists, and white collar offenders, would exhibit higher intelligence than many other kinds of lawbreakers, in that they are occupants of selective law-abiding occupations which draw from the college-trained in American society.

No systematic body of evidence is available on the question of intelligence differences among prisoners and nonincarcerated offenders, or among different criminal types. However, intelligence correlations may well exist. While it is one thing to deny causal significance to feeblemindedness or low mentality, it is another to claim that there are no intelligence correlations whatsoever. Their existence is very possible.

The XYY Chromosomal Pattern and Criminality

The most recent biological theory of criminality is the XYY, or extra chromosome, hypothesis, holding that certain kinds of criminals are inordinately drawn from the group in the population with this hereditary anomaly.[66] Much interest in this notion derives from a few spectacular cases, such as the mass murders and sexual assaults committed by Richard Speck in Chicago in 1966. Examination of Speck revealed that he had the XYY chromosomal pattern.

---

[65]Carl Murchison *Criminal Intelligence* (Worcester, Mass: Clark University Press, 1926); Simon Tulchin, *Intelligence and Crime* (Chicago: University of Chicago Press, 1939); see also Leslie D. Zeleny, "Feeblemindedness and Criminal Conduct," *American Journal of Sociology*, 38 (January 1933), 564–76.

[66]This theory and the evidence concerning it are admirably summarized in Richard G. Fox, "The XYY Offender: A Modern Myth?" *Journal of Criminal Law, Criminology and Police Science*, 62 (March 1971), 59–73; Theodore R. Sarbin and Jeffrey E. Miller, "Demonism Revisited: The XYY Chromosomal Anomaly," *Issues in Criminology*, 5 (Summer 1970), 195–207.

What is involved in chromosomal patterning and behavior? Richard Fox summarizes the matter:

In general terms, chromosomes are threads of complex molecules (DNA) containing the genetic material which transmits hereditary messages from generation to generation of both plant and animal life. These messages direct the development of the offspring after fertilization. The number of chromosomes to be found in each plant or animal cell varies according to species. There are, for instance, two chromosomes in each cell of a simple worm, fourteen in the garden pea, and forty-six in man. There is an exception to the general rule that each normal human cell has 46 chromosomes. The female ovum and male sperm cells respectively contain only 23 chromosomes but, on uniting at conception, they pool their chromosomes so that the fertilized ovum contains 46 chromosomes. These are arranged in 23 pairs. As the fertilized ovum grows by division into a new individual, each of the 46 chromosomes also divides so that eventually each normal cell (other than sperm and ovum) contains the same number of chromosomes. Of the 23 pairs of chromosomes in each cell one pair contains genes which determine, among other features, the primary sexual characteristics of the individual. In women this single pair of chromosomes are of similar size and are called X chromosomes or, in the biologists' shorthand, XX. In the male this pair of chromosomes are unequal in size; one of the pair is an X chromosome and is larger than the other which is called the Y chromosome. In the biologists' shorthand, the male's sex chromosomes are described as XY. The primary biological characteristics of masculinity are determined by the Y chromosome. From this it becomes obvious that the sperm of the father, not the ovum of the mother, determines the sex of the new individual. The character of the male sperm cell, X or Y, that fertilizes the ovum determines the sex of the child. If the sperm contains a Y chromosome the child will be male; if the sperm contains an X chromosome the child is normally female. If this process fails to operate effectively individuals may be born with either too few or too many chromosomes. Numerous chromosomal abnormalities are recognized. The XXY or Klinefelter Syndrome is one in which the person is usually found to be outwardly male but sterile, somewhat mentally retarded and suffering from some breast enlargement. This anomaly (which occurs in approximately one out of every 400–500 male births) has been linked with antisocial behavior, especially alcoholism and homosexuality, but as yet few findings of importance have been published. XXYY males have also been discovered. These persons generally exhibit the same physical features as XXY males but the view has been expressed that the additional Y chromosome may have a deleterious effect on the development of their personality and, as a consequence, on their behavior. It is, however, the XYY male who is presently of special interest to criminologists.[67]

[67]Fox, "The XYY Offender," p. 61.

The XYY chromosome hypothesis is of quite recent origin, for the first male with this pattern was not discovered until 1961. Additionally, that individual was *not* abnormal but, instead, was normal in behavior and of average physical structure and intelligence. Shortly after the discovery of this male, several dramatic cases of criminality came to light in Australia, France, and the United States, involving males with the chromosomal abnormality. In several criminal trials in 1968 and 1969 in the United States, the XYY chromosomal pattern has been offered as a defense but has not been upheld by the juries.[68]

As Fox notes, some authorities have contended that persons with an extra Y chromosome tend toward tall stature, long arms, severe acne, mental retardation, severe mental illness, and pronounced aggressive antisocial behavior of long duration. Clearly, if such a pattern were established, biological endowment would be linked to criminality.

Fox has also reviewed a series of studies showing that the XYY pattern is found in only about 0.15 percent of newborn male infants in the United States, Scotland, and Canada; it appeared in about 3 percent of the males in a Scottish maximum security mental hospital where offenders were incarcerated, and it was also found to be more frequent in some other samples of offenders.[69] Fox concludes that: "It cannot be denied that there is evidence that gross chromosomal abnormalities are found in small but unexpected numbers of males who become institutionalized for criminal or abnormal psychiatric behavior; but the stage at which it is meaningful to talk of an XYY syndrome . . . has certainly not been reached."[70]

The evidence at hand only indicates that somewhat larger numbers of incarcerated deviants than normal members of the population have the XYY pattern (although some males who have the XYY pattern are not abnormal or criminal). Regarding violent bizarre antisocial tendencies on the part of such individuals, the existing data indicate that "contrary to expectations generated by popular reports and mass media, the studies done thus far are largely in agreement and demonstrate rather conclusively that males of the XYY type are not predictably aggressive. If anything, as a group they are somewhat less aggressive than comparable XY's."[71] Existing evidence does not support notions that physical, neurological, and physiological abnormalities characterize XYY individuals.[72] Fox and several others also suggest that the apparent tendency for XYY persons to be relatively tall may be implicated in a social way in criminality; courts and psychiatrists may be biased in directing them toward

[68]These events are chronicled in *ibid.*, pp. 59–61.

[69]*Ibid.*, pp. 62–73.

[70]*Ibid.*, p. 66.

[71]*Ibid.*, pp. 72–73, Sarbin and Miller, "Demonism Revisited," p. 199.

[72]Fox "The XYY Offender," p. 370.

mental hospitals and prisons because their great build and height presents a frightening picture.

In summary, the XYY pattern is rare enough in the population that it cannot be a major factor in lawbreaking. Additionally, identified offenders who show this pattern seem not to be violent and aggressive individuals, contrary to popular views. Finally, how the XYY pattern produces deviant behavior, if indeed it does have this effect, remains unclear. Fox, as well as Theodore Sarbin and Jeffrey Miller, contends that this argument about XYY chromosomes is a modern version of demonism, in which fruitless attempts are made to locate the causes of crime in internal defects within the offender rather than in the operation of social and cultural factors.

SUMMARY

This chapter has dealt with a number of past endeavors to make sense out of criminality. Most of these have proved unrewarding. Whatever the explanation of lawbreaking, it is not to be found in defective heredity, biological taint, or in the other formulations presented in this chapter. But what of modern attempts to discover the causal processes in crime? The next several chapters turn to this topic. One of the most widely held views of crime is that it is the work of individuals with psychological or emotional problems. Chapter Seven is devoted to theories and evidence on psychogenic factors in criminal deviance.

7

PSYCHOGENIC APPROACHES

This chapter continues the overview of basic approaches to causal analysis begun in Chapter Six. This survey is aimed at showing the major directions of psychiatric and psychological views. We will comment on specific psychogenic theories and research as they bear on offender role patterns in the chapters on specific criminal types, so the present chapter is a general introductory statement.

In Chapter One, we noted that the psychogenic approach is devoted predominantly to social-psychological questions regarding criminality and delinquency so that it attempts to specify the factors that result in lawbreaking by particular actors. The central hypothesis is that the critical causal factors or variables center around personality problems to which criminal deviance is presumed to be a response. Regarding delinquent behavior, August Aichhorn, a pioneering figure in the development of this perspective, has declared: "There must be something in the child himself which the environment brings out in the form of delinquency."[1] Criminals and delinquents behave as they do because they are in some way "sick" or "maladjusted." Aichhorn's statement also indicates a second premise of psychogenic perspectives: the environment may act as a precipitating but never as a primary force in causation. However, as we shall see in later sections of this chapter, different psychogenic statements accord varying weight to the influences of environmental pressure. Thus, psychogenic arguments have given more or less attention to environmental or social factors.

Effort concentrated on social-psychological types of causal questions has introduced a fundamental ambiguity into psychiatric formulations. These arguments are nearly always mute regarding *rates* of deviance. Although we may concentrate our energies on some portion or body of causal questions and give less emphasis to other explanatory problems, in the interest of clarity we should identify partial answers and the hypotheses accounting for other parts of the phenomena to be explained. The issue here concerns the differen-

[1]August Aichhorn, *Wayward Youth* (New York: Meridian Books, 1955), p. 30.

151

tial rates of criminality among the different social classes and among other segments of the population. Official data regarding conventional criminality, to which psychogenic propositions are usually applied, suggest that this kind of illegality is heavily concentrated in lower-class groups, minority groups, and so forth. How are psychogenic claims, emphasizing personality problems of offenders, to be reconciled with the epidemiological observations?

Several possibilities make psychological hypotheses compatible with epidemiological observations. One proposition is that personality problems, however widespread or relatively uncommon, are not class concentrated. These personality pathologies lead to criminality under certain environmental stresses but eventuate in other responses in different environmental settings. We could argue that middle-class individuals solve their emotional tensions in noncriminal ways. Such a possibility is certainly plausible enough. Perhaps a severe condition of social deprivation is required to impel emotionally upset individuals toward criminality, whereas in a less stressful set of social circumstances emotional tensions can be discharged in noncriminal avenues.

A second argument holds that personality problems are common at all social class levels. Further, these personality dynamics result in criminality as a common response in all class groups, but differential law enforcement practices result in lower-status individuals becoming officially designated as offenders and middle-class persons remaining "hidden" criminals. A third proposition supposes that personality problems and criminality are both concentrated in lower-class groups so that middle-class persons are both noncriminal in behavior and well adjusted in terms of mental health.[2]

At this juncture, we are not concerned with adjudicating among these several possibilities. In fact, our bias is toward a fourth possibility: conventional offenders do not commonly exhibit personality problems at all. However, most psychiatric formulations have failed to be concerned with epidemiological issues, so they are ambiguous as to how such claims fit with the apparent facts of criminality.

The psychogenic perspective, largely the product of psychiatrists, has been a major theme in etiological analysis, with a large number of articles and books presenting causal theories and research in these terms. This approach has been the dominant influence in the development of treatment theories and processes. The rise of the rehabilitative orientation in correction has centered, for the most part, around the growth of individual treatment policies and theories arguing that offenders are emotionally "sick." Prison programs, probation services, guidance clinics, juvenile courts, and other treatment agencies

---

[2]Several studies have been conducted on the issue of class linkages and mental disorder, with results that are not entirely clear. See August B. Hollingshead and Fredrick C. Redlich, *Social Class and Mental Illness* (New York: John Wiley & Sons, 1958); Leo Srole, Thomas S. Langner, Stanley T. Michael, Marvin K. Opler, and Thomas A. C. Rennie, *Mental Health in the Metropolis: The Midtown Manhattan Study* (New York: McGraw-Hill Book Co., 1962).

have considered the lawbreaker as an emotionally disturbed person in need of psychotherapeutic treatment, almost to the exclusion of any other tactic.[3]

This chapter summarizes the basic outlines of the psychogenic perspective. This is no small job, so we need a taxonomic scheme if we are to present a satisfactory summary and critique of the many variants of psychogenic theory and research endeavors.

FORMS OF PSYCHOGENIC ANALYSIS

First, let us consider the now defunct concern with the hypothesis that criminals are to be explained as sufferers from some form of psychosis or some other marked pattern of mental disorder. This early idea failed to pass the test of evidence. The major portion of this chapter examines a number of contemporary psychogenic perspectives, which, in one form or another, advance the thesis that offenders respond to relatively subtle psychological forces rather than to some kind of gross pathology. The *psychoanalytic* position is one of these variants, growing out of the framework of psychoanalytic theory developed by Sigmund Freud and extended to crime and delinquency by Aichhorn, Friedlander, and others. In addition, a host of more *general arguments* regarding misbehavior and personality problems do not stem directly from psychoanalytic thought, such as the work of Healy and Bronner, Hewitt and Jenkins, the Gluecks, and many others. A third argument is that criminal deviance is the product of *psychopathic* or *sociopathic* personality structures.

In the following material, psychogenic statements regarding both criminals and delinquents will be noted. There are several reasons for discussing psychiatric claims about juvenile delinquents. Many of the most detailed versions of psychiatric viewpoints have been concerned with delinquents. Many psychogenic arguments imply that they hold for adult and juvenile lawbreakers alike. Finally, separation of adult from youthful offenders is often an arbitrary distinction, in that many juvenile delinquents eventually become adult criminals. If personality problems and emotional tensions are involved in juvenile misconduct, they are also indirectly implicated in the causation of adult criminality.

The concluding part of this chapter articulates some psychogenic considerations that we must attend to in the development of etiological theory. Our view is that certain psychological formulations are essential elements of crime

---

[3]For an analysis of the theoretical foundations of correctional treatment theory, see Don C. Gibbons, *Changing the Lawbreaker* (Englewood Cliffs, N.J.: Prentice-Hall, 1965). For two recent versions of psychiatric argument concerning causes and treatment of crime, see Karl Menninger, *The Crime of Punishment* (New York: The Viking Press, 1968); Seymour L. Halleck, *Psychiatry and the Dilemmas of Crime* (New York: Harper & Row, Publishers, 1967).

causation and we cannot overlook them if we are to explain criminality.[4] In some kinds of criminal behavior, emotional tensions play a highly significant causal role. However, as will become clear in the following discussions, a number of improvements are needed in psychogenic theory and research before psychogenic formulations can be amalgamated with sociogenic views.

MENTAL DISORDER AND CRIME

Following the demise of the feeblemindedness theory of criminality, the idea grew that criminality is often attributable to serious forms of mental disorder or impairment. In the early enthusiasm for this view, large proportions of offenders were diagnosed as suffering from mental pathology. Thus, 99.5 percent of the inmates at the Pontiac Reformatory in Illinois during the period from 1919 to 1929, were classified as psychiatrically abnormal, and most were diagnosed as "psychopathic."[5] Bernard Glueck's frequently cited study of Sing Sing inmates classified 12 percent of the prisoners as mentally diseased or deteriorated, along with 19 percent as "psychopathic personalities."[6] At the same time, a summary of surveys of the incidence of mental disorders among offenders, carried out before 1931, showed wide variations from one jurisdiction to another in the prevalence and forms of pathology reported.[7] This early work reveals more about the biases and preconceptions of the psychiatrists and other diagnosticians than it does about the actual characteristics of offenders.

After the first enthusiasm for the psychopathological hypothesis, inquiries into the extent of psychotic disorders and other gross forms of pathology among criminals involved estimates that these conditions are not much more common in offenders than among law-abiding citizens. One such investigation by the psychiatric clinic of the Court of General Sessions in New York between 1932 and 1935 involved nearly 10,000 felons, of whom only 1.5 percent were diagnosed as psychotic, 6.9 percent as psychoneurotic, 6.9 percent as psychopathic, and 2.4 percent as feebleminded.[8] Stated differently, 82.3 per-

[4]For one comment on this point, see Stanton Wheeler, "The Social Sources of Criminology," *Sociological Inquiry*, 32 (Spring 1962), 144–45.

[5]Paul W. Tappan, *Crime, Justice and Correction* (New York: McGraw-Hill Book Co., 1960), p. 117. Tappan has summarized a relatively large body of related studies of criminality and mental disorder in *Crime, Justice and Correction*, pp. 117–19.

[6]Bernard Glueck, "Concerning Prisoners," *Mental Hygiene*, 2 (April 1918), 177–218.

[7]Morris Ploscowe, *Some Causative Factors in Criminality*, vol. 1 of the Reports of the National Commission on Law Observance and Enforcement (Washington, D.C.: U.S. Government Printing Office, 1931).

[8]Walter Bromberg and Charles B. Thompson, "The Relation of Psychosis, Mental Defect and Personality Types to Crime," *Journal of Criminal Law and Criminology*, 28 (May–June 1937), 70–89; see also Walter Bromberg, *Crime and the Mind* (Philadelphia: J. B. Lippincott Co., 1948).

cent of the individuals passing through that court were diagnosed as "normal," although they were regarded as exhibiting mild forms of some kind of personality maladjustment. A similar report by Paul Schilder for the same court in 1937 indicated substantially the same thing, classifying 83.8 percent of the offenders as "normal."[9] H. Warren Dunham's study of over 500 males committed to the Illinois Security Hospital as criminally insane reached parallel conclusions.[10] According to Dunham, schizophrenia is a negligible factor in the causation of crime, although when criminal behavior and mental disorder occur together in the same person, schizophrenia is more often involved as the form of pathology than are other kinds of disturbance. In turn, schizophrenic disorders are most common in cases of crimes against persons. Results parallel to these were found in another investigation by M. H. Erickson.[11]

By now we might conclude that few criminals are psychotics. These are two different and independent forms of deviance. As this version of psychopathological theory has proved untenable, interest has shifted toward the hypothesis that offenders are responding to more subtle forms of pathology. One of these modern, currently popular views is the psychoanalytic, to which we now turn.

PSYCHOANALYTIC THEORIES

Before we begin our brief summary of Freudian arguments regarding human personality development and criminality, several disclaimers and cautionary remarks are in order.[12] Without doubt, the psychoanalytic position has been the single most influential nineteenth and twentieth century statement on human behavior.[13] It is an extremely complex body of thought, for psychiatrists and other theorists have modified and expanded the theory originally presented in a number of Freud's volumes. Similarly, psychoanalytic essays on crime and delinquency are numerous, lengthy, and complex. We could hardly do

---

[9]Paul Schilder, "The Cure of Criminals and Prevention of Crime," *Journal of Criminal Psychopathology*, 2 (October 1940), 152.

[10]H. Warren Dunham, "The Schizophrene and Criminal Behavior," *American Sociological Review*, 4 (June 1939), 352-61.

[11]M. H. Erickson, "Criminality in a Group of Male Psychiatric Patients," *Mental Hygiene*, 22 (July 1938), 459-76.

[12]For a brief outline of psychoanalytic views and the development of this perspective, see George B. Vold, *Theoretical Criminology* (New York: Oxford University Press, 1958), pp. 114-25; see also Richard R. Korn and Lloyd W. McCorkle, *Criminology and Penology* (New York: Holt, Rinehart and Winston, 1959), pp. 253-57.

[13]Richard T. LaPiere, *The Freudian Ethic* (New York: Duell, Sloan and Pearce, 1959). LaPiere makes a case for a pervasive influence of Freudian thought in twentieth century America, which he views as extremely unfortunate. However, the reviewers have not been altogether kind in their evaluation of this thesis. For example, see the review by Kaspar D. Naegele in *American Sociological Review*, 25 (June 1960), 422-23.

justice to either the general theory or applications of it to criminality in a few pages, so what we present here is a necessarily brief and terse summary.[14]

The Psychoanalytic Argument

Although psychoanalytic thought originated in the writings of Freud (1835-1939),[15] at present a number of versions of psychoanalytic theory exist, inasmuch as Freud's original arguments were elaborated and revised by himself and such persons as Carl Jung, Alfred Adler, Wilhelm Reich, Theodore Reik, and Karen Horney, among others. The basic thesis has been changed considerably over time. Some of the present-day versions remain orthodox and similar to Freud's original views; but others, such as the writings of Horney, represent drastic departures from some of the basic postulates.[16] What follows is a version of psychoanalytic theory in the direction of Freud's original views. This form has been dominant in the explanation of criminal and delinquent behavior.

Three propositions are at the heart of psychoanalytic thought. First, behavior is largely the product of unconscious psychological–biological forces ("drives" or "instincts"), which are not directly perceived or understood by the actor. Second, functional behavior disorders, including criminality, arise out of conflicts related to these basic drives. These behavioral pathologies may be the result of the repression of instinctual energy, which presses for recognition in disguised form, or they may be the product of inadequate socialization so that normal control over impulses is lacking. Third, to modify undesirable behaviors, the person must be guided toward insight into the unconscious roots of his responses so he can develop control over such impulses. Through psychoanalysis or some variant, a skilled psychoanalyst or therapist uncovers the basis of behavior through dream analysis, free associations, and other observations that point to unconscious motivational factors.

According to Freudians, human personality is made up of a trio of provinces or components. Newborn infants enter the world with an energy reservoir

---

[14]Hakeem has authored several critiques of Freudian notions, along with other psychiatric formulations in criminology. See Michael Hakeem, "A Critique of the Psychiatric Approach," in *Juvenile Delinquency*, ed. Joseph S. Roucek (New York: Philosophical Library, 1958), pp. 79-112; Hakeem, "A Critique of the Psychiatric Approach to Crime and Correction," *Law and Contemporary Problems*, 23 (Autumn 1958), 650-82.

[15]Sigmund Freud, *The Ego and the Id*, trans. Joan Riviere (London: Hogarth Press, 1927); Freud, *A General Introduction to Psychoanalysis* (New York: Boni and Liveright, 1920); Freud, *Civilization and its Discontents*, trans. and ed. A. A. Brill (New York: The Modern Library, 1938); A. A. Brill, *Freud's Contribution to Psychiatry* (New York: W. W. Norton and Co., 1944); Patrick Mullahy, *Oedipus: Myth and Complex* (New York: Hermitage Press, 1952); Bartlett H. Stoodley, *The Concepts of Sigmund Freud* (New York: The Free Press, 1959). For a relatively brief but lucid and careful summary of psychoanalytic thought, see Calvin S. Hall and Gardner Lindzey, "Psychoanalytic Theory and its Application in the Social Sciences," *Handbook of Social Psychology*, ed. Gardner Lindzey (Reading, Mass.: Addison-Wesley Publishing Co., 1954), pp. 143-80.

[16]For a summary of the various schools of psychoanalytic thought, see Ruth S. Monroe, *Schools of Psychoanalytic Thought* (New York: Dryden Press, 1955).

of instinctive, biological drives which are uncontaminated by external reality and undifferentiated in terms of object at birth. This component of personality is the *Id*, or instinctual forces, a major but not exclusive part of which centers around sexual drives in a broadly defined sense. At this point, the human organism is prepared to behave only in terms of the *pleasure principle*, toward the discharge of instinctual energy or tension whenever it arises.

However, soon after birth the *Ego* begins to develop. The autistic, self-absorbed infant begins to acquire an awareness of self as distinct from the surrounding environment and begins to adapt his drives to the exigencies of reality. Expression of instinctual drives may have to be temporarily postponed due to unavailability of a suitable outlet or the wishes of other persons in the immediate environment. The Ego represents that outgrowth of the Id which adapts the instinctual urges to one another and to the demands of reality. As such, the Ego operates as the executive of the personality. Under the influence of the external world, one part of the Id undergoes a special development to act as intermediary between the Id and the world of reality. This is the Ego, which determines whether an instinct shall be allowed to obtain satisfaction or be suppressed. The Ego reaches such decisions in terms of the *reality principle*; the Ego attempts to allow or postpone instinctual gratification so as to minimize pain. Initially, the Id and the Ego are not in conflict, for the Ego works under the guidance of the reality principle to get satisfactions for the Id.

The third component of personality, which develops out of Ego in childhood, is called the *Superego*. The Superego is the last part of the personality to be formed and consists in large part of morality or conscience. The Superego is formed out of the Ego from introjected standards and expectations of parents and other authority figures. In essence, the Superego represents the norms, values, and ideals of the society which the actor internalizes as his own. It functions to "police" the person by laying down rules and punishing him for failure to behave properly. This psychic punishment consists of guilt feelings and anxiety. The Superego limits the expression of instinctual energy, not in accordance with the reality principle but with the perfectionist standards of parents and authority figures.

In a well-balanced personality, these three components work in relative harmony. But in neurotic individuals and other abnormal cases, some imbalance and disharmony occurs. Superego may become dominant, so that a too-powerful and rigid Superego may create guilt feelings about repressed instinctual drives. Or repressed instinctual energy may press for recognition in disguised form, leading to "bizarre" behavior quite different from surface appearances. In particular, manifestations of the sexual instinct may appear in these forms. Still another possibility is that the Superego may not be sufficiently well developed and that antisocial behavior results as a consequence of poorly controlled instincts.

By and large, Freudians argue that parent–child interactions in early life produce personality balance or disharmony. In particular, variations in the way in which persons go through the stages of sexual development, from the oral stage of infancy, through the anal, phallic, and latency periods to adult heterosexuality have profound consequences for adult behavior. T. Benedek summarizes this idea:

> The integration of the *sexual drive* from its pre-genital sources to the *genital primacy* and to functional maturity is the axis around which the organization of the personality takes place. From the point of view of personality development, the process of interaction is the same in both sexes. Men and women alike reach their psychosexual maturity through the reconciliation of the sexual drive with the superego and through the adjustment of sexuality to all other functions of the personality.[17]

This paragraph highlights the important place instinctual energy of a sexual form occupies in Freudian thought. From such emphasis, it follows that many difficulties identified by psychoanalysts, which emerge in personality development, center around sexual tensions and problems.

Psychoanalytic Interpretations of Criminality

Applications of psychoanalytic notions to criminality grow directly out of the general theory. Vold summarizes the psychoanalytic view of criminality thus:

> Criminal behavior, under this general theoretical orientation, is to be understood, simply and directly, as a substitute response, some form of symbolic release of repressed complexes. The conflict in the unconscious mind gives rise to feelings of guilt and anxiety with a consequent desire for punishment to remove the guilt feelings and restore a proper balance of good against evil. The criminal then commits the criminal act in order to be caught and punished. Unconsciously motivated errors (i.e., careless or imprudent ways of committing the crime) leave "clues" so the authorities may more readily apprehend and convict the guilty, and thus administer suitably cleansing punishment.[18]

The earliest important application of psychoanalytic thought to the explanation of criminal behavior is found in the work of August Aichhorn, an Austrian psychiatrist and director of a correctional institution in that country in the early 1900s.[19] Out of his experience, he began applying Freudian theory to

---

[17]T. Benedek, "Personality Development," in *Dynamic Psychiatry*, ed. Franz Alexander and Helen Ross (Chicago: University of Chicago Press, 1952), p. 100.

[18]Vold, *Theoretical Criminology*, p. 119.

[19]Aichhorn, *Wayward Youth, passim*.

analysis of behavior problems of the boys in his institution. Aichhorn's book, *Wayward Youth*, which presented his line of reasoning, became the parent of a long line of psychoanalytic treatises on crime and delinquency. In addition, his work has played a considerable part in generating enthusiasm for psychiatric views among correctional works in the United States and elsewhere.

Aichhorn's writings describe several kinds of delinquents. Some are alleged to be similar to neurotic individuals; others are aggressive and lacking in Superego development. Some are said to have little capacity for repressing their instinctual drives; others are believed to have strong, distorted cravings for affection.[20]

We need not consider Aichhorn's theories in great detail here. His work is important now insofar as it has stimulated psychoanalytic analyses of criminality. His writings describe Austrian juveniles who may be quite unlike American youths. His descriptions are from more than thirty years ago, so we cannot easily argue that his propositions have much contemporary etiological relevance.

A plethora of psychoanalytic writings regarding crime and delinquency has emerged in the past several decades.[21] For example, Kate Friedlander has devoted an entire book to the exposition of this view.[22] In the main, she agrees with Aichhorn that delinquents are persons expressing antisocial impulses repressed in normal persons. Unfavorable environments play a part in lawbreaking, but only as a precipitating cause that calls out antisocial impulses from within the person.[23] In general, she also argues that the difference between neurotic and criminalistic persons is that the former are characterized by overly strict Superegos, whereas the latter show weak and defective Superegos stemming from early parental deprivations in childhood.[24]

The volume *Searchlights on Delinquency* presents another example of psychoanalytic theory.[25] This book, commemorating Aichhorn's seventieth birthday, includes an essay by Adelaide Johnson on the theme of Superego

[20]*Ibid.*, p. 115.

[21]Prominent examples of psychoanalytic writings on criminality include David Abrahamsen, *Crime and the Human Mind* (New York: Columbia University Press, 1945); Abrahamsen, *Who Are the Guilty?* (New York: Holt, Rinehart and Winston, 1952); Abrahamsen, *The Psychology of Crime* (New York: Columbia University Press, 1960); Franz Alexander and William Healy, *Roots of Crime* (New York: Alfred A. Knopf, 1935); Alexander and Hugo Staub, *The Criminal, the Judge, and the Public*, rev. ed. (New York: The Free Press, 1956); Lucien Bovet, *Psychiatric Aspects of Juvenile Delinquency* (Geneva: World Health Organization, 1951); Kate Friedlander, *The Psychoanalytic Approach to Juvenile Delinquency* (London: Routledge and Kegan Paul, 1947); Benjamin Karpman, *The Individual Criminal* (Washington: Nervous and Mental Disease Publishing Co., 1935); Robert M. Lindner, *Rebel Without a Cause* (New York: Grune & Stratton, 1944); Lindner, *Stone Walls and Men* (New York: Odyssey Press, 1946); William A. White, *Crimes and Criminals* (New York: Farrar and Rinehart, 1933); Gregory Zilboorg, *The Psychology of the Criminal Act and Punishment* (New York: Harcourt Brace Jovanovich, 1954).

[22]Friedlander, *The Psychoanalytic Approach to Juvenie Delinquency, passim.*

[23]*Ibid.*, pp. 7–10.

[24]*Ibid.*, pp. 116–17.

[25]K. R. Eissler, ed., *Searchlights on Delinquency* (New York: International Universities Press, 1949).

Lacunae, in which parents are considered to frequently encourage delinquent acts by their children so as to gratify their own forbidden impulses.[26] But the most striking impression that emerges from this symposium is of the great amount of disagreement and internal inconsistency among the different contributors; it is a mistake to suppose that there is only one psychoanalytic theory of criminality.

David Abrahamsen's writings constitute a final illustration of modern psychoanalytic commentary.[27] Although he concedes that environmental and social factors play some part in causation, Abrahamsen dismisses these as having only a precipitating, never primary, role in etiology. His theory of causation is indicated in these remarks: "In general we may say that the causes of a child's delinquent behavior may be traced to his parents, particularly to his mother's emotional attitude toward his early instinctual manifestations, which may be partly caused by her own personality makeup or by other elements from his environment. In addition, his antisocial attitude is also accentuated by the particular way his Ego and Superego [conscience] develop."[28] One of Abrahamsen's better known notions is what he terms a mathematical law expressing the relationship between factors in criminality. That "law" takes the form, $C = T + S/R$, in which C stands for crime, T for tendencies, S for the situation, and R for psychological resistances to impulses.[29] This law is nothing more than pseudomathematical shorthand, for the significant etiological factors in criminality are not likely to be reduced to as few as three mathematical terms.

Criticisms of the Psychoanalytic Position

General psychoanalytic formulations and applications to criminality have not suffered from a lack of criticism.[30] One line of attack centers around the vague, obscure language and circular reasoning at points in the argument that render many of the central propositions within the theory untestable because of claims about "unconscious" mind and other notions of that kind. For example, Vold declares: "A methodology [as in psychoanalysis] under which only the patient knows the 'facts' of the case, and only the analyst understands the meaning of those 'facts' as revealed to him by the patient, does not lend

---

[26]Adelaide M. Johnson, "Sanctions for Superego Lacunae of Adolescents," in Eissler, *Searchlights on Delinquency*, pp. 225–45. For a critique of this argument, see Hakeem, "A Critique of the Psychiatric Approach."

[27]Abrahamsen, *Crime and the Human Mind, passim.*

[28]Abrahamsen, *Who Are the Guilty?*, p. 27.

[29]*Ibid.*, pp. 67–72.

[30]For a discussion of some of these criticisms, see Hall and Lindzey, "Psychoanalytic Theory and its Application in the Social Sciences"; Robert E. L. Faris, *Social Psychology* (New York: The Ronald Press, 1952), pp. 11–33; Korn and McCorkle, *Criminology and Penology*, pp. 253–57; Vold, *Theoretical Criminology*, pp. 114–25.

itself to external, third person, impersonal vertificiation or to generalization beyond the limits of any particular case."[31]

Another group of criticisms deals with the substantive content of the theory, that is, the truth claims of psychoanalytic thought. Some of the most frequent and important of these are:

1. The theory is erroneous because it assumes biological motivation, particularly instincts. Evidence indicates that instincts or drives do not exist and that human behavior is not the product of biological forces.

2. The argument is defective because it stresses the impact of experiences of infancy and early childhood, particularly weaning, toilet training, and so on, for personality development. The data do not bear out these consequences of early and harsh toilet training and other experiences for later personality formation.[32]

3. The theory is flawed because it minimizes the influence of social factors on human behavior. Personality patterns develop out of variations in socialization experiences among cultures, and within a particular society, so that the influences of culture and social structure represent more than simply precipitating forces in their effects. However, variations exist among psychoanalysts regarding the role assigned to cultural variables in personality development; in addition, the fact that psychoanalysts do not pay much attention to cultural variables does not by itself invalidate psychoanalytic arguments.

4. The theory overemphasizes sexual aspects of behavior and motivation. The supposition that most human behavior is linked, directly or indirectly, to erotic sources of motivation is erroneous. In particular, the Freudian claims regarding infantile sexuality are open to serious question.[33]

These charges against Freudian theory apply to both the general argument and its applications to criminality. Several specific criticisms of psychoanalytic conceptions of delinquent and criminal behavior have also been offered. As we noted at the beginning of this chapter, these theories about so-called neurotic, "acting-out" offenders as opposed to conventional neurotic individuals are not clear. Both are alleged to result from the same causal dynamics. If so, why do two outcomes result from the same etiological processes? The conventional answer has been that criminal behavior is available in the environment for the "acting-out" offender to take over as a response. But this begs the question, for the existence of lawbreaking traditions in some areas and not in others must be explained.

[31]Vold, *Theoretical Criminology*, p. 125.

[32]This evidence is contained in Harold Orlansky, "Infant Care and Personality," *Psychological Bulletin*, 46 (January 1949), 1–48; Robert R. Sears, *Survey of Objective Studies of Psychoanalytic Concepts* (New York: Social Science Research Council, 1943); William H. Sewell, "Infant Training and the Personality of the Child," *American Journal of Sociology*, 58 (September 1952), 150–59.

[33]Faris, *Social Psychology*, pp. 25–26.

These criticisms persuade us to reject psychoanalytic views of criminality in favor of alternative theories that make better sense of the facts of lawbreaking. Irrational elements might sometimes enter into acts of criminality, and some offenders might sometimes only be dimly aware or totally oblivious of the reasons for their actions. In this sense, lawbreaking is "unconsciously" motivated. However, we submit that the particular formulations of unconscious mainsprings of human action found in psychoanalytic theories of criminality are erroneous. In addition, a major portion of the criminal population involves actors whose behavior is not to be attributed to unconscious elements of personality or personality aberrations of any kind, who are instead normal, well-socialized individuals. We agree with David Maurer, who argues that mental "conflicts" are absent among pickpockets, likening this situation to the Sioux Indians: "I venture to suggest that any psychiatrist who tried to give the participants in the Custer massacre insight into their 'guilt' feelings in connection with this event would have had rough going indeed. Those Sioux who exterminated Custer's force were behaving as they were expected to be in their culture; they enjoyed every bit of it, and derived status from it which they carried to their dying days."[34]

EMOTIONAL PROBLEMS AND CRIMINALITY

Beginning around 1900, psychiatrists and others have written much about personality problems or emotional disturbances and criminality, a great deal of which is independent of orthodox Freudian interpretations. The emotional dynamics they have identified are of many kinds, and they have alleged that the genesis of these problems involves a large variety of background situations, particularly parent–child tensions and distorted relationships. Hyman Grossbard claims that most delinquents exhibit inefficient or underdeveloped ego mechanisms, so they tend to act out conflicts instead of handling them by rational means or symptom formation, as do nondelinquents.[35] This view owes something to the psychoanalytic position, but it does not strictly follow Freudian theory.

Some Early Studies

Cyril Burt's allegation that 85 percent of the delinquents he studied were emotionally impaired is an early example of the general personality problems view.[36] Probably the most influential of the older studies of delinquency and emotional disturbance was the research of William Healy and Augusta Bronner, comparing 105 delinquents with 105 of their nondelinquent siblings in New

[34]David W. Maurer, *Whiz Mob* (New Haven, Conn.: College and University Press, 1964) pp. 16–17.
[35]Hyman Grossbard, "Ego Deficiency in Delinquents," *Social Casework*, 43 (April 1962), 171–78.
[36]Cyril Burt, *The Young Delinquent* (London: University of London Press, 1938).

Haven, Boston, and Detroit. After examining these children, Healy and Bronner concluded: ". . . it finally appears that no less than 90 percent of the delinquents gave clear evidence of being or having been unhappy and discontented in their life circumstances or extremely emotionally disturbed because of emotion-provoking situations or experiences. In great contradistinction we found similar evidence of inner stresses at the most in only 13 percent of the controls."[37]

These are impressive findings indeed. Nevertheless, this investigation has received critical attention as well as acclaim.[38] The critics have pointed out that the differences between the delinquents and nonoffenders were probably exaggerated, because the staff members who reported on personality characteristics of the subjects were psychiatrists and psychiatric social workers, predisposed to the view that the major causal variable in delinquency is emotional disturbance. Also, the clinical assessments were obtained by subjective methods, no attempt being made to conceal the identities of the subjects prior to the psychiatric examinations. Knowledge of the delinquent–nondelinquent status of the subjects may have colored their judgments. Moreover, the psychiatric workers were conducting a treatment program with the offenders and were in greater contact with them. The question arises: If they had spent an equvalent amount of time with the nonoffenders, would they have observed emotional problems originally overlooked? The critics have built such a damaging case against the Healy and Bronner investigation that we cannot accept the findings of this study as valid. At best other research results only partially support these psychogenic contentions.

Although not directly relevant to the study of criminality, the research of H. Hartshorne and M. A. May produced results that create grave problems for a simplified psychogenic thesis.[39] These researchers devised objective methods to study such hypothesized personality characteristics as "deceit," but their major finding was that apparently no general traits of this kind exist. Instead, traits are specific to particular situations—children steal under some circumstances and not others.

Advocates of psychogenic arguments must also contend with the findings of Karl Schuessler and Donald Cressey, who reviewed a large number of studies of personality characteristics of delinquents and criminals. They concluded: ". . . of 113 such comparisons, 42 percent showed differences in favor of the noncriminal, while the remainder were indeterminate. The doubtful validity of many of the obtained differences, as well as the lack of consistency in the combined results makes it impossible to conclude from these data that

[37]William Healy and Augusta F. Bronner, New Light on Delinquency and its Treatment (New Haven, Conn.: Yale University Press, 1936), p. 122.

[38]Hakeem, "A Critique of the Psychiatric Approach," pp. 89–95; Edwin H. Sutherland and Donald R. Cressey, Principles of Criminology, 8th ed. (Philadelphia: J. B. Lippincott Co., 1970), pp. 163–64.

[39]H. Hartshorne and M. A. May, Studies in the Nature of Character, vol. 1 (New York: The Macmillan Co., 1929); Hartshorne, May, and F. K. Shuttleworth, Studies in the Nature of Character, vol. 3 (New York: The Macmillan Co., 1930).

criminality and personality elements are associated."[40] More recently, Gordon Waldo and Simon Dinitz updated Schuessler and Cressey's survey and reviewed a series of studies done since 1950.[41] They too find no clear psychological factors associated with criminality, at least as these investigations indicate.

Recent Work

Hakeem has reviewed data from surveys of emotional disturbance among cases from an adolescents' court, a psychiatric clinic attached to a juvenile court, and a juvenile correctional institution.[42] The findings show a diversity of diagnostic decisions in each of the studies. One set of diagnostic labels categorized a number of offenders as suffering from psychoneurosis or neurotic character disturbances; in two other studies this category did not appear. Immaturity and mental conflict appear in one report but not in the others. In addition, in comparable diagnostic groups in the three investigations, the separate tabulations contain diverse proportions of offenders. Hence, Hakeem concluded that the results probably reveal more about the biases of the psychiatrists than about the characteristics of offenders. In addition, a number of the diagnostic categories in these three studies are of dubious validity. For example, in one, the diagnosis "conduct disorders" is used to classify about one-third of the cases. But were any identifiable characteristics of offenders used to recognize conduct disorders apart from the facts of involvement in delinquency? Quite likely, a tautological classification was involved; the delinquent activity of the juvenile was used to indicate the existence of a conduct disorder.

One report Hakeem cited is the Gluecks' investigation in *Unraveling Juvenile Delinquency.*[43] The delinquents and controls in this research were subjected to a psychiatric interview and Rorschach tests, a projective instrument designed to measure basic personality traits. The Gluecks report: "Considering first those traits in which the delinquents as a group significantly exceed the nondelinquents, we observed that they are to a much greater degree socially assertive, defiant and ambivalent to authority; they are more resentful of others, and far more hostile, suspicious and destructive; the goals of their drives are to a much greater extent receptive (Oral) and destructive-sadistic; they are more impulsive and vivacious, and decidedly more extroversive in their behavior trends."[44] A number of characteristics identified through

[40]Karl F. Schuessler and Donald R. Cressey, "Personality Characteristics of Criminals," *American Journal of Sociology,* 55 (March 1950), 476–84.

[41]Gordon P. Waldo and Simon Dinitz, "Personality Attributes of the Criminal: An Analysis of Research Studies, 1950–1965," *Journal of Research in Crime and Delinquency,* 4 (July 1967), 185–202.

[42]Hakeem, "A Critique of the Psychiatric Approach," pp. 86–89. Studies of psychological characteristics of delinquents are also summarized in Don C. Gibbons, *Delinquent Behavior* (Englewood Cliffs, N.J.: Prentice-Hall, 1970), pp. 76–89; Herbert C. Quay, *Juvenile Delinquency* (Princeton, N.J.: D. Van Nostrand Co., 1965), pp. 139–69.

[43]Sheldon Glueck and Eleanor Glueck, *Unraveling Juvenile Delinquency* (Cambridge, Mass.: Harvard University Press, 1951).

[44]*Ibid.,* p. 240.

the Rorschach test as more common among offenders are not clearly signs of maladjustment. Assertiveness, impulsiveness, and vivacity could indicate that the delinquents are better adjusted than the nondelinquents.

Psychiatric diagnoses of the offenders and nondelinquent controls brought out several points.[45] First, the differences between the two groups were not pronounced; about half of both groups showed no conspicuous mental pathology. Second, the delinquents classified as showing mental deviations exhibited a variety of disorders, whereas the disturbed nonoffenders were predominantly neurotic or showed neurotic trends. This finding runs counter to many psychogenic arguments in the criminological literature, which suggest that delinquency is a form of neurotic, acting-out behavior.

Another body of research data on the psychogenic thesis comes from studies using the Minnesota Multiphasic Personality Inventory.[46] The MMPI includes eight scales in which certain responses to questions in each scale are indicative of particular personality patterns. For example, persons with high scale points on the Pa, paranoia scale, of the MMPI give responses similar to those of individuals clinically diagnosed as suffering from paranoia.

One piece of research using this inventory involved its application to over 4,000 Minneapolis ninth grade pupils during 1948. In 1950, the same children were traced through the Hennepin County Juvenile Court and the Minneapolis Police Department to determine which had acquired records of delinquency. Of the boys, 22.2 percent had become delinquent, and 7.6 percent of the girls had become known to the court or the police. In analyzing the responses of delinquents and nonoffenders, the researchers found such results as these: 27.7 percent of the boys with high Pd (psychopathic deviate) scale points were delinquent, as were 25.4 percent with high Pa (paranoia) scale points. Of the boys with "Invalid" responses indicating uncooperativeness, lying, and so on, 37.5 percent were delinquent. Thus, delinquent boys tend to show disproportionate numbers in some of the scale areas of the MMPI, and substantially similar results were obtained with girls.

Starke Hathaway and Elio Monachesi are modest in the claims they make on the basis of these data. In the main, they argue only that the inventory

[45]Ibid., p. 239–43.

[46]Starke Hathaway and Elio D. Monachesi, eds., Analyzing and Predicting Juvenile Delinquency with the Minnesota Multiphasic Personality Inventory (Minneapolis: University of Minnesota Press, 1953); Hathaway and Monachesi, "The Minnesota Multiphasic Personality Inventory in the Study of Juvenile Delinquents," American Sociological Review, 17 (December 1952), 704–10; Hathaway and Monachesi, Adolescent Personality and Behavior—MMPI Patterns (Minneapolis: University of Minnesota Press, 1963); Dora F. Capwell, "Personality Patterns of Adolescent Girls: II. Delinquents and Nondelinquents," Journal of Applied Psychology, 29 (August 1945), 289–97; Elio D. Monachesi, "Some Personality Characteristics of Delinquents and Non-delinquents," Journal of Criminal Law and Criminology, 38 (January–February 1948), 487–500; Monachesi, "Personality Characteristics and Socio-Economics Status of Delinquents and Non-delinquents," Journal of Criminal Law and Criminology 40 (January–February 1950), 570–83; Monachesi, "Personality Characteristics of Institutionalized and Noninstitutionalized Male Delinquents," Journal of Criminal Law and Criminology, 41 (July–August 1950), 167–79; Thomas E. Hannum and Roy E. Warman, "The MMPS Characteristics of Incarcerated Females," Journal of Research in Crime and Delinquency, 1 (July 1964), 119–26.

possesses some discriminatory power. Nevertheless, critics have noted the problems of interpretation involved in the variability of results and have pointed out that a number of social factors correlate more highly with delinquency than do MMPI scores.[47]

One quite recent and sophisticated piece of work on personality characteristics of offenders concerns the Jesness Inventory.[48] This instrument, developed in the California correctional system, involves eight scales and a delinquency prediction score. The eight scales measure defensiveness, value orientation, neuroticism, authority attitude, family orientation, psychoticism, delinquency orientation, and emotional immaturity. Data from the development and validation studies of this inventory indicate that delinquents and nondelinquents do *not* differ significantly on defensiveness, value orientation, neuroticism, or family orientation. The two groups do vary on authority attitude, with delinquents exhibiting the greater hostility toward authority figures. They also differ on psychoticism, as the offenders are more suspicious and distrustful of other persons. Additionally, the two empirical scales, delinquency orientation and emotional immaturity, differentiate the delinquents from the nondelinquents. Compared to the nonoffenders, institutionalized delinquents are more concerned about being normal, exhibit more marked feelings of isolation, are less mature, lack insight, and tend to deny that they have problems.

John Conger and Wilbur Miller's relatively recent study deals with tenth grade students in Denver schools in 1956.[49] Youths who had appeared in juvenile court were identified as a subgroup among the students. Both delinquents and nondelinquents were studied retrospectively so that school records and teachers' ratings of the youths were examined. Conger and Miller found that teachers had viewed the delinquent youths as less well-adjusted than the nonoffenders as far back as the third grade. Additionally, personality tests administered to the two groups indicated that the delinquents were more immature, egocentric, impulsive, inconsiderate, and hostile than the nondelinquents.

A final case of psychogenic theorizing is the Interpersonal Maturity Levels (I-Levels) system currently in use in the juvenile correctional system in Califor-

[47]Clarence C. Schrag, review of Hathaway and Monachesi, *Analyzing and Predicting Delinquency with the Minnesota Multiphasic Personality Inventory*, American Sociological Review, 19 (August 1954), 490–91; Sethard Fisher, "The M.M.P.I.: Assessing a Famous Personality Test," *American Behavioral Scientist*, 6 (October 1962), 21–22. Fisher's main point, on which this book concurs, is that the M.M.P.I. is fundamentally inappropriate in the study of deviant roles. Instead, research needs to look for role-specific patterns of social-psychological characteristics.

[48]Carl F. Jesness, *The Jesness Inventory: Development and Validation*, Research Report No. 29 (Sacramento: California Youth Authority, 1962). See also Jesness, *Redevelopment and Revalidation of the Jesness Inventory*, Research Report No. 35 (Sacramento: California Youth Authority, 1963). The 1963 report presents somewhat different findings from applications of the Jesness Inventory to additional samples. However, the outlines of the Jesness Inventory results from this later study of delinquents and nondelinquents were not materially altered from those of the 1962 report, discussed here.

[49]John Janeway Conger and Wilbur C. Miller, *Personality, Social Class, and Delinquency* (New York: John Wiley & Sons, 1966).

nia.[50] The I-Levels argument contends that there are seven stages or levels of interpersonal maturity, through which persons move as they become socialized. Not all individuals reach the higher levels of interpersonal competence or maturity, remaining fixated at a lower level of development. According to the architects of the I-Levels formulation, delinquents are generally at lower or less developed levels of maturity as contrasted to nondelinquents. The I-Levels scheme further classifies juvenile lawbreakers into nine subtypes within three main interpersonal maturity levels, such as "immature conformist" or "neurotic, acting out." For each diagnostic type, the scheme specifies different patterns of treatment, carried on by different kinds of treatment agents.

The I-Levels theory is a complex formulation in tune with the common view that lawbreakers engage in deviant conduct because of flawed personality structure. However, practitioners have experienced difficulty in sorting real-life offenders into the diagnostic categories. More important, no firm evidence demonstrates that delinquents actually are less interpersonally mature than nonoffenders.

Voices of Dissent

The refrain that virtually all criminality and delinquency is the product of emotional disturbances continues unabated in many quarters, despite considerable evidence indicating that such claims do violence to the facts. At the same time, some psychiatrists have entertained doubts about the validity of psychogenic assertions. Aaron Esman argues, on the basis of impressionistic observations from a child guidance clinic, that a number of types of delinquency exist in the population of official offenders, only some of which fit the simple psychogenic model of the disturbed youngster acting out his problems illegally.[51]

A sophisticated version of psychiatric dissent from simple psychogenic notions is found in the work of Richard L. Jenkins.[52] His arguments are doubly impressive because many of them are solidly anchored in a foundation of careful and objective research rather than based on clinical impressions. Jenkins and several collaborators have been involved in a series of research inves-

[50]For a detailed critique of the I-Levels argument, see Don C. Gibbons, "Differential Treatment of Delinquents and Interpersonal Maturity Levels Theory: A Critique," *Social Service Review*, 44 (March 1970), 22–33.

[51]Aaron H. Esman, "Diagnostic Categories of 'Delinquency,'" *N.P.P.A. Journal*, 1 (October 1955), 113–17. For some other dissenters within psychiatry, see Hakeem, "A Critique of the Psychiatric Approach," p. 82.

[52]H. Hart, Richard L. Jenkins, Sidney Axelrad, and P. Sperling, "Multiple Factor Analysis of Traits of Delinquent Boys," *Journal of Social Psychology*, 17 (May 1943), 191–201; Richard L. Jenkins and Sylvia Glickman, "Common Syndromes in Child Psychiatry," *American Journal of Orthopsychiatry*, 16 (April 1946), 244–61; Jenkins and Glickman, "Patterns of Personality Organization Among Delinquents," *Nervous Child*, 6 (July 1947), 329–39; Lester E. Hewitt and Richard L. Jenkins, *Fundamental Patterns of Maladjustment, The Dynamics of Their Origin* (Springfield: State of Illinois Printer, 1947); Jenkins and Hewitt, "Types of Personality Structure Encountered in Child Guidance Clinics," *American Journal of Orthopsychiatry*, 14 (January 1944), 84–94.

tigations of delinquent types, out of which Jenkins has advanced two common forms of misbehavior—adaptive and maladaptive delinquency.[53] Jenkins claims that delinquent misconduct is not a form of neurotic behavior, for neuroticism involves a high level of inhibition, sense of duty, and introjected standards and strict superego control, whereas delinquency is frequently the direct opposite of such a pattern. According to Jenkins, most offenders are less neurotic than nonoffenders. In addition, only the maladaptive version or the unsocialized delinquent offender has a disturbed personality. The aggressive delinquent is poorly socialized, lacking in internalized controls, antagonistic toward his peers, and generally maladjusted. The more frequently encountered adaptive, or pseudosocial, violator is usually the product of lower-class slum areas and is reasonably well-socialized and "normal" among his peers and parents. He has attenuated inhibitions; his loyalty and group identification does not extend to the wider community beyond his local area and immediate peers. He engages in depredations against the community with relatively little guilt or concern. From the perspective of agents of law enforcement and social control, such behavior may be defined as abnormal, but in terms of the adaptive offender's immediate situation, his activities are rational and goal directed. His social adjustment, from this perspective, does not justify the judgment that he is maladjusted.

PSYCHOPATHY AND CRIMINALITY

What Is a Psychopath?

According to a popular psychogenic hypothesis, many delinquents and criminals exhibit a particular form of mental pathology, psychopathic personality (or sociopathic personality). The term *psychopath* usually refers to a pattern of pathology characterized by egocentricity, asocial behavior, insensitivity to others, hostility, and so on. Actually, the designation is only one of a number of synonymous terms used at different times, including psychopathic personality, constitutional psychopathic inferiority, moral imbecility, semantic dementia, sociopathy, and moral mania.[54]

What is a psychopath? The answer varies from one respondent to another. Hervey Cleckley provides one definition. He lists six general symptoms:

1. The psychopath is free from neurosis, psychosis, or mental defectiveness. He knows the consequences of his behavior but seems to have no inner feeling for what he verbalizes so rationally.

---

[53]Richard L. Jenkins, "Adaptive and Maladaptive Delinquency," *Nervous Child*, 2 (October 1955), 9–11; Jenkins, "Motivation and Frustration in Delinquency," *American Journal of Orthopsychiatry*, 27 (July 1957), 528–37; Jenkins, *Breaking Patterns of Defeat* (Philadelphia: J. B. Lippincott Co., 1954).
[54]Lindner, *Rebel Without a Cause*, p. 1.

2. The psychopath is habitually unable to adjust his social relations satisfactorily.

3. Punishment does not deter him; instead, he seeks it out.

4. He lacks motivation, or, if motivated, the motivation is not congruent with his behavior.

5. The psychopath expresses normal affective responses but shows a total lack of concern and callous indifference to others.

6. He has poor judgment and does not learn from experience, as is evident from his pathological lying, repeated crime, and other antisocial acts.[55]

Harrison Gough has offered another list of signs of the psychopath, which include overevaluation of immediate goals, unconcern for the rights and privileges of others, and impulsive behavior. Further characteristics of the psychopath are poor loyalty and social attachments, poor planning and judgment, no distress over his maladjustment, and projection of blame to others. Finally, Gough lists as common psychopathic patterns meaningless prevarication, lack of responsibility, and emotional poverty.[56] In both Cleckley's and Gough's descriptions, a picture emerges of a poorly socialized, indifferent, and uncooperative person.

Attempts to account for the genesis of psychopathic personalities have taken several directions. Some authorities have held that these persons are the product of genetic factors. However, the most common hypothesis is that the disorder stems from some defect of family relationships.[57]

If it exists, such a personality pattern might bear more than a slight relationship to criminality, for persons showing these traits might be less subject to the demands of society because they lack inner controls and are insensitive to contemporary conduct norms. However, if we are to make any use of the concept of psychopathic personality, we must first develop some way to recognize psychopaths. But this task is difficult because the concept has not been defined satisfactorily. Note that Gough's and Cleckley's definitions indicate a rather general and unspecific symptomology. Yet these are two of the clearer statements in the literature of psychopathy. Paul Preu, in examining how this concept has been used in practice, tells us: "The term, 'psychopathic personality' as commonly understood, is useless in psychiatric research. It is a diagnosis

[55]Hervey Cleckley, The Mask of Sanity (St. Louis: C. V. Mosby and Co., 1941); Cleckley, "Psychopathic Personality," in Encyclopedia of Criminology, ed. Vernon C. Branham and Samuel B. Kutash (New York: Philosophical Library, 1949), pp. 413–16; Cleckley, "The Psychopath, A Problem for Society," Federal Probation, 10 (October–December 1946), 22–26; see also Ben Karpman, "A Yardstick for Measuring Psychopathy," Federal Probation, 10 (October–December 1946), 26–31.

[56]Harrison G. Gough, "A Sociological Theory of Psychopathy," American Journal of Sociology, 53 (March 1948), 359–66.

[57]Harry R. Lipton, "The Psychopath," Journal of Criminal Law, Criminology and Police Science, 40 (January–February 1950), 584–96. For a general summary of the psychopath literature and hypothesized causes, see S. Kirson Weinberg, Society and Personality Disorders (Englewood Cliffs, N.J.: Prentice-Hall, 1952), pp. 260–97; William McCord and Joan McCord, Psychopathy and Delinquency (New York: Grune & Stratton, 1956).

of convenience arrived at by a process of exclusion. It does not refer to a specific behavioral entity. It serves as a scrapbasket to which is relegated a group of otherwise unclassified personality disorders and problems . . . delinquency of one kind or another constitutes the most frequently utilized symptomatic basis for the diagnosis of psychopathic personality."[58] The term can be used in this way, but if it is to be a synonym for criminality, it cannot be used to explain that same behavior. Other observers have reached much the same conclusion as Preu in indicating that in practical application, the concept has no stable referent and constitutes a psychiatric wastebasket.[59] Alfred Lindesmith points out that the term is frequently used in opiate addiction arguments as an etiological factor, but narcotic addiction itself is usually the evidence on which such a diagnosis depends.[60]

Psychopathy and Criminality

The results of investigations on psychopathy and criminality have been extremely confusing. Sutherland and Cressey have reviewed the evidence and concluded that no relationship has been shown to exist. They note that one psychiatrist at the Illinois State Penitentiary classified 98 percent of the inmates as psychopaths, but in a similar institution with different psychiatrists, only 5 percent of the prisoners were so diagnosed. Such variations tell us more about psychiatrists than they do about prisoners.[61] Other criminologists have reached similar conclusions about the uselessness of the psychopathy notion.[62]

On the other hand, a number of authorities accept the argument that psychopaths exist and that they appear in the population of offenders in inordinate numbers. But in none of these cases is any indication given of how common such personality problems might be in the population at large or in the population of offenders.[63]

In a rather remarkable piece of research on psychopathy,[64] Lee Robins traced the adult adjustments of 524 child guidance clinic patients in St. Louis 30 years after they had appeared in the clinic. She also conducted a follow-up study

[58]Paul W. Preu, "The Concept of Psychopathic Personality," in *Personality and the Behavior Disorders*, vol. 2, ed. J. McV. Hunt (New York: The Ronald Press, 1944), pp. 922–37.

[59]Oskar Diethelm, "Basic Considerations of the Concept of Psychopathic Personality," in *Handbook of Correctional Psychology*, ed. Robert M. Lindner and Robert V. Seliger (New York: Philosophical Library, 1947), p. 384; Weinberg, *Society and Personality Disorders*.

[60]Alfred R. Lindesmith, *Opiate Addiction* (Bloomington: Principia Press, 1947).

[61]Sutherland and Cressey, *Principles of Criminology*, p. 159.

[62]Hakeem, "A Critique of the Psychiatric Approach," p. 111. In his evaluation of McCord and McCord, *Psychopathy and Delinquency*, Hakeem states that the authors missed the important point that the concept of psychopath is useless for etiological explanation.

[63]Walter C. Reckless, *The Crime Problem*, 3rd ed. (New York: Appleton-Century-Crofts, 1961), pp. 292–95; Tappan, *Crime, Justice and Correction*, pp. 137–44; Harry Elmer Barnes and Negley K. Teeters, *New Horizons in Criminology*, 3rd ed. (Englewood Cliffs, N.J.: Prentice-Hall, 1959), pp. 105–11; Herbert A. Bloch and Frank T. Flynn, *Delinquency: The Juvenile Offender in America Today* (New York: Random House, 1956), pp. 144–49; Lewis Yablonsky, *The Violent Gang* (New York: The Macmillan Co., 1962).

[64]Lee N. Robins, *Deviant Children Grown Up* (Baltimore: The Williams and Wilkins Co., 1966).

of 100 normal school children in adulthood. Most of the guidance clinic juveniles had been sent by the juvenile court, for over 70 percent had been referred for "antisocial conduct," such as runaway behavior, truancy, and theft. The remarkable feature of this study is that the investigators managed to obtain interviews concerning 82 percent of those individuals who had lived to age 25, either from themselves or from their relatives.

The clinic patients who had been referred for neurotic symptoms showed satisfactory adult adjustments closely resembling those of the control subjects. However, the antisocial juveniles showed adult careers filled with frequent arrests for criminality and drunkenness, numerous divorces, occupational instability, psychiatric problems, and dependency on social agencies. For example, 44 percent of the male antisocial patients had been arrested for a major crime, but only 3 percent of the controls had serious criminal records. In short, the clinic subjects exhibited generally messed-up adult lives.

A major part of this research concerned the detailed study of sociopathic personality among the subjects in terms of adult behavior patterns. To be judged a sociopath, an individual had to exhibit symptoms of maladjustment within at least five of nineteen life areas. That is, he had to show some combination of poor work history, financial dependency, drug use, sexual misconduct, and so on. The final determination that a subject was sociopathic rested with the psychiatrists, who made clinical judgments from interview material. In all, 22 percent of the clinic subjects and 2 percent of the controls were designated as sociopaths.

Those skeptical about the sociopath concept will remain unimpressed by this study. Robins asserts that some kind of "disease" or personality entity is behind the symptoms that produces sociopaths, but no convincing evidence of this elusive entity appears in the report. Instead, the sociopathic argument looks tautological in form. Although this study emphatically shows that many youngsters who get into juvenile courts and guidance clinics live fairly disordered lives as adults, making a career out of failure, little evidence in this research indicates that these individuals are pathological personalities. Indeed, some findings tend to undermine the sociopath concept. For example, the data suggest that antisocial children who avoided the juvenile court or a training school were less likely to become sociopaths than those who had been through these agencies. Does the crude machinery of these organizations, rather than sociopathy, contribute to adult misfortune and botched lives? About a third of the sociopaths were judged to have given up much of their deviant activity by the time of the follow-up investigation. If sociopaths are supposed to be especially intractable, what happened to these sociopaths?

We regard any attempt to proceed further with the psychopathy–criminality line of inquiry a futile business. At present, we cannot answer questions about the relationship of criminality and psychopathy in the terms in which they are conventionally cast. However, Gough's work, to which we now turn, is one exception.

Gough's Contribution

Gough's work represents a singularly novel and fruitful approach to questions about psychopathy.[65] In a 1948 essay, he identified the major attitudes and characteristics of psychopathic personality and developed a role-taking theory to account for emergence of this syndrome. Briefly stated, the psychopath cannot look on himself as an object or identify with another's point of view—role-taking ability. Thus, the psychopath does not experience social emotions such as embarrassment, contrition, identification, or loyalty. When other persons look at the psychopath, they see him as asocial because he does not play the social game by the conventional rules. He is a "lone wolf," not a "team player."[66]

In subsequent elaborations of his views, Gough explicitly conceptualized psychopathy as a continuum rather than as dichotomous. Instead of viewing psychopathy as a clinical entity clearly marked off from "normal" individuals, he argues for a socialization continuum. Thus, a representative sample of the population at large would show personality patterns ranging from the exemplary citizen at one extreme, through persons with negative and positive traits, to the markedly asocial individual at the other extreme. In turn, these variations are the product of variations in the role-taking experiences of persons. Finally, Gough argues that correlations should be found when variations in socialization among persons are matched up with social behavior categories in which these persons are placed. We should expect relatively asocial individuals to be disproportionately criminals and other deviants, and well-socialized persons to occupy social positions of trust and repute. However, he notes: "... discrepancies are of course to be expected in individual instances between the sociological baseline and the psychological measurement, if for no other reason than that the culture will occasionally make mistakes, in putting some men in prisons and others in positions of trust and responsibility."[67]

Gough has developed measuring techniques and research to investigate this theory. His California Personality Inventory includes a number of scales to measure particular personality dimensions. One of these, the Socialization (So) Scale, was developed from the psychopathy theory. The following samples represent the kinds of items in this scale:

1. Before I do something I try to consider how my friends will react to it.
2. I often think about how I look and what impression I am making on others.

[65]Gough, "A Sociological Theory of Psychopathy"; Gough and Donald R. Peterson, "The Identification and Measurement of Predispositional Factors in Crime and Delinquency," *Journal of Consulting Psychology*, 16 (June 1952), 207–12; Gough, "Theory and Measurement of Socialization," *Journal of Consulting Psychology*, 24 (February 1960), 23–30.

[66]Gough, "A Sociological Theory of Psychopathy," *passim*.

[67]Gough, "Theory and Measurement of Socialization," p. 23.

3. I would rather go without something than ask for a favor.

4. I find it easy to drop or "break with" a friend.

Taken together, the 54 items in the scale are designed to provide indices of role-taking deficiencies, insensitivity to the effects of one's behavior on others, resentment against family, feelings of despondency and alienation, and poor scholastic achievement and rebelliousness.[68] These characteristics differentiate relatively asocial persons from relatively well-socialized individuals.

Gough has tested a number of samples of citizens on the So Scale, ranging from "best citizens" in a high school, through various occupational groups, to known delinquents and prison inmates. These groups exhibit clear differences in mean or average scores. Mean scores indicate average number of positive or "socialized" responses members of the different groups make. A group of "best citizens" in high school had a score of 39.44, a group of college students had a score of 37.41, and a collection of Selective Service inductees showed a mean score of 32.83. Various groups of deviants showed mean scores lower than any of the above: county jail inmates turned up with a score of 29.27, California prison inmates had a mean of 27.76, and a group of inmates in a federal reformatory showed a score of 26.23.[69]

These variations between offenders and nonoffenders have been established in other research studies as well.[70] One case is the work of Walter Reckless and associates, which examines the factors that "insulate" some boys who live in high delinquency areas from delinquent involvement. The potential offenders and nondelinquents in these studies differed in terms of So Scale responses in the expected direction.

In our opinion, Gough's research and companion studies that use Gough's techniques have much promise for the study of personality problems and criminality. One major implication of Gough's work is that the search for personality variations will only succeed insofar as the measuring instruments are specifically related to some explicit hypothesis under investigation.

THE FUTURE OF PSYCHOGENIC HYPOTHESES

What are we to make of this mass of psychogenic material? What are we to conclude from these theories and research findings? We have indicated that hypotheses that characterize offenders as suffering from such gross pathol-

---

[68]Gough and Peterson, The Identification and Measurement of Predispositional Factors in Crime and Delinquency, p. 209.

[69]Gough, "Theory and Measurement of Socialization," p. 25.

[70]Walter C. Reckless, Simon Dinitz, and Barbara Kay, "The Self Component in Potential Delinquency and Potential Non-delinquency," American Sociological Review, 22 (October 1957), 566–70; Reckless, Dinitz, and Ellen Murray, "The 'Good' Boy in a High Delinquency Area," Journal of Criminal Law, Criminology and Police Science, 48 (May–June 1957), 18–25.

ogies as psychoses are demonstrably false. The extent of psychotic disorders among criminals is no greater than among nonoffenders; indeed, psychoses may be less common among offenders. We have also unequivocally rejected conventional psychoanalytic formulations about criminality. These theories of behavior are hopelessly ambiguous, making rigorous scientific tests of the propositions of psychoanalytic thought impossible. Moreover, psychoanalytic hypotheses about criminality, even when liberally interpreted, seem clearly inconsistent with the facts. Most offenders are responding to observable motives different from those suggested by psychoanalysts. We do not deny that some instances of criminal deviation may represent the expression of dimly perceived motivational elements different from surface ones. For example, some arson cases may be related to certain sexual tensions on the part of the actor. But even here the motivational pattern and the social background from which it arose differ in important ways from the representations of psychoanalytic theory. More important, the vast majority of offenders seem guided in their conduct by observable motivational pressures of which they are at least dimly aware and which are relatively utilitarian in character. Only psychoanalysts are apparently capable of seeing evidence in support of psychoanalytic hypotheses about criminal motivation, and even they do not uniformly see the same things when looking at individual deviants.

Our evaluation of conventional notions about psychopaths and the extent of psychopathy among offenders is that the psychopath concept is worthless, both in general and in application to criminality. As used in analyses of lawbreakers, the psychopathy formulations represent nothing more than a deceptive form of name calling. However, we have suggested that Gough's unique treatment of psychopathy is meritorious and that the research resulting from his views has produced noteworthy findings. Along related lines, we indicated that most studies of general emotional problems have turned up negative or inconclusive results. Offenders do not differ from nonoffenders in many of the personality dimensions studied. Yet, at the same time, certain inquiries into personality dimensions of law violators, such as the research of Hewitt and Jenkins, the Gluecks, Jesness, and Conger and Miller, have reported positive evidence. To dismiss the possibility that certain forms of personality structure do bear a relationship to criminality would be premature.

We need to emphasize one major point regarding the results of the studies of the Gluecks, Jesness, Gough, and others: that *prison inmates, training school wards,* or other samples of *incarcerated* offenders turn out to differ from ostensibly noncriminal or nondelinquent individuals, particularly in terms of hostility, negativism, and antagonism toward authority figures, should cause little surprise. Observation of negligible differences would be reason for bemusement, for the experience of incarceration is unlikely to have neutral effects on the self-images and attitudes of prisoners. A common technique for warding off self-condemnatory feelings stemming from the experience of being segregated in an institution with other "bad" people might be to project blame and hostility on "the system" instead of on one's self. A frequent outcome of the experience of "doing time" may well be some deterioration of the actor's self-image as he takes on some of the invidious identity that society imputes to him. In the same way, other experiences with the social control machinery, such as placement on probation, may serve to create attitudinal and self-concept changes in individuals who go through this social apparatus. In short, some psychological characteristics observed in offenders, which differentiate them from nonoffenders, may be the *result* of involvement in deviance rather than a causal ingredient in the genesis of their misbehavior. The usual argument is that emotional factors produce deviance but the reverse is not so often entertained. We hold that much is to be said for the hypothesis that contacts with the "defining agencies"—the social control organizations—contribute to the development of deviant personalities or role conceptions. Chapter Ten examines this possibility at length.

Even if the social-psychological concomitants of deviant behavior are the product of deviance in some cases, the question still remains: Do predispositional patterns of personality structure contribute to at least some kinds of criminality? We think that such relationships may exist but they are much more subtle in character than present psychogenic theories suggest. To search for marked variations in emotional adjustment between some sample of officially designated criminals and another sample of presumed noncriminals is probably futile.

To begin with, the event of acquiring the official label or identity of criminal, or of avoiding such labeling, is often fortuitous. A great many individuals who are criminals in behavior have avoided apprehension, conviction, and detention.[71] Accordingly, comparison of prison inmates, probationers, or some similar group against noncriminals involves a contaminated sample. Even if we could find some way, using new investigative techniques, to obtain "pure" samples of criminals and noncriminals, we still should not expect marked personality variations between the two groups. The relatively obvious reason is that criminality is compounded of a heterogeneous assortment of behavioral forms having little in common other than a shared label. Good reasons exist for supposing that a great many "normal" individuals make their way into the criminal group. Some are accidental offenders with no great involvement in lawbreaking, for whom criminality is an isolated and atypical behavioral episode. Others are persons whose deviant behavior represents a response to organizational strains of some sort rather than to internal states of affairs. The white-collar criminal involved in law violations in the course of business activities is a case in point.

The noncriminal group includes "normal" individuals and others who are not so well-adjusted, some of whom may exhibit personality configurations

---

[71]For a discussion of this point, see Austin T. Turk, "Prospects for Theories of Criminal Behavior," *Journal of Criminal Law, Criminology and Police Science*, 55 (December 1964), 454-61.

parallel to those observed among some group of criminals. For example, some individuals may show a personality pattern of excessive dependence. Some may be naïve check forgers; others may be noncriminals but involved in alcoholism; and still others may be caught up in yet another pattern of adjustment. These varied outcomes in behavior may result from variations in "career contingencies" or in life experiences, which divert some individuals into one line of behavior and others along another pathway.[72] Most behavior patterns that different actors exhibit are the combined product of such personality elements as attitudes and self-images, as these interact with, or are conditioned by, differential social experiences. This is as true for deviant as it is for non-deviant roles. It may take an "addiction-prone" personality pattern and an opportunity structure of learning experiences with drugs, contacts with drug suppliers, and so forth for an individual to become caught up in the role of drug addict. In the same way, variations in social experience may impinge on individuals who share certain personality elements in common in such a way as to lead variously to deviant and nondeviant outcomes. On this matter of personality considerations, our views are related to those of Alex Inkeles, who argues:

> Sociologists have traditionally explained the fact that most people fulfill their major social obligations by referring to the system of sanctions imposed on those who fail to meet, and the rewards granted to those who do meet, the expectations of society. Performance is thus seen as largely dependent on factors "outside" the person. The only thing that need be posited as "inside," in this view, is the general desire to avoid punishment and to gain rewards. Important as such "drives" may be, they do not seem sufficient to explain the differences in the way people perform their assigned social roles. While accepting the crucial importance of the objective factors which determine social behavior, we must recognize that recruitment into occupational and other status-positions, and the quality of performance in the roles people are thus assigned, may, to an important degree, be influenced by personal qualities in individuals. It may be assumed, further, that this happens on a sufficiently large scale to be a crucial factor in determining the functioning of any social system. To the degree that this is true, to predict the functioning of a particular institution, of a small- or large-scale system, we need to know not only the system of status-positions but also the distribution of personality characteristics in the population at large and among those playing important roles in the system.[73]

Inkeles emphasizes the role of personality configurations as they affect the ways actors become allocated to positions in the social order. We concur

[72]Howard Becker, *Outsiders* (New York: The Free Press, 1963).

[73]Alex Inkeles, *What Is Sociology? An Introduction to the Discipline and Profession*, © 1964. Reprinted by permission of Prentice-Hall, Inc., Englewood Cliffs, N.J., p. 57. For commentary on this general issue of psychological elements in behavior, see chap. 4, pp. 47–61.

with Inkeles that personality formulations must be articulated with sociological ones, but at the same time we stress the conditioning effects of differential opportunities on the role-allocation processes by which individuals get sorted into social niches.

If the thrust of the foregoing remarks is on the mark, certain new directions are called for regarding psychogenic hypotheses in criminological analysis. More attention is required to explicate hypotheses that spell out the *specific* personality ingredients assumed to accompany some specific pattern of criminality. The theorist will have to indicate the factors that act on personality configurations to produce deviant or nondeviant outcomes in behavior. For example, certain notions currently fashionable hold that middle-class adolescent male delinquents commonly experience a good deal of anxiety about masculinity and that much of their behavior is to be understood as a response to masculinity stresses.[74] But to convert this unverified contention into a testable assertion, several theoretical improvements are required. The boundaries of the population to which this condition of masculine stress applies must be carefully delimited. Do all middle-class males experience masculinity problems, or are these more common among certain boys? Are all middle-class delinquents, including casual offenders and car thieves, to be explained in terms of this central variable? These are some of the specific issues involved. In addition, an adequte theory revolving around masculinity notions must be prepared to identify the various conditions that produce different behavioral outcomes on the part of individuals who exhibit the hypothesized masculinity concerns.

Edwin Lemert's research on "dependency" as a predispositional factor in alcoholism provides another illustration.[75] Lemert investigated the specific hypothesis that alcoholic individuals are frequently dependent in character prior to the onset of alcoholism. He discovered evidence of several kinds favoring this contention in a sizable proportion of the cases examined. The criminological significance of this study is that a related, intuitively derived "hunch" frequently advanced by correctional agents is that naïve check forgers are dependent individuals. Perhaps a personality configuration of dependency leads, under different circumstances, to these several outcomes. Still other examples of the type of theorizing are found in studies of delinquents by John Kinch and Sethard Fisher[76] and of sex offenders by Saul Toobert and others.[77]

[74]Talcott Parsons, *Essays in Sociological Theory*, rev. ed. (New York: The Free Press, 1954), pp. 304-5.

[75]Edwin M. Lemert, "Dependency in Married Alcoholics," *Quarterly Journal of Studies on Alcohol*, 23 (December 1962), 590-609.

[76]John W. Kinch, "Self Conceptions of Types of Delinquents," *Sociological Inquiry*, 32 (Spring 1962), 228-34; Sethard Fisher, "Varieties of Juvenile Delinquency," *British Journal of Criminology*, 2 (January 1962), 251-61.

[77]Saul Toobert, Kenwood Bartelme, and Eugene S. Jones, "Some Factors Related to Pedophilia," *International Journal of Social Psychiatry*, 4 (Spring 1959), 272-79.

This chapter is not the appropriate place for an extended discussion of the role of personality elements in specific patterns of criminality. In Chapters Twelve through Seventeen, specific offender role careers are the subject of attention. At that point, we shall resume this dialogue on personality elements in criminal deviance of different forms.

One final observation remains to be made before closing this chapter. As we have indicated, a number of improvements in criminological theory are required before we can conduct a completely definitive assessment of psychogenic factors. Some innovations in research procedure are also necessary.[78] For one thing, the search for psychogenic correlates of offender behavior calls for construction of research instruments specific to the hypotheses under study. Too often in the past, psychogenic students have proceeded in vacuum-cleaner fashion to administer indiscriminately a variety of personality tests to samples of offenders and nonoffenders, in an attempt to discover inductively significant differences between the two groups. Probably a great many of the personality measures bear no relationship to critical personality variations. For example, there is no reason to suppose that a scale measuring "masculinity–femininity" would differentiate between some group of offenders and another group of law-abiding citizens or between types of lawbreakers, because masculinity–femininity is a personality dimension uncorrelated with criminality. If we are to confirm specific psychogenic hypotheses, the instruments we use must be suitable to the formulation under investigation. In a number of instances, we may need to contrive instruments because appropriate ones do not exist.

Attempts to investigate psychogenic hypotheses will continue to be vitiated insofar as we fail to expand the samples studied so as to cover offenders-in-fact. Stated another way, researchers will need to follow the example of investigators of "hidden delinquency" by extending inquiry to representative cross-sections of the population and devising means to identify individuals as criminals or noncriminals without relying on official labels. We need to study uncontaminated samples of offenders and nondeviants.

A final modification in current research designs calls for longitudinal studies of lawbreakers. Whenever research focuses on samples of individuals at some fixed point in time, after those persons have progressed some distance through the social control machinery, observed differences between them and nonoffenders under investigation could be the consequence of correctional experiences rather than actual evidence of etiologically significant variations. The most conclusive demonstration that certain personality variables influence the subsequent behavior of individuals would be one in which the persons studied were followed chronologically from a point in time before the onset of deviant

---

[78]For some commentary related to this point, see Richard Quinney, "A Conception of Man and Society for Criminology," *Sociological Quarterly*, 6 (Spring 1965), 115-27.

careers. Although that kind of study would be costly and time-consuming, we can study individuals retrospectively so as to assess the likelihood that observed personality configurations did, in fact, precede the deviant behavior now under observation. At any rate, however accomplished, research will have to become more sensitive to untangling the process that generates criminality.

SUMMARY

This chapter necessarily ends on an inconclusive note. We have seen that the psychogenic theories about criminality are defective in a number of ways and that the research studies also leave much to be desired. Some basic revisions in theory and innovations in research design are needed if the role of psychological elements in lawbreaking is to be fully revealed. Among other things, psychogenic arguments must be meshed with those perspectives which focus on social and cultural influences. The next two chapters are concerned with these latter formulations; Chapter Ten brings some of these strands of thought together through the study of role careers in criminality.

8

SOCIOGENIC APPROACHES: SOCIAL STRUCTURE AND CRIMINALITY

We have examined a number of earlier approaches to crime in the form of biological theories, socialist arguments, and other hypotheses. The previous chapter considered a variety of psychogenic viewpoints regarding crime, in which criminals are thought to be pathological individuals. In this and the following chapter, our attention will turn to an analysis and critique of a variety of sociological perspectives. This chapter is concerned with a group of arguments devoted to the *sociology of crime*—the explanation of criminality and crime rate variations. Chapter Nine continues this exploration of explanatory frameworks, stressing the *social psychology of criminal careers,* factors and processes implicated in the development of criminal behavior patterns in specific persons.

These two chapters are concerned with general theories which attempt to account for crime or criminal behavior as a class of phenomena. Arguments of this sort identify some factor or set of conditions alleged to produce deviant behavior or criminality, such as "anomie," social disorganization, or value conflicts. These perspectives pay relatively little attention to different orders of deviance or criminality. Consequently, Chapters Twelve through Seventeen continue to explore sociological theories of crime and criminal behavior, but on a more detailed level, focusing on particular forms of behavior.

Consider what a fully developed scientific explanation of human action might look like. It would probably involve a collection of theories arranged on several levels of generality. On the first level, some overarching propositions, or "laws," might articulate the "causes" of deviant behavior, identifying key variables involved in every form of deviance. On a second level, criminological theories might be elaborated on the base of deviance theory, specifying additional factors and interrelationships that explain certain details about criminality. These criminological propositions might provide detailed and specific explanations of particular forms of criminality, stated in explicit and rigorous form so they could be subjected to research test. Hence, the task of a criminology textbook would be to direct the reader through successively more complex and detailed formulations, starting with deviance theories, moving on to general perspectives on criminality, and ending with accounts of the nature and genesis of particular orders of criminality.

The social sciences are a great distance away from formalized, axiomatic systems of interrelated theory. Existing theories of deviant behavior are incomplete and unfinished, representing what Carl Hempel has termed "explanation sketches."[1] Although they identify a collection of variables we cannot overlook in explaining some phenomenon, along with some crude propositions linking certain identified factors, they lack the logical rigor of formalized theories. Deviance theories are not clearly meshed with criminological theories, so the extent to which the latter are derivations from the former is not entirely apparent. The most appropriate term describing the existing situation regarding theories of deviance, criminality, and delinquency might be "disjointed."

In the following pages, a look at a number of theoretical perspectives having to do with deviant conduct precedes perusal of an assortment of views developed to account for criminality. Most contemporary views regarding deviance represent outgrowths from the pioneering works of Emile Durkheim, so we shall begin with his writings and follow with Robert Merton's subsequent elaborations.

THEORIES OF DEVIANT BEHAVIOR

Durkheim's Contributions[2]

French sociologist Durkheim (1858–1917) was responsible for at least two seminal themes on crime and deviance. He was one of the first to insist on the "normality" of criminality.[3] He maintained that the "normal" and the "pathological" are not intrinsically different froms of behavior but rather are labels standing for social distinctions men impose on behavior. Moreover, Durkheim

[1] For a discussion of this kind of theoretical statement, and for a fuller discussion of Hempel's notions, see William J. Wilson, Nicholas Sofios, and Richard Ogles, "Formalization and Stages of Theoretical Development," Pacific Sociological Review, 7 (Fall 1964), 74–80; Don C. Gibbons, Delinquent Behavior (Englewood Cliffs, N.J.: Prentice-Hall, 1970), pp. 65-71; see also Charles W. Lachenmeyer, The Language of Sociology (New York: Columbia University Press, 1971).

[2] Emile Durkheim, Suicide, trans. J. A. Spaulding and George Simpson (New York: The Free Press, 1951); Durkheim, The Rules of Sociological Method, ed. George E. G. Catlin (Chicago: University of Chicago Press, 1938). For excerpts from Durkheim's works relevant to the discussion here, see Lewis A. Coser and Bernard Rosenberg, eds., Sociological Theory: A Book of Readings, 2nd ed. (New York: The Macmillan Co., 1964), pp. 539-48, pp. 584-91; Emile Benoit-Smullyan, "The Sociologism of Emile Durkheim and His School," in An Introduction to the History of Sociology, ed. Harry Elmer Barnes (Chicago: University of Chicago Press, 1948), pp. 499–537; Nicholas S. Timasheff, Sociological Theory, rev. ed. (New York: Random House, 1957), pp. 106-18; Richard A. Cloward, "Illegitimate Means, Anomie, and Deviant Behavior," American Sociological Review, 24 (April 1959), 164-76; Richard R. Korn and Lloyd W. McCorkle, Criminology and Penology (New York: Holt, Rinehart and Winston, 1959), pp. 274-78.

[3] Durkheim, The Rules of Sociological Method, pp. 65-75; Coser and Rosenberg, Sociological Theory, pp. 584-91.

asserted that it is neither possible nor desirable for a society to repress criminality completely. To do so would be to create a situation inimical to innovation and desirable social changes. In this sense, criminality is functional or desirable behavior.

Why is criminality a natural and inevitable feature of social life? Durkheim points out that crimes are matters of social definition. Members of a society condemn behavioral deviations that depart markedly from prevailing norms, singling these out as crimes. The criminal serves as an identifying sign of the limits of permissible behavior. If these major violations of normative sentiments could be repressed, men would become sensitive to the less marked deviations they now overlook, and these acts would be regarded as crimes. In turn, if these were repressed, even slighter deviations would be elevated to the status of crimes, and so on, in an unending process of crime definition.[4] These increasingly intolerable demands for conformity, which would then be imposed on individuals not now thought of as criminal, would be detrimental to social progress, for "to make progress, individual originality must be able to express itself. In order that the originality of the idealist whose dreams transcend his century may find expression, it is necessary that the originality of the criminal, who is below the level of his time, shall also be possible. One does not occur without the other."[5]

Durkheim's second and most important contribution to the study of deviant behavior is in the theory of *anomie*, originally developed as an explanation of suicide.[6] According to Durkheim, the social needs or desires of humans are potentially insatiable, so collective order (social organization) is necessary as an external regulating force to define and control the goal-seeking of men. If the collective order is disrupted or disturbed, men's aspirations may increase to the point of outdistancing all possibilities of fulfillment. At this point, when traditional rules have lost their authority over behavior, a state of deregulation, normlessness, or anomie is said to exist. Durkheim claims that the regulatory functions of the collective order most commonly break down at the occurrence of sudden depression, sudden prosperity, or rapid technological change, when men are misled into aspiring to goals extremely difficult if not impossible to achieve. Sudden depressions have this effect because actors cannot adapt readily to a reduced state of existence: sudden prosperity is conducive to anomie because it lures some individuals into supposing that they can attain seemingly limitless wealth and achievement. Much the same

[4]Coser and Rosenberg, *Sociological Theory*, pp. 585–87.

[5]*Ibid.*, p. 588. For a somewhat related theme, holding that punishment of crime is functional for the affirmation of social solidarity, see George Herbert Mead, "The Psychology of Punitive Justice," *American Journal of Sociology*, 23 (March 1918), 585–92. For elaborations of this theme regarding functional consequences of deviance, see Lewis A. Coser, "Some Functions of Deviant Behavior and Normative Flexibility," *American Journal of Sociology*, 68 (September 1962), 172–81.

[6]Durkheim, *Suicide*, pp. 247–57; Cloward, "Illegitimate Means, Anomie, and Deviant Behavior," 164–66; Marshall B. Clinard, "The Theoretical Implications of Anomie and Deviant Behavior," in *Anomie and Deviant Behavior*, ed. Clinard (New York: The Free Press, 1964), pp. 3–10.

effect stems from rapid technological change, which instills in some persons imagination of boundless possibilities of achievement. According to Durkheim, these conditions engender pressures toward suicide, particularly in, Western, industrialized societies.[7]

Durkheim was not concerned about criminality in the theory of anomie. However, Robert K. Merton has modified and elaborated on Durkheim's original thesis. In the most widely used contemporary theory of deviant behavior, Merton has generated some specific applications to criminal conduct.

Merton and Anomie Theory[8]

American sociologist Merton has developed a rich body of elaborations on Durkheim's initial notions regarding the breakdown of regulatory norms and deviant behavior. In turn, others, principally Richard A. Cloward, have added to Merton's work in important ways. The resulting body of ideas has served as the most influential formulation in the sociology of deviance over the past twenty-five years, as attested to by copious citations in sociological textbooks. Merton has continuously enunciated the sociologist's operating premise that "some unknown but substantial proportion of deviant behavior does not represent impulses of individuals breaking through social controls, but, on the contrary, represents socially induced deviations—deviations which the culture and the social organization conjoin to produce."[9] His work mainly sketches out the details of the processes by which societally generated deviance comes about.

In his analysis, Merton distinguishes between two major elements of social and cultural structures—the culturally defined goals men are enjoined to pursue and the social structure that regulates and controls the acceptable modes or means for the pursuit of goals and interests. He notes that goals and institutionalized norms may vary independently of each other, sometimes leading

---

[7]For some important discussions and critiques of Durkheim's theory, see Marvin E. Olsen, "Durkheim's Two Concepts of Anomie," *Sociological Quarterly*, 6 (Winter 1965), 37—44; A. R. Mawson, "Durkheim and Contemporary Social Pathology," *British Journal of Sociology*, 21 (September 1970), 298–311; John Horton, "The Dehumanization of Anomie and Alienation: A Problem in the Ideology of Sociology," *British Journal of Sociology*, 15 (December 1964), 283–300.

[8]Robert K. Merton, *Social Theory and Social Structure*, rev. and enl. ed. (New York: The Free Press, 1957), pp. 131–94; Merton, "Social Conformity, Deviation, and Opportunity-Structures: A Comment on the Contributions of Dubin and Cloward," *American Sociological Review*, 24 (April 1959), 177–89; Merton, "The Social-Cultural Environment and Anomie," in *New Perspectives for Research on Juvenile Delinquency*, ed. Helen L. Witmer and Ruth Kotinsky (Washington, D. C.: U.S. Department of Health, Education and Welfare, 1955), pp. 24–50; Merton, "Anomie, Anomia, and Social Interaction: Contexts of Deviant Behavior," in Clinard, "Theoretical Implications of Anomie," pp. 213–42; Cloward, "Illegitimate Means, Anomie and Deviant Behavior"; Robert Dubin, "Deviant Behavior and Social Structure: Continuities in Social Theory," *American Sociological Review*, 24 (April 1959), 147–64; Albert K. Cohen, "The Study of Social Disorganization and Deviant Behavior," in *Sociology Today*, ed. Robert K. Merton, Leonard Broom, and Leonard S. Cottrell, Jr. (New York: Basic Books, 1959), pp. 461–66; Cohen, "The Sociology of the Deviant Act: Anomie Theory and Beyond," *American Sociological Review*, 30 (February 1965), 5–14; Clinard, "Theoretical Implications of Anomie," pp. 10–23.

[9]Merton, "The Social-Cultural Environment and Anomie," p. 29.

to malintegrated states, one extreme being the instance of inordinate stress on goals with little concern for prescribed means. In this case, a condition of "anything goes" prevails, with only considerations of technical expedience governing goal-striving behavior. Merton cites the example of unethical activities in college athletics, particularly football, as a situation in which institutionalized norms have become attenuated in favor of excessive concern with certain goals. The other polar case of goals–means malintegration involves undue emphasis on ritualistic conformity to norms. Between these two extremes are relatively stable societies, with a rough balance between goals and norms.[10]

Merton maintains that contemporary American society is anomic, for it represents the polar type in which success goals are emphasized without equivalent emphasis on institutionalized conduct norms. Merton asserts:

> The emphasis upon this set of culture goals is imperfectly integrated with organization of our society, which, as a matter of objective and generally recognizable fact, does not provide equal access to those goals for all members of the society. On the contrary, there are heavily graded degrees of access to this, in terms not only of class and ethnic origins, but also in terms of less immediately visible differentials.

> Given the composite emphasis of this uniform cultural value of success being enjoined upon all irrespective of origins, and given the fact of a social organization which entails differentials in the availability of this goal, pressure is exerted upon certain classes of individuals to engage in deviant behavior, particularly those classes or strata or groups which have the least direct access to the goal.[11]

Merton's thesis is that the cultural system of American society enjoins all men to strive for success goals by means of certain normatively regulated or approved forms of behavior. Yet, at the same time, opportunities to reach these goals through socially approved means are differentially distributed. According to Merton, in situations of this kind, "it is only when a system of cultural values extols, virtually above all else, certain *common* success-goals for the population at large while the social structure rigorously restricts or completely closes access to approved modes of reaching these goals, *for a considerable part of the same population*, that deviant behavior ensues on a large scale" (emphasis in the original).[12] Merton identifies five modes of adaptation to the situation of disjunction: *conformity, innovation, ritualism, retreatism, and rebellion*. The category of innovation is of particular interest to the criminologist, for it refers to cases in which actors continue to aspire

---

[10]Merton, *Social Theory and Social Structure*, pp. 131–36.
[11]Merton, "The Social-Cultural Environment and Anomie," p. 30.
[12]Merton, *Social Theory and Social Structure*, p. 146.

to approved goals, but by means of deviant or illegitimate techniques. In accounting for the adaptations or directions different individuals take, Merton strongly emphasizes variations in class-linked patterns of socialization, arguing that innovative responses are most common among relatively imperfectly socialized persons.

In several different ways, Richard A. Cloward has had an important role in the further development of anomie theory. Cloward has directed attention to the fact of differentials in *illegitimate* opportunities in addition to varied legitimate opportunity structures.[13] He points out that the forms of deviant behavior are conditional *both* on the situation of disjunction *and* on the opportunities to engage in deviant conduct. Just as the prospects for achievement of cultural goals through institutionalized means are differentially distributed, so are the opportunities for various kinds of careers in deviant conduct. For example, the use of drugs depends in part on contacts with suppliers of illicit narcotics. Similarly, development of a career as a professional criminal is partly contingent on contact with individuals who will induct the actor into this kind of deviant pattern.

Cloward has also been involved in two major applications of anomie theory to specific cases of social deviation. In the first, he studied a military prison in which the captors encouraged the prisoners to strive for restoration to active duty through certain approved forms of conduct summed up in the injunction, "Do your own time." However, the inmates quickly came to understand that the "open-class" ideology the administrators promulgated was a deception, for only 6 percent of the prisoners were actually restored to active duty, and even those individuals were given this status for reasons different from those the officials articulated. Cloward observed that this situation led some to conformist adaptations, whereas others followed the pattern of ritualism or passive noncooperation.[14] In essence, the Cloward prison report stands as a microcosmic illustration of the societal pattern described by Merton.

The other application of anomie theory is found in the explanation of subcultural delinquency by Cloward and Lloyd Ohlin,[15] an elaborate formulation we shall examine in some detail in Chapter Eleven. But the essentials of that theory are as follows: lower-class boys share a common American value com-

[13]Cloward, "Illegitimate Means, Anomie, and Deviant Behavior."

[14]Witmer and Kotinsky, *New Perspectives for Research on Juvenile Delinquency*, pp. 80–92.

[15]Richard A. Cloward and Lloyd E. Ohlin, *Delinquency and Opportunity* (New York: The Free Press, 1960). For an inventory of empirical and theoretical studies of anomie, see Stephen Cole and Harriet Zuckerman, "Appendix: Inventory of Empirical and Theoretical Studies of Anomie," in Clinard, "Theoretical Implications of Anomie," pp. 243–313. Many of the cited works are only tangentially linked to the Merton formulation. For ecological studies of delinquency and anomie, see Bernard Lander, *Toward an Understanding of Juvenile Delinquency* (New York: Columbia University Press, 1954); David J. Bordua, "Juvenile Delinquency and 'Anomie': An Attempt at Replication," *Social Problems*, 6 (Winter 1958–1959), 230–38; Roland J. Chilton, "Continuity in Delinquency Area Research: A Comparison of Studies for Baltimore, Detroit, and Indianapolis," *American Sociological Review*, 29 (February 1964), 71–83. These studies, as well as some other ecological investigations, are summarized in Gibbons, *Delinquent Behavior*, pp. 103–13.

mitment to "success," measured largely in material terms. But unlike middle-class youths, they do not have access to legitimate means or avenues to attain these success goals. If they do have access to legitimate means, they perceive their chances of success as limited. Thus, for many lower-class boys, a severe gap exists between aspiration levels and expectations. This goals–means disjunction generates pressures to engage in deviant behavior. In turn, the particular deviant adaptation that develops is a function of opportunity structures for deviant behavior, at least in part. Some lower-class areas are characterized by integration of criminalistic and conformist patterns of social organization, whereas others are lacking in stable criminalistic patterns. In the organized, criminalistic area, criminalistic gang subcultures develop in which boys are involved in instrumental acts of theft and in careers that often eventually lead to adult criminal behavior. In areas lacking criminalistic traditions, gang delinquency tends to take the form of "conflict" subcultural behavior, in which "bopping" (gang fighting) predominates. Finally, some boys, failures in both the legitimate and illegitimate opportunity structures, engage in retreatist behavior and become narcotic users.

The Mertonian schema regarding deviant behavior represents an elegant, plausible, and appealing formulation. However, the framework is amenable to, and in need of, further expansion and revision. Albert Cohen notes a number of points at which elaboration of the perspective is in order.[16] The unfinished nature of the argument is revealed in the fact that, for all of the popularity the theory has enjoyed, remarkably few applications have been made to specific instances of deviance. Instead, the propositions have been used most commonly as high level explanatory metaphor, with no real attempt to assess their theoretical usefulness through the formulation of specific hypotheses about forms of deviant conduct. Aside from Cloward's two cases, Mertonian theory has had little influence on criminological explanations.

Some unfinished business relative to anomie theory and deviance centers around the *boundary question*.[17] The argument is not yet sufficiently explicit

[16]Cohen, "The Sociology of the Deviant Act." For a harsher view of the needed modifications in anomie theory, see Edwin M. Lemert, *Human Deviance, Social Problems, and Social Control,* 2nd ed. (Englewood Cliffs, N.J.: Prentice-Hall, 1972), pp. 26–61; Jack D. Douglas, "Deviance and Order in a Pluralistic Society," in *Theoretical Sociology,* John C. McKinney and Edward A. Tiryakian, eds. (New York: Appleton-Century-Crofts, 1970), pp. 367–401.

[17]Scott and Turner have recently discussed some of the problems of Mertonian theory. They point out that the argument is ambiguous at a number of points. For one, "anomie" is not explicitly defined. Also, Merton makes no attempt to ascertain the range and variety of real-life forms of deviation or to fit the theory to these patterns. Instead, he selectively discusses forms of behavior that intuitively appear to be explained by the means–ends disjunction situation. Scott and Turner also contend that Merton's conception of anomie is actually closer to the ideas of Max Weber than to Durkheim's theories. That is, for Durkheim, anomie was the product of periods of rapid social change and dislocation. In Merton's theory, anomie centers about a relatively permanent state of affairs involving disjunction. Merton's deviants resemble Weber's Western men pursuing unlimited goals, whereas Merton's modes of adaptation parallel Weber's four types of social action. See Marvin B. Scott and Roy Turner, "Weber and the Anomic Theory of Deviance," *Sociological Quarterly,* 6 (Summer 1965), 233–40.

regarding the scope of the theory. Is anomie an explanation of all forms of deviance, or is it relevant to some kinds of noncomformist action but not to others? This argument does not account for all kinds of deviance. In a similar vein, more work on the *translation* of the view is necessary so as to coordinate the modes of adaptation (innovation, rebellion, retreatism, ritualism, conformity) with the social labels for deviance familiar in everyday life, such as "bums," "hoods," "pimps," "hustlers," "queers," or "beatniks." The empirical indicators of adaptations must be made explicit. In the case of criminality, more attention to the boundaries of anomie theory is called for so that forms of lawbreaking the theory does not cover can be distinguished from those included. To a limited extent, the analyses of specific forms of illegality in succeeding chapters will try to clarify this question.

Other Theories

Talcott Parsons presents another general theory of deviance.[18] Parsons has devoted much attention to explaining conformist conduct in a lengthy analysis that parallels much of Merton's commentary, but with additional information. No explicit applications of this argument have been made to particular forms of deviance, so although anecdotal reference is made to cases of deviant action, the viewpoint has not been given any specific empirical interpretation. Whether Parsonian insights have any explanatory prowess in application to criminality remains to be seen.

The theories of Merton and Parsons imply that a relatively clear value structure, violated by deviant or criminal behavior, characterizes American society. However, another perspective on social structure and deviance constitutes a nascent theory revolving around value pluralism. This emerging viewpoint, found in the writings of Jack Douglas[19] and Edwin Lemert[20] among others, suggests that American values are often less clear than Merton contends. Furthermore, those of a value pluralism persuasion claim that traditional theories have underestimated the number of values in modern society as well as paid insufficient attention to various subcultural values and value conflicts. Both Douglas and Lemert assert that deviance often arises as a positive response to one set of subcultural values that happen to be out of tune with another set. Accordingly, particular forms of deviance develop out of different societal dynamics rather than from a single state of anomie.

Two points regarding value pluralism formulations need further comment.

[18]Talcott Parsons, *The Social System* (New York: The Free Press, 1951), pp. 249–325; Cohen, "The Study of Social Disorganization and Deviant Behavior," pp. 466–74.

[19]Jack D. Douglas, "Deviance and Order in a Pluralistic Society," *loc. cit.*; Douglas, *American Social Order* (New York: The Free Press, 1971).

[20]Lemert, *Human Deviance, Social Problems, and Social Control*, pp. 3–30; Lemert, *Social Pathology* (New York: McGraw-Hill Book Co., 1951).

First, these views are only embryonic at present. They suggest some dimensions of value pluralism but do not provide any sort of inventory of the various patterns of values and value conflict. A full-blown alternative to anomie theory remains to be developed. Second, our analysis of lawbreaking represents an application of value pluralism notions. We shall consider a variety of patterns of criminality, along with etiological explanations that differ for the separate kinds of lawbreaking.

THEORIES OF CRIMINALITY

In countless textbooks on social disorganization, social problems, and criminology, sociologists have put their conceptual tools to work on the question of causal factors in crime and delinquency. The result is a bewildering accumulation of claims that initially projects a formidable image to the criminology student. However, nearly all sociological commentators follow some basic assumptions, to the effect that criminality is "normal" in all societies and lawbreaking is the product of various organizational features of particular nations.[21] Crime rates vary from country to country because of organizational or structural variations. Within a society, specific individuals become criminals or noncriminals as a consequence of their positions in that system, a result of variations in organizational components within societies. Beyond these presuppositions, most sociologists agree that the causes of criminality are found in value patterns, normative systems and conflicting patterns of conduct standards, social class influences of various kinds, family and peer group influences, and other identifiable social forms and variables.

In the following pages, we shall review a generous sample of the general theories regarding criminality. However, we shall single out those statements that, in our opinion, are the most significant, without attempting to cover the entire list of sociological theories of criminality.

Social Disorganization and Crime

The concept of social disorganization has an important place in sociology. The usual definition of social disorganization is a breakdown or disruption in the bonds of relationship, coordination, teamwork, and morale among groups of interrelated persons so as to impair the functions of the society

---

[21]For a good summary of sociological theories on crime, see Marshall B. Clinard, *The Sociology of Deviant Behavior*, 3rd ed. (New York: Holt, Rinehart and Winston, 1968), pp. 203–44; Paul B. Horton and Gerald Leslie, *The Sociology of Social Problems*, 4th ed. (New York: Appleton-Century-Crofts, 1970), pp. 152–72; Albert K. Cohen and James F. Short, Jr., "Crime and Juvenile Delinquency," in *Contemporary Social Problems*, ed. Robert K. Merton and Robert Nisbet, 3rd ed. (New York: Harcourt Brace Jovanovich, 1971), pp. 89–146.

or smaller social organization.[22] In this view, the United States and other Western nations are in various stages of disorganization, and their apparent high crime rates (and rates of deviation of other kinds) are to be attributed to that source.

Analysis of criminality from a social disorganization standpoint often begins with systems without serious manifestations of social disorganization, taken as a standard against which to measure the extent of disorganization in industrialized societies. Thus, the antithesis of modern, urban, criminalistic societies is the "folk society."

Robert Redfield describes the folk society in terms of small size, isolation from surrounding cultures, nonliterate population, dependence on folk knowledge, little unconventional behavior, homogeneity of personality types, complex kinship relations, dependence on folkways, and use of informal social controls rather than formal codes of law to control personal behavior.[23] Little nonconforming behavior exists, because culturally prescribed aspirations and socially structured ways of realizing them are in tune. Little personal insecurity or confusion is engendered, and only slight motivation toward deviant behavior is evident. The concept of folk society represents an ideal various cultures resemble in greater or lesser degree. Robert Faris describes the characteristics of successful social organizations, as opposed to modern, relatively disorganized systems, in much the same terms. He points out that they are characterized by high morale, little personal deviation, and a predominance of integrated customs and folk knowledge, along with informal controls.[24] Both Redfield and Faris find the closest approximations of folk societies mainly in the underdeveloped, agrarian nations of the world. American society probably never approached the ideal of folk society, but it has become even more unlike this organization with the passing decades.

Part of the foregoing argument is that in such a well-organized, consistent society, little personal inconsistency of behavior would be found. In comparison with urban society, personal deviation is uncommon. But we should not suppose that men are uniformly molded in one image even in folk societies or that deviations from conventional roles are nonexistent. Nicholas Demerath has reviewed studies of the distribution of schizophrenia among preliterates and maintains that the early reports by Elsworth Faris and others of an almost total absence of mental disorder are questionable, in light of the defective research methods on which these studies were based. Demerath indicates that studies have uncovered instances of mental disorder of various kinds

---

[22]Robert E. L. Faris, *Social Disorganization,* 2nd ed. (New York: The Ronald Press, 1955), pp. 3—83.

[23]Robert Redfield, "The Folk Society," *American Journal of Sociology,* 52 (January 1947), 293–308. For a detailed critique of the folk-urban argument, see Horace Miner, "The Folk-Urban Continuum," *American Sociological Review,* 17 (October 1952), 529-37.

[24]Faris, *Social Disorganization,* pp. 3-33.

among primitives. He also suggests that, although the present data are inadequate for any firm conclusions regarding relative incidence of mental disorder in one society or another, mental disorder is quite rare in truly primitive groups but increases with the processes of acculturation. As a formerly isolated folk group undergoes contact with other societies, certain persons react to culture conflict and marginality of status, with a resulting increase of serious mental aberrations.[25]

A recent study of a modern counterpart of the folk society, the Hutterites of North America, reveals that mental disorders are not unheard of there. The Hutterites are an Anabaptist religious sect who live a simple rural life, with a harmonious social organization and considerable economic security. A number of Hutterites had shown symptoms of mental disorder at some point in their lives, so although the authors of the study concluded that mental pathology is relatively rare among the Hutterites, even a well-organized society does not completely prevent deviant behavior.[26]

In contrast to the folk culture, the United States and other urbanized nations are complex, dynamic, materialistic, impersonal, and characterized by other features conducive to widespread crime and other kinds of deviant behavior. As Faris says:

> The essential feature in the social disorganization that underlies criminality appears to be partial failure of the normal mechanisms of social control. In a modern secular civilization this control is not as strong as in isolated and homogeneous primitive or peasant societies, or as in such religious societies as those of rural Quebec or the early Shaker or Mormon communities. In cities, and particularly in urban slums, the weakening of family and neighborhood controls may be so extreme as to constitute complete failure. In such a situation children who have not already acquired life-organizations based on habits of conventional behavior are, though not inevitably delinquent, at least easily subject to the positive influences of the boy gangs, "fences," and the organized rewards of underworld criminal organizations. . . .
>
> Generalized confusion of standards in our changing contemporary society is also a factor in the encouragement of criminal behavior. The underworld organization of professional criminals is provided with important support by the noncriminal citizen who vigorously insists upon his right to consume prohibited beverages or drugs, to engage in illegal gambling, to purchase

[25]Nicholas J. Demerath, "Schizophrenia Among Primitives," *American Journal of Psychiatry*, 98 (March 1942), 703–7.

[26]Joseph W. Eaton and Robert J. Weil, "The Mental Health of the Hutterites," in *Mental Health and Mental Disorder*, ed. Arnold Rose (New York: W. W. Norton, 1955), pp. 223–37; Eaton and Weil, *Culture and Mental Disorders* (New York: The Free Press, 1955); see also Herbert Goldhamer and Andrew W. Marshall, *Psychoses and Civilization* (New York: The Free Press, 1953).

goods in evasion of rationing and price regulations, and the like. "Rights" of different kinds and of different origins have come into conflict, and no unified code is accepted by the mass of the population. In this confusion it becomes easy to make and to rationalize moral decisions on the basis of individual interest.[27]

Unfortunately for the advancement of understanding in criminology, the concept of social disorganization is itself disorganized. Merton has provided one of the clearest definitions of social disorganization; he asserts: "Social disorganization refers to inadequacies or failures in a social system of inter-related statuses and roles such that the collective purposes and individual objectives of its members are less fully realized than they could be in an *alternative workable system*" (emphasis added).[28] Although this definition is exceptionally clear, it by no means assures us that examples of social disorganization are clearly recognizable. Application of this definition to real-life situations assumes that the collective purposes and individual objectives of members of a society are readily apparent to different sociologists. But many people would argue that purposes and objectives are problematic and by no means obvious. The question of alternative workable systems would be likely to provide considerable controversy among different observers. To classify American society as disorganized, using this definition, we must entertain some picture of a more harmonious and attainable system. Although such an alternative pattern of organization compatible with the major value orientations of American society might be structured, its outlines are certainly not lucidly visible to all. This leads to the conclusion that the concept of social disorganization is far from flawlessly objective.

Critics of social disorganization notions have also suggested that applications of the theory to real-life situations have often been tautological, the same behavior to be explained by disorganization being used to demonstrate the existence of that state of affairs. Lemert has charged that social disorganization theory has suffered from a poverty of subsidiary hypotheses so that few specific propositions to account for forms of pathological behavior have been derived from the general theory.[29] Cohen has charged that the concept is almost hopelessly ambiguous, but he has gone on to explicate a revised version eliminating ambiguities of the concept but also drastically restricting its uses. Cohen's revision has the effect of limiting application to small social systems rather than to the more traditional analyses of societal conditions.[30] Reece McGee has authored an essay on social disorganization in which the

[27]Faris, *Social Disorganization*, p. 246.

[28]Robert K. Merton, "Social Problems and Sociological Theory," in Merton and Nisbet, *Contemporary Social Problems*, pp. 819–20. See the entire discussion, pp. 818–38.

[29]Lemert, *Social Pathology*, pp. 7–10.

[30]Cohen, "The Study of Social Disorganization and Deviant Behavior," pp. 475–84.

term is retained while its customary meaning has been jettisoned. In McGee's work, social disorganization turns out to be another label for deviant behavior.[31]

Over the life history of social disorganization formulations, the major objection has been that the notions are judgmental. Nearly all sociologists agree that modern, industrialized societies represent an amalgam of competing value patterns and normative systems, different social strata with varied "life styles," and subcultures and contracultures of one kind or another. Consensus exists on the question of "differential social organization"; the diversified character of modern societies is not at issue. On this point, a number of authorities have argued that many of the conditions earlier considered as examples of disorganization or unorganization represent, instead, alternative systems of organization yielding satisfactions to the individuals who are their constituents.[32] The consequence is that evaluation of this state of affairs as disorganized involves more than simply an objective report of empirical observations.[33] For such reasons, the drift of thinking in recent decades has been away from disorganization views and toward stress on complexity and differential social organization.[34]

Differential Social Organization and Crime

We can find an abundance of examples of differential social organization views on criminality. Sutherland and Cressey have employed this perspective as a companion view to their theory of differential association which we shall examine in the next chapter. They argue that the social changes involved in the Industrial Revolution, with its emphasis on individualism, have produced conditions conducive to criminality. The social influences that play on individuals are inharmonious and inconsistent, and many persons become deeply involved in differential association with carriers of criminalistic norms and become criminals as a consequence.[35] Thorsten Sellin has advanced parallel views, with particular emphasis on the clash of cultural values resulting from immigration and mobility.[36] Milton Barron has aptly expressed the same theme in a textbook on delinquency entitled *The Juvenile in Delinquent Society.*[37]

[31]Reece McGee, *Social Disorganization in America* (San Francisco: Chandler Publishing Co., 1962).

[32]As a case in point, illustrating the functional utility of crime, see Daniel Bell, "Crime as an American Way of Life," *Antioch Review*, 13 (June 1953), 131–54.

[33]Clinard, *The Sociology of Deviant Behavior*, pp. 22–23.

[34]Books reflecting this view of deviant behavior include Clinard, *The Sociology of Deviant Behavior*; Russell R. Dynes, Alfred C. Clarke, Simon Dinitz, and Iwao Ishino, *Social Problems in America* (New York: John Wiley & Sons, 1960); Merton and Nisbet, *Contemporary Social Problems*.

[35]Edwin H. Sutherland and Donald R. Cressey, *Principles of Criminology*, 8th ed. (Philadelphia: J. B. Lippincott Co., 1970), pp. 93–112.

[36]Thorsten Sellin, *Culture Conflict and Crime* (New York: Social Science Research Council, 1938).

[37]Milton L. Barron, *The Juvenile in Delinquent Society* (New York: Alfred A. Knopf, 1955).

Finally Donald Taft and Ralph England have made a well-known statement of this position; they argue that the value conflicts, impersonality, individualism, disrespect for law and order, exploitiveness, and other ingredients central to the American way of life make widespread criminality an inevitable by-product of that cultural system.[38]

The Multiple-Factor Approach

Another trend of thought on questions of causation has flourished alongside the aforementioned theoretical endeavors. The multiple-factor view holds that causal analysis must be eclectic, providing room for a multitude of factors of different kinds, all bearing some relationship to crime and delinquency. Exponents of this view have often taken pride in their avoidance of dogmatism and rigidity and in their willingness to include biological, psychological, and social factors within some kind of explanatory porridge. Advocates of multiple-factor thinking have suggested that because the causes of criminality vary from individual to individual, lengthy inventories of these causes are needed in each instance of deviant conduct. According to this line of reasoning, the best explanatory system is a detailed set of variables or "categoric risks," all bearing some statistical association to criminality. Supporters of this viewpoint maintain that no one factor can be isolated to show an invariant relationship to criminality.

We reject such causal nihilism. Multiple-factor orientations as now structured are not explanations at all. To explain criminality scientifically, we will ultimately have to develop propositions of the form: "If conditions *A, B, C,* and *D* occur, criminality of some kind will also occur (and if these conditions are absent, noncriminality will be observed)." Although the operating principle of multiple-factor thinking is that such statements are outside the realm of the discoverable, we assume the opposite. We agree with Cohen, who has advanced an incisive critique of multiple-factor perspectives. He points out that the supporters of that framework confuse explanation by means of a *single theory* with explanation by means of a *single factor.* Few modern criminologists would hold that criminality is the result of one variable, although many would aver that some large but finite number of factors do combine to produce criminality. Efforts to develop sociological theories of criminality involve an extensive list of variables considered to play a role in criminal etiology.[39]

Not all etiological statements that involve a multiplicity of variables are examples of multiple-factor analysis. Instead, some excellent examples of theoretical work in which students of criminality and delinquency have endeavored to explicate complex theories take into account a large number of causal

[38]Donald R. Taft and Ralph W. England, Jr., *Criminology,* 4th ed. (New York: The Macmillan Co., 1964), pp. 277-79.

[39]Albert K. Cohen, discussed in Sutherland and Cressey, *Principles of Criminology,* pp. 59-61; see also George B. Vold, *Theoretical Criminology* (New York: Oxford University Press, 1958), pp. 309-10.

factors.[40] However, these cases differ from conventional multiple-factor views because they are etiological formulations that attempt to spell out some of the *ways these causal influences interact with one another to produce law-breaking.* These multivariate arguments illustrate the theoretical approach to questions of causation advocated in this book.

RACISM AND CRIME

As Chapter Five indicated, blacks in the United States have considerably higher rates of arrest for major crimes than do whites, particularly for such offenses as homicide, forcible rape, aggravated assault, robbery, weapons charges, prostitution, and gambling. How do we explain this apparent excessive criminality among blacks?

One line of sociological exposition holds that at least some significant portion of black offenders are the victims of *differential law enforcement.* As we saw in Chapter Four, a number of studies, such as those by Nathan Goldman,[41] Irving Piliavin and Scott Briar,[42] and Theodore Ferdinand and Elmer Luchterhand,[43] demonstrate that police deal with black youths more harshly than with white youngsters. A number of other crime differentials between blacks and whites are also likely to involve differential enforcement of the law. Prostitution and gambling arrests are cases in point; a good deal of commonsense observation suggests that the police differentially enforce the law against blacks involved in these forms of lawbreaking. Finally, as we saw in Chapter Four, blacks are frequently the targets of gratuitous physical force used against them by the police.

Arguments that stress differential application of the law do not deny that black citizens are involved in criminality but rather that arrest rates and other measures of involvement in lawbreaking are inflated for blacks because of racism, manifested in discriminatory operations of the police, courts, and correctional agencies.

Let us assume, as most authorities do, that even after we allow for differential law enforcement, American blacks do have higher rates of involvement in many kinds of crime than do whites. If so, how do we explain this excess?[44] Certainly not in terms of the patently false theory that black crime

[40]John M. Martin and Joseph P. Fitzpatrick, *Delinquent Behavior* (New York: Random House, 1964); Robert MacIver, *The Prevention and Control of Delinquency* (New York: Atherton Press, 1966).

[41]Nathan Goldman, *The Differential Selection of Juvenile Offenders for Court Appearance* (New York: National Council on Crime and Delinquency, 1963).

[42]Irving Piliavin and Scott Briar, "Police Encounters with Juveniles," *American Journal of Sociology,* 70 (September 1964), 206–14.

[43]Theodore N. Ferdinand and Elmer G. Luchterhand, "Inner-City Youth, the Police, the Juvenile Court, and Justice," *Social Problems,* 17 (Spring 1970), 510–27.

[44]For an excellent review of theories and evidence on racial variations in crime, see Edwin H. Sutherland and Donald R. Cressey, *Principles of Criminology,* 8th ed. (Philadelphia: J. B. Lippincott Co., 1970), pp. 132–50.

is racially determined. This contention holds that Negroes are members of a biologically primitive race, innately inclined toward crime. Because they cannot exercise control over their emotions, they engage in crimes of violence; because they lack moral commitment to property rights, they are uninhibited from engaging in property offenses. Views of this kind hardly square with observations that most American blacks show mixed racial heritage and are not members of a biologically pure type, that crime rates vary among different black social class groups, or that crime rates appear to be much lower among African blacks than among American blacks.

Those who reject biological explanations usually lean toward some version of theory holding that various forms of social and economic discrimination in American society are indirectly bound up in black criminality and represent the root causes of it. In its most dramatic expression of this argument, black crime is the product of endemic racism and oppression in American society.

What does it mean to say that the United States is a racist society? How does racial oppression lead to crime? These are extremely broad questions, but their answers lie in the following historical directions.

To begin with, oppression of blacks began with enslavement of Africans by Europeans in the fifteenth century. The first black slave was brought to America in 1619, and by the time of the Revolutionary War, several hundred thousand black slaves were in America.[45]

Black slaves in the United States were dealt with as property rather than as humans. Slavemasters deliberately broke up black families, creating family instability among blacks, which has persisted up to the present. As Andrew Billingsley observes:

> In short, there was the absence, in the United States, of societal support and protection for the Negro family as a physical, psychological, social, or economic unit. This crippled the development, not only of individual slaves, but of families, and hence of the whole society of Negro people. The consequences these conditions wrought for generations of Negroes under the slave system were direct and insidious. The consequences for succeeding and even modern generations of Negroes are, perhaps, less direct, but no less insidious.[46]

After slavery, various attempts were made to maintain blacks under conditions of oppression and to exclude them from the mainstream of society. In the South, the "separate but equal" system of schools and other social institutions worked to keep blacks mired in rural poverty and inferior social

[45]A lesser known fact of history is that a runaway Negro slave, Crispus Attucks, was the first person killed in the Boston massacre of 1770, an important incident leading up to the Revolutionary War.

[46]Andrew Billingsley, *Black Families in White America* (Englewood Cliffs, N.J.: Prentice-Hall, 1968), pp. 68–69. For a theory attributing delinquency to family instability among Negroes, see Walter B. Miller, "Lower Class Culture as a Generating Milieu of Gang Delinquency," *Journal of Social Issues,* 14, no. 3 (1958), 5–19.

status. Individuals who dared to fight against this system ran the risk of reprisals, such as a visit from Ku Klux Klan night riders. Intimidation, including the lynching of southern blacks, has been a continuing part of the postslavery experience, persisting even up to the present.[47] For example, between 1961 and 1965, 150 incidents of major violence were directed at blacks in Mississippi. During the summer of 1965 in that state alone, 35 shootings, 30 bombings, 35 church burnings, 80 beatings, and at least 6 murders were related to civil rights activities.[48]

"Racism" outside the South took other, more subtle but pervasive forms. Some authorities have characterized this situation as one of "colonization."[49] Robert Blauner argues:

There appear to be four basic components of the colonization complex . . . Colonization begins with a forced, involuntary entry. Second, there is an impact on the culture and social organization of the colonized people which is more than just a result of such "natural" processes as contact and acculturation. The colonizing power carries out a policy which constrains, transforms, or destroys indigenous values, orientations, and ways of life. Third, colonization involves a relationship by which members of the colonized group tend to be administered by representatives of the dominant power. . . . A final fundament of colonization is racism . . . by which a group seen as inferior or different in terms of alleged biological characteristics is exploited, controlled, and oppressed socially and psychologically by a superordinate group.[50]

Exploitation and oppression of American blacks outside the South has been manifested in a variety of ways. Blacks have been the victims of systematic discrimination in employment. Because of low incomes and discriminatory housing practices, blacks have become concentrated in the "Other America," to borrow Michael Harrington's phrase,[51] and receive inferior education in ghetto schools, which ill-equips them for success striving and upward mobility. Finally, the "sting of relative deprivation" suffered by contemporary blacks is probably more deeply felt because of rising general affluence, which has exacerbated the deprived condition of American blacks.[52]

[47]One famous, dramatic case of discriminatory justice directed at southern blacks was the Scottsboro incident. See Haywood Patterson and Earl Conrad, *Scottsboro Boy* (New York: Doubleday and Co., 1950).

[48]U.S. Commission on Civil Rights, *Law Enforcement: A Report on Equal Protection in the South* (Washington, D.C.: U.S. Government Printing Office, 1965); see also Don C. Gibbons, "Violence in American Society: The Challenge to Corrections," *American Journal of Correction*, 31 (March–April 1969), 6–11.

[49]Robert Blauner, "Internal Colonialism and Ghetto Revolt," *Social Problems*, 16 (Spring 1969), 393–408.

[50]*Ibid.*, p. 396.

[51]Michael Harrington, *The Other America* (New York: The Macmillan Co., 1962).

[52]Jackson Toby, "The Prospects for Reducing Delinquency Rates in Industrial Societies," *Federal Probation*, 27 (December 1963), 23–125.

These conditions of racism and exploitation provide the warrant for describing the situation of American blacks as "social disorganization" or for speaking of "criminogenic influences" within black society. The basic argument is plausible enough: these conditions exert massive pressure on blacks to engage in lawbreaking. Economic pressures are seen as the cause of property crimes among blacks; while crimes of violence are considered the outgrowth of neighborhood conditions of disorder and attenuated social ties among black citizens. In a broad and general way, this theory of racism and black crime is correct. Also, if this formulation captures the root causes of black crime, those causes are ultimately attributed to racial oppression and other defects of the encompassing society within which American blacks live. Black crime is a consequence of white racism.

The problem with such theorizing is that it is incomplete. We ultimately want to know more about the etiology of lawbreaking among black citizens. How do these conditions of discrimination and oppression get "inside the heads" of black offenders, so to speak? What are the more specific dynamics lying behind different forms of criminality that blacks engaged in? We shall take up such questions in detail in succeeding chapters, where we begin to examine the causal processes operating in particular forms of illegality.

GENERAL THEORIES: AN EVALUATION

The preceding pages enumerated some theories of deviant behavior which were then criticized on the grounds that they are not specific and detailed enough in application to criminality. We looked at social disorganization approaches to crime causation and found them defective in a number of ways. We also examined multiple-factor views but rejected these as a viable solution to etiological interests because such orientations deny the possibility of causal analysis.

On a more affirmative level, we hold that theories of criminality framed in differential social organization terms represent a valid approach to the explanation of lawbreaking. Much of the illegality rampant in American society in particular is related to features of social organization, including conflicts in basic values, a variety of social stratification influences including differentials in availability of legitimate means to attainment of cultural goals, widespread disrespect for law and order, the growing bureaucratization and impersonality of "mass society," and the racial and ethnic cleavages of a nominally democratic society. These factors make sense out of criminality.

But at the same time that we assert confidence in a broadly sociological account of crime causation, we hasten to add that these general theories are flawed by the same ambiguity, fuzzy boundary definitions, and other shortcomings enumerated earlier with regard to theories of deviance. The basic problem with theories of criminality is that the forms of conduct included are extremely varied. Consequently, any formulation which purports to explain crime must be more elegant, elaborate, and detailed than any conceptualization now extant. Not that existing general theories are false; rather, they are plausible but basically untestable. The criminality they are designed to explain is unidentified. In addition, they are not sufficiently specific in their claims of how particular factors conjoin to produce crime of one kind or another.

As an illustration of the deficiencies of current theories of crime, take the matter of social values and criminality. Robin Williams has tried to identify major value patterns, that is, interests or "things" that stand as principles individuals use in organizing their conduct. The values of a society are those pervasive interests men define as worth pursuing. Williams has suggested that American values emphasize achievement and success, stress activity and work, moral orientations, humanitarianism, efficiency and pragmatism, freedom and inequality, external conformity, secular rationality, and several others as well.[53]

If these are in fact dominant values of American society, they probably have something to do with criminality in the United States. But the value commitments that contribute to such activity as white-collar crime may be of a somewhat different order than the interests bound up in other forms of illegality. Accordingly, succeeding chapters will endeavor to advance the understanding of the role of cultural values in crime by paying attention to the contribution that particular values make to different kinds of lawbreaking.

Many commentators have suggested that the compulsive enactment of "manly" forms of behavior is endemic to males in the United States, owing to certain patterns of social organization, particularly family structure, which creates anxieties about masculinity in many males. This hypothesis is in need of testing, but assume for a moment that it is correct. If masculinity strivings are commonplace, they may play some role in crime and delinquency. At the same time, some kinds of lawbreaking may be quite unrelated to this factor, and others may be heavily influenced by masculinity concerns. At least two separate relevant hypotheses have been advanced, one suggesting that lower-class male delinquents are plagued with masculinity anxiety,[54] another maintaining that this experience is one which troubles middle-class delinquents.[55] Perhaps the problem of masculine identity is bound up in both forms of delinquency in somewhat different ways. If so, a complicated kind of theorizing is called for to unravel and clarify these causal strands and weave them into a larger etiological fabric.

---

[53]Robin M. Williams, *American Society*, 3rd ed. (New York: Alfred A. Knopf, 1970), pp. 438–504.

[54]Miller, "Lower Class Culture as a Generating Milieu"; Miller, "Implications of Urban Lower Class Culture for Social Work," *Social Service Review*, 33 (September 1959), 219–36.

[55]Talcott Parsons, "Certain Primary Sources and Patterns of Aggression in the Social Structure of the Western World," *Psychiatry*, 10 (May 1947), 167–81; Albert K. Cohen, *Delinquent Boys* (New York: The Free Press, 1955), pp. 161–69.

A third illustration of the complexities facing general theories of crime and delinquency centers on the hypothesized trend of Western societies in the direction of increased rates of criminality. Doomsayers in recent decades have repeatedly stated that Western societies are not only criminalistic, they are becoming even more so with the growth of "mass society." Although the epidemiological facts are not adequate to demonstrate conclusively or invalidate such notions, illegal conduct has become somewhat more pervasive in recent times. However, the long-range drift of things might well include countertendencies, with some kinds of deviant conduct becoming attenuated at the same time others are increasing. Certain kinds of organized prostitution, professional theft, and some other forms of lawbreaking apparently have been on the decline in the recent past. If there is a trend toward burgeoning criminality, certain kinds of illegality may have contributed most heavily to this increase. In particular, gang fighting, along with utilitarian forms of property crime among lower-class persons, may be on the rise,[56] as is middle-class delinquent conduct.[57] Some of the following chapters throw further light on these questions.

Finally, the development of criminological theory calls for more attention to certain kinds of criminality not included at all within existing general formulations. Sex offender behavior is one major case in point. Although sociologists have the potential to contribute to the understanding of sexual deviations, they have not begun to achieve that potential. Most existing arguments regarding criminality are written in such a way as to systematically ignore sex offenses. The result is theory that is not only overly general and ambiguous but also truncated. Somewhat the same observation can be made regarding organized crime in American society, for sociologists have had surprisingly little to say about that kind of criminality, other than to repeat some naïve conspiratorial descriptions of an assumed Mafia or Cosa Nostra organization.[58]

SUMMARY

This chapter has considered the present status of general sociological theories of crime. Our assessment of these notions is that the differential social organization perspective offers the most promise for criminological progress. However, explanations that locate the sources of lawbreaking in features of social structure should pay more attention to the forms criminality takes. The starting

[56]See, on this point, Toby, "The Prospects for Reducing Delinquency Rates."

[57]T. R. Fyvel, *Troublemakers* (New York: Schocken Books, 1962); Ralph W. England, Jr., "A Theory of Middle Class Juvenile Delinquency," *Journal of Criminal Law, Criminology and Police Science,* 50 (March–April 1960), 535–40; Joseph W. Scott and Edmund W. Vaz, "A Perspective on Middle-Class Delinquency," *Canadian Journal of Economics and Political Science,* 39 (August 1963), 324–35; Gibbons, *Delinquent Behavior,* pp. 142–71.

[58]One noteworthy exception is found in Bell, "Crime as an American Way of Life."

point for theories stressing differential social organization should be the variations of illegal deviance. We need theories sensitive to the forms of crime in all their richness and variety rather than formulations that try to force the facts of criminality into a preconceived scheme of analysis.

The second half of our review of sociological theories of crime concerns arguments attempting to indicate the factors that operate in the development of criminal behavior and attitudes on the part of individuals. Chapter Nine is concerned with these statements of the social psychology of criminal careers.

9

SOCIOGENIC APPROACHES: BECOMING AN OFFENDER

This chapter continues the overview of general theories of crime and criminality begun in Chapter Eight. Although the previous chapter was concerned with theories regarding *rates* of crime or the sociology of crime, the present discussion has to do with the social psychology of criminal careers. As indicated in the opening chapter, that phrase refers to hypotheses about the factors and experiences that lead to development of particular kinds of careers in law-violating deviant behavior.

We shall begin by inspecting certain frameworks advanced regarding the emergence of, and changes in, patterns of deviant behavior. The views of Edwin Lemert, Howard Becker, and other students of deviance provide some useful concepts and viewpoints to be applied to criminality. Ideally, the study of criminal role careers should be a specialized segment of the general exploration of deviant careers. Propositions regarding deviant conduct should be elaborated to account for criminal patterns. Although existing formulations about deviant patterns of action are not too well articulated, they do contain a number of concepts that should be highly useful in criminology.

This chapter also examines Edwin Sutherland's "theory of differential association," the most significant effort to date by a criminologist to spell out the nature of the learning processes by which individuals acquire criminal behavior. The theory is doubly significant, for Sutherland tried to use the same variables that explain the development of "normal" behavior. Sutherland believed that the study of criminal behavior belongs within the main body of sociological endeavors rather than at the periphery of the main currents of sociological thinking.

The last section of this chapter takes up a number of relatively circumscribed views that have been put forth regarding particular factors or sets of variables thought to play a major role in the development of criminal or delinquent careers. For example, certain patterns of family structure, such as broken or unhappy homes, have often been singled out in attempts to specify criminal producing processes. Other notions have assigned etiological importance to the influences of mass media and a host of other specific variables.

THE DEVELOPMENT OF DEVIANT CAREERS

Interactional and Labeling Theories of Deviance[1]

Chapter Eight examined several theories centering about the social-structural forces that produce deviance, with the anomie formulation singled out for the greatest attention. In these theories, deviance is thought to represent behavioral departures from a common cultural value system, which disrupts social equilibrium. Also in these arguments, central cultural values which are violated by deviant acts are thought to be relatively few in number and generally shared by citizens throughout the society. Then too, in these formulations, little attention is paid to reactions to deviance. Instead, the implicit assumption seems to be that societal responses are of little significance or interest to sociologists. These "structural-functional" formulations concerning deviance have sometimes been identified as constituting an "eastern" school of thought, in that they were most in vogue in universities in that part of the United States.

By contrast, a new and different set of themes or orientations about deviant behavior has sprung up in recent years, which is sometimes identified as the "western" or "Pacific Coast" school.[2] This newer and lively perspective on deviance is most commonly designated as the social interactional or labeling view. Although it would be misleading to claim that a single theoretical position can be identified as labeling theory, a sizable and growing body of sociologists do share a set of themes or viewpoints.[3] A generous supply of critical commentary has developed regarding this perspective.[4]

[1]For a critical examination of certain aspects of social-psychological and other approaches to deviance, see Don C. Gibbons and Joseph F. Jones, "Some Critical Notes on Current Definitions of Deviance," *Pacific Sociological Review*, 14 (January 1971), 20–37.

[2]These distinctions appear in David J. Bordua, "Recent Trends: Deviant Behavior and Social Control," *Annals of the American Academy of Political and Social Science*, 369 (January 1967), 149–63; Edwin M. Lemert, *Human Deviance, Social Problems, and Social Control*, 2nd ed. (Englewood Cliffs, N.J.: Prentice-Hall, 1972), pp. 14–15.

[3]For some of the major works that have advanced this perspective, see Lemert, *Human Deviance, Social Problems, and Social Control*; Lemert, *Social Pathology* (New York: McGraw-Hill Book Co., 1951); Howard S. Becker, *Outsiders* (New York: The Free Press, 1963); Jack D. Douglas, "Deviance and Order in a Pluralistic Society," in *Theoretical Sociology*, ed. John C. McKinney and Edward A. Tiryakian (New York: Appleton-Century-Crofts, 1970), 367–401; Douglas, *American Social Order* (New York: The Free Press, 1971); Douglas, ed., *Deviance and Respectability* (New York: Basic Books, 1970); Kai T. Erikson, "Notes on the Sociology of Deviance," *Social Problems*, 9 (Spring 1962), 307–14; John I. Kitsuse, "Societal Reaction to Deviant Behavior: Problems of Theory and Method," in *The Other Side*, ed. Howard S. Becker (New York: The Free Press, 1964), pp. 87–102; John Lofland, *Deviance and Identity* (Englewood Cliffs, N.J.: Prentice-Hall, 1969); David Matza, *Becoming Deviant* (Englewood Cliffs, N.J.: Prentice-Hall, 1969); Thomas J. Scheff, *Being Mentally Ill* (Chicago: Aldine Publishing Co., 1966); Edwin M. Schur, *Labeling Deviant Behavior* (New York: Harper & Row, 1971).

[4]These include Bordua, "Deviant Behavior and Social Control"; Ronald L. Akers, "Problems in the Sociology of Deviance: Social Definitions and Behavior," *Social Forces*, 46 (June 1968), 455–65; John DeLamater, "On the Nature of Deviance," *Social Forces*, 46 (June 1968), 445–55; Jack P. Gibbs, "Conceptions of Deviant Behavior: The Old and the New," *Pacific Sociological Review*, 9 (Spring 1966), 9–14; Edwin M. Schur, "Reactions to Deviance: A Critical Assessment," *American Journal of Sociology*, 75 (November 1969), 309–22; Don C. Gibbons, "Social Definitions of Deviance: Some Findings and Needed Research," paper presented at the annual meeting of the Pacific Sociological Association, April 1972.

What are the central arguments of the labeling view?[5] To begin with, the theorists of this persuasion remind us that deviance is problematic and a matter of social definition, in that the violated standards or norms are not universal or unchanging. Then, too, deviance is the result of social judgments that a social audience imposes on persons. Becker's view on this point is frequently cited:

> Social groups created deviance by making the rules whose infraction constitutes deviance, and by applying those rules to particular people and labeling them as outsiders. From this point of view, deviance is *not* a quality of the act the person commits, but rather a consequence of the application by others of rules and sanctions to an "offender." The deviant is one to whom that label has been applied; deviant behavior is behavior that people so label.[6]

Statements such as Becker's are sometimes taken to mean that only those persons involved in nonconformity and subjected to specific labeling or defining experiences are deviants. On the other hand, many labelers often speak of "secret deviants," who have not been publicly identified, or of "primary deviance," which has not received a societal reaction.[7] But all agree that nonconformists singled out by the police, mental health personnel, or other social audiences face adjustment problems centering about spoiled identity not encountered by "hidden" deviants. This proposition is at the center of the labeling orientation.

A second common theme in labeling views is that *deviance arises out of diverse sources* or circumstances. Labelers do not agree that some small core of cultural values and differentially available opportunity structures can account for the varied forms deviance takes in complex societies. Instead, these theorists stress the value pluralism of modern societies and underscore the significance of subcultural normative patterns in nonconformity. Deviant acts often develop in situations where individuals are pulled and tugged by competing interests and values. Whatever the circumstances producing norm violation, they cannot be subsumed under some all-embracing theory such as anomie.

Labelers agree that deviant behavior should be examined as a *social process*, in which the acts of nonconforming individuals are bound up with the responses of others to those deviations. Labelers draw attention to *careers*, in which persons who become caught up in nonconformity exhibit changes in behavior and self-concept patterns over time. In turn, careers arise and unfold in response to social reactions directed at the deviant person.

[5]For summaries of the main elements of labeling theory, see Schur, *Labeling Deviant Behavior*, pp. 7–13; Lemert, *Human Deviance, Social Problems, and Social Control*. pp. 16–25.

[6]Becker, *The Other Side*, p. 9.

[7]This point has been noted by Akers, "Problems in the Sociology of Deviance"; Gibbs, "Conceptions of Deviant Behavior"; and Bordua, "Deviant Behavior and Social Control," among others.

In many examples that labelers discuss, the actors often deny or disavow initial deviant acts so that their acts are "normalized." That is, for a time at least, the person defines his misbehavior as unimportant or as peripheral to his real self. But social reactions directed at the person ultimately undermine his claim to normality. At some point, the deviant is driven toward an altered social identity as a deviant or, less frequently, out of involvement in norm violation.

Labeling theorists draw attention to organizations and agencies that function ostensibly to rehabilitate the deviant or in other ways to draw him back into conformity. These theorists contend that various people-changing organizations often produce results quite different from their intentions, for they operate to seal off opportunities for the deviant to withdraw from deviance. These agencies stigmatize the actor and create other social impediments that stand in the way of rehabilitation. Labeling theorists are generally pessimistic about training schools, prisons, mental hospitals, and other such institutions, for they suspect that these places may often exacerbate the problems of the deviant.

We should note, however, that, to date, labeling views have been long on theory and short on empirical evidence. The labeling orientation currently stands as a set of plausible contentions about deviance rather than as a well-documented collection of empirical generalizations. For example, the labeling perspective on mental disorder does not seem to bear a close relationship to empirical facts currently at hand.[8] Along a similar line, we shall see in later chapters that the evidence regarding the operations of correctional organizations is less clear than labeling arguments imply.

Although labeling theories are designed to account for a variety of forms of deviance, many illustrative cases on which these arguments draw for support have to do with criminality and delinquency. We shall touch on these in the following pages. However, let us now examine certain labeling arguments in more detail.

Lemert's Contribution

Edwin Lemert's work represents a seminal version of the labeling theory. Lemert has written extensively on the processes by which persons are singled out as deviants, and by which the life careers of some become organized or individuated around deviant statuses.[9] Lemert's work is properly regarded as social-psychological in character in that he emphasizes deviant individuals and

---

[8]The labeling view of mental illness is most explicit in Scheff, *Being Mentally Ill*. For an evaluation of the empirical adequacy of this argument, see Walter R. Gove, "Societal Reaction as an Explanation of Mental Illness: An Evaluation," *American Sociological Review*, 35 (October 1970), 873-84.

[9]Lemert, *Social Pathology*; Lemert, *Human Deviance, Social Problems, and Social Control*. We should note that Lemert's writings on deviance date back to 1951, long before most other labeling theorists were active. One forerunner of modern labeling views is Frank Tannenbaum, *Crime and the Community* (Boston: Ginn and Co., 1938), pp. 19-21. In that work, Tannenbaum draws attention to "dramatization of evil," which was his term for the societal reaction experiences that drive the deviant further into misconduct.

their immediate social interactions with others rather than rates of deviance and the larger social structures producing these rates. Lemert's viewpoint is based on the assumption that "behavioral deviations are a function of culture conflict which is expressed through social organization."[10] As we noted in Chapter Eight, Lemert rejects structural–functional arguments, such as anomie, in favor of value pluralism, which emphasizes subcultural values and value conflicts as the sources of deviance.[11]

Lemert's writings distinguish between several contexts within which deviant conduct can arise. He suggests the categories of *individual, situational*, and *systematic* deviation to stand for these varied sources of origin.[12] Individual deviation refers to deviant acts that emanate from psychic pressures "within the skin," so to speak, whereas situational deviation is conduct that develops as a function of situational stresses or pressures. Acts of situational deviation are relatively independent of psychic pressures among actors so that different individuals placed in the same stressful setting would be expected to respond in similar deviant ways.

We can observe instances of deviation that approximate these limiting cases. For example, some kinds of sexual deviation can be explained only as the consequence of the wholly idiosyncratic motives of the offender. Along with other cases of this kind it is possible to point to nearly "pure" illustrations of situational deviation. Samples of the latter include the prison guard caught up in discordant role expectations making deviant acts unavoidable for him, the aircraft worker compelled to use deviant work practices to solve technological problems created by ill-fitting airplane assembly sections,[13] or individuals implicated in situations of cumulative, catastrophic financial stress such that theft appears the only problem-solving pattern of activity open to them. We shall have more to say about situational factors in criminality in a later section of this chapter.

As Lemert would acknowledge, these two categories represent polar extremes on a causal continuum, and many occurrences of deviant conduct arise as the joint product of pressures of social situations and factors from the inner life of the individual. In many real-life cases, the etiological task is evaluation of the relative contribution that each motivational source makes to the behavioral product under examination. This job is often at the heart of satisfactory explanation; many areas of deviant behavior need theoretical models that clarify and assign specific weights to these two factors. Take the case of deviant police conduct as illustrative of the substantive problem. In explaining these acts, the sociologist would probably have to examine variations in ethical standards, personality structure, and so on among police recruits, for these individuals probably vary in relevant ways at the time they enter into the social

[10]Lemert, *Social Pathology*, p. 23.
[11]Lemert, *Human Deviance, Social Problems, and Social Control*, pp. 26–61.
[12]Lemert, *Social Pathology*, p. 23.
[13]Joseph Bensman and Israel Gerver, "Crime and Punishment in the Factory: The Function of Deviancy in Maintaining the Social System," *American Sociological Review*, 28 (August 1963), 588–98.

system of the police department. Policemen vary in terms of involvement in deviant acts, partly as a result of personality differences they bring with them into police work. In explaining conduct violations among law enforcement persons, the sociologist would also need to examine the normative system of the organization to assess the part played in deviance by *organizational tolerance* for being "on the take" (petty graft), employing violence in contacts with citizens, and other infringements. Readers familiar with a different conceptual language will note that the issue in this illustration revolves around the extent to which psychogenic or sociogenic factors enter into acts of deviant conduct. We will have occasion to take up this central issue later. For example, in the analysis of embezzlement, we shall suggest that embezzlement is most likely to occur when certain kinds of personalities are collected in particular kinds of organizational structures. Similarly, in the discussion of semiprofessional property offenders we shall indicate some influences that deflect different individuals in stressful, working-class neighborhoods into careers as successful offenders, criminal failures, or law-abiding citizens. We shall argue that certain factors are "inside" the psyches of actors.

Lemert employs the term *systematic deviation* to refer to patterns of deviant behavior that take on the coloring of subcultures or behavior systems. He says: "When such communication [between deviants] carries specific content, when rapport develops between deviants and common rationalizations make their appearance, the unique and situational forms of deviation are converted to organized or systematic deviation."[14] Systematic or organized forms of deviance result from deviant conduct that was individual or situational in genesis. Lemert indicates that systematic deviation is most likely to occur in situations when society makes survival as a deviant person problematic for the individual unless he can become absorbed into some kind of protective social system. Accordingly, the existence of homosexual subcultures in American society is, at least in part, a consequence of the harassment and hostility the identified homosexual encounters in the United States.[15] One point Lemert makes is that most deviant subcultures follow a limited or circumscribed set of deviant mores, for most values of the members are those of the dominant culture.[16] Hence, drug addicts, homosexuals, or other social outcasts tend to hold allegiance to most conventional values of society, with a few specific deviant beliefs and conduct.

Much of Lemert's emphasis is on *processual* aspects of deviant behavior, in which he shows that deviant careers often undergo marked changes over time. In the past, the more usual model of explanation was of a simple stimulus–response kind, endeavoring to discover some set of influences that antedated the deviant behavior under study, often with a considerable time span

---

[14]Lemert, *Social Pathology*, p. 44.

[15]Maurice Leznoff and William A. Westley, "The Homosexual Community," *Social Problems*, 3 (April 1956), 257–63.

[16]Lemert, *Social Pathology*, pp. 48–50.

separating the causal factors and present behavior. Little attention was paid to changes in deviant careers, which flow out of differential experiences the deviant undergoes in his life history.

In Lemert's theorizing, initial acts of deviant behavior are frequently instances of "risk taking," representing tentative flirtations with proscribed behavior patterns.[17] Whatever the reasons for these actions, many become subjected to societal reactions. Someone else observes the acts and makes them the focus of concern. In this view, societal reations may influence the subsequent career experiences of the deviant more than anything else that has occurred prior to his involvement in disapproved conduct. Lemert notes that societal definitions and reactions in complex societies are often heavily *putative* so that beliefs become attached to deviant persons, which have no foundation in their actual behavior. The drug fiend" mythology, which holds that addicts are generally depraved and immoral, is a case in point.[18]

Lemert introduced a major distinction between *primary* and *secondary* deviation.[19] Primary deviation represents that state of affairs in which an individual engages in norm-violating conduct he regards as alien to his true self. Secondary deviation, on the other hand, involves cases in which the actor reorganizes his social-psychological characteristics around the deviant role. On this point, Lemert declares: "The deviant individuals must react symbolically to their own behavior aberrations and fix them in their sociopsychological patterns. The deviations remain primary deviations or symptomatic and situational as long as they are rationalized or otherwise dealt with as functions of a socially acceptable role."[20]

Sometimes primary deviation becomes secondary; in other cases it remains primary. Secondary deviation most often arises out of repeated acts of norm violation and the experience of societal reactions. A kind of feedback process often takes place in which repetition of misconduct or deviation triggers societal reactions to the behavior, which then stimulate further deviant acts. According to Lemert:

> The sequence of interaction leading to secondary deviation is roughly as follows: (1) primary deviation; (2) social penalties; (3) further primary deviation; (4) stronger penalties and rejections; (5) further deviation, perhaps with hostilities and resentments beginning to focus upon those doing the penalizing; (6) crisis reached in the tolerance quotient, expressed in formal action by the community stigmatizing of the deviant; (7) strengthening of the deviant conduct as a reaction to the stigmatizing and penalties; (8) ultimate acceptance of deviant social status and efforts at adjustment on the basis of the associated role.[21]

[17]Lemert, *Human Deviance, Social Problems, and Social Control*, pp. 38–40.
[18]Lemert, *Social Pathology*, pp. 55–57.
[19]Lemert, *Human Deviance, Social Problems, and Social Control*, pp. 62–92.
[20]Lemert, *Social Pathology*, p. 75.
[21]*Ibid.*, p. 77.

In his textbook analysis of forms of deviant behavior, Lemert shows the applicability of these theoretical notions to the varied forms misconduct and pathological behavior take. He also shows how development of deviant status results in a variety of limitations being imposed on the social participation of the deviant actor so that his economic activities, mobility experiences, and so on become markedly circumscribed as he progresses in deviant conduct. Lemert also applies these insights to research studies of alcoholic persons,[22] the development of paranoid social patterns,[23] and the genesis of certain forms of criminality.[24]

We have high regard for Lemert's conceptions and hypotheses. His viewpoints appear to explain a variety of forms of deviant conduct, with much to be gained from applying them to lawbreaking behavior. In the following chapters, we shall use some of the core ideas in Lemert's framework. We shall repeatedly focus on queries involving contexts of criminal action and inquire as to whether forms of criminality represent individual, situational, or systematic deviation. We shall also explore societal reactions to criminality in a number of places. In particular, Chapter Ten takes up a variant of societal reactions labeled "contacts with defining agencies." The commentary avers that varied experiences of offenders with various social control agencies operate as powerful influences on the course of their deviant careers. Finally, Lemert's distinction between primary and secondary deviation is incorporated into our categorizations of types of offenders. In the typological materials in Chapter Ten and in succeeding sections of the book, role-career patterns among offenders are distinguished in considerable measure in terms of attitudinal and self-image variations among these individuals.

Becker's Work

We should consider some other lines of commentary regarding the development of deviant careers. Becker's extended essay bears a good deal of similarity to Lemert's claims.[25] Becker points out that no automatic, fixed, and invariant relationship exists between behavioral acts and societal reactions to the conduct as deviant. Instead, the likelihood that behavioral occurrences will be identified publicly as aberrant varies in accordance with the time, place, and individuals who observe the conduct.[26] Becker notes that some individuals are falsely accused as deviants, for although they have been labeled outsiders,

[22]Lemert, "Dependency in Married Alcoholics," *Quarterly Journal of Studies on Alcohol*, 23 (December 1962), 590–609.

[23]Lemert, "Paranoia and the Dynamics of Exclusion," *Sociometry*, 25 (March 1962), 2–20.

[24]Lemert, "The Behavior of the Systematic Check Forger," *Social Problems*, 6 (Fall 1958), 141–49; Lemert, "An Isolation and Closure Theory of Naïve Check Forgery," *Journal of Criminal Law, Criminology and Police Science*, 44 (September-October 1953), 296–307.

[25]Becker, *The Other Side*.

[26]*Ibid.*, pp. 3–22.

their behavior has actually been conforming in character. Other persons represent secret deviants; although they misbehave, their misconduct does not come to the attention of any significant public. Still other individuals who acquire a public identity as "queer," "crazy," or in some other way deviant behave in ways that warrant this social judgment.

Becker stresses the temporal patterning of deviant behavior. He suggests that sociologists need to pay attention to *sequential models of deviance*, that is, to orderly changes in the actions of the deviant over time. He offers the concepts of *deviant careers* and *career contingencies* as explanatory tools. A career contingency is a factor or set of influences that results in the movement of a career incumbent from one position to another in a career pattern.[27] We have already incorporated the notion of career into our analysis. Moreover, Chapter Ten elaborates on these ideas at some length.

Regarding deviant careers, Becker suggests that interest be concentrated on the processes and variables that sustain a pattern of deviance over a lengthy time period rather than on isolated and fugitive deviant escapades. In a fashion similar to Lemert, he argues: "One of the most crucial steps in the process of building a stable pattern of deviant behavior is likely to be the experience of being caught and publicly labeled as a deviant. . . . The most important consequence is a drastic change in the individual's public identity."[28]

Other major insights in Becker's work center on the distinction between *master* and *subordinate* statuses, in which he argues that a particular deviant status, such as that of "hood," "fairy," or "hustler," may become superordinate over the individual's other statuses, with the result that the person's public identity as a deviant or discredited person colors his social relationships.[29] Finally, Becker, like Lemert, regards the development of deviant groups (subcultures or systematic deviation) as of profound importance as a determinant of the course of a deviant career.[30]

SUTHERLAND'S THEORY OF DIFFERENTIAL ASSOCIATION

Few scholars have played a more dominant role than sociologist Edwin H. Sutherland (1883–1950). Sutherland's best-known endeavors are in a study of professional theft as a behavior system,[31] the development of the concept of "white-collar crime" along with research studies of this activity,[32] and his theory of "differential association," which he attempted to apply to various kinds

[27]*Ibid.*, pp. 22–39.
[28]*Ibid.*, p. 30.
[29]*Ibid.*, pp. 31–34.
[30]*Ibid.*, pp. 36–39.
[31]Edwin H. Sutherland, *The Professional Thief* (Chicago: University of Chicago Press, 1937).
[32]Sutherland, *White Collar Crime* (New York: Dryden Press, 1949).

of criminality.[33] No major contribution to the sociological study of *adult* criminal behavior has been made in the two decades since Sutherland's untimely death, which serves as a testimonial to his signal place in criminology.

The framework called the theory of differential association with which we are concerned in this chapter emerged over an extended period of development. As Sutherland reported the gestation of this theory, his first ideas on criminological theory began to take shape around 1921, but not until 1939 did he develop the mature version of his differential association theory.[34] His aim in evolving the differential association perspective is stated in this passage: "I reached the general conclusion that a concrete condition cannot be a cause of crime, and that the only way to get a causal explanation of criminal behavior is by extracting from the varying concrete conditions things that are universally associated with crime."[35] In Sutherland's view, differential association is universally linked to criminal action.

We noted in Chapter Eight that Sutherland's arguments on crime causation were built from a foundation of notions on differential social organization. In his words: "Cultural conflict in this sense is the basic principle in the explanation of crime."[36] The social and economic changes involved in industrialization of the Western world are believed to have generated a pervasive individualism and other conditions conducive to criminality. The social influences persons encounter through their lifetimes are inharmonious and inconsistent so that many individuals become involved in contacts with carriers of criminalistic norms and become criminals as a consequence. This process is known as "differential association."

The elements of Sutherland's differential association theory as stated in 1939 and in subsequent editions of *Principles of Criminology* are:

1. *Criminal behavior is learned.* Negatively, this means that criminal behavior is not inherited, as such; also, the person who is not already trained in crime does not invent criminal behavior, just as a person does not make mechanical inventions unless he has had training in mechanics.

2. *Criminal behavior is learned in interaction with other persons in a proc-*

---

[33]Sutherland and Donald R. Cressey, *Principles of Criminology*, 8th ed. (Philadelphia: J. B. Lippincott Co., 1970). See also Albert K. Cohen, Alfred Lindesmith, and Karl Schuessler, eds., *The Sutherland Papers* (Bloomington: Indiana University Press, 1956) for a resume of the large number of other papers and studies by Sutherland. For other useful comments on differential association theory, see George B. Vold, *Theoretical Criminology* (New York: Oxford University Press, 1958), pp. 192-202; Donald R. Cressey, "Epidemiology and Individual Conduct: A Case from Criminology," *Pacific Sociological Review*, 3 (Fall 1960), 47-58.

[34]Cohen, Lindesmith, and Schuessler, *The Sutherland Papers*, pp. 13-29. This essay is highly recommended as an all too infrequent report on the "sociology of knowledge." In it, Sutherland presents a highly candid and characteristically modest account of the stages of thought through which he progressed and of the influences on his thinking, as he evolved the differential association view.

[35]*Ibid.*, p. 19.

[36]*Ibid.*, p. 20.

ess of communication. This communication is verbal in many respects but includes also "the communication of gestures."

3. *The principal part of the learning of criminal behavior occurs within intimate personal groups.* Negatively, this means that the impersonal agencies of communication, such as movies and newspapers, play a relatively unimportant part in the genesis of criminal behavior.

4. *When criminal behavior is learned, the learning includes (a) techniques of committing the crime, which are sometimes very complicated, sometimes very simple; (b) the specific direction of motives, drives, rationalizations, and attitudes.*

5. *The specific direction of motives and drives is learned from definitions of the legal codes as favorable or unfavorable.* In some societies an individual is surrounded by persons who invariably define the legal codes as rules to be observed, while in others he is surrounded by persons whose definitions are favorable to the violation of the legal codes. In our American society these definitions are almost always mixed, with the consequence that we have culture conflict in relation to the legal codes.

6. *A person becomes delinquent because of an excess of definitions favorable to violation of law over definitions unfavorable to violation of law.* This is the principle of differential association. It refers to both criminal and anti-criminal associations and has to do with counteracting forces. When persons become criminal, they do so because of contacts with criminal patterns and also because of isolation from anti-criminal patterns. Any person inevitably assimilates the surrounding culture unless other patterns are in conflict; a Southerner does not pronounce "r" because other Southerners do not pronounce "r." Negatively, this proposition of differential association means that associations which are neutral so far as crime is concerned have little or no effect on the genesis of criminal behavior. Much of the experience of a person is neutral in this sense, e.g., learning to brush one's teeth. This behavior has no negative or positive effect on criminal behavior except as it may be related to associations which are concerned with the legal codes. This neutral behavior is important especially as an occupier of the time of a child so that he is not in contact with criminal behavior during the time he is so engaged in the neutral behavior.

7. *Differential associations may vary in frequency, duration, priority, and intensity.* This means that associations with criminal behavior and also associations with anti-criminal behavior vary in those respects. "Frequency" and "duration" as modalities of associations are obvious and need no explanation. "Priority" is assumed to be important in the sense that lawful behavior developed in early childhood may persist throughout life, and also that delinquent behavior developed in early childhood may persist throughout life. This tendency, however, has not been adequately demonstrated, and priority seems to be important principally through its selective influence. "Intensity" is not precisely defined but it has to do with such things as the prestige of the source of a criminal

or anti-criminal pattern and with emotional reactions related to the associations. In a precise description of the criminal behavior of a person these modalities would be stated in quantitative form and a mathemetical ratio be reached. A formula in this sense has not been developed, and the development of such a formula would be extremely difficult.

8. *The process of learning criminal behavior by association with criminal and anti-criminal patterns involves all of the mechanisms that are involved in any other learning.* Negatively, this means that the learning of criminal behavior is not restricted to the process of imitation. A person who is seduced, for instance, learns criminal behavior by association, but this process would not ordinarily be described as imitation.

9. *While criminal behavior is an expression of general needs and values, it is not explained by those general needs and values since non-criminal behavior is an expression of the same needs and values.* Thieves generally steal in order to secure money, but likewise honest laborers work in order to secure money. The attempts by many scholars to explain criminal behavior by general drives and values, such as the happiness principle, striving for social status, the money motive, or frustration, have been and must continue to be futile since they explain lawful behavior as completely as they explain criminal behavior. They are similar to respiration, which is necessary for any behavior but which does not differentiate criminal from non-criminal behavior.[37]

The essence of Sutherland's argument is that criminal behavior is enacted by individuals who have acquired a number of sentiments in favor of law violation, sufficient to outweigh their prosocial or anticriminal conduct definitions. In turn, different actors get their varied congeries of prosocial and procriminal conduct standards through associations with others in their social environment. In general, contacts or associations with the greatest impact on persons are frequent, lengthy, early in point of origin, and most intense or meaningful. Sutherland suggests: "It is not necessary, at this level of explanation, to explain why a person has the associations he has; this certainly involves a complex of many things."[38] However, he maintains that the state of differential social organization characteristic of modern societies is responsible, in general terms, for the varied associational ties of different persons.

Sutherland's formulation has dominated criminology for two reasons. First, it is the major effort by a sociologist to state a theory regarding criminality in which a set of general propositions are enunciated as sufficient to explain the occurrence (or nonoccurrence) of criminal conduct. The differential association argument stands in contrast to multiple-factor orientations, for the latter are no more than descriptive inventories of a list of specific variables bearing some association to criminality, with few if any linkages indicated

[37]Sutherland and Cressey, *Principles of Criminology*, pp. 75–77.
[38]*Ibid.*, p. 82.

between them. Second, differential association claims are stated in terms of a small group of "core" concepts and arguments to which all sociologists owe allegiance. The "sociological perspective" advances an image of man as the product of his social experiences, which provide him with the definitions or standards of conduct and beliefs that stimulate and sustain his activities. Moreover, the sociological view is that the primary groups to which men belong (Sutherland's "intimate personal groups") exert the strongest influence. The sociologist sees man as driven by a "motor" the social process has placed inside him. No wonder that Sutherland's formulation won wide acceptance, for it is stated in the rhetoric and terminology of sociology. It includes no alien terminology from the psychologist's or psychiatrist's bag of words.

For all its merits, the theory of differential association is not without faults. As is true of most sociological exposition, the theory lacks clarity and precision. The problem is not that the claims are false but rather that they are overly ambiguous; they are rendered plausible but essentially untestable. For example, what are we to make of the contention that persons become criminal due to an excess of definitions favorable to law violation over prosocial sentiments? Perhaps some relationship is implied in which the sheer *number* of conduct definitions of one kind or another is the major determinant of conduct, with criminality resulting whenever the ratio of an individual's criminalistic attitudes to law-abiding ones becomes two to one, or some other ratio. Some conduct definitions could be more compelling than others, so a few criminalistic attitudes could, under certain circumstances, overpower a large number of conformist preferences. If we cannot agree as to which of these interpretations is correct and if we cannot spell out more adequately the relationship suggested by the theory, we cannot definitively test the argument.

The same point holds for other parts of Sutherland's statement. Are "associations" to be interpreted as identifiable, physical, group contacts in which individuals are enmeshed? The passages from *Principles of Criminology* rather clearly indicate that group associations of the individual are the important forces in behavior. However, some persons have interpreted Sutherland's statements to mean that associations are collectivities to which actors orient their conduct—their reference groups—so that some individuals are in differential association with social units other than those with which they are in physical contact.[39] But let us retain the interpretation of associations that Sutherland apparently intended. What kinds of associations are "intense" ones? The commonsense ring to the notion of intensity enables us to agree that somehow certain groups to which we belong are more important to us than are others. Yet it is quite another thing to operationalize the concept of intensity by settling on empirical indicators that measure the intensity of different group associations.

[39]Daniel Glaser, "Criminality Theories and Behavioral Images," *American Journal of Sociology*, 61 (March 1956), 433–44.

The foregoing suggestive objections have been leveled at Sutherland's differential association theory. The dialogue of criticisms and rejoinders has been so massive as to testify to the seminal role of Sutherland's conceptualization in the development of criminological theory. Whatever the final evaluation of this framework, the perspective has served criminology well in the role of an intellectual "pump primer."

Donald Cressey has prepared an extremely detailed and incisive account of the differential association controversy.[40] According to Cressey, allegations of defects in the differential association theory fall into two groups: those based on misinterpretations of the language of the theory or on ambiguities contained in it and those directed at substantive claims in the argument.

One erroneous interpretation holds that the theory suggests persons who associate with criminals become criminals in turn. But close examination of the argument shows that Sutherland maintained that criminality ensues from an excess of criminal associations over noncriminal ones. Another incorrect interpretation asserts that the theory says that criminality results from involvements with criminal persons, while the formulation actually refers to criminal *patterns,* many of which persons who are not gangsters or robbers carry and communicate. Other objections have been raised that the theory does not specify why individuals have the associations they have, even though Sutherland did give much attention to this question at other points in his work. Still another class of erroneous judgments stems from incorrect notions about the role of theoretical frameworks.[41]

Concerning substantive criticisms, Cressey notes that a number of criminologists have asserted that the theory fails to account for certain forms of criminality, but often without identifying the exceptional cases thought to be outside the boundaries of differential association. He notes that differential association has been said not to apply to rural offenders, violators of World War II OPA regulations, naïve check forgers, and certain other types of lawbreakers subjected to research investigation.[42]

Differential association theory has also been criticized for ignoring "personality traits" or "psychological variables." As Cressey makes clear, Sutherland wrestled at length with this objection. Sutherland believed that even if some personality traits are associated with forms of criminality (as distinct from being the *result* of deviant careers), so some kinds of offenders are uncommonly "aggressive," "introverted," or "anxious," differential association still determines which individuals with the personality patterns become criminal and which do not. We agree that this rejoinder is reasonable as far as it goes. Still, we are left with the major task of specifying linkages between offender patterns and predisposed personality constellations, as well as isolating and explicating ingredients of the processes by which individuals of some type get selectively recruited and canalized by social experience along different

[40]Cressey, "Epidemiology and Individual Conduct."
[41]*Ibid.,* 48–50.
[42]*Ibid.,* 51.

behavioral paths. This is major, unfinished theoretical business for criminology, but Sutherland cannot be held accountable for a failure to solve this question.[43]

Another substantive, conceptual problem with the theory centers about its failure to spell out the effects that experiences of the person at different age periods have on his behavior at any time. Some early life experiences may affect the *meaning* of later ones. They become influential in conditioning subsequent events, with persons who have encountered them reacting to certain adult associations and definitions significantly. At the same time, adult life events may have a neutral or insignificant impact on persons who have experienced a divergent set of earlier life happenings.[44] These possibilities resemble the statistician's notion of *stochastic processes*, in which the effects of any present experience or variable depend on an earlier transpiration in the life histories of the subjects under examination. Further, the probabilities of future events are likely to vary among actors, as they encounter variations in experiences that have not yet taken place. Becker's notions of "sequential models," "careers," and "career contingencies," discussed earlier in this chapter, represent this sort of view of deviant behavior.

The theory is also said to be defective because the ratio of learned behavior patterns used to explain criminality cannot be precisely studied in specific cases. Cressey offers a number of examples in which researchers have been unable to measure accurately definitions favorable, or unfavorable, to violation of law.[45] Finally, a number of critics have averred that the learning process for acquiring criminality or law-abiding behavior is more complex than the theory indicates. For example, it does not allow for the possibility that some individuals contrive their criminality apart from contact with criminal associations.[46]

We can find no better summary evaluation of the dialogue on differential association than Cressey's judgment. He says:

> On the other hand, it also seems safe to conclude that differential association is not a precise statement of the process by which one becomes a criminal. The idea that criminality is a consequence of an excess of intimate associations with criminal behavior patterns is valuable because, for example, it negates assertions that deviation from norms is simply a product of being emotionally insecure or living in a broken home, and then indicates in a general way why only some emotionally insecure persons and only some persons from broken homes commit crimes. . . . Yet the statement of the differential association process is not precise enough to stimulate

[43]A recent essay voicing this complaint about the absence of a dynamic view of personality in the differential association theory is S. Kirson Weinberg, "Personality and Method in the Differential Association Theory: Comments on 'A Reformulation of Sutherland's Differential Association Theory and a Strategy for Empirical Verification,'" *Journal of Research in Crime and Delinquency*, 3 (July 1966), 165–72.

[44]Cressey, "Epidemiology and Individual Conduct," 53.

[45]*Ibid.*

[46]*Ibid.*, 53–54.

rigorous empirical test, and it therefore has not been proved or disproved.[47]

Differential association should be acknowledged as a highly valuable point of view that has served as a beginning toward a mature version of criminological theory. To so describe it is in no sense to denigrate its importance. But according to Cressey's evaluation and our own, the task ahead is to elaborate on and revise the etiological beginnings Sutherland established. Several kinds of efforts are in order. Sutherland and Cressey suggest that research and theoretical labors might concentrate more on the study of specific orders or forms of criminality rather than on further elaboration of a general, overarching theory of crime such as differential association.[48] Such activity should perhaps begin to separate forms of criminality that arise out of some process akin to differential association from those that do not. Such theoretical endeavors should also introduce some clarity into the general theory of differential association by revealing the specific chains of variables or factors summed up in the general expression. Contemporary criminology needs elaborate formulations that are congruent with the complex character of social interaction as it is played out in real life.

Recently, several efforts have been made to revise and renovate the differential association theory so as to make it more serviceable. C. R. Jeffery criticizes the argument on the grounds that it is not stated in terms of modern learning theory.[49] Robert Burgess and Ronald Akers actually restate the differential association formulation in terms of modern learning theory from psychology.[50] Probably the most significant contribution to development of the theory is Melvin De Fleur and Richard Quinney's essay.[51] These sociologists, restating Sutherland's views in the language of set theory, have put the argument into a tightly logical form. They have turned up several points of ambiguity in the original formulation. De Fleur and Quinney's most important conclusion is that a testable version of differential association would have to be linked to an adequate taxonomy of criminal role patterns. We would then discover that a number of forms of differential association are related to different criminal patterns. In short, De Fleur and Quinney concur with our view that differential association is a label for an assortment of factors or experiences implicated in different forms of lawbreaking.

[47]Ibid., 57.

[48]Sutherland and Cressey, Principles of Criminology, p. 279. For other detailed remarks on this direction to theoretical activities, see Gibbons, Delinquent Behavior, pp. 21–73; Gibbons and Donald L. Garrity, "Some Suggestions for the Development of Etiological and Treatment Theory in Criminology," Social Forces, 38 (October 1959), 51–58; Gibbons and Garrity, "Definition and Analysis of Certain Criminal Types," Journal of Criminal Law, Criminology and Police Science, 53 (March 1962), 27–35; Gibbons, Changing the Lawbreaker (Englewood Cliffs, N.J.: Prentice-Hall, 1965).

[49]C. R. Jeffery, "Criminal Behavior and Learning Theory," Journal of Criminal Law, Criminology and Police Science, 56 (September 1965), 294–300.

[50]Robert L. Burgess and Ronald L. Akers, "A Differential Association-Reinforcement Theory of Criminal Behavior," Social Problems, 14 (Fall 1966), 128–47.

[51]Melvin L. De Fleur and Richard Quinney, "A Reformulation of Sutherland's Differential Association Theory and a Strategy for Empirical Verification," Journal of Research in Crime and Delinquency, 3 (January 1966), 1–22; also see Donald R. Cressey, "The Language of Set Theory and Differential Association," Journal of Research in Crime and Delinquency, 3 (January 1966), 22–26.

The discussions of different criminal role patterns in Chapters Twelve through Seventeen hint at the eventual shape causal theories may take. These theories show unmistakable signs of linkage to Sutherland's pioneering works.

SITUATIONAL FACTORS IN CRIMINALITY[52]

We described the differential association theory as providing an answer to the question: How does someone come to be the kind of person who commits a crime? This perspective asserts that offenders learn definitions favoring violations of law from their social associations. According to this framework, without motivation, deviation does not occur. But the differential association theory may be inaccurate for many lawbreakers. Differential association may be an answer to a defective question that assumes motivation to criminality must be inside individuals who engage in criminal conduct. Many offenders may not be any more motivated to engage in criminality than nonoffenders. Their lawbreaking behavior may arise out of some combination of situational pressures and circumstances, along with opportunities for criminality, which are totally *outside the actor*. Perhaps criminological attention should shift somewhat away from person-oriented perspectives toward more concern with criminogenic situations. Many offenders may be virtually indistinguishable from other citizens at the point of initial involvement in deviance so that traditional views of causal relationships may not hold for many contemporary criminals.

Ironically, Sutherland offered a major alternative perspective on etiology as well as differential association notions. He noted that differential association was a specific case of *historical* or *genetic* views of causation, which he contrasted to *mechanistic* or *situational* perspectives.[53] The genetic approach looks for factors operating in the earlier life history of the criminal or delinquent that can be linked to his lawbreaking. On the other hand, the mechanistic–situational–dynamic view examines processes occurring at or near the moment of the criminal event. In general, a situational perspective assumes that the causal process operating in some instance of criminality grew out of events closely tied in location and time to the deviant act.

Although he identified situational or mechanistic causation, Sutherland gave scant attention to this way of looking at etiology. He declared: "The objective situation is important to criminality largely to the extent that it provides an opportunity for a criminal act."[54] In his view, different persons will define the same objective situation differently; for some, the situation is conducive to criminality, but for others, it is not. Thus, only individuals motivated to engage in criminality will do so when confronted by particular situations. An historical or genetic explanation is required to explain how criminals define

[52]This section is an abridged version of Don C. Gibbons, "Some Observations on the Study of Crime Causation," *American Journal of Sociology*, 77 (September 1971), 262-78.

[53]Sutherland and Cressey, *Principles of Criminology*, pp. 74-75.

[54]*Ibid.*, p. 74.

current situations. Hence the image that emerges of the offender is of a person different, at least in social-psychological terms, from the nonoffender.

We argue that Sutherland overstated the matter by assuming that the earlier life experiences of offenders, extending over a lengthy time period, are always implicated in criminality. Contrary to his assumption, a long-term genetic process may not always operate with situational elements to create current lawbreaking. In many cases, criminality may be a response to nothing more temporal than the provocations and attractions bound up in the immediate circumstances out of which deviant acts arise.

Clearly, for some instances of criminality, historical or genetic factors are quite powerful and situational elements are of minor significance, such as certain types of deviant sexual conduct involving exhibitionism, voyeurism, or pronounced sexually aggressive acts. Concerning these forms of conduct, John Gagnon and William Simon assert: "In these cases, the causal nexus of the behavior appears to exist in the family and personality structures of the individual and is linked to the contingencies of his biography rather than those of social structure.[55] Aggressive lawbreaking often labeled "psychopathic" appears to be another form of criminality arising out of genetic factors, in this case, severe and early parental rejection. We shall take these forms of criminality up in more detail in Chapters Fifteen and Sixteen.

However, we can isolate other patterns of offender behavior composed primarily of situational elements, so probing about for genetic factors is unwarranted. As one concrete case, consider the report in *Tally's Corner*, that the incidence of burglary and other property crimes increases markedly during the winter in Washington, D.C., when Negro construction workers are laid off and turn to crime to eke out a living.[56] Little in that report suggests that criminality is a preferred pattern of behavior, that these persons are favorable to law violation, or that their lawbreaking is the outgrowth of a lengthy genetic process of differential socialization. Along the same line, Leroy Gould shows that the upsurge of car theft and bank robberies over the past several decades has directly been related to the growing abundance of these "victims."[57] Then, too, George Camp maintains that bank robberies are usually the work of desperate men, representing a last resort designed to solve some perceived crisis in the life of the robber.[58] They are not the acts of criminalistic gangs of "heavies" who make a career of carefully planned heists or whose lawbreaking has causal antecedents located in criminalistic associations that occurred years earlier.

We can isolate situational patterns of offender behavior, such as drunken driving and manslaughter. Then, too, Mary Cameron shows that "snitches"

[55]John H. Gagnon and William Simon, eds., *Sexual Deviance* (New York: Harper & Row, Publishers, 1967), p. 9.

[56]Elliot Liebow, *Tally's Corner* (Boston: Little, Brown and Co., 1967), pp. 29–71.

[57]Leroy Gould, "The Changing Structure of Property Crime in an Affluent Society," *Social Forces* 48 (September 1969), 50–59.

[58]George M. Camp, "Nothing to Lose: A Study of Bank Robbery in America" (Ph.D. thesis, Yale University, 1967).

or amateur shoplifters are "peripheral" criminals rather than "vocational" offenders.[59] They do not think of themselves, prior to arrest, as thieves, and no clear-cut genetic process emerges in the backgrounds of these offenders.

Another case of situational factors is found in Lemert's report on naïve check forgery, which he contends is an outgrowth of the process of "risk taking."[60] Risk taking is defined in the following terms: "This concept refers to situations in which persons who are caught in a network of conflicting claims or values choose not deviant alternatives but rather behavioral situations which carry risks of deviation. Deviation then becomes merely one possible outcome of their actions, but it is not inevitable.[61] The individual who writes a check while drinking, hoping to get to the bank with funds to cover it before the check reaches the bank, illustrates this process. Close examination of other kinds of criminality might show risk-taking elements as well.

To this point, we have argued that some forms of criminal behavior involve a heavy component of genetic etiology, wheras situational elements loom large in others. However, probably in a good many instances, genetic factors and situational contingencies are both significant. For example, acts of murder appear to be most frequent among individuals who have grown up in a "subculture of violence," who have been subjected to a number of disorganizing social influences over an extended period of time, and who look on others as potential assailants. At the same time, not all individuals who share these experiences commit acts of homicide. Those who do engage in murder often do so within situations of marital discord or tavern fights, in which a number of provocative moves and countermoves of interactional partners culminate in acts of homicide.[62] However, we should not assume that all participants in these short-lived sets of events intended them to have this criminal outcome, even a minute or so before the killing actually occurred.

This example of homicide is a criminological application of the "value-added" framework employed by Neil Smelser[63] and John Lofland and Rodney Stark[64] in the analysis of collective behavior and social movements. According to Smelser, the "value-added" process refers to a series of stages or events in which each must occur according to a particular pattern for a certain outcome to be produced. He notes: "Every stage in the value-added process, therefore, is a necessary condition for the appropriate and effective addition of value in the next stage. The sufficient condition for the final production, moreover, is the combination of *every* necessary condition, according to a definite pattern" (emphasis in the original).[65]

[59]Mary Owen Cameron, *The Booster and the Snitch* (New York: The Free Press, 1964).

[60]Lemert, *Human Deviance, Social Problems, and Social Control*, pp. 57–97.

[61]*Ibid.*, p. 11.

[62]Marvin E. Wolfgang, *Patterns of Criminal Homicide* (Philadelphia: University of Pennsylvania Press, 1958).

[63]Neil J. Smelser, *Theory of Collective Behavior* (New York: The Free Press, 1963).

[64]John Lofland and Rodney Stark, "Becoming a World-Saver: A Theory of Conversion to a Deviant Perspective," *American Sociological Review*, 30 (December 1965), 862–75.

[65]*Ibid.*, 13–14.

A value-added conception of homicide would assert that the experience of growing up in a subcultural setting where violence is a common theme is a precondition for violent acts but that specific instances of aggression and homicide do not occur until other events transpire, such as a marital dispute while drinking. Value-added ideas can also be applied to forcible rape. The available research evidence indicates that forcible rapists are usually working-class males who come from a social situation in which exploitative and aggressive themes regarding females are commonplace.[66] But only a small number of those males who regard sexual intercourse as something to be done *to* rather than *with* a female, or who express similar attitudes, become involved in forcible rape. An important factor in the value-added process, increasing the likelihood that forcible rape will occur, may be the situational one of sexually provocative interaction between a male and female during an evening of drinking.

A value-added analysis of criminality would produce a considerably different view of the relationship between genetic and situational factors than the one emphasized by Sutherland. As noted earlier, he argued that proximate situational influences were unimportant in criminality compared to conduct definitions acquired from genetic processes. We have suggested in the preceding commentary that situational influences may often be the crucial, final element in a value-added process that eventuates in lawbreaking. Without the presence of the situational correlates, the necessary and sufficient causes of at least some kinds of criminality fail to occur.

Much is to be said for the exploration of such familiar notions as "criminogenic culture" from a value-added position that looks for links between genetic and situational factors. For example, it may be the case that definitions favorable to law violation in the form of tolerant sentiments toward petty theft are widespread in American society and much less common in some other nation, so persons in this country commonly do learn these attitudes from some kind of genetic socialization experience. If so, these genetically acquired definitions would account partly for cross-cultural variations in crime rates. They would be etiologically significant, even though additional factors would have to be identified to uncover the complete causal pattern producing criminally deviant acts on the part of specific individuals.

We have argued that criminology has given inordinate attention to motivational formulations and genetic processes and insufficient weight to situational factors in criminality. In the future, more concern should be given to identification of those cases in which one or another or both of these sets of influences are operating, to explication of the relationships between these factors, and to determination of the relative weights assigned to these factors in particular cases of criminality.

Some sense of the directions to be explored is contained in the preceding

---

[66]See Chapter Sixteen. Also see Menachem Amir, "Forcible Rape," *Federal Probation*, 31 (March 1967), 51–58.

pages. Situational elements are probably involved in a good many nontrivial instances of criminality; not just the speeding motorist responds in a lawbreaking fashion to the inducements of the moment. Thus, the prisons may be filled with many persons who became enmeshed in criminality more out of adverse situations than out of differential learning. Along this line is Bruce Jackson's recent account of the life style of a contemporary Texas "character" (criminal argot for a police character, that is, an offender well-known to law enforcement agencies).[67] This thief is a safe robber from an upper-middle-class background who drifted into deviance after becoming detached from familial ties rather than being inducted into it through some kind of associational learning. Once involved in the thief life, he discovered that he enjoyed stealing and the "wine, women, and song" life style that accompanies it.[68] Another instructive case is Gilbert Geis' analysis of the occupational cross-pressures under which participants in the heavy electrical equipment antitrust cases of 1971 found themselves. Situational inducements to law violation appeared to have more to do with this behavior than did any kind of learning of antisocial sentiments through differential association.[69]

We could enumerate at length examples illustrating the need for attention to situational elements in lawbreaking. However, systematic attention to etiological theory rather than the multiplication of illustrations is required. We shall return to this matter at a number of points in Chapters Twelve through Seventeen, where we examine the causal processes operating in various forms of criminality.

FAMILY FACTORS AND CRIMINALITY

The opening remarks in this chapter indicated that certain formulations about the influence of single factors or causal patterns in criminality have enjoyed a good measure of popularity. Most have been points of view or lines of emphasis rather than rigorous instances of theorizing. Doubtless the most important of these orientations assigns a crucial etiological role to intrafamily experiences. A great many psychiatrists, psychologists, and sociologists generally agree that the family dimension is critical in the genesis of patterns of lawbreaking. Beyond this consensus, however, a variety of interpretations of the precise significance attached to home factors exist. Some people claim that the family variable is *the* crucial one; others take a much more cautious position, arguing that it is only one of a number of important considerations and not always the most critical.

[67]Bruce Jackson, *A Thief's Primer* (New York: The Macmillan Co., 1969).

[68]I have discussed Jackson's book with a criminologist and friend of mine who has served a lengthy sentence in a California prison. He avers that a number of thieves with whom he is acquainted express positive enjoyment of stealing and the thrills accompanying it once they become enmeshed in that activity.

[69]Gilbert Geis, *White Collar Criminal* (New York: Atherton Press, 1968), pp. 103-18.

The rationale behind heavy emphasis on home factors in criminality is easily stated. Take first the matter of delinquency and the role of parental family processes in it. In almost every society, the family has the most intense and consistent contact with children from infantile dependence through at least the preadolescent stage of life. Even in American society, where other social structures invade childrearing, no other social institution has the same degree of control over the socialization process as does the family. Thus, primary group interaction within family settings probably greatly influences the behavior of all youngsters, delinquent or nondelinquent. As a consequence, much interest has centered on relationships among home conditions, childrearing practices, and delinquent conduct.

The family is an important force in adult criminality, but for somewhat different reasons. Some forms of adult lawbreaking may result from distortions and pathologies in the offender's childhood experiences in his family. But nearly all adult persons eventually leave the family of orientation or parental family situation and move into a marriage, where they become engaged in the creation and maintenance of a new family system. At any point in time, most adult Americans are either married or in transition between marriages. A wealth of evidence indicates that the family is the major anchorage point for most adults; given that an individual is in a stable family unit, his behavior is likely to be conventional. On the other hand, since disruptions of marital relationships often seem implicated in a host of forms of aberrant, deviant, or otherwise unusual behavior, some kinds of criminality may represent responses to distorted family relationships. Examples of father–daughter incest, acts of victim-precipitated homicide carried out on marital partners, and exhibitionism are instances wherein family variables may be importantly involved.

As far as investigations of the role of family dynamics in criminality are concerned, the bulk of research has concentrated on juvenile delinquents. Regarding such studies, Sutherland and Cressey have summarized the generalizations involving home conditions and delinquency. They indicate that delinquents tend to come from homes characterized by one or more of the following conditions: other members of the family are criminal, delinquent, or alcoholic; one or both parents are absent from the home through divorce, desertion, or death; the home is marked by a lack of parental control; home uncongeniality is evidenced by such things as domination by one member, favoritism, oversolicitude, overseverity, neglect, or jealousy; racial or religious differences in conventions and standards, foster home or institutional home situations; and economic pressures stemming from unemployment or insufficient income.[70]

The Gluecks' study of 500 delinquents and 500 nonoffenders represents a major source of data regarding home factors.[71] From this research, they re-

---

[70]Sutherland and Cressey, *Principles of Criminology*, p. 204. See their chapter on family patterns, pp. 203–218, for a discussion of the supportive data behind these contentions.

[71]Sheldon Glueck and Eleanor Glueck, *Unraveling Juvenile Delinquency* (Cambridge, Mass.: Harvard University Press, 1951).

ported that 49.8 percent of the delinquents but only 28.8 percent of the nonoffenders were from broken homes.[72] Moreover, 60.4 percent of the delinquents and 34.2 percent of the nondelinquents had at some time prior to the study lived in a home broken by separation, divorce, death, or prolonged absence of one parent.[73] The offenders were more commonly from homes in which the parents had a history of serious physical ailments, mental retardation, emotional disturbance, drunkenness, or criminality.

The social climate of the delinquents' homes was wretched in other ways, too. According to the Gluecks, the parents of the delinquents were not good managers of income, were relatively poor planners of home routine, and exhibited less self-respect than parents of the nonoffenders. The same parents were less ambitious, had poorer conduct standards, and poorer conjugal relations. The mothers of the delinquents gave poor supervision to their children, and the parents showed less cohesiveness than did those of nondelinquents.[74] Marked differences were seen between parental affection exhibited toward delinquent children as compared to nondelinquents.[75] The parents of the offenders were also more frequently lax, overstrict, or erratic in disciplining their children than were the parents of the nondelinquents.[76]

From this amalgam of factors, the Gluecks concluded that defective family patterns represent the major causal dimension in delinquency. It would be hard to ignore this generalization, given these supportive findings. However, two points come to mind regarding this conclusion. First, other variables, such as peer group relationships, could loom equally large in the etiology of delinquency, as other findings of the Gluecks tend to indicate. Second, different family relationships among delinquents might be observed if the focus of attention were to shift away from working-class, gang delinquents to other types of juvenile offenders. The evidence from studies of middle-class offenders and certain other kinds of adolescent lawbreakers points to a different constellation of parent–child relationships.

Broken homes have received a great deal of emphasis as an important variable in delinquency, with much research directed toward discovering the relationship between this factor and juvenile misconduct. Estimates of the proportion of broken homes among delinquents vary from one study to another, but in general they range from 30 to 60 percent of the offenders, with lesser numbers of broken homes for nondelinquents.[77]

One contrary piece of evidence on broken homes comes from the work of Clifford Shaw and Henry McKay, who compared the incidence of broken

[72]*Ibid.*, p. 88.
[73]*Ibid.*, p. 122.
[74]*Ibid.*, pp. 108–16.
[75]*Ibid.*, pp. 125–26.
[76]*Ibid.*, p. 131.
[77]For a discussion of these estimates, see Harry M. Shulman, "The Family and Juvenile Delinquency," *The Annals of the American Academy of Political and Social Science*, no. 261 (January 1949), pp. 21–31; P. M. Smith, "Broken Homes and Juvenile Delinquency," *Sociology and Social Research*, 39 (May–June 1955), 307–11.

homes among Chicago schoolboys and male juvenile delinquents.[78] They found that the broken-home rate of offenders was 42.5 percent as compared to 36.1 percent for the nondelinquents, an insignificant difference. However, Jackson Toby has shown that evaluation of broken homes as inconsequential in delinquency is valid for older male delinquents but not for male preadolescents or female offenders.[79] He indicates that the Shaw and McKay study did not include girls, and other research shows that female delinquents do come from broken homes in considerable numbers.[80] Furthermore, he shows that in terms of broken homes the difference between preadolescent delinquents and nondelinquents is rather marked; the broken home does have some causal impact on both girls and preadolescent boys.

The most common research design regarding family variation and delinquent conduct has compared a group of offenders against a sample of nondelinquents. The Glueck study is one example of this kind. In most cases, the results have been somewhat ambiguous, leading to a confused picture of family relationships for both lawbreakers and nondelinquents. Perhaps another kind of procedure is in order. If a variety of offender behavior patterns exist in the total population of delinquents (or criminals), then assorted constellations of family factors are probably related to them. Several instances of research have generally confirmed this contention. Richard Jenkins and Lester Hewitt studied a group of guidance clinic cases in which three patterns of maladjustment were identified: unsocialized aggressive children, pseudosocial or gang offenders, and overinhibited youngsters. The investigators found that the aggressive youths were from backgrounds of parental rejection, whereas pseudosocial offenders were from situations of parental neglect and exposure to delinquency patterns. The pattern of overinhibited, shy, withdrawn youngsters appeared to be the result of situations of parental repression and overcontrol.[81]

Another investigation by Albert Reiss produced similar results. Reiss examined the social backgrounds of 1,110 juvenile court probationers in Cook County, Illinois, who court workers classified as relatively integrated delinquents, offenders with defective superego controls, or delinquents with weak ego controls. The study of social correlates of these types indicated a number of differences among them, some of the major ones having to do with family variations.[82]

[78]Clifford Shaw and Henry D. McKay, "Social Factors in Juvenile Delinquency," *Report on the Causes of Crime*, National Commission on Law Observance and Enforcement, vol. 2 (Washington, D.C.: U.S. Government Printing Office, 1937), pp. 261–84.

[79]Jackson Toby, "The Differential Impact of Family Disorganization," *American Sociological Review*, 22 (October 1957), 505–12.

[80]See, for example, Don C. Gibbons and Manzer J. Griswold, "Sex Differences Among Juvenile Court Referrals," *Sociology and Social Research*, 42 (November–December 1957), 106–10; William Wattenberg and Frank Saunders, "Sex Differences Among Juvenile Offenders," *Sociology and Social Research*, 39 (September–October 1954), 24–31.

[81]Richard L. Jenkins and Lester E. Hewitt, "Types of Personality Structure Encountered in Child Guidance Clinics," *American Journal of Orthopsychiatry*, 14 (January 1944), 84–94.

[82]Albert J. Reiss, Jr., "Social Correlates of Psychological Types of Delinquency," *American Sociological Review*, 17 (December 1952), 710–18.

Our concluding comment on home factors and delinquency is much the same as our summary assessment of a number of other arguments, such as those involving emotional disturbance or deteriorated neighborhoods. The influence of family patterns on delinquent conduct cannot be gainsaid. However, to argue that family variables always have primacy over all other factors would be to draw a caricature of real life. Claims that some particular family pattern is found in all forms of criminality are equally erroneous. Parental influences may well vary in significance in different types of criminality, just as parental factors or marital relationships important in one type of deviance may not be significant in another. Consequently, such factors need to be examined within the context of specific offender role careers. In Chapters Twelve and Seventeen, we shall explore the place of family factors in the causation of various forms of criminal conduct.

OTHER PARTICULARISTIC HYPOTHESES

By now, we have covered most of the major general and specific theories on criminality. Some other particularistic, single-factor arguments have been made in addition to those previously enumerated. For example, some attention has been given to the role of mass media in criminality, parallel to the vulgarized form of this contention popular with the general public. However, the major share of these specific claims are concerned with delinquents rather than with adult criminals.

Evaluation of single-variable contentions should be fully apparent. Insofar as single variables have merit, it is only as components of more complex, multivariate formulations. Stated differently, any narrowly delimited causal variable operates in a complex interrelationship with many others, and the criminologist's theoretical task is to explain these etiological congeries.

Particularistic notions also need to be narrowed to types of deviant careers in which they are most influential. The general situation is parallel to that of family factors and criminality, family influences being of different kinds and entering in different ways into forms of criminality. Accordingly, the meaningful approach to particularistic factors is directed at specific role patterns, which is the procedure in the chapters to come on offender careers.

SUMMARY

This chapter has concluded the comprehensive probing into the body of existing theoretical formulations on criminality. The most fruitful attack on etiological questions in criminality pays close attention to the different forms of conduct that the population of lawbreakers practice. The time has now come for a close look at this orientation to criminology, the subject of Chapter Ten.

10

THE STUDY OF BEHAVIOR PATTERNS AND ROLE CAREERS

Chapters Seven, Eight, and Nine consistently stressed that progress in causal analysis in criminology depends on a shift in attention toward the study of specific forms of criminality and away from inquiries into "crime" or "delinquency." Chapter Seven contended that offenders are motivated, striving, feeling beings so that personality dynamics, including varieties of pathological personality structure, are implicated in crime causation. The major thrust of that discussion was that the interlocking patterns of social and personality variables that activate criminal or noncriminal forms of conduct can only be clarified through study of different offender role careers. Chapter Eight asserted that existing sociological formulations, which aim to account for *rates* of criminality, are overly broad. Another level of theorizing is required in which middle-range theories directed at particular orders of criminality would supplement generic formulations about crime. Chapter Nine concluded on the note that propositions regarding social-psychological processes in deviant and criminal careers are similarly in need of further exposition in which the permutations of these views would be developed for particular forms of criminal behavior.

Now we should take a detailed look at the perspective on criminality usually called the "typological" approach. This chapter outlines a typological framework.[1] Chapters Twelve through Seventeen apply these views to the study of particular forms of criminality.

Criminals or delinquents might be classified or "typed" in almost an infinite number of ways, but these taxonomies may not all be equally useful for explanatory purposes. For example, one simple scheme for sorting offenders into types would be on the basis of specific legal offenses with which they are charged. However, such a system has several problems. Processes of "plea copping," in which the person pleads guilty to a lesser charge than the original one, mean that legal categories do not accurately distinguish various offender

---

[1]For an earlier, detailed version of the viewpoint laid out in this chapter, see Don C. Gibbons, *Changing the Lawbreaker* (Englewood Cliffs, N.J.: Prentice-Hall, 1965).

patterns. Even more important, legal offense categories often fail to reflect significant dimensions or aspects of the social behavior that has been the subject of social control agency attention. The legal category of "rape" includes quite varied patterns of deviant activity; some rape involves force, violence, and unwilling participation by the victim, whereas these elements are missing in other cases.

Another problem with legal offense categories as the basis of classification is that in many cases offenders do not consistently commit only a single kind of deviant act; a person labeled a "burglar" today may become a "larcenist" tomorrow. A more serious difficulty is that legal classifications do not identify theoretically significant types. There is little reason to suppose that persons characterized as "burglars" or typed in terms of some other specific legal offense are the product of a uniform etiological process.

Violators can be classified in terms of a multitude of variables: offense, hair color, race, urban–rural residence, ad infinitum. The criminologist who hopes to settle on a causally significant classification of offenders must take a calculated risk. He must choose one system from the many available. Hopefully, his choice will be significant so that when offenders are sorted out in terms of the selected scheme, the result will be homogeneous types in which the etiological process is the same for all members of the category. But no obvious or right way to classify violators jumps out at the observer from the facts of criminality. The decision to sort out deviants by means of variable X rather than variable Y can be made only in terms of some logic or rationale, some argument in defense of a particular choice of variables. We cannot be certain, in advance of research test, that a particular classificatory scheme is causally significant. This part of taxonomic and other theoretical work warrants use of the term "calculated risk."

THE DEVELOPMENT OF TYPOLOGICAL VIEWS

Movement in the direction of study of variations among types of lawbreakers and away from analysis of "crime" and "delinquency" is a major trend in criminology. Recent textbooks by Bloch and Geis,[2] Sutherland and Cressey,[3] and Clinard[4] are structured around the viewpoint that "crime" and "delinquency" represent heterogeneous forms of behavior. No single theory of crime or delinquency is sufficient to account for the various forms these phenomena

[2]Herbert A. Bloch and Gilbert Geis, *Man, Crime, and Society*, 2nd ed. (New York: Random House, 1970), pp. 167–379.

[3]Edwin H. Sutherland and Donald R. Cressey, *Principles of Criminology*, 8th ed. (Philadelphia: J. B. Lippincott Co., 1970), pp. 278–92.

[4]Marshall B. Clinard, *Sociology of Deviant Behavior*, 3rd ed. (New York: Holt, Rinehart and Winston, 1968), pp. 245–301.

take, so it is generally argued that causal theories specific to particular forms of deviant conduct will have to be developed.[5]

A sizable body of theory and research has focused on patterns of behavior held to represent offender types. Theories have been stated regarding "embezzlers," "gang delinquents," "automobile thieves," "naïve check forgers," and a number of other types of criminals and delinquents. Research investigations have also been conducted on a number of kinds of juvenile or adult illegality. However, a broad, organizing theory has not guided most studies of narrowly defined types; most patterns that have been the subject of investigation have been defined ad hoc. There are nearly as many versions of specific types as there are persons who have conducted research studies. Although the empirical data accumulated from these researches are important, they do not have the same cumulative impact as would a collection of findings structured in terms of a single, overall theoretical view of the range of offender patterns.

Consider a series of studies by Julian Roebuck and his associates, based on a sample of 1,155 inmates in the District of Columbia reformatory.[6] Roebuck sorted these offenders into such categories as "Negro armed robbers," "Negro drug addicts," and "Negro 'short con' men." His typology was based on legal categories of offense behavior studied within the framework of *criminal careers*. He sorted prison inmates into classes on the basis of their overall crime record as revealed in official records. Roebuck identified thirteen patterns of criminal careers in all.

After he constructed this typology, Roebuck went on to compare single types with the balance of the offender group. For example, Negro armed robbers were compared with the rest of the inmates to uncover significant differences between the robbers and the other prisoners. In the main, the robbers were from more disorganized home backgrounds and more deterio-

---

[5]For another recent typological statement, see Albert Morris, "The Comprehensive Classification of Adult Offenders," *Journal of Criminal Law, Criminology and Police Science*, 56 (June 1965), 197–202; see also Edwin D. Driver, "A Critique of Typologies in Criminology," *Sociological Quarterly*, 9 (Summer 1968), 356–73. For a more adequate attempt to develop an offender typology, see Marshall B. Clinard and Richard Quinney, eds., *Criminal Behavior Systems* (New York: Holt, Rinehart and Winston, 1967), pp. 1–19. These authors advance a system made up of eight "types": violent personal crime, occasional property crime, organized crime, political crime, public order crime, conventional crime, organized crime, and professional crime. These investigators discuss a number of dimensions along which these patterns vary. However, a number of the specific forms of criminality included within each of the eight rubrics show a good deal of variation from one another so that the eight categories slur over some important differences among lawbreakers.

[6]Julian B. Roebuck and Mervyn L. Cadwallader, "The Negro Armed Robber as a Criminal Type: The Construction and Application of a Typology," *Pacific Sociological Review*, 4 (Spring 1961), 21–26; Roebuck, "The Negro Drug Addict as an Offender Type," *Journal of Criminal Law, Criminology and Police Science*, 53 (March 1962), 36–43; Roebuck and Ronald Johnson, "The Negro Drinker and Assaulter as a Criminal Type," *Crime and Delinquency*, 8 (January 1962), 21–33; Roebuck and Johnson, "The Jack-of-all Trades Offender," *Crime and Delinquency*, 8 (April 1962), 172–81; Roebuck, "The Negro Numbers Man as a Criminal Type: The Construction and Application of a Typology," *Journal of Criminal Law, Criminology and Police Science*, 54 (March 1963), 48–60; Roebuck and Johnson, "The 'Short Con' Man," *Crime and Delinquency*, 10 (July 1964), 235–48; Roebuck, *Criminal Typology* (Springfield, Ill.: Charles C Thomas, 1966).

rated and criminalistic areas of urban communities than were the other criminals. They were also characterized by a kind of short-run hedonism, having no long-term plans and relatively spontaneous and uncommitted attitudes.

These commendable reports comprise part of the intellectual capital out of which a theory of crime might be evolved. Nonetheless, this material has some problems, among which is the ethnic orientation of this typological system. Ethnic background is probably not an important variable for sorting out homogeneous types of offenders. There is little reason to suppose that *Negro* armed robbers or other kinds of criminals are much different from their *Caucasian* counterparts.

The major objection to Roebuck's and other investigators' methodology of specific types is that the inductive discovery of types could go on forever. Because persons can be classified in many different ways, such causal analysis would be forced to contend with hundreds of specific types of offenders. Perhaps a system of types can be stated a priori, involving a limited number of types that subsume most patterns arrived at inductively. Indeed, our major thesis is that formulation of a structure of offender types is possible and highly desirable.[7]

TOWARD A TYPOLOGICAL PERSPECTIVE

What are the prospects for making the typological orientation something more than a crude heuristic or organizing device? The major outlines of a coherent typological structure for causal analysis can be carved out. We shall present a set of basic assumptions behind a role-career view of offender types; then we shall discuss in some detail the ingredients of a role-career analysis. Finally, Chapters Twelve through Seventeen will collate a large body of theoretical contentions and empirical claims regarding offenders within a role-career conceptualization of criminal types. Taken as a whole, we might term this network of arguments and propositions a criminological theory, although we would do just as well to withhold that label from our following presentation. Criminology is already plagued with a number of incompletely formed views to

[7]This chapter has not considered a large number of efforts to develop typologies of juvenile delinquents. See Theodore N. Ferdinand, *Typologies of Delinquency* (New York: Random House, 1966); National Clearinghouse for Mental Health Information, *Typological Approaches and Delinquency Control: A Status Report* (Washington, D.C.: U.S. Department of Health, Education and Welfare, 1967); Don C. Gibbons, *Delinquent Behavior* (Englewood Cliffs, N.J.: Prentice-Hall, 1970); John W. Kinch, "Continuities in the Study of Delinquent Types," *Journal of Criminal Law, Criminology and Police Science*, 53 (September 1962), 323–28; Kinch, "Self-Conceptions of Types of Delinquents," *Sociological Inquiry*, 32 (Spring 1962), 228–34; Sethard Fisher, "Varieties of Juvenile Delinquency," *British Journal of Criminology*, 2 (January 1962), 251–61; Richard L. Jenkins and Sylvia Glickman, "Patterns of Personality Organization Among Delinquents," *Nervous Child*, 6 (July 1947), 329–39; Lester E. Hewitt and Jenkins, *Fundamental Patterns of Maladjustment, The Dynamics of Their Origin* (Springfield: Illinois State Printer, 1947); Jenkins and Hewitt, "Types of Personality Structure Encountered in Child Guidance Clinics," *American Journal of Orthopsychiatry*, 14 (January 1944), 84–94; Albert J. Reiss, "Social Correlates of Psychological Types of Delinquency," *American Sociological Review*, 17 (December 1952), 710–18.

which the term *theory* has been prematurely applied.[8] These presentations, like the one in this book, are "explanation sketches," which identify some critical variables implicated in criminality, along with some incompletely formed propositions representing a first stage of theorizing, and they lack the substantive detail and logical elegance of mature theories.[9]

SOME BASIC ASSUMPTIONS

The following seventeen claims represent a set of exceedingly broad assumptions that stand as a sample of one sociologist's notions about the causation of crime and delinquency. They constitute, as well, a set of contentions on which most criminologist–sociologists would agree. These statements are listed to identify in one place the major premises and hypotheses that form the bases for the more detailed remarks about particular forms of criminality in succeeding chapters. A number of these notions are derived from theories of deviant or criminalistic behavior examined in previous chapters. Some are also drawn out of existing data on criminality, so the specific discussions in later chapters should demonstrate the accuracy of some of these propositions.

Some of the first assumptions are typical of basic sociology textbook propositions and may appear pedestrian. Nonetheless, there are different perspectives from which deviant behavior could be examined, and one's presuppositions should be brought into the open for public scrutiny. Some of the seventeen claims are also extremely simple. Take assumption six, which argues that "badness" tends to be specific rather than general in form. In other words, there is no reason to suppose that individuals who are "bad guys" as far as criminality is concerned are also "bad guys" in all other ways. There are no grounds for supposing that offenders also beat their wives and abuse their children, belong to the Communist Party, or verbalize atheistic beliefs. However, the opposite assumption about generic "badness" is often involved in commonsense beliefs about deviants.

The seventeen assumptions are these:[10]

1. The members of a society are the carriers of an organization of social roles, that is, behavior patterns reflecting different social statuses or positions. (In other words, it is meaningful to approach the description of the behavior of individual persons by paying attention to the related

[8]One illustrative case is the "containment theory." See Walter C. Reckless, *The Crime Problem*, 4th ed. (New York: Appleton-Century-Crofts, 1967), pp. 469–83.

[9]William J. Wilson, Nicholas Sofias, and Richard Ogles, "Formalization and Stages of Theoretical Development," *Pacific Sociological Review*, 7 (Fall 1964), 74–80; Charles W. Lachenmeyer, *The Language of Sociology* (New York: Columbia University Press, 1971); Gibbons, *Delinquent Behavior*, pp. 60–68.

[10]Originally stated in Don C. Gibbons, *Changing the Lawbreaker*, The Treatment of Delinquents and Criminals, © 1965. Reprinted by permission of Prentice-Hall, Inc., Englewood Cliffs, New Jersey, pp. 44–47.

but independent component activities or roles making up their behavior.)

2. Social roles are the product of social organization and socialization, that is, of the ongoing structure of society and of learning processes in primary groups. (In other words, the developmental process in human behavior centers around the acquisition, by the person, of a collection of social roles made available to him by the society in which he is found.)

3. Various patterns of social organization and socialization exist in complex societies so that, in turn, a variety of statuses and roles exist in them. There is a variety of nondeviant roles as well as a great many deviant ones (radical, homosexual, criminal, and so forth).

4. All people play criminal or delinquent roles at one time or another, if only symbolically. (In other words, petty violations of law are engaged in by nearly every person in the course of his lifetime. Also, many individuals entertain deviant and criminalistic motives but do not act upon them; thus they play deviant roles symbolically.)

5. Sociologically, "criminals" or "delinquents" are persons who play criminalistic roles heavily and/or who are identified by "society" as criminals or delinquents. (Persons who come to be tagged as offenders by the legal processes are frequently ones who are involved in repetitive and serious acts of law violation; but individuals who engage in petty and isolated acts of illegality are also sometimes reacted to as violators. Both of these groups are "criminals" or "delinquents" because they have been so labeled by the official machinery of social control.)

6. Criminal or delinquent behavior is one social role, but not the only one, that persons play. Criminal or delinquent individuals also play roles as "citizen," "father," "employee," and so forth.

7. Among persons identified as criminals or delinquents, there are variations in the character and intensity of the deviant role. These include variations in both (a) actual deviant role behavior and (b) role-related social-psychological characteristics. The illegal acts carried on by offenders vary from one individual to another. Also, some persons have no self-image as a deviant, whereas others exhibit such self-definitions. In turn, among individuals with deviant or nondeviant self-conceptions, variations are exhibited in the particular kind of image held ("tough guy," "right guy," "smart hustler," and so on).

8. Stable patterns of criminal or delinquent roles, involving recurrent forms of deviant activity accompanied by uniform social-psychological role characteristics, can be observed in the population of offenders. In these terms, it can be said that types of criminalistic deviance exist.

9. Although behavioral and social-psychological changes occur in specific criminal or delinquent roles during the development of the role, these changes are limited, orderly, and identifiable. As a result, it is possible to define specific, stable criminal and delinquent role-careers. Offend-

ers do not engage in random and unpredictable patterns of role-behavior; they do not "play the field" of offenses.

10. The specific etiological process that leads to one particular kind of criminalistic role behavior involves a number of causal variables and differs from that which produces another criminal role. In this sense, criminal and delinquent behavior is the product of multiple-causation. At the same time, it is possible to identify the different etiological processes which are implicated in the various forms of criminalistic deviance.

11. The learning of criminal and/or delinquent roles is maximized in a criminalistic society, and the United States is such a society.

12. Much, but not all, criminal and delinquent behavior in the competitive, materialistic American society is societally generated and takes the form of assaults upon property. Property crime is not usually the expression of hidden motives but, rather, of surface ones. (Offenders steal to "make a living" rather than to commit symbolic incest and so on.)

13. Crime and delinquency in complex societies are encouraged in a variety of ways by that complexity. For example, police ineffectiveness is a correlate of a democratic, complex, urban social organization. In turn, ineffectual police work aids in the commission of crime and is an encouragement to criminality. (In a society which demands that law enforcement agents behave according to strict rules of arrest, search and seizure, interrogation, and the like, many offenders are inevitably going to avoid apprehension or conviction for crimes. Additionally, in a society in which relatively few policemen are employed to maintain surveillance over a large population living in metropolitan communities, the law enforcement persons are not going to be able to observe most illegal acts that occur. As a result, the risk of being apprehended for deviant acts will appear to be slight to many individuals.)

14. Some criminalistic roles are mainly the consequence of social-class variations in socialization and life experiences, along with other social-structural variables. In particular, situations in which legitimate avenues to the attainment of common American goals or values are blocked are importantly involved in certain forms of crime and delinquency.

15. Some criminalistic roles are produced by family and other socialization experiences which are not class-linked or class-specific. Among these are "parental rejection," "deviant sexual socialization," and others. These kinds of experiences occur at all social class levels.

16. The "defining agencies" (police, probation services, courts, and so forth) play a part both in the definition of deviants and in the continuation of deviant roles. The result of apprehension and "treatment" may be quite contrary to the expected result. In other words, although one official function of correctional agencies and processes is the reformation of the offender, the actual outcome is often the isolation of the person, reinforcement of the deviant role, and rejection of society by the offender, the final result being nonreformation.

17. Variations can be seen in societal reactions to criminality of different kinds. Personal offenses and crude, visible attacks upon property are likely to be severely dealt with and punitively handled. Accordingly, embezzlers and similar persons are reacted to differently than gas station stick-up artists or strong-arm robbers. In addition, societal reactions to criminal deviants are based upon other characteristics of the individual than criminal role behavior. Middle-class delinquents, for example, are accorded a societal reaction different from that directed toward working-class individuals involved in similar delinquent behavior. In turn, these reactions have implications for involvement in, and continuation in, criminality.

The user of such contentions is committed to a certain view of crime and delinquency causation. The first six claims enunciate some major ingredients of social role analysis. Propositions seven through nine suggest the major dimensions for studying law violators as incumbents of criminal roles. Finally, statements ten through seventeen point to some major causal factors in criminality. The causal framework in the set of assumptions emphasizes multiple causation at the same time it implies that scientific explanations of criminality are attainable. In other words, the argument is that the etiological factors in criminality are numerous and operate in different patterns of conduct in different ways and with varying degrees of influence. At the same time, these variables are also finite or limited so that ultimately propositions such as "If A, B, C, D, and E occur, criminality of type X will result" can be stated.

These terse propositions represent a skeleton version of a causal presentation. Because the perspective contained in them requires elaboration, let us first take up the role-career portion.

DEVIANT STATUSES AND ROLES[11]

The assumption that the total behavior of individuals can be meaningfully examined as a *pattern* of *social roles* lies at the heart of the sociological analysis of many kinds of behavior. Social roles represent how persons interact with others in terms of various statuses or positions within social systems. Statuses are "jobs" in a social division of labor (social system) involving a pattern of normative expectations or rules that the status incumbent is expected to follow in pursuit of some interactional end or objective. The task of professor in an academic institution is an example of a status, for it involves a set of expectations that any particular teacher will behave in specified ways toward students, colleagues, and the general public. The actual performance activity of a specific professor represents role behavior within this particular status. The core of this point is that the sociological perspective on behavior is not a

[11]For a general treatment of deviant statuses and roles, see Clinard, *Sociology of Deviant Behavior*, pp. 65–79.

disguised version of the study of personality systems. Statuses are not labels for characteristics internal to the actor but are identified in terms of the expectations of persons in the external situation in which the status incumbent is placed. A status and related role activities of any individual are not descriptive of that actor as a totality but of only a part of the total behavior of the person.

Status and role concepts are easily seen as useful in analysis of social behavior when applied to such activities as school superintendent, physician, and a variety of other occupational or social positions. However, status and role analysis may not be so quickly perceived as relevant to the study of such deviant patterns as homosexuality, narcotics addiction, political radicalism, or criminality. Even though criminal and delinquent statuses often involve expectations that persons in these positions will behave in ways some social groups evaluate negatively, criminalistic behavior can, nonetheless, be tackled within a status-role perspective. As a matter of fact, many statuses and roles in addition to the criminalistic are negatively defined by some group or groups.[12] Moreover, invidious evaluation of criminal or delinquent statuses is relative to particular group standards. Within associations of offenders, deviant statuses are frequently evaluated positively; the "old-time box man" (skilled safecracker) is deemed an exemplary person by his criminal peers. Illustrations of this kind could be multiplied indefinitely, for many "tough" prisoners in institutions are highly esteemed by other inmates, narcotic users are fondly regarded by other drug users, and so forth.

Criminal statuses and roles constitute only one of many statuses and roles in which persons find themselves. However, in many cases criminality may well become what Becker has termed a *master status*, the separate social niches occupied by the offender becoming heavily colored by his involvement in criminalistic role behavior.[13] As one example, the occupational activities of the ex-convict are often so greatly influenced by the "parolee" identity he has acquired that he finds the task of obtaining a job exceedingly difficult.[14] Employment instability as a social consequence of being identified as "bad" and "criminal" may create further distortions in the actor's marital role and other facets of his life as well so that to be a criminal is to be the occupant of a highly significant status.

Even though deviant statuses may color or affect other statuses, we can hardly infer that delinquent or criminal individuals differ in all important ways

[12]Two studies of deviant roles other than criminal ones are Thomas J. Scheff, *Being Mentally Ill* (Chicago: Aldine Publishing Co., 1966); Robert B. Edgerton, *The Cloak of Competence* (Berkeley: University of California Press, 1967).

[13]Howard S. Becker, *Outsiders* (New York: The Free Press, 1963), pp. 31–34.

[14]For a revealing investigation of this matter, see Richard D. Schwartz and Jerome H. Skolnick, "Two Studies of Legal Stigma," in *The Other Side*, ed. Howard S. Becker (New York: The Free Press, 1964), pp. 103–17. Another incisive analysis of the role problems of parolees is John Irwin, *The Felon* (Englewood Cliffs, N.J.: Prentice-Hall, 1970). His discussion centers about the desires of the parolee to find a postprison noncriminal role that involves a measure of dignity to him.

from nonoffenders. There is little reason to assume that offenders are less patriotic or less committed to family values than nonoffenders or that criminals differ in total personality structure from nondeviants. Although this point may seem obvious, much research has proceeded on an implicit assumption that the deviant is a generally different person from the nondeviant. Failure of investigators to discover traits that distinguish criminals from noncriminals is probably attributable principally to the invalidity of this built-in assumption about deviants and nondeviants. Investigations that have attempted to sweep up evidence of pervasive differences between the two groups have failed because they were unguided by explicit theory spelling out the salient factors in which the two groups might differ.

Description of offender roles must include the social context within which behavior occurs. Indeed, the concept of role is relatively meaningless when divorced from the network of role expectations of others. Thus, in addition to indicating that an offender engages in role activity taking the form of burglary, we also need to ask about the social circumstances of that behavior. Were the criminal acts carried on in isolation? Or did that behavior take place within the structure of a group of participating role players (other burglars)? Or, finally, is the activity of the person part of a pattern of responses within a deviant subculture in which other individuals encourage deviant acts? Although behavioral acts that identify a person as a law violator are necessary components of any description of offender types, we should also consider the components of role behavior as well as the particular form of illegal activity. Some deviant roles, such as embezzlement, are enacted surreptitiously, because nonembezzlement is defined as the appropriate behavior within the system of action in which defalcations occur. Other kinds of criminality represent role activities that associates of the offender evaluate positively, even though the larger social organization may define the acts negatively. Along a somewhat related line, some kinds of criminality grow out of situations in which the victim was initially an interactional partner of the offender—for example, murder of one's spouse, or rape. In other instances, the victim has had no prior contact with the lawbreaker; and in still other situations no specific victim can be identified—for example, forms of white-collar crime, shoplifting, and kindred other offenses. All of these matters need to be attended to in a sociological description and analysis of criminality.

CRIMINAL ROLE BEHAVIOR AND ROLE CAREERS

In an examination of role incumbents, we can identify two basic components of social roles: *behavioral acts* (role behavior) and *role conceptions* (self-image patterns and role-related attitudes). This distinction is illustrated in everyday life when predictions are made about the future conduct of an individual.

For example, knowledge that an actor has committed an assault is not sufficient evidence on which to predict that additional episodes of violence will occur in the future. Confidence in such a prediction is enhanced with the observation that the assaultive individual defines himself as a "tough guy" and regards other persons as "mean" and not to be trusted. Quite a different estimate would be in order with observations that the assaulter acted under conditions of severe personal stress and is now contrite and repentant in posture.

We can find many other illustrative cases wherein ostensibly similar behavior by separate persons has quite different meanings for the individuals. We should not assume that in every case of criminal role behavior of a common kind, similar role conceptions exist for all the actors. This distinction between role behavior and role conceptions is closely parallel to Lemert's notions of *primary* and *secondary* deviation discussed in Chapter Nine.[15] Lemert notes that deviant behavior is often primary in character, for the person views the behavior as atypical on his part, and he lacks a self-image as a deviant. Some deviant roles become secondary in form because the actor ultimately integrates his aberrant activity into his total personality organization. In this process, he eventually undergoes a measure of personality reorganization in which deviant behavior becomes a role verbalized by such self-reference statements as: "I am a 'hype' " or "I am a thief" or "I am a 'lush.' "[16] Although primary deviation precedes development of secondary deviation, the latter does not always follow from involvement in primary deviance. One obvious illustration of this point, at least in degree, is the "Square John" inmate in prison who persistently alleges that he is not a "real criminal."[17]

[15]Edwin M. Lemert, *Social Pathology* (New York: McGraw-Hill Book Co., 1951), pp. 73–98; see also Becker's discussion of the concept of "commitment" in Howard S. Becker, *Sociological Work* (Chicago: Aldine Publishing Co., 1970), pp. 261–87; Albert K. Cohen, *Deviance and Control* (Englewood Cliffs, N.J.: Prentice-Hall, 1966), pp. 97–101.

[16]For an excellent illustrative case of secondary deviation, centered about a criminal identity, see Bruce Jackson, *A Thief's Primer* (New York: The Macmillan Co., 1969); see also Henry Williamson, *Hustler!* (New York: Doubleday and Co., 1965).

[17]Relatively little systematic attention has been given to role behavior and role conceptions on the part of offenders because little is known regarding the question: "What do offenders *do*?" Much evidence on the criminal behavior of lawbreakers comes from individual accounts of specific offenders, such as those in footnote 16. Similarly, the matter of self-concept variations among offenders has not received the search attention it deserves. The most systematic body of data on this topic is found in the work of Reckless and associates, dealing with favorable self-concept as an "insulator" against delinquency. See Walter C. Reckless, Simon Dinitz, and Ellen Murray, "Self-Concept as an Insulator Against Delinquency," *American Sociological Review*, 21 (December 1956), 744–56; Reckless, Dinitz, and Barbara Kay, "The Self-Component in Potential Delinquency and Potential Non-delinquency," *American Sociological Review*, 22 (October 1957), 566–70; Reckless, Dinitz, and Murray, "The 'Good Boy' in a High Delinquency Area," *Journal of Criminal Law, Criminology and Police Science*, 48 (May–June 1957), 18–25; Dinitz, Kay, and Reckless, "Group Gradients in Delinquency Potential and Achievement Scores of 6th Graders," *American Journal of Orthopsychiatry*, 28 (July 1958), 598–605; Jon Simpson, Dinitz, Kay, and Reckless, "Delinquency Potential of Pre-Adolescents in High Delinquency Areas," *British Journal of Delinquency*, 10 (January 1960), 211–15; Frank R. Scarpitti, Murray, Dinitz, and Reckless, "The 'Good Boy' in a High Delinquency Area: Four Years later," *American Sociological Review*, 25 (August 1960), 555–58; Dinitz, Scarpitti, and Reckless, "Delinquency Vulnerability: A Cross Group and Longitudinal Analysis," *American Sociological Review*, 27 (August 1962), 515–17. For criticisms of this work, see Michael Schwartz and Sandra S. Tangri, "A Note on Self-Concept

Offender roles can also be analyzed profitably in longitudinal terms as *role-careers*. Many nondeviant roles, such as occupational ones, continue over extremely long periods and involve a series of behavioral changes as particular social situations alter. A medical career illustrates this point nicely, for this career originates when a person makes an initial decision to become a doctor and undertakes activity to implement his choice. Medical school is a further episode in the medical career, and professional employment as a physician a still further involvement. Medical role incumbents exhibit behavior patterns that are somewhat different at each stage. They also exhibit role conceptions that are not identical in each of these periods.[18] Nonetheless, these varied behavior patterns and role conceptions are parts of a long-term career, for they "hang together" in obvious ways. In these cumulative events, advanced stages of occupational involvement are built on experiences occurring in earlier parts of the occupational history.

Although the notion of careers is most familiar in occupational analysis, we can also analyze other roles, including deviant ones, in this manner. The alcoholism career, extending over several decades during which the drinker becomes progressively more involved in deviant drinking as well as in other altered social relationships flowing out of his alcoholism, comes to mind as one illustration of a complex deviant career pattern. In the area of criminality, the collection of life experiences beginning with petty delinquent episodes of gang members in slum areas stands as an example of an offender career. With advancing age, this career line leads into more systematic involvement in utilitarian thefts, and still later it culminates in a sustained pattern of adult episodes of property crimes interrupted by periodic prison terms. The career finally terminates when the offender withdraws (or "retires") from active participation in criminality in middle age, as he comes to evaluate continued lawbreaking as too fraught with such hardships as long penal commitments.[19]

We can make some further observations about deviant role careers, including the variation of role careers over time. In some criminal roles, an isolated illegal act intruding into an otherwise exemplary life history represents role performance, whereas in other criminal roles, involvement in sustained deviance continues over several decades, as in the instance of professional criminals. Although in some ways persons who commit one fugitive act of lawbreaking hardly qualify as criminals, many do acquire a public identity as violators. Some end up in penal institutions and other correctional settings, or they encounter other societal reactions directed at them as "bad persons"

---

as an Insulator Against Delinquency," *American Sociological Review*, 30 (December 1965), 922–26; James D. Orcutt, "Self-Concept and Insulation Against Delinquency: Some Critical Notes," *Sociological Quarterly*, 11 (Summer 1970), 381–90.

[18]Howard S. Becker, Blanche Geer, Everett C. Hughes, and Anselm L. Strauss, *Boys in White* (Chicago: University of Chicago Press, 1961).

[19]For one of the best discussions, see Irwin, *The Felon*.

so that their idiosyncratic acts of deviance do make a difference. Also, in Chapter Five, we saw that many persons found in arrest tabulations have been involved in relatively petty acts of lawbreaking. Quite probably, many of these individuals have been involved in transitory careers in criminality. Thus, short-lived careers in criminal misbehavior are commonplace.[20]

Another point regarding offender roles is that some delinquent patterns lead to adult criminal careers, whereas other patterns are terminal and do not culminate in adult criminality. In turn, some criminal careers begin with juvenile delinquent behavior, whereas other forms of adult lawbreaking develop in adulthood and do not result from prior delinquent conduct. On this matter, one major argument is that a role-career perspective promises to untangle the web of relationships between juvenile and adult criminality. The durable shibboleth that "the delinquent of today is the criminal of tomorrow" is frequently false, for although some delinquents become adult offenders, others do not.

Some role careers involve more changes in component episodes of the pattern than do others. For example, the career of a semiprofessional property offender begins with minor peccadilloes in early adolescence. These frequently lead to more serious forms of delinquency with advancing age, which in turn result in repeated police contacts, commitment to juvenile institutions, "graduation" into adult forms of crime, and more contacts with law enforcement agencies and correctional institutions. Over this lengthy developmental sequence, the social-psychological characteristics of offenders also change. The degree of hostility toward policemen and correctional agents the adult semiprofessional criminal exhibits is likely to be considerably greater than the enmity he demonstrates at an earlier age. The same point holds for other changes in self-image, attitudes, and kindred other characteristics.

To summarize, we contend that criminal or delinquent roles usually involve more than a specific kind of illegal act but that criminal behavior is *patterned* rather than comprised of random behavioral activities. Some evidence supports the notion of stability among deviants, at least regarding illegal activities. The findings of Roebuck[21] are cases in point, as is a report by Harold Frum.[22]

This point of view regarding role careers and its significant behavioral dimensions provides the foundation for a typological analysis of criminality. The descriptions of criminal role careers in Chapters Twelve through Seventeen categorize offenders according to the patterns of illegal role behavior they exhibit and also in terms of the social context of their deviant acts. Offenders are also classified along two other dimensions: self-image patterns

[20]For further, detailed evidence on this point, see Don C. Gibbons, "Crime in the Hinterland," *Criminology*, forthcoming.

[21]Roebuck, *Criminal Typology*.

[22]Harold S. Frum, "Adult Criminal Offense Trends Following Juvenile Delinquency," *Journal of Criminal Law, Criminology and Police Science*, 49 (May-June 1958), 29-49.

and role-related attitudes. Finally, observations about temporal changes in deviant roles are provided in a summary of the characteristics of the role career.

The result of the assumptions and role-career arguments is a typology of criminals, which contends that lawbreakers can be sorted so that some are "semiprofessional property offenders," "embezzlers," or "naïve check forgers," whereas others are "nonviolent sex offenders," "professional thieves," or members of some other category. An individual is labeled a "naïve check forger" or some other role-career incumbent if he shows the pattern of deviant behavior and the social-psychological characteristics specified in the typology.

TYPOLOGIES AND THE REAL WORLD

The categories of an adequate typology, whether of criminality or some other kind of behavior, should provide *accurate* descriptions of actual persons or events. Secondly, the typology should be relatively *comprehensive* so that most of the actual cases of behavior the typology is supposed to describe fall within the scheme.

In the early stages of development of a criminal typology, descriptions of offender types stand as contentious hypotheses about the real world. The typology claims that real people exist who resemble those persons described in the typology. The typology of offenders used in this book is one of those initial ventures into criminal taxonomy, so its empirical status is to some degree indeterminate. A body of research evidence provides direct or tangential support for some of the descriptive claims about offenders, and Chapters Twelve through Seventeen are concerned with the study of that material. But at the same time, some patterns of criminality, such as deviant sexual activities, have been little studied. Accordingly, remarks about these types are more speculative than some of the other characterizations of offenders. In short, the typology here qualifies both as a collation of existing knowledge *and* as a programmatic essay that suggests a number of lines of further research evidence.

As a word of caution, this approach may be pushed beyond heuristic usefulness, so that these classification schemes might lead to an oversimplified and distorted picture of criminal behavior, perceiving types as more crystallized and distinct than they are in fact. This state of affairs might come if criminologists choose behavioral observations to fit a typological perspective and ignore discordant data.

A recent study by Clayton Hartjen and the author is germane to this point.[23] The investigators subjected a modified version of the typology in this book to empirical examination in a probation setting. Only about half the proba-

---

[23]Clayton A. Hartjen and Don C. Gibbons, "An Empirical Investigation of a Criminal Typology," *Sociology and Social Research*, 54 (October 1969), 56–62.

tioners fell within one or another typology category. The other half of the probation sample was sorted into some crude types, such as nonsupport cases, petty property offenders, and so on. However, these types were not entirely clear cut; the offenders did not appear to differ much from one another in terms of social backgrounds or to be different from the run-of-the-mill citizen. Much of this lawbreaking appeared to be of the "folk crime" variety, in which the offenders were not involved in a long-term criminal career.[24] For example, one quarter of these persons were nonsupport cases who had failed to comply with a civil court order to provide child support. These kinds of offenders do not get much attention in contemporary versions of typologies, and they are not the subject of most causal arguments currently fashionable in criminology. But if they exist in the real world, their existence will ultimately have to be reflected in criminological thinking.[25]

The thrust of this commentary is that we should acknowledge the existence of a broad class of offenders who might be labeled "situational–causal" criminals. These persons are involved in various forms of short-run criminality such that they do not fall into any clear-cut role career. In short, the typological characterizations in this book have counterparts in the real world of criminality, but not all real-life offenders fall within these categories.

TYPOLOGIES AND CAUSATION

A criminal typology is a collection of statements asserting that "this is the way offenders are—these are the ways they behave." As such, it says nothing about causation, or "how they got that way." Contentions about the etiology of different criminal role careers constitute a separate body of hypotheses. All the claims about patterns of criminality and causal factors would make up a complex theory of criminal behavior. The structure of a typological theory is shown in Figure 6.

In the typological sketches of offender careers in the next few chapters, we shall comment about causal factors as well as factors that enumerate the behavioral aspects of deviant roles. These remarks will indicate some major background characteristics of offender types, organized within four relatively large categories or dimensions: social-class variations, family background pat-

---

[24]H. Laurence Ross, "Traffic Law Violation: A Folk Crime," *Social Problems*, 9 (Winter 1961), 231–41.

[25]Similar findings to those of Hartjen and Gibbons showed up in a study of federal probationers by Moore and Gibbons. Several hundred probationers were sorted into such types as mixed property offenders, selective service violators, income-tax offenders, and car thieves. But these types seemed not much different from one another or different from law-abiding citizens. Most of them had been involved in transitory criminal episodes, and most of them became reestablished in law-abiding citizen roles while on probation. See Robin Moore and Don C. Gibbons, "Offender Patterns in a Federal Probation Caseload," Center for Sociological Research, Portland State University, mimeographed. Also see Gibbons, "Crime in the Hinterland."

Offender Typology

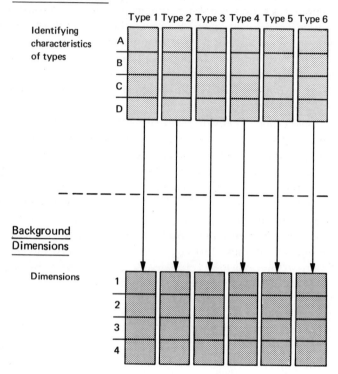

FIGURE 6 The Structure of Typological Arguments

terns, peer group associations, and contacts with defining agencies. These categories arise from the same rationale that underlies the focus on role careers.

Social Class, Family, and Peers

One obvious fact of life which is frequently ignored in discussions of etiological elements in criminality is that the immediate social circumstances in which persons are enmeshed are part of larger patterns of social organization. Individuals are not only members of families and peer associations, they are also situated in distinctive neighborhood and social-class locations. These structures impinge on their conduct, and as a consequence we find offender types distributed in varied ways within social-class levels. For example, gang offenders are nearly all working-class boys, whereas joyriders are often from comfortable economic areas, as are naïve check forgers and certain other kinds of lawbreakers. Other juvenile and adult types are distributed in still other ways within the class structure of American society. The suspicion arises that these are not chance variations, that something about the social life of different social class groups may bring forth particular kinds of misbehavior. In succeeding chapters, we shall return to the question of what aspect of social stratification contributes to forms of criminality.

Another elementary fact is that development of a specific person's role behavior is a direct function of the processes of socialization. Socialization refers to the complex processes of social interaction through which an individual learns habits, skills, beliefs, and standards of conduct. Not all interaction is equally important to the individual, so his self-conception, his attitudes, and his behavioral motives are most likely to be the product of primary group interaction. Family and peer group associations are two kinds of primary groups, and the great attention social psychologists give to interactional processes within these groups is not accidental.

Whatever else it might be, criminality is learned behavior, so we shall look closely at family and peer groups as sources of causally significant experiences in the development of criminal role careers. We could identify a plethora of specific family-oriented relationships that enter into different forms of criminality. For one, the family is a vehicle through which social-class phenomena are expressed, that is, social-class values are imparted to persons through family interaction experiences, at least in part. On this point, Walter Miller argues that the "focal concerns" of lower-class society are such as to encourage illegal behavior. He claims that lower-class value emphases on "toughness," "having a good time," and related interests cause many working-class males in particular to engage in deviant activities.[26] If this argument is correct, "focal concerns" exert an influence over specific persons only to the extent that they have been communicated through social interaction. The family is a major setting for such learning, and communication takes place.

Although "class-linked" behavior patterns do exist, the behavior of individual members of particular social classes varies quite markedly because of differences in the interactional processes in particular family groups. The values or focal concerns of a social class may be given different emphases in particular families, so the family situation works to condition the impact of class phenomena on individuals.

Families who share a relatively uniform life style of a particular social class vary in other important ways. Within working-class families, some parents reject their children, others neglect their offspring, spouses interact in varied ways with each other, and other families carry on still other idiosyncratic forms of existence. A number of patterns of criminality are closely related to interac-

[26]Walter B. Miller, "Lower Class Culture as a Generating Milieu of Gang Delinquency," *Journal of Social Issues*, 14, no. 3 (1958), 5–19; Miller, "Implications of Urban Lower Class Culture for Social Work," *Social Service Review*, 33 (September 1959), 219–36.

tional processes and difficulties between family members, particularly between spouses. Incest behavior, assaults, and homocides come readily to mind as cases in point.

The comments about the mediating influence of family structure hold as well for peer group associations so that broad class-linked influences often have their effects on specific persons through the particular kinds of peer group relationships within which those individuals participate.

In this analysis of offender types, the interactional context of deviant acts, including peer associations, is discussed as part of offense behavior in role-careers. Peer group processes are also included in the body of causally related dimensions. As one illustration, pressures to engage in white-collar criminality are in many cases directed at business employees by their fellow workers. We can uncover numerous other illustrations in which the offender's associates have had a large part to play in his deviant behavior.

Before leaving this matter of peer group and family relationships, let us recall the discussion of situational factors in causation in Chapter Nine. That commentary argued that, contrary to conventional aasumptions that law-breakers must be different in terms of social experiences from nonoffenders, they may sometimes differ little from noncriminals. Thus their peer group and family relationships may not be much different from those of nonoffenders.

Contact with Defining Agencies

What about the causal consequences of contacts with defining agencies? Defining agencies are official and semiofficial agencies responsible for detecting, apprehending, punishing, and rehabilitating offenders. The discussion of deviant careers and the effects of societal reactions on them, centering about the contributions of Lemert and Becker, suggested that agency contacts may be of major significance. One of the major factors that may drive juveniles toward delinquency as a systematic role is the extent to which community organizations have defined the individual as a "delinquent" and "bad boy." We have already taken note of a study pointing out that identified adult criminals may be driven further into criminality as a result of employment difficulties they encounter because of their social stigma.[27] In other cases, contacts with defining agencies or kindred groups may have positive effects, as with amateur female shoplifters or "snitches." In a study in Chicago, Mary Owen Cameron found that women shoplifters rarely repeated the act after store personnel had apprehended and compelled them to admit they were "thieves" and "criminals." Apparently, the painful social-psychological trauma involved in admitting their deviance served to repress these individuals from further behavior of this nature.[28]

[27]Schwartz and Skolnick, "Two Studies of Legal Stigma."

[28]Mary Owen Cameron, "Department Store Shoplifting" (doctoral dissertation, Indiana University, 1953); Cameron, *The Booster and the Snitch* (New York: The Free Press, 1964).

Such etiological factors have been given short shrift in research. Customarily, the search for causal variables has paid little or no attention to career processes and agency experiences as career contingencies. However, some years ago, Frank Tannenbaum argued that the effects of official dealings with deviants, ostensibly therapeutic, constitute instead a process of "dramatization of evil." He asserted that the outcome of official handling in the courts and related circumstances was frequently contrary to the intended purposes of such actions. Instead of deflecting the actor away from a deviant career, such experiences alert citizens in the community to the presence of an "evil" person in their midst. Once he becomes singled out as "evil" an individual is likely to be thought of as "bad" in the future, quite apart from how he actually behaves. If his deportment does not change, the original diagnosis is validated in the eyes of the community. If for some reason he does modify his behavior, the change is seen as a devious attempt to hide his true nature. Either way, the offender cannot win, so his possibilities for action become narrowly circumscribed. In many instances, the deviant develops sentiments of being dealt with unjustly, which operate as rationalizations for his conduct. As a result, the end product of treatment is reinforcement of the very behavior the correctional agents are attempting to reduce.[29] Tannenbaum's thesis is polemic in tone, so there is room for argument concerning the extent to which his dismal implications are warranted. Nonetheless, this provocative hypothesis deserves more attention than it has received. Although Lemert and Becker have touched on the effects of societal reactions on deviants, relatively little work has been done on the specifics of these factors in criminality.[30]

Contacts with defining agencies could be positive in impact, so as to deflect the deviant away from further misconduct. Or they could be harmful in effect, driving the actor into further violations in response to his changed social identity. A third possibility is that such experiences could be of neutral significance, neither deterring nor harmfully affecting the individual.

Bits of empirical evidence seem to indicate that each of these three possibilities does occur. Cameron's study shows that contacts with defining agencies can lead to deterrence of further deviation. But some findings from the Highfields project point to deleterious consequences of contacts with treatment agencies. The Highfields institution is a small, intensive treatment facility for

---

[29]Frank Tannebaum, *Crime and the Community* (Boston: Ginn and Co., 1938), pp. 19–21. For a more general essay on these processes, see Harold Garfinkel, "Conditions of Successful Degradation Ceremonies," *American Journal of Sociology*, 61 (March 1956), 420–24; see also Erving Goffman, *Stigma* (Englewood Cliffs, N.J.: Prentice-Hall, 1963); John I. Kitsuse, "Societal Reaction to Deviant Behavior: Problems of Theory and Method," *Social Problems*, 9 (Winter 1962), 247–56.

[30]One notable exception is found in the theory of Cloward and Ohlin, which examines and extends Tannenbaum's claims to gang delinquents. See Richard A. Cloward and Lloyd E. Ohlin, *Delinquency and Opportunity* (New York: The Free Press, 1960), pp. 124–43. For a major statement on the role of societal reactions in mental disorder, see Scheff, *Being Mentally Ill*. For a contrary view and evidence, see Walter R. Gove, "Societal Reaction as an Explanation of Mental Illness: An Evaluation," *American Sociological Review*, 35 (October 1970), 873–83; Milton Mankoft, "Societal Reaction and Career Deviance: A Critical Analysis," *Sociological Quarterly*, 12 (Spring 1971), 204–18.

delinquent boys in New Jersey. As part of a research program associated with the institution, a projective personality test was given to Highfields boys and to inmates of a conventional reformatory in New Jersey at the time of admission and at a later point in their institutional stay. The test results indicated that the reformatory youths moved toward bleaker, darker outlooks on life during their stay in the reformatory and may have become resigned to further deviation as a life career; the Highfields boys showed movement in an opposite direction.[31] In this case, a double conclusion seems appropriate: traditional penal facilities operate in harmful ways as concerns contributions to criminality, but different results can be achieved within an atypical correctional program.

Knowledgeable criminologists are rarely sanguine about the rehabilitative potential of prison. Indeed, many criminologists have estimated that two-thirds or more of the prisoners released from penal institutions return to criminality. If these figures are correct, they certainly imply that correctional institutions play a major role in binding persons to deviant careers. However, a massive investigation by Daniel Glaser indicates that these pessimistic judgments about prisoner recidivism are grossly exaggerated and that recidivists are more likely to make up about a third of all prisoners rather than comprising a large majority of them.[32] Glaser's detailed study of the workings of the federal prison and parole system demonstrates that, although recidivists in that system are not as common as are men who refrain from further criminality, the whole matter of correctional effects is exceedingly complex. There is not one relationship of criminality, correctional experience, and the like, to reinvolvement in deviance; there are many specific and varied patterns.[33]

From these discordant reports on the effect of contacts with defining agencies, intervening variables clearly seem to be interposed in the situation. The outcome of agency intervention is dependent on a number of added factors, at least four of which come to mind. *Personality variations* exist among subjects who are the focus of agency concern. By virtue of certain personality patterns, some persons would probably be responsive to even innocuous experiences with agencies and their personnel, whereas others might find such events of no important personal consequence.

A second factor has to do with variations in *societal definitions* of behavior. Consider violations of traffic laws. Little public condemnation is attached to such deviance, so the person involved with agencies for this reason runs little risk of societal or agency hostility being directed at him. Other kinds of crimi-

[31]Lloyd W. McCorkle, Albert Elias, and F. Lovell Bixby, *The Highfields Story* (New York: Holt, Rinehart and Winston, 1958), pp. 122–26.

[32] Daniel Glaser, *The Effectiveness of a Prison and Parole System* (Indianapolis: Bobbs-Merrill Co., 1964), pp. 13–35. See also Stanton Wheeler, "Socialization in Correctional Institutions," *Handbook of Socialization Theory and Research*, ed. David A. Goslin (Chicago: Rand McNally and Co., 1969), pp. 1005–23.

[33]*Ibid.*, pp. 504–13.

nality are defined as serious by agencies but are regarded in a more tolerant light by the general public. Persons engaged in these forms of conduct are in a sense insulated from markedly negative repercussions from contacts with agencies because of public tolerance.

Not only do societal reactions vary for different forms of lawbreaking, but different segments of the general community react to the same behavior in discrepant ways. Thus, a third factor that probably influences the effects of agency experiences has to do with *exposure to antisocial environments*. The person who has grown up in an antisocial subculture in which antipolice attitudes and other hostile sentiments are endemic is not likely to be traumatized by any specific contact with defining agencies. That same individual is immunized against agency pressures by a supportive peer system, which assists him in warding off invidious definitions of himself that flow from these agency contacts. On the other hand, a person who is a product of middle-class, prosocial social circumstances is much more likely to react to experiences with the police or courts as profoundly important.

Finally, *agency climate* is a fourth factor influencing the impact of agency contacts. Some organizations take a punitive and hostile attitude toward persons who come into their hands, whereas others adopt a more positive posture. We might expect the effect of being apprehended by an abusive police officer to be different from interaction with a polite and pleasant officer. In the same way, correctional institutions vary in their social atmosphere and may have different influences on offenders, as the findings concerning Highfields and a state reformatory suggest.

One thing is certain from this brief discussion: the impact of agency contacts is not the same for all who enter into these contacts. Fragments of tangential evidence suggest some of the differential effects of agency experiences, but definitive findings gathered through carefully conducted research are sorely needed. The discussion of role careers in criminality in succeeding chapters will speculate about the part these processes play in types of offender behavior, which is all we can do in the face of a paucity of hard evidence.

CRIMINAL TYPOLOGY: AN ILLUSTRATION

An earlier work by the author presented a typology of nine delinquent role careers and another involving fifteen forms of adult criminality.[34] In this book, typological descriptions of offender patterns, stemming from the perspective enunciated in this chapter, will be interwoven with other materials on crime causation. To close this chapter on a proper note of completeness, let us

[34]Gibbons, *Changing the Lawbreaker*, pp. 75–125.

examine one typological characterization at this point: the pattern of naïve check forger.[35]

Definitional Dimensions

Offense Behavior. A naïve check forger engages in unsophisticated forms of forgery. He normally passes "NSF" ("Not Sufficient Funds") checks on his personal checks, written on his own bank accounts. In some cases he passes personal checks signed with some fictitious name. But in neither instance does the forger resort to such skilled activities as passing fraudulent payroll checks. Normally, the naïve check forger has no prior record of delinquency and may have a record of only minor adult crimes. The naïve forger often passes a bad check a number of times; that is, naïve forgery is not a "one shot" form of crime.

Interactional Setting. The offender acts alone in check passing, which is usually carried out in liquor stores, supermarkets, and other retail business agencies. Not infrequently the check forger passes "NSF" checks at a business location where he is personally known, such as a neighborhood bar.

Self-concept. Naïve check forgers do not view themselves as "real criminals." They tend to exhibit stereotyped rationalizations of the form: "You can't kill anyone with a fountain pen" or "No one is hurt by forgery because supermarkets make great profits and don't miss a little money lost through bad checks." Although the forger admits that passing bad checks is outside the range of conventional and acceptable behavior, he argues that special circumstances have compelled him to commit these acts.

Attitudes. The naïve check forger exhibits attitudes generally prosocial but somewhat atypical of law-abiding citizens. The check forger indicates commitment to conventional work roles and marital activities but exhibits dissatisfaction, bitterness, and resentment concerning his participation in such activities. He often shows a pattern of occupational and marital instability, which precedes involvement in forgery.

Role Career. The role career of the naïve check forger normally begins in adulthood and is not preceded by delinquency. Difficulties in employment, marriage, and general social participation precede the role career. The check forger gets involved in forgery after he has become significantly isolated from stable social ties. Once he has embarked on check forgery, repeated instances are not uncommon. The forger is often handled informally and outside the framework of criminal courts for his first episodes of forgery. When he is dealt with in a court, he is frequently placed on probation. Probation violation rates are quite high for this class of offender, many of them ultimately making their way into correctional institutions.

[35]*Ibid.,* pp. 108–10.

Background Dimensions

Social Class. The check forger is not exclusively from a single economic or class background. However, many are categorized as middle class, for they have had relatively comfortable economic circumstances and have been employed at white-collar jobs or similar occupational levels.

Family Background. There is little reason to suppose that the naïve check forger comes from an extremely disordered or unconventional family setting. The check forger does not appear to have experienced severe or atypical parental contacts. Additionally, the check forger's adult family background is relatively conventional. Many naïve forgers are married, but disruptions in marital relationships often play some part in the development of check forgery. The marital situation of the check passer is frequently not entirely harmonious prior to the forgery activities.

Peer Group Associations. Peer group associations in naïve forgery play no clearly significant role. Certainly the forger does not participate in a supportive subculture of forgers. Instead, the naïve forger commonly discovers for the first time in prison that other offenders behave in similar ways.

Contact with Defining Agencies. Check forgers tend to be dealt with informally for initial violations of the law and then handled in the least punitive way when processed through the courts; for example, they are often placed on probation. Swift and rather dramatic action by defining agencies in the first instance of check forgery might be positive in its consequences. Stated differently, conventional procedures now employed with check forgers may contribute to continuation of this behavior. They may lead the forger to assume that forgery can be carried on with relative impunity. Perhaps a more traumatic and earlier confrontation with the defining agencies would result in a different career outcome in this case.

SUMMARY

The previous three chapters, along with the present one, have been directed at various approaches to understanding of criminalistic deviance. Chapter Eleven brings these lines of commentary together in one place. Chapters Twelve through Seventeen examine a number of different criminal behavior patterns. The discussion of each behavior pattern includes some attention to the place of these forms of lawbreaking within American social structure. Additionally, the social-psychological concepts useful in the study of criminal role careers are applied to these patterns of conduct.

CAUSAL
ANALYSIS:
AN
ASSESSMENT

The preceding four chapters have presented a bewildering array of theories and research data concerning the etiology of criminality and criminal behavior. We might well ask at this point: "What does it all mean?" This brief chapter presents a reprise of these discussions, with an explication of some of the major dimensions of causation as they have emerged from the preceding chapters. Chapter Ten has already presented one overview of etiological processes, in the form of seventeen assumptions underlying the typological perspectives of this book. The reader should reexamine those claims about the social sources of criminality before proceeding further in this chapter.

Figure 7 offers a representation of some of the major forces in the development of lawbreaking behavior, focusing on the actions of persons. Although we often try to account for patterns of criminality or crime rates involving a collectivity of actors, the behavior of individuals is the ultimate unit we must explain. Individual offenders added together make up rates of burglary, rape, or other kinds of misconduct.

In brief, Figure 7 suggests that lawbreaking is related to a variety of *basic factors*, centering about some major ingredients of social structure, including cultural values, social-class patterns, racism, and other aspects of the collective order. These root causes of criminality impinge on nearly all citizens within a particular society. However, a number of *intervening variables* mediate or influence these forces. These factors differentiate members of society and partially determine the different lines of activity they pursue. For example, family interaction patterns vary among even those who grow up in the same social-class group and, in turn, shape, to some extent, the social roles these individuals play.

Figure 7 also shows that *precipitating factors*, which are the immediate sources of criminality, join basic factors and intervening variables. One set of precipitating influences includes attitudes and motives favorable to law violation, but other precipitators of lawbreaking exist as well.

Figure 7 summarizes the typological argument previously presented. Criminality takes myriad forms, each of which is the product of a separate chain

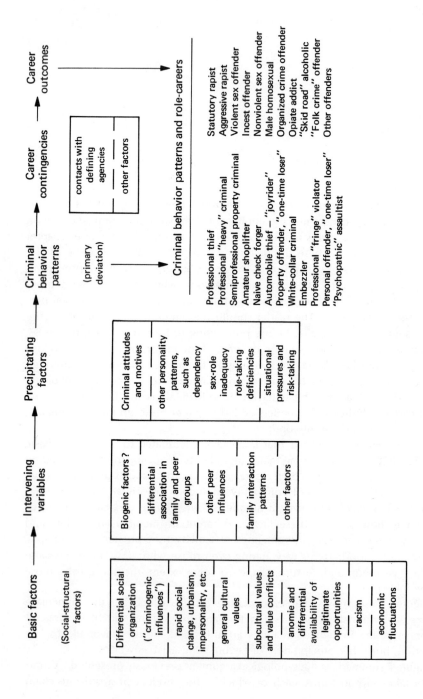

FIGURE 7 Causal Processes in Criminal Behavior

The chart, read left to right, presents the following stages and their associated factors:

Basic factors (Social-structural factors)

- Differential social organization ("criminogenic influences")
- rapid social change, urbanism, impersonality, etc.
- general cultural values
- subcultural values and value conflicts
- anomie and differential availability of legitimate opportunities
- racism
- economic fluctuations

↑

Intervening variables

- Biogenic factors ?
- differential association in family and peer groups
- other peer influences
- family interaction patterns
- other factors

↑

Precipitating factors

- Criminal attitudes and motives
- other personality patterns, such as dependency
- sex-role inadequacy
- role-taking deficiencies
- situational pressures and risk-taking

↑

Criminal behavior patterns (primary deviation) → Criminal behavior patterns and role-careers

- Professional thief
- Professional "heavy" criminal
- Semiprofessional property criminal
- Amateur shoplifter
- Naive check forger
- Automobile thief — "joyrider"
- Property offender, "one-time loser"
- White-collar criminal
- Embezzler
- Professional "fringe" violator
- Personal offender, "one-time loser"
- "Psychopathic" assaultist

↑

Career contingencies

- contacts with defining agencies
- other factors

↑

Career outcomes →

- Statutory rapist
- Aggressive rapist
- Violent sex offender
- Incest offender
- Nonviolent sex offender
- Male homosexual
- Organized crime offender
- Opiate addict
- "Skid road" alcoholic
- "Folk crime" offender
- Other offenders

of etiological influences. Figure 7 lists twenty-three patterns of criminal behavior. The last two categories, " 'folk crime' offender" and "other offenders," are broad and include a host of persons caught up in transitory episodes of lawbreaking.

The causal process outlined in Figure 7 also indicates that various *career contingencies*, which occur to persons who engage in initial or primary acts of criminal deviance, exert considerable influence on the subsequent course they take. Correctional experiences, difficulties in employment that arise out of "ex-con" status, and kindred other experiences may play a major role in deflecting some offenders out of lawbreaking or in preventing others from withdrawing from deviance.

The preceding four chapters have already discussed particular basic factors, intervening variables, precipitating factors, career contingencies, and criminal behavior patterns at some length. However, let us take a closer look at the entries under these rubrics in Figure 7.

BASIC FACTORS—SOCIAL-STRUCTURAL
VARIABLES

Differential Social Organization

As the remarks in Chapter Eight and Ten make clear, we agree, as do nearly all other criminologists, with Sutherland and Cressey's contention that "crime is rooted in the social organization and is an expression of that social organization."[1] Further, we have appropriated their term *differential social organization*, which stands as a general or abstract label for a variety of social-structural factors generating criminality ("criminogenic influences"). Concerning differential social organization, Sutherland and Cressey say:

> This condition of normative conflict is ordinarily considered "social disorganization" or "unorganization," because the social pressures for conformity on the part of the person are not uniform or harmonious. . . . Actually, the social conditions in which the influences on the person are relatively inharmonious and inconsistent are themselves a kind of social organization. Such social organization is characteristic of all except the earliest societies and the most isolated contemporary societies, although there are wide variations in the degree of heterogeneity and in the pervasiveness of the normative inconsistencies.[2]

Normative conflict takes a variety of forms. In American society, some societal pressures toward lawbreaking revolve around anomie or the unavaila-

---

[1]Edwin H. Sutherland and Donald R. Cressey, *Principles of Criminology*, 8th ed. (Philadelphia: J. B. Lippincott Co., 1970), p. 77.

[2]*Ibid.*, p. 95.

bility of legitimate opportunities for the achievement of common success values. Unequal access to law-abiding routes to upward mobility and material success is particularly pronounced for some groups within society. Earlier, we examined this component as racism in American society.

Other social-structural influences in criminality have to do with subcultural value patterns that encourage lawbreaking. Some theorists have spoken of a "subculture of violence" in the United States, in which the group members are inordinately suspicious of one another and prone to use physical aggression in interpersonal interaction. Along the same line, others have claimed that subcultural attitudes toward sexuality and physical force have much to do with the social-class concentration of forcible rape among working-class groups. As we have already noted, some observers have identified this situation of value conflicts and subcultural value patterns as constituting "value pluralism."

According to another claim about the criminogenic impact of growing social complexity, impersonality and loose social bonds among citizens characterize modern societies; hence, persons are less inhibited from criminality as a result.[3]

Differential social organization in contemporary United States is usually attributed to historical processes centering about rapid social change, stress on material success, the growing "scale" of modern social structure, pronounced urbanism, population heterogeneity flowing out of mass movements of foreignborn into the country in earlier periods, and other such occurrences. For example, many people have claimed that contemporary American lawlessness grew out of frontier traditions in which violence predominated as a means of settling disputes. Others have linked some of the current problems of criminality to traditional American values that stress individual freedom and developed with the founding of the nation.

Let us reiterate our conclusion about social-structural factors stated in Chapter Eight. Although these forces doubtless do play a fundamental role in criminality, we need to articulate in more detail how specific social-cultural influences are bound up with intervening and precipitating factors so as to result in specific kinds of lawbreaking. Chapters Twelve through Seventeen endeavor to spell out some of these patterns.

INTERVENING VARIABLES

The number of variables intervening between basic social-structural processes and the occurrence of criminal acts must be large indeed. Figure 7 only hints at some of these factors. For example, one collection of intervening influences

[3]For some evidence on this point, see Erwin O. Smigel, "Public Attitudes Toward Stealing as Related to the Size of the Victim Organization," in *Crimes Against Bureaucracy*, ed. Smigel and H. Laurence Ross (New York: Van Nostrand Reinhold Co., 1970), pp. 15–28; see also Smigel, "Public Attitudes Toward 'Chiseling' with Reference to Unemployment Compensation," in *ibid.*, pp. 29–45.

centers about opportunities for lawbreaking actions. For example, an employee who works on an assembly line would be hard pressed to embezzle any of the firm's funds, no matter how motivated he might be to do so. Similarly, middle-class citizens have less chance to satisfy any curiosity they might have about narcotics than do individuals who frequent the "Tenderloin" area of the community, where opportunities to pursue various "vices" are considerably more commonly encountered.

Are There Biogenic Influences in Criminality?

Our earlier perusal of the literature on biological factors in criminal behavior failed to turn up any evidence to support hypotheses of that sort. We noted that theoretical and methodological inadequacies of one kind or another have flawed much of the criminological work in that area. The most recent of these arguments, concerning XYY chromosomal abnormality, is unconvincing. From the material in Chapter Six, we might conclude that no biological influences exist in criminality. But that conclusion is not warranted. All that we can say about biological arguments is that, to date, no proof of these hypothesized relationships has been uncovered. Conceivably, although perhaps unlikely, future investigations might turn up evidence supporting biological assertions.

Differential Association

Chapter Nine included a detailed examination of differential association theory. In our discussion we acknowledged the crucial role that theoretical argument played in the development of modern criminology. At the same time, we argued that some processes similar to those Sutherland described as differential association are probably involved in some forms of criminal conduct and absent in others. In the following pages, devoted to the analysis of specific forms of criminal behavior, we shall see that some kinds of lawbreaking are the outgrowth of lengthy episodes of differential association with carriers of criminal norms. On the other hand, in some forms of criminal deviance, association with criminalistic individuals is not implicated. In short, differential association is a label for one extremely important set of intervening variables, although other intervening factors exist as well. The following chapters sort out cases of criminality that involve differential association from those that do not.

Other Peer and Family Interaction Patterns

Chapter Nine has already acknowledged the impact of various kinds of family interaction patterns on criminality. We noted that particular kinds of lawbreaking are related to distorted parent–child relationships, as in the case of incest;

parent-child tensions, as involved in some forms of juvenile delinquency; and husband-wife disharmony, as in homicide and assault. In general we hold that social and cultural forces have their effects on individuals only as they are mediated through the groups in which persons interact.

PRECIPITATING FACTORS

Criminal Attitudes, Motives, and Personality Patterns

We have noted that according to the traditional criminological view, lawbreaking is the result of an etiological process in which the social experiences certain persons encounter produce criminal attitudes and motives, which in turn lead them to engage in deviant acts. In our discussion of differential association theory, we conceded that this kind of etiological process probably is accurate for some kinds of offenders. In some criminal careers, the actors have acquired criminalistic attitudes out of protracted involvement in differential association, broadly defined. Chapters Twelve through Seventeen examine a number of kinds of offender behavior in which this etiological pattern is evident.

At the same time, much of the argument to this point has contended that some kinds of lawbreaking arise out of other precipitating factors, some of which involve personality patterns or attributes that differentiate offenders from nonoffenders. The evidence examined in Chapter Seven failed to support the broad claim that most forms of criminality involve personality pathology. But those data did not by any means rule out the possibility that personality deviations are implicated as precipitating elements in some specific instances of offender behavior. We would be hard pressed to ignore such a hypothesis when considering the violent sex offender or "psychopathic" assaultist, instances of criminal conduct we shall examine later in more detail.

Earlier, we contended that psychological patterns are probably involved as precipitating forces in many instances of criminal behavior, in addition to instances involving personality pathology. For example, the hypothesis that certain check forgers are drawn into this behavior because of an overly-dependent personality structure is worthy of further examination. Similarly, some of the commentary on other specific forms of offender behavior in the following chapters will explore the possibility that personality dynamics such as sex-role inadequacy may be implicated.

Situational Pressures and Risk Taking

Chapter Nine devoted much discussion to situational pressures as precipitating forces in lawbreaking. We should emphasize that traditional criminological views of lawbreaking have tended to stress social-structural factors and intervening variables, along with criminal attitudes and motives, as the necessary combination of elements for criminality to occur. In short, we have viewed the offender as different from the nonoffender because of the offender's motivation to engage in lawbreaking. Situational factors have been relegated to a minor place in traditional criminological perspectives. By contrast, our remarks in Chapter Nine accorded heavier emphasis to risk-taking processes and situational influences in criminality. In the following pages, we shall examine particular cases of situational factors in more detail.

CRIMINAL BEHAVIOR, CAREER CONTINGENCIES, AND CAREER OUTCOMES

Forces leading up to or producing initial or primary acts of lawbreaking may not determine the course that criminal involvement takes. In many cases, experiences with police or correctional agencies may play a major part in career outcomes. In some instances, these contingencies may deter the person from more than a single flirtation with deviance. In other cases, the actor may become further entangled in misbehavior, partly as a consequence of his experiences with correctional processes.

Chapters Twelve through Seventeen discuss offender role careers and attempt to identify the impact of career contingencies on lawbreakers. In addition, Chapters Eighteen through Twenty-Two analyze the effects of correctional processes on criminal careers. However, in actuality relatively little is known about the impact of imprisonment on specific offenders or about other experiences of that kind. Although there are numerous polemic essays about prisons as "crime schools," hard evidence concerning the effects of the penitentiary on particular offender careers is not abundant. The same is true of other correctional structures and processes.

SUMMARY

This brief chapter has been devoted to a broad synthesis of the etiological elements identified in earlier chapters. The commentary in this chapter and the preceding ones is a general theoretical exposition on crime causation. At this point, we have laid out a general perspective on etiology; we turn to a more detailed examination of particular forms of criminal conduct. Chapter Twelve begins this task.

12

INTRODUCTION TO PROPERTY OFFENDER CAREERS

Acts defined as crimes tend to be those that most grossly offend the major values or sentiments of particular societies. In America, property and material goods are revered, so it is not surprising that a number of forms of conduct centering around violation of property rights have been singled out as crimes. In this and the following chapter, we shall examine a number of different property offender patterns. Chapter Twelve takes up professional thieves, professional "heavy" criminals, and semiprofessional property criminals; Chapter Thirteen discusses property offender "one-time losers," automobile thieves, naïve check forgers, and amateur shoplifters.

We shall see that professional thieves develop out of relatively comfortable economic circumstances, whereas "heavies" and semiprofessionals are often the adult counterparts of urban, slum-area gang delinquents. Accordingly, we shall examine much recent theory and research on working-class gang delinquency. A major argument in favor of the typological viewpoint is that it tends to illuminate the otherwise murky question of relationships between juvenile delinquency and crime. Some criminals arise out of delinquency backgrounds; others do not.

PROFESSIONAL THEFT AS A WAY OF LIFE

We begin our examination of types of crime with the colorful group of offenders who call themselves "grifters," "boosters," "carnies," or other argot terms and who sociologists term "professional thieves." Professional thieves engage in a variety of nonviolent and frequently complex forms of property crime, usually involving some element of the "con" or manipulation of the victim or victims. Although some might quarrel with the designation of professional attached to these lawbreakers, such criminals do exhibit a long period of training, complex occupational skills, and a shared set of occupationally oriented attitudes—elements usually regarded as central to professional status.[1] Professional thieves also engage in full-time pursuit of illicit incomes through criminality; "grifting" is a way of life with them. The following discussion presents a typological characterization of professional thieves, followed by some comments about the research evidence regarding thieves, and other remarks.

THE PROFESSIONAL THIEF ROLE CAREER

Definitional Dimensions

Offense Behavior. Individuals other criminals recognize as professional thieves or "grifters" engage in a diversity of specific acts of criminality. Some are involved in the "big con," which is an elaborate form of swindle involving a number of players or con men. Other thieves are "short con" men, who carry out crimes of lesser duration, which also involve fewer participants and result in smaller profits to the offenders. Other thieves shoplift, pick pockets, "hotel prowl," or are involved in related activities. Finally, some thieves are implicated in petty, low-ranked forms of crime, such as "carnival grifting." Cutting through this diversity of behavior, however, is the central element of nonviolent criminality. In many cases "wits," or the ability to manipulate victims, counts heavily in successful acts of grifting. Sophisticated, nonviolent conduct is the essential element of professional theft as a form of criminality.

Interactional Setting. Certain kinds of professional theft, such as the "big con," involve a number of participants in a complex, highly staged presentation into which "marks," or victims, are drawn by the thieves. Swindles depend heavily on larcenous motives on the part of marks. Victims of con games are led to believe that they are in a position to defraud someone else through a "get rich quick" scheme offered by the con man. Something of the same sort is involved in "short con" episodes. However, other forms of professional theft, such as pickpocket behavior, involve victims who are not active participants in the illegal events, as is true also of shoplifting, sneak thieving, and hotel prowling.

In most instances, grifters carry out their criminal endeavors in collaboration with one or more confederates. Pickpockets work in groups called "troupes" or "whiz mobs." These associational networks among offenders often extend into the noncriminal segments of their lives, involving many persons in a generalized pattern of differential association with other thieves. A highly devel-

---

Everett Cherrington Hughes, *Men and Their Work* (New York: The Free Press, 1958), p. 33. See Hughes' commentary, pages 78-87, for some problems with the designation of forms of criminality as professional in character.

oped and esoteric argot or specialized language is characteristic of thieves and is one of the central features of a criminal subculture of thieves.

Self-concept. Professional thieves define themselves as "thieves" or "grifters" and disassociate themselves from other criminals they regard as amateurs and of markedly lower social standing. Among thieves, status or prestige distinctions exist on the bases of criminal skills and profit derived from illegality; "big con" men are accorded highest rank and consider themselves the elite of the criminal world. Grifters as a group judge themselves to be clever criminals in a world populated by devious, scheming, corrupt individuals. In this view, "everyone has a racket," and grifters regard themselves as basically no worse than the "marks" they defraud.

Attitudes. Professional thieves exhibit relatively positive attitudes toward most individuals in their social environment. They tend to view the criminal world as composed of thieves like themselves, certain other professional criminals with whom they have common interests, and the balance of the offender population, whom they regard as amateurs and aliens to their world. In the view of thieves, the noncriminal population is made up of "marks" who deserve to be victimized because of their larcenous motives, law enforcement persons who perform necessary tasks of regulating the affairs of society but represent an occupational hazard to be neutralized through bribes or avoided, and other noncriminal citizens. Thieves tend not to demonstrate extreme hostility toward any of these individuals; instead they simply regard themselves as different from and superior to these others. Grifters take considerable pride in their criminal skills and view themselves as incumbents of professional roles.

Role Career. Professional thieves enter into grifting relatively early in life. Some become involved in learning experiences as neophyte grifters in their teens; others enter into thievery at a later age from occupational backgrounds peripheral to the criminal underworld. Professional theft is a way of life pursued over an extended period of time and in a relatively uninterrupted fashion. Because of the skilled nature of their criminality, professional grifters are rarely found in prison populations. Also, the victims of thieves are frequently reluctant to report being victimized to the police authorities, so many cases of theft go unreported. It is likely that many thieves ultimately retire voluntarily from theft activity as they come to regard the frequent traveling and other features of theft behavior as overly burdensome. Still, professional theft is a form of criminality that probably represents an atypically long career pattern.

Background Dimensions

Social Class. Professional thieves appear to be drawn from a variety of social class backgrounds. Most of them do not seem to be from extremes of poverty, so professional theft is not a form of criminality that commonly draws its members from lower-class populations. According to the evidence on professional grifters, many are inducted into this activity from occupational categories or situations peripheral to the criminal underworld. The recruitment process often involves bartenders, taxicab drivers, bellhops, and kindred occupational types who interact with grifters and various other deviant individuals in the course of their occupations. Such persons begin in tangential or minor roles of grifting. Ultimately, many move into full-time involvement in grifting; the end product of the training process is professionalized crime skills.

Family Background. It is likely that professional thieves often derive from unexceptional family backgrounds, though some may have grown up in somewhat disturbed or deviant family settings. On this point, one line of argument holds that certain situations of tension between family members produce a "budding grifter" personality type. According to this view, the manipulative, devious personalities generated in such situations frequently make their way into professional thievery as a life's work. However, probably a good many grifters have grown up in family settings in which they have become alienated from other family members and detached from parental ties relatively early in life. In turn, these actors have come into contact with carnival grifters or other mobile groups of thieves and have become grifters.

Peer Group Associations. There is little basis for supposing that the peer group relationships in which professional thieves were involved before they became grifters have played a significant role in causation of their behavior. Whatever its etiology, professional theft does not appear to be a function of any kind of peer influence. However, once an individual is engaged in grifting activity, peer relations take on critical significance. The complex, subtle crime skills of professional theft cannot be acquired by any other technique than direct tutelage of other criminals. In addition, the life of professional grifting is a behavior system or subcultural way of life, so differential association with criminal peers is much a part of this form of crime. Hence, the thief is in a situation of constant reinforcement of his deviant self-notions and attitudes through interaction with like-minded individuals.

Contact with Defining Agencies. The contacts thieves have with law enforcement and correctional agencies do not appear to be major forces in their criminality. Thieves do not look on such organizations with great hostility. One reason for their relatively mild attitudes toward the police and correctional personnel is that they have little contact with such persons. Professional theft is a low-risk crime in that grifters are rarely apprehended for their illegal acts. They often enjoy relatively congenial relations with members of defining agencies. Thieves are usually articulate, charming persons, they do not shoot at or assault policemen, and they are not antagonistic toward them. On those infrequent occasions when a grifter "falls" (is arrested), the experience is not likely to be particularly traumatic for him.

Some Evidence

The greatest portion of the data regarding professional theft concerns the criminal activity in which grifters engage.[2] Police officers have compiled lengthy collections of case material on the *modus operandi* of thieves,[3] and several social scientists have also spent some of their energy cataloguing the details of professional grifting.[4] What emerges from all of these accounts is a picture of criminality that demonstrates the esoteric and complex nature of grifting as a kind of crime.

Considerably less is known about the backgrounds and causal situations from which professional thieves derive than is apparent about the criminality in which they engage. Our typological remarks suggested that thieves are often recruited from certain occupations in which contact with underworld figures is fairly common and that, in addition, grifters may often be drawn from a cohort of individuals with particular personality patterns. On this first point, Sutherland's report on professional offenders indicated that many of these persons were originally active in occupational pursuits peripheral to criminalistic ones.[5]

Psychiatrist Richard L. Jenkins contends that thieves have "budding grifter" kinds of personality structures.[6] He suggests that "budding grifters" are specialists in deceit who have developed interpersonal betrayal into a fine art. Rather than experiencing guilt over their devious activities, they exhibit a professional pride in their workmanship and may feel chagrin and humiliation in instances where their manipulative endeavors go awry.

According to Jenkins, elements or experiences that may contribute to the development of "budding grifter" personalities include:

1. Experiences (as of unusual hardship) during the formative period which put a high premium upon material success.

[2]Herbert A. Bloch and Gilbert Geis, *Man, Crime, and Society,* 2nd ed. (New York: Random House, 1970), pp. 173-85; Walter Bromberg and Sylvan Keiser, "The Psychology of the Swindler," *American Journal of Psychiatry,* 94 (May 1938), 1441-58; Walter B. Gibson, *The Bunco Book* (Holyoke, Mass.: Sidney H. Radner, 1946); Richard L. Jenkins, *Breaking Patterns of Defeat* (Philadelphia: J. B. Lippincott Co., 1954), pp. 148-58; John C. R. McDonald, *Crime is a Business* (Stanford, Calif.: Stanford University Press, 1939); David W. Maurer, *The Big Con* (Indianapolis: Bobbs-Merrill Co., 1940); Maurer, *Whiz Mob* (New Haven, Conn.: College and University Press, 1964); Julian R. Roebuck and Ronald Johnson, "The 'Short Con' Man," *Crime and Delinquency,* 10 (July 1964), 235-48; Edwin M. Schur, "Sociological Analysis of Confidence Swindling," *Journal of Criminal Law, Criminology and Police Science,* 48 (September-October 1957), 296-304; Edwin H. Sutherland, *The Professional Thief* (Chicago: University of Chicago Press, 1937); Robert Louis Gasser, "The Confidence Game," *Federal Probation,* 27 (December 1963), 47-54.

[3]McDonald, *Crime Is a Business.*

[4]Maurer, *The Big Con;* Roebuck and Johnson, "The 'Short Con' Man."

[5]Sutherland, *The Professional Thief,* pp. 211-14; also see Gasser, "The Confidence Game."

[6]Jenkins, *Breaking Patterns of Defeat,* pp. 148-58.

2. Early experiences which force a close self-protective attention to the emotional reactions of intermittently or constantly hostile adults.
3. Early experiences which tend toward the development of distrust and the expectation of betrayal.
4. Attitudes on the part of those emotionally important to the child which sanction unreliability, or which laud deceit or betrayal as an adaptation and means of getting on in the world. In some instances this involves definite teaching or coaching in the art of betrayal.
5. Early and repetitive gain from the use of deceit.
6. Attitudes and experiences which lead to the development of verbal facility, social charm and ingratiating ways.[7]

Social settings likely to culminate in learning of deceit and reward for its practice include disharmony and marital tension between the parents of the child. In this situation, the parents compete for the allegiance of the child, attempting to win his loyalty and alienate him from the other marital partner. The "budding grifter" learns to turn this situation to his advantage by playing each parent against the other.

These claims of Jenkins represent a series of clinical hunches derived from psychiatric practice, rather than hard facts from careful research. Moreover, the hypothesis advanced in this case is broad, holding that the "grifter" personalities these experiences generate subsequently make their way into a variety of social circumstances. Because Jenkins does not argue that all or most of them become professional criminals, we might expect to find "budding grifters" at work on used car lots, selling vacuum cleaners or aluminum siding, or in myriad other settings.

At least one corroborative study has revealed that grifters do exhibit unique personality configurations. Julian Roebuck and Ronald Johnson have reported that the "short con" men they examined were of above average intelligence and that most of them exhibited the personality marks of the grifter suggested by Jenkins.[8]

Although facts are hard to come by, we estimate that professional theft has always been a relatively uncommon form of criminality in American society. Moreover, there is reason to suppose that grifting is generally on the decline. Certain forms of grifting, in particular, have become nearly obsolete, probably as a consequence of certain broad changes that have occurred in societal conditions in the United States. For one, the practice of the "big con" has probably waned as a result of changes in banking procedures, the growing sophistication of "marks," and other trends of that sort. Carnival grifting is perhaps a vanishing form of illegality because of the general disappearance of the carnival as a feature of small-town life in this country. Certain other

---

[7]*Ibid.*, p. 150.
[8]Roebuck and Johnson, "The 'Short Con' Man," pp. 238–41.

forms of grifting have survived to the present; "boosting" (shoplifting) and certain "short con" games persist as forms of professional theft. But even these surviving patterns are probably infrequent in comparison to the "garden variety" forms of lawbreaking.

What is the significance of professional theft? Two points stand out in any evaluation of the criminological salience of grifting. First, professional theft is an extreme illustration of the extent to which a pattern of deviant conduct may become elaborated into a complex interactional pattern, behavior system, or subculture, in which the members are bound together by a variety of social ties in addition to their involvement in criminal acts. Moreover, these deviant actors are players in a complex social system in which they are implicated in symbiotic ties with a variety of "noncriminals," including policemen, tipsters, fences, cab drivers, and other related types. Professional theft is a significant case of deviant conduct transmitted from generation to generation; much of the content of activity originated well before the birthdates of contemporary thieves.

The second observation to be made about criminality, stemming from the study of grifting, has to do with the interconnections of illegality to other features of organized social life. For example, Edwin Schur suggests that professional theft cannot be understood apart from consideration of basic values of American society, which encourage or condone swindles, frauds, "sharp" business practices, and unethical conduct of various kinds.[9] The United States exhibits a cultural climate in which profit motives, salesmanship, and "something for nothing" interests stand out. The professional thief is a skilled worker who turns this situation of tolerance for devious conduct to his advantage. Grifters claim that in England grifting is difficult if not impossible because of the lesser emphasis on risk-taking, acquisitive actions in that nation. In the same way, they frequently assert the impossibility of "conning" or victimizing an honest man; the mark must have "larceny in his soul" to be swindled. In short, the case of professional thieves is an illustration of the impossibility of sustaining the clear distinctions between the "good guys" and the "bad guys" in American society. The law violator is no less a product of society than the moral, upright citizen, and both of them have much more in common than they are likely to acknowledge.

PROFESSIONAL "HEAVY" CRIMINALS

The typological descriptions around which the content of this text is organized suggest the existence of a number of relatively clear-cut types of property offenders. Professional "heavy" criminals who engage in robberies and burgla-

---

[9]Schur, "Sociological Analysis of Confidence Swindling."

ries are distinguished from semiprofessional property offenders and "one-time loser" property criminals who also engage in robberies and related offenses. One major basis for separating these offender role careers is that the three vary markedly in terms of the criminal expertise the respective role incumbents demonstrate.

However, we should make clear that the distinction between professional "heavy" criminals and semiprofessional property offenders is actually one of degree rather than kind. The dividing line between professional and semiprofessional property offenders is somewhat arbitrary. On the whole, professional "heavies" are highly competent lawbreakers who reap large sums of money from their illegal activities and work at this occupation full time. Semiprofessionals tend to be relatively unskilled, poorly paid for their criminal endeavors, and work at crime in some cases on a part-time basis. Doubtless many offenders would fall clearly into one or another of these types, but some criminals might be difficult to categorize in that technical skill, amount of profit from crime, and involvement in criminality are matters of degree rather than of different qualitative attributes of offenders.

Numerous descriptions of professional "heavy" crime are in existence, including several in the form of the life stories of professional criminals.[10] One useful account of professional crime, which might serve as a comparison to other instances, is the famous Brink's robbery that occurred in Boston in 1950. The following excerpt from the Federal Bureau of Investigation report of the Brink's robbery clearly communicates the flavor of professional crime:

> The Brink's robbery was a product of a combined thought and criminal experience of men who had known one another for many years. The gang spent more than a year in planning the robbery and they started a systematic study of the Brink's organization after it moved to its present site on Prince Street in Boston.
>
> Before the robbery was carried out, all the participants were well acquainted with the Brink's premises. Each had surreptitiously entered the building on several occasions after the Brink's employees had left for the day and they made a study of Brink's schedules and shipments.
>
> The planning for the robbery included several "trial runs" in which the gang members practiced their approach to the building in a truck and their flight over the "getaway" route. The gang abandoned plans to carry out the robbery several times when conditions were not favorable.
>
> During these occasions one gang member was stationed on the roof of

---

[10]Everett DeBaun, "The Heist: The Theory and Practice of Armed Robbery," *Harper's*, 200 (February 1950), 69–77; Quentin Reynolds, *I, Willie Sutton* (New York: Farrar, Straus & Giroux, 1953); John Bartlow Martin, *My Life in Crime* (New York: Harper & Row, Publishers, 1952); Jack Black, "A Burglar Looks at Laws and Codes," *Harper's*, 160 (February 1930), 306–13; Black, *You Can't Win* (New York: The Macmillan Co., 1926); Bruce Jackson; *A Thief's Primer* (New York: The Macmillan Co., 1969).

a building on Prince Street overlooking Brink's. He signaled the others with a flashlight. The last of these "false" approaches took place on the evening before the robbery.

During the early evening of January 17, 1950, members of the gang met in the Roxbury section of Boston and entered the rear of a Ford stake-body truck which had been stolen in Boston in November, 1949, to be used in the robbery.

Including the driver, this truck carried nine members of the gang to the scene of the robbery. During the trip from Roxbury seven of the men donned Navy-type peacoats and chauffeur's caps. Each of the seven also was given a pistol and Halloween-type mask. Each had gloves and wore either crepe-sole shoes or rubbers so their footsteps would be muffled.

As the men approached the Brink's building, they looked for a signal from the "lookout" on the roof of a Prince Street building. The "lookout" previously had arrived in a stolen Ford sedan.

After receiving the "go ahead" signal, seven members of the gang left the truck and walked through a playground which led to the Prince Street entrance to Brink's. Using the side-door key they had previously obtained, the men quickly entered and donned the masks.

Other keys in their possession enabled them to proceed to the second floor, where they took five Brink's employees by surprise. The seven robbers ordered the employees to lie face down on the floor, tied their hands behind them, and placed adhesive tape over their mouths. Before fleeing with the loot, the seven armed men attempted to open a metal box containing the payroll of the General Electric Co., but they had brought no tools and were unsuccessful.

Immediately upon leaving, the gang loaded the loot into the stolen truck. As the truck sped away with nine members of the gang, the "lookout" departed in the stolen sedan. The truck was unloaded at the home of one of the participants in Roxbury that same evening. Some members of the gang made a preliminary effort to count the loot, but they quickly dispersed to establish alibis for themselves.

On the night of the robbery, approximately $380,000 of the loot was removed from the house in Roxbury for security reasons. Additionally, the equipment used in the robbery was taken by a gang member for disposal. On January 18, 1950, another gang member took the remainder of the loot from the house; and several weeks later it was divided among the eleven men.

In addition to the cash and securities, the robbers took four pistols from Brink's. One of these was recovered by a Somerville, Mass., police officer on February 5, 1950. It had been found by a group of boys near the Mystic River in Somerville.

Descriptions of the truck used in the robbery were obtained from persons in the vicinity of the crime scene. Pieces of an identical truck were found at a dump in Stoughton, Mass., March 14, 1950. This truck had been cut up with an acetylene torch.

During the F.B.I.'s six-year investigation thousands of possible suspects were eliminated. Thousands of other persons, possible witnesses and individuals who could furnish background information concerning matters arising in various phases of the investigation were interviewed. Circulars concerning a $100,000 reward offered by Brink's were distributed to all parts of the country and no tip was loverlooked.[11]

In many of its details, this illustration parallels the *modus operandi* of the "heist" former robber Everett DeBaun enumerates.[12]

The following sections present a typological description of professional "heavy" offenders, followed by a typological characterization of semiprofessional criminals. As these discussions indicate, the social backgrounds of both types of lawbreakers seem relatively similar so that relatively unskilled offenders and technically proficient ones alike appear to develop from gang delinquent origins. Most of these individuals have lived in urban communities, frequently in slum neighborhoods. Highly skilled professional "heavies" appear to be former gang offenders of above-average intelligence who have been in social situations where they have been able to acquire special skill in criminality, usually through differential association with other professional violators. Semiprofessionals, on the other hand, are the less able deviants, probably of only average intelligence, and have been deprived of criminal learning opportunities.

Following the typological description of these two kinds of offenders, we shall examine the available theories and evidence regarding their etiological backgrounds. We shall pay particularly close attention to recent theoretical contentions regarding working-class, subcultural delinquency and to the research evidence regarding these lines of argument.

THE PROFESSIONAL "HEAVY" ROLE CAREER[13]

Definitional Dimensions

Offense Behavior. Professional "heavy" criminals engage in armed robbery, burglary, and other direct assaults on property. They are highly skilled at crime, so although the element of coercion and threat of violence is involved here,

---

[11]*Seattle Times,* January 11, 1957.

[12]DeBaun, "The Heist: The Theory and Practice of Armed Robbery."

[13]Don C. Gibbons, *Changing the Lawbreaker,* The Treatment of Delinquents and Criminals, © 1965. Reprinted by permission of Prentice-Hall, Inc., Englewood Cliffs, New Jersey, pp. 102-4.

they rarely use actual force. The *modus operandi* of professional "heavy" criminals involves a relatively lengthy period of detailed planning prior to execution of the criminal offense. The actual burglary or robbery is accomplished swiftly, with the offenders employing the element of surprise to avoid the risk of apprehension.

Interactional Setting. Most activities of professional "heavy" criminals are carried on as team or "mob" operations. Although on some occasions a single offender can carry out a robbery, professional burglaries and robberies involve a number of partners. The crime partners are involved in specialized roles; one participant may be the "rod man," while another is the "wheel man," a specialist in driving getaway cars.

Self-concept. Professional "heavies" define themselves as criminals and as professionals in criminality. They exhibit pride in their specialized skills and view crime as a lucrative, satisfying way of life. Professionals draw clear distinctions between themselves and other offenders they regard as amateurs.

Attitudes. The attitudes of the professional "heavy" toward the police range from scorn for inept policemen regarded as "clowns" to respect for competent police workers. In either event, the professional does not exhibit great hostility toward the police, who are regarded as necessary persons with a job to do. The professional "heavy" shows somewhat negative attitudes toward conventional work roles, inasmuch as crime seems to him a preferable way of earning a livelihood.

Role Career. Professional "heavies" are normally from urban, lower-class backgrounds. Most of them began their criminal careers as predatory gang delinquents. However, predatory gang offenders do not necessarily become professional "heavies"; but rather "heavies" are selected out of a large group of gang delinquents. The "heavy" usually goes through a process of increasing differential involvement with older professionals from whom he learns necessary crime skills. Persons who engage in professional property offenses tend to continue criminal activities into middle age, whereupon many of them ultimately retire into noncriminal occupations.

Background Dimensions

Social Class. Offenders of this type have usually resided for long periods of time in working-class (lower-class) neighborhoods in urban areas. They frequently lived as youngsters in deteriorated neighborhoods in which patterns of adult criminality were often readily observable. As adults, some of them have moved into more "respectable," middle-class neighborhoods, while at the same time maintaining their previous social ties to working-class friends.

Family Background. As juveniles, most of these offenders experienced family backgrounds of parental neglect and exposure to delinquency patterns. Intense interfamily tension did not usually characterize the family structure. Family members were on relatively good terms with one another, but the offender commonly was not subjected to close parental supervision. On occasion, this type had experienced a family background in which siblings were also delinquent or involved in criminality. In addition, the parents were on occasion involved in forms of criminality; hence, differential association with deviant family members played a significant part in career development.

Adult "heavy" professional offenders are usually involved in stable marital relationships and parental ties to offspring. Involvement in deviant behavior tends not to be disruptive of family relationships, for "heavy" criminals are rarely caught up in the correctional machinery that might create family disorganization.

Peer Group Associations. As a juvenile, this type of offender was involved in interaction within the structure of delinquent gangs or differential association with delinquent peers. In some cases, these delinquent peers form a recognizable gang, whereas in others they represent a loose confederation of offenders. In either case, the offender exhibited differential avoidance of nondelinquent juveniles in his community. Commonly, this type associated with a group of youths known in the area as troublemakers and delinquents, all of whom shared such characteristics as expulsion from school and unemployment. The peer structure provided group support for his hostile and cynical attitudes. The peer structure also provided social rewards for prowess in delinquent acts, in that peers often accorded high status to the most delinquent boys.

Adult "heavy" professional criminals continue to associate differentially with criminal peers. They may number among their friends many other "heavy" professionals. However, these individuals do not usually constitute a stable "mob" carrying on repeated acts of criminality. Instead, "mobs" or groups of lawbreakers are formed on the occasion of a specific criminal offense and disbanded at its conclusion. The constituent members of these "mobs" vary, so professional "heavies" are only loosely organized into a criminal confederation.

Contact with Defining Agencies. This type usually exhibited early involvement with the police. In many instances, his police contacts are considerably more common than his official record indicates. This type was also well-known to the juvenile court. His record is likely to show several juvenile probation experiences, culminating in placement in a correctional institution. Persons who dealt with the offender as a juvenile usually viewed him as a "tough kid," lacking insight and unconcerned about his delinquent conduct. In turn, the offender usually viewed law enforcement and correctional agents as "phonies."

The early adult history of this type is likely to show several commitments to penal institutions. Commonly, some of the criminal skills the person exhibits were acquired in this learning environment. As the developing professional acquires expertise in deviance and becomes more enmeshed in the world of professional criminality, prison becomes an occupational hazard he infrequently encounters. Accordingly, the correctional machinery has an insignificant effect on mature professional "heavy" criminals.

THE SEMIPROFESSIONAL PROPERTY CRIMINAL
ROLE CAREER[14]

Definitional Dimensions

Offense Behavior. Semiprofessional property offenders engage in strong-arm robberies, holdups, burglaries, larcenies, and similar direct assaults upon personal or private property. They employ crime skills which are relatively simple and uncomplicated. For example, strong-arm robbery does not involve much detailed planning and careful execution of the crime, but rather application of crude physical force in order to relieve a victim of his money. This is referred to as semiprofessional crime, because even though technical skill is not characteristic of these offenders, most of them attempt to carry on crime as an occupation.

Interactional Setting. Many of the offenses of the semiprofessional offender are two-person affairs involving an offender and a victim, for example, strong-arm robbery and liquor store and gas station stickups. On occasion, semiprofessionals operate in collections of several crime partners, as in instances of burglary and safe-robbery. In either event, the criminal act tends to be direct and unsophisticated, a complex interactional pattern rarely being involved.

Self-concept. Semiprofessional property offenders view themselves as criminals. Additionally, the semiprofessional sees himself as an individual who has few alternatives to criminal behavior and as a victim of a corrupt society in which everyone has a "racket." Thus the semiprofessional is relieved from any sense of guilt regarding his criminality by deflecting blame onto "the system."

Attitudes. The attitudes of the semiprofessional offender toward the police tend to be more hostile and antagonistic than is the case with professional "heavies." Doubtless this is in considerable part a function of the greater number of contacts with police agents experienced by this offender. In the same way, the semiprofessional's views of the courts and correctional agents are more hostile than those of the professional "heavy." Semiprofessionals also denigrate conventional occupations as a way of life, holding that "only slobs work." They frequently show a diffuse set of bitter and resentful atti-

[14]Don C. Gibbons, *Changing the Lawbreaker*, The Treatment of Delinquents and Criminals, © 1965. Reprinted by permission of Prentice-Hall, Inc., Englewood, Cliffs, New Jersey, pp. 104-6.

tudes toward, not only the police and correctional agents, but their parents, social agencies, and schools.

Role Career. Semiprofessional property offenders represent the more usual outcome of patterns of predatory gang delinquency, as contrasted to the professional "heavy" adult outcome. That is, most adult semiprofessional offenders exhibit juvenile backgrounds of predatory gang behavior, and many juvenile gang offenders continue in criminality as semiprofessionals. As an adult, the semiprofessional rapidly accumulates an extensive "rap sheet," or record of crimes and institutional commitments. Because of the low degree of skill involved in the criminality of the semiprofessionals, the risks of apprehension, conviction, and incarceration are high. Many semiprofessionals spend a considerable part of their early adult years in penal institutions, where they are likely to be identified as "right guys," or antiadministration inmates. It does not appear that conventional treatment efforts are successful in deflecting many of these persons away from continuation in crime. On the other hand, many of them ultimately do withdraw from crime careers upon reaching early middle age.

Background Dimensions

Social Class. See description of professional "heavy" criminals. Semiprofessionals are from similar social class origins.

Family Backgrounds. See description of professional "heavy" criminals. Semiprofessionals are from similar family backgrounds.

Peer Group Associations. See description of professional "heavy" criminals. Semiprofessionals experience similar peer group associations. However, semiprofessionals have usually been restricted in their interactional experiences to associations with other relatively unskilled offenders, so they have not had opportunities to learn the more esoteric or complex crime skills. In addition, semiprofessional offenders usually interact as adults with kindred types of individuals, rather than with professional criminals. That is, the noncriminal endeavors of these persons as they act out their general social roles take place within collectivities of noncriminal citizens or semiprofessional offenders.

Contact with Defining Agencies. See description of professional "heavy" criminals. Semiprofessionals experience similar agency contacts, particularly as juveniles. However, adult semiprofessional offenders spend major portions of their lives in penal institutions. Many are recidivists who enter, leave, and reenter prisons, so they are treatment failures. It appears that many of them become progressively more hostile in attitude and fixed in behavior as they undergo these recurrent prison commitments; contacts with defining agencies play a contributory role in the development of their deviant careers.

Some Evidence

One study indirectly related to the role-career descriptions in this chapter is Leroy Gould's statistical analysis of trends in car theft and bank robbery over the past several decades in the United States.[15] Gould indicates that the upsurge in these two forms of criminality has directly been related to the growing abundance of these "victims." Also, his data suggest that as these kinds of property increased, more amateur offenders than professionals tended to commit these crimes. Along a somewhat related line, in a study of a sample of bank robbers incarcerated in federal prisons, George Camp indicates that about half the robbers were amateurs rather than professional criminals.[16] This finding is in contrast to an earlier situation, in which bank robberies were usually the work of skilled criminals. Camp also found that both amateur and professional robbers in prison had usually robbed a bank as an act of desperation rather than as the result of careful planning.

Descriptive data on the characteristics of professional and semiprofessional offenders are available in considerable quantity, so certain contentions in the foregoing typological sketches are well supported. We have already noted a group of biographical and autobiographical reports concerning the social origins of offenders and their participation in crime.[17]

In an inquiry concerning armed robbery, Werner Einstadter studied several dozen paroled California robbers.[18] His report maintains that professional armed robbers usually go about lawbreaking in transitory partnerships; they do not band together into diffuse and persisting criminal collectivities made up of criminal friends. Einstadter also notes that "viewed as a type, the individual careerist assumes the posture of a man whose round of life never quite seems to meet the standards of middle-class convention. . . . Typically, the careerist represents one who lives on the fringes, more a 'night' dweller than a 'day' dweller. In his circle of intimate acquaintances are the hustler, the bookie, the gambler, and the pimp; the bartender, the taxidriver, and the bellhop."[19]

---

[15]Leroy C. Gould, "The Changing Structure of Property Crime in an Affluent Society," *Social Forces,* 48 (September 1969), 50–59.

[16]George M. Camp, "Nothing to Lose: A Study of Bank Robbery in America," (Ph.D. thesis, Yale University, 1967).

[17]See footnote 10. See also Donald MacKenzie, *Occupation: Thief* (Indianapolis: Bobbs-Merrill Co., 1955); Hutchins Hapgood, *Autobiography of a Thief* (New York: Fox, Duffield, 1930); John E. Conklin, *Robbery and the Criminal Justice System* (Philadelphia: J. B. Lippincott Co., 1972), pp. 59–78. Conklin presents a relatively crude typology of robbers: the professional robber, the opportunist robber, the addicted robber, and the alcoholic robber.

[18]Werner J. Einstadter, "The Social Organization of Armed Robbery," *Social Problems,* 17 (Summer 1969), 64–83.

[19]*Ibid.,* p. 82.

Numerous detailed investigations of semiprofessional offenders have been carried out. In one such research study, Sheldon and Eleanor Glueck examined the backgrounds and criminal histories of 500 Massachusetts Reformatory inmates who had been released from the institution in 1921–22. The Gluecks traced individuals up to 1926–27 and asserted that 80 percent had not been rehabilitated.[20] This early study seemed to point unequivocally to the conclusion that penal institutions are dismal failures. However, less than half the group was alleged to have committed felonies or other serious acts of lawbreaking. Recent evidence suggests that prisons are considerably more effective than formerly supposed.[21]

Study of the social backgrounds of these 500 offenders indicated that most of them had developed in disorganized families in slum areas and had experienced relatively wretched life situations. For example, about 75 percent of the inmates had backgrounds in which other family members were involved in criminality.[22]

John Gillin conducted another inquiry into the backgrounds of institutionalized offenders in Wisconsin.[23] In his investigation, Gillin compared murderers, sex offenders, and property criminals. Unfortunately, he lumped a variety of types of property criminals within the single category that he compared with sexual offenders and the murderers, and as a result his report presents a confused picture of the social origins of property violators.[24]

Norman Hayner provides a more theoretically satisfactory piece of work, in which he tested a series of hunches regarding five hypothesized offender types, one of which was the "heavy."[25] In this study, Hayner examined the case records of inmates in Washington State institutions to determine if certain types, including "alcoholic forgers" and "heavies," do exist. The study identified "heavies" as prisoners over twenty-five years old, who had been engaged in robbery or burglary as a crime pattern, so they were apparently semiprofessionals. Hayner discovered that these individuals had frequently attempted to escape from prison, exhibited antisocial personalities, and were defined as "right guys" by other inmates in the prison. The "heavies" had poor work records outside the institution, were often from families in which other members were delinquent or criminal, and were generally from lower socio-

---

[20]Sheldon Glueck and Eleanor Glueck, *500 Criminal Careers* (New York: Alfred A. Knopf, 1930).

[21]Daniel Glaser, *The Effectiveness of a Prison and Parole System* (Indianapolis: Bobbs-Merrill Co., 1964), pp. 13–35.

[22]Glueck and Glueck, *500 Criminal Careers*, pp. 112–13.

[23]John L. Gillin, *The Wisconsin Prisoner* (Madison: University of Wisconsin Press, 1946).

[24]*Ibid.*, pp. 14–16.

[25]Norman S. Hayner, "Characteristics of Five Offender Types," *American Sociological Review*, 26 (February 1961), 96–102.

economic status groups. As a result of this accumulation of unfavorable social characteristics, they were usually given long prison sentences.

The results of investigations by Clarence Shrag and his associates run parallel to the findings of Hayner. Schrag reported the social characteristics of "antisocial" prisoners known as "right guys" in the argot of prison culture.[26] Antisocial inmates are recidivists who show an evolving career pattern in lawbreaking that began with truancy and expressive theft during the adolescent period and developed into semiprofessional property criminality in adulthood. These prisoners show a background of low socioeconomic status and associations with delinquent companions or criminalistic siblings. They often come from relatively warm, stable family backgrounds, which are generally criminogenic because of the involvement of family members in deviance.

Roebuck conducted still another study that turned up findings compatible with those already enumerated.[27] He investigated the social backgrounds of a group of black offenders in the Washington, D.C., Reformatory by comparing these persons with inmates who had engaged in other kinds of criminality. The armed robbers were older than most of the other felons, had grown up in urban areas and in slum neighborhoods, had been inducted into delinquency early in their lives, and exhibited average intelligence ratings. Most of them had experienced dismal home conditions in which their families frequently depended on public assistance for support. Most were members of migrant families from the south. These characteristics are the sort enumerated in the typologies in this chapter, although these specific black robbers were perhaps from somewhat more deteriorated social surroundings than would be true of other samples of semiprofessional criminals, because the subjects were black and, as a consequence, were recipients of special kinds of social and economic discrimination.

Still other reports concerning semiprofessional property offenders are those by Richard Peterson et al.[28] and by Harold Frum,[29] who both discovered stable deviant careers. Collectively, these investigations all identify a type of criminal career, which we have labeled semiprofessional property crime. Although some specific items in the characterizations of semiprofessional offenders

---

[26]Clarence C. Schrag, "Some Foundations for a Theory of Correction," in *The Prison*, ed. Donald R. Cressey (New York: Holt, Rinehart and Winston, 1961), pp. 346–56; Schrag, "A Preliminary Criminal Typology," *Pacific Sociological Review*, 4 (Spring 1961), 11–16.

[27]Julian B. Roebuck and Mervyn L. Cadwallader, "The Negro Armed Robber as a Criminal Type: The Construction and Application of a Typology," *Pacific Sociological Review*, 4 (Spring 1961), 21–26.

[28]Richard A. Peterson, David J. Pittman, and Patricia O'Neal, "Stabilities in Deviance: A Study of Assaultive and Non-Assaultive Offenders," *Journal of Criminal Law, Criminology and Police Science*, 53 (March 1962), 44–48.

[29]Harold S. Frum, "Adult Criminal Offense Trends Following Juvenile Delinquency," *Journal of Criminal Law, Criminology and Police Science*, 49 (May–June 1958), 29–49.

might be debatable, the general accuracy of this portrait does not seem to be in question.

GANG DELINQUENCY AND ADULT PROPERTY CRIME

A rich body of empirical data is available on gang delinquency backgrounds out of which semiprofessional offenders develop in addition to evidence on their adult activities. Indeed, along with the large theoretical and research literature that has accumulated in recent years, Frederic Thrasher, Clifford Shaw, Henry McKay, and others provide detailed investigations of the gang world. The following sections provide a brief overview of sociological inquiry into gang delinquency.[30]

Early Work

The largest single study of gangs ever attempted is Thrasher's pioneering work in Chicago, in which he examined the activities of 1,313 male gangs. One of his conclusions, which has stood relatively unquestioned to the present, is that *"gangland represents a geographically and socially interstitial area in the city"* (emphasis in the original).[31] By "interstitial," Thrasher meant those spaces (interstices) that intervene between sections of the urban fabric, areas thought to be socially disorganized. Although we might argue against the characterization of the gangland as socially disorganized rather than as differentially organized, juvenile gangs are most frequently encountered in slum, deteriorated, working-class sections of the city.

Paralleling Thrasher's work in Chicago are the many reports of Shaw, McKay, and others.[32] Shaw and McKay presented a series of ecological studies demonstrating that gang delinquency tends to be concentrated in "delinquency areas" of the city, which are also slum neighborhoods characterized by high rates of social breakdown. They also contributed a number of detailed descriptions of delinquent *behavior* of urban gangs. These commentaries indicated that

[30]For a detailed review of this material, see Don C. Gibbons, *Delinquent Behavior* (Englewood Cliffs, N.J.: Prentice-Hall, 1970), pp. 102–41.

[31]Frederic M. Thrasher, *The Gang* (abridged and with a new introduction by James F. Short, Jr.) (Chicago: University of Chicago Press, 1963), p. 20.

[32]Clifford Shaw, *The Jack Roller* (Chicago: University of Chicago Press, 1930); Shaw and Maurice E. Moore, *The Natural History of a Delinquent Career* (Philadelphia: A Saifer, Publisher, 1951); Shaw, Henry D. McKay, and James F. McDonald, *Brothers in Crime* (Chicago: University of Chicago Press, 1938); Shaw and McKay, *Juvenile Delinquency in Urban Areas* (Chicago: University of Chicago Press, 1942); Shaw and McKay, *Social Factors in Juvenile Delinquency, Report on the Causes of Crime for the National Commission on Law Observance and Enforcement*, vol. 11 (Washington, D.C.: U.S. Government Printing Office, 1931).

most delinquent boys lack personality pathologies and are the products of learning situations in which criminal endeavors are initially learned as forms of hedonistic "fun." As they progress through careers in delinquency, deviant acts come to take on a more utilitarian character so that many of the boys ultimately acquire the skills and criminal sophistication of semiprofessional offenders.

Finally, in this collection of early works on delinquency are several other ecological investigations of delinquency rates and social conditions in urban areas.[33] These confirm contentions about linkages of gang delinquency to low socioeconomic status and other, related conditions.

Recent Theory and Research on Delinquent Subcultures[34]

Although gang delinquency has been a subject of persistent interest to sociologists since the 1920s, relatively little theorizing or research on gang misconduct was carried out in the interval between the aforementioned Chicago work and the 1950s. Publication in 1955 of Albert K. Cohen's *Delinquent Boys* triggered an impressive resurgence of speculative and empirical attention to delinquent gang activity. A massive body of argument and counterargument has grown out of Cohen's initial insights. In the same way, a large and valuable collection of research evidence produced in the past dozen years represents research material initially stimulated by Cohen's work. Clearly, his theoretical contributions are of great significance because of the seminal role they have played in the growth of *subcultural* theory and research. In the following pages, we shall examine some major developments in this area of inquiry, roughly in chronological order.

Cohen and Delinquent Subcultures

In his initial essay on gang delinquency, Cohen indicated that he was interested in accounting for the emergence of delinquent subcultures in working-class areas of American cities.[35] According to Cohen, a delinquent subculture may

[33]Bernard Lander, *Toward an Understanding of Juvenile Delinquency* (New York: Columbia University Press, 1954); David J. Bordua, "Juvenile Delinquency and 'Anomie': An Attempt at Replication," *Social Problems,* 6 (Winter 1958-59), 230–38; Roland J. Chilton, "Continuity in Delinquency Area Research: A Comparison of Studies for Baltimore, Detroit, and Indianapolis," *American Sociological Review,* 29 (February 1964), 71–83; Richard Quinney, "Crime, Delinquency, and Social Areas," *Journal of Research in Crime and Delinquency,* 1 (July 1964), 149–54. Additional ecological studies are discussed in Gibbons, *Delinquent Behavior,* pp. 103–13.

[34]For a summary of theory and research concerning gang delinquency, see Gibbons, *Delinquent Behavior,* pp. 102–41.

[35]Albert K. Cohen, *Delinquent Boys* (New York: The Free Press, 1955). On the issue of the social-class distribution of subcultural gang delinquency, Cohen argues: "It is our conclusion, by no means

be defined as "a way of life that has somehow become traditional among certain groups in American society. These groups are the boy's gangs that flourish most conspicuously in the 'delinquency neighborhoods' of our larger American cities."[36] The delinquent subculture revolves around *nonutilitarian, malicious,* and *negativistic* behavior. That is, Cohen asserts that interests other than rational utilitarian gain motivate much of the stealing and other behavior of gang delinquents so that gang offenders steal "for the hell of it." The malicious and negativistic character of gang behavior is revealed in a variety of ways, most commonly in observations that gang members reap enjoyment from discomfort they have caused others and take pride in reputations for "meanness."[37] Cohen also characterizes subcultural misbehavior in terms of *short-run hedonism,* indicated by a lack of long-term goals or planning on the part of gang members. Finally, *group autonomy* is a hallmark of subcultural deviance, and delinquent gangs are said to be solidary collectivities.[38]

Why did the delinquent subculture develop among lower-class boys? In brief, Cohen's answer is that working-class gang delinquency represents a social movement among juvenile delinquents. This subculture arose as a solution to *shared* problems of low status among working-class youths. In his words, "The crucial condition for the emergence of new cultural forms is the existence, *in effective interaction with one another,* of a number of actors with *similar problems of adjustment*" (emphasis in the original).[39]

The shared problem of low status or esteem among gang boys arises as a consequence of their placement in the social order: working-class youths experience status threats when they are evaluated in terms of a middle-class measuring rod—a set of social expectations of "good boys," centering about such traits as ambition, individual responsibility, possession of talents, asceticism, rationality, manners and courtesy, and control of physical aggression.[40] The exemplary youth, in the eyes of middle-class teachers and other important citizens, embodies most or all of these social characteristics. But the working-class boy has inadequately been socialized in these notions of proper behavior, so he finds himself at a competitive disadvantage in classrooms and other social arenas as he competes with middle-class peers for adult recognition. Again, to cite Cohen: "The delinquent subculture, we suggest, is a way

---

novel or startling, that juvenile delinquency and the delinquent subculture in particular are overwhelmingly concentrated in the male, working-class sector of the juvenile population" (*Delinquent Boys,* p. 37).

[36]*Ibid.,* p. 13.
[37]*Ibid.,* pp. 25–30.
[38]*Ibid.,* pp. 30–32.
[39]*Ibid.,* p. 59.
[40]*Ibid.,* pp. 84–93.

of dealing with the problems of adjustment we have described. These problems are chiefly status problems: certain children are denied status in the respectable society because they cannot meet the criteria of the respectable status system. The delinquent subculture deals with these problems by providing criteria of status which these children can meet."[41] These boys who withdraw from such situations of social hurt as the school find their way into the subculture of the gang, which provides them with a social setting insulating them against assaults on their self-esteem.

Cohen's original picture of gang delinquency was painted with a broad brush, relatively small areas of factual data being joined with big strokes of speculation. No wonder that a number of critics detected what they felt to be errors in this initial formulation. In their criticism, Gresham Sykes and David Matza contend that delinquents are at least partially committed to the dominant social order, experience guilt or shame when they engage in deviant acts, and contrive rationalizations or justifications for their acts of lawbreaking to assuage their guilt feelings.[42] Sykes and Matza then enumerate some of these "techniques of neutralization," which include denial of responsibility for one's behavior, denial of injury, and condemnation of the condemners. These notions represent a useful contribution in their own right, in that they direct attention to some of the ways offenders define the situation to exculpate themselves from guilt regarding violations of norms they regard as valid "in principle." However, a close reading of Cohen's theory indicates that he was not inattentive to the delinquent boy's sensitivity to middle-class ethical standards; the Sykes–Matza argument is compatible with that of Cohen.

Harold Wilensky and Charles Lebeaux have noted other defects in the Cohen theory,[43] and John Kitsuse and David Dietrick charged that Cohen failed to make a compelling case for the argument that working-class boys care about middle-class persons' views of them.[44] Kitsuse and Dietrick maintain that working-class boys are not oriented to status in middle-class systems. Accordingly, in their view, Cohen's notion of the delinquent subculture as a "reaction formation" is seriously undermined. They also contend that Cohen's description of delinquent subcultures is faulty, in that real-life delinquents are more businesslike in action and less directly malicious toward "respectable" persons than the theory suggests. Finally, they claim that the theory is ambiguous on the issue of how subcultures are maintained once they come into existence.

[41]*Ibid.*, p. 121.

[42]Gresham M. Sykes and David Matza, "Techniques of Neutralization: A Theory of Delinquency," *American Sociological Review,* 22 (December 1957), 664–70.

[43]Harold L. Wilensky and Charles N. Lebeaux, *Industrial Society and Social Welfare* (New York: Russell Sage Foundation, 1958), pp. 187–207.

[44]John I. Kitsuse and David C. Dietrick, *"Delinquent Boys:* A Critique," *American Sociological Review,* 24 (April 1959), 208–15.

Kitsuse and Dietrick propose an alternative formulation to that of Cohen, arguing that the original motives of delinquent actors for participation in gangs are varied. Once they get involved in the subculture, hostile responses by respectable adults, correctional agents, and others are directed at them. In turn, the offenders reject their rejectors through further deviant conduct. Thus, according to these authors, "the delinquent subculture persists because, once established, it creates for those who participate in it, the very problems which were the bases for its emergence."[45]

David Bordua also raises a series of questions about theories of subcultural delinquency, including Cohen's theory.[46] Bordua notes that, in most of these theories, the image of the delinquent is markedly different from that advanced by Thrasher many years ago. Although Thrasher's boys were caught up in the attractiveness of delinquent "fun," the delinquents of contemporary theorists are "driven" by stresses and anxieties emanating from a prejudicial and harsh social environment.[47] In addition, Bordua contends that Cohen's theory places undue emphasis on the nonutilitarian character of gang misconduct. Bordua also suggests that Cohen, as well as a number of other subcultural theorists, has failed to accord sufficient weight to family, ethnic, and certain other social variables in delinquency causation. In particular, Bordua suggests that class-linked family patterns may be the source of much of the stress delinquent boys experience. The relatively loosely structured parent–child relationships, absentee fathers, and other common characteristics of many working-class families may have much to do with the development of problems and, subsequently, delinquency in lower-class boys.[48]

Cohen has responded to some of these criticisms of his work. In a paper with James F. Short, he offers rejoinders to a number of critical points, including the assertion that more than one form of working-class gang delinquency exists.[49] Cohen and Short agreed with this view and suggested that lower-class subcultures include the parent–male subculture, the conflict-oriented subculture, the drug addict subculture, and semiprofessional theft subculture. The characteristics of the parent–male subculture are enumerated in *Delinquent Boys*. Cohen and Short use the label of "parent subculture" to suggest that other gang forms are specialized offshoots from it, thus "it is probably the

[45]*Ibid.*, 215.

[46]David J. Bordua, *Sociological Theories and their Implications for Juvenile Delinquency*, Children's Bureau, Juvenile Delinquency, Facts and Facets, no. 2 (Washington, D.C.: U.S. Government Printing Office, 1960); Bordua, "Delinquent Subcultures: Sociological Interpretations of Gang Delinquency," *Annals of the American Academy of Political and Social Science*, 338 (November 1961), 119–36; Bordua, "Some Comments on Theories of Group Delinquency," *Sociological Inquiry*, 32 (Spring 1962), 245–60.

[47]Bordua, "Delinquent Subcultures."

[48]Bordua, "Some Comments on Theories of Group Delinquency," 249–56.

[49]Albert K. Cohen and James F. Short, Jr., "Research in Delinquent Subcultures," *Journal of Social Issues*, 14, no. 3 (1958), 20–37.

most common variety in this country—indeed, it might be called the 'garden variety' of delinquent subculture. . . ."[50]

In endeavoring to account for the development of these different subcultural forms in individual neighborhoods, Cohen and Short laid much stress on an earlier paper by Solomon Kobrin,[51] who pointed out that areas vary in the extent to which conventional and criminal value systems are mutually integrated so that in some areas criminality is meshed with the local social structure. Adult criminals are prestigious citizens, active in local businesses, fraternal organizations, politics, and so on. They serve as local "heroes" or role models for juvenile apprentice criminals. In other neighborhoods, criminality is individualistic, uncontrolled, and alien to the conventional social organization. We shall see these notions reappearing in the work of Richard Cloward and Lloyd Ohlin.

Delinquency and Opportunity Structures

Chapter Eight has already traced the development of anomie theory originating with Durkheim, through the work of Merton, to the application of this argument to delinquency in the contentions of Cloward and Ohlin. Let us briefly reexamine these latter claims.[52]

This body of theory represents a full-scale alternative rather than some exceptions to parts of the Cohen argument. For Cloward and Ohlin, the raw material for delinquent gangs consists of boys concerned about economic injustice rather than with middle-class status. They aver: "It is our view that many discontented lower-class youth do not wish to adopt a middle-class way of life or to disrupt their present associations and negotiate passage into middle-class groups. The solution they seek entails the acquisition of higher position in terms of lower-class rather than middle-class criteria."[53]

Cloward and Ohlin argue that working-class gang delinquent subcultures are to be understood in the following terms. Lower-class boys share a common American value commitment to "success," measured largely in material terms. But these youths are at a competitive disadvantage compared to their middle-status counterparts. Either they do not have access to legitimate or conventional means to reach these success goals, or if they do have objective opportunities for achievement, they perceive their chances of success as circumscribed. Accordingly, for many working-class boys, a severe disjunction

[50]*Ibid.*, p. 24.

[51]Solomon Kobrin, "The Conflict of Values in Delinquency Areas," *American Sociological Review*, 16 (October 1951), 653–61.

[52]Richard A. Cloward and Lloyd E. Ohlin, *Delinquency and Opportunity* (New York: The Free Press, 1960).

[53]*Ibid.*, p. 92.

exists between aspiration levels and expectations or between what they want out of life and what they anticipate they will receive. This goals–means discrepancy in turn generates pressure to engage in deviant behavior.[54] Cloward and Ohlin summarize their position thus:

> Our hypothesis can be summarized as follows: The disparity between what lower-class youth are led to want and what is actually available to them is the source of a major problem of adjustment. Adolescents who form delinquent subcultures, we suggest, have internalized an emphasis upon conventional goals. Faced with limitations on legitimate avanues of access to these goals, and unable to revise their aspirations downward, they experience intense frustrations; the exploration of nonconformist alternatives may be the result.[55]

Opportunity structures for deviant behavior greatly influence the particular adaptation working-class youths assume. Borrowing from the insights of Kobrin, Cloward and Ohlin argue that integration of criminal and conformist patterns of social organization characterize some lower-class areas; whereas stable criminal networks are lacking in others. In the organized, criminal neighborhood, "criminalistic" gang subcultures develop in which boys are involved in instrumental acts of theft and in careers that often lead eventually to adult criminal behavior. This community produces the "budding gangster." In areas lacking in criminal traditions, gang delinquency tends to take the form of "conflict" subcultural behavior in which gang fighting ("bopping" and "rumbles") predominates. Some boys who are failures in both the legitimate and illegitimate opportunity structures disengage from the competitive struggle and withdraw into the "retreatist" subculture of the drug addict.

Reactions to the Cloward and Ohlin theory have generally been extremely favorable. A number of action programs for the prevention and amelioration of juvenile crime have been formulated on the basis of opportunity structure theory.[56] Still, a series of critical comments have been advanced on this theory.[57] Cloward and Ohlin's definition of subcultures has been said to limit their theory to a minority of all delinquents. Critics have contended that much gang delinquency in working-class areas is more spontaneous and unstructured than Cloward and Ohlin would have us believe. One authority has termed many of these deviant collectivities "near groups," to highlight their shifting

[54]*Ibid.*, pp. 77–143.

[55]*Ibid.*, p. 86.

[56]Gibbons, *Delinquent Behavior*, pp. 179–82.

[57]Bordua, "Delinquent Subcultures," "Some Comments on Theories of Group Delinquency"; David Matza, review of *Delinquency and Opportunity, American Journal of Sociology*, 60 (May 1961), 631–33; Clarence C. Schrag, "Delinquency and Opportunity: Analysis of a Theory," *Sociology and Social Research*, 46 (January 1962), 167–75.

membership, ambiguous role definitions, lack of group identifications, and other characteristics.[58] Regarding this objection, the definition of subcultures could be liberalized without abandoning the major ingredients of the theory.

Bordua and others have assessed the opportunity structure formulation and raised questions about its failure to deal systematically with variations in working-class family structures, racial factors, and other background variations among different working-class groups.[59] This body of commentary has suggested that real-life social structure in a society such as the United States is exceedingly complex, comprised of interwoven social variables, which in combination produce behavioral outcomes such as delinquency. In short, existing theories of gang delinquency are not yet rich or elaborate enough to encompass the varieties of real-life experience.

Lower-Class Focal Concerns and Delinquency

Walter B. Miller has proposed another explanation of gang behavior, which is strikingly at variance with that of Cohen.[60] For Miller, the structure of lower-class life plays the dominant role in bringing forth gang delinquency—the product of long established, durable cultural traditions of lower-class life rather than the result of responses to conflicts with middle-class values.

One of the major structural patterns in lower-class society is what Miller calls a female-based household, in which one or more adult females provide the stability of the family unit. The mother and older daughters play multiple roles, providing economic support for the family unit as well as discharging the household and affectional duties. This kind of family structure results from the practice of serial monogamy, in which women are involved in repetitive sequences of mate-finding, legal or common-law marriage, and divorce or desertion. One result is that the household may be made up of a number of children, each of whom has been born to the same mother but a different father.

For the male who grows up in the female-dominated family, life is fraught with anxieties about sex-role identification. Verbal assertions that men are "no damn good" assault the young male on all sides. Because of this situation,

[58]Lewis Yablonsky, "The Delinquent Gang as a Near-Group," Social Problems, 7 (Fall 1959), 108–17.

[59]Bordua, "Some Comments on Theories of Group Delinquency," 250–52.

[60]Walter B. Miller, "Lower Class Culture as a Generating Milieu of Gang Delinquency," Journal of Social Issues, 14, no. 3 (1958), 5–19; Miller, "Implications of Urban Lower Class Culture for Social Work," Social Service Review, 33 (September 1959), 219–36; Miller, "Preventive Work with Street Corner Groups: Boston Delinquency Project," Annals of the American Academy of Political and Social Science, 322 (March 1959), 97–106; Miller, "The Impact of a 'Total-Community' Delinquency Control Project," Social Problems, 10 (Fall 1962), 168–91; William C. Kvaraceus and Walter B. Miller, Delinquent Behavior: Culture and the Individual (Washington, D.C.: National Education Association, 1959).

the boy is concerned about becoming a "real man" as quickly as possible. The male adolescent peer group, territorially located in the urban streets, provides the training ground and milieu in which lower-class males seek a sense of maleness, status, and belonging.

These elements, along with the pervasive sense of material and social deprivation common to lower-class citizens, result in life patterns and experiences organized around what Miller calls focal concerns, which represent a series of broad themes that condition the specific acts of lower-class persons. The focal concerns of lower-class society include "trouble," "toughness," "smartness," "excitement," "fate," and "autonomy." Trouble refers to a dominant concern about avoiding entanglements with the police, social welfare agencies, and similar bodies—encounters that are an ever-present possibility in this segment of society—whereas toughness denotes a concern for continued demonstrations of bravery, daring, and other traits denoting masculinity and "hardness." Smartness is a label for such things as the ability to dupe or outwit others, live by one's wits, and earn a livelihood through a "hustle" (pimping and the like). Excitement is a generic concern for seeking out weekend activities to disrupt the monotony of weekday routine jobs; and fate has to do with definitions by lower-class citizens that forces over which they have little control rule their lives, that "luck" plays a major part in their life chances. Finally, autonomy refers to a profound concern about avoiding control or domination by others.

These structural elements and focal concerns combine in several ways to produce criminality. Those who respond to some of these focal concerns automatically violate the law through their behavior. In situations where they have a choice of alternative lines of conduct, lower-class persons select a deviant form of activity as the most attractive. In summary, Miller argues that to be lower class in contemporary American society is to be in a social situation that contains a variety of direct influences toward deviant conduct, one form of which is juvenile delinquency.

Miller's notions have not escaped criticism.[63] First, Miller fails to account for the varieties of gang delinquency other students have posited. Some offenders steal, some "rumble," and some "shoot dope," but Miller does not offer much explanation for these variations. Miller also fails to spell out the detailed variations observed in patterns of lower-class culture. His characterization seems to be most applicable to certain urban, slum area groups, particularly blacks, and hardly descriptive of such other lower-class groups as Italian or Chinese. Specifically, the picture of serial monogamy and female-based households is accurate principally for blacks but does not hold for other low income, disadvantaged groups. A third claim centers about the danger of tautology in the focal concerns Miller uses to account for delinquent con-

---

[63]Bordua, "Some Comments on Theories of Group Delinquency," "Delinquent Subcultures."

duct. Miller is not always careful to distinguish between observations about these interests and evidence of the behavior they are designed to explain. Finally, Bordua has observed that Miller has not effectively refuted Cohen's contention that working-class boys are sensitive to middle-class standards.[64] In Bordua's view, both Cohen and Miller could be partially correct. Perhaps many lower-class boys do not initially internalize middle-class norms as part of their socialization, but when they get into schools and other competitive situations, these status-measuring standards are forced on them. These experiences may then alienate lower-class boys, driving them into delinquent subcultures. Note the similarity of this line of conjecture to that of Kitsuse and Dietrick.

We agree with Bordua, who suggests that the description of lower-class focal concerns stands as a detailed ethnography of working-class life, which fills in some of the descriptive gaps in the Cohen and Cloward and Ohlin statements.[65]

Other Voices

The three lines of analysis we have examined to this point are the best-known and influential theories regarding working-class delinquency, but other views have been put forth. Herbert Bloch and Arthur Niederhoffer claim that a cross-cultural perspective on youth behavior is needed to correct the ethnocentric bias in Cohen's theory.[66] They contend that adolescent crises centered about the transition from childhood to adulthood occur in all societies, and ganging is the universal response to these problems. In this sense, lower-class delinquent gangs have much in common with middle-class ones, and they in turn share many ingredients with peer collectivities in other lands.

Bloch and Niederhoffer make a good deal of sense when commenting on structural similarities among adolescent groups in various locales. However, anthropological observations of questionable accuracy flaw their thesis in a number of places, as do highly suspect assertions regarding American society, such as the claim that class or status differentials are disappearing in this country.[67] Most important, although they raise some challenges to parts of Cohen's description of gang behavior, the cornerstone of his argument remains

[64]Bordua, "Delinquent Subcultures," pp. 129–30.

[65]For one effort to reconcile these discrepant views on lower-class values, see Hyman Rodman, "The Lower-Class Value Stretch," *Social Forces*, 42 (December 1963), 205–15. Rodman argues that lower-class persons have a wider range of values than others within the society. They share general societal values with members of other classes, but additionally they have stretched these values or developed alternative ones that help them to adjust to their deprived circumstances. See also Herbert H. Hyman, "The Value Systems of Different Classes: A Social Psychological Contribution to the Analysis of Social Stratification," in *Class, Status and Power*, ed. Reinhard Bendix and Seymour Lipset (New York: The Free Press, 1953), pp. 426–42.

[66]Herbert A. Bloch and Arthur Niederhoffer, *The Gang* (New York: Philosophical Library, 1958).

[67]*Ibid.*, p. 175.

undisturbed: serious, repetitive, organized, subcultural delinquency is a particularly peculiar working-class phenomenon in the United States, qualitatively different from peer behavior in other strata or in most other cultures. In consequence, more than an adolescent crisis theory is needed to account for the particular form working-class adolescent conduct takes.

Another discordant voice is that of Lewis Yablonsky, who maintains that the central figures in working-class gangs are sociopaths—socially deficient boys who cannot manage the social struggle as adequately as other lower-class youths but who find in the gang a social structure in which they can survive.[68] Critics of Yablonsky's view have not treated him kindly, charging that he has little or no evidence for the sociopathy hypothesis independent of the aggressive delinquency it is supposed to explain.[69]

One final contribution, which represents something of an antidote to certain theories of delinquency, is that of Matza and Sykes, which stresses the role of "subterranean" values in delinquency.[70] They suggest that the view of middle-class culture, which emphasizes ascetic devotion to thrift, hard labor at a work task defined as a calling, and so on, is one-sided. Many conventional citizens have pursued other respectable but subterranean or unpublicized values, such as hedonistic fun or tolerance for certain kinds of aggression and violence. Thus, the delinquent's search for "kicks," disdain for work, desire for the "big score," and posture of aggressive toughness make him an exaggerated and immature version of many middle-class citizens. The substance of these ideas is that delinquency may have considerable positive appeal to youngsters at all social-class levels, including those in the working class, who for one reason or another are indifferent to or alienated from schools, adult role-preparation, and so forth.

Research on Delinquent Subcultures[71]

These varied lines of explanation for gang delinquency present a bewildering pattern of conflicting claims. Each theory is plausible, at least until we hear the criticisms or we are confronted with a theoretical competitor. Clearly, a mass of hard evidence is necessary to adjudicate among these theoretical

[68]Lewis Yablonsky, *The Violent Gang* (New York: The Macmillan Co., 1962).

[69]Solomon Kobrin, review of *The Violent Gang*, *American Sociological Review*, 28 (April 1963) 316–17.

[70]David Matza and Gresham M. Sykes, "Juvenile Delinquency and Subterranean Values," *American Sociological Review*, 26 (October 1961), 712–19; Matza; *Delinquency and Drift* (New York: John Wiley & Sons, 1964).

[71]Several collections of research on delinquent subcultures are available, including James F. Short, Jr., ed. *Gang Delinquency and Delinquent Subcultures* (New York: Harper & Row, Publishers, 1968); Malcolm W. Klein, ed. *Juvenile Gangs in Context* (Englewood Cliffs, N.J.: Prentice-Hall, 1967). See Klein's introduction, pp. 1–12, for a good brief assessment of the current state of affairs regarding subcultural research.

contenders. Let us look at some of the data produced on working-class delinquency. A word of warning is in order before we turn to this material. The research findings will not magically reduce the argument about gang delinquency to one set of straightforward propositions. Rather, the evidence is likely to make an explanation of gang delinquency even more complex, in that it reflects the diversity and richness of real life.

What do lower-class boys do in the way of delinquent conduct? Is subcultural deviance patterned as Cohen and Short, and Cloward and Ohlin suggest? Gerald Robin conducted an investigation in Philadelphia in which he studied the official and unofficial police records of over 700 black male members of 27 gangs in that city.[72] Most of these youths came to the attention of the police before they were fifteen years old. They showed progressive movement toward deviant acts of increasing seriousness, which in many cases culminated in adult criminal careers. Robin maintains that although most of these subjects had committed a diversified collection of delinquent acts, about two-thirds had engaged in at least one offense involving physical violence. He interprets this finding as support for the claims of Cloward and Ohlin concerning the existence of a conflict subculture in delinquency.[73]

In two separate studies, Irving Spergel has provided evidence that seems to confirm the Cloward and Ohlin description of different delinquent subcultures.[74] His research in Chicago indicated that delinquency and crime tended toward a criminalistic form in a relatively stable black slum area, but in a more unstable neighborhood criminality was untrammeled and violent.[75] In his New York City investigation, Spergel indicates that conflict behavior was most common in Slumtown, a disorganized area, whereas criminal delinquency was oriented around theft activities in one relatively integrated neighborhood and around racketeering in another community area heavily populated by Italian-Americans.[76] Spergel's material suggesting that criminalistic delinquency comes in several varieties provides a footnote to the Cloward and Ohlin framework.

Studies in Chicago by James Short and others provide a rich body of empirical evidence on gang behavior.[77] In one investigation they examined the delin-

[72]Gerald D. Robin, "Gang Member Delinquency: Its Extent, Sequence and Typology," *Journal of Criminal Law, Criminology and Police Science*, 55 (March 1964), 59–69.

[73]*Ibid.*, pp. 64–65.

[74]Irving Spergel, "Male Young Adult Criminality, Deviant Values, and Differential Opportunities in Two Lower Class Negro Neighborhoods," *Social Problems*, 10 (Winter 1963), 237–50; Spergel, "An Exploratory Research in Delinquent Subcultures," *Social Service Review*, 35 (March 1961), 33–47; Spergel, *Rocketville, Slumtown, Haulburg* (Chicago: University of Chicago Press, 1964).

[75]Spergel, "Male Young Adult Criminality."

[76]Spergel, *Racketville, Slumtown, Haulburg*.

[77]James F. Short, Jr., "Gang Delinquency and Anomie," in *Anomie and Deviant Behavior*, ed. Marshall B. Clinard (New York: The Free Press, 1964), pp. 98–127; Short and Fred L. Strodtbeck, *Group Process and Gang Delinquency* (Chicago: University of Chicago Press, 1965).

quent and nondelinquent conduct of about 600 members of Chicago gangs, in which street workers maintained detailed records of the day-to-day activities of these boys. The findings indicate that most of the offenders are involved in a wide range of deviant and nondeviant acts rather than in the narrowly focused patterns Cloward and Ohlin suggest. Short and his colleagues argue that an undifferentiated "parent delinquent subculture" exists from which more specialized deviant groups emerge. In other words, they suggest that the generic form of gang behavior involves behavioral versatility and that, from this broad form, cliques and sub-groups branch off into more specialized careers in deviant conduct.[78]

A study by Albert Reiss provides a final bit of information on gang behavior of a group of lower-class delinquent males in Nashville, Tennessee.[79] Their activities included participation in a complex structure of relationships with adult homosexuals in which the boys submitted to adult fellators in exchange for pay, an interaction pattern they conceptualize as strictly a business transaction.

These seemingly contradictory characterizations of gang delinquency, indicating existence of different subcultures in some but not in others, can perhaps be reconciled. Gang misconduct may take a number of forms, both in terms of the degree of organization among the deviant actors and in the kind of activity in which they engage. We suggest that relatively crystallized forms of conflict delinquency may be most common in large cities and quite uncommon in smaller communities. Gang structure may be influenced by ethnic variables, variations in neighborhood organization and community structure, and other contingencies of this sort. The variability in the descriptive data may be a reflection of the diversity of behavior in the real world of delinquents.

Another research problem attacked recently is the matter of social-class correlates of delinquency, neighborhood characteristics and deviant patterns, and related topics. Reiss and Albert Rhodes have thrown much light on the relationships between delinquent conduct and socioeconomic position.[80] In a study dealing with a large number of juvenile males in the Nashville metropolitan area, they found that no simple or uniform linkage exists between social-class position and delinquency. Although those boys most frequently encountered in the population of officially designated delinquents are from

[78]Short, "Gang Delinquency and Anomie," pp. 103–5; Short, Ray A. Tennyson, and Kenneth I. Howard, "Behavior Dimensions of Gang Delinquency," in Short and Strodtbeck, Group Process and Gang Delinquency.

[79]Albert J. Reiss, Jr., "The Social Integration of Queers and Peers," Social Problems, 9 (Fall 1961), 102–20.

[80]Albert J. Reiss, Jr., and Albert Lewis Rhodes, "The Distribution of Juvenile Delinquency in the Social Class Structure," American Sociological Review, 26 (October 1961), 720–32.

the lower class, delinquency life chances or risks are not the same for all working-class youths. Juvenile misconduct is most common in homogeneous lower-class neighborhoods and less usual in mixed social status neighborhoods. Accordingly, Reiss and Rhodes maintain that social class structure and cultural traditions of the community areas condition the behavior of working-class boys. Youths whose parents are working-class individuals have a high risk of delinquent involvement if they live in areas populated largely by other lower-class persons, but they are not so likely to become offenders if they live in neighborhoods of mixed or predominantly middle-class socioeconomic status.

In his New York City study, Spergel claims to have identified separate theft, racketeering, and conflict subcultures existing in distinct lower-class neighborhoods.[81] Spergel describes Slumtown, the locale of conflict behavior, as an area with a Puerto Rican and black population suffering from extremely low socioeconomic status and the highest index of social breakdown as shown by public assistance caseloads, venereal disease rates, and other indicators of social liabilities. Haulburg, the community area in which theft behavior predominated, was populated by second generation Americans of European ancestry and stood highest of the three in measures of socioeconomic status, occupational structure, and absence of social breakdown. Racketville was intermediate on most of these measures of community structure. These results generally confirm the claims of Cloward and Ohlin regarding neighborhood variations in illegitimate opportunity structures, although some ambiguity exists as to how Spergel identified these neighborhoods and what techniques he used to develop these descriptions.[82]

A number of lines of evidence have also accumulated regarding social-psychological characteristics of gang delinquents.[83] One test of the Cloward and Ohlin formulation regarding delinquents' hypothesized disjunction between occupational aspirations and expectations, in other words, between what boys want and what they expect to get out of life, is found in Spergel's New York City study.[84] He reports that delinquent boys in Slumtown and Haulburg had a marked disparity between aspirations and expectations,

[81]Spergel, *Racketville, Slumtown, Haulburg*, pp. 2–28.

[82]See also Erdman B. Palmore and Phillip E. Hammond, "Interacting Factors in Juvenile Delinquency," *American Sociological Review*, 29 (December 1964), 848–54. This study showed that delinquency was most common in New Haven, Connecticut among black youngsters who were school failures and who lived in situations of high family and neighborhood deviation. Palmore and Hammond view these data as consistent with the Cloward and Ohlin view that delinquency should be most frequent among youths who are cut off from legitimate opportunities and who live in circumstances in which illegitimate opportunities are common.

[83]John W. Kinch, "Self-Conceptions of Types of Delinquents," *Sociological Inquiry*, 32 (Spring 1962), 228–34; Sethard Fisher, "Varieties of Juvenile Delinquency," *British Journal of Criminology*, 2 (January 1962), 251–61.

[84]Spergel, *Racketville, Slumtown, Haulburg*, pp. 93–123.

whereas the young Racketville deviants had aspirations and expectations in close harmony. Thus, these results partially confirm the Cloward and Ohlin theory, although Spergel's cases were so few as to require that the findings be interpreted with caution. Delbert Elliott has also reported on the question of perceptions of legitimate opportunities on the part of delinquent boys.[85] He found that *both* middle-class and lower-class delinquents in his sample perceived their life chances as more limited than did the nondelinquent youths.

The Chicago material of Short and others presents the most detailed and comprehensive data regarding position discontent, delinquent norms and values, and related matters.[86] On the question of aspirations contrasted to perceptions of opportunities, these findings show that delinquents exhibit greater discrepancies between occupational aspirations and expectations than do nondelinquents. More delinquent boys view educational opportunities as closed to them than do nonoffenders. But these relationships are far from clear, for black boys who show the greatest divergence between their aspirations and expectations, compared to the achievements of their fathers, are at the same time least delinquent. Also, contrary to the hypotheses in the Cloward and Ohlin theory, those boys who had high educational aspirations but poor school adjustment or perceived educational opportunities as relatively closed were less delinquent than those youths with low educational aspirations.[87] Short interprets these results in the following way: "A possible explanation of findings reported in this paper lies in the hypothesis that for our boys, high aspirations are indicative of identification with conventional values and institutions. The stake in conformity thus indexed serves to protect the boys from delinquency involvement."[88]

Short and his colleagues have also examined the question of value commitments of delinquent boys. They find that, contrary to theories contending

[85]Delbert S. Elliott, "Delinquency and Perceived Opportunity," *Sociological Inquiry*, 32 (Spring 1962), 216–27.

[86]Short, "Gang Delinquency and Anomie"; Short and Strodtbeck, *Group Process and Gang Delinquency*.

[87]Short, "Gang Delinquency and Anomie," pp. 105–15.

[88]*Ibid.*, p. 115. On the question of "insulation" from delinquency, see also Walter C. Reckless, Simon Dinitz, and Ellen Murray, "Self Concept as an Insulator Against Delinquency," *American Sociological Review*, 21 (December 1956), 744–56; Reckless, Dinitz, and Barbara Kay, "The Self Component in Potential Delinquency and Potential Non-delinquency," *American Sociological Review*, 22 (October 1957), 566–70; Reckless, Dinitz, and Murray, " 'The Good Boy' in a High Delinquency Area," *Journal of Criminal Law, Criminology and Police Science*, 48 (May–June 1957), 18–25; Dinitz, Kay, and Reckless, "Group Gradients in Delinquency Potential and Achievement Scores of Sixth Graders," *American Journal of Orthopsychiatry*, 28 (July 1958), 598–605; Jon Simpson, Dinitz, Kay, and Reckless, "Delinquency Potential of Pre-Adolescents in High Delinquency Areas," *British Journal of Delinquency*, 10 (January 1960), 211–15; Frank R. Scarpitti, Murray, Dinitz, and Reckless, "The 'Good' Boy in a High Delinquency Area: Four Years Later," *American Sociological Review*, 25 (August 1960), 555–58; Dinitz, Scarpitti, and Reckless, "Delinquency Vulnerability: A Cross Group and Longitudinal Analysis," *American Sociological Review*, 28 (August 1962), 515–17.

that subcultural delinquents are in rebellion against middle-class ideals, individual offenders verbalize allegiance to such middle-class values as cohesive family life, stable jobs, and conformist behavior.[89] However, the structure of gang life inhibits youngsters from expressing those sentiments openly so that a state of "pluralistic ignorance" prevails in which gang members see each other in distorted terms. Finally, and most important, Short argues that although gang behavior is not a direct revolt against middle-class values or a protest against generalized invidious rankings of the boys by the wider society, status considerations are nevertheless of major importance in comprehending lower-class delinquency. He contends that delinquent activities are often a response to the real or imagined status threats boys experience and that most of these status deprivations emanate from the more immediate social world, including the threats to the boys' status as males, gang members, and so on.[90]

Several theorists have argued that gang delinquency is not a response to strongly held motivation or social position discontent. For example, Matza offers a portrait of delinquents as "drifters" into misconduct whose attachment to prosocial norms has been temporarily broken by various circumstances and neutralizing rationalizations so that they can engage in misbehavior.[91] Similarly, Scott Briar and Irving Piliavin propose a picture of delinquency causation stressing lack of commitment to conformity rather than positive motivation to delinquency.[92] As we have indicated, the research of Short and Strodtbeck confirms much of this picture of drifting, uncommitted delinquents. Some other lines of evidence also support this interpretation of delinquency, which links it to negative life circumstances and lack of commitment, including Downes' study in London, England.[93] Then, too, Travis Hirschi has turned up a measure of support for this characterization of delinquents as lacking in commitment to conformity, with attenuated attachments to parents, school, and peers.[94]

An Evaluation

At this point, the reader may well ask, "What does it all mean?" By way of a brief summing up, these things can be said about gang delinquency. First, gang delinquents frequently become adult criminals, although many working-class deviant youngsters drift out of delinquency and into conventional

---

[89]Short, "Gang Delinquency and Anomie," pp. 115-21. For some parallel findings, see Edward Rothstein, "Attributes Related to High School Status: A Comparison of the Perceptions of Delinquent and Non-delinquent Boys," *Social Problems*, 10 (Summer 1962), 75-83.

[90]Short, "Gang Delinquency and Anomie," pp. 117-27.

[91]Matza, *Delinquency and Drift*.

[92]Scott Briar and Irving Piliavin, "Delinquency, Situational Inducements, and Commitment to Conformity," *Social Problems*, 13 (Summer 1965), 35-45.

[93]David Downes, *The Delinquent Solution* (New York: The Free Press, 1966).

[94]Travis Hirschi, *Causes of Delinquency* (Berkeley: University of California Press, 1969).

life patterns. Second, the ecological habitat of gang behavior is the lower-class neighborhood of the city. Third, explanations of the development and persistence of gang misbehavior are not easily evaluated. Most of the formulations examined in these pages are polemic in tone, putting forth an overdrawn and incomplete version of the mainsprings of subcultural delinquency. The empirical world resists being forced into the patterns existing theories represent.

We are tempted to take refuge in a fuzzy eclecticism by arguing that all the variables identified in the different theories play their part in delinquency. But we do not counsel that course of action. Instead, we suggest that although the motivations that lead boys into gang delinquency vary, they are identifiable. A complete census of these psychological sources of involvement in youthful deviance would probably indicate that existing theories have already identified a good many of them. Some lower-class juveniles are in gangs because of social status concerns stemming from their placement at the bottom of the social order. For some youths, the pervasive deprivations of lower-class life provide the psychological fuel that propels them toward gangs. For others, the status problems that lead toward deviant peer groups are more immediate, centering about the need to be protected by the gang from assaults by other boys, masculinity anxieties, and so on. These different motivational dynamics are of varied importance in separate cohorts of lower-class youths, so boys in black slums may face problems different from lower-class whites in smaller cities. There is not one route to the gang; there are several.

In addition, the preceding pages have suggested that we need to examine a series of intervening variables if we are to understand how this boy became a delinquent while another one, similar to the first, became an exemplary citizen. One intervening variable alluded to at various points is the influence of variations in family structure.[95] Highly cohesive lower-class families probably turn out juveniles with a marked stake in conformity. These boys encounter adversity in the school system and elsewhere, but instead of becoming delinquent they zealously pursue success. Along a somewhat different line, we need to be more sensitive than has been customary to fortuitous factors and feedback processes in delinquency. Conceivably, one contingency that influences the development of delinquent careers of working-class boys is the experience of early police apprehension, often an almost chance happening. We need also to examine the matter hinted at in several of the foregoing studies, that delinquency begets more delinquency. We may well find that, as boys get caught up in flirtations with deviant behavior, they encounter societal rejection which then impairs their adjustment to school and other social institutions, so they are driven further into delinquent conduct. This

[95]Family factors in delinquency are discussed in Chapter Nine. See also Gibbons, *Delinquent Behavior*, pp. 132–35 for a review of evidence on family patterns and delinquency. See Gibbons, *Delinquent Behavior*, pp. 135–38 for a review of school factors and delinquency.

adds up to an extremely detailed picture of delinquency. To portray it otherwise would be to do violence to the facts.

SUMMARY

In this chapter we have taken a detailed look at three of the kinds of offenders most people have in mind when they think of crime and criminals. Chapter Thirteen continues this study of property offenders but pays attention to some kinds of illegality not so widely attended to as those in this chapter. However, as we shall see, certain of these undramatic forms of criminality may well be more costly in terms of monetary losses to the public than the criminality considered to this point.

13

ADDITIONAL PROPERTY OFFENDER CAREERS

The preceding chapter considered three kinds of lawbreaking that the man on the street thinks of as "crime." In this chapter, we turn to some additional forms of illegality involving property that are not so widely known or are less subject to public denunciation as criminality. Two of these, amateur shoplifting and naïve check forgery, are extremely common forms of predatory conduct usually directed at retail stores and other business concerns. The evidence seems to indicate that shoplifting and "bad checks" are normal events in business life, in that merchandisers expect a large volume of this conduct to take place. In turn, they adopt pricing policies anticipating business losses from thefts and checks that "bounce" (as well as from pilferage by employees). Those cases reported to the police represent only a fraction of the instances known to store personnel or which occur but are undetected even by the business establishment. "Nice people" from moderate economic circumstances carry on a good many of these acts of shoplifting or check forgery. They do not fit the image of the slum area "tough guy," which probably has much to do with the infrequent referral of such persons to the police.

This chapter also takes up the matter of automobile theft—"joyriding"—as still another form of property crime. Joyriders are young adults who steal cars for recreational purposes rather than to "strip" them and sell the parts for profit. Finally, this chapter is concerned with the property offender, "one-time loser." This role career is represented by relatively naïve and unsophisticated offenders who do not shoplift, forge checks, or steal cars, but steal some amount of property from an individual or from an organization other than a retail store. The label "one-time loser" suggests the nature of this kind of lawbreaking. Large numbers of persons manage to find their way into isolated but frequently serious instances of illegal conduct in which they commit a single burglary or theft. Although much deviant behavior of this kind no doubt goes unreported, some is not ignored. Indeed, some culprits involved in this kind of idiosyncratic criminality are in state prisons serving relatively long sentences.

Each of these forms of criminal conduct will be taken up in some detail.

However, several general lines of causal commentary regarding much of this behavior might be advanced at this point. In Chapter Nine, we reviewed some of the contentions of Edwin Lemert regarding the development of deviant careers.[1] Two sources of deviant conduct he identifies seem particularly relevant to much of the criminal behavior under discussion. One has to do with value pluralism in the United States, in which groups holding one set of standards find they must conform to another, discordant set of values. Insofar as these persons violate the alien standards, their actions come to be labeled deviant.[2] Lemert offers a number of illustrations of this form of deviance, including the case of "totin' " or petty theft by rural black migrants. We suggest that petty thievery is a not uncommon kind of activity that is at least tolerated, if not actually supported, by value preferences in many rural areas in the United States. Thus, amateur or casual offenders may define a good many isolated acts of larceny as "borrowing" so that such activities are fairly commonplace. Nonetheless, some of these persons are unlucky enough to be sternly dealt with in the correctional process and receive prison sentences for their actions.

The second etiological hypothesis that Lemert advances centers about "risk taking," in which individuals get involved in deviant behavior as a result of embarking on a line of conduct having several potential outcomes, one of which is a deviant form.[3] This kind of nonconforming behavior cannot be called the product of clear-cut motivational elements driving the actor, for the individual did not specifically intend to become involved in deviance at the beginning of the behavioral events. Commenting on the suicide behavior of residents of the island of Tikopia, Lemert says: "This analysis of suicide suggests the more general possibility that there are many instances in which people do not elect deviant solutions to problems but instead initiate lines of behavior which, according to how circumstances unfold, may or may not become deviant."[4] He then shows that, in his research on naïve check forgery, he found a number of persons who were not motivated to pass bad checks but simply took chances that a check they authored might not be honored or that they might not be allowed to cover the check if it "bounced."[5]

The major value of Lemert's contentions regarding the risk-taking origins of deviance is that they warn us against the automatic assumption that criminal conduct is always "motivated," in the sense of being related to relatively long-standing attitudes and psychological concerns of the individual. All too frequently, we presume that criminal deviance stems from "antisocial" orien-

[1]Edwin M. Lemert, Human Deviance, Social Problems, and Social Control, 2nd ed. (Englewood Cliffs, N. J.: Prentice-Hall, Inc., 1972), pp. 26-61.

[2]Ibid., pp. 64-66.

[3]Ibid., pp. 71-73.

[4]Ibid., p. 72.

[5]Ibid., p. 29.

tations within the actor, which are the product of some set of experiences that occurred much earlier in his life career. Without denying that many kinds of criminality do show such a form, we hold that many are probably instances of situational risk taking that emerge out of ongoing processes.

Likely examples of risk-taking criminality are abundant. One illustration is felonious drunken driving in which the offender did not deliberately set out to become intoxicated. The majority of episodes in which individuals become involved in a situation they define as being "drunk" probably represent one of several possible outcomes of social drinking. At the beginning of the drinking activity, the prospect of becoming intoxicated was an eventuality the drinker least anticipated so that his drunkenness in this sense was unintentional. With the drunk driver, becoming intoxicated was an unplanned outcome of social drinking. In turn, the individual who drives while in a drunken condition does not intend to drive erratically and certainly does not plan to have an accident or injure anyone. However, with his driving ability impaired by alcohol, these results can eventuate if the driver is "unlucky," that is, if certain contingent events occur. Doubtless most drivers perceive these risks, at least dimly, when they drive while intoxicated.

Risk-taking processes may play a major role in the assaultive conduct of lower-class groups. In Chapter Twelve, we examined some of Walter Miller's arguments regarding the "focal concerns" of lower-class culture.[6] One of his hypotheses is that the weekly round of activities of working-class persons is frequently made up of the unrelieved boredom of weekday work routines, punctuated in dramatic fashion on weekends by the hedonistic pursuit of "fun" and "excitement." These weekend events center about drinking and provocative interaction with others, including members of the opposite sex. Although avid pursuit of fun does not lead directly to deviant or criminal behavior, it is a potential outcome of unrestrained hedonism. Flirtatious interaction with another person's wife or girl friend may culminate in a "cutting," that is, a knife assault. Similarly, when a group of individuals who have been drinking are brought together in close contact, assaultive acts are likely to occur over a variety of interactional difficulties. Again, these kinds of criminality stand as risks in a larger pattern of social class life. They cannot be understood as events that grow out of idiosyncratic but long-standing psychological characteristics of the offenders who commit them.

"One-time loser" property offenders, to be examined in more detail later in this chapter, also become involved in risk taking. Examination of descriptive materials in probation case files and elsewhere reveals that many of these persons get involved in petty acts of crime as part of a sequence of activities

---

[6]Walter B. Miller, "Lower Class Culture as a Generating Milieu of Gang Delinquency," *Journal of Social Issues*, 14, no. 3 (1958), 5–19.

that were not initiated as criminalistic ventures. For example, Skid Road transients often find themselves in the hands of the police as a result of petty burglaries carried out after becoming markedly intoxicated in a drinking bout with alcoholic companions, for falling into a drunken sleep in the bathtub of a cheap hotel, or for other ventures into risk situations. Other minor instances of theft may be a function of situational opportunities rather than deep-seated motivational elements of the offenders. Many individuals may manage to suspend their normal feelings of condemnation toward crime and steal petty articles of property when the immediate situation appears conducive to such behavior, particularly when the victim is a relatively large and impersonal organization. The processes that operate may have something in common with the activities of campers and picnickers who litter campgrounds with beer cans and rubbish in blatant disregard for fellow campers. These same individuals would probably hesitate to throw beer cans into the yards of neighbors in the residential areas in which they live. They would also give verbal allegiance to the general principle that one should keep picnic grounds clean.

Risk-taking hypotheses also apply to many instances of amateur shoplifting, by both juveniles and adults. Quite probably, the original motive for entering a retail store was either to purchase some item or to "look around," to examine merchandise and possibly buy some of it. Shoplifting actions are emergent as the sojourn through the store takes place. The impulse to pilfer some item develops as the shopper perceives the immediate situation as conducive to stealing—salespersons who might observe him are absent from the particular section of the store. The act of shoplifting by an adult thief may also be related to some immediate budgetary problem, the stolen articles allowing the individual to spend some of his money on things he would not otherwise be able to purchase. In any event, monetary problems do not fully explain an individual's behavior, for such problems do not always lead to thievery. The majority of shoppers with financial difficulties probably never resort to shoplifting, so something more than economic need is involved in this form of criminality.

So much for these general remarks. In the following pages our attention turns to amateur shoplifters, naïve check forgers, automobile thief-"joyriders," and property offender, "one-time losers."

THE AMATEUR SHOPLIFTER ROLE CAREER

The typological sketch of the amateur shoplifter, or the "snitch," as this person is known in the language of the retail store, is something of a caricature. The description is more or less accurate for the variety of amateur thieves who roam through retail stores, but it is most characteristic of adult, women thieves. Small children and juveniles who steal from stores depart in certain ways from the following characterization.

Definitional Dimensions

Offense Behavior. Amateur shoplifters or "snitches" steal amounts of property that vary in cost, so some steal petty items and others steal quite costly merchandise. Amateur shoplifters also vary in terms of crime skills, some of them employing "booster bags" and other criminal paraphernalia, whereas others exhibit only rudimentary techniques of crime. Further, these offenders vary in their degree of involvement in crime, for some steal only once or twice and others are caught up in recurrent acts of deviance. The distinguishing mark of the amateur as contrasted to the professional "booster" is that the former steals merchandise for personal use. The "booster," on the other hand, converts the results of his thievery into cash by selling the stolen goods to other persons.

Interactional Setting. Amateur shoplifters carry out their criminal acts in large department stores and variety stores in urban communities. Their deviant activities are enacted by individuals operating alone, as contrasted to professional "boosters" who commonly engage in team operations with other shoplifters.

Self-concept. Amateur shoplifters consider themselves to be honest, upright citizens. They do not think of themselves as thieves, and they do not exhibit other sorts of deviant self-image patterns.

Attitudes. Amateur shoplifters exhibit ordinary prosocial sentiments. They verbalize sentiments indicating that they are opposed to crime and thievery, in principle.

Role Career. Amateur shoplifters frequently engage in repetitive acts of theft, so their careers are often more than "one-shot" affairs. Most amateur "snitches" are eventually apprehended by store personnel, although few are subsequently reported to the police. Store officials are reluctant to refer other than the most serious cases of shoplifting to the authorities. Instead, store detectives and other employees handle many of the cases informally. The offender is compelled to confess his wrongdoing and promise to refrain from futher stealing. The apparent consequence of this kind of handling is to deter the person from further criminality.

Background Dimensions

Social Class. The Social-class origins of shoplifters are somewhat varied; both lower- and middle-class "snitches" come to the attention of store personnel. However, amateur shoplifting does not appear to be class-linked in any important degree.

Family Background. The family backgrounds of shoplifters are quite mixed in character, although most store thieves are from relatively common and conventional family backgrounds. Most adult shoplifters are married.

Peer Group Associations. There is nothing particularly unusual or striking about the peer associations of amateur shoplifters, either as juveniles or adults. These individuals receive no peer group support or encouragement for criminal acts.

Contact with Defining Agencies. As previously indicated, most detected cases of amateur shoplifting are handled informally by personnel of the victimized store. The offender is led to confess his criminality and promise not to repeat the behavior. Store officials threaten various dire consequences if they apprehend him again. These experiences are apparently so traumatic in their impact on the offender that they deter him from further criminality. The principal factor seems to be that criminality is inconsistent with the person's self-conception. Once he is forced to acknowledge participation in activities discordant with his self-image, he avoids repetition of those actions. The socially-psychologically painful aspects of the confrontation process make the offender unwilling to experience that process again. To avoid the pain, the individual avoids shoplifting.

Some Evidence[7]

The opening remarks of this chapter indicated that shoplifting rarely becomes a matter of public knowledge. Shoplifters are infrequently observed in the act, so those who become known to the victim store or business concern represent only a fraction of those actually involved in stealing from it. Individuals who shoplift are most likely to be apprehended in stores that employ private police or protective personnel. Other factors that condition the likelihood of shoplifters being detected include variations in the operating procedures of store detectives, racial biases of protective officers which lead them to scrutinize more closely the movements of blacks in the stores, reluctance to confront "respectable" people with accusations of criminality, and special attention to juveniles who are thought to be particularly theft prone.[8]

Known shoplifters constitute a minority of all thieves who direct their predatory activities at retail stores. In addition, most offenders known to store personnel are not reported to the police, so officially labeled shoplifters represent an even smaller sample of all store thieves. As we shall see, shoplifters who become publicly identified as criminals through court proceedings are in no sense representative of known thieves or of all shoplifters.

[7]Mary Owen Cameron, *The Booster and the Snitch* (New York: The Free Press, 1964); Loren E. Edwards, *Shoplifting and Shrinkage Protection for Stores* (Springfield, Ill.: Charles C Thomas, Publisher, 1958); Gerald D. Robin, "The American Customer: Shopper or Shoplifter?" *Police* (January–February 1964); Robin, "Patterns of Department Store Shoplifting," *Crime and Delinquency*, 9 (April 1963), 163–72.

[8]Cameron, *The Booster and the Snitch;* pp. 24–32.

How much shoplifting takes place in the United States? How much money is lost through the criminality of store thieves? A variety of estimates have been advanced, not all in agreement. However, they all indicate that shoplifting is a far from inconsequential kind of lawbreaking. For example, one claim has been made that shoplifters stole $247,000,000 of merchandise from drug and department stores, grocery stores, and variety stores in the United States in 1948.[9] Another contention has been that twelve department stores in New York City suffered over $10,000,000 in shoplifter losses in 1951, and still another authority has argued that each year shoplifters take over $1,700,000,000 from retailers in the United States.[10] A final estimate of the magnitude of shoplifting is derived from a report of the National Commission on Food Marketing, established by Congress. That commission set the annual cost of shoplifting at $300,000,000 per year, or 2 percent of total sales. The commission survey profiled the average shoplifter as between eighteen and thirty years of age, stealing predominantly on Thursday, Friday, or Saturday, between 3 P.M. and 6 P.M., and stealing about $3.75 worth of goods. The commission urged that all shoplifters except pregnant women, senile aged, and "kleptomaniacs" be prosecuted.[11]

According to store protective agents, most losses are inflicted on stores by amateur shoplifters or "snitches," rather than by professional "boosters," although the average amount stolen is apparently larger in cases of professional shoplifting than in amateur stealing.[12] In general, criminal skills used by professionals exceed those of "snitches," although the latter often show some degree of sophistication in their criminality. Many use "bad bags" (well-worn shopping bags issued by the victim store), are equipped with scissors or razor blades for snipping price tags from stolen merchandise, sometimes carry lists of items they intend to steal, and often plan their offenses in advance.[13]

An important parenthetical note is that even though it is commonplace, shoplifting makes a relatively small contribution to the total losses suffered by stores. Protection agencies estimate that about 75 percent of all pilferage in stores is the work of employees rather than customer thieves.[14]

Mary Owen Cameron has conducted a detailed study of shoplifters involving analysis of records on a sample of shoplifters apprehended in a Chicago department store between 1943 and 1950, along with a sample of women charged with "petty larceny, shoplifting" in Chicago courts between 1948 and 1950.[15] Cameron discovered that shoplifters in "Lakeside Company" were gen-

[9]Robin, "The American Customer: Shopper or Shoplifter?"
[10]Cameron, The Booster and the Snitch, pp. 9–15.
[11]National Council on Crime and Delinquency, NCCD News, 45 (March–April 1966), 1.
[12]Cameron, The Booster and the Snitch, p. 56.
[13]Ibid., pp. 58–60, 70–84.
[14]Ibid., pp. 11–15.
[15]Ibid., pp. 24–38.

erally apprehended for relatively small thefts averaging about six dollars, juveniles stole amounts of merchandise of lesser value than did adults, and male shoplifters were caught with fewer stolen items in their possession than was true of women. About one-fifth of the apprehended adult thieves were men. The much higher number of shoplifting women is attributable to most department store customers being women, as well as to women's stealing more items than men and thus running a greater risk of being observed.[16]

Cameron's findings from "Lakeside Company" indicate that the shoplifters are a cross-section of the Chicago population in terms of socioeconomic status, although they are of somewhat lower status than the over-all customer group in the store. Black shoplifters are found in about the same proportion as in the Chicago population, but black shoplifters are much more likely to be reported to the police. Moreover, black offenders convicted in court tend to receive stiffer penalties than do white shoplifters.[17]

Cameron's results make abundantly clear that officially recognized shoplifters make up only a small part of all store thieves. She indicates that between 1943 and 1949 the Chicago Police Department tallied an average of 633 women per year charged with larceny of all kinds. At the same time, "Lakeside Company" apprehended about 400 women each year for shoplifting, although only about 10 percent were turned over to the police. Thus, Cameron declares: "One department store, in other words, *arrested* for shoplifting about 60 percent of the total number of women per year as were officially charged with all types of larceny (including shoplifting) in the entire city of Chicago" (emphasis in the original).[18]

Many factors are involved in the decision to prosecute, such as refusal of the suspected thief to confess and difficulties of getting speedy court action at any particular time. As already noted, stores are more likely to report black offenders to the police as well as to turn over professional "boosters" to the authorities. The result of these decisions is that court cases of store thieves are ecologically concentrated in areas with generally high crime rates and low socioeconomic status, although the total group of known thieves is not so distributed.[19] Shoplifting stands as a prominent example of differential law enforcement, with official rates of shoplifting bearing little relationship to the true distribution of such behavior.

Cameron effectively demolishes hypotheses about shoplifting which would explain this behavior as a result of psychiatric disturbances, compulsiveness, or "kleptomania." The contention that store theft is a compulsive psychiatric aberration is inconsistent with her evidence that most shoplifters stopped stealing after getting caught, even though they had engaged in repetitive acts

---

[16]*Ibid.,* pp. 70–88.
[17]*Ibid.,* pp. 91–96, 136–44.
[18]*Ibid.,* p. 123.
[19]*Ibid.,* pp. 132–33.

of criminality up to that point.[20] "Kleptomania" turns out to be nothing more than a social label hung on "nice people" who steal and withheld from "bad people" who are simply "crooks"! The label is a social identity akin to that of "sick alcoholic," which is accorded the middle-class drinker and denied the Skid Road "drunk." Cameron's interpretation of her findings is that amateur female shoplifters are women who steal items their limited budgets will not allow them to buy without depriving other family members. These women have no self-conception as thieves and offer a variety of rationalizations to "explain" their deviance. When apprehended by store detectives, they are forced to acknowledge that they are thieves. These women are without any ingroup support for their stealing, so they have no way of buffering themselves against social condemnation. Consequently, they refrain from further shoplifting because they cannot accommodate themselves to a revised self-definition as a "thief."[21]

The most important single conclusion from Cameron's data probably has to do with the observation that "normal," respectable people can and do engage in systematic criminality. As Howard Becker has suggested, these findings call into question notions that use "middle-class morality" as an explanation for conformity of middle status individuals. A deeply introjected set of values probably guides the conduct of fewer respectable citizens than is sometimes supposed. Instead of being kept on a consistent course of conformity by an internal gyroscope of ethical standards, many reinterpret values to fit particular situations and invoke countervailing rationalizations that allow them to deviate under certain circumstances. Their law-abiding conduct may frequently be a result of fear of being caught and punished rather than deeply held values of upright conduct.[22]

In a report on department store shoplifting, Gerald Robin[23] examined data on 1,584 persons apprehended for shoplifting in three of the five largest department stores in Philadelphia in 1958. Most of his findings run parallel to those of Cameron; for example, he discovered that the stores are both cautious and informal in their handling of detected thieves. Juvenile thieves are almost never turned over to the authorities for official action, and only about one-fourth of the adult shoplifters are prosecuted.[24] Individual thefts that were detected usually involved relatively small losses, about half of them of merchandise valued at less than $10. Juveniles were responsible for smaller losses on the average than were adult thieves.[25] However, these two studies do differ

---

[20]Ibid., pp. 115-17, 154-57; the psychiatric theme concerning shoplifting is expressed in Fabian L. Rouke, "Shoplifting: Its Symbolic Motivation," NPPA Journal, 3 (January 1957), 54-58.

[21]Cameron, The Booster and the Snitch, pp. 159-70.

[22]Howard S. Becker, review of Cameron, The Booster and the Snitch, American Journal of Sociology, 70 (March 1965), 635-36.

[23]Robin, "Patterns of Department Store Shoplifting."

[24]Ibid., pp. 169-70.

[25]Ibid., pp. 167-69.

in some respects. Robin notes that nearly half the shoplifters in the Philadelphia stores were black, although blacks make up considerably less of the total city population. Women thieves outnumbered male shoplifters, but not so strikingly as in Cameron's materials. Juvenile thieves constituted about 60 percent of all shoplifters, thus they were more frequent than in Cameron's data.[26]

One major observation that emerges from both Robin's and Cameron's research is that juvenile shoplifting is most commonly *group* activity, whereas adult thieves usually engage in surreptitious and individualistic thievery.[27] Among juveniles, many of the youngsters act as "aiders" or "abettors" who act as lookouts for their peers. Cameron suggests that adult thieves are probably often persons who engaged in group stealing as adolescents and learned their crime skills in that setting; in other words, the juvenile thieves of today become the adult shoplifters of tomorrow. This may be a dubious hypothesis, for juvenile theft could be a peer-supported kind of conduct developing out of some temporally circumscribed influences of a "youth culture" and terminated as youngsters move out of this age period. At any rate, the hypothesis needs more study, for its accuracy is presently indeterminate.

Robin indicates that a major factor influencing the decision to prosecute cases of shoplifting is size of theft, so few individuals who pilfer less than $20 worth of merchandise are reported to the police, but nearly all those who steal items valued at over $60 are prosecuted.[28]

Robin's observations also have a bearing on contentions that psychological aberrations or compulsions drive amateur shoplifters to steal. He shows that thefts are markedly more common during the months of October, November, and December than they are at any other time of the year.[29] If compulsions impel individuals toward thievery, rates of stealing should be much the same the year round, for compulsions should not wax and wane with the seasons. Clearly, these fluctuations have more to do with seasonal budgetary strains than with psychological tensions. Along the same line, Robin cites an instance of a power failure in Chicago's Loop area in which, during the thirty minutes of darkness, thousands of dollars of merchandise was stolen by "normal" persons.[30] Finally, he notes that a study of 698 "food lifters" in Chicago supermarkets in 1951 showed that nearly all were ordinary citizens, mainly housewives, who had enough money to pay for the stolen items found in their custody.[31] These bits of evidence seem to confirm Cameron's argument that amateur shoplifters steal to stretch their budgets, doing so deliberately

[26]*Ibid.,* p. 166.
[27]*Ibid.,* p. 170; Cameron, *The Booster and the Snitch,* pp. 101-4.
[28]Robin, "Patterns of Department Store Shoplifting," pp. 169-70.
[29]*Ibid.,* pp. 170-71.
[30]Robin, "The American Customer: Shopper or Shoplifter?"
[31]*Ibid.*

and rationally, after conjuring up rationalizations that allow them to continue to think of themselves as honest, law-abiding citizens. These thieves steal when they evaluate the elements of immediate situations to be most conducive to successful deviance.

Paula Newberg conducted another investigation of shoplifting in national food chain stores in the Chicago area.[32] She reports that the company estimated its losses through shoplifting and employee theft at over $2,500,000 out of a net profit of $25,000,000 in 1958. Newberg also found that the individual stores in the chain had different rates of shoplifting, produced by differing actions on the part of store personnel toward shoplifters. That is, in some food stores, employees dealt with shoplifters differently from other stores.

George Won and George Yamamoto conducted a study of shoplifting in Honolulu, dealing with the social characteristics of about 500 persons who had been apprehended for shoplifting in a major supermarket chain.[33] The major finding of their inquiry centered about the middle-class social status of the thieves, for these lawbreakers were numerically and proportionately middle-class in background. Here again, the data indicate that shoplifting is often a criminal act carried on by "respectable people."

THE NAÏVE CHECK FORGER ROLE CAREER

We have every reason to believe that the writing and passing of "bum checks" is an extremely commonplace and costly form of American crime. The significance of checks in modern society is indicated by Herbert Bloch and Gilbert Geis, who report that over 90 percent of the money transactions in the United States at present take place by means of checks rather than through cash transactions.[34] No wonder that numerous endeavors by professional criminals toward obtaining money through fraudulent checks occur, for forgery and check passing is relatively easy in a cultural situation in which check transactions are normal activities arousing little suspicion. As a part of growing up, nearly every adult citizen learns to handle his affairs through checking accounts. The amateur offender in need of emergency funds has acquired simple skills he can easily turn toward forgery.

The naïve check forger is one of two relatively distinct kinds of check passers. The other is the professional forger who engages in check passing as a means of livelihood and exhibits fairly complicated and well-developed

[32]Paula Newberg, "A Study in Deviance: Shoplifting," *International Journal of Comparative Sociology*, 9 (June 1968), 132–36.

[33]George Won and George Yamamoto, "Social Structure and Deviant Behavior: A Study of Shoplifting," *Sociology and Social Research*, 53 (October 1968), 44–55.

[34]Herbert A. Bloch and Gilbert Geis, *Man, Crime, and Society*, 2nd ed. (New York: Random House, 1970), p. 178.

crime skills.[35] Professionals manufacture and pass checks in bunches, frequently in an elaborate fashion involving the printing of impressive looking payroll checks from a nonexisting company. Professional forgers often pass fictitious checks made to look authentic through the use of a stolen check-printer. Offenders of this kind are not discussed in the commentary on naïve forgers. Instead, professional check passers stand as a case of "grifting," a variant of professional theft. The previous chapter contained an analysis of professional thieves, and the reader is directed back to that section for further remarks regarding professional forgers.

Chapter Ten has already presented a role-career description of the naïve check forger. This offender was characterized as a person with simple crime skills who thinks of himself in prosocial terms. Check forgery was seen as developing out of certain situations of social stress. The role-career description from Chapter Ten need not be repeated, but the reader is referred back to page 242 for that presentation.

Some Evidence

The analysis of Uniform Crime Reports statistics for the United States in Chapter Five provided some indication of the widespread nature of forgery. Another measure of the extent of this kind of illegality can be found in reports in the state of California. For example, in 1963, of the 27,222 persons referred to probation departments for consideration for probation, 4,668 were charged with forgery and check offenses.[36] But we have every reason to suppose that these known cases are a small fraction of all check violations. For one thing, many instances of behavior that qualify technically as forgery probably go unreported because they are suspected of being accidental. Persons do fairly commonly write checks that "bounce" unintentionally because they have miscalculated the amount of money in their checking accounts. As a result, the demarcation point between mistakes and willful misconduct is hazy. The deliberate or intentional forger has this defense available to employ against the aggrieved merchant. He can assert that the "NSF" check was an accidental miscalculation, and the businessman may well find himself forced to honor this explanation for fear of alienating the customer. That same offended merchant may be deterred from responding to the forger's misconduct as crime out of feelings of identification and sympathy for the actor, particularly if the forger is a person of middle-class position and a long-standing customer of

[35]For evidence on aspects of professional forgery see Edwin M. Lemert, "The Behavior of the Systematic Check Forger," Social Problems, 6 (Fall 1958), 141–49; David Maurer, "The Argot of Forgery," American Speech, 16 (December 1941), 243–50; Julius L. Sternitzky, Forgery and Fictitious Checks (Springfield, Ill.: Charles C Thomas, Publisher, 1955); Norman S. Hayner," Characteristics of Five Offender Types," American Sociological Review, 26 (February 1961), 96–102.

[36]State of California, Delinquency and Probation in California, 1963 (Sacramento: Bureau of Criminal Statistics, 1963), p. 179.

the victim's establishment. Finally, the merchant may be loath to report the case to authorities for fear of getting entangled in time-consuming court appearances and also out of anticipation that he will then be unable to gain recompensation for the financial loss he has suffered.

One bit of evidence probably symptomatic of the differential handling of forgers comes from the author's work.[37] Interviews with the manager of a suburban chain drug store in the San Francisco area disclosed that large numbers of check forgers victimized this establishment each week, even though it takes elaborate steps to prevent such incidents. Nearly all the checks that "bounce" and are returned to the store by banks are handled informally. The drug store endeavors to collect its losses from the check passers and in many cases succeeds in doing so. But the store does not always manage to recoup its losses; the manager reported that "chiselers" who pass bad checks for small amounts frequently refuse to make good on them. They predicate their actions on the assumption that the store will not be willing to go through the cumbersome, time-consuming steps required to prosecute. These forgers are usually correct in this assumption, for the management rarely engages in formal actions against check passers. Cases that are prosecuted normally involve a large amount of money lost to the store.

The most detailed and revealing investigation of amateur check forgers now available is by Edwin Lemert.[38] His research was designed to investigate the theory that "naive check forgery arises at a critical point in a process of social isolation, out of certain types of social situations, and is made possible by the closure or constriction of behavior alternatives subjectively held as available to the forger."[39] Lemert examined the case records of over 1,000 naïve forgers in the Los Angeles area and conducted interviews with a sample of these individuals. The subjects had little or no contact with criminal individuals, were nonviolent persons with a marked repugnance for forms of crime other than forgery, and appeared to be likable and attractive but impulsive individuals. The forgers were predominantly white males, older on the average than other probationers, and with higher intelligence ratings and better occupational status than other offenders.[40]

Lemert's hypothesis about social isolation as the prelude to forgery was borne out by his observations. Most of the check writers had been involved prior to their criminality in unemployment, gambling losses, alcoholic sprees, difficulties in military service, or estrangement from their families. Marital disruptions appear to play a particularly critical role as an isolating experience,

[37]Interview material in the author's personal files.

[38]Edwin M. Lemert, "An Isolation and Closure Theory of Naive Check Forgery," *Journal of Criminal Law, Criminology and Police Science,* 44 (September–October 1953), 296–307.

[39]*Ibid.,* p. 298.

[40]*Ibid.,* pp. 299–300.

for about 40 percent of the forgers were divorced. In general, Lemert concludes that these various experiences tend to be progressive in character and mutually reinforcing, so the person caught up in them becomes more and more alienated from conventional social bonds.[41]

According to Lemert, the social experiences most of these persons get involved in immediately prior to check forgery are what he terms "certain dialectical forms of social behavior."[42] He means that the individual usually embarks on a course of action or events having a clear beginning and end, so considerable impetus is built up to carry the activities through to their conclusion. An alcoholic "spree" is a case in point, in which initial involvement in drinking pressures the actor to continue until he has been intoxicated for a lengthy period of time. In the event that he prematurely exhausts his funds, considerable tension may arise, provoking him to seek some solution that will bring the action pattern to its terminal point.

Lemert argues that the forger finds relief from this situational tension by a social-psychological process of "closure."[43] Check forgery is selected as a way to bring finality to the dialectical events. The choice of check writing comes about in part because the individual is unaware of less deviant solutions; he feels he cannot borrow money from anyone and cannot employ other alternatives. Moreover, forgery is "in the culture," learned as part of becoming an adult, so no special skill is required to commit this act. It is also nonviolent and can be rationalized through such arguments as, "You can't kill anyone with a fountain pen."

This work by Lemert is the most significant study of naïve forgers. In addition, the argument should be evaluated for its broader implications regarding models of causation in criminology. Lemert's account of the development of check forgery stands as an illustration of his concept of "situational deviation," which we examined in Chapter Nine. The isolation and closure conception of check forgery can also be offered as an example of a mechanistic or situational explanation of criminality, which Edwin Sutherland and Donald Cressey contrast to historical or genetic models of etiology.[44] A situational view of causal dynamics accounts for some kind of behavior in terms of processes operating at the moment of the criminality, as compared to genetic formulations, which look for the roots of ongoing behavior in earlier experiences, often separated by a lengthy interval of time. Although some causal elements that contribute to forgery are probably genetic, check writing cannot be understood without reference to problems of the immediate situation or to Lemert's dialectical endeavors.

[41]*Ibid.*, pp. 301–4.
[42]*Ibid.*, pp. 303–4.
[43]*Ibid.*, pp. 304–5.
[44]Edwin H. Sutherland and Donald R. Cressey, *Principles of Criminology*, 8th ed. (Philadelphia: J. B. Lippincott Co., 1970), pp. 74–75.

Several other studies of naïve forgers reveal findings parallel to those of Lemert. Maurice Gauthier discovered that forgers in Kingston Penitentiary in Canada were older males of above average education and from "good" middle-class families.[45] He suggests that these offenders engage in forgery as a technique for relieving inner tensions of the kind Lemert proposed. Irwin Berg's comparison of forgers and other inmates in Southern Michigan Penitentiary turned up similar results: the check offenders had higher intelligence ratings than the other inmates, were older than the other convicts, and were less criminally involved than the other felons.[46] John Gillin's report on Wisconsin criminals in the state prison noted that forgers were from middle-income backgrounds and were older and more intelligent than other felons.[47] Several case histories Gillin cited present a picture of check writing that meshes with the isolation and closure formulation. Finally, Norman Hayner contrasted professional or "con forgers" and naïve or "alcoholic forgers" with other prisoner types in the Washington State penal institutions. The naïve forgers turned out to have higher than average intelligence.[48] Many were from situations of social isolation; 45 percent were divorced. According to Hayner, alcoholic forgers are frequently "dependent" persons—a judgment he arrived at by examining case record materials available on the prisoners.

This last contention is worthy of further exploration. The claim that check writers are commonly dependent, passive individuals is one the author has frequently heard correctional agents in California and elsewhere advance.[49] The same argument turns up in Hayner's data. The problem is that such a finding could emerge from case records as an artifact of the belief systems of correctional persons rather than as an accurate indicator of true characteristics of forgers. In other words, if correctional treatment workers regard check writers as dependent individuals, they may report such observations in case documents, even though the forgers do not fit this characterization. A more carefully controlled kind of inquiry is needed to search out evidence on the psychological correlates of check writing behavior. Lemert's study of dependency on the part of alcoholic individuals offers a model of the kind of investigation required.[50] In summary, at present this dependency claim is contentious.

[45]Maurice Gauthier, "The Psychology of the Compulsive Forger," *Canadian Journal of Corrections*, 1 (July 1959), 62–69.

[46]Irwin A. Berg, "A Comparative Study of Forgery," *Journal of Applied Psychology*, 28 (June 1944), 232–38.

[47]John L. Gillin, *The Wisconsin Prisoner* (Madison: University of Wisconsin Press, 1946), pp. 167–73.

[48]Hayner, "Characteristics of Five Offender Types," pp. 96–102.

[49]For a discussion of this matter, see Don C. Gibbons, *Changing the Lawbreaker* (Englewood Cliffs, N.J.: Prentice-Hall, 1965), pp. 267–70.

[50]Edwin M. Lemert, "Dependency in Married Alcoholics," *Quarterly Journal of Studies on Alcohol*, 23 (December 1962), 590–609.

THE AUTOMOBILE THIEF–"JOYRIDER" ROLE CAREER

That form of car theft called "joyriding," in which the offenders steal automobiles to provide short-run recreation rather than to deprive the owner permanently of his property, is an extremely commonplace kind of illegality in the United States. In addition, joyriding behavior spans juvenile delinquency and adult criminality. Joyriding car theft is often carried on by persons from about thirteen to twenty years of age. Many of these individuals get apprehended and diverted into juvenile courts, thereby becoming "delinquents" in point of legal fact, whereas others are remanded to criminal courts and acquire the legal status of "criminal." The following typological description characterizes a "juvenile delinquent" as well as a "criminal."[51] Moreover, the research findings on car thieves reported in the succeeding section refer principally to samples of car thieves from juvenile court or training school situations.

Definitional Dimensions

Offense Behavior. Joyriders steal cars for recreational or joyriding purposes, not to "strip" or for other profit motives. The customary activity is to steal automobiles by the technique of "hot wiring," ride around in them for a short time, and then abandon the cars undamaged. Car thieves are sometimes known in the community as "wild" boys who drink and associate with "wild" girls. However, their delinquent activities tend to center around auto theft, and they are not usually involved in other kinds of property offenses.

Interactional Setting. Joyriders steal cars within a loosely structured group of fellow joyriders. On any particular occasion, an individual car thief engages in these acts with several other delinquents. Over a series of joyriding incidents, the participants in such acts vary somewhat; on one occasion, cars are stolen by boys A, B, and C, whereas another time they are stolen by boys A, D, E, and F. Consequently these boys, A, B, C, D, E, and F, do not constitute a well-structured gang, but represent individuals who associate differentially with each other, that is, "birds of a feather." As a group, they are likely to be juveniles (or young adults) with adjustment problems in school and elsewhere.

Self-concept. These offenders define themselves as nondelinquents or noncriminals and distinguish themselves from "real delinquents" or "real criminals." They are youths who frequently exhibit a considerable psychological investment in self-notions as "tough" and masculine. In general, they regard their delinquent activities as evidence that they are "tough" and "cool."

---

[51]Don C. Gibbons, *Changing the Lawbreaker*, The Treatment of Delinquents and Criminals, © 1965. Reprinted by permission of Prentice-Hall, Inc., Englewood Cliffs, New Jersey, pp. 88–90.

Attitudes. Joyriders exhibit essentially prosocial attitudes in that they show conventional attitudes toward work and reveal other conventional norms. Their views of the police are not so much hostile as they are notions that the police are stupid and inefficient.

Role Career. The role career of the joyrider begins in adolescence with automobile theft. It may persist over several years and involve a number of instances of joyriding. Repetitive acts of car theft are likely to result in arrest of the offender, adjudication as a delinquent or adult felon, and placement on probation. Some of these youths eventually end up in training schools or reformatories, where they make a reasonably stable adjustment. Most car thieves terminate these actions in the late teen-age years and become law-abiding citizens.

Background Dimensions

Social Class. Joyriders are juveniles who specialize in this kind of activity, as distinct from juveniles who occasionally steal cars but whose acts are normally in the direction of predatory theft. Car thieves of the first sort are usually from middle-class, comfortable economic backgrounds. They live in single-family dwellings in middle-income areas. Their parents are usually white collar or other types of middle-class workers.

Family Background. The family situation out of which joyriders emerge is one of relatively close supervision and discipline. However, joyriders frequently indicate a lack of intense interaction with their fathers. It may be that the fathers of the car thieves fail to provide completely adequate models of adult, masculine behavior to their sons. Another not uncommon characteristic of the families of joyriders is a relatively high degree of occupational and residential mobility. This pattern may sometimes contribute to the marginal status of the boys in the community in terms of peer group membership.

Peer Group Associations. Joyriders exhibit relatively adequate peer group adjustments. However, although they interact with nondelinquent peers, they exhibit differential association with other car thieves, most of whom have reputations as "wild" and somewhat deviant. To some extent, the joyrider appears to be a marginal member of conventional peer groups.

Contact with Defining Agencies. Contact with defining agencies in the case of joyriders seems to confirm the person's status as a "tough" individual in his own eyes. Repeated contacts with the police and courts tend to produce negative attitudes toward these groups. However, these contacts do not usually lead the offender to a commitment to adult patterns of criminality. Instead, the joyrider is sufficiently socialized to conventional norms that he ultimately gets a job, gets married, and assumes the behavior of a conventional law-abiding citizen.

Discussion and Research Findings[52]

The preceding portrait of the juvenile or young adult joyrider suggests the following causal dynamics. First, car thieves are relatively well-adjusted boys on good terms with most of their peers, particularly fellow joyriders with whom they steal cars. These boys are predominantly middle-class youths who have grown up in a relatively stable family setting but with problems of masculine identity for adolescent males. Further, boys who steal cars often show family backgrounds involving some mild degree of parent–child tension. Out of all middle-class males who show social-psychological problems surrounding masculinity, the ones most likely to get involved in automobile theft are perhaps those involved in situations of "marginality" of one kind or another. Marginality is our term for a variety of conditions that prevent the boy from working out his problems of masculinity in nondeviant ways. The pimply lads who have communication difficulties with girls and other persons, the boys who are too small to engage in high school athletics, or the ones whose families move frequently within the city, so that the youngsters have difficulties in becoming socially integrated into school life, are the kinds of youths who are candidates for delinquent careers in joyriding. Through this multifaceted process, certain middle-class boys are drawn into car theft.

This hypothesized etiological background in joyriding is an elaboration of a line of analysis regarding "middle class delinquency" first advanced by Talcott Parsons[53] and subsequently enunciated by Albert Cohen.[54] Cohen has succinctly summarized the ingredients of this set of notions:

> Because of the structure of the modern family and the nature of our occupational system, children of both sexes tend to form early feminine identifications. The boy, however, unlike the girl, comes later under strong social pressure to establish his masculinity, his *difference from* female figures. Because his mother is the object of the feminine identification which he feels is the threat to his status as a male, he tends to react negativistically to those conduct norms which have been associated with mother and therefore have acquired feminine significance. Since mother has been the principal agent of indoctrination of "good," respectable behavior, "goodness" comes to symbolize femininity and engaging in "bad" behavior acquires the function of denying his femininity and therefore asserting his masculinity. This is the motivation to juvenile delinquency (emphasis in the original).[55]

[52]This section is a slightly revised version of Don C. Gibbons, "Problems of Causal Analysis in Criminology: A Case Illustration," *Journal of Research in Crime and Delinquency*, 3 (January 1966), 47–52.

[53]Talcott Parsons, "Certain Primary Sources and Patterns of Aggression in the Social Structure of the Western World," *Psychiatry*, 9 (May 1947), 167–81; Parsons, "Age and Sex in the Social Structure of the United States," *American Sociological Review*, 7 (October 1942), 604–16.

[54]Albert K. Cohen, *Delinquent Boys* (New York: The Free Press, 1955), pp. 157–69.

[55]*Ibid.*, p. 164.

Parsons and Cohen both maintain that the middle-class boy has the most severe masculinity difficulties, because the father works at some distant locale and his son cannot observe him as a role model. The work tasks of the father are also relatively abstract and intangible so that the boys cannot easily identify with them.

We have added to this argument the two ingredients of parent–child tensions and marginality to form an overarching rubric for a series of specific contingencies some middle-class, adolescent or young adult males encounter. One British student of delinquency has also offered this masculinity hypothesis to account for car thieves he studied, holding that these boys were from families characterized by fathers who failed to serve as adequate role models.[56]

Since our remarks so far have been phrased in speculative terms, we might now ask: How well do these propositions stand up in the face of empirical evidence? Are these contentions about masculine protest, marginality, and the like, true? Unfortunately, available research materials do not provide unequivocal answers to these questions. The existing data are only tangentially relevant to the preceding lines of theoretical exposition.

Empirical investigations of car theft conducted to date stand as dramatic illustrations of the poverty of results that comes from studies unguided by explicit theory and dependent on information reported in official records. The record-keeping systems of most official agencies involve only a limited number of facts about offenders, such as age, sex, and official charge for which the person had been apprehended. Not uncommonly, even these sparse items are unreliably or unsystematically recorded. But most important, these fact-gathering procedures are usually insensitive to the accumulation of data on theoretically significant dimensions of concern to the investigator. Few facts are recorded on such critical matters as the structure of the social behavior, which has resulted in the offender's being labeled as a deviant. For example, statements about victims and their relationship to the offender are usually absent from official records. An investigator can draw out of official reports only those facts agency officials put there, and in many cases he will be lucky if some of these happen to be related to the concepts and categories in which he is interested. This is particularly true of instances where the researcher is investigating some complex dimension or process, such as marginality or Lemert's "isolation" in the case of naïve forgery. These concepts are not simply equivalents of the commonsense categories used in correctional record keeping. Significant research in the future will involve testing specific theories through collection of firsthand observations explicitly linked to concepts in a theoretical argument.

We do not suggest that existing pieces of inquiry are of no use whatsoever; evidence at hand is superior to no evidence at all and, in addition, such ma-

---

[56]T. C. N. Gibbens, "Car Thieves," *British Journal of Delinquency*, 8, no. 4 (1958), 257-68.

terial does help to delineate promising etiological hypotheses for future studies.

Leonard Savitz[57] and Jerome Hall [58] have made detailed surveys of the existing information regarding car theft. In discussing joyriding car theft as distinguished from those automobile larcenies in which the car is "stripped" or permanently stolen, Savitz notes that many jurisdictions have created special legislation to cover this form of behavior. He notes that early efforts to prosecute joyriders under general larceny statutes were often unsuccessful because the offenders had not intended to deprive the owners of their automobiles permanently.[59] As a result an offense usually labeled "Taking a Motor Vehicle Without the Owner's Permission" was invented to cover the activities of joyriders. Along a somewhat related line, Hall notes that some courts have resorted to administrative procedures dealing with joyriders under a statute which, technically, did not apply to them, rather than under the relevant law covering theft of cars, to prevent these persons from being harshly punished for relatively minor criminal acts.[60]

The essays by Savitz and Hall indicate that the crime techniques or *modus operandi* of car thieves are varied; some employ technically simple tactics of lawbreaking, whereas others use more esoteric skills.[61] These authors also observed that about 90 percent of the vehicles reported stolen are ultimately recovered, usually undamaged, and usually within a short time interval.[62] Reports of the San Francisco Police Department show that, of the cars stolen in the nine different police districts of that city, more than half were recovered within the same district in which they had been stolen.[63]

Savitz has also enumerated some major characteristics of car thieves indicated in available reports and studies.[64] He notes that most of them are young males, usually under twenty years of age and single. Large cities have the highest rates of automobile theft, probably due in part to anonymity and other features that provide opportunities for vehicles to be stolen easily and with slight risk.

One of the major studies using firsthand evidence regarding joyriders is that of William Wattenberg and James Balistrieri.[65] These investigators exam-

---

[57]Leonard D. Savitz, "Automobile Theft," *Journal of Criminal Law, Criminology and Police Science,* 50 (July–August 1959), 132–43. Several older studies of car thieves, not discussed in this book, are noted in Savitz's paper.

[58]Jerome Hall, *Theft, Law and Society,* 2nd ed. (Indianapolis: Bobbs-Merrill Co., 1952), pp. 233–88.

[59]Savitz, "Automobile Theft," p. 132.

[60]Hall, *Theft, Law and Society,* pp. 262–75.

[61]Savitz, "Automobile Theft," pp. 139–40; Hall, *Theft, Law and Society,* pp. 250–56.

[62]Savitz, "Automobile Theft," p. 133; Hall, *Theft, Law and Society,* pp. 240–45.

[63]"An Analysis of Auto Thefts and Recoveries by Police District," mimeographed, in the author's files.

[64]Savitz, "Automobile Theft," pp. 133–35.

[65]William W. Wattenberg and James Balistrieri, "Automobile Theft: A 'Favored-Group' Delinquency," *American Journal of Sociology,* 58 (May 1952), 575–79.

ined the detailed case records of over 200 white boys the Detroit police apprehended in 1948 for car theft, and they compared these youths with several thousand other white youngsters arrested for different delinquencies. Black car thieves were not studied because they were infrequently encountered, at least by the police, even though blacks constituted a sizable portion of the Detroit population.

The major impression that emerges from the comparisons of car thieves with other delinquents centers about the "favored group" status of the former. Car thieves were from neighborhoods the police rated as "above average," from uncrowded single-family dwellings, from houses in good physical condition, and from racially homogeneous neighborhoods. They were also from families with only one employed parent. The car thieves were older boys on good terms with their peers. Although the automobile thieves were considered rambunctious gang members, the police frequently evaluated these youngsters as "responsive." Finally, the parents' involvement in their sons' recreation was judged to be "occasional" rather than "seldom" or "regular."[66] Wattenberg and Balistrieri interpret this pattern of results as an indication that car thieves are the product of a permissive upbringing, which results in an "other-directed" personality structure. These boys are thought to be easily drawn into peer-supported patterns of antisocial conduct; at the same time they are unresponsive to larger social entities and their values.[67]

In his report on juvenile car thieves, Charles Browning compared fifty-six car thieves, sixty-three truants, and fifty-eight control group nondelinquent juveniles.[68] The offenders were Los Angeles County probation wards. Both groups of offenders were from broken homes in greater numbers than were the control group boys. The auto thieves and controls were more commonly from medium income backgrounds than were the truants. Similarly, the car thieves and nondelinquents showed better community and personal adjustment than did the truant youngsters. Considerably more car thieves had backgrounds of residential mobility than did the other two groups; about three-fourths of the car thieves had lived for less than five years at their present address. In general, these findings parallel those of Wattenberg and Balistrieri, particularly with regard to the "favored group" status of car thieves.

An investigation by Erwin Schepses involves boys in the New York state training school at Warwick.[69] Schepses compared twenty-two boys who were "pure" car thieves, that is, with records solely of vehicle theft, with fifty-nine

[66]*Ibid.*, pp. 577–78.

[67]*Ibid.*, pp. 578–79.

[68]Charles J. Browning, "Differential Social Relations and Personality Factors of Parents and Boys in Two Delinquent Groups and One Nondelinquent Group" (Doctoral dissertation, University of Southern California, 1954).

[69]Erwin Schepses, "Boys Who Steal Cars," *Federal Probation*, 25 (March 1961), 56–62; Schepses, "The Young Car Thief," *Journal of Criminal Law, Criminology and Police Science*, 50 (March–April 1960), 569.

"mixed" car thieves who had engaged in other delinquencies as well, and eighty-one control group cases of training school wards charged with offenses other than automobile theft. He observed that, in most cases, joyriding is a group form of deviance, for most of the thieves had been apprehended with at least one other offender or "fall partner."[70]

The other major results turned up in this inquiry involve the following observations. First, car thieves are more frequently white boys, rather than black or Puerto Rican, even though black car thieves are fairly common in the Warwick population. This finding differs from that of Wattenberg and Balistrieri, who encountered few black joyriders in their sample. Car thieves were generally more intelligent and advanced in reading skills than were the other delinquent boys. They were also more commonly from comfortable economic circumstances than were the control youngsters. The "pure" automobile thieves were principally from unbroken homes, whereas the "mixed" car thieves and the control group boys were from broken homes in over half the cases.[71] According to Schepses, the car thieves exhibited a wide variety of family constellations: some had passive fathers; some had authoritarian parents; others showed various other family backgrounds. In his view, theories alleging that a specific kind of nuclear, middle-class family pattern leads to joyriding are incorrect.[72]

One indicator of the differences between the social process leading boys into car theft and the process drawing youngsters into other forms of delinquency is found in Schepses' observation that the car thieves were older at their first court appearance than were the other delinquents. His materials also indicate some slight tendency for car thieves to make a poorer institutional adjustment than the other wards; for example, more of them have records as runaways from the school.[73] Finally, the three groups differed slightly in post-release adjustment.[74]

Martin Dosick provides some further evidence on automobile thieves, derived from a study of federal Dyer Act violators.[75] He hypothesizes that car theft takes three general forms—joyriding by juveniles, along with "short history" and "long history" patterns of car theft among young adults (seventeen to twenty-one years old, predominantly). "Long history" thieves have engaged in a variety of criminal acts, are criminally sophisticated, and are enmeshed in delinquent subcultures. "Short history" offenders have been less involved in criminality. In Dosick's view, the young adult car thieves steal

[70]Schepses, "Boys Who Steal Cars," pp. 58–59.
[71]Ibid.
[72]Ibid., pp. 58–60.
[73]Ibid., pp. 60–61.
[74]Ibid., pp. 60–62.
[75]Martin L. Dosick, "Statement for Presentation to the Subcommittee to Investigate Juvenile Delinquency, United States Senate, January 17, 1967," mimeographed.

cars for "instrumental" reasons but for motives that differ between "short history" and "long history" offenders. "Long history" thieves steal cars for various impulsive reasons, which are usually illegitimate; but "short history" offenders steal cars as an illegitimate route to legitimate or conventional goals, such as a new job. Interviews and questionnaire responses on 200 Dyer Act violators generally confirmed these hypotheses. The "long history" car thieves had stolen cars to display masculine daring and toughness or to obtain other short-run delinquent goals. The "short history" offenders had taken cars to go to another area in search of a job or for other reasons of that kind. More were concerned about upward mobility and other middle-class goals than were the "long history" cases. Dosick concluded: "My data, then, points to some men who stole cars as incidents in delinquent careers, and to other men who took cars to help solve the problem of educational and job-based transition into male adulthood." [76]

Several other studies of violators of federal auto theft laws are available for examination. In one of these studies, a sample of auto offenders in federal institutions in 1964 was studied. [77] The researchers discovered that 49 percent of these lawbreakers had previously been convicted for auto theft, and 20 percent had stolen two or more cars in their last offense. The reasons for car theft seemed varied; 52 percent of the offenders had stolen cars for transportation, 32 percent had taken them for joyriding, and only 5 percent had stolen the auto to sell or strip it. However, 71 percent of the offenders under the age of seventeen had taken cars for joyriding purposes.

Larry Karacki investigated a group of 632 federal offenders charged with auto theft and compared them with 369 prisoners who had committed other offenses. [78] The car thieves showed greater residential mobility than the other lawbreakers; 59.3 percent of them had moved three or more times in the previous five years. More auto thieves had been in military service or confinement prior to their offense than was true of the other inmates. More auto thieves had poor work records than did the other offenders. The institutional adjustments of car thieves were poorer, more of them having been involved in disciplinary incidents, escapes, transfers to other institutions, or close or maximum confinement. The auto thieves showed poorer post-release records; 63.8 percent of them had violated parole in the two years after release, as contrasted to 46.3 percent of the other prisoners. Karacki concluded that these findings suggest that car thieves are from more unfavorable backgrounds than most other offenders, a conclusion different from most of the claims made about auto thieves.

The observation that emerges most consistently from these studies is the "favored group" character of joyriding. However, these reports are not entirely

[76]Ibid., p. 5.
[77]Federal Bureau of Prisons, "Auto Theft Offenders," 1964, mimeographed.
[78]Larry Karacki, "Youthful Auto Theft Offender Study," Federal Bureau of Prisons, 1966, unpublished.

consistent in this regard and are even less uniform on such matters as the ethnic backgrounds of car thieves. Most have little to say about specific contentions regarding family patterns in joyriding. At this point, we return to our initial observation that further investigations are needed that test specific hypotheses about automobile thieves, through the use of firsthand data gathering and measures specifically relevant to the dimensions of personality, family life, and so on, identified in the theoretical claims. Not much more can be said about car thieves until such studies are conducted.

THE PROPERTY OFFENDER, "ONE-TIME LOSER" ROLE CAREER[79]

As we have seen, casual offenders who do not define themselves as lawbreakers engage in various kinds of illegality. Some shoplift; some write "bad checks"; others steal cars. Still another kind of miscreant, the "one-time loser" property offender, commits isolated acts of petty or major larceny. We commented earlier on the applicability of risk-taking notions to these individuals who engage in idiosyncratic instances of lawbreaking. But let us examine these commonly encountered offenders in greater detail.

Definitional Dimensions

Offense Behavior. This category refers to offenders who commit a single property crime, frequently relatively serious in nature, such as grand theft. It excludes embezzlers, who also frequently commit only a single, isolated criminal act. One-time losers normally show little skill in criminality, so arrests are frequent.

Interactional Setting. The criminal acts of one-time losers are often carried out by the offender acting alone. In those cases in which several crime partners are involved, all are likely to be amateur offenders.

Self-concept. Individuals of this type exhibit noncriminal self-images. The offender usually admits readily that he has been involved in a serious deviant act, but maintains that it was atypical and that he is not a "real criminal." When seen in a correctional institution, he maintains that he is different from most of the inmates in the institution. In turn, he is seen as different by the inmate group. One-time losers are regarded as "square Johns" by other prisoners, that is, aliens in the criminalistic subculture of the prison.

Attitudes. These offenders verbalize prosocial sentiments. In prison, this offender is likely to be planning to resume a law-abiding career upon release.

---

[79]Don C. Gibbons, *Changing the Lawbreaker*, The Treatment of Delinquents and Criminals, © 1965. Reprinted by permission of Prentice-Hall, Inc., Englewood Cliffs, New Jersey, pp. 106–8.

In most cases, he was working at some conventional occupation before arrest. His attitudes toward conventional work roles are the same as those of law-abiding citizens. Similarly, individuals of this type are usually married and exhibit conventional attitudes regarding marital roles.

Role Career. The one-time loser property offender usually shows no delinquency record and no prior criminal record other than such minor law violations as drunkenness or disturbing the peace. Such persons are frequently placed on probation, and usually complete the probation period satisfactorily. Some who have committed a property offense involving large financial loss to the victim are sentenced to prison. Their adjustment there is satisfactory, they are infrequently involved in conduct infractions, and they gain early paroles. They complete the parole period satisfactorily and do not reenter the offender population.

Background Dimensions

Social Class. These violators are from several social class levels, but the most common is lower middle class. Many one-time losers are persons who earn modest incomes from skilled or semiskilled occupations and are normally from nonslum areas or relatively rural small towns.

Family Background. Most individuals in this type are from relatively stable and conventional family backgrounds. Behavior of this kind cannot be linked to any critical kind of family background situation.

Peer Group Associations. There is nothing particularly unusual or striking about the peer associations of one-time losers, either as juveniles or adults. These offenders receive no peer support or encouragement for criminal acts.

Contact with Defining Agencies. Contacts with defining agencies are not causally significant except perhaps in a minor but positive way. These offenders have the same interpretation of their criminal acts as do law enforcement agencies. The individual views crime as atypical for him. Although he may develop rationalizations which excuse this atypical, "bad" act, such rationalizations are not powerful enough to counteract other prosocial attitudes. Accordingly, these offenders do not usually repeat their deviant activities, quite apart from any rehabilitative programs in which they might have participated.

Some Evidence

Supporting evidence for the characterization of one-time loser property offenders is available in some abundance. Analyses of the records of adult probationers show that many offenders were involved in isolated, nonrecurrent acts of illegality. They also show these individuals to be quite conventional in appearance, without antisocial attitudes or criminogenic backgrounds.

In one of the most detailed of these studies, Ralph England examined the records of 500 federal probation cases who had completed the probationary period.[80] Most of the probationers were white, older, married males. They had been sentenced for a variety of offenses, although nearly half had been convicted of liquor law violations. The remainder had committed a large variety of crimes; but forgery, draft evasion, mail fraud, and assorted kinds of theft were also commonly found. Most of these probationers had records of law-abiding behavior prior to the offense. About 80 percent had remained free of recidivism for five years after being released from probation. In another study of these persons, England demonstrated that few had received any significant amount of casework on probation, so their successful adjustment must be attributed to general lack of criminal orientation.[81]

In another report concerned with prison inmates in Washington State, Clarence Schrag noted that prosocial "square Johns" are individuals who have been sentenced for some kind of larceny.[82] These felons lack serious records of criminality, they are not from particularly disordered or criminogenic backgrounds, and their actions seem attributable to various kinds of situational stresses.

This material reveals that many individuals whom the detached observer might judge as petty lawbreakers nonetheless are considered to be fairly serious law violators. Those who encounter certain contingent risks end up as probationers and prison inmates, so the legal consequences of their behavior are far from petty.

SUMMARY

The lawbreakers considered in Chapter Twelve tend to be those "bad guys" citizens have in mind when they discuss "the crime problem." The common man less often thinks of the behavior patterns discussed in this chapter as crime, although some of these activities are serious and costly kinds of illegality. In the next chapter, we shall turn to some cases of criminality carried

---

[80]Ralph W. England, Jr., "A Study of Postprobation Recidivism Among Five Hundred Federal Offenders," *Federal Probation*, 19 (September 1955), 10–16; see also England, "What is Responsible for Satisfactory Probation and Postprobation Outcome?" *Journal of Criminal Law, Criminology and Police Science*, 47 (March–April 1957), 667–76; Don C. Gibbons, "Probation: Theory and Reality," *Canadian Journal of Corrections*, 1 (January 1959), 10–18; Albert Wahl and Daniel Glaser, "Pilot Time Study of the Federal Probation Officer's Job," *Federal Probation*, 27 (September 1963), 20–25.

[81]England, "What is Responsible for Satisfactory Probation and Postprobation Outcome?"

[82]Clarence C. Schrag, "A Preliminary Criminal Typology," *Pacific Sociological Review*, 4 (Spring 1961), 11–16; Schrag, "Some Foundations for a Theory of Correction," in *The Prison*, ed. Donald R. Cressey (New York: Holt, Rinehart and Winston, 1961), pp. 346–56; see also Gillin, *The Wisconsin Prisoner*, passim.

on by businessmen and influential citizens. These forms of misconduct, such as white-collar crime, are rarely included in the laymen's complaints against lawlessness. Yet, as we shall see, some of these "hidden" forms of crime are much more costly and serious than all the "garden variety" crimes.

14

CRIMINALITY AMONG "RESPECTABLE CITIZENS"

Imagine the case of a suburban resident named John Smith who returns home late in the evening from a weekend excursion, only to discover that the lock on the back door of his house has been broken. Imagine further that he surprises a total stranger inside the house and that the intruder has a cloth bag filled with silverware and other items belonging to the Smith family. What will Smith do now? In all probability he will call the police, for he senses that he is the victim of a "burglary." The police will have no hesitation about arresting the apprehended stranger, for they recognize a "burglar" when they see one. When the offender is convicted of the crime, he will find the condemnation of the community directed at him, for he is clearly a "criminal person." The same could be said of acts of assault, rape, and various forms of property crime, and of the persons who do these things. Nearly all people consider such behavior as "crime." These are usually crude, highly visible attacks on persons or private property carried on by offenders who are undistinguished in appearance and unknown to the victims. Laymen, lawyers, and criminologists rarely ask whether these are "really" crimes or whether the actors are "really" criminals. In legal theory, these crimes are termed *mala en se,* in that they are seen as behavioral deviations uniformly condemned in the community. Criminal laws regarding these activities are viewed as the formal expression of conduct definitions described "in the mores." Such crimes stand in contrast to those that are *mala prohibita*—technically illegal actions that do not offend basic moral values or common public sentiments.

Is this all there is to crime? Are these nondescript persons who carry out crude actions the sum total of our criminals? What about respectable citizens who engage in "antisocial" or "unethical" conduct? What shall we say about "suede shoe" salesmen who use trickery and deceit to sell merchandise to unwary customers? What of violations of antitrust statutes, labor–management regulations, or related rules? Should criminologists be concerned with such things as fee-splitting and abortions or with embezzlement of large sums of money by trusted employees? Perhaps a sociological conception of crime that focuses on "socially harmful" conduct should be developed.

The most prominent development in this direction in the past several decades has centered about the concept of "white-collar crime," Edwin Sutherland's term for violations of laws designed to regulate conduct of business affairs. Used in this fashion, white-collar crime refers to a relatively homogeneous form of behavior involving actions undertaken by individuals to contribute to the financial success of the organization. They violate the law *for* the firm. However, as we shall see, the term has been loosely defined and indiscriminately employed since it was first introduced.[1] Even Sutherland failed to use it consistently. The net result is that the label is often attached to such actions as embezzlement, which bear little relationship to violations of regulatory provisions in business. Embezzlers are "enemies within" who surreptitiously steal the assets of the organization and make no contribution to the economic health of the business concern. Many other forms of conduct to which the term has been applied have even less in common with the original meaning of the concept.[2]

Blanket application of a single term to unrelated kinds of activity will not do; neither will an attempt to analyze all forms of criminality under a single encompassing label, as though these activities had a good deal in common. Some distinctions must be made regarding unlike forms of behavior by respectable people. These disparate acts must be sorted into relatively homogeneous behavioral units if causal progress is to be made. Incidentally, we use the term "respectable people" merely to draw attention to a group of criminal activities that are not often the target of public condemnation; the persons who carry on these actions are not considered as criminals in the common view. In point of legal fact, the behavior under discussion is illegal and those who engage in it are criminals From a sociological standpoint, one of the most interesting questions about this criminality concerns the reasons why the conduct does not discredit the perpetrators. How do they stay "respectable" while committing crimes?

In the following pages, we shall examine several categories of criminality conducted by respectable people. First, we will reserve the term "white-collar crime" for violations of business regulations or occupational roles carried on as contributory to the business or occupational enterprise. An offense will be said to be a white-collar one insofar as it represents violation of a legal rule constructed to govern business affairs or occupational practice and insofar

---

[1] The conceptual anarchy involved in applications of this term has been discussed by Geis. See Gilbert Geis, "Toward a Delineation of White-Collar Offenses," *Sociological Inquiry*, 32 (Spring 1962), 160–71. See also Geis, ed., *White-Collar Criminal* (New York: Atherton Press, 1968). This volume is a useful compilation of works on white-collar crime, including many of the studies and discussions herein cited.

[2] The concept is used in this way in connection with embezzlement in the popular literature. As a case in point, see Norman Jaspan with Hillel Black, *The Thief in the White Collar* (Philadelphia: J. B. Lippincott Co., 1960); see also Frank Gibney, *The Operators* (New York: Harper & Row, 1960).

as the law violation took place as part of the conduct of regular business or occupational activities. By this definition, misrepresentation in advertising is a white-collar crime, embezzlement is not. White-collar offenses are also distinguished from the common or conventional crimes of persons of comfortable economic circumstances. Acts of murder, manslaughter, rape, or drunk driving by high-status individuals need no special label, and these lawbreakers will not be discussed in this chapter. Embezzlement, in which employees are involved in stealing from the organization, is not a white-collar crime because it is not lawbreaking as a part of regular business practice. Finally, we shall separate from these other matters a group of offenses, such as abortion, engaged in by professional persons. These are discussed as "fringe" violations because they are frequently regarded with some condemnation within the professions in which they occur. Although these criminal acts use professional skills, they are occupationally deviant and are often committed by marginal figures within the professional group. They are usually endeavors of individuals acting alone rather than organizational events involving a collection of fellow deviants.[3]

WHITE-COLLAR CRIME

The White-Collar Criminal Role Career

The discussions of criminality in preceding chapters have begun with descriptions of offender role careers, organized in terms of definitional and background dimensions. In the case of white-collar offenders, we shall depart from that format. The following brief characterization amalgamates a series of different claims about these lawbreakers into a two-paragraph sketch. In an earlier book, the author presented this picture of white-collar violators:

> White collar crime means those criminal acts in which employees steal or violate the law for the benefit of their employer (although the individual employee may benefit from these violations too). Such crimes as embezzlement represent stealing *from* the employer. The employer does not encourage or sanction such activities, and they are not properly classified as white collar crime. . . . The white collar criminal category is comprised of those persons in business and corporate organizations who violate state and fed-

---

[3]These distinctions were first presented by the author in Don C. Gibbons and Donald L. Garrity, "Definition and Analysis of Certain Criminal Types," *Journal of Criminal Law, Criminology and Police Science*, 53 (March 1962), 34–35; they were elaborated in Don C. Gibbons, *Changing the Lawbreaker* (Englewood Cliffs, N.J.: Prentice-Hall, 1965), pp. 110–16. Geis has commented on this same matter and suggested that embezzlement should be separated from white-collar crime. See Geis, "Toward a Delineation of White-Collar Offenses," pp. 170–71.

eral regulatory statutes. The violations are usually processed by such federal regulatory agencies as the Federal Trade Commission, the Securities and Exchange Commission, and the Attorney General's office. Informal or civil court disposition of these cases is common, because of the difficulties of criminal prosecution. That is, partly because many of these activities are complex in character, it is often difficult to demonstrate that a clear-cut violation of law has occurred.

"Ignorance of the law" is not, in most cases, an important factor in white collar violations. That is, the offenders were involved in activities which they recognized as illegal or probably illegal. What does appear to be significant in these cases is a process in which business and corporate groups have come to define violations of regulatory statutes as acceptable or necessary conduct. Many white collar criminals acknowledge the moral superiority of regulatory provisions over prevailing business ethics, but legitimacy is withdrawn from these regulatory norms on the grounds that violation of such laws is necessary in order to survive in business, in order to regularize competition, and so on. In other words, it is likely that many white collar violators would prefer to conform to the law, but at the same time, they define the economic situation as demanding deviant conduct. If this line of argument is correct, explanations seeking to locate the genesis of white collar criminal acts in the backgrounds and personalities of the offenders would be misguided. Instead, white collar criminals are normal, conventional persons who come to learn definitions of the situation favorable to violation of law in the course of involvement in business or corporate organization.[4]

Development of the Concept

A variety of sociologists in the past half-dozen decades have made relatively inarticulate observations about the criminality of respectable citizens. Recurrent reports in the mass media concerning criminality and unethical conduct by businessmen, professionals, and other high status persons have also stimulated interest in this phenomenon. For example, Reader's Digest conducted an informal survey in 1941 of illegal or questionable business tactics among auto repairmen, radio repairmen, and automobile mechanics, which turned up evidence of widespread "crookedness."[5] In the same way, a former retail furniture salesman has revealed some of the hazards the customer runs in patronizing "borax houses" selling inexpensive furniture.[6] However, Sutherland turned the

[4]Don C. Gibbons, Changing the Lawbreaker, The Treatment of Delinquents and Criminals, © 1965. Reprinted by permission of Prentice-Hall, Inc., Englewood Cliffs, N.J., pp. 111-12.

[5]This survey is summarized in Herbert A. Bloch and Gilbert Geis, Man, Crime, and Society, 2nd ed. (New York: Random House, 1970), p. 315.

[6]Lee Nugent, "Here's How I Gyp You," Saturday Evening Post (June 29, 1957), pp. 25-76.

behavioral deviations of high-status persons into an important sociological category.[7]

Sutherland offered several accounts of what he meant by "white-collar crime." In one place, he declared: "White-collar crime may be defined approximately as a crime committed by a person of respectability and high status in the course of his occupation."[8] Another time, he said: "The white collar criminal is defined as a person with high socioeconomic status who violates the laws designed to regulate his occupational activities."[9] The first of these definitions implies that embezzlers are included, while the second suggests that they should not be so designated. In yet another discussion, Sutherland mentioned "robber barons" and other rapacious early figures in American commerce and industry as white-collar criminals. He declared that Philip Musica, alias Donald F. Coster, who stole a huge sum of money from the McKesson-Robbins drug company while its president, was a white-collar criminal, as were other individuals of this ilk, such as Insull, Kruger, and Sinclair. In that essay, he also named abortions, fee-splitting, political graft, and embezzlement as forms of white-collar crime.[10]

Many persons who adopted Sutherland's term to their own uses showed an even more cavalier attitude toward precise definitions. No wonder a number of critics of this concept have warned that objective analysis of criminality could deteriorate into denunciatory comments by the criminologist directed at activities that offend his private sensibilities but have little or nothing in common with crime.[11] The term might be reduced to a pejorative one rather than a scientific concept.

Although it has been loosely defined, the concept has not been so recklessly employed in actual research studies. The several major investigations of white-collar crime have all directed attention at a relatively consistent body of violations of regulatory provisions designed to control business operations. It seems clear that these are the kinds of behavior to which Sutherland intended the term to apply. At any rate, we think the concept should properly concern these forms of conduct.

[7]Edwin H. Sutherland, "White Collar Criminality," *American Sociological Review*, 5 (February 1940), 1–12; Sutherland, "Crime and Business," *Annals of the American Academy of Political and Social Science*, 217 (September 1941), 112–18; Sutherland, "Is 'White Collar Crime' Crime?" *American Sociological Review*, 10 (April 1945), 132–39; Sutherland, "The White Collar Criminal," in *Encyclopedia of Criminology*, ed. Vernon C. Branham and Samuel B. Kutash (New York: Philosophical Library, 1949), pp. 511–15; Sutherland, *White Collar Crime* (New York: The Dryden Press, 1949); Sutherland "Crime of Corporations," in *The Sutherland Papers*, ed. Albert Cohen, Alfred Lindesmith, and Karl Schuessler (Bloomington: Indiana University Press, 1956), pp. 78–96.

[8]Sutherland, *White Collar Crime*, p. 9.

[9]Sutherland, "The White Collar Criminal," p. 511.

[10]Sutherland, "White Collar Criminality."

[11]For a good resumé of the controversy surrounding this concept, see Frank E. Hartung, "A Critique of the Sociological Approach to Crime and Correction," *Law and Contemporary Problems*, 23 (Autumn 1958), 722–25.

Studies of White-Collar Crime

Sutherland's Research. Sutherland's investigation of the violations of corporations is probably the best-known study of this kind.[12] He examined the corporate life histories of the seventy largest namufacturing, mining, and mercantile corporations in the United States, which had been in existence for an average of forty-five years. He assembled the data on violations of regulations in the categories of restraint of trade, misrepresentation in advertising, infringement of patents, trademarks, and copyrights, unfair labor practices, rebates, financial fraud, and trust violations, violations of wartime regulations, and certain miscellaneous offenses.

Sutherland argues that these kinds of behavior represent criminality because the regulations or rules they violate meet the two basic criteria of crimes: a legal description of acts as socially injurious, and legal provision of a penalty for violations.[13] Moreover, he notes that many of the regulatory statutes state explicitly that the forbidden acts are "crimes" or "misdemeanors," and many of the laws have logical roots in the common law so that false advertising is an extension of common law fraud. Sutherland was forced to concede that the criminal status of certain of these activities was in question. In the instance of patent, trademark, and copyright infringements, federal statutes do not explicitly define some forms of infringement as crimes, nor do the laws provide criminal penalties, such as punitive damages. Sutherland admitted that of 222 decisions on infringements included in his data, 201 appeared not to constitute acts of criminality.[14]

Records of the corporations regarding violations of law indicated that the seventy had been involved over their organizational lifetimes in 980 violations (including the aforementioned 201 infringement cases). The most "criminal" corporation had been implicated in fifty decisions, whereas the least "criminal" had been involved in a single decision. These organizations had an average of fourteen adverse decisions in their careers.

Differential implementation of the law emerged most strikingly from the corporation records, in that only 158 (16 percent) of the 980 decisions had been reached in criminal courts. In other words, only 16 percent of these cases were "crimes" in the technical sense that they had been so labeled in a criminal tribunal. Of the rest, 425 had been reached in civil or equity courts, and 397 had been produced informally through commission orders or other procedures.[15] In Sutherland's view, the use of civil or informal, rather than criminal, proceedings against business organizations is related to the high

---

[12]Sutherland, *White Collar Crime.*

[13]Sutherland, "Is 'White Collar Crime' Crime?"; Sutherland, "The White Collar Criminal," p. 511; Sutherland, *White Collar Crime,* pp. 29–55.

[14]Sutherland, *White Collar Crime,* pp. 36–38, 95.

[15]*Ibid.,* pp. 22–25.

status of businessmen, the general trend away from harsh punishments, and relatively unorganized public resentment regarding these activities.[16]

The Black Market. In his study of World War II black market operations, Marshall Clinard provides another major collection of findings regarding white-collar crime.[17] Like Sutherland, Clinard felt compelled to defend labeling as "crime" the violations of rationing and economic control regulations imposed during the war. He argued that nearly all these rules defined the relevant behavior as offenses and allowed the use of criminal penalties in case of violations. However, the criminal status of certain behavioral forms Clinard studied is not clear; for example, civil rule violations that were unintentional and to which criminal sanctions were not applied. Additionally, the criminal status is ambiguous in certain violations of administrative orders of governmental agencies, rather than statutory rules, which were handled under contempt proceedings.[18]

However one might label the activities Clinard studied, the rules violated were clearly required during wartime. He makes a convincing case for the importance of these regulations in maintaining an equitable distribution of scarce goods and minimizing the long-term costs of the war.[19] He shows that violations of these regulations were so widespread that the war effort was jeopardized on more than one occasion. For example, during a nine-month period in 1944–45, counterfeit gasoline stamps involving 88 million gallons of gas were discovered, along with stamps for great quantities of rationed sugar and meat.[20] Price-ceiling violations, tie-in sales, and mislabeling and quality violations were similarly commonplace.

How can we explain these violations in the face of strong public support for price controls and rationing during wartime?[21] Who were the offenders engaged in these violations? According to Clinard, the black market offenders were principally conventional businessmen, many of whom were carrying on forms of business conduct closely akin to tactics they had used prior to wartime and the imposition of controls. The major exception, in which conventional criminals were involved, was the counterfeiting of rationing stamps.[22] Clinard attributed these law violations to a combination of factors, one of which was the generally lenient penalties handed out for violations. These were not sufficient to act as a deterrent to illegality.[23] He also maintained that the

[16]*Ibid.,* p. 46.
[17]Marshall B. Clinard, *The Black Market* (New York: Holt, Rinehart and Winston, 1952); Clinard, "Criminological Theories of Violations of Wartime REgulations," *American Sociological Review,* 11 (June 1946), 258–70.
[18]Clinard, *The Black Market,* pp. 226–63.
[19]*Ibid.,* pp. 1–7.
[20]*Ibid.,* pp. 28–50.
[21]*Ibid.,* pp. 89–114.
[22]*Ibid.,* pp. 156–63.
[23]*Ibid.,* pp. 151–53.

process of differential association among businessmen, in which group support was provided for hostile attitudes toward the regulations, was a major determinant of lawbreaking. He also believed that personality differences among businessmen must have played some part in their behavior, for some disobeyed the laws whereas others, similarly situated in the business world, refrained from violations.[24]

Hartung's Study. The third investigation in this survey was conducted by Frank Hartung and concerned violations of wartime regulations in the wholesale meat industry in Detroit.[25] Between 1942 and 1946, regulatory agencies in Detroit processed 122 cases of price violations and other illegal acts. Only two of the offenders had prior records of criminality, so these were predominantly acts of lawbreaking by respectable businessmen. The offenders paid $132,811 in damages and nearly $100,000 in fines; a few were given jail terms as well. A major conclusion from this investigation centers about the discrepancy between the generally lenient penalties invoked and the seriousness of the activities, measured in monetary terms and other ways as well.

Consumer Fraud. The principle of *caveat emptor,* or "Let the buyer beware," has always been dominant in merchandising relationships in the United States. Business tradition has always maintained that the customer should protect himself from the merchant. A good deal of evidence indicates that this tradition remains viable and that consumer fraud is endemic in the United States. For example, David Caplovitz has directed a large-scale study of consumer practices in four low-income housing project areas in New York City.[26] He found that the poor do pay more, for among other things, customers were often charged whatever the merchant thought he could obtain for his goods, with fixed prices being a rarity. Furthermore, the merchants often charged the poor exorbitant prices for inferior quality items and sold them used merchandise that was supposedly new. Although this activity is essentially unethical, much of it is also specifically illegal. Low-income citizens are frequently the victims of commercial crime directed at them by merchants and businessmen.

Other investigations all over the United States have turned up findings parallel to those of Caplovitz. Supermarkets, for example, have been observed charging higher prices to ghetto residents than to suburbanites for comparable items. Warren Magnuson and Jean Carper have drawn a large variety of these dismal facts together in a book documenting the widespread extent of consumer fraud in the United States.[27] For example, they report on the large

---

[24]*Ibid.*, pp. 285-389. See also Clinard, "Criminological Theories of Violations of Wartime Regulations," pp. 267-70. In this essay, Clinard indicates that the size of the firm is unrelated to rates of violation.

[25]Frank E. Hartung, "White-Collar Offenses in the Wholesale Meat Industry in Detroit," *American Journal of Sociology,* 56 (July 1950), 25-32.

[26]David Caplovitz, *The Poor Pay More* (New York: The Free Press, 1967).

[27]Warren G. Magnuson and Jean Carper, *The Dark Side of the Marketplace* (Englewood Cliffs, N.J.: Prentice-Hall, 1968).

number of complaints that have been directed at a nationally franchised transmission repair company for practices such as "lo-balling" in which a repair service is advertised at an extremely low price to lure a customer, and then the company gouges the unsuspecting person for unneeded repairs. The Magnuson and Carper book also documents the widespread selling of various unsafe products to American customers.

William Leonard and Marvin Weber provide still another report on consumer fraud.[28] In studying market pressures to which automobile manufacturers subject franchised new car dealers, these authors confirm the widely voiced suspicion of citizens that car dealers conduct unethical and illegal sales practices. These practices include compelling customers to purchase unwanted accessories, gouging customers on repairs, and providing illegal finance charges.

In addition to the direct consequences of consumer fraud, we should also note the indirect ramifications of this criminality. The argument that this activity is one of the criminogenic forces in other lawbreaking is meritous. Perhaps, because of their perceptions that businessmen often fail to observe proper standards of business conduct, many citizens show less allegiance to the law than they might otherwise. As we have previously noted: "Although definitive evidence on this matter is lacking, it is possible to gather up an abundance of statements by articulate criminals and delinquents in which these individuals allude to the facts of white-collar crime as one basis for their grievances against 'society.' "[29]

Is "White-Collar Crime" Crime?

The relatively strict definition of white-collar crime embodied in the previous three studies and contained in the perspective of this book has come under a barrage of critical attack, separate from that directed at the more omnibus usages of the term. Some persons would exclude the study of violations of regulatory statutes in business from criminological attention.[30] Paul Tappan has sometimes been identified as one of these abolitionists, although he has disclaimed some of the views attributed to him. He has criticized individuals who would make white-collar crime the study of "unethical" or "immoral" behavior, much of it outside legal codes. He has declared:

> The author wishes to make it clear here, since there has been some misconstruction of his view in literature on the subject, that he believes white-collar crime, properly and precisely defined, to be not only a legitimate

[28]William N. Leonard and Marvin Glenn Weber, "Automakers and Dealers: A Study of Criminogenic Market Factors," *Law and Society Review*, 4 (February 1970), 407-24.

[29]Gibbons, *Changing the Lawbreaker*, p. 271.

[30]For a good discussion of these criticisms, as well as rejoinders to them, see Donald R. Cressey, Foreword to 1961 edition of Sutherland, *White Collar Crime* (New York: Holt, Rinehart and Winston, 1961).

but an important phase of criminological inquiry. He deplores the loosely normative connotations that have been attached to the concept by some of Sutherland's interpreters, and he believes that they have resulted in some confusion so far as needed empirical research in this area is concerned.[31]

Robert Caldwell is another critic of white-collar ciminologists. Several of his remarks are not entirely clear, but one does have merit. He pointed out that decisions of civil courts and administrative agencies are often arrived at by procedures that have less regard for strict due process than do criminal court proceedings. Consequently, some question exists as to whether the actions processed in these ways would have been declared criminal if they had been dealt with in a criminal court.[32] These remarks underscore the persistent ambiguity inherent in the phenomenon of white-collar crime, even when it is carefully defined.

One of the most well-known attacks on the narrow conception of white-collar crime is that of Ernest Burgess, which we noted in Chapter Two. In a comment on Hartung's research, Burgess maintained that meat violations were not crimes because the offenders did not define themselves as criminals and the public did not regard them as criminals. Moreover, he held that because mores did not support the regulations, little social condemnation was directed at the violators. He also said these were not crimes because great numbers of citizens were involved in them.[33] Burgess believed that these may have been criminal acts in legalistic but not in sociological terms, for: "A criminal is a person who regards himself as a criminal and is so regarded by society. He is the product of the criminal-making process."[34] Most of Burgess's factual contentions are highly questionable; for example, Hartung notes that many people did, in fact, support price controls in wartime.[35] As we will see later, white-collar offenders view themselves as implicated in wrongful and criminal conduct. But even if Burgess had been correct in these assertions about white-collar crime, the general conception of crime and criminals he promoted must be declared nonsense. Countless offenders in prison do not think of themselves as criminals, although some citizens regard them as criminals. Are we to declare that they are not criminals? What is the "criminal-making process" of which Burgess speaks? Probably the clearest example would be the judicial process through which lawbreakers get tagged as criminals! There seems to be no single process through which law violators are manufactured. In summary, to follow Burgess's advice would be to enter a conceptual maze from which one might never escape.

[31]Paul W. Tappan, Crime, Justice and Correction (New York: McGraw-Hill Book Co., 1960), p. 7.

[32]Robert G. Caldwell, "A Reexamination of the Concept of White-Collar Crime," Federal Probation, 22 (March 1958), 30–36.

[33]Ernest W. Burgess, "Comment," American Journal of Sociology, 56 (July 1950), 32–33; Hartung, "White-Collar Offenses"; Hartung, "Rejoinder," pp. 33–34; Burgess, "Concluding Comment," p. 34.

[34]Burgess, "Concluding Comment."

[35]Hartung, "Rejoinder."

A second complaint that white-collar crime is somehow not "real" crime is that of George Vold, who has argued that because mores do not condemn these activities, the public does not resent the acts. Vold has declared: "There is an obvious and basic incongruity involved in the proposition that a community's leaders and more responsible elements are also its criminals."[36] We readily agree that the situation of high-status persons committing acts of criminality does seem incongruous. Vold would have us define these activities out of criminology. But we maintain that the low visibility of such crimes, lack of social condemnation, and the ability of offenders to maintain positions of social prestige while violating the law all represent critical matters for inquiry rather than topics to be conceptually jettisoned from criminological study.

Some Other Views

A number of others share our position that the ambiguities of business violations, differential treatment of these activites, and so on are fundamental problems for criminological analysis rather than matters to be excluded and subsequently disposed of. Donald Newman has argued that we should examine the problems of value conflicts, power relations, social control, and other matters revealed in white-collar crime.[37] Vilhelm Aubert has made much the same judgment, advising:

> For purposes of theoretical anlysis it is of prime importance to develop and apply concepts which preserve and emphasize the ambiguous nature of the white-collar crimes and not to "solve" the problem by classifying them as either "crimes" or "not crimes." Their controversial nature is exactly what makes them so interesting from a sociological point of view and what gives us a clue to important norm conflicts, clashing group interests, and maybe incipient social change.[38]

Aubert has illustrated the kinds of research he believes white-collar crime demands. In one study of the attitudes of Norwegian businessmen toward regulatory statutes, he found that they held allegiance in principle to law-abiding conduct but that they also felt a commitment to the special norms of the business group, which defined law violations of business regulations as acceptable behavior. In another case, he examined the character of a new Norwegian law governing the working conditions of domestic help. He found that the law provided criminal sanctions but was practically unenforceable because of the private nature of the violations. The law was a legislative hybrid,

[36]George B. Vold, *Theoretical Criminology* (New York: Oxford University Press, 1958), p. 253.

[37]Donald J. Newman, "White Collar Crime," *Law and Contemporary Problems*, 23 (Autumn 1958), 735–53.

[38]Vilhelm Aubert, "White-Collar Crime and Social Structure," *American Journal of Sociology*, 58 (November 1952), 266.

designed to pacify several interest groups who were making divergent demands on the lawmakers.[39]

Gilbert Geis has echoed some of these same sentiments with a call for more attention to the analytical problems embodied in white-collar crime.[40] Although he contends that the concept of white-collar crime is valuable, Geis notes that a number of improvements in its application are in order. Separate studies of relatively homogeneous forms of business crime are urgently needed for the encompassing class of white-collar offenses. Closer attention to internal variations would involve exploration of forms of corporate organization, patterns of corporate ethics, differential involvement of corporation officials in lawbreaking, and so on. The general theme is that white-collar analysis has tended to make uncritical generalizations about the behavior of corporations as entities without sufficient awareness of variations in the internal workings of these organizations.[41] Rather than more epidemiological documentation of the extent of white collar crimes, causal analysis detailing with the morphology of business crime is needed.

Geis made much of the facts regarding the electrical conspiracy case revealed in 1961, for these facts tell us a good deal about the complex character of lawbreaking in corporate organizations.[42]

The electrical conspiracy case refers to an antitrust criminal action taken by the federal government against twenty-nine corporations and forty-five corporation officials who had conspired to rig bids on electrical products and carry out other price-fixing schemes. The individual defendants were found guilty, a number were given jail terms, and the court fines totaled nearly two million dollars. General Electric received a $337,500 fine, and Westinghouse was fined $72,500. Additionally, these concerns are liable to civil actions by victims seeking recovery of the illegal profits.[43]

Richard Smith studied in detail the workings of the conspiracy within General Electric. He indicated that the price-fixing was not a new innovation, for the circuit-breaker division of General Electric had been involved in price-rigging for about twenty-five years before the criminal action was filed.[44] In his view, one condition that led to price-fixing in that corporation was the decentralization inaugurated in 1950. The corporation was broken into twenty-seven autonomous divisions made up of 110 small companies, thus

[39]*Ibid.*, pp. 268–70.

[40]Geis, "Toward a Delineation of White-Collar Offenses."

[41]*Ibid.*, pp. 161–68. Another statement that takes Sutherland to task for uncritical discussions of corporations as "criminal," as though they represented homogeneous entities, is Thomas I. Emerson, book review, *Yale Law Journal*, 59 (February 1950), 581–85.

[42]Richard Austin Smith, "The Incredible Electrical Conspiracy," Part I, *Fortune*, 63 (April 1961), 132–218; Part II, 63 (May 1961), 161–224. See also John Herling, *The Great Price Conspiracy: The Story of the Antitrust Violations in the Electrical Industry* (Washington, D.C.: Robert B. Luce, 1962).

[43]Smith, "The Incredible Electrical Conspiracy," Part I, pp. 132–34.

[44]*Ibid.*, Part I, p. 137.

reducing surveillance of the corporation from the top of the organizational hierarchy. A number of "collusionists" among the corporation executives looked on antitrust violations as illegal but necessary for economic survival, and therefore not unethical. Most of them engaged in conspiratorial tactics reluctantly but felt that the erratic features of the electrical business demanded violation of the law to stabilize the market. Without doubt, they were clearly aware of the illegal nature of their activities, for they took great precautions to conduct their conspiratorial affairs in secrecy and to disguise their activities. At the same time, other company officials refused to engage in price-fixing, holding that such practices were clearly unethical. These observations undermine the picture of the corporation as a monolith of like-minded individuals.[45] Examples of corporation officials who were either ignorant of the conspiracy or refused to participate in it were also observed in other of the corporations.[46]

There is more to the explanation of price-fixing in this case than the association of criminally-inclined executives. Smith indicates that there were variations in the extent of lawbreaking in different parts of the corporation as well as fluctuations in the degree of criminality within organizational units. During several periods of "white sale" waves of discounting prices, pressures to engage in price stabilization became particularly acute. The price-rigging conspiracies were revived at these times after they had been relatively dormant.[47]

In a final comment on this price-fixing case, Smith argues:

The problem for American business does not start and stop with the scofflaws of the electrical industry or with anti-trust. Much was made of the fact that G.E. operated under a system of disjointed authority, and this was one reason it got into trouble. A more significant factor, the disjointment of morals, is something for American executives to think about in all aspects of their relations with their companies, each other, and the community.[48]

The Ethics of Businessmen

Some other pieces of evidence exist on the question of business ethics, corporate organization, and allied matters. Robert Lane studied patterns of labor relations violations and misrepresentation cases in the New England shoe industry.[49] One issue he examined was the question of ignorance of the law as a factor of criminality. His findings suggest that this factor is not a major consideration, for shoe manufacturing concerns with the largest employee

[45]*Ibid.*, Part I, pp. 134–35.
[46]Geis, "Toward a Delineation of White-Collar Offenses," pp. 168–69.
[47]Smith, "The Incredible Electrical Conspiracy," Part I, pp. 132–218.
[48]*Ibid.*, Part II, p. 224.
[49]Robert E. Lane, "Why Business Men Violate the Law," *Journal of Criminal Law, Criminology and Police Science*, 44 (July–August 1953), 151–65. See this article for further data on the extent of white-collar offenses.

groups were more involved in lawbreaking than those with fewer workers. This finding is the reverse of what we might expect if ignorance plays a part in violations, in that large firms can avail themselves of more legal counsel and advice than small ones and should thus be better able to maintain a law-abiding record.[50] Some support for a differential association interpretation of law violations exists, for Lane observed that violation rates varied from community to community. Moreover, many of the individuals implicated in law violations also read materials hostile toward governmental regulations. Finally, illegality was more common in smaller manufacturing towns, where businessmen with antiregulatory attitudes might conceivably be in common contact with one another.[51] In another publication dealing at length with the attitudes and values of businessmen, Lane contends that an older business ideology involving such beliefs as the sacredness of private enterprise and the inalienable rights of industry has been undermined, without a newer ethical code taking complete form. Accordingly hostility toward business regulations may be a transitional stage, to be succeeded by a revised ethical system.[52]

A second study of the ethical standards of businessmen is by Raymond Baumhart, involving a sample of 1,700 executives in various business organizations in the United States.[53] These officials were given a detailed questionnaire that probed a variety of matters having to do with ethical beliefs and practices in business. Although much of the behavior reported in that study had to do with activities and practices that were not clearly illegal, the responses shed considerable light on the question of antiregulatory attitudes of businessmen as a factor in white-collar crime.

According to the findings of this study, most businessmen verbalized sentiments of general concern for ethical business behavior. Nearly all said that businessmen should be concerned with goals additional to profit making, and 85 percent declared that a manager who operates solely in terms of his stockholders' interests would be unethical. Only about 20 percent agreed with the principle of *caveat emptor*. Nearly all said that use of call girls as a business tactic or "padding" of expense accounts would be clearly unethical.

However, many of these executives disagreed on the specifics of "ethical" or "unethical" conduct. Moreover, many of them professed a higher level of ethical aspiration and conduct for themselves than they were willing to concede for the "average businessman." Baumhart argues that the judgments made about the probable behavior of other executives are probably closer to the actual conduct of affairs in business than are the claims these people make about themselves. In other words, executives may put forth an exagger-

[50]*Ibid.*, pp. 155–58.
[51]*Ibid.*, pp. 158–61.
[52]Robert E. Lane, *The Regulation of Businessmen* (New Haven, Conn.: Yale University Press, 1954).
[53]Raymond C. Baumhart, "How Ethical are Businessmen?" *Harvard Business Review*, 39 (July –August 1961), 6–176.

ated picture of themselves, reporting on the kind of organizational official they would prefer to be rather than the kind they actually represent.[54]

These officials not only expressed considerable cynicism about the ethical behavior of other organization executives, in addition many of them asserted that unethical practices, many of which are also illegal, were widespread. Although the practices varied from one industry to another, the use of call girls, granting of gratuities, price violations, and dishonest advertising were among those often identified as common in industry.

The responses of the officials in this study suggest that one major influence determining the degree of unethical behavior in organizations is the model of conduct those at the top of the executive pyramid set. The "behavior of company superiors" was ranked as the most important variable for ethical or unethical conduct. Baumhart employed an "organization man" kind of theory to interpret these results, arguing that organizations vary in the degree to which individual executives are in differential association with carriers of unethical beliefs or practices.[55] Interestingly, the majority of the persons studied argued that an industrywide ethical code would be desirable as a means of reducing unethical activities, but they favored systems of code enforcement without "teeth," such as self-policing within the industry. Only about 4 percent of them thought that a government agency should have charge of enforcing a code of ethics.[56]

White-Collar Crime and Public Opinion

We have seen the common contention that white-collar crime is not really crime because the public does not regard it as criminality. We also observed that certain studies of citizen opinion, particularly with regard to wartime rationing and price-control regulations, indicated that citizens supported these laws and condemned violations. This critical question needs more attention as a part of the broader interest in public attitudes toward laws in general. Chapter Two drew attention to one illustrative case of the kind of research required.[57] Newman examined laymen's views of violations of the Federal Food, Drug and Cosmetic Act of 1938. In this investigation, a sample of citizens was asked to select the punishments thought appropriate in cases of product misbranding and food adulteration. Their selections were then compared to the penalties actually invoked in the cases studied. About 80 percent of the consumer respondents felt that the penalties for these offenses should have been more severe than the ones levied. At the same time, the citizens favored

---

[54]Ibid., pp. 16-19.
[55]Ibid., pp. 156-57.
[56]Ibid., pp. 166-72.
[57]Donald J. Newman, "Public Attitudes Toward a Form of White Collar Crime," Social Problems, 4 (January 1957), 228-32.

sanctions that were less harsh than those used for such conventional crimes as burglary. In general, their penalty choices were within the range of punishments allowable in existing statutes. Thus, these citizens seemed generally satisfied with existing legislation, and their dissatisfaction was with the administration of the statutes.

Concluding Comment

This book is allied with criminological arguments that favor examination of white-collar crime. The preceding commentary has stressed a number of complex problems that will continue to plague investigation of this kind of criminal conduct. For example, we shall continue to find instances of business or occupational behavior that are not clearly criminal or noncriminal, owing to the administrative procedures by which the activity was handled, the complexity of the behavior, and other factors. But excluding these difficulties from scrutiny will not "solve" them. Instead, careful attention to such matters as clear specification of categories of business behavior will allow us to make progress in the study of white-collar crime. A number of the studies previously cited stand as models of the kind of inquiry that should be pursued in criminology.

Throughout most of the preceding passages, we have spoken of business and occupational offenses as making up white-collar crime. Nearly all the empirical evidence on this kind of lawbreaking has centered about the behavior of corporations and large businesses. But there is no logical reason why the deviant acts of professional persons and workers in small-scale occupational settings should not also be studied. Earl Quinney's investigation of prescription violations among retail pharmacists provides one case of this sort of research.[58] Quinney studied the extent and nature of prescription law violations among druggists in Albany, New York. Twenty pharmacists detected in prescription violations were compared with another group of sixty druggists who had not been so involved.

Quinney points out that retail pharmacy combines elements of both a professional and a business pursuit, so the druggist should experience some degree of role strain as a consequence. He identified four role orientations among the pharmacists he studied: some saw themselves as professionals, some as businessmen, some as involved in both roles, and a few were indifferent to these matters. Prescription violations were significantly related to the role orientations of the druggists, in that 75 percent of the business-oriented persons had committed violations, whereas none of the professionally-oriented persons had. Generally, the more professionally oriented the pharmacist, the lower the likelihood of occupational deviance. Quinney con-

[58]Earl R. Quinney, "Occupational Structure and Criminal Behavior: Prescription Violation by Retail Pharmacists," *Social Problems*, 11 (Fall 1963), 179–85.

tends that the professional orientation of the druggists provided internal social controls that constrained them from deviant activity, where these standards did not influence the business-oriented persons. Quinney suggests that we might find the same phenomena of role strains and deviant conduct in other professions and occupations, such as dentistry, optometry, chiropody, osteopathy, real estate, and accounting, which combine elements of business and profession.

EMBEZZLEMENT AND EMBEZZLERS[59]

The opening remarks of this chapter characterized embezzlers as "enemies within," who are engaged in financial subversion, rather than as organizational warriors who make positive contributions to the business firm or concern. These are furtive and secretive enemies, the extent of their surreptitious deviations almost impossible to identify with much accuracy. Instead, wildly divergent estimates of the total financial cost of employee pilfering and embezzlement have been advanced. Nevertheless, these employee thieves are clearly responsible for huge financial losses incurred by the organization.

One indication of the magnitude of this kind of crime has been provided by Norman Jaspan, who noted that thefts and embezzlements by employees may total more than $4,000,000 per day in the United States. He also indicated that bonded losses from thefts in 1946 amounted to $13,000,000, whereas in 1957 such losses totaled $35,000,000. The significance of these figures is that only about 10 percent of the private business firms in the United States are covered by theft insurance, so the total losses must have been greatly in excess of these figures.[60] Jaspan also observed that his own business protective agency unearthed $60,000,000 of employee dishonesty in 1959 alone; again, this kind of deviant activity must be extensive indeed.[61] Jaspan's account on employees who steal is filled with case history documents which seem to show that dishonest workers are an extremely varied bag of individuals who steal out of a diverse set of motives.

Another well-researched statement on embezzlement and theft set the amount of employee larcenies at $500,000,000 in 1956, but also indicated that some experts regard this figure as too low, contending that the losses from employee criminality are probably in excess of one billion dollars per year.[62] One expert has claimed that the total cost of this kind of crime is nearer three billion dollars than these lower estimates. To gauge the importance of

[59]For a detailed bibliography of studies on embezzlement, see Donald R. Cressey, *Other People's Money* (Belmont, Calif.: Wadsworth Publishing Co., 1971), pp. 159–66.

[60]Jaspan, *The Thief in the White Collar*, p. 234.

[61]*Ibid.*, p. 10.

[62]"Embezzlers, the Trusted Thieves," *Fortune*, 56 (November 1957), 142–88.

these amounts, consider the FBI estimate that the total loss from burglaries, armed roberies, auto thefts, and incidents of pickpocket activity was only about $440,000,000 in 1956. Employees steal at least twice this amount from their employers. This same discussion noted that embezzlement is a crime of growing magnitude, for fidelity insurance losses increased by about 250 percent between 1946 and 1956, although insurance in force grew only by about 70 percent. This article pointed out that bank losses through misappropriations of funds have been increasing steadily in recent decades. In 1951, the Federal Deposit Insurance Corporation had 608 reports of defalcations in insured banks, involving 759 employees from various employee levels. These figures would be considerably higher at the present.

Finally, in her research on shoplifting, Cameron found that twelve department stores in New York City set their losses from shoplifting and employee pilferage combined at ten million dollars in 1951. She also noted that store protection agencies estimate that employee thefts make up three-fourths of all the "inventory shrinkage" stores suffer.[63] One writer has argued that the increase in employee criminality is linked to the changing "scale" of modern societal organization, growing impersonality within organizations, and attenuation of attitudes holding wealth sacred.[64] Whatever the causes, these findings indicate that respectable employees involved in stealing from their employers are legion.

THE EMBEZZLER ROLE CAREER[65]

Definitional Dimensions

Offense Behavior. This type involves persons who violate positions of trust by stealing from an employer, excluding those employees who pilfer small amounts of merchandise. The embezzler is an employee who converts a large sum of his employer's money to his own uses, usually through some form of alteration of business records.

Interactional Setting. The interactional setting of embezzlement is one in which the violator ostensibly performs a conventional occupational task while, in secrecy, he engages in criminal acts. The embezzler takes great pains to keep his illegal activities minimally visible. Normally, the criminal actions of the embezzler are unknown to the employer, the spouse of the offender, and other associates of the deviant.

[63]Mary Owen Cameron, *The Booster and the Snitch* (New York: The Free Press, 1964), pp. 9–11.
[64]David Cort, "The Embezzler," *The Nation,* 188 (April 18, 1959), 339–42.
[65]Don C. Gibbons, *Changing the Lawbreaker,* The Treatment of Delinquents and Criminals, © 1965. Reprinted by permission of Prentice-Hall, Inc., Englewood Cliffs, New Jersey, pp. 114–16.

Self-concept. The embezzler exhibits a noncriminal self-image, but shows relatively elaborate rationalizations for his conduct when discovered in embezzlement. These often include allegations that he was only "borrowing" the money, not stealing it. It appears that such rationalizations are contrived by the offender *before* he begins to embezzle. They allow him to square deviant activities with his self-image as a law-abiding person. When the embezzler is sent to prison upon conviction, he is likely to argue that, unlike the other inmates, he is not a "real"criminal.

Attitudes. The embezzler is characterized by conventional, prosocial attitudes. The offender indicates that he acknowledges the "bad" character of such acts, but has rationalizations which excuse him from culpability for these "bad" and "evil" actions.

Role Career. The embezzler is normally a person without any delinquent or criminal record prior to involvement in embezzlement. One reason is, of course, that persons with criminal records are not able to obtain positions of trust in the first place. A great many detected embezzlers are dealt with informally by their employers or by bonding agencies, so that only a small and perhaps biased sample is handled within criminal courts. Those offenders who are convicted and sentenced to institutions tend to make a good adjustment in that setting. Upon release, further violations of the law are unlikely. However, it is probable that many paroled embezzlers find readjustment to civilian society somewhat difficult insofar as their criminal records create impediments for them. A paroled embezzler is likely to have some trouble obtaining another position of trust.

Background Dimensions

Social Class. Embezzlers tend as a group to be persons from relatively comfortable, middle class backgrounds.

Family Background. The parental background of the embezzler appears to be of little significance in the explanation of deviation. Embezzlers do not develop out of any specific parent–child interaction pattern. On the other hand, the offender's adult family pattern does have some significance, for some of his "nonshareable" problems, often described as "wine, women, and song" difficulties, relate to patterns of family activity. It is likely that many acts of embezzlement develop as attempts to sustain a standard of living and to live according to a pattern of expectations for which legitimate income is insufficient.

Peer Group Associations. The peer associations of embezzlers are of little significance in the development of this behavior. Such offenders do not learn attitudes favorable to embezzlement or how to embezzle from their associates. Peer associations may play some part in embezzlement in that the offender is unable to communicate about certain "nonshareable" problems with his peers.

Contact with Defining Agencies. Contacts with the police, courts, and correctional agencies do not seem to be highly significant for embezzlers. In prison, the embezzler is regarded by other inmates as a "square John." He associates differentially with other "square Johns," and such associations tend to reinforce the offender's conception of himself as a law-abiding citizen.

Some Evidence

The typological description of embezzlers describes individuals who steal relatively large sums of money, often in increments over an extended time period. The typological sketch said nothing about other employees who pilfer small amounts and often steal only once or twice. One major reason for emphasizing the serious cases of embezzlement is that a more complex chain of events may be required to produce this form of conduct than is the case in petty thefts. Large-scale embezzlements may be responses to emergency situations the actor faces, whereas pilfering may often be spur-of-the-moment behavior. Perhaps workers who carry away small items or petty amounts of cash do not face a major social-psychological problem of reconciling this conduct with their self-conception, for they may be able to dismiss it as innocuous and "not really criminal." The large-scale thief may go through a more elaborate process of contriving face-saving rationalizations. A second reason for the stress on costly embezzlement is that most of the data from which the typological characterization has been drawn are based on major cases of trust violation.

Clearly embezzlement is a form of illegality that rarely results in criminal prosecution. Jerome Hall has suggested that only about 1 percent of the cases of trust violation are dealt with as criminal actions.[66] He enumerated a number of factors responsible for infrequent prosecution, one of which is the embezzler's deviation in appearance and demeanor from the stereotype of the "crook" or "bad guy." In addition, organizations fear adverse public reactions to "cold-hearted" companies that prosecute their employees. Management often feels some loyalty to the worker, particularly if he is an "old-timer." Along a similar line, the actor's lawbreaking is often related to a dire emergency he faces, so the embezzler is often the beneficiary of sympathetic understanding. Still other factors include costs and uncertainty associated with prosecutions, as well as the difficulties of obtaining restitution. Finally, according to Hall, too much scrutiny of employee behavior may throw unwelcome investigative light into other dark corners and turn up evidence of peccadilloes by management.[67]

[66]Jerome Hall, *Theft, Law and Society,* 2nd ed. (Indianapolis: Bobbs-Merrill Co., 1952), pp. 304–6.
[67]*Ibid.,* pp. 306–12.

Several studies of embezzlers have been conducted, one of which was by Elizabeth Redden, who examined 7,629 cases from fidelity insurance company records and classified them into a half-dozen commonsensical categories, including such types as "the little-fellow embezzler," "the grab-and-run-embezzler," and so on.[68]

The best sociological study of embezzlers to date was carried out by Donald Cressey.[69] In his opening comments, Cressey distinguishes between investigations of *systematic* and *genetic* causation. Systematic causation refers to a definable conjuncture of events operating at the time of an offense. It is the person–situation complex in existence just preceding a deviant act; an example might be drinking and quarreling, which eventuates in a husband–wife assault case. Genetic causation refers to the prior life experiences that have propelled the individual into his present circumstances. In the case of trust violators, the study of systematic causation asks: "What goes on at about the time a person embezzles?" while genetic investigations probe into the early life experiences which may produce a "budding grifter" or an individual predisposed to thievery.[70] Cressey identified his inquiry as a case of systematic etiology.

Cressey employed the method of analytic induction, in which hypotheses are formulated and then examined in application to a group of embezzlers. These hypotheses are rejected if found defective, until a hypothesis is discovered that accounts for the cases under study.[71] Although the research began as a study of embezzlement, it was quickly changed to an investigation of "criminal violation of financial trust." Cressey discovered that some persons in his group of 133 prisoners from Joliet Prison, Illinois, Chino in California, and the federal penitentiary at Terre Haute, Indiana, who were charged with embezzlement had actually been involved in such offenses as confidence swindles. For a subject to be included in the study as a violator of financial trust, he must have accepted a position of trust in good faith and then violated that trust by criminality.[72] Note that "criminal violation of financial trust" is not a category derived from statutory law. It is behavioral and groups similar individuals who may have been formally charged with a variety of specific offenses.

Cressey rejected several initial formulations about the dynamics of trust violation, including one that violations occur when employees learn that theft is defined as acceptable behavior within the organization. Another hypothesis

<hr>

[68]Elizabeth Redden, "Embezzlement: A Study of One Kind of Criminal Behavior with Prediction Tables Based on Fidelity Insurance Records" (Doctoral dissertation, University of Chicago, 1939).

[69]Donald Cressey, *Other People's Money* (Belmont, Calif.: Wadsworth Publishing Co., 1971).

[70]*Ibid.*, pp. 12-14.

[71]*Ibid.*, pp. 13-17. For criticisms of this method, see Ralph H. Turner, "The Quest for Universals in Sociological Research," *American Sociological Review*, 18 (December 1953), 604-11; W. S. Robinson, "The Logical Structure of Analytic Induction," *American Sociological Review*, 16 (December 1961), 812-18.

[72]Cressey, *Other People's Money*, pp. 19-26.

that failed the test of evidence was that violations of trust take place when individuals experience financial emergencies. Some offenders had encountered grave financial difficulties earlier in their occupational careers but had not "solved" these by theft. The final version of Cressey's generalization about embezzlement is: "Trusted persons become trust violators when they conceive of themselves as having a financial problem which is nonshareable, are aware that this problem can be secretly resolved by violation of the position of financial trust, and are able to apply to their own conduct in that situation verbalizations which enable them to adjust their conceptions of themselves as trusted persons with their conceptions as users of the entrusted funds or property."[73] The entire process must occur before trust violation takes place.

We should emphasize two major aspects of this process: the role of *nonshareable* problems in trust violation and the development of justificatory rationalizations *in advance* of the deviant act. Cressey's concept of nonshareable problems is an inclusive label for a plethora of difficulties about which the actor cannot communicate to others, so he cannot resolve them by legitimate means. One kind of nonshareable problem centers about the sort of activity the layman calls "booze, bookies, and blondes," in which an individual gets entangled in unconventional or discrediting experiences that must be kept hidden from others. Many of Cressey's subjects had nonshareable problems involving attempts to "live up to one's position; as in the case of bank employees who felt compelled to affect life styles for which their incomes were not adequate. In general, most of the problems of the trust violators related to status-seeking or status-maintaining behaviors, which created financial problems for them.[74]

Cressey's analysis of the role of rationalizations in trust violation represents a major contribution to etiological understanding. His point is that these justificatory arguments must be developed *before* embezzlement can occur, which is markedly different from conventional views of rationalizations. He asserts:

> The rationalizations which are used by trust violators are necessary and essential to criminal violation of trust. They are not merely *ex post facto* justifications for conduct which already has been enacted, but are pertinent and real "reasons" which the person has for acting. When the relationship between a personal non-shareable problem and the position of trust is perceived according to the bias induced by the presence of a rationalization which makes trust violation in some way justified, trust violation results.[75]

The significance of this argument extends well beyond trust violation. The process wherein actors develop rationalizations before they engage in deviance

[73]*Ibid.*, p. 30.
[74]*Ibid.*, pp. 33–76.
[75]*Ibid.*, pp. 136–37.

probably also occurs in other forms of lawbreaking. Gresham Sykes and David Matza contend that juvenile delinquents contrive neutralizing beliefs allowing them to violate norms they uphold in principle. These techniques of neutralization precede deviant activities rather than follow from them.[76]

Critics of Cressey's generalizations have stressed several points thought to be defects in his work. Karl Schuessler has complained that one can hardly imagine an adequate test of the argument, for a cross-section of the general population would have to be examined. In that way, it might be possible to determine whether all individuals who have nonshareable problems and appropriate rationalizations engage in trust violations.[77] Clinard has also expressed disappointment with Cressey's research, arguing that some of Cressey's techniques are questionable. However, Clinard's major contention is that the behavioral sequence lacks predictive meaning. We can only predict occurrence of trust violation at the moment that the complete process has transpired. Clinard contends that other studies could perhaps discover particular personality configurations or social situations that are indicators of the onset of trust violation, and would be operative some time prior to trust violation.[78] But Clinard may well be in error. Perhaps trust violation is a kind of criminality in which genetic and systematic aspects of causation merge into a single process. There may not be any clear-cut personality dynamics that predispose persons to embezzlement so that the etiology of this behavior may begin with involvement in nonshareable predicaments, and not before. If this is the case, the search for long-term genetic influences or causes would be an illusory goal.

Most of the commentary on embezzlement to date, other than that of Cressey, has emphasized the traits and characteristics of the violator. Little or no attention has been paid to situational contexts that may contribute to trust violation. As a result, we cannot point to much evidence showing the influence of social situations. However, one bit of material regarding the organization of a bank lends itself to speculation in this direction. Chris Argyris has reported that one bank he studied went about hiring employees thought to be "the right type." These workers were passive, quiet, obedient, and careful individuals. Once employed, they avoided each other's conversation and remained on cordial but distant terms. These employees rarely communicated any complaints and opinions about the work situation to their superiors, and bank officials did not try to deal with human relations problems in the bank.[79]

---

[76]Gresham M. Sykes and David Matza, "Techniques of Neutralization: A Theory of Delinquency," *American Sociological Review*, 22 (December 1957), 664-70.

[77]Karl F. Schuessler, review of *Other People's Money, American Journal of Sociology*, 49 (May 1954), 604.

[78]Marshall B. Clinard, review of *Other People's Money, American Sociological Review*, 19 (June 1954), 362-63.

[79]Chris Argyris, *Human Relations in a Bank*, Labor and Management Center, Reprint No. 21 (New Haven, Conn.: Yale University, 1954); Argyris, "Human Relations in a Bank," *Harvard Business Review*, 32 (September-October 1954), 63-72.

Although this research had nothing directly to do with embezzlement, such a work situation could easily contribute to the nonshareable character of employee problems.

Another set of observations on this point has to do with the extremely low rate of employee thefts among postal workers. Embezzlement and thefts in United States Post Offices appear to be rare, particularly given the opportunities for criminality present in that situation. Hall has indicated that, in 1951, only 531 workers were apprehended for mail theft and only 144 employees detected in embezzlement out of a work force of over a half-million employees. However, 569 of these 675 were prosecuted and convicted. Hall suggested that several factors operate to repress employee crimes, including the plethora of postal inspectors, which maximizes likelihood of detection, and the frequent prosecution of detected offenders, which deters other potential thieves. On the positive side, postal employees have relatively high morale and identification with the postal service, which may affect their behavior, too.[80] Any organization that desires to repress employee pilfering and embezzlement might pay close attention to these situational variables.[81]

Erwin Smigel's study of public attitudes toward stealing from organizations of varied size also has implications for embezzlement control. He discovered that most citizens say they disapprove of stealing from organizations of any size. But when forced to choose the organization from which they would steal with least reluctance, most said they would do so first from large business firms, then from governmental agencies, and from small businesses last. Apparently two considerations influenced most of these persons: the relative risks of detection and the principle of least evil. They regarded stealing from large businesses as less reprehensible and less harmful than other thefts. We might argue that this willingness to steal from large businesses stems from views that regard such organizations as cold and impersonal.[82] At any rate, these kinds of contentions regarding situational influences in employee theft are worthy of further exploration.

THE PROFESSIONAL "FRINGE" VIOLATOR ROLE CAREER[83]

The last group of lawbreaking respectable citizens to be considered in this chapter is that of professional "fringe" violators. This category designates

[80]Hall, Theft, Law and Society, pp. 326–30. For a discussion which indicates that postal workers are involved in a good deal of "deviance" which is not criminal in nature, see Dean Harper and Frederick Emmert, "Work Behavior in a Service Industry," Social Forces, 42 (December 1963), 216–25.

[81]For a technical discussion of methods of controlling embezzlement in business, see Albert E. Keller, Embezzlement and Internal Control (Washington, D.C.: Warner-Arms Publishing Co., 1946).

[82]Erwin O. Smigel, "Public Attitudes Toward Stealing as Related to the Size of the Victim Organization," American Sociological Review, 21 (June 1956), 320–27.

[83]Don C. Gibbons, Changing the Lawbreaker, The Treatment of Delinquents and Criminals, © 1965. Reprinted by permission of Prentice-Hall, Inc., Englewood Cliffs, New Jersey, pp. 112–14.

those who engage in law violations in which their professional skills are centrally involved. Professional colleagues regard their activities as unacceptable forms of behavior. Yet at the same time, fringe violators are often involved in symbiotic ties with more law-abiding fellow professionals so that the deviants perform services for the nondeviants. The doctor-abortionist who gets his referrals from other physicians who are themselves loath to commit abortions is the clearest case of a violator who occupies a marginal or fringe position within a professional group.

Definitional Dimensions

Offense Behavior. Professional fringe violators are members of legitimate professions who employ professional skills in the commission of crimes not regarded as legitimate activities within the profession. Illegal abortions by physicians represent the clearest cases, particularly those instances of "abortion mills" in which the physician is involved in full-time, systematic practice of abortion. Also included would be illegal practices occasionally found among members of the legal profession. This type does not include ordinary crimes committed by persons who incidentally happen to be professional persons.

Interactional Setting. Professional fringe violators are normally involved in two-person crimes involving the offender and a "victim." In the instance of abortions, no victim in the usual sense is involved, for the pregnant female has sought out the services of the abortionist. Although fringe violators are regarded by other professionals as engaged in behavior which is beyond the pale, many of these offenders are at the same time abetted in their activities by other professional persons. In the case of abortion, for example, many abortionists commit these illegal acts upon females who have been referred to them by other physicians who are themselves unwilling to perform abortions.

Self-concept. Fringe violators regard themselves as legitimate professional persons, not as criminals. Although the offender acknowledges the illegal character of his actions, he normally offers some explanation or rationalization by which he attempts to square criminality with his noncriminal self-image.

Attitudes. Fringe violators exhibit conventional, prosocial attitudes. Many abortionists would argue that they are performing a service which is technically illegal but necessary. They maintain that the proper solution to the problem of abortion would be to modify the legal statutes which define such acts as criminal.

Role Career. In the nature of this form of criminality, fringe violators begin their criminal careers late in life. Some of them commit only a single law violation, others engage in several episodes of criminality, still others are involved in systematic criminal practice. Most of these law violations do not result in detection or prosecution. Among offenders who are prosecuted, different outcomes develop. Some desist from further crimes of this kind, whereas in other cases prosecution and incarceration fail to deter the offender from further deviant acts.

Background Dimensions

Social Class. By definition, professional fringe violators are middle income, middle class persons. Law violations of this kind are likely to be differentially common among professional persons in urban areas and less common among rural or small-town professionals.

Family Background. Professional fringe violators are in most cases from relatively conventional family backgrounds.

Peer Group Associations. Peer associations are relatively unimportant in this type of crime, except insofar as professional peers have failed to maintain the behavior of the offender within professional norms and standards. As suggested earlier, members of professional groups in which these kinds of violations occur tend to be somewhat ambivalent toward certain illegal activities involving professional skills. Lack of strong moral censure for these acts plays some part in the behavior of fringe violators.

Contact with Defining Agencies. Fringe violators tend to have few contacts with defining agencies. It appears that, for those professionals who are apprehended, convicted, and sentenced to institutions, such experiences have a relatively neutral impact. Individuals who desist from further law violations are more likely responding to concerns about their standing within the professional group than anything else. It is unlikely that offenders who commit further offenses do so as a consequence of contacts with correctional agents or other defining agencies.

Some Evidence

Occupational deviations of the fringe variety have been little studied, particularly by sociologists. The professional person who commits these violations has not been subjected to much investigation, so little is known of the occupational career line that leads the doctor into abortion or other professionals into marginal activities.

One recent study of unethical and illegal activities by lawyers stands as a model of the sort of research needed into fringe violations. Kenneth Reichstein investigated "ambulance chasing" (solicitation of cases) in personal injury cases in Illinois.[84] Among other things, he discovered that Chicago lawyers are not all in agreement in their opinions of personal injury solicitation, even though Bar Association ethical canons and state law as well forbid such activity. In general, attorneys who worked in small firms or independently

---

[84]Kenneth J. Reichstein, "Ambulance Chasing: A Case Study of Deviation and Control Within the Legal Profession," *Social Problems,* 13 (Summer 1965), 3–17.

and served low-status clients looked on solicitation tolerantly, whereas lawyers from large, successful firms practicing corporation law viewed "ambulance chasing" unfavorably. Reichstein also indicated that lawyers who had been brought before the Illinois Supreme Court on disciplinary charges involving solicitation were dealt with relatively leniently. All of this goes to suggest the ambiguous line between proper and improper behavior in the legal profession.

A second inquiry involving occupational deviations is that of Jack Ladinsky concerning legal careers among Detroit area attorneys. Ladinsky points out that lawyers who engage in "solo" work, as contrasted to group practice in a law firm, were usually sifted earlier in their careers into relatively poor law schools. They were barred from entry into high prestige law schools because of ethnic considerations or other variables that influence the selection process. These same "solo" lawyers do the "dirty work." The less desirable, poorer paying legal tasks are allocated to them, such as criminal court defense work, personal injury cases, and parallel chores.[85] Some of these individuals might easily drift into unethical or illegal practices if their legal careers were to deteriorate, in that they are already vulnerable to occupational and financial vicissitudes by virtue of their occupational detachment from the organized practice of law.

On the subject of abortion and abortionists, Edwin Schur has provided an admirable summary of the literature on this matter.[86] One question he addressed concerns the extent of abortions in the United States. He noted that the Kinsey investigations indicated that about one-quarter of the married women in that study had experienced at least one induced abortion before they were forty-five years of age. Estimates of the extent of abortion in 1955 indicated that at least 200,000, and perhaps as many as 1,200,000, are performed in the United States annually. These abortions are illegal under many existing state laws. The females who are aborted are a cross-section of the population; so that some are married, others single, from various economic, religious, and ethnic groups.[87]

Schur pointed out that most state laws permit induced abortions only when necessary to preserve the life of the mother. The practical effect of such statutes is to make abortion nearly always illegal, for pregnancies today almost never endanger the mother's life, due to advances in modern prenatal care. Therapeutic abortions performed in hospitals by physicians are often technically illegal, even though the law enforcement authorities do not usually take

[85]Jack Ladinsky, "Careers of Lawyers, Law Practice, and Legal Institutions," *American Sociological Review*, 28 (February 1963), 47-54; further evidence on this point is contained in Jerome E. Carlin, *Lawyers on their Own* (New Brunswick, N.J.: Rutgers University Press, 1962). Carlin's study of 93 Chicago attorneys who were solo practitioners revealed that they were often compelled to engage in "dirty work," such as "fixing" cases, bribing officials, and so on. See also Arthur Lewis Wood, *Criminal Lawyer* (New Haven, Conn.: College and University Press, 1967).

[86]Edwin M. Schur, *Crimes Without Victims* (Englewood Cliffs, N.J.: Prentice-Hall, 1965), pp. 11-66.

[87]*Ibid.*, p. 12.

action in these cases. A number of abortions are performed in cases where the pregnant woman has contracted German measles, because this experience often results in various malformations, such as cataracts, lesions, and mental abnormality, of the newborn infant. Other abortions are carried out for psychiatric reasons or because pregnancy is the result of rape or incest.[88]

Physicians are not now able to anticipate the consequences that might ensue if they perform an abortion for a reason not recognized as legitimate in existing laws, because of the uncertainty surrounding existing police and court procedures. One device that has been contrived as a way of protecting doctors both from entreaties of patients and prosecution by authorities is the abortion committee in hospitals. The committee makes the decision as to whether a female will be allowed an abortion, so the responsibility is spread around among a number of doctors.[89]

The hospital abortion committee does not completely solve the problem for many doctors, and it certainly does not alleviate the difficulties of the woman with an unwanted pregnancy. She may continue to demand an abortion, even after committee refusals. Schur suggests that many doctors faced with an insistent patient either perform the abortion or refer the person to an abortionist-doctor. The Kinsey findings indicate that most of the women in that study who reported an abortion said they were aborted by a physician.[90]

Evidence regarding the characteristics of doctors who commit abortions is obviously hard to uncover. However, Schur argued that the physicians who practice abortions are frequently marginal figures in one way or another. Some are doctors who have lost their licenses; some are foreign-trained physicians who have not been admitted to practice in this country; still others may be unsuccessful doctors who are attracted by the lucrative financial aspects of abortion.

One indication of the symbiotic links between these fringe figures and other doctors is in the case of a Baltimore doctor who had performed abortions over a twenty-year period and indicated that he had received referrals from 353 other physicians.[91] Schur indicates that the practice of abortion in American cities appears to be an elaborate *sub rosa* form of medical practice rather than an ephemeral form of sporadic deviance. Abortion "mills" have been discovered involving doctors in full-time abortion practices, with various assistants and an elaborate network of referral sources including other doctors, drugstore personnel, and so on.[92]

[88]*Ibid.*, pp. 13–14.
[89]*Ibid.*, pp. 18–21.
[90]*Ibid.*, p. 21.
[91]*Ibid.*, pp. 25–31.

[92]*Ibid.*, pp. 31–34. For a detailed account of abortion practices in New York, see Jerome E. Bates, "The Abortion Mill: An Institutional Study," *Journal of Criminal Law, Criminology and Police Science*, 45 (July–August 1954), 157–69.

SUMMARY

This chapter has examined several kinds of "hidden crime" involving law-breaking by respectable citizens. Throughout the discussion, questions and controversies point to the need for further research. Some major changes in criminological analysis are likely to come about as these matters receive more attention in the future. Accumulation of evidence on the pervasive character of criminality and the interweaving of illegal conduct into the fabric of social and economic life will compel us to abandon those comforting notions that crime is restricted to only a relatively few daring "bad guys." The study of criminality turns out to be a major task in sociological inquiry, for lawbreaking is often a central feature of the day-to-day activities of citizens everywhere in American society.

Beginning with the next chapter, we turn away from property offenses and toward some role careers involving assaults and other interpersonal actions. Chapter Fifteen is addressed to assaultive and homicidal behavior, and Chapter Sixteen focuses on patterns of sexual deviation.

15

MURDERERS
AND
ASSAULTISTS

In this and the following chapter, our attention moves away from property offenders and property crime. We shall take up murder and assaultive behavior in this chapter and examine a variety of kinds of sexual criminality in Chapter Sixteen. Both chapters deal with forms of conduct that appear to many laymen to be particularly bizarre, deviant, or unusual activity, as contrasted to the endeavors of thieves, robbers, or business offenders. To those uninformed about criminality, the taking of a human life, violent assault by one person on another, or coercion of a female into sexual intercourse appear extremely unusual events. The murderer, assaultist, or sexual offender is often presumed to be an individual with markedly idiosyncratic personal characteristics. In the public view, rapists must be "fiends" with pathological personalities, for how else can their actions be explained? Laymen often invoke an explanation of homicides emphasizing situations of extreme social stress as the mechanism triggering violent acts.

In this chapter, we shall discover that most murders and assaults depart markedly from the popular image of activities carried on by clever, scheming individuals and involving complex techniques by which persons are killed or assaulted. For every publicized case in which some person contrives a complicated and elaborate scheme for murder, countless other cases exist in which one person kills another on the spur of the moment and in dismal surroundings. From another perspective, if the facts were known to citizens, garden variety homicides and assaults would appear strange and virtually inexplicable. In the eyes of the middle-class individual, homicides and assaults would seem to arise out of extremely trivial circumstances. The files of municipal police departments are filled with cases in which one person killed another over a slighting remark or a seemingly innocuous, socially inappropriate action, such as a flirtatious gesture toward the murderer's spouse. Indeed, the mundane character of much assaultive conduct would bewilder individuals who live outside situations in which interpersonal violence is relatively commonplace.

THE LAW OF HOMICIDE AND ASSAULT

In law, the term *homicide* is generic, referring to the killing of one person by another.[1] Culpable homicides, which result in criminal prosecution, are differentiated from *justifiable* homicides and *excusable* homicides. Justifiable homicide constitutes killings performed as a result of legal demands, such as a police officer's shooting a fleeing suspect. In this instance, the homicide occurred while the officer was discharging his legal responsibility to pursue the criminal. Another case of justifiable homicide is in occurrences where jail or prison guards kill prisoners attempting to escape from confinement. Excusable homicide is the term for deaths that result accidentally from lawful acts performed by lawful means. The death of a child from medicine the parent administered in the course of an illness would be treated as excusable homicide.

Culpable homicides for which persons are held criminally responsible are normally differentiated in law into *murder* in the *first* or *second degrees* and *manslaughter*. In turn, these distinctions rest on degrees of *premeditation* and *malice aforethought*. Premeditation designates intent to violate the law formulated prior to the activity; in other words, a decision to commit a crime, planning the execution of it, and so on. Malice aforethought refers to the simple presence of intent to kill at the time of the act. For a person to be convicted of murder in the first degree, both premeditation and malice aforethought must be established. In second degree murder, only malice aforethought must be proved. Statutes define manslaughter as culpable homicide in which neither premeditation nor malice aforethought are present. Manslaughter is unintended or unwitting homicide. Degrees of manslaughter are usually recognized in law; first degree manslaughter designates that a prudent person could reasonably anticipate a fatal outcome to a set of behavioral events. The accidental death of a passenger in an automobile driven in a reckless manner by an intoxicated driver would be a case in point.

Although the laws draw relatively clear distinctions among forms of homicide, these distinctions are often blurred in judicial practice. A host of conditions influence the decision to process a case of criminality as first- or second-degree murder or manslaughter, in addition to the similarity of the conduct to legal definition. Many acts of homicide that could be prosecuted as first-degree murder are instead processed as second-degree murder or manslaughter. For instance, an individual may "cop a plea," that is, agree to plead guilty to a homicide in return for reduction in the charge from second-degree murder to manslaughter. Accordingly, we would be unwise to assume that court statistics on first- and second-degree murder and manslaughter cor-

[1]For a discussion of homicide law, see Herbert A. Bloch and Gilbert Geis, *Man, Crime, and Society*, 2nd ed. (New York: Random House, 1970), pp. 222–24.

rectly indicate the distribution of cases technically fitting the legal definitions of these terms.

Assault in common law and statute law, both in the United States and in England, is usually defined as an attempt to commit a battery, which is the unlawful application of physical force to another person. Assaults can and frequently do culminate in two separate kinds of actions against the offender. The injured party can endeavor to obtain redress in civil action, and the assaulter is also liable to criminal court prosecution for the criminal violation of law. Criminal laws usually distinguish degrees of assault; *aggravated assault* is the most serious form and involves such actions as assault with a deadly weapon or assault with intent to kill. Aggravated assault is a felony carrying more severe penalties than common or ordinary assault. The latter is a misdemeanor involving lesser punishments.

The kinds of persons who commit homicides or assaultive acts and the situations in which they engage in these are considerably more varied than the categories of murder, manslaughter, and assault recognized in statute law. As a consequence, any meaningful discussion of crimes against persons must concentrate on the major dimensions along which these vary. Students of homicide have made several attempts to provide taxonomies of forms of murder or murderers. Manfred Guttmacher found that there are normal, sociopathic, alcoholic, and avenging murderers, as well as schizophrenic killers and those who are temporarily psychotic.[2] Still other murderers include homosexuals, passive aggressive killers, and sadistic murderers. Doubtless, the population of killers includes each of these kinds of individuals, but Guttmacher's classification is too anecdotal and descriptive to be of much use in explanations of homicide behavior. Paralleling Guttmacher's scheme, W. Lindesay Neustatter uses case histories to illustrate schizophrenic, hysteric, and mentally defective murderers.[3] Neustatter also contends that some killers are paranoiac, epileptic, or suffering from organic brain damage. Other murderers are sadistic, psychopathic, melancholic, or suffering from hypoglycemia. Much the same comment applies to Neustatter's scheme as to Guttmacher's, for both are relatively descriptive and anecdotal.[4]

The following discussion offers no detailed classification of forms of homicide or assault. Instead, it presents a generalized description of the role career of a personal offender, "one-time loser." Following this discussion, we shall examine a body of theory and research on homicide and assault. The role-career statement is a sort of standard against which empirical cases can be

[2]Manfred S. Guttmacher, *The Mind of the Murderer* (New York: Farrar, Straus and Giroux, 1960), pp. 13–106; for another eclectic discussion of murder, see John M. MacDonald, *The Murderer and his Victim* (Springfield, Ill.: Charles C Thomas, Publisher, 1961).

[3]W. Lindesay Neustatter, *The Mind of the Murderer* (New York: Philosophical Library, 1957).

[4]For a more recent, sophisticated attempt to delineate types of violence-prone persons, see Hans Toch, *Violent Men* (Chicago: Aldine Publishing Co., 1969).

contrasted. For example, assaultists come in several varieties so that certain of them are more similar to the role-career description than are others.

THE PERSONAL OFFENDER, "ONE-TIME LOSER" ROLE CAREER[5]

Definitional Dimensions

Offense Behavior. This type includes offenders involved in major crimes of a personal and normally violent nature. Murder, negligent homicide, and serious assaults are the forms of behavior included. Some of these violators have prior records of other assaultive activities so that, strictly speaking, they are not "one-time losers" or first offenders. However, individuals who commit violent acts while in the course of carrying out other criminal offenses, such as those involved in "felony-murder," are not included in this category.

Interactional Setting. Personal offender, one-time losers are normally engaged in offenses with a victim who is well-known to the offender, or at least has been in interaction with the violator. Homicide in which the victim is the offender's spouse is the classic case. In instances where the offender and victim are members of the same family group, the criminal act is often the culmination of a long period of tense relationships. In some cases of wife-murder, the offender has been involved in wife-beating for a long time. Finally, he administers a beating to his wife which turns out to be fatal.

Self-concept. One-time loser personal offenders exhibit noncriminal self-images. Frequently the violator himself reports his behavior to the police, due to the fact that, after it has occurred, he is contrite, guilt-ridden, and repentant.

Attitudes. The attitudes of the one-time loser are conventional and prosocial. In prison, these persons are designated by other inmates as "square Johns," prisoners who are aliens in the criminal subculture.

Role Career. Most personal offenders show no extensive delinquency record or previous pattern of criminality. On occasion, the offender has been involved in minor offenses, such as drunkenness or wife-beating. Criminals of this type receive long prison sentences. When they are released on parole, as many are, their adjustment is normally quite satisfactory.

Background Dimensions

Social Class. One-time loser personal criminals do not come exclusively from one specific social class background. However, rates of homicide and assault

[5]Don C. Gibbons, *Changing the Lawbreaker,* The Treatment of Delinquents and Criminals, © 1965. Reprinted by permission of Prentice-Hall, Inc., Englewood Cliffs, New Jersey, pp. 116–17.

are considerably higher among lower class groups than any other in the American population. Furthermore, those who are from lower class backgrounds have often been involved in aggression preceding the major violent episode, partly because of the subcultural approval of interpersonal violence in lower class groups.

Family Background. It does not appear that there is a specific family background of parent–child interaction which leads to a "violence prone" personality type. The early family backgrounds of these persons are quite varied. On the other hand, the adult family situation is much involved in the illegal behavior of the person. Cases of extreme violence normally develop out of a marital situation in which tensions have existed for a long time between the victim and the offender.

Peer Group Associations. Attitudes which support the use of physical force in marital relationships or in settling interpersonal difficulties are probably acquired primarily within peer groups. Additionally, those subcultural views which link masculinity to physical aggressiveness are also communicated to persons within same-sex peer groups.

Contact with Defining Agencies. The contacts of the one-time loser personal offender with defining agencies are of neutral significance. The person has the same definition of his behavior as do the defining agencies, and tends to agree that he should be punished for his deviant act. Correctional institutions appear to have little effect, positive or otherwise, upon such individuals.

FOUR STUDIES OF HOMICIDE

Examination and comparison of four relatively extended studies of homicide may help provide a reasonably full understanding of homicide behavior. Although not strictly parallel in every detail, these investigations provide evidence on a number of points in common. The first study, by Marvin Wolfgang, involves information on all 588 criminal homicides known to the police which occurred in Philadelphia between 1948 and 1952.[6] Wolfgang's inquiry stands as the most comprehensive single examination of empirical evidence on homicide in the United States. The second piece of research, by Robert Bensing and Oliver Schroeder, concerns 462 homicides in Greater Cuyahoga County (Cleveland), Ohio, between 1947 and 1953.[7] Bullock's examination of all cases of homicide in Houston between 1945 and 1949 is the third souce of evidence,[8]

[6]Marvin E. Wolfgang, *Patterns of Criminal Homicide* (Philadelphia: University of Pennsylvania Press, 1958). Wolfgang's volume provides a rich source of materials on homicide in the United States and elsewhere.

[7]Robert C. Bensing and Oliver Schroeder, Jr., *Homicide in an Urban Community* (Springfield, Ill.: Charles C Thomas, Publisher, 1960).

[8]Henry A. Bullock, "Urban Homicide in Theory and Fact," *Journal of Criminal Law, Criminology and Police Science*, 45 (January–February 1955), 565–75.

and Alex Pokorny's replication of Wolfgang's Philadelphia work, carried on in terms of Houston homicides between 1958 and 1961, is the final study.[9] We shall consider the findings of all four investigations in the following sections dealing with different aspects of violent behavior.

Temporal and Ecological Characteristics

In the Philadelphia study, homicides were found to occur most frequently on weekends: 66 percent occurred between Friday and Sunday, and 32 percent took place on a Saturday.[10] Bensing and Schroeder found that 62 percent of the homicides in Cleveland took place on the same three days,[11] and, similarly, Bullock reported that most homicides occur on weekends.[12] To locate the occurrence of acts of violence more specifically, in both the Philadelphia and Cleveland cases these criminal events were most common between 8 P.M. and 2 A.M.[13] In each of these cases, the temporal fluctuation in violence appears related to cycles of weekday labor and weekend leisure pursuits. Proximity of persons, increased use of alcohol, and so on, on weekends serve to increase the potential for violent outbursts.

Homicides do not occur randomly throughout the urban community, for Bullock found that over 70 percent of those in Houston took place in 18 percent of the census tracts in that city.[14] Similarly, the Cleveland data show that two-thirds of the crimes took place in 12 percent of the city of Cleveland.[15] Both of these studies located the urban centers of homicidal acts in predominantly black areas characterized by dense populations and overcrowding, physical deterioration, and other manifestations of urban slum conditions.

Wolfgang found that homicides were about evenly divided between the home and places outside the home, in terms of specific locale, which was also true of the Houston homicides investigated by Bullock and Pokorny.[16] Incidents of violence occurring outside of residences were mainly in streets adjacent to taverns or eating places.

---

[9]Alex D. Pokorny, "A Comparison of Homicides in Two Cities," *Journal of Criminal Law, Criminology and Police Science*, 56 (December 1965), 479–87; see also Pokorny, "Human Violence: A Comparison of Homicide, Aggravated Assault, Suicide, and Attempted Suicide," *Journal of Criminal Law, Criminology and Police Science*, 56 (December 1965), 488–97.

[10]Wolfgang, *Patterns of Criminal Homicide*, pp. 96–119.

[11]Bensing and Schroeder, *Homicide in an Urban Community*, pp. 8–10.

[12]Bullock, "Urban Homicide in Theory and Fact," p. 566.

[13]Bensing and Schroeder, *Homicide in an Urban Community*, pp. 8–10; Wolfgang, *Patterns of Criminal Homicide*, pp. 96–119.

[14]Bullock, "Urban Homicide in Theory and Fact," pp. 567–69.

[15]Bensing and Schroeder, *Homicide in an Urban Community*, pp. 105–37.

[16]Wolfgang, *Patterns of Criminal Homicide*, pp. 120–33; Bullock, "Urban Homicide in Theory and Fact," pp. 570–75; Pokorny, "A Comparison of Homicides in Two Cities," pp. 481–82.

Motives, Situations, and Methods

The offender's private motives are always difficult to determine, particularly when police reports of motives are relied on instead of interviews with the culprits. Nonetheless, several of these studies enumerated the most commonly identified motives in police files and other official records and tell us a good deal about the social situations leading up to acts of violence. Records on the weapons employed in these behavioral episodes also provide useful information.

In the Philadelphia materials, 37 percent of the offenses were attributed to altercations of one kind or another, whereas domestic quarrels accounted for 13 percent and jealousy for another 11 percent. The parties to the crime were close friends in 28 percent of the cases and family relatives in another quarter of the homicides.[17] Pokorny's evidence for Houston shows the same pattern, with the parties to homicide being close friends or family relations in most instances.[18] The Cleveland homicides were most frequently linked to petty quarrels, marital discord, and sexual disputes.[19] In each of these cases, the circumstances that appear to trigger homicides might well strike the outsider as petty.

These investigations of homicide are not in complete agreement on the question of methods of killing. In Wolfgang's data, stabbing was the leading technique, accounting for 39 percent of the homicides. Blacks were particularly likely to use knives, whereas white offenders more commonly beat their victims to death. Women most frequently employed cutting instruments, usually a kitchen knife.[20] In Cleveland, guns accounted for 55 percent of the homicides, whereas only 27 percent were accomplished with knives.[21]

Racial and Sexual Variations

One of the most striking findings of all these inquiries is the high rate of homicide among blacks in American cities. Wolfgang found that 73 percent of the victims and 75 percent of the offenders in Philadelphia were blacks, although blacks made up only 18 percent of the 1950 population of that city. Homicides were also concentrated among males, for 76 percent of the victims and 82 percent of the offenders were males, although males comprised only 48 percent of the population. Women were infrequently involved in homicide; although females represented only 18 percent of the offenders, they constituted 24 percent of the victims. *However, the racial concentration was more marked than the sexual one.* The rate of homicide for black males (41.7 of-

[17]Wolfgang, *Patterns of Criminal Homicide*, pp. 185-89, 203-21.
[18]Pokorny, "A Comparison of Homicides in Two Cities," p. 483.
[19]Bensing and Schroeder, *Homicide in an Urban Community*, pp. 72-77.
[20]Wolfgang, *Patterns of Criminal Homicide*, pp. 79-95.
[21]Bensing and Schroeder, *Homicide in an Urban Community*, p. 84.

fenses per 100,000 population) was many times greater than that for white males (3.4 homicides per 100,000 population). In addition, the homicide rate for black females (9.3 per 100,000 population) also exceeded that for white males. Racial lines were crossed in only 6 percent of the homicides, so blacks nearly all kill other blacks, and whites nearly all kill other whites.[22] The Cleveland homicides were distributed in the same fashion, for 76 percent of the offenders were black, although only 11 percent of the Cuyahoga County population was made up of blacks.[23] Pokorny reported that Houston blacks made up only 23 percent of the population of that city, but they contributed 63 percent of the offenders.[24]

Age, Social Class, and Criminal Backgrounds

Several of these studies indicated that variations exist in the ages of offenders and victims. Wolfgang noted that the killers are generally younger than the victims; the majority of offenders were between twenty and thirty years of age, whereas the victims were on the average about five years older.[25] Bensing and Schroeder indicated that relatively young persons carried out most homicides, 72 percent of whom were between twenty-one and forty-five years of age.[26]

The preceding material on the ecological distribution of homicides clearly indicates that this activity is more common among working-class groups than any other. Both the Philadelphia and Cleveland studies confirm these socioeconomic differentials in violence; rates of homicide for lower-class individuals of all ethnic backgrounds were found to exceed those for persons of higher economic status.[27]

The Philadelphia material contains some data on the criminal backgrounds of offenders and victims. Wolfgang indicated that 64 percent of the offenders and 47 percent of the victims had a record of prior offenses. Those with criminal backgrounds had usually been involved in earlier incidents of violence, for 66 percent had been implicated in crimes against persons.[28] Finally, Wolfgang noted that alcohol was present in 64 percent of the homicide occurrences and that both parties to the act had been drinking in 44 percent of the cases.[29]

[22]Wolfgang, Patterns of Criminal Homicide, pp. 31–35.
[23]Bensing and Schroeder, Homicide in an Urban Community, p. 41.
[24]Pokorny, "A Comparison of Homicides in Two Cities," pp. 480–81.
[25]Wolfgang, Patterns of Criminal Homicide, pp. 65–78.
[26]Bensing and Schroeder, Homicide in an Urban Community, pp. 70–71.
[27]Ibid., pp. 128–29; Wolfgang, Patterns of Criminal Homicide, pp. 36–39.
[28]Wolfgang, ibid., pp. 168–74.
[29]Ibid., pp. 134–67. On this point, see also MacDonald, The Murderer and his Victim, pp. 18–20. He summarized a series of studies which show that a third or more of the offenders in homicide cases had been drinking prior to the act of violence.

Victim-Precipitated Homicide

One of the most important innovations in the study of homicide is Wolfgang's notion of "victim-precipitated homicide"—a term for acts of violence in which the victim initiated the fatal outburst by making the first menacing gesture or striking the first blow. As we have seen, a good many homicides take place between persons who have been in social interaction with each other, but victim-precipitated killings involve more than prior interaction. In the victim-precipitated case, the victim induced his death through his own menacing actions. Wolfgang's examination of victim-precipitated homicides shows that these more commonly involve black victims and offenders, with the victim being male and the offender female. The victim is often the husband of the offender and is commonly stabbed in circumstances in which he has been drinking. Finally, the victim frequently had a prior record of assaultive conduct.[30]

SUBCULTURES OF VIOLENCE

According to Bullock's findings in Houston: "The basic ecological process of urban segregation centralizes people of like kind, throws them together at common institutions, occasions their association on levels of intimacy, and thereby paves the way for conflicts out of which homicides occur."[31] In other words, the urban community shows concentrations in particular areas of groups whose life styles are especially productive of homicides and assaultive acts. This argument has recently been advanced under the rubric of "cultures of violence," in which the life circumstances of certain groups are claimed to trigger violence as a relatively commonplace outcome of social interaction.[32]

Subcultures of violence made up of groups quick to use force in interpersonal relations appear to be centralized in urban slum areas, which the preceding four studies indicated as the places where homicide rates are high. Frequently, these neighborhoods are populated by lower income blacks and are residential ghettos. According to many sociologists, the grinding poverty, unstable community organization, and disorganized family life in such areas lead to the emergence of certain lower-class values or focal concerns.[33] Miller identifies one of these concerns as "trouble," which refers to suspicion of

[30]Wolfgang, *Patterns of Criminal Homicide*, pp. 264–65.

[31]Bullock, "Urban Homicide in Theory and Fact," p. 575.

[32]For a valuable discussion and resumé of the literature on this topic, see Frank E. Hartung, *Crime, Law and Society* (Detroit, Mich.: Wayne State University Press, 1965), pp. 136–66; see also Marvin E. Wolfgang and Franco Ferracuti, *The Subculture of Violence* (New York: Barnes and Noble, 1967).

[33]Miller has provided the richest description of these ingredients of lower class life. See Walter B. Miller, "Lower Class Culture as a Generating Milieu of Gang Delinquency," *Journal of Social Issues*, 14, no. 3 (1958), 5–19; Miller, "Implications of Urban Lower Class Culture for Social Work," *Social Service Review*, 33 (September 1959), 219–36.

others and generalized anticipation of difficulty from policemen, welfare agencies, schools, and fellow citizens. Another focal concern is "excitement," which has to do with pursuit of hedonistic pleasures, particularly on weekends, to counteract the dullness of weekday pursuits. Actors with these motivations thrown together in close contact heighten the potential for violent incidents. The contention is that this subcultural situation goes far toward accounting for high rates of homicide among lower-class citizens. This argument makes it unnecessary to invoke notions of personality pathology to account for homicides.

One interesting bit of evidence on this point comes from a study by Leroy Schultz in St. Louis.[34] Schultz reviewed a series of investigations maintaining that blacks commonly carry weapons and that the arrest rates for weapons offenses are much higher among blacks than whites. He conducted interviews with fifty black offenders convicted of charges centering about possession of dangerous weapons. These violators offered a number of reasons for carrying guns—some did so to commit crimes; others did so to force payment of debts owed them. However, 70 percent declared that they carried weapons because they anticipated attack from others in their environment. Carrying a weapon was a defensive or anticipatory act. Schultz indicated: "This group voiced a chronic concern about being attacked and the need for self-defense and assumed automatically that others in their environment were also carrying weapons, or if not actually carrying weapons, 'acted as if they were.' "[35]

SOME OTHER STUDIES

We should briefly note several other studies of murder in the United States. One investigation, by John Gillin, involves inmates in a Wisconsin prison, in which he observed that 44 percent of the murderers studied had committed their crime in connection with another offense, whereas 24 percent had killed in conjunction with an immediate quarrel and another 32 percent had murdered someone with whom they had been carrying on a long-standing feud.[36] In addition, Gillin reported on the background characteristics of the incarcerated killers. They were more frequently from rural areas than were the sex offenders or property criminals. More of them had contributed to the support of their families at an early age than had the other prisoners. More killers had foreign-born parents, more were from lower income backgrounds, more had left school

[34]Leroy G. Schultz, "Why the Negro Carries Weapons," *Journal of Criminal Law, Criminology and Police Science*, 53 (December 1962), 476-83.

[35]*Ibid.*, p. 479.

[36]John L. Gillin, *The Wisconsin Prisoner* (Madison: University of Wisconsin Press, 1946), pp. 56-60; see also Gillin, "Murder as a Sociological Phenomenon," *Annals of the American Academy of Political and Social Science*, 284 (November 1952), 20-25.

prematurely, and more had unsteady employment records than was the case with the other prisoners. Finally, the murderers had less frequently been involved in prior offenses than had the other convicts.[37] These findings add up to a picture of Wisconsin murderers as "Square John" criminals, so although they were commonly detached and alienated individuals, they were also relatively conventional persons.

Another study of a group of imprisoned murderers, by Stuart Palmer, deals with fifty-one offenders in New England penal institutions who were compared with their noncriminal siblings.[38] Palmer found that most of these murders were unplanned, shooting was the leading technique of homicide, and alcohol was not usually present. One difference between Palmer's data and that of the foregoing four studies is that the victims of these murderers were strangers or slight acquaintances in 67 percent of the cases. The murderers were persons with low educational attainment and low socioeconomic status.[39] Based on interviews with the mothers of the offenders, Palmer concluded that the killers had been subjected to uncommonly frequent frustrations in their lives, in contrast to their siblings. However, the observations of the mothers could be erroneous as they attempted to report retrospectively the experiences of their sons.

In concluding this section we should mention Harwin Voss and John Hepburn's study dealing with homicides in Chicago in 1965.[40] Their investigation was a replication of the Wolfgang's research. In addition, they found that nonwhites far exceeded whites in rates of homicide, occurrences of homicide were most frequent on weekends, most of them took place in the home, and alcohol was associated with them in over half the cases. Voss and Hepburn also observed that about one-third of the homicides were victim-precipitated. One point at which their data differed from that of Wolfgang was on the matter of methods of killing, in that about half the Chicago victims had been shot rather than stabbed.

HOMICIDE IN OTHER SOCIETIES

Homicide occurs at markedly varying rates in different countries. In general, African societies have low homicide rates, as do many Asiatic nations and most European countries. The United States has comparatively large numbers of violent deaths, as do Ceylon, Finland, and a number of other nations. Computations made in England between 1940 and 1949 of rates per 1,000,000

[37]Gillin, The Wisconsin Prisoner, pp. 9–11.

[38]Stuart Palmer, A Study of Murder (New York: Thomas Y. Crowell Co., 1960).

[39]Ibid., pp. 21–37.

[40]Harwin L. Voss and John R. Hepburn, "Patterns in Criminal Homicide in Chicago," Journal of Criminal Law, Criminology and Police Science, 59 (December 1968), 499–508.

population give some indication of worldwide variations in homicide. England and Wales show a rate of 4.0 and New Zealand a rate of 7.2, whereas in the United States rates vary from 13.6 in Massachusetts to 167.3 in Georgia. In all these cases, we are led to suspect that something about the social structure of different nations influences their homicide rates.[41]

Although detailed data on homicide in other nations are not available in abundance, several revealing investigations have been conducted on this topic. Paul Bohannan has reported on homicide in a number of African societies.[42] He notes that one of the forms of killing in Africa is nonculpable homicide in dangerous but legal institutions. Hunting with poisoned arrows falls into this category, for deaths frequently occur as a consequence of the risk courting in such activities. These nonculpable homicides have American parallels in such activities as auto racing, where the participants cause unintended deaths. A second form of nonculpable homicide is institutionalized killing such as jural homicide (executions) or ritual killings. Finally, culpable homicides occur in African societies in which the offender is held criminally accountable.[43]

One of the most significant facts about African homicide centers about discordant definitions of culpable and nonculpable homicide. Bohannan indicates that African tribes often defined thief-killing, witch-killing, and killing of adulterers as nonculpable acts. However, these are regarded as criminal actions in British law, which has been injected into African affairs. The conflict between tribal norms and Western law is reduced through compromises; hence, judges tend to be lenient in the sentences handed down to native killers. In some instances, the charge against the violator is reduced from murder to manslaughter.[44]

Another highly significant finding on African criminality is that homicide rates among natives are extremely low compared to rates for American blacks. The Philadelphia blacks in Wolfgang's study had a rate of 24.6 homicides per 100,000 population during the period between 1948 and 1952, whereas according to Bohannan's reports African tribes had rates of less than 12 homicides per 1,000,000 population. These African rates, among the lowest in the world, demolish effectively any hypotheses linking high homicide rates of American blacks to biological or racial factors.[45]

A third observation on African homicide is that the proportion of female offenders in the population of killers is even smaller than that for the United States and other Western nations. However, in several African tribes, females

---

[41]For an analysis of the high homicide rate in Finland, see Veli Verkko, *Homicides and Suicides in Finland and Their Dependence on National Character* (Copenhagen: G. E. C. Gads Forlag, 1951).

[42]Paul Bohannan, ed., *African Homicide and Suicide* (Princeton, N.J.: Princeton University Press, 1960).

[43]*Ibid.*, pp. 230–34.

[44]*Ibid.*, p. 233.

[45]*Ibid.*, pp. 236–37.

comprise 45 to 60 percent of the victims, whereas in the United States, women are homicide victims in only about one-quarter of the cases.[46]

Bohannan's material points to still another homicide variation from Western patterns. In the United States, when a family member is killed, the victim is likely to be a spouse; in Denmark, the victim is likely to be a child; but in African countries, a wide variety of different kinsmen are the victims of homicide. Clearly, this tendency has much to do with the extended family patterns more common in African nations than in Western ones.[47]

Homicide in Ceylon has received the attention of several investigators. Some years ago, Jacqueline Straus and Murray Straus observed that the relatively high rate of homicide in Ceylon is principally the result of killing among the lowland Sinhalese in that country rather than among the Tamil group. Because they have experienced the most contact with European cultural influences, the Sinhalese live in a less rigid class structure than the Tamil. According to these investigators, the looser social ties among the Sinhalese are responsible for their greater contribution to the homicide rate.[48]

In a more recent study of homicide in Ceylon, Arthur Wood examined and confirmed two hypotheses.[49] The first contended that homicide should be most common in the lowest ranks of an achieved status system, particularly when members of these groups perceive themselves to be externally restrained from achieving their goals. This argument is similar to Cloward and Ohlin's notions of "opportunity structures," which hold that lower-class youths are disproportionately represented in the population of delinquents because they see themselves as constrained from achieving their goals by an unjust social order.[50] A social structure that theoretically provides open opportunities for all is perceived as hypocritically restricting the life chances of working-class individuals. Wood's second hypothesis was that homicide is more frequent among alienated, demoralized persons, who show reactions of hostility. Supporting evidence for both hypotheses was uncovered in this investigation.

Interpersonal relationships between victims and offenders in homicides have been the subject of two studies in Denmark and in India. Kaare Svalastoga observed that, in Danish homicides for the periods 1934–39 and 1946–51, family members were victims in 57 percent of the cases, friends and acquaintances were victims in 31 percent, and strangers were killed in only 12 percent of the homicides.[51] Along the same line, Edwin Driver notes that in Indian

[46]Ibid., pp. 237–39.

[47]Ibid., p. 242.

[48]Jacqueline H. Straus and Murray A. Straus, "Suicide, Homicide, and Social Structure in Ceylon," American Journal of Sociology, 58 (March 1953), 461–69.

[49]Arthur L. Wood, Crime and Aggression in Changing Ceylon (Philadelphia: Transactions of the American Philosophical Society, 1961); Wood, "A Socio-Structural Analysis of Murder, Suicide, and Economic Crime in Ceylon," American Sociological Review, 26 (October 1961), 744–53.

[50]Richard A. Cloward and Lloyd E. Ohlin, Delinquency and Opportunity (New York: The Free Press, 1960).

[51]Kaare Svalastoga, "Homicide and Social Contact in Denmark," American Journal of Sociology, 62 (July 1956), 37–41.

homicides the partners to the offense are usually kinsmen or close associates of the same sex, religion, or caste. Prior to the actual killing, the interactional partners have been caught up in situations of heightened enmity flowing out of sexual disputes, arguments about property, or kindred quarrels.[52]

In summary, homicide is a universal form of crime. Although similarities in homicide exist throughout the world, some data indicate that homicidal activities in different nations take on certain characteristics or the coloration of the host social system.

PATTERNS OF AGGRESSION

A good deal of evidence points to the existence of two general forms of assaultive conduct. The first is situational or subcultural in character, in which some individuals who reside in certain urban neighborhoods get involved in violence largely in response to the exacerbated tensions and disorder of their social situation. This kind of assaultive conduct bears a close similarity to the homicides occurring in subcultures of violence; indeed, both are the product of the same general social variables.

A second form of criminally aggressive behavior is psychogenic or individualistic in form, rather than subcultural. The evidence indicates that certain kinds of socialization experiences produce individuals with atypically hostile psychological orientations. These persons, variously called "unsocialized aggressives," "psychopaths," or "sociopaths," find their way into the population of offenders as a result of attacks on others. Many commit property violations as well as assaultive acts, but in any event their conduct is marked by a violent and aggressive posture as a central feature of their personalities. These offenders are from a variety of social-class backgrounds, for the conditions that generate the offense are not class-linked.

In the following discussion, we shall first study some findings on situational assault. Then we shall consider a typological characterization of the "psychopathic" assaultist role career, along with some supporting evidence on this form of criminality.

SITUATIONAL AGGRESSION

An important study of assaultive conduct, by Richard Peterson, David Pittman, and Patricia O'Neal, concerns St. Louis police arrest cases.[53] These investigators determined that because most of the apprehended offenders had relatively

---

[52]Edwin D. Driver, "Interaction and Criminal Homicide in India," *Social Forces*, 40 (December 1961), 153–58.

[53]Richard A. Peterson, David J. Pittman, and Patricia O'Neal, "Stabilities in Deviance: A Study of Assaultive and Non-Assaultive Offenders," *Journal of Criminal Law, Criminology and Police Science*, 53 (March 1962), 44–48.

stable patterns of deviance, individuals arrested for crimes of violence had rarely been involved in property crimes earlier in their careers. Conversely, most of the property offenders had avoided use of violence in their criminal careers. The assaultive offenders were from more seriously disrupted homes and, at the same time, had higher levels of generalized hostility than did the property criminals.

A more recent investigation of assaultive behavior, by Pittman and William Handy, also centers in St. Louis.[54] The study tests Wolfgang's hypotheses to determine if assaults show patterns similar to those for homicide. By and large, their observations about the morphology of assault closely parallel Wolfgang's analyses of homicide. For example, 132 of the 241 aggravated assault cases investigated in this study occurred between 6 P.M. Friday and 6 A.M. Monday, most taking place on Saturday. The assaults occurred in a variety of places; but 45 percent were on streets, whereas 38 percent transpired in homes. No seasonal variation in assaultive acts was observed. About one-half of the assaults involved knives; but physical force was more common among white assaultists, whereas Negro offenders used weapons. The victim reported many of the offenses to the police, and nearly all offenders were cleared by arrest. In only three cases was another crime involved.[55]

Most of Pittman and Handy's information duplicated that of Wolfgang. The majority of acts of violence occurred within an offender–victim dyad, in most of the cases the participants were similar in age, most of the parties to violence were "blue-collar" workers, interracial assaults were uncommon, and most of the offenders with criminal records had backgrounds of petty criminality. The majority of the assaults developed out of quarrels and arguments immediately prior to the violent outbursts.[56]

In another piece of evidence on assaultive offenders, Julian Roebuck and Ronald Johnson compare the social backgrounds of forty black felons charged with assault and drunkenness with the backgrounds of 360 other persioners.[57] The violent offenders had developed out of more rigid, fundamentalist family backgrounds and had stricter, more dominating fathers than the other inmates. But they also showed closer primary group ties in childhood and adulthood than the other prisoners, and were from less criminogenic social circumstances.

These investigations seem to add up to a picture of assault carried on in relatively disorganized social settings by individuals who are not particularly bizarre or pathological in personality organization. For this reason, we can properly call this kind of criminality situational. For the most part, this material confirms our argument about subcultures of violence.

---

[54]David J. Pittman and William Handy, "Patterns in Criminal Aggravated Assault," *Journal of Criminal Law, Criminology and Police Science*, 53 (December 1964), 462–70.

[55]*Ibid.*, pp. 463–67.

[56]*Ibid.*, pp. 467–68.

[57]Julian Roebuck and Ronald Johnson, "The Negro Drinker and Assaulter as a Criminal Type," *Crime and Delinquency*, 8 (January 1962), 21–33.

THE "PSYCHOPATHIC" ASSAULTIST ROLE CAREER

Chapter Seven included a discussion of etiological hypotheses linking criminality to certain kinds of atypical individuals called "psychopaths" or "sociopaths." Abundant psychiatric literature holds that a clinical entity or personality type called a "psychopath" does exist. Such a person is said to be poorly socialized, unconcerned about the privileges of others, insensitive to social influences, and frequently violent in disposition. According to this view, such persons develop out of certain atypical social backgrounds and, in particular, are the product of disordered family experiences. It is a small jump to the corollary contention that psychopaths are inordinately common in the population of criminal deviants, for their personality characteristics are thought to impel them toward lawbreaking or other deviant paths.

Chapter Seven also alleged that customary applications of psychopathy formulations are defective, for the concept is used too loosely in most cases. Specific indicators of psychopathic personality patterns are not usually enumerated. Instead, the term is applied *ex post facto* to persons already identified as deviants, such as criminals, homosexuals, or political radicals. Used in this way, the concept is circular in definition, and proof of psychopathy turns out to reside in the same deviant conduct the label is supposed to explain.

Perhaps the psychopathy hypothesis might be useful if it were not relied on to account for all manner of socially aberrant individuals. The following role-career description characterizes psychopathic assaultists who exhibit fairly clear and identifiable traits of aggressiveness and violence in social relations. We retain the term *psychopath* because the offenders included in this pattern frequently receive this label in correctional diagnostic processes.

Definitional Dimensions

Offense Behavior. Psychopathic assaultists are adults who engage in violent and seemingly meaningless assaults on others. On occasion, these applications of force are in conjunction with the commission of another crime, but in such cases the assaults are characterized as "senseless." The violent actions go well beyond the degree of force that might be required to carry off the criminal act, so the behavior has the appearance of irrationality in the eyes of others. These offenders often show records of juvenile misconduct involving unprovoked assaults on their peers and, on occasion, on adults or animals. Acts of extreme cruelty toward other humans or animals are characteristic of such offenders.

Interactional Setting. Psychopathic or overly aggressive offenders are "lone wolves." They rarely engage in sustained forms of cooperative criminality, for their involvement in diffuse forms of aggression alienates them from others.

Self-concept. These offenders exhibit defiance, a kind of chip-on-the-shoulder attitude, and the view that people are not to be trusted. Because of their suspicion of others, they lash out with the intent of striking the first blow before others suspected of having bad motives can punish or harm them. At the same time, psychopathic assaultists show a marked psychological investment in notions of themselves as "tough" and "manly."

Attitudes. The attitudes of psychopathic assaultists make up a collection of diffuse sentiments of hostility toward persons and society.

Role Career. These offenders frequently show records of early incarceration as juveniles in correctional institutions. Their adult lives are likely to be filled with recurrent episodes of commitment to penal institutions along with prison sentences of increasing length. Because they are often defined as "hopeless" criminals not amenable to treatment, psychopathic assaultists are generally kept in custody for long periods of time.

Background Dimensions

Social Class. Psychopathic assaultists do not come from any single social-class background.

Family Background. Although specific family experiences of overly aggressive offenders vary somewhat, in nearly every case some kind of early and severe parental rejection appears to be the prelude to aggressive behavior. The psychopathic offender was usually an illegitimate or unwanted pregnancy, rejected and abandoned by his parents at an early age. As a youngster he may have undergone severe parental rejection within the home if he was not physically separated from his parents. Many have lived for extended periods of time in foster homes, orphanages, and so on rather than with their natural parents.

Peer Group Associations. Intensive interaction with peers is uncommon among overly aggressive offenders because of two factors. First, most aggressive offenders refrain from initiating relationships with peers because they are socially inept and because of their hostile views of people. Second, most eligible peers avoid contacts with with aggressive psychopaths because of the potentially violent consequences.

Contact with Defining Agencies. As children, overly aggressive offenders exhibit considerable contact with police, courts, and child guidance clinics, and they show hostile attitudes toward such agencies and persons. These attitudes are not the product of such experiences, however; they are the result of diffuse feelings of hostility the aggressive person directs toward people generally. In adult life, psychopathic assaultists continue this career line, spending lengthy periods of time in prison. Parole violation rates are consistently high for such offenders, quite independent of the amount of time spent in incarceration. In prison, these offenders are feared and avoided by other inmates, so they are not central figures in the inmate subculture.

Some Evidence

Let us examine a few of the important strands of data on psychopathic assault-ists. A good deal of evidence indicates that a small band of violent and socially maladjusted individuals does exist in prison, and these individuals are designat-ed in the inmate language system as "hard guys," "outlaws," "gorillas," "toughs," or some similar appellation. Sykes has noted that inmates in a New Jersey state prison single out "gorillas" as persons to be avoided, for such prisoners are quick to use coercion to extract favors from other convicts. Certain other individuals labeled "toughs" also are also avoided because of their touchiness and willingness to employ physical violence in settling minor disputes.[58] Both of these argot roles or inmate types look much like a within-prison variant of psychopathic assaultists. Much the same picture emerges from Clarence Schrag's studies in which asocial prisoners called "outlaws" by their peers have been reported. "Outlaws" have been imprisoned for a variety of offenses, but they have frequently employed violent and bizarre techniques of criminality. They exhibit records of excessive recidivism and are usually the product of backgrounds of early and severe parental and social rejection.[59] Donald Garrity has observed that "outlaws" exhibit high rates of parole viola-tion, which seem little influenced by the amount of time spent in custody.[60] These reports appear to be concerned with roughly the same kind of offender, so the different labels of "outlaw," "gorilla," "hard guy," and "tough" are apparently simply a reflection of regional variations in prison argot.

An abundance of revealing data is available on the childhood social back-grounds of overly aggressive persons.[61] The specific socialization experiences such individuals have undergone vary considerably, but one recurrent thread throughout these case histories is early and severe parental rejection. For example, Jenkins examined numerous aggressive children, nearly all of whom had been abandoned by their parents or suffered some other severe form of rejection, including repeated physical assaults by their parents. As a con-sequence, they developed into relatively unsocialized individuals who engaged in myriad forms of aggression against human and animal targets.[62]

[58]Gresham M. Sykes, *The Society of Captives* (Princeton, N.J.: Princeton University Press, 1958), pp. 84–108.

[59]Clarence Schrag, "Some Foundations for a Theory of Correction," in *The Prison*, ed. Donald R. Cressey (New York: Holt, Rinehart and Winston, 1961), pp. 346–56; Schrag, "A Preliminary Criminal Typology," *Pacific Sociological Review*, 41 (Spring 1961), 11–16.

[60]Donald L. Garrity, "The Prison as a Rehabilitation Agency," in *The Prison*, ed. Cressey, pp. 375–78.

[61]R. L. Jenkins and Lester E. Hewitt, "Types of Personality Structure Encountered in Child Guidance Clinics," *American Journal of Orthopsychiatry*, 14 (January 1944), 84–94; Jenkins, *Breaking Patterns of Defeat* (Philadelphia: J. B. Lippincott Co., 1954), pp. 9–28; Albert J. Reiss, Jr., "Social Correlates of Psychological Types of Delinquency," *American Sociological Review*, 17 (December 1952), 710–18; John W. Kinch, "Self-Conceptions of Types of Delinquents," *Sociological Inquiry*, 32 (Spring 1962), 228–34; Fritz Redl and David Wineman, *The Aggressive Child* (New York: The Free Press, 1960); Leonard Berkowitz, *Aggression* (New York: McGraw-Hill Book Co., 1962); Albert Bandura and Richard H. Walters, *Adolescent Aggression* (New York: The Ronald Press Co., 1959).

[62]Jenkins, *Breaking Patterns of Defeat.*

Another detailed study of aggressive youngsters, by Albert Bandura and Richard Walters, involves delinquents who were not as poorly socialized or aggressive as those reported in the psychiatric literature.[63] School authorities or juvenile court workers had singled out these boys as aggressive because they had engaged in frequent fights with other children, or for other reasons of that sort. According to Bandura and Walters, children on this end of a continuum of aggressive behavior are the product of relatively stable and intact homes. Their early socialization has produced dependency needs. However, they have cold and indifferent fathers who fail to nurture these dependency needs, and instead they are encouraged to solve their problems by themselves. Additionally, the youngsters are encouraged in aggressive actions by parents who take some pride in the ability of the child to fight successfully with other children. These same parents tend to be relatively lax in the demands and restrictions they impose on their children. A developmental chronology in these cases begins with adequate early socialization of the child, leading to the development of dependency yearnings and then to frustration by the father in particular. The aggressive child is then allowed to express hostility outside the home and restrictions are not imposed on him within the home setting. At some point, he gets into difficulties with the schools or juvenile courts as a result of aggressive acts.

Unfortunately, longitudinal studies that follow such persons from childhood through adult life are not available. We lack information about the effects of commitment to guidance clinics, training schools, reformatories, or kindred experiences. Nevertheless, these life events seem to exacerbate the hostile perspectives of the offender so that he becomes cumulatively more aggressive and hostile as he encounters a variety of kinds of social rejection. Accordingly, the psychopathic assaultist is probably something more than the aggressive child grown up, for these career contingencies also influence his adult behavior.

SUMMARY

This chapter represents half of our analysis of forms of crime against persons. The foregoing pages have shown that interpersonal violence is many-faceted, taking a number of forms. In the same way, the etiological influences behind assaultive acts are diverse. This picture of assaultive behavior will be paralleled by the admixture of behavioral forms taken up in Chapter Sixteen, which is concerned with sexual deviation in its many forms. We shall see that sexual misconduct ranges from pedestrian and unexceptional actions to some extremely violent and bizarre deviant behavior.

[63]Bandura and Walters, *Adolescent Aggression*.

16

PATTERNS
OF
SEXUAL
DEVIATION

Sociological analyses of criminality have not devoted equal attention to all forms of lawbreaking. Much work has been done on property crimes at the same time that little has been said about other illegality, particularly sexual misconduct. This relative inattention to sexual criminality probably stems from an impression that this behavior is the result of causal factors of a different sort from those identified in social-structural explanations of property violations. Because it does not seem to fit conveniently within the usual frames of reference of the sociologist, sexual deviation is systematically ignored.

Sociologists have done a fair amount of work on certain matters having to do with sexual behavior, but they have had relatively little to say about sexual deviations of one kind or another.[1] This silence regarding patterns of deviant sexual activity can be linked to the lack of a socialization model concerning sexual development against which to measure departures from "normal" sexual socialization.

Nevertheless, interest in sociological analysis of sexual misconduct seems to be growing. Stanton Wheeler's critique of sex offense statutes contains a number of insights regarding the sociological analysis of sexual behavior and sexual deviation.[2] He hints at several provocative hypotheses concerning social interactional backgrounds out of which certain forms of sexual deviation may develop. William McCord, Joan McCord, and Paul Verden have reported on the family backgrounds of sexual deviants in one of their siftings of the Cambridge–Somerville Youth Study data.[3] Albert Reiss has illuminated the topic

---

[1] This point has been made regarding homosexuality by Howard S. Becker, in his review of Hendrik M. Ruitenbeek, ed., The Problem of Homosexuality in Modern Society (New York: E. P. Dutton and Co., 1963), in American Journal of Sociology, 70 (July 1964), 130.

[2] Stanton Wheeler, "Sex Offenses: A Sociological Critique," Law and Contemporary Problems, 25 (Spring 1960), 258–78.

[3] William McCord, Joan McCord, and Paul Verden, "Family Relations and Sexual Deviance in Lower-Class Adolescents," International Journal of Social Psychiatry, 8 (Summer 1962), 165–79. This is a somewhat defective study; for one thing, some relatively novel definitions of "sexual deviance" are employed so that juvenile masturbators are labeled as "perverted" deviants. Also, no data are provided regarding the adult outcomes of these juvenile patterns, so it is not entirely clear what kinds of persons are the subject of attention here.

of adolescent sexual deviation through a thoughtful examination of American values, adolescent status structure, and related variables.[4] He notes a number of ways contemporary values and adolescent status contribute to patterns of sexual behavior. He also directs attention to the varied societal definitions of adolescent sexual conduct related to age, race, socioeconomic status, and other variables. We shall examine other cases of this sort in this chapter.

American sexual values seem to be in the process of rapid change, at least as far as a growing openness of discussions of sexuality is concerned. John Gagnon and William Simon note that the psychiatric view of sexuality and sexual deviations has begun to replace the more traditional public perspective which viewed deviation as "immoral."[5] Also indicative of the changing sexual morality in the United States is the dramatic proliferation of "adult book stores," "skin flick" movie houses, and other operations of that kind in recent years. Quite probably the changes in the general public's attitude toward sexual questions have had something to do with the increased interest in the study of sexuality and deviant sexual conduct within sociology in recent years. Nonetheless, great gaps in sociological knowledge still exist in this area.

On the whole, until recently, sociologists have ignored the developmental processes by which persons come to be homosexuals, exhibitionists, child molesters, or to engage in other forms of sexual conduct. One common tendency in the study of deviance and criminology has been to default on the etiological issues regarding sexual deviation by turning this matter over to psychiatrists.[6] For example, this kind of behavior is often attributed to "compulsions," which supposedly drive the deviant. Sex offenders are seen as persons whose actions are not rationally motivated, and hence they are thought to lie outside the purview of sociological commentary.[7] But we need to alter this viewpoint. Sexual conduct, deviant or otherwise, is learned behavior. As such it is no less "sociological" than most of the other phenomena with which we have been concerned.

---

[4]Albert J. Reiss, "Sex Offenses: The Marginal Status of the Adolescent," *Law and Contemporary Problems*, 25 (Spring 1960), 309-33.

[5]John Gagnon and William Simon, "Sexual Deviance in Contemporary America," *Annals of the American Academy of Political and Social Science*, 336 (March 1968), 106-22. See this entire issue, "Sex and the Contemporary American Scene," for a series of useful articles on sex in American society. Other useful anthologies are Edward Sagarin and Donal E. J. MacNamara, eds., *Problems of Sex Behavior* (New York: Thomas Y. Crowell Co., 1968); John H. Gagnon and William Simon, eds., *Sexual Deviance* (New York: Harper & Row, Publishers, 1967).

[6]One example of psychiatric analysis of sexual deviation is Anthony Storr, *Sexual Deviation* (Baltimore: Penguin Books, 1964).

[7]For an incisive analysis of the compulsive hypothesis, see Donald R. Cressey, "The Differential Association Theory and Compulsive Crimes," *Journal of Criminal Law, Criminology and Police Science*, 45 (May-June 1954), 29-40. Cressey notes that offenders to whom the label "compulsive" is attached, such as "kleptomaniacs," are motivated in the same way that other criminals are motivated. They select places in which to carry out their acts, plan their crimes in advance, and behave in other ways indicating deliberate, rational thought. Cressey suggests that application of the "compulsive crime" label most frequently occurs when the subject is not able to verbalize about his behavior in terms of current, popular, and sanctioned motives.

SEXUAL SOCIALIZATION

What have social psychologists had to say about sexual socialization in terms of a model of "normality" against which to contrast deviant sexual behavior and roles? Gagnon and Simon have expressed the need for a theory of sexual socialization regarding the etiology of homosexuality: "It is our current feeling that the problem of finding out how people become homosexual requires an adequate theory of how they became heterosexual; that is, one cannot explain homosexuality in one way and leave heterosexuality as a large residual category labelled 'all other.' Indeed, the explanation of homosexuality in this sense may await the explanation of the larger and more modal category of adjustment."[8]

In a summary of the social-psychological state of interest in sexual issues, Irvin Child declares:

> But while socialization variables are thus shown by elimination to have great importance as antecedents to adult sexual behavior, we do not yet have an adequate scientific basis for stating the exact relationships involved. Nor do we have as yet an adequate basis for judging the extent to which variations in adult sexual behavior are to be ascribed directly to variables in sexual socialization, and to what extent they are instead to be considered as indirect effects of variables originally pertinent to other systems of behavior.[9]

From what sources shall a conception of sexual learning be drawn? The most well-known approach to sexual development is in psychoanalytic theories.[10] These arguments stress the assumed role of instinctual sources of sexual motivation in behavior and advance a number of claims about early life experiences and sexuality that are difficult or impossible to test scientifically. Accordingly, we must look elsewhere for directions regarding sexual socialization theory. Some psychiatrists, such as Harry Stack Sullivan, have offered interpretations of sexual behavior that are rooted in learning theory and symbolic-interactional perspectives on human behavior.[11] Similarly, psychiatrists have conducted studies of sexual conduct that provide behavioral data for social-psychological interpretations; that is, these materials can be understood in interactional terms.[12]

[8]William Simon and John H. Gagnon, "Homosexuality: The Formulation of a Sociological Perspective," *Journal of Health and Social Behavior*, 8 (September 1967), 177–85.

[9]Irvin L. Child, "Socialization," in *Handbook of Social Psychology*, vol. 2, ed. Gardner Lindzey (Reading, Mass.: Addison-Wesley Publishing Co., 1954), p. 667.

[10]For examples of psychoanalytic theory applied to sex offenders, see Bernard Glueck, Sr., "Sex Offenses: A Clinical Approach," *Law and Contemporary Problems*, 25 (Spring 1960), 279–91; Clifford Allen, *A Textbook of Psychosexual Disorders* (London: Oxford University Press, 1962).

[11]Harry Stack Sullivan, *The Interpersonal Theory of Psychiatry* (New York: W. W. Norton and Co., 1953), pp. 263–96.

[12]Irving Bieber, Harvey J. Dain, Paul R. Dince, Marvin G. Drellich, Henry G. Grand, Ralph H. Gundlach, Malvina W. Kremer, Alfred H. Rifkin, Cornelia B. Wilbur, Toby B. Bieber, *Homosexuality* (New York: Basic Books, 1962).

Manford Kuhn has offered some observations that suggest the directions a symbolic interactional view of sexual behavior would take. He points out that sex acts, sexual objects, and sexual partners are *social objects* that have meaning to persons because social definitions have been assigned to them through language and communication. The physiology of man does not explain his behavior, sexual or otherwise. Kuhn asserts that sexual roles are social; hence, although physiology sets limits on the role behavior, the learning process creates sexual motives, designates partners, and determines the kinds of behavior to be engaged in to reach sexual objectives.[13]

Kuhn's observations offer a starting point for development of a social-psychological theory of sexual socialization and sex roles. Patterns of sexual behavior—sex roles—are learned.[14] A wide range of stimuli has the potential to call out sexual responses, so individuals could react, in theory at least, in ways they define as sexual (ejaculation and so on) to such varied stimuli as heterosexual intercourse, homosexual mouth, genital, or anal contacts, animal contacts, burglary of dwelling units, firesetting, and a plethora of seemingly "nonsexual" stimuli. Nearly all the potential sexual stimulus–response patterns are actually observed in any large population of adults. All the varied forms of sexual role behavior are learned through some kind of socialization experience.

One major observation is that an individual's relatively permanent sexual role behavior is largely a function of his sexual self-concepts. For example, evidence from the Kinsey studies shows that many males experience homosexual contacts at some point in their lives but do not adopt homosexuality as an adult, preferred pattern of sexual adjustment.[15] On this same point, studies by David Ward and Gene Kassebaum and by Rose Giallombardo in two women's prisons indicate that a number of the prisoners become involved in a transitory pattern of homosexual activity, becoming known by the other prisoners as "jail house turnouts."[16] Interestingly, most of these women continue to define themselves as heterosexual and apparently return to the heterosexual patterns of response on release from prison. Impressionistic observations from male prisons suggest that similar homosexual liaisons occur among male inmates without leading to homosexuality as a preferred sexual role outside of prison walls. Reiss' data on delinquent boys who "play

---

[13]Manford H. Kuhn, "Kinsey's View of Human Behavior," *Social Problems*, 1 (April 1954), 123.

[14]For a general review of existing writings and research in the anthropology and sociology of sex, see Winston Ehrmann, "Social Determinants of Human Sexual Behavior," in *Determinants of Human Sexual Behavior*, ed. George Winokur (Springfield, Ill.: Charles C Thomas, Publisher, 1963), pp. 142–63.

[15]Alfred C. Kinsey, Wardell B. Pomeroy, and Clyde E. Martin, *Sexual Behavior in the Human Male* (Philadelphia: W. B. Saunders Co., 1948); for a review and critique of the Kinsey studies, see "Sexual Behavior in American Society," *Social Problems*, 1 (April 1954). This issue contains a series of papers centered around the Kinsey studies.

[16]David A. Ward and Gene G. Kassebaum, "Homosexuality: A Mode of Adaptation in a Prison for Women," *Social Problems*, 12 (Fall 1964), 159–77; Ward and Kassebaum, *Women's Prison* (Chicago: Aldine Publishing Co., 1965), Rose Giallombardo, *Society of Women* (New York: John Wiley & Sons, 1966).

the queers" indicate that these youths participate in homosexual mouth-genital contacts without adult heterosexual roles being impaired.[17]

We are not concerned so much with how persons come to engage in certain forms of overt behavior, but rather with how actors come to define themselves as "normal" (and subsequently engage in heterosexual acts). In the same way, we need to inquire as to how persons adopt role conceptions of themselves as "gay," "dikes," "sexually inadequate," and so on and thereafter come to engage in various forms of deviant conduct.

In a general way, individuals usually appear to see themselves as "normal," heterosexual males or females out of a variety of sex role experiences beginning early in life. Probably the most critical are those experiences that contribute to the development of a stable, *generalized* conception of self as male or female. That is, the specific sexual conception of self and the sexual response preferences that develop represent the relatively natural outgrowth of acquisition of a broad set of cultural definitions centering around gender roles.

The kinds of experiences involved in normal sexual socialization are those in which parents consistently deal with the child within the guidelines of culturally prescribed parent–child interactional norms. The clinical literature on sexual behavior indicates that an atmosphere of tolerance for forms of sexual experimentation, such as masturbation, and an open-minded and "natural" parental attitude regarding sexual matters have important consequences for the individual's degree of sexual adjustment. The literature suggests that "deviant" sexual adjustment patterns, particularly homosexual ones, are commonly the product of atypical socialization experiences in which the individual is dealt with in sexually inappropriate ways or fails to acquire an appropriate pattern of identification with his parents. This clinical material shows that the occurrence of a number of markedly unconventional, "seductive" parent–child experiences sometimes leads to markedly deviant sexual role conceptions and behavior patterns.

Sexual learning is unduly complicated and dangerous in American society because of the peculiarity of American sexual values, which define sexuality as evil or "dirty" and not to be discussed openly. According to Gagnon, a pronounced lack of consensus regarding sexual behavior and sexual experiences exists in the United States. For the most part, value agreements concerning sexuality are evolved between such sexual pairs as husbands and wives largely in terms of subtle cues and gestures rather than explicit communicational dialogues. As a result of this secretive and unshared character to sexuality, parents are required to work out by themselves solutions to parent–child interactional concerns in the sexual area.[18] Because sexuality is

[17]Albert J. Reiss, Jr., "The Social Integration of Queers and Peers," *Social Problems*, 9 (Fall 1961), 102–20.

[18]John H. Gagnon, "Sexuality and Sexual Learning in the Child," *Psychiatry*, 28 (August 1965), 212–28; see also Daniel G. Brown and David B. Lynn, "Human Sexual Development: An Outline of Components and Concepts," *Journal of Marriage and the Family*, 28 (May 1966), 155–62; Clark

a forbidden topic, parents normally fail to provide their children with a vocabulary for interpreting and integrating sexuality and allied matters, and widespread "nonlabeling" occurs. In turn, Gagnon holds that "given this framework of repression and avoidance by parents, it is not surprising that the child gets the bulk of his sexual information, though not his attitudes, through peer relationships."[19]

Our discussion so far suggests that we should look for clues regarding the plethora of sexual difficulties in which Americans are enmeshed in the general area of early interactional experiences. Such distortions of sexuality as frigidity might be traced to overly repressive parent–child experiences, and impotency or sexual fears are probably linked to identifiable interactional experiences. Idiosyncratic socialization experiences are probably frequently at the heart of homosexual role behavior. Some markedly atypical experiences, including seductive interaction, also probably contribute to the development of instances of violent sexual conduct in which the victim is mutilated, beaten, and otherwise abused by the offender. In brief, early interactional experiences condition the long-term sexual activity of the adult and lead to particular sexual self-notions that, in turn, result in adoption of some specific sexual role pattern.

Some forms of sexual behavior, particularly deviant ones, probably emerge out of adult life experiences. Moreover, in some cases, the person's sexual self-image is likely to have emerged *after* some initial, exploratory playing of a new sex role. For example, exhibitionism and child molesting are carried on by individuals who have gone through a conventional socialization experience and are "normal" in sexual orientation. But in later life certain of these persons have undergone alterations in family relationships or other experiences, which culminate in self-concept changes toward notions of "inadequacy." Their behavior appears to be related to these relatively current experiences and cannot be traced back to initial sexual socialization.

A parallel line of argument is that investigation of homosexual behavior might profit from attention to the risk-taking, processual conceptualization of the development of deviant careers advanced by Edwin Lemert.[20] Homosexual roles may sometimes grow out of situations in which tentative and exploratory flirtations with homosexual activities lead to social identification of the person as a "queer" or "fairy." This altered social identity cuts the person off from reentry into the world of "normals," so he is prevented from reestablishing his heterosexual self-image. A "mechanistic" causal pattern could conceivably be operating here, instead of the commonly assumed genetic process

---

E. Vincent, ed., *Human Sexuality in Medical Education and Practice* (Springfield, Ill.: Charles C Thomas, Publisher, 1968).

[19]Gagnon, "Sexuality and Sexual Learning in the Child," p. 223.

[20]Edwin M. Lemert, "Social Structure, Social Control, and Deviation," in *Anomie and Deviant Behavior*, ed. Marshall B. Clinard (New York: The Free Press, 1964), pp. 57–97.

in which early life experiences result in early sexual identities which then determine adult role behavior.[21]

On the point of mechanistic or situational causation, Wheeler holds that a good deal of the behavior labeled as "normal" rape, in which force is employed in sexual intercourse but mutilation and other aberrant actions are absent, is carried on by "normal" individuals.[22] These instances of deviation often develop out of a pattern of interaction in which the "victim" is initially a willing and voluntary participant in the actions. The activities of the two interactional partners become "rape" only at a later point, when the offender's sexual demands exceed the expectations of the "victim," as for example when he requests anal intercourse with the "victim." Some evidence is at hand to indicate that cases of "pedophilia" (child molesting) are carried on by relatively "normal" individuals who have come to develop feelings of sexual and interpersonal inadequacy out of relatively recent life events.[23] Deteriorated relationships between marital partners might contribute to genesis of this kind of behavior in several obvious ways. Finally, data on father–daughter incest contain indications that this activity is carried on by males with relatively conventional sexual orientations. Involvement in sexual behavior with "inappropriate" partners seems related to unavailability of more appropriate sexual partners, due to illness of the spouse, social and physical isolation of the family unit, and related factors. In some cases, seductive interaction between father and daughter may contribute to development of incestuous acts, as may covert collaboration of the wife in the relationship, as she encourages the father to refrain from sexual acts with her and "winks at" sexual contact between him and his daughter.

We shall use these broad outlines of a social-psychological perspective on sexual development to elaborate on learning processes in normal and deviant sexual conduct.

SEX AND LAW IN AMERICAN SOCIETY

The schizoid character of American social structure as it has to do with sexual conduct is readily apparent to any literate citizen in the United States. The major cultural heroes of American society include the Hollywood actress sex symbol who serves as an erotic object in the fantasies of millions of males. This society couples a kind of *Playboy* mentality and an emphasis on youthfulness, eroticism, and sexual attractiveness with laws that restrict the display of sexual conduct to marriage. Even there, laws of various states attempt to regulate the particular forms of sexual activity in which marital partners may

[21]Laud Humphries, *Tearoom Trade* (Chicago: Aldine Publishing Co., 1970).

[22]Wheeler, "Sex Offenses: A Sociological Critique."

[23]Saul Toobert, Kenwood F. Bartelme, and Eugene S. Jones, "Some Factors Related to Pedophilia," *International Journal of Social Psychiatry*, 4 (Spring 1959), 272-79.

engage. In short, sexual behavior occupies a central place in the scheme of American values, coexistent with puritanical sentiments which would severely circumscribe the citizen's opportunities to engage in sexual activity.

American criminal laws regarding sexual misbehavior are extremely ubiquitous. In general, these laws endeavor to regulate the degree of consent in sexual acts, the nature of the sexual object, the nature of the act, or the setting in which the act occurs.[24] Wheeler argues that these statutes embody conflicting aims: Some express the moral condemnation of the community, such as laws directed at homosexuals; others are concerned with sex acts viewed as socially harmful, and still others endeavor to control individuals thought to be psychopathological in personality organization.[25] This situation of large numbers of laws directed at sexual behavior means that nearly all sexual acts other than specific forms of heterosexual intercourse in marriage are forbidden by law.

Of course, the fact that criminal laws are broadly defined does not mean that the majority of persons who violate them are dealt with as criminals. Quite the contrary, for a great many forbidden acts are voluntarily engaged in within situations of privacy and go unobserved and unreported. Laws against fornication would be a case in point, for it is doubtful that more than a negligible share of the adult fornicators ever become subjected to the criminal law.

American sex laws are not without critics; it has been widely argued that these statutes improperly and unwisely extend the concern of criminal law to innocuous matters of private morality, such as homosexual acts between consenting adults.[26] The critics would revise these prohibitions to narrow the kinds of behavior they proscribe to acts that are unequivocally harmful to society. Sex laws in the United States are also extremely inconsistent from one jurisdiction to another. For example, adultery laws vary between different states both in definitions of adultery and in penalties associated with these acts; mutual masturbation is a criminal offense in some states and not in others; penalties for consensual homosexual acts range from fines or jail sentences to life imprisonment. Clearly, the uniformity criminal law is presumed to contain is missing in the case of sex statutes.[27]

Existing laws defining sex offenders have several major implications for the study of causation. First, the etiological task cries out for some kind of tax-

---

[24]Wheeler, "Sex Offenses: A Sociological Critique," pp. 258–59.

[25]Ibid., pp. 259–61.

[26]Homosexual acts between consenting adults are illegal in all states except Illinois and Oregon.

[27]For an excellent summary of American laws, with particular emphasis on the variations in these laws, see Morris Ploscowe, "Sex Offenses: The American Legal Context," Law and Contemporary Problems, 25 (Spring 1960), 217–24; see also Karl M. Bowman and Bernice Engle, "A Psychiatric Evaluation of Laws of Homosexuality," American Journal of Psychiatry, 112 (February 1956), 577–83; Karl M. Bowman, "Review of Sex Legislation and Control of Sex Offenders in the United States of America," in Final Report on California Sexual Deviation Research, State of California, Department of Mental Hygiene (Sacramento: State of California, 1954), pp. 15–40; John Drzazga, Sex Crimes (Springfield, Ill.: Charles C Thomas, Publisher, 1960).

onomy of sex offender patterns that will allow us to reduce the variety of criminal activities to an orderly set of types amenable to explanation. A number of efforts to evolve meaningful systems for categorizing sex offenders are discussed in the following pages. We shall consider a number of descriptions of offender role careers designed to identify homogeneous patterns of sexual criminality.

The second causal consequence of existing criminal statutes is that an adequate formulation concerning sexual criminality will have to be sufficiently multifaceted and complex to explain extremely disparate kinds of behavior. Some kinds of criminality represent behavior patterns that differ little or not at all from conventional patterns of sexual behavior, such as statutory rape, which involves consenting individuals both of whom are sexually although not chronologically mature. In this case, the explanatory problem is in accounting for social contingencies that result in some persons falling into the hands of the police rather than accounting for personal idiosyncracies of the offenders. At the polar extreme from this kind of illegality stand bizarre and violent incidents of sexual crimes. Because these actions are probably not carried on by individuals who are the product of normal sexual socialization, a strikingly different explanation of behavior must be uncovered.

We shall identify six types of offender behavior in the following sections. We shall discuss statutory rapists, aggressive rapists, violent sex offenders, nonviolent sex offenders (child molesters and exhibitionists), incest cases, and homosexuals. Role-career descriptions will be provided for all of these types.

Before turning to examination of role careers, let us take an overview of several major studies of sex offenders.[28] A summary presentation of these pieces of research should be useful in acquiring a sense of sex offenders in the aggregate. Moreover, most research in the past has been oriented to inductive discovery rather than being informed by a body of theory. Because these investigations have not endeavored to test propositions about sex offender role careers, they are difficult to interpret in typological terms.

STUDIES OF SEX OFFENDERS

One older study of sex offenders concerned deviants referred to Bellevue Hospital in New York for psychiatric investigation.[29] The researchers indicated that these criminals had been involved in a wide variety of sex crimes, including incest, forced sexual relations, child molesting, and homosexual acts. Most of the offenders had prior records of criminality, but this is to be expected in view of the special character of the sample.

[28]For a somewhat incoherent but rather complete summary of studies, see Benjamin Karpman, *The Sexual Offender and His Offenses* (New York: The Julian Press, 1954).

[29]Benjamin Apfelberg, Carl Sugar, and Arnold Z. Pfeffer, "A Psychiatric Study of 250 Sex Offenders," *American Journal of Psychiatry*, 100 (May 1964), 762-70.

In an older investigation concerned with Wisconsin prisoners,[30] John Gillin reports that of the 279 sex offenders incarcerated in the institution, 127 had been convicted of rape, 25 had been charged with statutory rape, and the remaining 127 had committed a wide variety of other sex offenses. The sex offenders as a group were predominantly from backgrounds of low socioeconomic status, had poor school records and relatively low intelligence, poor marital ties, and generally bland personalities.

Another report on sex offenders, by Manfred Guttmacher, concerns 172 persons referred to a court-connected psychiatric clinic in Baltimore.[31] Some of the major findings in this material are that blacks were underrepresented in the group of sex offenders, and persons of low intelligence were overrepresented. Slightly over half the offenders were categorized as showing "neurotic character disorders." This is not surprising, given the kind of sample involved in this study.[32]

Albert Ellis and Ralph Brancale have examined a somewhat more representative sample of sex offenders in an investigation in New Jersey.[33] As a result of legislation passed in 1949 in that state, all persons charged with rape, sodomy, incest, lewdness, indecent exposure, dealing in obscene material, indecent communications to females, or carnal abuse were to be referred to the New Jersey Diagnostic Center.[34] This study reported on the characteristics of the first 300 persons sentenced to the center. These offenders were a mixed bag of individuals, for 20 percent had committed statutory rape, 17 percent had been involved in sex relations of other kinds with minors, 29 percent had engaged in exhibitionism, and 16 percent had been apprehended for homosexuality. Only 3 percent of the offenders had been involved in forcible rape, whereas incest cases made up only 4 percent of the group. Clearly, the majority of sex offenders who fall into the hands of the police and courts in New Jersey are relatively petty or nonviolent individuals.[35] In comparing the center commitments with inmates at the state prison, the former appeared to include many more relatively petty deviants, whereas the prison received the more disordered or violent individuals.

About one-half of the sex offenders were under thirty years of age, nearly one-half were single, 44 percent had less than eighth grade educational attainment, and nearly 70 percent were from low income backgrounds.[36]

---

[30]John L. Gillin, *The Wisconsin Prisoner* (Madison: University of Wisconsin Press, 1946), pp. 11–13, 88–131.

[31]Manfred S. Guttmacher, *Sex Offenses* (New York: W. W. Norton and Co., 1951).

[32]*Ibid.*, pp. 58–104.

[33]Albert Ellis and Ralph Brancale, *The Psychology of Sex Offenders* (Springfield, Ill.: Charles C Thomas, Publisher, 1956); for a summary of this study, see Brancale, Ellis, and Ruth R. Doorbar, "Psychiatric and Psychological Investigations of Convicted Sex Offenders: A Summary Report," *American Journal of Psychiatry*, 109 (July 1952), 17–21.

[34]Ellis and Brancale, *The Psychology of Sex Offenders*, pp. 11–12.

[35]*Ibid.*, p. 31.

[36]*Ibid.*, p. 12.

The Ellis and Brancale data lend themselves to two general conclusions. First, the vast majority of sex offenders appear to be petty criminals who are relatively normal in personality structure. They do not fit the "sex fiend" image in any important way. For example, only about 5 percent of these offenders had used force in their crimes. Additionally, 78 percent were diagnosed as "normal," "mildly neurotic," or "severely neurotic," whereas only 3 percent were judged psychopathic. Over one-half of these violators were deemed to be sexually inhibited, with 72 percent of the exhibitionists and 66 percent of the child molesters being so classified. These findings vary markedly with sex fiend notions citizens in American society currently hold.[37]

The second major impression from this study is that apprehended sex offenders tend to be socially disadvantaged individuals of generally low intelligence and economic position. It looks as though persons identified as sex offenders are often picked out of the population because of their social backgrounds rather than as a direct result of their criminality. In this sense, the case of apprehended sex offenders parallels that of property offenders, many of whom appear unluckier than other persons rather than distinctly more criminalistic than nonoffenders.

Another large-scale study in sexual deviation, carried on in the 1950s in California, noted that felony sex crimes in 1952 constituted only 2.5 percent of all reported felonies in that state.[38] Of the 3,705 felony sex crimes in 1952, 1,941 were cases of forcible or statutory rape, whereas 1,764 were other kinds of sex offenses. Extreme force and violence was rare, even in felony crimes; hence, only 9 percent of the persons prosecuted in San Francisco on rape charges were convicted of forcible rape. The investigators reported that most of the sex offenses known to the police in California were petty misdemeanor offenses.[39] They concluded: "These data therefore show that the majority of all convicted sex offenders commit socially-offensive but nondangerous acts, and the majority of all convictions occur at the level of misdemeanor."[40]

Other findings from this research include the observation that incarcerated sex offenders had less extensive records of prior criminality than other kinds of criminals and also showed lower parole violation rates than other prisoners.[41] In a separate part of this study, a group of violators who had been placed in Metropolitan State Hospital as "sexual psychopaths" were examined. These individuals were a somewhat varied collection of sex deviants, but most had been sexually involved with children. The clinical staff classified a group of these offenders as either *minor sexual deviants* who had histories of commonplace sexual acts or *major sexual deviants* who employed aggression and

[37]*Ibid.*, pp. 26–63.
[38]State of California, Department of Mental Hygience, *Final Report on California Sexual Deviation Research.*
[39]*Ibid.*, pp. 94–98.
[40]*Ibid.*, p. 99.
[41]*Ibid.*, p. 100.

force in their criminality and were characterized by compulsive pursuit of bizarre sexual activities. The researchers subjected these persons to psychological testing, using the Minnesota Multiphasic Personality Inventory. They found that a scale of twenty-one items from that personality inventory did separate the two groups of deviants: the major sexual deviants generally had different scores on this scale than the minor deviants. This evidence appears to confirm the findings of other studies which show that many sex offenders are relatively normal individuals but that some relatively disturbed individuals who commit atypically deviant sexual acts are to be found in the population of sexual criminals.[42]

The most recent study of sex offenders, as well as the most complex and detailed investigation to date, is by the Kinsey-founded Institute for Sex Research, Inc.[43] The report of that investigation is nearly 1000 pages in length, representing a vast compendium of findings on sexual deviants. However, the study is impressive negatively as well, for it demonstrates the relative paucity of results from inductive, fact-gathering inquiry. This work was not guided by a set of theoretical propositions around which evidence was gathered. Instead, it endeavored to discover significant facts about sex offenders through examination of great amounts of descriptive information.

This study dealt with a sample of 1,356 convicted sex offenders, primarily from prisons in Indiana and California, who were interviewed during 1941–45 and 1953–55. These sex offenders were compared to a sample of 888 prison inmates convicted of nonsexual offenses and a control group of 477 noncriminal citizens.[44]

Because of the wide range of activities engaged in by the sex offenders, the researchers found they had to categorize the offenders and their actions in several major dimensions. The sexual offenses were classified in terms of the sex of the victim or co-participant to recognize heterosexual and homosexual behaviors. In addition, sexual actions were divided into forced as opposed to consensual, and victims or co-participants were categorized as children, minors (persons between twelve and fifteen years of age), and adults. Combinations of these dimensions yielded twelve possible types of behavior, but patterns of forced homosexual relations were excluded because they were rarely encountered among the offenders. Finally, the researchers sorted sex offenders into three additional incest types based on age of victim or co-participant, as well as into two other categories, peepers and exhibitionists. In all, they singled out fourteen types of sex misbehavior for study.[45]

The general strategy in this research centered about examination of a

[42]*Ibid.*, pp. 136–47.
[43]Paul H. Gebhard, John H. Gagnon, Wardell B. Pomeroy, and Cornelia V. Christenson, *Sex Offenders* (New York: Harper & Row, Publishers, 1965).
[44]*Ibid.*, pp. 27–53.
[45]*Ibid.*, pp. 10–11.

number of kinds of experiences in the lives of each person involved in the fourteen kinds of sexual activity. Facts on early life experiences, masturbation, sex dreams, heterosexual petting, premarital coitus, marital experiences, extramarital coitus and postmarital coitus, animal contacts, criminality of the offenders, and a number of other matters were reported. Although much of this factual and statistical material tends to obscure more than it reveals, some significant facets of sexual misconduct do emerge from this information. For example, almost none of the heterosexual offenders against children said they preferred young girls as sex objects, so their behavior appears to be more the result of situational contingencies than pathological motivation.[46] Regarding heterosexual acts with minors or adults, the data indicate that the victim was frequently active in initiation of the sex behavior and that the offenders were quite normal and conventional persons.[47] Another finding was that those who used force in heterosexual offenses against adults were not markedly unconventional individuals, except with regard to their willingness to use coercion in achieving sexual ends.[48] Finally, the investigators reported that exhibitionists and peepers were meek, sexually inadequate persons rather than sex fiends.[49] We shall refer to more of this material when we examine offender role careers in greater deatil.

PATTERNS OF SEXUAL CRIMINALITY

Our earlier comments indicated that sex offenders are a mixed bag of deviants who need to be sorted out into behavioral types. The foregoing studies also pointed to variability among these criminals, so classificatory efforts have repeatedly been involved in these investigations. Without doubt, we could recommend various meritous ways of classifying sex offenders. However, we will treat as relatively distinct types six forms of sexual deviation. In general, our distinctions between offenders are drawn in terms of character of the sexual acts and role of the victims in the behavior. Statutory rapists and aggressive rapists represent two categories similar in the sense that both involve relatively "normal" heterosexual conduct, but they differ in the degree of force and coercion employed in attaining sexual ends. We hold that these two kinds of offenders are fundamentally different from violent sexual assaultists who exhibit idiosyncratic and bizarre sexual motives centering about violence and cruelty. In turn, nonviolent offenders who engage in child molesting or exhibitionism differ from the preceding three types, both in terms of their behavior and in their sexual inhibitions. Of course, nonviolent offenders also vary from

[46]Ibid., p. 66.
[47]Ibid., pp. 83–102.
[48]Ibid., pp. 177–206.
[49]Ibid., pp. 358–99.

the others in the sense that the general public is likely to define them as "perverted" or in other ways markedly unusual. Their behavior is hard to identify with, either because the activity appears peculiar or the victims seem markedly inappropriate as sexual objects. Incest behavior is a fifth kind of sexual deviancy that appears to be the product of a relatively specialized form of motivational process and background situation. Finally, we shall single out male homosexuals as a sixth group; within this category important variations exist in sexual behavior, participation in homosexual subcultures, and so on. The six types discussed here are viewed as sufficiently homogeneous to warrant separate discussion, although more detailed differentiations are possible within the role-career categories.[50]

THE STATUTORY RAPIST ROLE CAREER[51]

Definitional Dimensions

Offense Behavior. Persons in this category are adult males who engage in sexual intercourse with minor females. The "victim" is a willing and voluntary participant in the sexual activities.

Interactional Setting. Statutory rape cases develop in a variety of ways. Some offenders are persons such as sailors apprehended "shacking-up" with a minor female in a downtown hotel, for example. Other cases involve adult males who have been carrying on a long-term relationship with a minor female and have been apprehended for sexual acts with that person. In either instance, the essential character of statutory rape is that two individuals have entered into a cooperative, voluntary sexual relationship which happens to be illegal because of the age of the female. The girl in cases of statutory rape which result in detection is usually dealt with in a juvenile court.

Self-concept. Statutory rapists regard themselves as law-abiding citizens. They usually view themselves as unlucky persons who were simply doing what everyone else is doing, but got caught. There is, of course, considerable truth in that claim.

Attitudes. The attitudes of statutory rapists tend to be conventional and prosocial.

Role Career. These persons usually are without any prior record of delinquency or adult criminality. They are essentially law-abiding citizens who have fallen into the hands of the police and courts for technically illegal but culturally widespread acts. Many apprehended and convicted statutory rapists are placed on probation, where they are good risks. Those sent to correctional

---

[50]Female prostitution and lesbianism are not considered in this chapter. For some useful discussions of these matters, see Gagnon and Simon, "Sexual Deviance in Contemporary America," in Gagnon and Simon, *Sexual Deviance.*

[51]Don C. Gibbons, *Changing the Lawbreaker,* The Treatment of Delinquents and Criminals, © 1965. Reprinted by permission of Prentice-Hall, Inc., Englewood Cliffs, New Jersey, pp. 122–23.

institutions make good adjustments and tend to play the role of "square Johns" in the institution.

Background Dimensions

Social Class. There is little reason to suppose that statutory rape is a class-linked form of behavior. However, there may be some tendency for law-enforcement agencies to take more stringent actions against detected lower class offenders than against other statutory rapists.

Family Background. The family backgrounds of statutory rapists are usually normal and conventional, lacking in any kind of major interactional problems among family members.

Peer Group Associations. The peer group affiliations of statutory rapists are conventional. They are usually involved in peer associations in which sexual activities are highly regarded, but this is in no way an atypical peer group value.

Contact with Defining Agencies. Contacts with defining agencies are relatively neutral in effect. Some offenders probably feel some degree of hostility toward the police and courts because they view themselves as merely "unlucky" rather than deviant. But it is doubtful that this hostility leads to any reorganization of the person's self-image or to continuation in criminality.

Discussion

Several of the studies discussed earlier contain evidence on the characteristics of statutory rapists. The investigation by Gebhard, et al. contains a number of findings that generally confirm the foregoing role-career description. These investigators report that the median age of men convicted of heterosexual offenses with minor partners (females between twelve and sixteen years of age) was twenty-five years of age. Four-fifths of these individuals were first offenders; few were pathological persons. In most cases, the "victim" did not discourage the sexual activity, and in most cases, she failed to report the sexual behavior to anyone. Instead, a third party originated the complaint against the offender.[52]

Much the same picture emerges regarding offenders involved in heterosexual acts with adults. Most of the female "victims" were under twenty-five years of age, and three-fifths were under eighteen years of age.[53] Because no unusual characteristics on the part of the offenders emerge from the data, the authors concluded: "One is left with the over-all impression of an uneducated, opportunistic, and basically goodhearted soul who takes his pleasure where he finds it and lets the future take care of itself."[54]

[52]Gebhard et al., *Sex Offenders*, pp. 83–105.
[53]*Ibid.*, pp. 106–32.
[54]*Ibid.*, p. 132.

THE AGGRESSIVE RAPIST ROLE CAREER

Definitional Dimensions

Offense Behavior. Aggressive rapists are persons usually charged with "rape" rather than "statutory rape" when apprehended. They employ varying degrees of force to coerce a physically adult female into sexual activity. The amount of force varies in cases of aggressive rape, and, in addition, interpretations of the offender and the victim regarding the coercion involved in the event frequently differ. Aggressive rapists often argue that they have been convicted on a "bum beef" in that the victim was actually more cooperative than she was willing to admit. At any rate, aggressive rape differs from statutory rape because both participants did not freely enter into the sexual activity. In most instances of aggressive rape, the sexual activity centers about heterosexual intercourse. Occasionally, aggressive rapists compel the victim to engage in other sexual acts, such as fellatio, which are commonly defined as "perversions" but are nonetheless fairly commonplace forms of sexual behavior among "normal" persons. In short, this behavior is deviant because the offender employs force.

Interactional Setting. Aggressive rape is a form of criminality that often represents a disruption of ordinary interactional patterns. In a good many cases, aggressive rape is the end result of a pattern of social intercourse between a "victim" and an offender, which began with voluntary involvement of the two persons in some kind of social activity. An example of this kind of sequence would be a "pickup" in a cocktail bar. Initially, the two individuals engage in drinking, and both anticipate that the evening will end on a sexual note. But as events unfold, the offender makes sexual demands that exceed the expectations of the "victim," so coercion is employed. At that point, fornication is converted into "rape." Aggressive rape also sometimes involves instances in which persons unknown to the victim seize her and force her into sexual acts; but this kind of rape probably occurs less frequently.

Self-concept. Aggressive rapists do not define themselves as criminals. Although they acknowledge involvement in a criminal act, they offer a variety of arguments to minimize the seriousness of their behavior, such as the contention that the victim acted in provocative and seductive ways toward them. These offenders view their acts of deviance as essentially alien or unimportant aspects of their conduct.

Attitudes. The attitudes of aggressive rapists are relatively conventional, except perhaps for a relative insensitivity to the feelings of the victim.

Role Career. Aggressive rapists show backgrounds of little or no prior criminality. If they have been involved in earlier episodes of lawbreaking, these are usually relatively petty offenses. Rapists are not particularly prone to parole violation and recidivism. Instead, most of them serve long prison sentences and are released, whereupon they are absorbed back into the population of law-abiding citizens.

Background Dimensions

Social Class. Aggressive rapists are commonly lower-class or lower middle-class individuals. Apparently, the general disposition to employ force in interpersonal relations is most common in this social stratum, so aggressive rape is a manifestation of class-linked toleration of violence.

Family Background. Aggressive rapists are not from markedly unusual family situations, although some do show backgrounds of relatively early alienation from family bonds. This estrangement from conventional social ties probably contributes to the willingness of the offender to infringe on the rights of others in the area of sexual conduct.

Peer Group Associations. The peer group relationships of the aggressive rapist do not appear to contribute in any marked way to the development of this behavior, at least in the sense of effecting the genesis of sentiments in favor of rape. Of course, in instances of gang rape, the stimulus of group contacts immediately preceding the rape probably contributes something to these episodes.

Contact with Defining Agencies. Experiences such as imprisonment apparently have a relatively neutral effect on these offenders. These contacts do not seem to impel them in the direction of further involvement in criminality.

Discussion

Data directly relevant to the preceding role-career description are hard to obtain, particularly in the case of contentions about the interactional processes leading to rape. Unfortunately, criminologists have devoted insufficient attention to systematic collection of information concerning the social nature of the behavior. This deficiency in the literature of criminology is particularly apparent in the area of sexual misconduct. We need a good deal more descriptive material that indicates the social circumstances in which incest, rape, and other sexual offenses occur.

One bit of data regarding rape comes from a study by Asher Pacht, Seymour Halleck, and John Ehrmann, who examined 1,605 offenders committed to the Department of Public Welfare in Wisconsin for psychiatric diagnosis.[55] The Wisconsin Sex Crimes Law requires a psychological investigation in all cases of rape, attempted rape, or indecent sex behavior with a child. Slightly less

[55]Asher R. Pacht, Seymour L. Halleck, and John C. Ehrmann, "Diagnosis and Treatment of the Sexual Offender: A Nine-Year Study," *American Journal of Psychiatry,* 118 (March 1962), 802–8.

than half these offenders were judged to be "not deviated" in psychological makeup. Additionally, these researchers indicated that, of the persons committed to prison, only 17 percent subsequently violated parole. These findings confirm the picture of the aggressive rapist as a person without marked pathology.

The New Jersey study by Ellis and Brancale also contributes to an understanding of rape behavior.[56] These investigators reported that in 66 of the 300 cases examined at the diagnostic center, some degree of force had been involved in the sexual offense. They suggest that reports of coercion in rape cases are sometimes exaggerated because the victim frequently endeavors to minimize her complicity in the offense. This same study noted that sexual assaultists and rapists had relatively low recidivism rates in comparison to petty sex offenders.

The inquiry into sex offenses by Gebhard et al. also contains some material germane to the case of aggressive rapists. The heterosexual aggressors who had been involved with minors (females between twelve and sixteen years of age) were relatively young men. Many were somewhat impulsive persons from relatively disorganized backgrounds. The heterosexual aggressors against adult females were relatively nondescript individuals who were unusual only in the sense that they had used force in sexual activities.[57]

A recent study by Menachem Amir represents a beginning of the kind of research needed on rape and other sexual offenses.[58] The investigation dealt with 646 cases of forcible rape that occurred in Philadelphia in 1958 and 1960. It examined the social backgrounds of the 646 victims and 1,292 offenders, as well as the circumstances surrounding the acts of forcible rape.

The findings of the research show that most forcible rapes were intraracial events rather than acts occurring between persons of different racial background. Rapes were significantly more frequent among blacks than whites, for the rape rates were twelve times higher among black than white females. Of course, these observations should be treated with some caution, in that they may reflect differentials in crime reporting and law enforcement practices as well as real racial variations in forcible rape.

Most forcible rape offenders in this report were between fifteen and twenty-five years of age, and the majority of victims were also young women. Most offenders were unmarried, which was also true of the victims. However, Amir rejected any sort of demographic imbalance explanation of rape, for the sex ratio of unmarried persons in Philadelphia was not unbalanced. Most offenders and victims were from lower income backgrounds, and many were unemployed. About half the rapists had prior records of criminality, and about

---

[56]Ellis and Brancale, *The Psychology of Sex Offenders*, pp. 32–37.
[57]Gebhard et al., *Sex Offenders*, pp. 155–206.
[58]Menachem Amir, "Forcible Rape," *Federal Probation*, 31 (March 1967), 51–58.

a quarter of the victims had been in difficulties with the law or acquired tarnished reputations.[59]

Amir discovered no appreciable relationship between rape and season of the year. However, marked variations existed in the distribution of forcible rapes by days of the week, for most occurred on the weekends, particularly on Saturday. The peak hours for rape were from 8:00 P.M. to 2:00 A.M. Alcohol appeared to be a factor in only about one-third of the cases.

Most rapists and their victims lived within the same general area of the community, and the acts of sexual assault occurred within this same neighborhood. About half the offenders and victims had been involved in a primary relationship with each other before the sexual assault, so these findings seriously undermine the stereotype of the wild-eyed rapist who assaults a total stranger.

The types of coercion or violence employed in the rape incidents were classified and tabulated. In 15 percent of the incidents, no force was used; in another 29 percent offenders were rough. Brutal beatings or choking accompanied forcible rapes in only about 30 percent of the cases. Here again, forcible rape seems to depart from some of the public stereotypes about this behavior. Amir found that the victims were submissive and put up no resistance in over half the rape incidents. The rapists subjected the victims to "sexual humiliation" (fellatio, cunnilingus, or repeated intercourse), in only about a quarter of the cases. Multiple rape by two or more offenders was involved in 276 of the 646 rape cases.

One point relevant to the typological characterization of rapists is that, in 122 of the incidents, the rape appeared to be victim-precipitated. That is, the victim deported herself in such a way as to encourage sexual assault. She had agreed to engage in intercourse but had later recanted, or she had acted in a sexually provocative manner.

Taken on balance, these findings support the typological description of aggressive rape. This kind of criminality apparently departs from conventional sexual conduct mainly in the use of threats or force. The participants in aggressive rape do not appear to be pathological types. The strong suggestion emerges from Amir's research that forcible rape may be an occasional legal outcome of situations in lower-class areas where casual and transitory sexual episodes are commonplace. Quite probably, a large number of the sexual liaisons that take place are not very different from the forcible rapes.

Richard Jenkins has offered a set of theoretical contentions about rape and other sexual assaults in American society, which is congruent with the foregoing findings.[60] He maintains that the bulk of sexually assaultive conduct in

[59]Fairly parallel findings are reported for Denmark by Svalastoga. See Kaare Svalastoga, "Rape and Social Structure," *Pacific Sociological Review*, 5 (Spring 1962), 48–53.

[60]Richard L. Jenkins, "The Making of a Sex Offender," in *Criminology: A Book of Readings*, eds. Clyde B. Vedder, Samuel Koenig, and Robert E. Clark (New York: The Dryden Press, 1953), pp. 293–300.

the United States involves the use of fairly minor degrees of force by relatively normal persons. At the same time, he claims that at the other end of the scale of violence, pathological actors engage in unprovoked sexual assaults of a bizarre and extraordinary kind. We shall turn to these offenders in the following section.

Jenkins' central thesis is that because American society involves the association of violence with sexuality, themes or motives that join eroticism and cruelty are often learned in sexual socialization. The results of this kind of socialization frequently show up in mildly sadistic acts, which do not become subject to official attention. If Jenkins is correct, we would expect marital partners to report such incidents fairly regularly. However, when these associations with sexuality occur in persons hostile to others, a potential rapist can be observed. According to Jenkins, the extreme example of hostility and sadistic orientations to sexual behavior can be recognized in lust murderers. Jenkins contends that aggressive rapists are not a particularly unusual or aberrant group of individuals. He avers: "The difference between the law-abiding man and the rapist lies typically not in a difference of sex impulse but in a difference of inhibition and consideration for the personality of others."[61]

One piece of confirmatory evidence bearing on this claim that aggression and sexuality are often joined in American society comes from Clifford Kirkpatrick and Eugene Kanin's study of dating behavior on a college campus.[62] Over half the girls interviewed said that they had been offended by sexual aggression directed at them in the previous year. Moreover, the 162 girls who were the targets of aggression reported 1,022 such episodes of gratuitous force. Nearly one-quarter of the girls claimed that their dates had tried to coerce them into sexual intercourse.

THE VIOLENT SEX OFFENDER ROLE CAREER

We have already seen that sex offenders taken en masse represent an extremely diverse group of criminals. Within this class of lawbreakers are a good many who direct their attention to adult females. But even this subgroup is heterogeneous, for, as we have observed, statutory rapists are unlike aggressive rapists in a variety of ways. Scattered among the offenders who engage in sex offenses against mature females is a third and much smaller group of lawbreakers referred to here as violent sex offenders. They carry out such violent actions against female victims that homicides often result from their behavior. There is no denying that these offenders are numerous, for newspapers periodically report incidents of criminality that fit this characterization, and a reading of

[61]*Ibid.,* p. 295.

[62]Clifford Kirkpatrick and Eugene Kanin, "Male Sex Aggression on a University Campus," *American Sociological Review,* 22 (February 1957), 52–58.

case-history materials in penal institutions turns up persons who fit this role-career description. Nonetheless, the following role-career commentary must be treated as speculative and contentious, for no detailed evidence has been collected on offenders of this kind. Some indication of the nature of this criminal pattern can be obtained from a work by J. Paul de River, which contains a series of extremely disagreeable photographs of victims of these crimes, but de River's book has few other redeeming features. It does not contain evidence on the causal backgrounds out of which these offenders develop.[63] The studies of sex offenders we previously examined are also of little use as far as violent sex offenders are concerned, for these investigations made no attempt to separate out such lawbreakers for special attention. Instead, violent sex offenders have been intermingled with more conventional murderers and sex offenders.[64]

Definitional Dimensions[65]

Offense Behavior. Violent sex offenders engage in attacks on female victims which are ostensibly sexual in character. The assault is usually accompanied by acts of extreme and bizarre violence, such as slashing of the victim, cutting off of breasts, and other activities. This behavior is in no sense conventional statutory rape in which the "victim" is a willing participant in sexual intercourse but below the age of consent. Neither is this conventional aggressive rape, for violent sexual offenders use extreme forms of aggression against a victim, sometimes culminating in homicide. In some cases, normal sexual acts are not part of the actions of the person.

Interactional Setting. Violent sex assaults are two-person affairs between a victim and an offender. Victims are chosen in several ways. Some are casual pickups; others are ambushed or surprised by the offender. In either case, the victim has not been in interaction with the offender for any lengthy period of time prior to commission of the criminal act.

Self-concept. Violent sex offenders think of themselves as noncriminal, law-abiding citizens, but they are likely to exhibit some self-awareness that they are "different" from other persons.

Attitudes. The attitudinal structure of violent sex assaultists is conventional, except in the rather private area of sexual attitudes. These are attitudes which are not highly "visible" or likely to be noticed prior to commission of a violent sex act.

Role Career. Most violent sex assaultists have no delinquency record or

[63]J. Paul de River, *The Sexual Criminal*, 2nd ed. (Springfield, Ill.: Charles C. Thomas, Publisher, 1956).
[64]Gebhard et al., *Sex Offenders*, pp. 197–205.

[65]Don C. Gibbons, *Changing the Lawbreaker*, The Treatment of Delinquents and Criminals, © 1965. Reprinted by permission of Prentice-Hall, Inc., Englewood Cliffs, New Jersey, pp. 118–19.

history of involvement in criminality. On occasion, the violent sex offender has been involved in episodes of "peculiar" conduct, such as minor stabbings of females. The offender is normally apprehended after the commission of the crime, convicted, and sentenced to prison. He is normally incarcerated for a lengthy period of time, so recidivism is unlikely in many cases.

Background Dimensions

Social Class. Violent sex criminals seem not to be the product of any single social class background. The etiological factors which lead to this form of criminality are not class-linked in any important way.

Family Background. Although there is considerable confusion about the causal backgrounds which lead to this form of behavior, certain patterns of parent–child interaction are significantly involved. It is likely that the violent sex assaultist is the product of a family pattern of repressive sexual notions, seductive mother–son interaction, or similar conditions.

Peer Group Associations. Patterns of peer group interaction have no specific significance for behavior patterns of this kind.

Contact with Defining Agencies. This violator's contacts with defining agencies are apparently of neutral significance. Such contacts appear not to be harmful, but neither does any treatment seem to have an impressively positive effect.

Discussion

The need for a typological orientation that would divide this heterogeneous population of sex offenders into meaningful units, as well as for an improved form of sexual socialization theory from which deviant departures could be studied, is readily apparent in the case of violent sex offenders. Research investigations of these persons are not available, and the direction an explanation of their behavioral development should take is not clear. However, the role-career description hints at some notions about these lawbreakers that might be hypotheses for investigation. The thrust of these claims is that violent sex offenders probably grow up in simultaneously seductive and repressive family environments. The developing person acquires out of this situation a basic heterosexual orientation centered about the expression of conventional erotic motives. A variety of sexually provocative overtures of the mother further arouses or stimulates this orientation. Case-history documents often note such experiences as the mother sleeping with the son or bathing with him long after he has become a physically mature young male. It would be surprising if the offender could repress completely any feelings of sexual arousal that emanate from these experiences. At the same time, the youth is prevented from overt demonstrations of arousal, partly because of the incest taboo that strongly forbids sexuality directed at the mother. The mother in many cases verbally treats sexual responsiveness as dirty, evil, and something not to be openly acknowledged. This sort of interactive process may well produce individuals who are carriers of combined themes of lust and aggression in pronounced form. Their hostility-charged sexual actions represent the extreme form of the erotic-aggressive syndrome described by Jenkins.

THE NONVIOLENT SEX OFFENDER ROLE CAREER

Probably the most abhorred sexual offender, in the eyes of both the general public and prison inmates, is that person who engages in exhibitionism or child molesting. These individuals are regarded as "perverts" because of their involvement in sexual activities that depart strikingly from conventional heterosexual intercourse with adult partners. In the following role-career sketch, exhibitionists and child molesters (pedophiles) are described as one pattern of criminality. Even though the specific acts of lawbreaking in which they engage differ, both child molesters and exhibitionists share a good many characteristics in common.

Definitional Dimensions[66]

Offense Behavior. This category includes offenders involved in exhibitionism, child molesting, and related offenses, such as peeping or making lewd telephone calls. A comment is in order regarding the term "nonviolent." It is true that, on occasion, the victims of child molesters are killed by the offenders. However, this is frequently the result of a panic reaction in which the person fears that the victim will report him, and is not an act motivated by interest in homicidal behavior or violence. Thus persons in this category who commit homicides differ in two ways from violent sex offenders. The former commit sex acts against physically immature victims and show no basic motivational component of violent and aggressive interests. The point should be underscored that the majority of acts of child molesting are restricted to fondling of the child, are psychologically insignificant events as far as trauma to the victim is concerned, and do not culminate in violence of any sort.

Interactional Setting. The interactional settings in which these crimes occur vary somewhat. In the case of exhibitionism, "victims" are usually persons unknown to the offender, chosen somewhat randomly. Exhibitionism tends to occur at places where female observers are likely to be present—schools, parks, and so on. In child molesting, some victims are unknown to the offender

---

⁶⁶Don C. Gibbons, *Changing the Lawbreaker*, The Treatment of Delinquents and Criminals, © 1965. Reprinted by permission of Prentice-Hall, Inc., Englewood Cliffs, New Jersey, pp. 119-21.

and chosen rather randomly, but others are youngsters well-known to the deviant—neighborhood children, children of friends, children of relatives, and so on.

Self-concept. The self-image of the nonviolent sex offender is noncriminal in form. Some offenders vehemently deny that they are "real" criminals. Some also deny that they did, in fact, commit the acts for which they are imprisoned. Others admit that they engaged in the acts for which they have been charged, but for reasons quite different from the apparent ones. Child molesters, for example, sometimes contend that the victim initiated the sexual activity. Denial of involvement in sex crimes and avowal of righteous religious sentiments is a common characteristic of nonviolent sex criminals.

Attitudes. The attitudes of nonviolent sex offenders are for the most part conventional and prosocial.

Role Career. Most criminals in this category are without delinquency records or backgrounds of other criminal activities. Persons engaged in this kind of sexual deviation are usually apprehended, convicted, and sentenced to long prison terms. Those released on parole appear to get reinvolved in such activities in a number of cases.

Background Dimensions

Social Class. This form of crime is not class-linked so such offenders come from a variety of social class origins.

Family Background. It does not appear that the early parental backgrounds of nonviolent sex offenders are of major significance. These background experiences may play some contributory role in that the offender is characterized by a timid, retiring personality which resulted from early experiences. However, it appears that the more significant family variables by far have to do with the adult marital situation of the offender. In most cases, a pattern of long-term sexual inadequacy on the part of the individual seems to precede involvement in sex crimes, particularly exhibitionism and child molesting. Sexual inadequacy appears to be a part of a larger constellation of husband–wife characteristics in which the husband is dominated by a physically and socially more aggressive spouse. The husband has been troubled by the "man or mouse" question, in which he has experienced chronic, nagging doubts about his adequacy as a male.

Peer Group Associations. Peer group interaction patterns are not of major importance in development of this kind of behavior, except insofar as the person's associations have contributed to his sense of inadequacy through joking or ridicule directed at him. Such experiences may play a contributory role in development of behavior patterns of this kind, but they do not play a central part in such activities.

Contact with Defining Agencies. Nonviolent sex offenders rather frequently get into the hands of the defining agencies. These organizations tend to share the same extremely negative views of such offenders as do citizens generally. Doubtless such notions are communicated to the offender, so that he experiences considerable difficulty in preserving any kind of self-image as a "normal" person. In prison, nonviolent sex offenders are assigned the status of "ding" and "rapo," terms referring to the lowest social positions occupied by inmates. All of these experiences create difficulties for the criminal, but it is also probable that he would encounter great problems of identity protection even if he were to receive rather different reactions from the defining agencies, given the general scorn, revulsion, and hostility directed at him by the general public.

Discussion

For the most part, evidence concerning the role-career description of nonviolent sex offenders forms a consistent picture. However, Paul Gebhard and John Gagnon have presented some findings concerning male sex offenders against young children in which the subjects were relatively young adult males.[67] This finding is not consistent with other accounts, which report that pedophiles are usually older men.

An investigation some years ago by Benjamin Apfelberg, Carl Sugar, and Arnold Pfeffer noted that child molesters were the oldest group among six different kinds of sex offenders held for psychiatric examination at Bellevue Hospital in New York. This same study reported that exhibitionists showed inferiority feelings of a variety of kinds, including concerns about sexual adequacy.[68] The more recent work of Gebhard and others revealed that sex offenders against children infrequently had serious records of prior criminality and that those with previous involvement in lawbreaking had usually been involved in sex offenses. These investigators also pointed out that about 60 percent of the victims were known to the offenders before the sex acts had occurred.[69] This inquiry also uncovered evidence of heterosexual difficulties on the part of exhibitionists. These offenders were described as sexually inadequate; hence, their acts of exhibitionism served as affirmations of masculinity.[70] "Peeping Toms" also appeared to be inhibited individuals with inadequate heterosexual lives.[71] Bernard Glueck examined a number of homosexual pedophiles in Sing Sing Prison and compared these offenders with incarcerated rapists and a general sample of other inmates. He contended that the homosexual child molesters exhibited attenuated heterosexual interests and also showed

[67]Paul H. Gebhard and John H. Gagnon, "Male Sex Offenders Against Very Young Children," *American Journal of Psychiatry*, 121 (December 1964), 576-80.

[68]Apfelberg, Sugar, and Pfeffer, "A Psychiatric Study of 250 Sex Offenders."

[69]Gebhard et al., *Sex Offenders*, pp. 54-82.

[70]*Ibid.*, pp. 380-99.

[71]*Ibid.*, pp. 358-79.

self-images centering about feelings of inadequacy.[72] The New Jersey study discussed earlier also turned up evidence that exhibitionists and child molesters are sexually inhibited individuals rather than hypersexed "fiends."[73] Toobert and others subjected a large group of San Quentin Prison pedophiles to the Minnesota Multiphasic Personality Inventory, with the result that the child molesters appeared more distrustful, effeminate, and passive than the control group prisoners.[74] These researchers contended: "Most typically the pedophile is a person who is sexually dissatisfied, who has rather strong religious interests, who feels inadequate in his interpersonal relations, who expresses a good deal of guilt, and who is highly sensitized to the evaluations of others."[75] J. H. Conn observed that a group of exhibitionists placed on probation were uncommonly meek, passive, sexually inhibited males who were married to domineering, aggressive, "castrating" females.[76]

The innocuous character of child molesting has been the subject of comments by Lauretta Bender and Abram Blau[77] and by John Gagnon.[78] In both cases, the sexual experiences usually had only a slight effect on the victim; and moreover, the children frequently played an initiatory role in the sexual activities.

Charles McCaghy has produced another study of child molesters, dealing with incarcerated molesters, as well as those on probation in two counties in Wisconsin.[79] His findings indicate that most of the offenders were unskilled or semiskilled workers. The average age of the molesters was 37.3, whereas that of the victims was 9.0. Over two-thirds of the molesters had been at least casually acquainted with the victims prior to the offense; in three-fourhs of the cases the molester did not use overt coercion and restricted contact mainly to acts of genital manipulation. However, McCaghy also argues that child molesters are a somewhat mixed group:

> . . . we tentatively suggest six types of molesters who appear to be relatively distinct from one another with regard to several characteristics, only the most prominent of which are mentioned here: (1) high interaction molester (whose characteristics have been described above); (2) incestuous molester

[72]Bernard C. Glueck, Jr., "Psychodynamic Patterns in the Homosexual Sex Offender," *American Journal of Psychiatry*, 112 (February 1956), 584–90; see also N. K. Rickles, *Exhibitionism* (Philadelphia: J. B. Lippincott Co., 1950); Alex J. Arieff and David B. Rotman, "One Hundred Cases of Indecent Exposure," *Journal of Nervous and Mental Disease*, 96 (November 1942), 523–28.

[73]Ellis and Brancale, *The Psychology of Sex Offenders*, pp. 41–44.

[74]Toobert et al, "Some Factors Related to Pedophilia."

[75]*Ibid.*, p. 278.

[76]J. H. Conn, "The Psychiatric Treatment of Certain Chronic Offenders," *Journal of Criminal Law and Criminology*, 32 (March–April 1942), 631–35.

[77]Lauretta Bender and Abram Blau, "The Reaction of Children to Sexual Relations with Adults," *American Journal of Orthopsychiatry*, 7 (October 1937), 500–518.

[78]John H. Gagnon, "Female Child Victims of Sex Offenses," *Social Problems*, 13 (Fall 1965), 176–92.

[79]Charles H. McCaghy, "Child Molesters: A Study of Their Careers as Deviants," in *Criminal Behavior Systems*, ed. Marshall B. Clinard and Richard Quinney (New York: Holt, Rinehart and Winston, 1967), pp. 75–88.

(whose victim is related and living in his residence); (3) asocial molester (whose molesting offense is but one segment of a lawbreaking career); (4) senile molester (whose older age and low educational level distinguish him from other molesters); (5) career molester (whose current offense does not represent his only arrest for molesting); and (6) spontaneous-aggressive molester (whose offense characteristics are opposite those of the high interaction molester).[80]

Alex Gigeroff, J. W. Mohr, and R. E. Turner have presented some summary observations about exhibitionists, which show these individuals to be relatively young persons.[81] The average age of the exhibitionists they studied was about twenty-five, with the peak period for this lawbreaking in the early to middle twenties. Because the social backgrounds of the offenders did not appear to be markedly unusual, these researchers argue that the behavior is a response to stress situations in the individual's personal and social relations rather than a manifestation of mental illness or impairment.

The final group of research observations about nonviolent sex offenders has to do with the outcast status of these persons among other prisoners in correctional institutions. Studies of prison communities have indicated that most convicts avoid social contacts with a large group of fellow prisoners known in the inmate argot as "dings." Many of these outcasts are assigned this outcast status because of their bizarre or unpredictable patterns of behavior. "Dings" who receive the special label of "rapos" are nonviolent sex offenders held in contempt by other prisoners because of the nature of their sexual crimes.[82] One investigation of "rapos" by Walter Martin confirmed the commonplace assertion by inmates that nonviolent sex offenders are the major recruits into the prison religious program. Martin observed that "rapos" frequently verbalized religious sentiments in the institution and most frequently attended church.[83]

THE INCEST OFFENDER ROLE CAREER

Criminal statutes in the United States which define the offense of incest show a good deal of variation from state to state. Intercourse between father and daughter, mother and son, and brother and sister are prohibited everywhere; but some states extend the meaning of incest to sexual intercourse between first cousins. Brothers and sisters of half blood are sometimes included within

[80]*Ibid.*, p. 87.

[81]Alex K. Gigeroff, J. W. Mohr, and R. E. Turner, "Sex Offenders on Probation: The Exhibitionist," *Federal Probation*, 32 (September 1968), 18–21.

[82]Clarence C. Schrag, "Social Types in a Prison Community" (Master's thesis, University of Washington, 1944); Peter G. Garabedian, "Social Roles and Processes of Socialization in the Prison Community," *Social Problems*, 11 (Fall 1963), 139–52.

[83]Walter T. Martin, "The Religious Attitudes of the Prison Sex Offender" (Master's thesis, University of Washington, 1944).

the purview of incest legislation, as are fathers and adopted daughters. Other states do not prohibit sexual relations between these individuals, at the same time that some forbid such pairs of individuals to marry. These statutory variations are of little importance in one major respect, for, in practice, father–daughter incest is almost the sole form of forbidden sexual intercourse that results in prosecution as "incest." This is not to say that sexual intercourse never occurs between mothers and sons or between siblings. These acts occur but are rarely reported, unlike father–daughter incest. In the latter case, the mother often acts as complainant against the father. In other instances, the daughter becomes pregnant and is induced to identify her father as the person responsible for her pregnancy.

Definitional Dimensions

Offense Behavior. Incest offenders are normally fathers who have been charged with sexual intercourse with a daughter. Most commonly, the daughter is an adolescent or older, so that the sexual acts between the two consist of sexual intercourse. The deviant character of the behavior resides in the inappropriateness of the sexual partners rather than in the behavior itself.

Interactional Setting. Acts of intercourse between father and daughter tend to develop in situations of physical and social isolation, where the daughter represents the only sexual partner available to the father. Not infrequently, the daughter is a relatively willing participant in the sexual activity, in which case the behavior may extend into a number of sexual incidents over time. In many cases, the father and mother have become estranged although they continue to live in the same household. In some instances, the sexual activity between father and daughter is apparent to the mother, who tolerates the situation in order to avoid the sexual demands of the father.

Self-concept. Incest offenders lack criminalistic self-images and often deny their involvement in incest. Some offer justificatory arguments for their conduct in which they contend that they were motivated to engage in incest for reasons other than erotic ones. They assert that they were carrying out a parental obligation to educate their children, or advance other claims of this sort. In prison, incest offenders are sensitive to the low esteem in which they are held by other prisoners.

Attitudes. The attitudes of incest offenders are relatively conventional. These lawbreakers do not verbalize criminalistic attitudes.

Role Career. Incest offenders do not exhibit extensive records of criminality before being apprehended for incest. Most of them refrain from further involvement in crime after release from prison. However, they tend to receive exceedingly long prison sentences because of the general abhorrence of such behavior in American society.

Background Dimensions

Social Class. These individuals are predominantly from lower-class backgrounds. The conditions of physical and social isolation that contribute to attenuation of internalized prohibitions against incest tend to be most common in lower-class populations.

Family Background. There apparently is no important link between early life family experiences and incest behavior. However, the adult life family situation in which incest occurs plays a directly contributory role in this form of deviance. Incest offenders are frequently in marital situations marked by tension and social distance between the husband and wife. On occasion, the offender's spouse is physically disabled so as to be incapable of fulfilling the offender's sexual demands. Distorted interactional patterns in families in which incest occurs lead the lawbreaker to focus upon a daughter as a sexual substitute for the wife.

Peer Group Associations. The peer associations of the incest violator do not play any direct part in this behavior. However, isolation from the controlling influence of peers does sometimes contribute to the genesis of this behavior.

Contact with Defining Agencies. The experiences of the incarcerated incest offender with correctional agencies do not appear to impair his ability to refrain from recidivism upon release. For one thing, the long prison sentences these persons serve have the effect of altering their family situation, making repeated episodes of incest unlikely. That is, the offender serves a long prison term, during which time his female children grow into adulthood and leave the parental family. By the time the offender is released from prison, there are no children remaining at home with whom he might resume incestuous activities. Although the paroled incest case returns to the community heavily stigmatized, he often goes back to a situation of social isolation from others, so their hostile views are of little import to him.

Discussion[84]

Much evidence on incest confirms the characterization of this role career in the preceding section. Svend Riemer has reported on a number of father-daughter incest cases in Sweden.[85] He indicated that incest occurs most frequently among agricultural laborers or other similarly disorganized groups of industrial workers. These persons generally came from broken homes or experienced early separation from their family because of tension in relationships

[84]For a review of materials on incest, see R. E. L. Masters, *Patterns of Incest* (New York: The Julian Press, 1963).

[85]Svend Riemer, "A Research Note on Incest," *American Journal of Sociology*, 45 (January 1940), 566–75.

with their parents. Entry into the labor market early in life restricted their educational attainment. As a consequence, their adult life showed frequent job changes and employment instability. Shortly preceding the incest episode, these persons had been involved in marked employment difficulties or other disruptions of social routine. Riemer contends that the incest offenders had been in situations of sexual frustration prior to occurrence of the crime, in that their wives had become incapacitated or had refused to engage in intercourse. Riemer holds that incest is thus a result of indifference toward social responsibilities on the part of the actor along with extreme sexual frustration. The choice of a sexual partner outside of the family was limited; so although the offender had no special sexual interest in his daughter, she was the only sexual partner available to him.

A study of Illinois offenders by S. Kirson Weinberg involved predominantly father–daughter incest cases.[86] Weinberg argued that the offender's behavior is a manifestation of personal instability and retarded emotional development. According to Weinberg, incest offenders are of two general types. Some show schizophrenic characteristics; they are involved in such ingrown family relationships that they have difficulty in relating effectively to persons outside of the family. The others exhibit "psychopathic" characteristics and have insufficiently internalized guilt and aversion toward sexual relations with family members. Individuals in the latter category were involved in relatively disorganized family relationships in which effective social constraints against incest were absent. Throughout his analysis, Weinberg presents case materials that point to social isolation and family disorganization as major precipitating factors in the onset of father–daughter incest.

Noel Lustig and others have conducted research on incest that also emphasizes the disorganized character of family situations in which incest occurs.[87] In the same way, Irving Kaufman and others have studied a small group of incest cases involving fathers and daughters in which this portrait of family patterns also emerges.[88] The fathers in these cases were lower-class individuals involved in poverty, alcoholism, and employment instability; hence, they resembled the individuals Riemer describes. The sex offender research of Gebhard and others reported that prisoners convicted of incest with children were ineffectual, nonaggressive, dependent individuals who drank heavily and were employed sporadically.[89] Much of the same pattern of personal characteristics

[86]S. Kirson Weinberg, *Incest Behavior* (New York: Citadel Press, 1955).

[87]Noel Lustig, John W. Dresser, Seth W. Spellman, and Thomas J. Murray, "Incest," *Archives of General Psychiatry*, 14 (January 1966), 31–40.

[88]Irving Kaufman, Alice L. Peck, and Consuelo K. Tagiuri, "The Family Constellation and Overt Incestuous Relations Between Father and Daughter," *American Journal of Orthopsychiatry*, 24 (April 1954), 266–77; see also Hector Cavallin, "Incestuous Fathers: A Clinical Report," *American Journal of Psychiatry*, 122 (April 1966), 1132–38.

[89]Gebhard et al., *Sex Offenders*, pp. 207–29.

and social situations was uncovered in the case of incest offenders involved with minor or with adult daughters.[90]

THE MALE HOMOSEXUAL ROLE CAREER

Those persons who engage in acts of sexual conduct with members of the same sex represent one of the most widely discussed groups of deviants in American society. There has been no shortage of commentary directed at homosexuals, ranging from objective analyses on one extreme to denunciatory attacks in moral terms on the other. At the same time, sociologists have paid little attention to homosexuality, so a major share of the literature is psychiatrically-oriented and has been produced by psychiatrists.

In the following sections, we shall focus exclusively on male homosexuals. This is not to say that female homosexuals are uncommon in the United States, for there is reason to believe that lesbians are about as numerous as male homosexuals. But nearly all arrests of individuals for homosexual conduct involve males. Although the police have considerable difficulty in apprehending male homosexuals, they would encounter even greater obstacles were they to attempt to round up a large number of lesbians. Homosexual acts among women are carried out in private places to which the police do not have access and so are less "visible" than acts of male homosexuality. Additionally, there is probably a general disbelief in the possibility of homosexuality among women, so agents of social control do not feel compelled to ferret out such persons. This situation is in contradistinction to male homosexuality, which the police go about detecting through a variety of techniques, such as vice squad work by plainclothesmen who make themselves available for homosexual advances and then arrest the offender who makes such overtures.

All types of hypotheses have been advanced to account for homosexual behavior. One prominent school of thought contends that homosexuality is constitutional in nature, having its base in physiological factors. This same line of argument often holds that homosexuals represent a fairly distinct personality type.[91] Edmund Bergler is a prominent exponent of the view that homosexuality is always the result of a neurotic distortion of personality structure.[92] Persons who advance this contention tend to be emphatic in stating this claim without offering much persuasive evidence in its support.

A growing body of opinion asserts that homosexuality is the outcome of certain kinds of sexual socialization rather than the product of faulty biology.

[90]*Ibid.*, pp. 230-71.

[91]For an example of this thesis, see Herbert Greenspan and John D. Campbell, "The Homosexual as a Personality Type," *American Journal of Psychiatry*, 101 (March 1945) 682-89.

[92]Edmund Bergler, *Homosexuality: Disease or Way of Life?* (New York: Hill and Wang, 1956).

Abram Kardiner has averred that male homosexuality develops in family settings in which individuals develop incapacitating fears of females and other, related characteristics conducive to homosexual involvement.[93] Clara Thompson[94] and Donald Cory,[95] among others, have also enunciated this social perspective, which we shall follow in our role-career description. We shall also examine some evidence consistent with a social learning approach to homosexuality.

Another prefatory comment should also be made. Much of the work on homosexuality has proceeded in terms of implicit assumptions picturing the homosexual as a person dominated by his sexual patterns and preferences and generally ignoring his other social roles and activities. In much of the scientific literature, the homosexual is portrayed as a person apart from "normals," living a bizarre and idiosyncratic life style. But in the view of Simon and Gagnon, this literature has grossly exaggerated the deviant component in the total behavior of persons who happen to be homosexual, presenting the deviant in a social landscape that has been stripped of everything but his deviant commitment. In their perspective on homosexuality, these authors contend that homosexuality is a heterogeneous category, representing many different sexual styles, and that homosexuals also occupy nonsexual roles. They also suggest that much more attention should be paid to the life cycle and career adjustments homosexuals go through after having become engaged in this line of sexual behavior, with less concern for the question of etiology.[96]

Definitional Dimensions

Offense Behavior. Male homosexuals get into the hands of the police or the criminal courts under a variety of charges but frequently for a misdemeanor offense such as "lewd conduct" or "disorderly conduct," owing to difficulties the police encounter in making arrests for specific illegal sexual acts. However, the offender becomes the subject of official attention because he is presumed to be involved in homosexuality. The specific sexual acts are quite numerous, encompassing a variety of masturbatory acts, oral and anal contacts, as well as other sexual responses.

Interactional Setting. The social context in which homosexual acts are conducted tends to vary. Some individuals engage in transitory episodes of homosexuality with male "hustlers" and other casual sexual partners; others are found in differential social and sexual association with members of a homosexual subculture. Homosexuals who "cruise" for casual pickups run the

[93]Abram Kardiner, "The Flight from Masculinity," in *The Problem of Homosexuality in Modern Society*, ed. Hendrik M. Ruitenbeek (New York: E. P. Dutton and Co., 1963), pp. 17-39.

[94]Clara Thompson, "Changing Concepts of Homosexuality in Psychoanalysis," in Ruitenbeek, *The Problem of Homosexuality in Modern Society*, pp. 40-51.

[95]Donald Webster Cory, *The Homosexual in America* (New York: Greenberg, Publisher, 1951).

[96]William Simon and John H. Gagnon, "Homosexuality: The Formulation of a Sociological Perspective."

greatest risk of detection by vice squad detectives. They are also most in danger of being assaulted by "rough trade" sexual partners.

Self-concept. Many adult homosexuals who have been engaged for any length of time in homosexuality define themselves as homosexuals and as "gay." However, most regard themselves as noncriminals who are unfairly harassed by the social control agencies. Many would argue that they are engaged in a harmless form of deviance, both to themselves and to "society."

Attitudes. The attitudes of homosexuals are for the most part conventional and prosocial, the only major exception being that they exhibit tolerance and positive attitudes toward homosexuality.

Role Career. Adult male homosexuals often compile a lengthy record of arrests for homosexually-related charges during their lifetimes. However, most of them show little or no involvement in other crimes.

Background Dimensions

Social Class. Homosexuals can be discovered at all social class levels in American society.

Family Background. Although adult homosexuals have experienced somewhat mixed family background patterns, certain kinds of sexual socialization and parent–child relations are inordinately common in their life histories. In particular, maternal domination is a frequently reported pattern in the family origins of these offenders.

Peer Group Associations. The peer associations of homosexuals do not appear to play an important contributory role in the genesis of their behavior. However, for adult members of homosexual subcultures, differential association with homosexual peers operates as a major social support in the offenders' attempts to establish a *modus vivendi* with the "straight" or nonhomosexual society.

Contact with Defining Agencies. Encounters adult homosexuals have with policemen and other social control agents are not congenial. But their attachment to this role career is more conditioned or influenced by considerations other than the effects of societal reactions as mediated through defining agencies.

Some Research on Homosexuality

In our view, the research of Bieber et al. represents one of the most revealing etiological studies of male homosexuality.[97] This investigation involved a sample of 106 homosexuals undergoing psychoanalytic treatment in metropolitan New York City, along with a sample of 100 nonhomosexual "controls." The

[97]Bieber et al., *Homosexuality.*

data of the study consisted of observations on these persons, which the psychiatrists treating them recorded on questionnaires.[98]

Bieber and his associates reported that most of these homosexual subjects were the product of peculiar family backgrounds. In particular, nearly 70 percent had been reared by "close-binding-intimate" (CBI) mothers who accorded them preferential treatment. These same mothers were overcontrolling in their dealings with their sons; many also behaved seductively toward their sons.[99] The authors concluded:

> A seductive CBI configuration emerges from these data. Such mothers over-stimulated their sons sexually within the context of an overclose, overintimate relationship, and at the same time, through antisexual attitudes, prohibitions, and demasculinizing behavior toward their sons, compelled them to conceal all manifestations of sexuality. Thus, the sons were caught in a double-bind: *Maternal seductiveness—maternal sexual restriction* (emphasis in the original).[100]

The remaining homosexual subjects in this study showed a variety of relationships with their mothers. The researchers observed that the fathers of most of the homosexuals were detached, hostile, minimizing, and openly rejecting figures.[101] The most frequently observed family pattern was a triangular system involving the homosexual, a close-binding mother, and a detached-hostile father dominated by the mother. At the same time, these families showed a good deal of structural variation, indicating departures from this pattern.[102]

Inquiring into the developmental backgrounds of the homosexual subjects, these researchers observed that many subjects were excessively afraid of injuries in childhood, growing up dependent on their mothers and isolated from their peers. A number of them showed early involvement in homosexual conduct.[103]

One interesting part of this study concerned evidence of heterosexual inclinations on the part of many of the homosexuals. These persons reported that they had made attempts to engage in heterosexual intercourse and also had experienced dreams with heterosexual content.[104]

These investigators concluded that their findings add up to a picture of homosexuality as an adaptation to hidden but incapacitating fears of the op-

[98]*Ibid.*, pp. 21–29.
[99]*Ibid.*, pp. 44–84.
[100]*Ibid.*, p. 53.
[101]*Ibid.*, pp. 85–117.
[102]*Ibid.*, pp. 140–72.
[103]*Ibid.*, pp. 173–206.
[104]*Ibid.*, pp. 220–54.

posite sex. In their view, homosexuality is a pathological alternative to heterosexuality.[105]

McCord, McCord, and Verden conducted a study[106] that confirmed the results of Bieber et al. The "feminine" deviants who were homosexually oriented were from families dominated by repressive, authoritarian mothers. Their mothers were also sexually anxious, and their fathers were physically punitive. Lauretta Bender and Samuel Paster came up with somewhat similar findings in an investigation of homosexual children.[107] More recently, Gebhard et al. have claimed that homosexual offenders are frequently from disordered families. They also maintained that their subjects usually began their homosexual activities at a relatively early age.[108]

Evelyn Hooker has probably accumulated the most detailed body of descriptive data on homosexuals and their sexual patterns.[109] In one of her reports, she observed that male homosexuals engage in varied and changeable forms of sexual activity so that categorizations of such persons as "fellators," "insertees," "passive," or "active," oversimplify the real world.[110] Her most critical set of observations concerns the psychological adjustment of homosexuals. Hooker has shown that a group of thirty overt male homosexuals apparently did not vary in psychological well-being from a sample of nonhomosexuals.[111] This finding is markedly at variance with the frequently stated opinion that homosexuals are neurotic or in some other way abnormal.

Certainly not all homosexuals fit the picture that emerges from the study of Bieber et al. In the introductory portion of this chapter, we suggested that acts of sexual deviation, including homosexuality, may sometimes be the product of situational causation. Some support for this argument comes from Laud Humphries' study of men who patronize "tearooms," (public restrooms) to engage in impersonal homosexual acts with other men.[112] Over half of the men Humphries observed were married and living with their wives. For many

---

[105]Ibid., pp. 303–19.

[106]McCord, McCord, and Verden, "Family Relations and Sexual Deviance in Lower-Class Adolescents."

[107]Lauretta Bender and Samuel Paster, "Homosexual Trends in Children," American Journal of Orthopsychiatry, 11 (October 1941), 730–43.

[108]Gebhard et al., Sex Offenders, pp. 272–357.

[109]Evelyn Hooker, "Male Homosexuality," in Taboo Topics, ed. Norman L. Farberow (New York: Atherton Press, 1963), pp. 44–55; Hooker, "Male Homosexuals and Their Worlds," in Sexual Inversion, ed. Judd Marmor (New York: Basic Books, 1965), pp. 83–107; Hooker, "An Empirical Study of Some Relations Between Sexual Patterns and Gender Identity in Male Homosexuals," in Sex Research: New Developments, ed. John Money (New York: Holt, Rinehart and Winston, 1965), pp. 24–52; Hooker, "The Adjustment of the Male Overt Homosexual," Journal of Projective Techniques, 21 (March 1957), 18–31.

[110]Hooker, "An Empirical Study of Some Relations Between Sexual Patterns and Gender Identity in Male Homosexuals."

[111]Hooker, "The Adjustment of the Male Overt Homosexual."

[112]Humphries, Tearoom Trade.

of them, involvement in acts of fellatio represented a quick, inexpensive, and impersonal alternative sexual outlet, additional to sexual intercourse with their wives. Most of the participants in these sexual acts refrained from any kind of sustained social intercourse with their sexual partners, to the point of avoiding even verbal communication with them. Finally, Humphries' data suggest that many of the participants in "tearoom" sex are without homosexual self-images.

The organized world of homosexuals in American society has been the subject of fictional treatment[113] as well as objective scrutiny by social researchers. The latter includes observations by Donald Cory and John LeRoy[114] and by James Reinhardt.[115] Maurice Leznoff and William Westley studied the homosexual community in a Canadian city and observed the existence of both "secret" and "overt" homosexuals.[116] Helmer's description of the homosexual subculture in New York City also pointed to the existence of an organized set of social relations among homosexuals in that city.[117] All of these materials agree that American cities include a component population group of homosexuals who frequent "gay bars," restaurants catering to "gay" individuals, and clothing stores that feature particular lines of apparel. The homosexuals who patronize these "gay" enterprises also restrict much of their social interaction to other homosexuals. Finally, Reiss,[118] Raven,[119] and Ginsburg[120] have described the behavior patterns of "hustlers" who sell sexual services to homosexuals.

SUMMARY

This chapter has endeavored to illuminate a number of questions concerning patterns of sexual criminality in American society. Throughout the discussion, we have commented on the dearth of attention paid to these forms of law-breaking. At a number of points, our analysis has been hampered by the lack of solid empirical works. Hopefully, sociological inquiry will become more concerned with sexual deviation so that future discussions of such matters

[113]John Rechy, *City of Night* (New York: Grove Press, 1963); Hubert Selby, *Last Exit to Brooklyn* (New York: Grove Press, 1964).

[114]Donald Webster Cory and John P. LeRoy, *The Homosexual and His Society* (New York: Citadel Press, 1963).

[115]James M. Reinhardt, *Sex Perversions and Sex Crimes* (Springfield, Ill.: Charles C Thomas, Publisher, 1957), pp. 17–77.

[116]Maurice Leznoff and William A. Westley, "The Homosexual Community," *Social Problems*, 3 (April 1956), 257–63.

[117]William J. Helmer, "New York's Middle-Class Homosexuals," *Harper's*, 266 (March 1963), 85–92.

[118]Reiss, "The Social Integration of Queers and Peers."

[119]Simon Raven, "Boys Will Be Boys: The Male Prostitute in London," in Ruitenbeek, *The Problem of Homosexuality in Modern Society*, pp. 279–90.

[120]Kenneth N. Ginsburg, "The 'Meat-Rack': A Study of the Male Homosexual Prostitute," *American Journal of Psychotherapy*, 21, (April 1967), 170–85.

will be able to marshal a larger body of supporting evidence. In particular, a role-career or typological perspective on sexual offenders is surely in order.

Our efforts to comprehend the variety of forms of criminal conduct are not yet finished. Certain major patterns of criminality remain to be examined. In particular, drug addiction, chronic drunkenness, and organized crime have to be considered. Chapter Seventeen considers these forms of lawbreaking.

17

PATTERNS OF "VICE": SUPPLIERS AND USERS

In this concluding chapter on causation, we turn to organized crime, gambling, drug addiction, and drunkenness. The chapter title speaks of "vices," for laymen often see gambling, drug use, and chronic alcoholism as indicators of wickedness on the part of those who engage in them. A discussion combining organized crime and drug addiction makes considerable sense, for the illegal traffic in narcotics is a major part of the activities of contemporary organized crime. Although organized criminals do not distribute alcohol, organized crime first became a flourishing form of crime during the Prohibition period when the sale and consumption of alcohol were illegal. During that period, many famous gangsters, such as Al Capone, Johnny Torrio, and Dion O'Bannion, arose to prominence in bootlegging.

This chapter is not devoted to some relatively unimportant "tag ends" of deviant behavior. Quite the contrary, the kinds of illegality discussed here involve important costs of various kinds, either to general society or to the person engaged in these patterns of lawbreaking.

ORGANIZED CRIME

Organized Crime in American Society

The flamboyant cowboy gunfighter is frequently alleged to be a unique cultural type, found only in the United States and symbolizing a variety of cultural values. Yet *vaqueros* and other kinds of cowboys are common in South America. A better candidate as a unique American type would be the gangsters engaged in racketeering or providing illicit services to the general public. Various authorities have pointed out that organized criminals embody major cultural values in their activities and scarcely differ from their fellow citizens with regard to the ends they pursue. The gangster and the businessman are

413

both engaged in single-minded pursuit of material success, so they differ primarily in terms of the services they render and the techniques they use.[1]

The image of organized criminals or gangsters on television is of evil malefactors against whom the police are relatively powerless. These "bad guys" are pictured as involved in extortion, violence, and other crimes directed against an innocent public that is offended by such behavior but at the same time intimidated by these malevolent figures.

This conception of organized crime has two fundamental flaws. Gangsterism has normally involved collusion among the criminals, police, and city officials. Cooperation rather than conflict among these groups has been commonplace, so the notion of society at war with gangsters is more of a caricature than anything else.[2]

In addition, popular views of organized crime hold that this criminality exists *despite* the wishes of the public rather than *as a consequence* of citizen demands for illegal goods or services. Someone has to pay hoodlums to engage in union busting and similar violence; someone must be willing to purchase sexual intercourse for prostitution to succeed as a business; customers must exist for illegal liquor if bootlegging is to flourish; and at least two persons are required in gambling, one of them a citizen who wishes to place a bet or draw a card. In short, organized crime exists to provide for the satisfaction of widely demanded, but legally prohibited, activities or products.

Daniel Bell has incisively identified the cultural roots of organized crime.[3] He argues:

Americans have had an extraordinary talent for compromise in politics and extremism in morality. The most shameless political deals (and "steals") have been rationalized as expedient and realistically necessary. Yet in no other country have there been such spectacular attempts to curb human appetites and brand them as illicit, and nowhere else such glaring failures. . . . Crime as a growing business was fed by the revenues from prostitution, liquor and gambling that a wideopen urban society encouraged and which a middle-class Protestant ethos tried to suppress with a ferocity unmatched in any other civilized country.[4]

His theme has been echoed by Gus Tyler, who notes that American attempts

---

[1]Alfred R. Lindesmith, "Organized Crime," *Annals of The American Academy of Political and Social Science*, 217 (September 1941), 119-27.

[2]For some commentary on this matter, see Robert K. Merton, *Social Theory and Social Structure*, rev. ed. (New York: The Free Press, 1957), pp. 72-82.

[3]Daniel Bell, "Crime as an American Way of Life," *Antioch Review*, 13 (June 1953), 131-54.

[4]*Ibid.*, p. 132.

to suppress "immorality" have provided the seed bed out of which organized crime has grown.[5] On this point, he indicates:

> Our puritanism creates a whole range of illegal commodities and services, for which there is a widespread demand. Into the gap between what people want and what people can legally get leaps the underworld as purveyor and pimp, with gambling tables, narcotics, and women. Puritanism gives the underworld a monopoly on a market with an almost insatiable demand.[6]

Such commentary emphasizes the point that organized crime is not some kind of alien "sickness" afflicting an otherwise healthy social organism. Instead, organized criminality is as natural a part of society as various kinds of socially esteemed behavior. Three basic groups of citizens are bound together in the complex comprising organized crime: the criminals who engage in organized crime, the police and city officials with whom they are in collusive cooperation, and the citizens who purchase the services of racketeers, gamblers, and other related types.

Trends in Organized Crime

Although organized criminality has been in existence for a long time, most students of this problem identify passage of the Volstead Act (the Eighteenth Amendment) as the primary reason for the pronounced growth of organized crime after 1920 in the United States.[7] During the fourteen years of Prohibition in which consumption of alcohol was outlawed, gangsters such as Al Capone were prominent figures in every American city. These organized criminals in the 1920s and 1930s earned lucrative sums from bootlegging, labor racketeering such as strikebreaking, and prostitution.

Humbert Nelli produced a detailed historical analysis of the shift in the character of organized crime, dealing with the involvement of Italians and Italian-Americans in crime in Chicago between 1890 and 1920.[8] He indicates that the public furor regarding Italian criminality in the period before 1920 obscured a number of facets of that lawbreaking, including the fact that organized criminality by the Black Hand society was mainly directed at other immigrants *within* the Italian colony in Chicago. The growth of various forms of extortion and other criminal practices within the Italian community provid-

---

[5]Gus Tyler, ed., *Organized Crime in America* (Ann Arbor: University of Michigan Press, 1962).

[6]*Ibid.*, p. 48.

[7]For a history of organized crime, see Bell, "Crime as an American Way of Life"; Herbert A. Bloch and Gilbert Geis, *Man, Crime, and Society*, 2nd ed. (New York: Random House, 1970), pp. 194–97.

[8]Humbert S. Nelli, "Italians and Crime in Chicago: The Formative Years, 1890–1920," *American Journal of Sociology*, 74 (January 1969), 373–91.

ed the groundwork for the dominance of Italians in organized crime in Chicago after 1920. The decline of immigration into the United States after 1920 virtually put an end to criminal victimization of Italians, but the passage of Prohibition legislation presented vast new opportunities for gangsters. Many persons who had been involved in crime within the Italian community then moved into the mainstream of American gangsterism.

The organized crime of this period was noteworthy for its grossness, among other things. Prostitution was openly carried on in houses of prostitution within organized vice districts. Similarly, physical violence predominated in labor racketeering. Kenneth Allsop has indicated that during the fourteen years of Prohibition, at least 700 gang murders occurred as a consequence of intergang conflicts.[9] Probably no period in American history exceeded this one in terms of violent lawlessness. The television and movie image of the Prohibition-era gangster in odd clothing, equipped with a submachine gun, racing through the streets in an open black touring car with machine gun blazing, is based on fact, even though other elements of this picture are not accurate.

Prostitution as carried on in American cities in early decades of this century provides a clear illustration of the symbiotic linkages between elements of the population involved in organized crime. Prostitution was almost exclusively conducted in segregated "red light" districts. These areas of the city, usually near the downtown section, were filled with houses of prostitution peopled by a madam and a collection of prostitutes. Clients either found their way there by themselves or were delivered to the vice district by taxicab drivers. The fact that prostitution was the major activity of the area was an open secret.

Prostitutes employed in houses turned their earnings over to the madam and were paid a share of their total earnings in wages. The metropolitan police were involved in the regulation of this business rather than in its suppression. In return for tolerating the vice operations, and in payment for their actions in controlling unruly clients and other contingencies of this sort, the police extracted a sizable share of the proceeds from the persons operating the prostitution outlets. This "payoff" was then redistributed among various policemen, politicians, city officials, and other citizens.

Public attitudes were frequently tolerant during these years of organized prostitution in vice districts. Arguments were advanced on the positive social functions prostitution was alleged to perform. Prostitution was held to be a stimulant to business through attracting visitors to the city, or it was said to provide an outlet for sex deviants who would otherwise rape "decent" women. Reform campaigns would occasionally direct negative attention to

[9]Kenneth Allsop, *The Bootleggers and Their Era* (Garden City, N.Y.: Doubleday and Co., 1961), p. 14; see also Alson J. Smith, *Syndicate City* (Chicago: Henry Regnery and Co., 1954).

prostitution, so a call for police suppression would sporadically be heard. On these occasions, conventional police practice was to stage token raids of houses of prostitution. A few days later, business would be back to normal, with prostitution running at full speed.

Part of the mythology of organized prostitution was that girls were forcibly abducted into sexual bondage by "White Slavers"; thus the prostitute was seen as a female who had been physically coerced into a fate worse than death! The truth is that prostitutes usually engaged quite voluntarily in this activity. Most saw that work career as less obnoxious and more lucrative than the alternatives open to them, such as waitress or sales clerk positions. Once involved in the practice of prostitution, the girls became caught up in an occupational pattern in which they were periodically moved from one community to another to provide variety to the customers of the houses.[10]

In a number of ways, organized crime in the United States mirrors the changes that have occurred in the host society. Take prostitution as an example. Although vice districts still exist in some American cities, prostitution has generally undergone radical changes in form. With the decline of political corruption in American cities, particularly since World War II, the police have suppressed organized prostitution in segregated vice districts. Prostitutes no longer work in large whorehouses with a dozen or so fellow employees. The new forms of prostitution involve individual women who act as "pickups" and "hustle" out of cocktail bars, other kinds of independent streetwalkers, or "call girls" who engage in sexual transactions involving relatively large amounts of money. Prostitution has also become a major source of income to be used for drug purchases by female addicts. This kind of prostitution is much less visible to the general public. Moreover, this form of vice activity does not depend on police collusion for its success. It creates some complicated law enforcement problems for the police, which were not encountered in the days of organized vice districts.[11]

Daniel Bell has noted the changes in the shape of organized crime in the United States. He contends that as organized prostitution and industrial racketeering have declined, other forms of criminality have flourished. According to Bell, "in the last decade and a half, industrial racketeering has not offered much in the way of opportunity. *Like American capitalism itself, crime shifted its emphasis from production to consumption*" (emphasis in the original).[12] He contends that organized crime has become more "civilized" and technologically complex in recent decades. Wire-service betting on horseracing, with

---

[10]For a description of this operation on the west coast, see Robert Y. Thornton, "Organized Crime in the Field of Prostitution," *Journal of Criminal Law, Criminology and Police Science*, 46 (March–April 1956), 775–79.

[11]See Jerome H. Skolnick, *Justice Without Trial* (New York: John Wiley & Sons, 1966), pp. 96–111.

[12]Bell, "Crime as an American Way of Life," p. 152.

its telegraph communication of race results, network of bookies, and arrangements for "lay-off" betting, in which gamblers share the risks of financial losses, illustrates this transition nicely. Organized criminals have profited from the increasing subtlety of crime and have become more respectable figures.[13]

Bell believes that in the future organized crime will be less prominent as the social sources for it are eroded away. He avers:

> With the rationalization and absorption of some illicit activities into the structure of the economy, the passing of an older generation that had established a hegemony over crime, the general rise of minority groups to social position, and the break-up of the urban boss system, the pattern of crime we have discussed is passing as well. Crime, of course, remains as long as passion and the desire for gain remain. But big, organized city crime, as we have known it for the past seventy-five years, was based on more than these universal motives. It was based on certain characteristics of the American economy, American ethnic groups, and American politics. The changes in all these areas mean that it too, in the form we have known it, is at an end.[14]

In this passage Bell sounds the death knell for labor racketeering, extortion, prostitution, and certain other kinds of organized crime. However, the newer forms of organized lawbreaking, particularly gambling and narcotics traffic, are likely to be with us for a long time. Bell's forecast seems less valid for these kinds of organized criminality.

Evidence regarding current patterns of organized crime has been uncovered in greatest detail by two investigative committees of the United States Senate. The first of these was the Committee to Investigate Crime in Interstate Commerce, commonly known as the "Kefauver Committee" and chaired by the late Senator Estes Kefauver. This group, investigating organized crime in the late 1940s, found widespread evidence of gambling and other forms of racketeering in a number of American cities.[15] More recently, the Select Committee on Improper Activities in the Labor or Management Field, often designated as the "McClellan Committee" and led by Senator John L. McClellan, turned up a vast amount of information about corrupt practices in American labor unions. This committee uncovered a large number of instances in which gangsters and racketeers were influential in the conduct of union affairs.[16]

---

[13]Geis has also remarked on the decline of violence as a style among organized criminals. Gilbert Geis, "Violence and Organized Crime," *Annals of The American Academy of Political and Social Science*, 364 (March 1966), 86–95.

[14]Bell, "Crime as an American Way of Life," p. 154.

[15]Estes Kefauver, *Crime in America* (Garden City, N.Y.: Doubleday and Co., 1951); see also Morris Ploscowe, ed., *Organized Crime and Law Enforcement*, two vols. (New York: The Grosby Press, 1952); Marshall B. Clinard, *Sociology of Deviant Behavior*, 3rd ed. (New York: Holt, Rinehart and Winston, 1968), pp. 282–92.

[16]Robert F. Kennedy, *The Enemy Within* (New York: Harper & Row, Publishers, 1960).

The most recent survey of organized crime in the United States is presented in the report of The President's Commission on Law Enforcement and Administration of Justice.[17] The commission indicates that estimates of the amount of money spent on illegal gambling in the United States range from $7 billion to $50 billion per year. Loan sharking is alleged to be a widespread form of organized crime, although no figures are offered regarding the profits involved. Narcotics traffic is held to result in $21 million in profits per year to importers and distributors of drugs. The commission also claims that organized criminals have reinvested much of their money in legitimate businesses indirectly controlled by gangsters. Finally, labor racketeering is said to remain an important form of organized crime. According to the commission, organized crime exists in all sections of the United States, in small cities as well as in large ones.[18]

Mafia: Myth or Reality?

One of the most widely held notions among the mass audience in the United States is that organized crime in this country is under the control of a national and international criminal conspiracy, ruled from Sicily and known as the Mafia. According to this view, Italian-American criminals such as Frank Costello, Albert Anastasia, and Joey Adonis are linked to "Lucky" Luciano and other members of the Mafia hierarchy in Sicily. The Kefauver Committee gave great credence to this hypothesis; on the basis of testimony before his committee, Senator Kefauver contended: *"A nationwide crime syndicate does exist in the United States of America, despite the protestations of a strangely assorted company of criminals, self-serving politicians, plain blind fools, and others who may be honestly misguided, that there is no such combine"* (emphasis in the original).[19] Kefauver's discussion of this claim is somewhat equivocal, for he went on to indicate that the nationwide syndicate is elusive and furtive. Nonetheless, he continued by asserting: *"Behind the local jobs which make up the national crime syndicate is a shadowy, international criminal organization known as the Mafia, so fantastic that most Americans find it hard to believe it really exists"* (emphasis in the original).[20]

Supporters of the Mafia interpretation of organized crime make much of a supposed "summit meeting" of gangsters held in 1957. In November of that year, fifty-eight persons from all over the United States converged on the Apalachin, New York, residence of Joseph Barbara, a wealthy beverage distribu-

[17]The President's Commission on Law Enforcement and Administration of Justice, *The Challenge of Crime in a Free Society* (Washington, D.C.: U.S. Government Printing Office, 1967), pp. 187–209.
[18]*Ibid.*, pp. 188–91.
[19]Kefauver, *Crime in America*, p. 12.
[20]*Ibid.*, p. 14.

tor. These fifty-eight individuals all drove expensive automobiles, carried extraordinarily large sums of money on their persons, had extensive criminal records, and were of Italian extraction. They explained their presence at the small village of Apalachin as guests at a barbecue—an explanation that surely lacks the ring of plausibility! Twenty of these persons were subsequently convicted in a federal court in December 1959 of conspiring to obstruct justice by lying about the purpose of their meeting. However, in 1960 an appellate court overturned this conviction on the grounds that the federal government had failed to prove that any improper conduct had taken place at that meeting. Hence, this whole affair is sufficiently ambiguous to be interpreted either as support for the Mafia argument or as contrary to that contention.

That the Mafia existed as a corrupt quasi-political organization in certain parts of Sicily is not debated, for a number of investigators have thrown light on that phenomenon.[21] At issue is the body of claims advanced by such persons as Harry Anslinger, former Director of the Federal Bureau of Narcotics, to the effect that an international Mafia controls the traffic in narcotics, gambling, and other forms of organized crime in America. Edward Allen,[22] Frederic Sondern,[23] and Ed Reid[24] have also stridently enunciated this view of the Mafia and organized crime.

The report of The President's Commission on Law Enforcement and Administration of Justice contains a modified version of the Mafia argument, which is probably closer to the truth. This description portrays the system of organized crime as made up of a number of loosely coordinated regional syndicates. According to the commission, organized crime in America has the following features:

Today the core of organized crime in the United States consists of 24 groups operating as criminal cartels in large cities across the Nation. Their membership is exclusively Italian, they are in frequent communication with each other, and their smooth functioning is insured by a national body of overseers. To date, only the Federal Bureau of Investigation has been able to document fully the national scope of these groups, and FBI intelligence indicates that the organization as a whole has changed its name from the Mafia to La Cosa Nostra. . . .

In individual cities, the local core group may also be known as the "outfit," the "syndicate," or the "mob." These 24 groups work with and control other racket groups, whose leaders are of various ethnic derivations. In addition, the thousands of employees who perform the street-level func-

[21]For accounts of the Sicilian Mafia, see Norman Lewis, The Honored Society (New York: G. P. Putnam's Sons, 1964); Giovanni Schiavo, The Truth About the Mafia (New York: Vigo Press, 1962).
[22]Edward J. Allen, Merchants of Menace—The Mafia (Springfield, Ill.: Charles C Thomas, Publisher, 1962).
[23]Frederic Sondern, Jr., Brotherhood of Evil: The Mafia (New York: Farrar, Straus & Giroux, 1959).
[24]Ed Reid, Mafia (New York: Random House, 1952).

tions of organized crime's gambling, usury, and other illegal activities represent a cross section of the Nation's population groups. . . .

The highest ruling body of the 24 families is the "commission." This body serves as a combination legislature, supreme court, board of directors, and arbitration board; its principal functions are judicial. Family members look to the commission as the ultimate authority on organizational and jurisdictional disputes. It is composed of the bosses of the Nation's most powerful families but has authority over all 24. The composition of the commission varies from 9 to 12 men. According to current information, there are presently 9 families represented, 5 from New York City and 1 each from Philadelphia, Buffalo, Detroit, and Chicago.

The commission is not a representative legislative assembly or an elected judicial body. Members of this council do not regard each other as equals. Those with long tenure on the commission and those who head large families, or possess unusual wealth, exercise greater authority and receive utmost respect. The balance of power on this nationwide council rests with the leaders of New York's 5 families. They have always served on the commission and consider New York as at least the unofficial headquarters of the entire organization.[25]

Robert Anderson's discussion of the changing character of organized crime presents a similar view of the Mafia or Cosa Nostra:

The Mafia as a traditional type of formal organization has disappeared in America. Modern criminals refer to its successor as *Cosa Nostra*, "Our Thing." The Cosa Nostra is a lineal descendant of the Mafia, but it is a different kind of organization. Its goals are much broader as it exploits modern cities and an industrialized nation. The real and fictive kinship ties of the Old Mafia still operate among fellow Sicilians and Italians, but these ties now coexist with bureaucratic ones. The Cosa Nostra operates above all in new and different terms. The new type of organization includes elaboration of the hierarchy of authority; the specialization and departmentalization of activities; new and more pragmatic, but still unwritten, rules; and a more developed impartiality. In America, the traditional Mafia has evolved into a relatively complex organization which perpetuates selected features of the older peasant organization but subordinates them to the requirements of a bureaucracy.[26]

Still another description of the contemporary structure of the Cosa Nostra comes from Donald R. Cressey, who prepared the report on organized crime

[25]The President's Commission on Law Enforcement and Administration of Justice, *The Challenge of Crime in a Free Society*, pp. 192–95.

[26]Robert T. Anderson, "From Mafia to Cosa Nostra," *American Journal of Sociology*, 71 (November 1965), 10.

for The President's Commission on Law Enforcement and Administration of Justice. He contends:

1. A nationwide alliance of at least twenty-four tightly knit "families" of criminals exists in the United States. (Because the "families" are fictive, in the sense that the members are not all relatives, it is necessary to refer to them in quotation marks.)

2. The members of these "families" are all Italians and Sicilians, or of Italian and Sicilian descent, and those on the Eastern Seaboard, especially, call the entire system "Cosa Nostra." Each participant thinks of himself as a "member" of a specific "family" and of Cosa Nostra (or some equivalent term).

3. The names, criminal records, and principal criminal activities of about five thousand of the participants have been assembled.

4. The persons occupying key positions in the skeletal structure of each "family"—consisting of positions for boss, underboss, lieutenants, (also called "captains"), counselor, and for low-ranking members called "soldiers" or "button men"—are well known to law-enforcement officials having access to informants. Names of persons who permanently or temporarily occupy other positions, such as "buffer," "money mover," "enforcer," and "executioner," also are well known.

5. The "families" are linked to each other, and to non–Cosa Nostra syndicates, by understandings, agreements, and "treaties," and by mutual deference to a "Commission" made up of the leaders of the most powerful of the "families."

6. The boss of each "family" directs the activities, especially the illegal activities, of the members of his "family."

7. The members of this organization control all but a tiny part of the illegal gambling in the United States. They are the principal loan sharks. They are the principal importers and wholesalers of narcotics. They have infiltrated certain labor unions, where they extort money from employers and, at the same time, cheat the members of the union. The members have a virtual monopoly on some legitimate enterprises, such as cigarette vending machines and juke boxes, and they own a wide variety of retail firms, restaurants and bars, hotels, trucking companies, food companies, linen-supply houses, garbage collection routes, and factories. Until recently, they owned a large proportion of Las Vegas. They own several state legislators and federal congressmen and other officials in the legislative, executive, and judicial branches of government at the local, state, and federal levels. Some governmental officials (including judges) are considered, and consider themselves, members.

8. The information about the Commission, the "families," and the activities of members has come from detailed reports made by a wide variety of police observers, informants, wire taps, and electronic bugs.[27]

---

[27]Donald R. Cressey, *Theft of the Nation* (New York: Harper & Row, Publishers, 1969), pp. x–xi.

Those who argue against the Mafia theory begin by stipulating that Italian-Americans are inordinately frequent among organized criminals in the United States. However, they maintain that organized crime consists of a number of loosely coordinated regional syndicates in the United States rather than a single network of criminal associations. They would not be entirely convinced of the accuracy of The President's Commission description of an all-powerful "commission." Furthermore, critics of the Mafia hypothesis suggest that organized crime and participation of Italian-Americans in it is an indigenous feature of American life. Daniel Bell, one of these disbelievers, argues that heavy involvement of Italians in organized crime must be seen as a consequence of the late arrival of Italian immigrants into the United States.[28] Most of them came to this country after the beginning of the present century and found many of the routes to upward mobility and wealth closed to them. Many of these individuals turned to illicit avenues of mobility, such as bootlegging; others found their way into relatively unconventional occupations, which offered the promise of success, such as boxing; and still others entered urban politics. The latter were frequently aided by the criminals, who provided much financial support for Italian political hopefuls. As a result of these developments, a number of Italian-Americans did rise to positions of political importance in city government, at the same time that others became prominent in criminal mobs and gambling. Within the Italian-American community, gangsters and mobsters were viewed with a good deal of respect and admiration, for their careers represented "success," even though by somewhat unconventional means.[29] All of this is a far cry from a nationwide conspiracy controlled from Sicilian soil. Moreover, as Bell noted, this interlocking structure of Italian politicians and criminals is probably on the wane with the assimilation of Italian-Americans into more conventional opportunity structures.

Giovanni Schiavo is another student of the Mafia who contends that those who have put forth this argument regarding American organized crime are deluded.[30] He contends that the Mafia did exist in Sicily but virtually disappeared after 1927 when the Italian dictator, Mussolini, forcibly disbanded it. Moreover, Schiavo argues that no evidence supports the existence of either an American or an international Mafia in control of organized crime.

What shall we make of these divergent claims about the Mafia? We suspect that the facts will ultimately show that organized crime is an American way of life, managed by local or regional criminal "power structures" bound together into loose and relatively informal larger organizations or associations.

[28]Bell, "Crime as an American Way of Life."

[29]Cf. Nelli, who contends: "At the time when 'American' Italians were arriving at maturity only to find economic advancement made difficult (but not impossible) by inadequate education, social and ethnic background, lack of political connections, a new field of endeavor appeared, requiring as qualifications only ambition, ruthlessness, and loyalty." Nelli, "Italians and Crime in Chicago," p. 389.

[30]Schiavo, The Truth About the Mafia.

Presumably, the Apalachin gathering represented a meeting of members of this criminal structure.

Ramsey Clark, former Attorney General of the United States, has voiced a similar view.[31] He acknowledges that a good deal of organized crime exists in America, but he also contends that "the Mafia exists in the United States. It was first identified on our soil in the 19th century and came here with immigrants, principally from Sicily. In terms of the power it wields, the extent of its operations, the numbers of its membership and their capacity for violence, it is probably less significant today than in the 1920's, the 30's or the 40's. Gang wars of the 1920's and 1930's exceeded anything we have witnessed since World War II."[32] Clark argues that although a Mafia does exist, no one massive organization manages all the organized crime in the United States. Finally, he contends that the tactic of the federal strike force begun in 1967, in which a number of law enforcement agencies working together made coordinated attacks on organized crime in a single city, has had considerable impact on organized crime.[33] More known members of the Cosa Nostra were indicted in 1967 and 1968 as a result of task force operations than had been indicted during the entire preceding dozen years.

Gambling in the United States

The discussion earlier in this chapter suggested that gambling and other forms of consumptive activity have emerged as prominent contemporary forms of organized crime in America.

Although facts regarding the extent of gambling in this country are difficult to ascertain, all the available estimates indicate that gambling is "big business."[34] For example, Kefauver suggested that over 50,000,000 adult Americans gamble in some way or another and spend $30,000,000,000 per year in this activity. Of this sum, $6,000,000,000 represent the profit to syndicates and gambling entrepreneurs. This figure is greater than the annual profits of all the largest industrial enterprises combined in the United States.[35] Fred Cook has offered a similar staggering estimate of the profits in gambling; he asserts that this activity nets $10,000,000,000 per year in profits to those who control gambling.[36]

[31]Ramsey Clark, *Crime in America* (New York: Simon and Schuster, 1970), pp. 68–84.

[32]*Ibid.*, p. 75.

[33]*Ibid.*, pp. 75–80.

[34]For a useful review of materials on gambling, see Robert D. Herman, *Gambling* (New York: Harper & Row, Publishers, 1967); for an analysis of gambling in Nevada, where it is legal, see Wallace Turner, *Gambler's Money* (Boston: Houghton Mifflin Company, 1965).

[35]Herbert A. Bloch, "The Dilemma of American Gambling: Crime or Pastime? in *Crime in America*, ed. Bloch (New York: Philosophical Library, 1961), p. 335.

[36]Fred J. Cook, "Gambling, Inc.," *The Nation*, 191 (October 22, 1960), 260. This special issue of *The Nation* was devoted to a lengthy and revealing essay on American gambling by Cook.

What accounts for the involvement of hordes of Americans in gambling? On a general level, Herbert Bloch has argued that gambling of various kinds meets some deep-seated human needs.[37] Among other things, it introduces an element of hope into lives otherwise filled with failure and despair. The chance of winning through gambling offers the working-class person an opportunity to demonstrate some mastery over his life. Furthermore, Bloch contends that gambling finds a particularly tolerant audience in the United States, for it is little different in principle from various kinds of socially approved forms of risk taking and tampering with fate, such as stock market speculation.

Irving Zola has made some concrete observations of this contention regarding the social functions of gambling.[38] He studied horse race betting in a lower-class bar and discovered that this behavior represents a method by which the working-class person can "achieve" and gain some recognition by "beating the system" and demonstrating that one's fate is not solely a matter of "luck." The horse players who had highest status among their peers were those who at least occasionally won and employed betting systems, handicapping techniques, and so on.

Gambling serves other social functions as well. The persistence and popularity of "numbers" or "policy" gambling in urban areas is due in part to the fact that this form of gambling operates as a kind of welfare aid. Although the numbers player has a slight likelihood of winning when he places a wager on some number or numbers he predicts will turn up in a drawing of some sort, when he does occasionally win, his earnings allow him to purchase goods and services he could not otherwise obtain. Policy winnings make possible enjoyment of hedonistic pleasures that he cannot obtain through "legitimate" welfare services provided by local or state government. Thus, numbers profits make the difference between dull monotony and an occasional moment of novelty and pleasure. Local residents of urban slum areas have relatively sanguine views of policy gambling.[39]

In their detailed examination of the workings of the numbers racket in Chicago's "Black Belt" area, St. Clair Drake and Horace Cayton indicate that it was one of the major businesses in that neighborhood, providing employment for a good many local residents. Their analysis documents the linkages between organized crime and the police. Chicago blacks prominent in policy enjoyed high status as "race leaders" and "race heroes" in the community.[40]

In locales where the playing of numbers is commonplace, it is often bound up with magical practices and other elaborations. George McCall has shown

<hr />

[37]Bloch, "The Dilemma of American Gambling."

[38]Irving Kenneth Zola, "Observations on Gambling in a Lower-Class Setting," in The Other Side, ed. Howard S. Becker (New York: The Free Press, 1964), pp. 247–60.

[39]For a detailed account of the numbers racket, see St. Clair Drake and Horace R. Cayton, Black Metropolis (New York: Harcourt Brace Jovanovich, 1945), pp. 470–94.

[40]Ibid.

that numbers and hoodoo religion are intertwined in black communities, so the players' choices of numbers on which to bet are made in terms of superstitions, religious omens, and so on.[41]

These kinds of observations about gambling in the United States suggest that it is likely to persist as one of the more enduring forms of organized crime in America. In a society of growing affluence, which at the same time produces a marked sense of alienation in many citizens, gambling may well continue as an outlet for numerous frustrations and hostilities.[42]

DRUG ADDICTION

Those persons who exhibit "vices" in which they ingest chemicals of various kinds arouse a variety of indignant and hostile sentiments on the part of the general public in the United States.[43] Witness the furor in recent years over LSD and other hallucinatory drugs, which resulted in the passage of criminal laws making the use of such substances illegal in California and certain other states. At the same time, citizen attitudes are clearly far from consistent on these matters. A case in point is marijuana; "pot" smoking is a criminal act, widely regarded as particularly dangerous and immoral. The fact is that marijuana is relatively innocuous; it is not addictive, it is not accompanied by harmful physiological effects, and it does not produce bizarre or exaggerated behavior. Marijuana use stands in marked contrast to tobacco smoking or alcohol consumption, both of which are associated with distinctly harmful physical effects on the person engaged in them. Yet alcohol and tobacco are not illegal and are not viewed as "vices."

William Simon and John Gagnon, among others, have pointed out that we live in a drug age or drug culture, in which the majority of citizens use one or another kind of stimulant, drug, tranquilizing agent, or other chemical substance, to face the demands of modern living.[44] Accordingly, not just the "pot" smoker or opiate user represents the drug user; instead, these are only two relatively uncommon forms of drug use that the law and criminal justice system have singled out for attention. Table 1 indicates the range of drugs Americans use in addition to alcohol.

Doubtless there are a number of reasons behind the rise of "drug fiend" stereotypes, in which users of marijuana, opiates, or certain other drugs have

[41]George J. McCall, "Symbiosis: The Case of Hoodoo and the Numbers Racket," in Becker, *The Other Side*, pp. 51–66.

[42]For one case illustration of this point, see William Barry Furlong, "Out in the Bleachers, Where the Action Is," *Harper's* 233 (July 1966), 49–53.

[43]For some data on public attitudes toward drug addicts, see Elizabeth A. Rooney and Don C. Gibbons, "Social Reactions to 'Crimes Without Victims,'" *Social Problems*, 13 (Spring 1966), 400–410.

[44]William Simon and John H. Gagnon, "Children of the Drug Age," *Saturday Review*, 51 (September 21, 1968), 60–78.

Table 12 CLASSIFICATION OF PSYCHOACTIVE DRUGS, WITH MEDICALLY ADDICTIVE PROPERTIES AND EXAMPLES OF EACH TYPE[45]

Drug Effects*	Opiate Narcotics	Stimulants	Minor Tranquilizers (Sedative hypnotics and depressants)	Major Tranquilizers	Antidepressants	Hallucinogenic (Psychotogenic or "mind expanding")	Cannabis
Physical dependence	+	-	+	-	-	-	-
Tolerance	+	+	+	-	-	+	-?
Psychological dependence	+	+	+	-	-	-	+
Examples of each drug type	Heroin Morphine Meperidine (demerol) Methadone (dolophine) Hydromorphine (dilaudid) Codeine Paregoric	Cocaine Amphetamine (dexedrine, benzedrine) Metham-phetamine (methedrine)	Barbiturate (pentobarbital, phenobarbital, amytal, seconal) Glutethamide (doriden) Meprobamate (equanil, miltown) Chlordiazepoxide (librium) Chloral hydrate Peraldehyde Alcohol	Phenothiazines (thorazine, mellaril, stelazine)	Imipramine (tofranil) Amitriptyline (elavil)	LSD STP DMT Mescaline (peyote) Psilocybin Morning glory seeds	Marijuana Hashish

*In considering the medically addictive properties of each drug type, "-" represents slight or no effect; "+" that the property is present, and "?" that the effect is not clearly established.

[45]From Donald D. Pet and John C. Ball, "Marijuana Smoking in the United States," Federal Probation, 32 (September 1968), 8-15.

become the target of hostile public attitudes and efforts to "criminalize" their behavior through passage of laws proscribing the use of these substances. Howard Becker has identified the Federal Narcotics Bureau, acting in the role of *moral entrepreneur*, as a major force in promulgating hostile views of addicts.[46] Federal and state narcotics enforcement personnel have been the principal source from which definitions of the seriousness of drug use and of the drug addict have been derived, so these groups have contributed heavily to current attitudes.

In the years since passage of the Harrison Narcotic Act of 1914, making the possession of opium derivatives illegal in most circumstances, drug use has become a subject of considerable scientific interest and investigation. At present, voluminous literature on drug use of various kinds is available. Our discussion will touch only briefly on most of this material.[47]

First, how frequent is use of illegal narcotics in the United States? Although detailed and highly accurate statistics are impossible to obtain, various estimates of the magnitude of this phenomenon have been made. John Clausen contends that there are probably between 100,000 and 200,000 opiate users in the United States.[48] Most of them are concentrated in metropolitan areas within New York, Illinois, and California, with others gathered in Washington, D.C., Detroit, St. Louis, Dallas, and a few other metropolitan areas.

Clausen has also provided estimates on the number of marijuana users in the United States, arguing that marijuana smoking has increased dramatically since 1960. He contends that at least 10 million individuals in the United States today have smoked marijuana at least a few times.[49] Some further indication of the rapid spread of marijuana use is provided in figures from the state of California, indicating that only 248 juvenile drug arrests were recorded in that state in 1962, but the number grew to 3,869 in 1966.[50] Additionally, recent FBI arrest figures show that 232,690 persons were arrested by 4,759 reporting agencies for narcotic drug law violations, principally marijuana, in 1969.[51] In the period between 1960 and 1969, drug law arrests increased by 491 percent,

---

[46]Howard S. Becker, *Outsiders* (New York: The Free Press, 1963), pp. 121–46. See also Troy Duster, The *Legislation of Morality* (New York: The Free Press, 1970), pp. 3–28.

[47]For valuable summaries of this literature, see Edwin M. Schur, *Crimes Without Victims* (Englewood Cliffs, N.J.: Prentice-Hall, 1965), pp. 120–68; John A. Clausen, "Drug Use," in *Contemporary Social Problems*, ed. Robert K. Merton and Robert A. Nisbet, 3rd ed. (New York: Harcourt Brace Jovanovich, 1970), pp. 185–226; Clinard, *Sociology of Deviant Behavior*, pp. 302–42; Alfred R. Lindesmith, *The Addict and the Law* (Bloomington: Indiana University Press, 1965); Earl Rubington, "Drug Addict as a Deviant Career," *The International Journal of the Addictions*, 2 (Spring 1967), pp 3–20; John A. O'Donnell and John C. Ball, eds., *Narcotic Addiction* (New York: Harper & Row, Publishers, 1966); on marijuana, see David E. Smith, ed. *The New Social Drug* (Englewood Cliffs, N.J.: Prentice-Hall, 1970).

[48]Clausen, "Drug Use," p. 205.

[49]*Ibid.*, pp. 201–2.

[50]James T. Carey, *The College Drug Scene* (Englewood Cliffs, N.J.: Prentice-Hall, 1968), p. 45.

[51]Federal Bureau of Investigation, U.S. Department of Justice, *Crime in the United States: Uniform Crime Reports, 1969* (Washington, D.C.: U.S. Government Printing Office, 1970), p. 112.

contrasted to an increase of only 24 percent for all kinds of offenses.[52] Finally, the FBI figures for 1969 indicate that over half the drug arrests were of persons under twenty-one years of age, and about one quarter of them involved individuals under eighteen years of age.

By contrast with any other Western nation for which figures are available, the United States is clearly the only country with a narcotic "problem." Yet the majority of drug users are marijuana smokers, most of whom do not graduate into opiate addiction. Although American opiate addicts are more numerous than those in other countries, they constitute a numerically small portion of all criminals in the United States.

Drug *use* should be distinguished from drug *addiction*, for the latter represents a special case of the former. Drug addiction involves three elements: overpowering compulsion to take a drug, development of a need for increased dosages of the drug over time, and psychic dependence on the drug.[53] Based on this definition, marijuana is not an addicting drug, whereas opiates are markedly addicting in character. Individuals can engage in sporadic smoking of marijuana without developing any pronounced craving for the drug or tolerance to it. Opiate users, on the other hand, exhibit compulsive use of the drug, tolerance, and also exhibit an *abstinence syndrome*. That is, persons who have become involved in continued use of opiates invariably experience a marked degree of physiological distress involving lacrimation, cramps, tenseness, sweating, and other physical responses when they withdraw from opiate use. The opiate addict furnishes the model on which public views of narcotic use are based; his "habit" becomes progressively more costly as he requires increased dosages of heroin or other opiates to feel "normal." The opiate addict is also the subject of books and movies such as *The Man With the Golden Arm*, which portrays the physical agony of an addict unable to acquire drugs to maintain his "habit." The opiate user rather than the "pot" smoker engages in petty theft, prostitution, and other forms of criminality to maintain a supply of narcotics. No wonder criminologists minimize the seriousness of marijuana and stress opiate addiction. In the following sections, we shall pay most attention to the opiate addict role career, with only passing concern for marijuana use.

The opiate addict role career describes *criminal* addicts, that is, individuals normally from slum backgrounds who are the subject of law enforcement agency attention. But we should mention the narcotic addict who escapes the criminal label and correctional processing. A relatively large number of physicians and other medical personnel are narcotic addicts. Charles Winick claims that the addiction rate among doctors is one in 100 physicians, compared to a rate of one addict among 3000 citizens in the general population.

[52]*Ibid.,* p. 113.
[53]Clausen, "Drug Use," pp. 190–91.

He studied nearly 100 doctors who had been drug addicts and attributed their addiction to a number of factors, one of which is relatively easy access to narcotics. These addict physicians also exhibited role strain, in that many were relatively unenthusiastic about medical careers. They were also frequently passive individuals with self-images centering about omnipotent views of themselves. According to Winick, such doctors are most likely to find medical practice particularly stressful and seek some relief from occupational pressures in drug use.[54]

THE OPIATE ADDICT ROLE CAREER

Definitional Dimensions

Offense Behavior. Most criminal opiate addicts are young men who specialize in the use of narcotics as deviant behavior. Many begin by experimenting with marijuana as juveniles, progressing in turn to occasional use of heroin or other opium derivatives, and ending by becoming heavily involved in addiction. Many of them engage in other criminal acts, particularly forms of petty property crime or "hustling" (pimping, and so on), but only to obtain funds to purchase drugs.

Interactional Setting. Juvenile and young adult drug users are not normally members of large delinquent gangs. Although drug users are sometimes recruited from delinquent gangs, involvement in patterns of "heavy" drug use normally results in expulsion of the user from more conventional delinquent peer groups or voluntary withdrawal of the addict from such groups. Other delinquents often view narcotic users as undependable and bizarre personalities. Drug users are often members of an addict subculture, which sometimes takes the form of a "cat" culture. Differential association with other drug users occurs for several reasons. Association with narcotic addicts involves a system of mutual aid in which users inform one another about drug sources, illicit means to obtain narcotics, and so on.

Self-concept. The narcotic user usually exhibits a self-image as a drug addict rather than as a "delinquent" or "criminal." He maintains that drug use is no more deviant than the various other "kicks," such as drinking or smoking, noncriminals resort to. The narcotic addict views himself as a person who has plenty of justification in his life circumstances for drug use. He argues that he should be allowed to use narcotics and that, if he were, few problems would exist for him and society. Some narcotic addicts view themselves as

[54]Charles Winick, "Physician Narcotic Addicts," *Social Problems*, 9 (Fall 1961), 174–86.

"cats," individuals who are "cool" and able to make a living through various forms of "hustle." In turn, "cats" evidence considerable disdain for "squares" or noncriminal persons.

Attitudes. The heroin user alleges that he is being harassed by a society that provides few satisfying experiences for persons of his kind. The narcotic user reacts negatively toward work, but his principal antagonism is directed toward the police. This reaction is understandable, of course, considering the addict frequently comes in contact with the police and is continually under surveillance by narcotic agents.

Role Career. Narcotic addicts are sometimes juveniles who began their delinquent careers as members of conventional gangs but ultimately branch off from such groups as they become caught up in narcotic use. On other occasions, the drug user drifted into narcotic use outside the framework of conventional gangs. The juvenile drug user often continues in drug use into adulthood and becomes an adult, criminal drug user.

Background Dimensions

Social Class. Drug users are usually from urban, slum area, lower-class backgrounds. They appear to have pronounced feelings of low status, lack of opportunity, and inability to extricate themselves from situations of extreme stress and unpleasantness.

Family Background. Drug users tend to be from lower-class families in which close parent–child ties are absent. Family life tends to be relatively meaningless and unimportant for the drug user.

Peer Group Associations. Narcotic addicts normally associate differentially with other addicts. They usually learn the use of drugs and norms defining narcotics as pleasant from interaction with other addicts. When the "budding addict" becomes seriously involved in drug use, he usually withdraws into almost exclusive isolation from nonaddicts and into interaction with other users. This interaction has important consequences for his continuation in drug use, for these persons share a set of norms that define narcotic use as acceptable and suggest that cures for addiction are nonexistent.

Contact with Defining Agencies. Drug users experience numerous contacts with defining agencies during the course of their deviant careers. On the one hand, involvement in programs of conventional treatment in which the user is incarcerated, withdrawn from dependence on narcotics, and given psychiatric treatment does not appear to have any pronounced rehabilitative effect. Instead, drug users tend to resume drug habits soon after release from treatment. But, on the other hand, contact with defining agencies does not appear to play any direct role in drug relapse. Such contacts have only a neutral impact on drug users.

Discussion

This role-career description stands as a set of propositions about opiate users. But what of the supporting evidence for this characterization? Let us examine some of the data at hand regarding opiate addicts.

In the years since passage of the Harrison Act, certain major trends have occurred regarding the social characteristics of addicts. In earlier decades, only about 10 percent of the addicts received at the U.S. Public Health Service Hospital, Lexington, Kentucky, which treats drug users, were blacks, whereas in recent years about two-fifths of the addict patients have been blacks. Although two decades ago only about 10 percent of the addicts were under twenty-five years of age, in recent years over one-third of them were under twenty-five years of age.[55]

Present-day criminal drug addicts tend to come from certain urban social areas in largest numbers. These neighborhoods show a concentration of indices of social breakdown—high crime and delinquency rates, high rates of prostitution and illegitimacy, high infant mortality, and large numbers of broken homes. They are also areas of marked population density, with a great deal of population turnover among the heterogeneous groups who live there.

One major study that documents the wretched character of the neighborhoods from which addicts come was carried out by Isidor Chein and others in New York City.[56] Their evidence shows that, in addition to the social and physical deterioration characteristic of these areas, two cultural themes pervade the social life of high delinquency–high addiction neighborhoods. The residents commonly exhibit negative perspectives on life along with a deepseated sense of futility.[57]

Although delinquency and drug addiction are commonplace in such communities, they are not causally related. Juvenile street gangs are not active in the spread of drugs through a process of differential association. Some drug users may have been in gangs at an earlier point in their lives but dropped out of gang life when they became involved in drug use. Addicts are poorly regarded by delinquent gang members, for they are viewed as unreliable and are thus shunned. Contrary to current stereotypes of the addiction process, most juvenile drug users are *not* initiated into drug use by adult "pushers." Instead, they usually began using drugs at the urging of a peer.[58]

Recent studies have shown that young opiate addicts have frequently begun the use of drugs by experimenting with marijuana. Chein and his associates

---

[55]Clinard, *Sociology of Deviant Behavior,* pp. 312–16.

[56]Isidor Chein, Donald L. Gerard, Robert S. Lee, and Eva Rosenfeld, *The Road to H* (New York: Basic Books, 1964), pp. 47–77.

[57]*Ibid.,* pp. 78–108.

[58]*Ibid.,* pp. 3–16.

assert that 86 percent of the young adults they studied had begun by smoking marijuana, most frequently around the age of fifteen.[59] At first glance, this finding seems to indicate that marijuana use is a prelude to opiate addiction. In a sense, this notion is true, but these observations do not reveal that a great many individuals in slum areas and elsewhere who smoke marijuana never progress to opiate addiction. Thus, marijuana smokers who become opiate addicts represent a small subclass of all marijuana users.

Opiate addiction cannot be explained solely in terms of the socioeconomic and physical deficiences of slum areas and the ideological themes of futility and negativism found there. Residents of such areas demonstrate a variety of life patterns; some are criminals, many are noncriminals, and fewer are drug addicts. There must be something additional to the factors identified so far, which diverts some youths into drug addiction. That factor is widely held to be a pattern of disordered and inadequate home life which produces persons with pronounced personality pathology. These individuals are in the market for the special solution to life's problems that heroin promises.

This psychogenic contention about addicts is found in the theoretical work of Cloward and Ohlin, who contend that drug users make up a special subculture of "retreatists," or "double failures." These youths have not managed to find a niche for themselves in either the world of nondelinquent conformists or the delinquent street gang. Presumably, such boys are "double failures" because they are crippled by personality deficiencies that alienate them from more normal youngsters.[60] Support for this view of the addict is found in the Chein study, for these investigators report that users are youths with a variety of personality problems. These pathologies fall into four major groupings: ego pathology, narcissism, superego pathology, and problems of sexual identity.[61] These personality attributes are not the by-product of involvement in deviant behavior. The personality disturbances preceded drug use and were the outgrowth of situations of family pathology. In comparison with nonusers from the same neighborhoods, the drug users much more commonly come from homes marked by absence of a father figure, conflict between marital partners, and inadequate parental standards.[62]

Julian Roebuck conducted another study which turned up similar findings. He compared fifty Negro addicts in the District of Columbia Reformatory with a large group of nonaddict inmates. According to Roebuck, the users were predominantly "passive-dependent–dependent" personalities who had grown up in home situations of maternal dominance. However, the addicts in this

[59]Chein et al., The Road to H, p. 149.
[60]Richard A. Cloward and Lloyd E. Ohlin, Delinquency and Opportunity (New York: The Free Press, 1960), pp. 178-86.
[61]Chein et al., The Road to H, pp. 193-226.
[62]Ibid., pp. 251-75.

study were from social and economic backgrounds more favorable in some ways than those from which the nonaddicts came.[63]

Further confirmation of many of the claims in the role-career description of addicts can be found in a Chicago study by Harold Finestone. The drug users in his research were young black males who had become enmeshed in a "cat" culture, centered about pursuit of hedonistic pleasures and supported by a variety of illicit, nonviolent "hustles," such as pimping.[64]

Nearly all the commentary to this point has dealt with *male* opiate addicts, and for good reason. Although female addicts were estimated to outnumber males before passage of the Harrison Act, in recent decades women users have comprised less than 20 percent of all addicts. Chein and his associates have indicated that female drug users show much the same pattern of disordered home life, low socioeconomic status, and so on, as male opiate users.[65]

Drug addiction is perhaps the most pronounced case of criminality in which recidivism is extremely common. This high rate of relapse into drug use is noted in the addict's assertion: "Once an addict, always an addict." Estimates of the relapse rate for addicts treated in the major specialized treatment facilities, such as the hospital at Lexington, Kentucky, noted that at least 75 percent and perhaps 95 percent or more of the treated addicts relapse into drug use.[66] Miserable social circumstances, intensified personality problems, and stigmatization come together to make it extremely difficult for the treated addict to maintain his commitment to the role of nondeviant.[67]

One claim in the role-career description had to do with the association of drug use and other forms of criminality. John O'Donnell carried out an investigation in which he examined the criminal activities after release from treatment of nearly 300 addicts who had been patients at the U.S. Public Health Service Hospital at Lexington.[68] The follow-up data on these users were compared with results from other studies of the criminality of addicts. O'Donnell's major conclusions were that addicts have increasingly been recruited from the ranks of persons with prior criminal records in recent decades. These persons commit more crimes after becoming addicted than they would have otherwise. But, in fact, many addicts do not have criminal records, either before or after becoming addicted.[69]

[63]Julian B. Roebuck, "The Negro Drug Addict as an Offender Type," *Journal of Criminal Law, Criminology and Police Science*, 53, (March 1962), 36–43.

[64]Harold Finestone, "Cats, Kicks, and Color," *Social Problems*, 5 (July 1957), 3–13; see also the narrative on New York juvenile addicts by Robert Rice, "Junk," *New Yorker*, 41 (March 27, 1965), 50–142.

[65]Chein et al., *The Road to H*, pp. 299–319.

[66]Schur, *Crimes Without Victims*, p. 146.

[67]For a study of the relapse process in drug addiction, see Marsh B. Ray, "The Cycle of Abstinence and Relapse Among Heroin Addicts," in *The Other Side*, ed. Howard S. Becker (New York: The Free Press, 1964), pp. 163–77.

[68]John A. O'Donnell, "Narcotic Addiction and Crime," *Social Problems*, 13 (Spring 1966), 374–85.

[69]*Ibid.*, p. 385.

O'Donnell reached the same conclusion of other investigators: drug addiction per se does not produce criminality. Rather, petty thievery and other forms of instrumental criminality represent secondary consequences of addiction to which the addict is driven because of the illegality of drug use. Presumably, if the user were not a target of law enforcement agents but free to ingest drugs if he so chose, he would not be involved in criminality to support his addiction.

ALCOHOLISM AND AMERICAN SOCIETY

No statistics are required to demonstrate that drinking of alcoholic beverages is extremely widespread in the United States. That fact is obvious to any adult American, although the precise extent of drinking may not be so clear. One detailed indication of the ubiquity of alcohol comes from Harold Mulford's study involving a nationwide sample of persons over twenty-one years of age.[70] Nearly three-fouths of these persons reported themselves as drinkers; hence, more than 80,000,000 adult Americans appear to consume alcoholic beverages. Of these drinkers, 11 percent said they were "heavy drinkers," and 10 percent admitted that they had experienced difficulties in managing their drinking behavior.

These exceedingly commonplace drinkers, ranging over a spectrum from moderate drinkers to chronic alcoholics, are the subject of massive literature dealing with the chemical, biological, psychological, legal, and sociological facets of drinking. For example, the *Quarterly Journal of Studies on Alcohol* is devoted entirely to reports and discussions on aspects of alcohol behavior. An abundance of books also deals with various features of drinking.[71] In this text, we shall peruse only a small sampling of this storehouse of material.

Drinking behavior is of interest to criminologists for several reasons, but the most important is that arrests for drunkenness are extremely common in the United States. Police arrest figures for 1969 indicate that of 5,773,988 arrests reported to the Federal Bureau of Investigation, 1,982,149 were for drunkenness.[72] "Skid Road" alcoholics, who contribute most of these arrests, represent "garden variety" offenders constituting a major class of lawbreakers. We should probably add to this figure for drunk arrests some sizable part of the arrests for vagrancy and disorderly conduct, offenses that frequently involve

---

[70]Harold A. Mulford, "Drinking and Deviant Drinking, U.S.A., 1963," *Quarterly Journal of Studies on Alcohol,* 25 (December 1964), 634–50.

[71]For a summary of much of this material, see Clinard, *Sociology of Deviant Behavior,* pp. 388–455. For a representative sample of essays that touch on a number of dimensions of alcohol behavior, see David J. Pittman and Charles R. Snyder, eds., *Society, Culture, and Drinking Patterns* (New York: John Wiley & Sons, 1962).

[72]Federal Bureau of Investigation, *Uniform Crime Reports for the United States, 1965,* p. 112.

excessive drinkers. In addition, drunkenness is associated with other forms of criminality such as petty thievery and, less frequently, homicidal actions.[73]

The report of The President's Commission on Law Enforcement and Administration of Justice contains some information about drunkenness arrests in the United States. The commission indicates that not only are arrests for drunkenness and allied offenses exceedingly common, many offenders are chronic repeaters, turning up repeatedly in arrest statistics over an extended period of time. The commission also notes that communities vary markedly in their arrest policies for drunkenness. In a comparison of Washington, D.C., St. Louis, and Atlanta, widely discrepant figures emerge regarding the percentage drunk arrests comprise of all arrests. In Washington, 76.5 percent of all arrests in 1965 were for drunkenness, disorderly conduct, and vagrancy, whereas 76.7 percent of the total arrests in Atlanta were for these reasons. In St. Louis, on the other hand, which had a tolerant policy toward drunks, only 18.9 percent of all arrests were for these offenses.[74]

We can discern two basic types of alcoholics, one of which is a "criminal" drinker and the other is usually a nonoffender. The latter is represented by the chronic drinker, usually a middle-class individual found in such private alcoholism treatment settings as "Alcoholics Anonymous" or psychiatric counseling, or processed through civil court commitment into a public treatment organization. These individuals are often labeled "inebriate" or "alcoholic," so they are not stigmatized as "criminals."

The evidence regarding middle-class alcoholics indicates that their drinking has been solitary activity, often conducted surreptitiously so as to avoid detection by associates. E. M. Jellinek and other investigators have identified a process of involvement in alcoholism through which these persons go, starting with social drinking that leads progressively to more pathological forms of drinking. These phases in the drinking career usually extend over a fifteen or twenty year period. This alcoholic career is one of gradual change from *primary* to *secondary* deviation; the middle-class alcoholic does not adopt a self-orientation as a "lush" or "alcoholic" until he reaches an advanced stage of this pattern.[75] The noncriminal alcoholic also endeavors to drink at the same time that he discharges the role obligations of his conventional roles as a parent, employee, and so on, although at some point his drinking begins to have serious ramifications for successful performance of these roles. Along a related line, several researchers have turned up evidence showing that families in which this kind of alcoholism develops go through several stages of

---

[73]Marvin E. Wolfgang and Rolf B. Strohm, "The Relationship between Alcohol and Criminal Homicide," *Quarterly Journal of Studies on Alcohol*, 17 (September 1956), 411–25.

[74]The President's Commission on Law Enforcement and Administration of Justice, *The Challenge of Crime in a Free Society*, 233–37.

[75]E. M. Jellinek, "Phases of Alcohol Addiction," in Pittman and Snyder, *Society, Culture, and Drinking Patterns*, pp. 356–68.

adjustment. The role structure of the family unit undergoes changes as the members adapt to the presence of an alcoholic in their midst.[76] The personality characteristics of middle-class alcoholics have been studied, as illustrated in Lemert's investigation of "dependency" on the part of married alcoholics. In that analysis, Lemert obtained measures of dependency among alcoholics from observations on domination of the person by his spouse, economic dependence of the alcoholic on others, and dependence imputed to the person by his wife. He uncovered indications of dependency existing prior to the onset of drinking problems in about two-fifths of the cases.[77]

The middle-class alcoholic does sometimes become involved with law enforcement agencies and the courts on charges of "public intoxication." But the second type of alcoholic, the denizen of "Skid Road," is of most concern to criminologists.[78] In the folklore of American society, these individuals are sometimes thought to be similar to middle-class alcoholics. They are seen as persons who have experienced a "fall from grace" in which they eventually drifted to the "Skid Road" area of homeless men and drinking as a life career. According to this romanticized version of "Skid Road" alcoholism, we should expect to find numerous ex-professors, lawyers, and other persons of that sort whose drinking resulted in their social degradation. But most "Skid Roaders" originated out of humble backgrounds and have been isolated from conventional patterns of social life for most of their adult lives. They show a career in alcoholism that differs in important ways from the pattern of middle-class problem drinkers.

THE "SKID ROAD" ALCOHOLIC ROLE CAREER

Definitional Dimensions

Offense Behavior. The lives of "Skid Road" alcoholics center about drinking. They show patterns of multiple arrests for "public intoxication," "vagrancy," "disorderly conduct," and other related offenses.

Interactional Setting. "Skid Roaders" are frequently involved in drinking

---

[76]Joan K. Jackson, "The Adjustment of the Family to the Crisis of Alcoholism," *Quarterly Journal of Studies on Alcohol,* 15 (December 1954), 562–86; Edwin M. Lemert, "The Occurrence and Sequence of Events in the Adjustment of Families to Alcoholism," *Quarterly Journal of Studies on Alcohol,* 21 (December 1960), 679–97.

[77]Edwin M. Lemert, "Dependency in Married Alcoholics," *Quarterly Journal of Studies on Alcohol,* 23 (December 1962), 590–609.

[78]In the literature on alcoholism, the homeless men area of the city is referred to as both "Skid Road" and "Skid Row." The label "Skid Road" originated in Seattle and preceded the term "Skid Row." As used initially, "Skid Road" had reference to logging roads constructed of small logs laid side by side, over which larger logs were "skidded" to a loading area. The term was applied to the area of homeless men and transients because a good many of the residents of that area were heavy drinking loggers.

activities and other social endeavors in "bottle clubs" made up of fellow drinkers. Many of them engage in forms of socialization and mutual aid with other alcoholics, although "Skid Road" also contains drinkers who are isolates and social rejects.

Self-concept. These individuals view themselves not as "criminals" but as persons who drink as their major life activity.

Attitudes. "Skid Roaders" are characterized by generally prosocial attitudes. However, they exhibit disinterest in stable occupational or marital ties or other conventional social activities. These individuals view the police as persons to avoid but do not see the police in markedly hostile terms. In general, "Skid Roaders" are reconciled to recurrent contacts with law enforcement persons, jail personnel, or public alcoholic treatment agency workers.

Role Career. The "Skid Road" alcoholic usually becomes involved in this kind of alcoholism relatively early in life, as he severs his connections with his family and other conventional social ties. "Skid Road" life becomes a pattern of day-to-day drinking, interrupted from time to time as the alcoholic is sentenced to a short jail term. The "Skid Roader" repeatedly passes through a correctional "revolving door." This role career is eventually terminated when the drinker dies from tuberculosis, cirrhosis of the liver, or other hazards related to a life of alcoholism.

Background Dimensions

Social Class. These individuals are usually from relatively lower-class origins.

Family Background. These offenders are often from relatively conventional family backgrounds, although they commonly become estranged from their parental family as young men. Many "Skid Roaders" have never been married, whereas others were at one time married. The latter have customarily been isolated from their spouses for a long time through divorce or desertion.

Peer Group Associations. The early life peer group ties of these drinkers are apparently not of major importance in the genesis of their deviant behavior. However, the peer ties many of these drinkers establish with other "Skid Roaders" have considerable influence on them. These social ties provide reinforcement for many of the offender's attitudes about drinking, treatment agencies, and other matters.

Contact with Defining Agencies. These alcoholics have numerous contacts with the police and other defining agents. Their interactions with policemen tend not to be laden with hostility, either on the part of the officers or the drinkers. Policemen normally regard "Skid Roaders" more as nuisances than as "bad guys." The drinker often views the policeman who patrols a "Skid Road" beat as something of a friend, even though the policeman does occasionally arrest the alcoholic. Not uncommonly, the beat patrolman acts to promote the welfare of the drinker, as when he removes him from an alley during a cold night, thus preventing the alcoholic from freezing to death. In a similar way, the alcoholic takes a relatively bland view of judges and other correctional agents, for he sees them as duty bound to interfere with his drinking. The pronounced recidivism of these offenders is due to factors other than harmful effects of correctional processes.

Discussion

Supporting evidence for the foregoing characterization of the "Skid Roader" can be found in a number of studies, one of which is by David Pittman and C. Wayne Gordon, who gathered detailed data on 187 chronic police case inebriates in the Monroe County Penitentiary in Rochester, New York.[79] The sociocultural profile of these persons indicated that they were older than males in the general population, with a mean of 47.7 years of age. A high percentage of the inebriates were blacks, whereas Irish and English comprised the largest nationality groups. Nearly 60 percent of the alcoholics had been married at some time, but almost none was living with spouses at the time of the study. These offenders were from disadvantaged social backgrounds, for 70 percent had not gone beyond grammar school, whereas 68 percent were unskilled workers. The majority of these individuals showed backgrounds of great residential instability. Most of them had been arrested many times, so they had a mean number of 16.5 arrests.[80]

Pittman and Gordon reported that the alcoholics they studied were products of early family life situations marked by inadequate socialization. According to these investigators, "Skid Roaders" were ill-equipped by virtue of their backgrounds to embark on stable adult lives.[81] As a result, most of them had experienced unsatisfactory marriages and had failed in their occupational endeavors.[82] Many of them then became caught up in "Skid Road" life, and a number of them had been institutionalized for lengthy periods of their lives. On "Skid Road" they turned to daily wine drinking, often with small groups of other alcoholics.[83]

Another study that produced results similar to those of Pittman and Gordon is by Lois Grote, concerning "inebriates" who were alcoholics handled in civil court proceedings and "arrested drinkers" who had been criminally processed.[84] Grote found that these two groups of individuals in Oakland, Califor-

---

[79]David J. Pittman and C. Wayne Gordon, *Revolving Door* (New York: The Free Press, 1958).
[80]*Ibid.*, pp. 16–58.
[81]*Ibid.*, pp. 78–93.
[82]*Ibid.*, pp. 109–24.
[83]*Ibid.*, pp. 59–77.
[84]Lois P. Grote, "Inebriates, Arrested Drinkers and Other Offenders: An Exploratory Study" (Master's thesis, San Francisco State College, 1962).

nia, were dissimilar types of alcoholics. The "inebriates" were from relatively stable, middle-class origins, whereas the arrested drinkers were "Skid Roaders" from lower-class backgrounds. These arrested drinkers were concentrated in three tracts that make up the homeless man area.[85]

A third report of this sort compared workhouse inmates incarcerated for drunkenness with a group of alcoholic patients in a volunteer clinic. The workhouse inmates were "Skid Roaders" who differed markedly from the volunteer patients, for the former were either unmarried or divorced, had begun drinking early in their lives, and had been isolated from conventional social ties for a long time.[86]

Additional studies of "Skid Road" alcoholics and other "Skid Road" residents have been conducted in Minneapolis,[87] Philadelphia,[88] Chicago,[89] New York,[90] and most recently, in San Francisco[91] and Seattle.[92] On the whole, these reports include findings that support the sketch of "Skid Roaders" in this book.

The social life of "Skid Road" has also been the subject of sociological attention. Joan Jackson and Ralph Connor have investigated this matter in Seattle, where they report that two groups of residents populate "Skid Road": nonalcoholics and alcoholics. The alcoholic group is further divided into types recognized in the argot of the drinkers, for they speak of such persons as "bums," "characters," "winos," "rubby-dubs," and "lushes." "Bums" and "characters" violate group norms about drinking or exhibit bizarre forms of behavior. "Winos" and "lushes," on the other hand, band together in social groups devoted to drinking and forms of mutual aid.[93] W. Jack Peterson and Milton Maxwell have also analyzed the social life of "Skid Road" and have shown that many alcoholic residents are involved in a rich, although deviant, interactional network of social ties.[94] Jacqueline Wiseman's study reveals many details of life on "Skid Road"; many of the alcoholics she studied were involved in

---

[85]*Ibid.*, p. 65.

[86]Francis E. Feeney, Dorothee F. Mindlin, Verna H. Minear, and Eleanor E. Short, "The Challenge of the Skid Row Alcoholic," *Quarterly Journal of Studies on Alcohol*, 16 (December 1955), 645–67.

[87]Theodore Caplow, Keith Lovald, and Samuel Wallace, *A General Report on the Problem of Relocating the Population of the Lower Loop Redevelopment Area* (Minneapolis: Minneapolis Housing and Redevelopment Authority, 1958); Lovald, "From Hobohemia to Skid Row" (Ph.D. thesis: University of Minnesota, 1960); Wallace, *Skid Row as a Way of Life* (Totowa, N.J.: Bedminster Press, 1965).

[88]Leonard Blumberg, Irving Shandler, and Thomas E. Shipley, Jr., *Relocation Services to Skid Row Men* (Philadelphia: Greater Philadelphia Movement and Redevelopment Authority of the City of Philadelphia, 1966).

[89]Donald Bogue, *Skid Row in American Cities* (Chicago: University of Chicago Press, 1963).

[90]Howard M. Bahr, *Homelessness and Disaffiliation* (New York: Bureau of Applied Social Research, Columbia University, 1968).

[91]Jacqueline P. Wiseman, *Stations of the Lost* (Englewood Cliffs, N.J.: Prentice-Hall, 1970).

[92]James P. Spradley, *You Owe Yourself a Drink* (Boston: Little, Brown and Co., 1970).

[93]Joan K. Jackson and Ralph Connor, "The Skid Road Alcoholic," *Quarterly Journal of Studies on Alcohol*, 14 (September 1953), 468–86.

[94]W. Jack Peterson and Milton A. Maxwell, "The Skid Road 'Wino,'" *Social Problems*, 5 (Spring 1958), 308–16.

a recurrent pattern of incarceration in county jail, commitment to a state mental hospital, and residency in a Salvation Army facility.[95] James Spradley's study also provides a number of insights into the relationships between "Skid Roaders" and the police, courts, and jails.[96]

SUMMARY

This chapter has brought a variety of materials together concerning organized crime, drug addiction, and alcoholism. At this point, we have completed our analysis of offender types, and we now turn to the correctional processing of lawbreakers.

One point should be made before we begin consideration of correctional reponses. The experiences of criminals within correctional organizations are normally considered different from causation, that is, from the factors that get these persons into the correctional machinery. In this view, causal processes are restricted to matters we have already reviewed. But as we will see in the following pages, correctional reactions directed toward lawbreakers may often operate as influences that impel some of these persons toward further involvement in criminality. Quite probably, the study of etiological influences cannot be neatly restricted just to experiences that occurred to offenders before they became the subjects of penological handling.

The mass of material we have studied to this point makes abundantly clear that criminality comes in many forms. We should not be surprised to find that the correctional and punitive reactions toward it have been of many varieties as well. Chapter Eighteen surveys some of the dispositions that have been made of offenders in past eras as well as actions taken against them in contemporary society. Chapters Nineteen through Twenty-two also look at features of correctional experiences offenders encounter in prisons, probation, and other settings.

[95]Wiseman, *Stations of the Lost, passim.*
[96]Spradley, *You Owe Yourself a Drink, passim.*

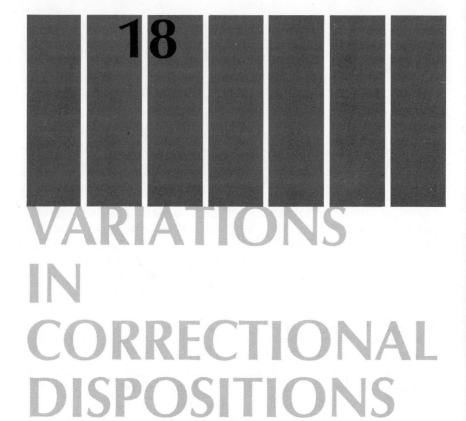

18

VARIATIONS
IN
CORRECTIONAL
DISPOSITIONS

This chapter takes up some matters originally introduced in Chapters Three and Four dealing with the processing of offenders by the police, courts, and related agencies. Chapter Eighteen is concerned with an overview of the various dispositions that can be made of lawbreakers who have been convicted in a criminal court. The chapter is divided into two parts, the first dealing with the ways criminals have been disposed of in earlier historical periods, the second having to do with contemporary correctional proceedings. The remaining chapters of the book take up various facets of current correctional procedures in greater detail.

A BRIEF HISTORY OF CORRECTIONAL PRACTICES

During the long, complex history of correctional actions against criminals, all manner of reactions have been employed at one time or another. Offenders have been subjected to death or torture, social humiliation such as the pillories and stocks, banishment and transportation, imprisonment, and financial penalties. In general, responses toward lawbreakers were originally retributive, compelling the criminal to make amends in some way. Later, restraint and punishment became the principal form of reaction to deviants, and this approach is still dominant in Western societies and elsewhere in the world. Most recently, a rehabilitative philosophy has begun to emerge, maintaining that some form of corrective action should be taken against criminals to deflect them from deviant pathways.

Large-scale societal devices and procedures for dealing with criminals are of recent origin. For example, the United States prison system, in which over 200,000 adults are incarcerated at any one time, developed within the past 100 years. The entire world population numbered only about 450,000,000 in 1650, although it exceeds three billion at present. Thus, until the last several centuries, individual societies were generally small and characterized by un-codified and informal techniques of social control. In this sense, the history of corrections extends only over the past several centuries.[1]

Some formalized legal codes and state-administered procedures of justice can be uncovered in ancient times. The earliest known system of laws was the Code of Hammurabi, developed by King Hammurabi of Babylon in the eighteenth century B.C. This code was exceedingly complicated, designed to regulate a wide variety of human affairs. Concerning crime, the ruling principle of the code was the retributive *lex talionis,* or "an eye for an eye, a tooth for a tooth." Death was a frequently employed means of dealing with law-breakers, as was mutilation and monetary compensation. Mosaic law and the legal codes of the Roman Empire are other cases of formalized legal codes and criminal proceedings in antiquity.

In small, preliterate societies, both past and present, secular offenses not thought to offend the spirits were handled as private wrongs. These acts were usually left to family or clan groups to settle as they saw fit, commonly by means of retaliatory blood feuds.[2] For example, the Germanic conquerors of Rome were organized into tribal groups in which retaliation by victims was seen as a hereditary right that the offended family could exercise if it so chose. In this system of private vengeance, society played a secondary role. Eventual-ly, pecuniary compensation replaced blood feuds. At the beginning of the Christian era, the Teutonic tribes of Northwest Europe took vengeful retaliation on offenders by extracting monetary compensation. Still, the injuries for which persons were forced to make compensation were regarded as private matters. The Germanic groups recognized only a limited number of tribal crimes, as contrasted to private wrongs.[3] In the same way, until about the twelfth century, England was divided into shires presided over by sheriffs who assisted in ob-taining compensation from violators to be paid to injured parties.

During the twelfth century in England, the crown gradually assumed control over administration of justice, so compensation began to be paid to the king rather than to the wronged party. As the crown intruded into the regulation of these matters, a system of punishment slowly began to emerge. Briefly

[1]The history of correctional practices is reviewed in Edwin H. Sutherland and Donald R. Cressey, *Principles of Criminology,* 8th ed. (Philadelphia: J. B. Lippincott Co., 1970), pp. 303–19; Richard R. Korn and Lloyd W. McCorkle, *Criminology and Penology* (New York: Holt, Rinehart and Winston, 1959), pp. 358–414; Harry Elmer Barnes and Negley K. Teeters, *New Horizons in Criminology,* 3rd ed. (Englewood Cliffs, N.J.: Prentice-Hall, 1959), pp. 285–347; U.S. Bureau of Prisons, *Handbook of Correctional Institution Design and Construction* (Washington, D.C.: U.S. Bureau of Prisons, 1949), pp. 16–25; Elmer H. Johnson, *Crime, Correction, and Society,* rev. ed. (Homewood, Ill.: The Dorsey Press, 1969), pp. 296–310.

[2]For a discussion of regulation of private feuding by the larger society, see E. Adamson Hoebel, *The Law of Primitive Man* (Cambridge, Mass.: Harvard University Press, 1954).

[3]For an account of changes in Germanic legal systems, see Korn and McCorkle, *Criminology and Penology,* pp. 384–88.

defined, punishment involves pain or suffering produced by design and inflicted on a member of a group by that group or society in its corporate capacity. Punishment is directed at persons viewed as having wronged the group as well as the victim. As we shall see, punitive policies developed and flourished well before the emergence of a clear-cut philosophy of punishment that rationalized this posture toward offenders.

The forms of punishment most common in Europe in the middle ages and in the period up to the nineteenth century involved various kinds of corporal punishment or banishment; imprisonment is a relatively recent invention. European jails in the middle ages were places for the confinement of prisoners awaiting trial or punishment rather than custodial institutions in which punishment was meted out. These jails were frequently maintained in castle towers and similar locations, managed by private citizens, and were usually wretched places in which persons of both sexes and all ages were indiscriminately thrown together. In the sixteenth and seventeenth centuries, offenders were often sentenced to labor in the galleys, but this form of punishment was more an expedient for providing laborers in the ships than a conscious effort to contrive a kind of imprisonment.

Houses of correction established in England in the 1500s constitute forerunners of imprisonment as a form of punishment. A house of correction known as "Bridewell," opened in London in 1557, was used for incarceration of vagrants and other idle persons. This was a congregate institution, as were other English houses of correction, so the inmates were not maintained in separate cells. Those vagrants, unemployed persons, orphans, and other individuals kept therein were put to work at various kinds of labor, and their services were frequently contracted out to private citizens. Such institutions were constructed in some number on the European continent in the 1600s and 1700s. The most famous of these was a workhouse at Ghent, Belgium, opened in 1773. This institution featured individual cells and certain other characteristics to become common in modern prisons. Some other prototypes of modern correctional institutions were found in Italy in the 1700s. However, prisons and penitentiaries in which offenders are incarcerated for extended periods of time and subjected to various punitive or corrective measures did not become widespread until the nineteenth century.

At various points in human history, banishment was a technique for dealing with malefactors. Between 1597 and 1776, England transported as many as 100,000 criminals to America. After England was compelled to discontinue transporting offenders to America, criminals were banished to Australia; from 1787 to 1875, over 135,000 lawbreakers were disposed of in that manner.[4] Many

[4]Barnes and Teeters, New Horizons in Criminology, pp. 294–305.

of these criminals eventually became influential citizens in Australia and, along with other Australians, were ultimately successful in forcing England to discontinue the policy of transportation. France and other nations have also banished offenders to other lands and penal colonies at various times in the past.

Capital punishment was another procedure for handling offenders and was widely used in Europe in past centuries. For example, England had only about seventeen capital crimes in the early 1400s; but by 1688 the number of capital offenses had increased to fifty, and by 1780, 350 separate crimes carried the death penalty. Between 1327 and 1509, six statutes were enacted which carried the death penalty; between 1509 and 1660, thirty more capital crimes were defined; and from 1660 to 1819, 187 additional capital offenses were created. Moreover, creation of new capital offenses at an accelerated pace during the eighteenth century was not an empty ritual, for large numbers of executions were carried out in accordance with this legislation. Many of these executions were of persons convicted of property crimes, so these penalties were grossly severe by contemporary standards. Life was cheap, and society had little hesitation in spending that of criminals. The excesses of this period eventually ran their course, for by 1830 the number of capital offenses had been reduced back to only seventeen.

As noted earlier, punitive responses to offenders grew in advance of tightly reasoned philosophies of punishment. The first full-blown argument in defense of punishment is found in the classical school of thought that developed out of the writings of Locke, Hume, Voltaire, Montesquieu, Rousseau, and others.[5] The most prominent classical theorist was the Italian nobleman Cesare Bonesana, Marchese de Beccaria (1738–1794), while others involved in this school of thought were Blackstone, Eden, and Romilly in England. Beccaria's book, *An Essay on Crimes and Punishment*, written in 1764, grew out of his agitation regarding widespread abuses and inequities in prevailing legal practices. He was disturbed by the secret accusations, inadequate defense of accused persons, arbitrary and capricious exercise of powers by judges, and barbarous penalties commonplace in the Europe of his time.

The classical position on punishment revolved around a conception of men as rational animals who deliberately and willfully chose the courses of action they pursued. According to this view, the ruling principle by which men orient their behavior was *hedonism*, or pursuit of pleasure and avoidance of pain. Criminals were seen as individuals who made a conscious choice to behave in a lawbreaking manner but could be coerced into conformity. Nondeviant

---

[5]For a summary of classical, neoclassical, and positivist views on punishment, see George B. Vold, *Theoretical Criminology* (New York: Oxford University Press, 1958), pp. 14–40. The rise of classical views is discussed briefly in Barnes and Teeters, *New Horizons in Criminology*, pp. 322–27, and in detail in Leon Radzinowicz, *A History of English Criminal Law and its Administration from 1750*, 3 vols. (New York: The Macmillan Co., 1948–1957).

behavior was to be obtained through application of a finely calculated measure of suffering; the offender would make a hedonistic decision to refrain from crime in the future. Beccaria endeavored to introduce order into the punitive system and to modify the situation in which offenders were frequently punished in a harsh and violent fashion well beyond the quantity of suffering required to tip the hedonistic balance toward law-abiding conduct. He was also concerned about ending the practices through which some more fortunate law violators escaped punishment altogether. Many of Beccaria's suggestions for reform of punishment were embodied in the French Penal Code of 1791 as well as in the revisions of correctional practice in nineteenth century England.[6]

According to the classical position on punishment and criminality discussed in Chapter Six, the initial reforms in criminal law that grew out of classical arguments made little provision for discretionary handling of lawbreakers. The French Penal Code of 1791 ignored individual differences among kinds of criminals and treated adults and minors, intelligent persons and mentally defectives, sane persons and psychotics, as all equally competent to stand trial. All were held equally responsible for their criminality. Subsequent revisions in punitive theory, usually identified as neoclassical reforms, granted judges some freeedom to modify sentences on the basis of extenuating circumstances. Neoclassical reforms also made exceptions in correctional practices for children and incompetents.[7] By and large, underlying behavioral presumptions of contemporary criminal laws and procedures are the same as those in neoclassical thought. Additionally, the penalty structure built into criminal codes in Western societies has remained relatively unmodified in the past century. Such developments as probation and parole have served to introduce a measure of variability into correctional practice without making any fundamental changes in neoclassical punitive philosophy.

Another distinct philosophy of punishment arose in the latter part of the nineteenth century in the positivist school of thought associated with Lombroso, Ferri, Garofalo, and others. Lombroso's views have already been noted in Chapter Six. He and his followers believed that a multiplicity of factors cause criminality. The positivist position denied that offenders were responsible for their deeds, thus claiming that a punitive posture toward them is unjustified. Instead, lawbreakers were to be treated if they were treatable; but those who could not be reclaimed from criminality were to be segregated from their fellowmen.

Vold has argued that modern criminology is positivist, in the sense that criminologists contend that criminality can and should be studied by the meth-

---

[6]Radzinowicz, A History of English Criminal Law.
[7]Vold, Theoretical Criminology, pp. 24-26.

ods of science. Contemporary criminology is also positivist in that some version of behavioral determinism is contained within the theoretical assumptions of most criminologists.[8] Positivism is involved in contemporary correctional methods as well but to a lesser extent; rehabilitative endeavors that have grown are allied with behaviorist conceptions of criminality. Most correctional workers involved in treatment activities are followers of a positivist perspective on criminality. However, it would be a mistake to suppose that the "new penology," which endeavors to rehabilitate offenders rather than punish them, is much in evidence in the United States and elsewhere.[9]

Returning to historical developments in correctional practice, we should note that penitentiaries are an American invention that arose in the early years of American history.[10] The first forerunner of the modern prison was the Walnut Street Prison opened in Philadelphia in 1776, under the urging of Pennsylvania Quakers. This institution was followed by the Pennsylvania Prison at Cherry Hill, opened in 1829. These penitentiaries operated on the *solitary system.* The Pennsylvania system prisons, as they are often called, were characterized by a distinct architecture intended to isolate prisoners from one another. Inmates were kept in single cells in which they took their meals, engaged in individual forms of labor, exercised, and contemplated the error of their ways. This prison program and architecture attracted a good deal of attention from European observers. Many were persuaded that this system would reform, and as a result a number of solitary institutions were created in Europe.

However, the Pennsylvania system had a major competitor in the United States. Auburn Prison in New York was opened in 1819, followed a few years later by Sing Sing Prison in the same state. These institutions provided the architectural model for nearly all penitentiaries and reformatories constructed in the United States until the last several decades. The Auburn—Sing Sing system was sometimes referred to as a *silent system.* These prisons were walled institutions in which inmates were incarcerated in cells in multitiered cell blocks. The prisoners worked together and took their meals in a common dining room. However, nearly total silence among convicts was maintained within a repressive regime featuring striped uniforms, lock-step marching, and severe punishment for violations of rules.

Advocates of the Auburn—Sing Sing prison model won out in the United States. Until a decade or so ago, nearly all prisons and reformatories constructed in this country were based on the same general physical plant design.

---

[8]*Ibid.,* pp. 39–40.

[9]The undeveloped state of a treatment-oriented correctional practice is discussed in Don C. Gibbons, *Changing the Lawbreaker* (Englewood Cliffs, N.J.: Prentice-Hall, 1965), pp. 190–96.

[10]Brief discussions of the historical origins of American prisons can be found in Barnes and Teeters, pp. 328–47; Johnson, *Crime, Correction, and Society,* pp. 477–94. A more detailed essay is David J. Rothman, *The Discovery of the Asylum* (Boston: Little, Brown and Co., 1971.).

These places are surrounded by high walls on which guard towers are placed at various points, they include a number of multitiered cell houses with inside cells housing one or more prisoners, and they have dining halls and work areas in which inmates are handled in congregate fashion. Most of these institutions had additions made in relatively haphazard fashion, with new cell houses or other buildings occasionally built within the original walled area to alleviate the pressures of a growing inmate population. As a consequence, these foreboding-looking penal institutions are actually difficult places in which to maintain close security over prisoners, and escapes from them are fairly common.

The rapid growth of prisons in this country is indicated in a publication of the American Correctional Association.[11] That report shows that, of the ninety state penal institutions for males in the United States in 1957, fifteen were constructed before 1850, and fifty-two were opened before 1900. Only sixteen new institutions were built between 1930 and 1957. Many of these facilities are large, for forty-eight of the ninety institutions had inmate populations exceeding 1,000. Eighteen of the penal facilities held over 2,000 inmates; of these, San Quentin Prison in California, Joliet–Statesville Prison in Illinois, and Southern Michigan Prison at Jackson each held over 4,000 prisoners.

Over the decades since the beginnings of imprisonment in the United States, institutions have gradually become less severe and more humane places. The lock-step, rules of silence, physical punishments for rule infractions, isolation of recalcitrant prisoners in "the hole," strict limits on visiting privileges of inmates, and so on have been abandoned or eased. These changes in prison life represent humanitarian reforms designed to lessen the pains of imprisonment.[12] Prisoners in contemporary prisons are allowed to listen to radios in their cells and see movies regularly; they are also permitted visitors each month, are fed well, and receive good medical and dental care. In these ways, doing time has been made less painful. However, some authorities maintain that little has been done to relieve the psychological pains of imprisonment, which inevitably accompany the experience of doing time.[13] We shall have more to say about this question in a later chapter.

In passing, we should note several other major developments in correctional practices. Probation has become a widely used technique for handling juvenile offenders and many relatively petty adult criminals. Probation in this country originated with the work of a Boston shoemaker, John Augustus, who interceded with the courts to take on the informal supervision of offenders in that city in the middle of the nineteenth century. Probation ultimately became

[11]American Correctional Association, *State and National Correctional Institutions of the United States of America, Canada, England and Scotland* (New York: American Correctional Association, 1957). Minimum security institutions and farms were not counted in these tabulations.

[12]On the rise of humanitarianism, see Gibbons, *Changing the Lawbreaker*, pp. 130–34.

[13]Gresham M. Sykes, *The Society of Captives* (Princeton, N.J.: Princeton University Press, 1958), pp. 63–83.

a state-sponsored program with passage of enabling legislation in Massachusetts in 1878. In the past century, probation services have become standard in all states and in the federal correctional system. Parole programs have also become commonplace in the United States within the last century; currently about 95 percent of all adult offenders sentenced to institutions are eventually released on parole, under supervision.

Innovations of various kinds continue to be attempted in correctional work. In recent years, halfway houses to which parolees are released from prisons have been suggested as a device for curbing parole failure. Along a somewhat related line are work-release programs developed in some county jails, in which prisoners work at conventional jobs during the day and return to the jail at night. Still other innovations can be found in private correctional endeavors such as Synanon, a residential treatment facility for drug addicts. These activities are the subject of extended discussion in later chapters where attention turns to contemporary correctional programs.

PUNISHMENT: SOME GENERAL CONSIDERATIONS

What does it mean to punish criminals? Sutherland and Cressey offer the following definition of the ingredients of punishment as a form of social control: "Two essential ideas are contained in the concept of punishment as an instrument of public justice. (a) It is inflicted by the group in its corporate capacity upon one who is regarded as a member of the same group. . . . (b) Punishment involves pain or suffering produced by design and justified by some value that the suffering is assumed to have."[14]

The Aims of Punishment

What purposes does the infliction of suffering on lawbreakers serve? Paul Tappan has offered an incisive summary of the purposes of punishment. He notes that punishment is designed to achieve the goal of *retribution* or *social retaliation* against the offender.[15] Punishment also involves *incapacitation,* which prevents the violator from misbehaving during the time he is being punished. Additionally, punishment is supposed to have a *deterrent* effect, both on the lawbreaker and on potential misbehavers. *Individual* or *specific* deterrence may be achieved by intimidation of the person, frightening him against further midsbehavior, or it may be effected through reformation, in

---

[14]Sutherland and Cressey, *Principles of Criminology,* p. 298.

[15]Paul W. Tappan, *Crime, Justice and Correction* (New York: McGraw-Hill Book Co., 1960), pp. 241-61.

which the lawbreaker changes his deviant sentiments. *General deterrence* results from the warning offered to potential criminals by the example of punishment directed at a specific miscreant.

Tappan warns against the misleading supposition that the retributive function of punishment is disappearing. Instead, he avers that retribution has been and continues to be a major ingredient of penal law and correctional systems. Thus, he contends that "it appears likely that the effects of a retributive legal and moral tradition will persist for a long time, though mixed increasingly with other purposes of correctional treatment."[16]

Deterrence: General and Specific

What do the sizable recidivism rates, which we shall examine later in this book, mean? What conclusions can we draw from the fact that the correctional system fails to prevent many of the offenders it processes from further involvement in criminality? One naïve conclusion on the basis of these data is that punishment is a failure, both as a specific and a general deterrent. But as Tappan cautions us: "A complete failure of legal prevention cannot be inferred from the serious crimes committed by a small percentage of the population any more than its success by the law obedience of the great preponderance of men."[17]

Tappan's view of the evidence is that punishment does achieve a significant level of general deterrence. He contends that punishment may bring about deterrence through the fear of unpleasant consequences it instills in potential lawbreakers, but it may also operate to strengthen the public's moral code, bringing about deterrence through inhibition of wayward impulses and formation of conformist habits.[18]

The issue of general deterrence has often been posed in terms of half-truths, such that some have argued the case against deterrence in terms of the specific experience of the death penalty. Homicide rates are higher in the United States than in many other nations, where the death penalty does not exist; therefore, it is argued, punishment of any kind fails to deter. But special conditions surrounding homicide make it a form of criminality least amenable to deterrence. Any comprehensive and adequate discussion of the deterrent effects of punishment would have to examine the effects of different kinds of punishment on the diverse forms of crime as well as the various kinds of persons who may be potential lawbreakers. Specific penalties may deter some kinds of criminality and potential lawbreakers, whereas punishment may have little influence on other kinds of misbehavior. Then, too, the effectiveness of punishment may vary with its certainty and severity. Punitive sanctions,

[16]*Ibid.,* p. 242.
[17]*Ibid.,* p. 246.
[18]*Ibid.,* pp. 248–49.

no matter what their severity, tend to be most effective when they are relatively certain in application.[19]

The deterrent effects of punishment, if any, are still largely unknown. The empirical study of sanctions as curbs to lawbreaking has hardly begun; this subject has been restricted principally to philosophers and others of a speculative mind.[20] Doubtless one obstacle to such research has been the enormous complexity of the phenomena to be investigated. In probably the most succinct and lucid statement of the problems of analysis so far produced, Franklin Zimring has provided some idea of the range of considerations that must be kept in mind in the study of deterrence.[21] He draws attention to a number of important distinctions, such as that between partial deterrence and marginal deterrence. The former refers to threats or punishment that reduce the magnitude of the threatened or punished behavior but without curbing it entirely. Zimring argues that a number of partial deterrents may curtail lawbreaking. Marginal deterrence is the degree to which some specific punishment reduces the rate of illegal behavior below that produced by some lesser penalty. For example, marginal deterrence is in operation in the instance of prison sentences that reduce the rate of reinvolvement in criminality from that brought about by placing offenders on probation.

Zimring's analysis also identifies a number of different ways threats of punishment may operate as deterrents. He further suggests that research on the deterrent impact of sanctions will have to accommodate various forms of punishment. Perhaps punishments of one degree of severity have quite different effects on lawbreakers than do sanctions of lesser or greater severity. Finally, the study of deterrence must consider the variations among lawbreakers. No wonder, then, the study of deterrence is in its infancy.

Some Studies of Punishment

Although studies of deterrence are not available in great quantity, some recent inquiries have been conducted. In one study on a midwestern university campus, William Chambliss found a significant reduction in parking violations after an increase in the severity and certainty of penalties.[22] In another recent investigation, Jack Gibbs calculated indexes of the certainty and severity of punishment for homicide in the United States. He found considerable evi-

---

[19]*Ibid.*, pp. 251-53.

[20]For several excellent sociological essays dealing with many of the issues here, see Alexander L. Clark and Jack P. Gibbs, "Social Control: A Reformulation," *Social Problems*, 12 (Spring 1965), 398-415; Gibbs, "Sanctions," *Social Problems*, 14 (Fall 1966), 147-59.

[21]Franklin E. Zimring, *Perspectives on Deterrence* (Washington, D.C.: National Institute of Mental Health, 1971).

[22]William J. Chambliss, "The Deterrent Influence of Punishment," *Crime and Delinquency*, 12 (January 1966), 70-75.

dence to indicate that homicide was least frequent where apprehension was relatively certain and where prison sentences were severe.[23]

Charles Tittle's study of crime rates and punishment parallels that of Gibbs, but it deals with a series of criminal offenses.[24] Tittle found strong and consistent negative relationships between certainty of punishment and crime rates for different states, as measured in terms of the ratio between felony admissions to state prisons and the total crimes known to the police in different states. Those states with the lowest crime rates had a proportionately larger number of incarcerated persons. On the other hand, severity of punishment bore no marked relationship to crime rates. Tittle's findings led him to conclude that measures to improve the efficiency of police work probably would have significant effects on crime rates but that increasing the severity of punishment would be of limited effectiveness.

A final report on the effects of punitive sanctions comes from Donald Campbell and H. Laurence Ross's study dealing with a "crackdown" on speeding motorists.[25] Following a rash of highway fatalities in Connecticut in 1955, the governor ordered that persons convicted of speeding be deprived of their licenses for thirty days on the first offense, with more serious penalties for repeaters. The researchers found that traffic fatalities decreased after the changes in enforcement policies. However, they noted that the period of high traffic fatalities preceding the crackdown was atypical of long-term trends in the state. Thus, the later reduction in accidents may have had relatively little to do with changes in punitive policies.

VARIATIONS IN CONTEMPORARY DISPOSITIONS[26]

Criminals in the United States and other Western societies are disposed of in one of several major ways.[27] A few who have committed felonies are executed, but most felons are imprisoned or placed on probation. Those guilty of

[23]Jack P. Gibbs, "Crime, Punishment, and Deterrence," *Southwestern Social Science Quarterly,* 28 (March 1968), 515-30.

[24]Charles R. Tittle, "Crime Rates and Legal Sanctions," *Social Problems,* 16 (Spring 1969), 409-23.

[25]Donald T. Campbell and H. Laurence Ross, "The Connecticut Crackdown on Speeding: Time-Series Data in a Quasi-Experimental Analysis," *Law and Society Review,* 3 (August 1968), 33-53.

[26]For a valuable, up-to-date survey of contemporary correctional dispositions in the United States, see The President's Commission on Law Enforcement and Administration of Justice, *The Challenge of Crime in a Free Society* (Washington, D.C.: U.S. Government Printing Office, 1967), pp. 159-85; see also The President's Commission on Law Enforcement and Administration of Justice, *Task Force Report: Corrections* (Washington, D.C.: U.S. Government Printing Office, 1967).

[27]Contemporary correctional practices outside the United States are surveyed in John P. Conrad, *Crime and Its Correction* (Berkeley: University of California Press, 1967).

lesser crimes are put on probation, fined, or sentenced to relatively short terms in jail. Although the major outlines of criminal handling are clear, the details are not so apparent. We shall examine some of these specifics of correctional handling, such as variations in use of imprisonment as a disposition.

The enormous size of the correctional workload in the United States is revealed in figures of the President's Commission on Law Enforcement and Administration of Justice. Table 13 shows data the commission obtained in a nationwide survey of the correctional caseload. The offenders listed as being in institutions were in jails, reformatories, penitentiaries, and other custodial facilities. Individuals listed in the community were offenders on probation or parole.

Correctional work represents a major employment category, as Table 13 indicates. However, we should not suppose that the 121,000 persons employed in this activity in 1965 were principally involved in rehabilitation and treatment. Only 24,000, or 20 percent of the correctional workers, were engaged

Table 13 SOME NATIONAL CHARACTERISTICS OF CORRECTIONS, 1965[28]

	Average Daily Population of Offenders	Total Operating Costs	Average Cost of Offender per Year	Number of Employees in Corrections	Number of Employees Treating Offenders
Juvenile corrections					
Institutions	62,773	$ 226,809,600	$3613	31,687	5,621
Community	285,431	93,613,400	328	9,633	7,706
Adult felon corrections					
Institutions	221,597	435,594,500	1966	51,866	3,220
Community	369,897	73,251,900	198	6,352	5,081
Misdemeanant corrections					
Institutions	141,303	147,794,200	1046	19,195	501
Community	201,385	28,682,900	142	2,430	1,944
Total	1,282,386	$1,005,746,500	——	121,163	24,073

[28]The President's Commission on Law Enforcement, The Challenge of Crime, p. 161.

in some treatment capacity in institutions or the community. The time of the remaining 80 percent was taken up with custodial or maintenance tasks.[29]

Capital Punishment

In general, capital punishment is commonly authorized in most nations in cases of homicide.[30] However, crimes that constitute capital homicides vary considerably around the world. In the United States, all states that employ capital punishment do so in the instance of first-degree murder, that is, premeditated and intentional homicide. In addition, treason, espionage, and rape carry the death penalty in federal law. Kidnapping is a capital offense in thirty states, treason carries the death penalty in twenty-four states, and rape is so defined in twenty-one states; persons can be executed for robbery in nine states, for arson in five, and for burglary or train wrecking in four states.

Although the death penalty is not widely used, it is employed more frequently in the United States than elsewhere. For example, 632 persons were executed in England and Wales between 1900 and 1940. Between 1930 and 1960, 3,724 executions were held in the United States. Even though the American population is much larger than that of England and Wales, the relative number of executions was still far greater in the former. Of these American executions, 3,225 were in cases of murder, 434 were for rape, 23 for armed robbery, 18 for kidnapping, 11 for burglary, and 13 for other crimes. Only 31 of these executions were for federal offenses, and only 31 involved female offenders.

There are some pronounced patterns in capital punishment in the United States. Of the 3,724 executions between 1930 and 1960, nonwhites were executed in 50 percent of the murders, 90 percent of the rapes, and 46 percent of the other offenses. One of the principal arguments against capital punishment is that it is highly discriminatory, so offenders from lower-income backgrounds and disadvantaged ethnic groups are most likely to be executed. Capital punishment is also more common in some sections of the country than in others—60 percent of the executions occurred in the seventeen southern states. All but two of the executions for rape and all burglary executions took place in southern states. This contrast is also revealed by the observation that only one execution occurred between 1940 and 1960 in New Hampshire, although Georgia executed 358 individuals. These figures partially reflect regional variations in occurrence of capital offenses, but the southern states also show a greater willingness to snuff out the lives of criminals.

One trend in capital punishment in the United States has been toward

[29]Ibid., p. 162.

[30]A useful sourcebook on capital punishment is Thorsten Sellin, ed., Capital Punishment (New York: Harper & Row, Publishers, 1967).

a reduced number of executions. Table 14, which shows the number of persons executed in individual years since 1952, indicates that capital punishment has infrequently been employed in recent decades. In the period from 1930 to 1934, the average annual number of executions in this country was 155, whereas in the 1956–60 period, the yearly average was 57, and between 1962 and 1966, the average was 18.

Other developments in capital punishment include the slight trend toward abolition of the death penalty; nine states were without capital punishment in 1965. The California State Supreme Court ruled in 1972 that capital punishment is unconstitutional in that state. The death penalty has also become permissive rather than mandatory, in that it is optional in capital cases except in the District of Columbia. The number of capital crimes has also been reduced in the United States. There are currently twelve capital offenses in the fifty states combined; but fourteen states have only one capital crime, two offenses carry the death penalty in eight states, and only nine states have six or more capital crimes. Executions have also become private events rather than public spectacles, and the techniques of executions have become relatively swift and painless.[31] The most widely used means of carrying out the penalty is electrocution.

Arguments against capital punishment are several, including the ethical position that the practice is morally wrong. Opponents of the death penalty stress its inequitable features, pointing to the large proportion of lower-class and nonwhite individuals executed. In addition, abolitionists note that execution is irrevocable and cannot be undone once it is carried out. Doubtless there have been cases of persons wrongfully convicted and executed.

Enemies of the death penalty contend that the major argument for its use, its presumed deterrent effect, is erroneous. If capital punishment reduces the

Table 14 EXECUTIONS, UNITED STATES, 1952–1971

Year	Number of Executions	Year	Number of Executions
1952	88	1962	47
1953	62	1963	21
1954	82	1964	15
1955	76	1965	7
1956	65	1966	1
1957	65	1967	0
1958	48	1968	0
1959	49	1969	0
1960	57	1970	0
1961	42	1971	0

[31]Sutherland and Cressey, Principles of Criminology, pp. 303–8.

occurrence of capital offenses, its impact should be observed in comparisons of crime rates. Instead, statistical studies show that yearly homicide rates are about the same for contiguous states that are socially and economically similar, even though the death penalty is used in one state and not in another. The long-term trends in homicide rates are also similar in adjoining states even though some use capital punishment and others do not. In cases where the death penalty has been introduced, abolished, or reintroduced in a state, the homicide rate has not fluctuated as proponents of capital punishment suggest it should. Finally, the rates of homicide involving policemen are no higher in states without capital punishment than in states with the death penalty.

Imprisonment

Although most American citizens go through their lives without ever seeing the inside of a correctional institution, imprisonment befalls more persons in the United States than in most other nations. Herbert Bloch and Gilbert Geis note that the imprisonment rate in this country is about 120 persons out of each 100,000 population. In other words, each year about this number of individuals serve time in penal institutions. When the number of persons serving time is calculated to include lengthy jail sentences, the rate of imprisonment increases to 178 persons per 100,000. By contrast, the imprisonment rate in England and Wales is 65 persons, and in Japan 89 persons, per 100,000 population.[32] The number of adult prisoners in state and federal prisons and reformatories in recent years is shown in Table 15.

The figures in Table 15 do not reveal the high turnover of prisoners in institutions. For example, during 1964, 75,096 new prisoners were received in state prisons. Thus, of the 192,647 persons in these places at the end of

Table 15 PRISONERS IN STATE AND FEDERAL PRISONS AND REFORMATORIES*

Year	Federal Institutions	State Institutions	Total	Rate per 100,000 Population
1960	23,218	189,907	213,125	118.7
1961	23,696	196,453	220,149	120.8
1962	23,944	194,886	218,830	118.3
1963	23,128	194,152	217,280	115.7
1964	21,709	192,647	214,356	112.4
1965	21,040	190,111	211,151	109.6
1966	19,245	180,409	199,654	102.7
1967	19,579	176,100	195,679	—

*Prisoners on December 31 of each year.

[32]Herbert A. Bloch and Gilbert Geis, Man, Crime, and Society, 2nd ed. (New York: Random House, 1970), p. 465.

the year, about 40 percent had not been there one year earlier. Over an extended period of time, this high population mobility means that a sizable segment of the population experiences penal commitment. In addition, Table 15 does not include delinquents incarcerated in juvenile facilities. On April 1, 1960, 45,695 youngsters were in custody in juvenile institutions in this country.

A large number of custodial institutions is required for all persons incarcerated. According to an American Correctional Association publication, there were 118 state prisons and reformatories for males in the United States in 1957, along with 29 women's institutions and 117 honor farms or camps. The federal penal system involved an additional six penitentiaries, four reformatories, four juvenile and youth institutions, seven correctional institutions, four camps, one detention facility, and a medical center. State juvenile facilities included seventy-five training schools for boys, fifty-six schools for girls, and twenty-nine camps.[33]

Some indication of the magnitude of incarceration in the larger states can be obtained from statistics for California. In July 1965, California population was approximately 18,602,000. On December 31, 1965, the state had 26,325 adult prisoners in penal institutions.[34] In addition, 6,377 juvenile delinquents were in Youth Authority institutions as of that date.[35] At about the same time, county and city jails held 16,233 persons in custody, and an additional 9,763 were in county and city operated camps. Of the 25,996 county and city prisoners, 16,897 were sentenced offenders serving time in these places.[36] Clearly, in states such as California, the local and state governments represent major employers, for large numbers of correctional workers are required to keep these prisoners occupied at various tasks.

Other Dispositions

As we have noted, probation and other dispositions are widely employed at present as alternatives to incarceration. Unfortunately, recent statistics on the extent of probation as a form of disposition are not available. The U.S. Bureau of the Census discontinued collection of these data in 1946. However, statistics for 1945 indicated that probation was used across the country in 31.6 percent of major offenses. Probation was granted in only 13.0 percent of the serious crimes in Iowa, but was employed in 64.6 percent of the instances in Rhode Island. The trend is apparently toward greater use of probation, for in 1935 probation had been employed in only 28 percent of the serious cases of crime. Data from New York show that probation was granted in 34.6 percent of the

[33]American Correctional Association, *State and National Correctional Institutions.*

[34]State of California, *Crime and Delinquency in California, 1965* (Sacramento: Bureau of Criminal Statistics, 1966), p. 134.

[35]*Ibid.*, p. 197.

[36]*Ibid.*, p. 131.

felony cases in 1945 but in 39.8 percent of the cases in 1951.[37] In the same way, evidence indicates that probation was employed in 32.8 percent of the felony cases in California in 1945 but in 44.2 percent in 1955. In both 1964 and 1965, probation was granted in California in 50.8 percent of the felony cases.[38]

Some further details on the use of probation and other dispositions are available from detailed statistics gathered in California. Convictions were given to 84.2 percent of the felony defendants before the courts in 1965 in that state, while 62.3 percent of them were convicted through pleas of guilty or *nolo contendere*.[39] Probation was not granted to these convicted offenders at the same rate throughout the state. As few as 4 percent were placed on

Table 16 SENTENCES IMPOSED ON FELONY DEFENDANTS, CALIFORNIA, 1965

Offense	Imprisonment	Probation	Jail	Other*
Murder	94.8	2.6	—	2.6
Manslaughter	51.3	42.3	1.7	4.7
Manslaughter, vehicle	11.2	79.4	6.9	2.5
Robbery	63.4	20.1	1.9	14.6
Assault	18.7	56.5	19.9	4.9
Burglary	25.4	46.0	18.4	10.2
Theft, except auto	13.9	56.3	24.8	5.0
Auto theft	17.5	41.1	25.4	16.0
Receiving stolen property	14.2	62.4	17.7	5.7
Forgery and checks	26.6	53.6	16.6	3.2
Rape	16.8	63.3	12.2	7.7
Lewd and lascivious conduct	28.0	70.5	0.4	1.1
Other sex offenses	11.8	76.2	9.5	2.5
Narcotics and dangerous drugs	25.4	65.6	2.8	6.2
Deadly weapons	23.6	41.5	29.8	5.1
Drunk driving	5.1	81.7	10.0	3.2
Failure to render aid	5.0	81.4	9.1	4.5
Escape	59.9	6.5	30.8	2.8
Bookmaking	0.6	85.2	6.2	8.0
Contributing	—	75.2	22.0	2.8
All other	7.9	63.3	21.5	7.3

*Includes transfer to Youth Authority jurisdiction.

[37]Tappan, *Crime, Justice, and Correction*, pp. 559-60.
[38]State of California, *Crime and Delinquency in California, 1965*, p. 80.
[39]*Ibid.*, p. 67.

probation in one county, but in another county 70.6 percent of the convicted persons received probation. Probation granting also varies in terms of the offenses for which persons are charged. Table 16 indicates the sentences imposed on felony defendants in California in 1965.[40]

Table 16 contains few surprises. Although California courts are loath to grant probation in homicide cases and instances of gross and coercive crime such as robbery, nonviolent offenses frequently culminate in probation. The low percentage of sex offenders imprisoned might surprise the layman, but these figures probably reflect that the majority of sex offenses are innocuous, petty acts.

This discussion of contemporary dispositions of offenders would not be complete without some mention of decisions in the cases of juveniles. The subject of juvenile handling was touched on in Chapter Three, where we noted that police throughout the United States settle informally most delinquency cases they encounter in the community. As a consequence, juveniles who end up in the juvenile courts represent only a fraction of those known to the police or other groups in the community. Some further details regarding the juvenile correctional machinery are available from reports in the state of California. In 1965, the police reported 277,649 arrests of juveniles, of which 21.6 percent were for major law violations, and the remainder were on charges of minor law violations or "delinquent tendencies." The police reported 45.7 percent of the total cases to juvenile courts, referring 72.4 percent of the major law violations and only 39.5 percent of the "delinquent tendencies" instances.[41]

That a youngster is referred to a juvenile court does not mean that he will become officially labeled a "juvenile delinquent" or be incarcerated. In the California referrals in 1965, 49.6 percent of the cases were closed at intake or turned over to other agencies, and an additional 13.6 percent were placed on informal probation. Petitions, the juvenile court parallel of indictments or informations, were filed in only 36.8 percent of the cases.[42] The sorting processes continue beyond the petition-filing stage, for although 35,614 petitions were filed in juvenile courts, only 6,174 youths were committed to the California Youth Authority in 1965.[43] The other juveniles were either assigned to probation supervision or incarcerated in county operated institutions. These statistics indicate that a pronounced shrinkage of cases exists at every point, from initial police contact of juveniles through institutionalization of some in state training schools.

[40]*Ibid.*, p. 81.
[41]*Ibid.*, p. 144.
[42]*Ibid.*, p. 163.
[43]*Ibid.*, p. 197.

SUMMARY

This chapter has been concerned with the different events after offenders have been convicted or adjudicated in the courts. In the next chapter, we shall examine the social workings of the agencies and institutions to which these individuals are consigned. We shall discover that most of these agencies and institutions operate in ways not accurately described in organizational charts or brochures stating the purposes or workings of these structures. In particular, we shall find that prisons and other correctional institutions often constitute social communities at cross-purposes with their official aims.

19

CORRECTIONAL SOCIAL ORGANIZATION

The preceding chapter indicated that as societies have grown in size and complexity, particularly in the past few centuries, relatively permanent organizational structures have been invented for dealing with lawbreakers. Some of these, such as prisons, are physically separated from the societies they serve, whereas others, such as police agencies or probation organizations, exist within the community and impinge more directly on the activities of citizens. In either case, these law enforcement and correctional devices represent prominent social forms in modern societies.

In the past decade or so, sociologists have begun to subject these structures to research scrutiny so that at present a large and growing literature exists on "the sociology of correctional organizations."[1] This phrase refers to the body of sociological work that attempts to discover the social processes and patterns characteristic of correctional organizations. The sociologist approaches prisons and other custodial institutions as particular cases of "total institutions" or as a subtype of the larger class of formal, complex organizations.[2]

Analysis of the social workings of legal and correctional agencies encompasses a wide variety of organizations, not all of which are discussed in this chapter. Inquiries into the social structure of the police represent one case of the sociology of correctional organizations, but Chapter Three has already dealt with the police. Studies of social values and attitudes regarding crime have been reported in Chapter Two,[3] and the question of social stigma resulting

[1] The growth of this area of interest is reflected in Don C. Gibbons, "Bibliography on the Sociology of Correctional Organizations," mimeographed. This collection of materials on prisons, police, and other correctional organizations runs to nearly 200 titles, most of which have appeared in the past decade or so. For an anthology containing a generous sample of this material, see Lawrence E. Hazelrigg, ed., *Prison Within Society* (Garden City, N.Y.: Doubleday and Co., 1968).

[2] For a discussion of the characteristics of "total institutions," see Erving Goffman, "On the Characteristics of Total Institutions: The Inmate World," and "On the Characteristics of Total Institutions: Staff-Inmate Relations," in *The Prison*, ed. Donald R. Cressey (New York: Holt, Rinehart and Winston, 1961), pp. 15–106.

[3] For data on citizen views of corrections, see Joint Commission on Correctional Manpower and Training, *The Public Looks at Crime and Corrections* (Washington, D.C.: Joint Commission on Correctional Manpower and Training, 1968).

from legal handling has also been examined earlier.[4] This chapter is devoted to sociological aspects of prisons, training schools, and other custodial institutions, as well as probation and parole agencies.[5]

Sociologists have not subjected all the various correctional devices extant in modern society to equal research treatment: jails and certain police systems have generally been ignored. We shall note various gaps and deficiencies in the literature on correctional social organization at various points in the following material.

PRISON SOCIAL ORGANIZATION

In a number of ways, prisons are unlike any other kind of institution or organization in modern society. They are foreign to the experience of most citizens, for few individuals other than prisoners and their keepers ever see the inside of a prison. Although life in a penal institution can be described to persons who have not been in one, such a description can hardly portray all the atmosphere of the place. It fails to capture the noises of clanging cell doors; the mean, harsh, "grey" flavor of institutional living, even in the most humane penitentiary; and many other elements that make life in the penal institution unique as a human experience. Nonetheless, the following pages provide some glimpses of social life behind prison walls, beginning with an examination of similarities and variations among prisons.[6]

Prison Similarities and Variations

One characteristic all prisons share is that they are places where one group of men devote their attention to managing a group of captives. Prisoners do not enter penitentiaries voluntarily; they are forcibly brought there and restrained by prison workers whose main product is social order among inmates. Prisons are also similar in the sense that inmates who enter them are alike; hence, prisons everywhere work with much the same raw material. Most reformatories and penitentiaries in the United States are walled institutions with inside cell blocks and other features of the Auburn–Sing Sing physical plant. Most inmates depart from penal facilities through the device of parole. Finally,

[4]Richard D. Schwartz and Jerome H. Skolnick, "Two Studies of Legal Stigma," in *The Other Side,* ed. Howard S. Becker (New York: The Free Press, 1964), pp. 103–17.

[5]This chapter is a revised and expanded version of material which first appeared in Don C. Gibbons, *Changing the Lawbreaker* (Englewood Cliffs, N.J.: Prentice-Hall, 1965), pp. 189–227.

[6]One of the best reports on the flavor of prison life is contained in a prison novel. See Malcolm Braly, *On the Yard* (Boston: Little, Brown and Co., 1967). See also John Irwin, *The Felon* (Englewood Cliffs, N.J.: Prentice-Hall, 1970), for a lucid sociological analysis of prison life as experienced by the felon.

prisons are devoted to the same general functions—administering some punishment to lawbreakers while keeping them securely in custody, and with certain other aims.

Some important differences among penal institutions probably condition the kind of social structure that grows in them. For one, prisons vary considerably in size of physical plant and inmate population. As noted in Chapter Eighteen, American prisons range in size from some holding several hundred men to several with over 4,000 men.

Although the Auburn–Sing Sing style of architecture is the most commonly encountered in the United States, some penal institutions in this country have been constructed along different lines. A major variant in physical design is the so-called "telephone pole" physical plan, in which all the institutional buildings are connected to one central corridor. This architectural style evolved relatively recently and has provided the model for most of the newer institutions in this country. One major advantage of this kind of physical plant is that control over inmates does not demand the inordinate amount of time and energy devoted to that task in the older Auburn–Sing Sing kind of prison, with its hodgepodge of poorly designed and poorly located structures.

Penal institutions also vary in the financial resources they can call on for implementation of their programs. For example, in some states, guards receive extremely low wages; in some other states correctional officers receive fairly reasonable salaries. Another variation among prisons has to do with the kind of administrative organization within which they are placed. In some states, a Department of Corrections or similar agency exercises continued jurisdiction over the individual institutions and usually provides a degree of stability to the correctional program. In other areas, prisons are autonomous operations subjected to the vicissitudes of political interference.

Custodial institutions show some differences in the kinds of inmates with which they deal. Reformatories usually handle relatively young prisoners, most of them under twenty-five years of age, whereas prisons and penitentiaries hold an older, more mature offender population. In all likelihood, institutions with youthful populations are subjected to more violent and erratic behavior by inmates than is true of those places with an older convict population. Certain states, such as California, have moved far in the direction of establishing diversified institutions, each holding a relatively homogeneous group of prisoners. The institution at Chino holds minimum security inmates, while San Quentin Prison is restricted to dangerous, criminally mature offenders. In many states with a smaller total population of prisoners, one prison handles the entire heterogeneous mixture of felons.

Penal institutions seem to mirror various features of the societies in which they are found. Accordingly, the student of prison life might expect to find variations in these places from one country to another. Indeed, several studies of European prisons have turned up discrepancies between them and American institutions.[7] Similarly, Donald Cressey and Witold Krassowski have identified some features of Soviet labor camps not found in American institutions.[8]

Prisons and the "Host" Society

Prisons are sometimes seen as "total institutions" in which the prisoner's life events occur. This label implies that penal facilities exist in isolation from the society they serve, but such a view is partially erroneous. Most of the day-to-day concerns of prisoners center about life inside the walls, and they are painfully aware that they have been isolated from other citizens. Yet convicts are not completely cut off from contact with the outside world. Visitors and tours frequently pass through the institution. Inmates are allowed to listen to radios and read newspapers so that they do not lose complete contact with the world outside the prison. They sometimes seize on such devices as riots and disturbances to dramatize their complaints against the institution to an audience in the free community.

Prisons are less than "total" in another sense, since the persons who run these places are restrained by interests outside the institution. What kinds of restraints operate on prison administrators? Citizens generally appear to be ignorant and diffident about prisons. One study of public knowledge about correctional practices in California indicated that most citizens were unaware of the bases on which persons are committed to prisons as well as ignorant of the number, variety, or character of penal institutions in that state. Most laymen knew that executions take place by means of gas at San Quentin Prison, but they showed little awareness of most other facets of the correctional program.[9]

Although laymen do not appear to have any sustained or informed interest in penitentiaries, it would be a mistake to suppose that the public plays no part in the programs of prisons. Various community groups interested in penal operations function as pressure groups that endeavor to influence institutional programs. For example, social worker associations pressure the prison to establish therapy programs, and various industry and labor organizations attempt to force the institution to curtail manufacture of goods that compete with products of private industry. We cannot understand such prison phenomena as the widespread idleness endemic in American institutions without taking into account the activities of outside pressure groups, which have forced institutions to restrict their production to "states-use" goods.

---

[7] Terence and Pauline Morris, *Pentonville* (London: Routledge and Kegan Paul, 1963); Hugh J. Klare, *Anatomy of Prison* (Baltimore: Penguin Books, 1962); Thomas Mathiesen, *The Defences of the Weak—A Sociological Study of a Norwegian Correctional Institution* (London: Tavistock Publications, 1965).

[8] Donald R. Cressey and Witold Krassowski, "Inmate Organization and Anomie in American Prisons and Soviet Labor Camps," *Social Problems*, 5 (Winter 1957-58), 217-30.

[9] Gibbons, "Who Knows What about Correction?" *Crime and Delinquency*, 9 (April 1963), 137-44.

The interest groups that intrude into prison policies are such a mixed collection that different ones often press for conflicting ends. Correctional administrators can sometimes manage the disruptive potential of these claims on the system because much of the activity of these groups is intermittent. Administrators sometimes deal with interest groups by "giving" one institution to one group and another to a different pressure group. In other words, treatment is stressed in one facility to reduce agitation from welfare workers, whereas a repressive regime is established in a second prison to assuage proponents of punitive themes.[10]

Prison Programs

A brief sketch of the workings of the prison as revealed in casual observations would include some of these elements. The prison is nominally under the control of an administrator, usually called a warden or superintendent, who is assisted by one or more associate wardens responsible for the custodial or treatment programs of the institution. The custodial staff is by far the largest group of employees, comprised of a captain of the guards and his lieutenants, along with the guards. The latter are sometimes called "correctional officers" by administrators and are usually termed "bulls" or "screws" by the inmates.

A second group of prison employees consists of a business manager along with various clerical persons and bookkeepers. These individuals have the task of managing the flow of goods and supplies into and out of the prison community.

The third group of workers in the modern prison is made up of individuals presumed to be working at the rehabilitation of the prisoners. Most prisons have some kind of classification office that gathers detailed facts about newly arrived prisoners. This information is then used in making custodial assignments and other program decisions about inmates. Institutions also maintain a school program and a number of teachers who attempt to continue the education of some of the convicts. A variety of vocational training is often found in modern penal facilities, so some prisoners learn typewriter repair or other skills of that kind. However, the bulk of the inmates work during the day in various kinds of prison industries that have no vocational consequences for them. Prisoners assist in kitchen duties, make clothing or shoes for other state institutions, manufacture road signs and license plates, or engage in other, related kinds of prison labor. Supervisory employees are responsible for these activities, along with guards who also maintain surveillance of the inmates during the day. The institution employs social workers to engage in various kinds of "helping" activity with the convicts.

[10]For a discussion of correctional interest groups, see Donald R. Cressey, "Prison Organizations," in *Handbook of Organizations*, ed. James G. March (Chicago: Rand McNally and Co., 1965), pp. 1030–32.

Correctional administrators often distribute descriptions of their prisons that imply orderly, efficient, coherent systems in which the various facets of correctional activity coverge on the inmate to convert him into a law-abiding citizen. But how accurate is the official description of the prison? Recently accumulated evidence on the social workings of penal organizations indicates that the official view of penal operations is more fiction than fact.

Prison Social Structure

The general description of prison organization that follows is drawn from the existing literature and should be viewed as most descriptive of maximum security prisons and as more or less accurate for institutions that vary in the ways suggested in the preceding pages.

Members of the general public have often thought of prisons as autocratic.[11] Custodial officers *give orders* and inmates *obey* them. Prisoners are totally managed persons whose opportunities for self-direction and independent action are almost completely circumscribed. Penal institutions are monoliths with a singularity of purpose in which all responsibilities of members of the system are clearly and specifically defined. Prisons are well-oiled, smooth-running, people-punishing, and people-changing social machines. In this view, all prison employees, from the warden down to the guards, agree on their tasks of maintaining, disciplining, and sometimes treating inmates. Prisons are frequently believed to be models of autocratic and rational bureaucratic structures.

This image is greatly distorted, for prisons normally depart rather markedly from this monolithic model. Cressey has devoted a good deal of attention to a discussion of the organizational cross-currents built into modern prisons.[12] He has pointed out that as basic concepts of prison purposes and institutional management have changed, new activities have been added to the institutional operation but without being integrated with the earlier forms of administrative structure. Accordingly, nearly all modern penal facilities have three principal administrative hierarchies, relatively independent of one another, and devoted to keeping, serving, and using inmates. In other words, prisons have a number of employees who maintain custody over prisoners, another group which supervises inmates in their work activities, and a third collection of workers who endeavor to rehabilitate the prisoners.[13] Of course, in many institutions, that part of the system supposedly devoted to treatment is a small segment of the organization, but at least a token effort to develop a rehabilitative program has been made in many penal institutions in recent years. Cressey also notes

[11]For an analysis of prisons as autocracies, see Norman A. Polansky, "The Prison as an Autocracy," *Journal of Criminal Law and Criminology*, 33 (May–June 1942), 16–22.

[12]Cressey, "Prison Organizations," pp. 1023–70.

[13]*Ibid.*, p. 1024.

that in the general shift in the past century, away from the view that persons are sent to prison *for* punishment to the perspective that imprisonment alone is punishment enough, "mere incarceration" has not been consistently defined. Over the decades, prisons have vacillated from repressive regimes to periods in which they have been loosely run and less punitive and harsh. Still, most contemporary prisons continue to place prisoners in some degree of physical discomfort, so "mere incarceration" tends to refer to a mean existence unrelieved by many of the diversions of normal living.[14]

Cressey has summarized the somewhat contradictory ingredients of the mandate under which modern prisons operate:

> . . . at present there are three popular and sanctioned reactions to crime in contemporary American society. One is hostility, with insistence that the criminal be made to suffer in prison, whether the suffering is physical or psychological. Another reaction is one of humanitarian concern that the punishments in prisons not be too harsh, severe, cruel, or inhuman. A third is inquiry designed to secure comprehension of the social and psychological processes in criminal behavior, so that control can be based on knowledge.[15]

The responsibility of the prison to maintain secure custody over prisoners so they cannot escape, and at the same time refrain from brutalizing the inmates, creates grave difficulties for the institution. The prisoners are not in the institution voluntarily and do not accord legitimacy to the official norms or prescriptions of the organization. The situation of prisoners is different from that of persons in a military autocracy, for in the latter case most members of the system have internalized the authority of the rules, even though somewhat grudgingly. Most are motivated to conform to military regulations and procedures, even though they may regard conformity as personally unpleasant. The same cannot be said for many (but not all) prison inmates.

Autocratic rule over hostile and uncooperative inmates could theoretically be obtained at a price. Prisoners could be isolated, physically abused and coerced, and put under continual and pervasive surveillance. In theory, they could be maintained under conditions of marked anomie and demoralization. However, these possibilities do not actually exist, for prison officials are expected to deal with their charges in a humane fashion. They are obligated to minimize the physical and social isolation of inmates, rather than maximize it, and are forbidden to abuse physically or coerce prisoners. These are real limitations, for institutions do come under periodic scrutiny by the outside world. In addition, constant surveillance of prisoners by correctional officers to detect rule violations is impossible for two reasons: most prisons are not

[14]*Ibid.,* pp. 1026–30.
[15]*Ibid.,* pp. 1029–30.

physically constituted in such a way as to allow continual supervision and observation of convicts, and not enough observers are available. Although guards comprise the largest single class of employee, the prisoners greatly outnumber them.[16]

In theory, officers are expected to maintain social distance from prisoners and give orders inmates are presumed to obey because they are powerless to do otherwise. But as we previously indicated, prison guards do not have techniques of physical coercion available to obtain compliance from recalcitrant prisoners. Moreover, even if it were legitimized, physical force as a technique for managing convicts would be self-defeating in the long run. Because of the disproportionate number of inmates to guards, extensive use of force would produce convict reprisals, uprisings, and other negative consequences.

One technique contrived for control of uncooperative prisoners has been to urge them to put themselves into voluntary isolation from other convicts, to "do your own time," and pursue incentives and privileges as rewards for conformity. In turn, if an inmate violates rules, he loses privileges.[17] However, this mechanism has severe limitations. Deprivation of privileges tends to have little effect within the harsh environment of institutions because the prisoners are already severely deprived. They are cut off from sexual relations and many kinds of freedom of action as to choice of clothing, companionship, and so on. To be denied the privilege of attending a movie tends not to be viewed as a severe loss. Prisoners have redefined such incentives as reduction of the inmate's sentence for good behavior as "rights" rather than rewards, so the administration tends to tamper with "good time" credits only in extreme cases. Furthermore, they are accorded to the inmate at the start of his sentence rather than at points in his institutional career as rewards for appropriate institutional conduct. Thus, they do not operate as important incentives and are normally awarded routinely to nearly all inmates except those who have had extemely troublesome and violent institutional careers.

The modern prison must find some way of maintaining a reasonable degree of order without extreme physical coercion and manipulation of meaningful rewards for conformity. The solution of this problem of how to keep the peace with and among uncooperative inmates takes the form of "corruption of authority" in many prisons.[18] Corruption of authority assumes several forms. One refers to liaisons, relationships, "deals," and other informal *sub rosa* ties, which develop between inmates and administrators and are not defined as

---

[16]For one incisive commentary on the limits of "total power" in prisons, see Gresham M. Sykes, *The Society of Captives* (Princeton, N.J.: Princeton University Press, 1958), pp. 40-62; Sykes, "The Corruption of Authority and Rehabilitation," *Social Forces,* 34 (March 1956), 257-62; Clarence Schrag, "Some Foundations for a Theory of Correction," in Cressey, *The Prison,* pp. 338-39.

[17]Richard A. Cloward, "Social Control in the Prison," in Cloward, Donald R. Cressey, George H. Grosser, Richard McCleery, Lloyd E. Ohlin, Gresham M. Sykes, and Sheldon L. Messinger, *Theoretical Studies in Social Organization of the Prison* (New York: Social Science Research Council, 1960), pp. 20-48.

[18]Sykes, *The Society of Captives,* pp. 52-62.

legitimate or proper within the formal definitions of prison procedures. Penal administrators and prisoner "elites" enter into informal relationships that provide special privileges to these leaders. In turn, they take over the job of coercing other inmates into minimally disruptive behavior. As Richard Korn and Lloyd McCorkle have indicated, "far from systematically attempting to undermine the inmate hierarchy, the institution generally gives it covert support and recognition by assigning better jobs and quarters to its high-status members providing they are 'good inmates.' In this and other ways the institution buys peace with the system by avoiding battle with it."[19] Being a "good inmate" in this context means refraining from direct assaults on the administrative system. It does *not* mean "doing your own time," for elites interfere with other inmates, control them, and demand special privileges and favors from less powerful prisoners. They are covertly aided in these activities by the prison administration, which pretends not to see this interaction among the convicts.

A second form of corruption of authority extends to inmate–guard relationships generally, in which correctional officers obtain a measure of cooperation and obedience from inmates by discretionary action in which they overlook some conduct infractions. In turn, in a *quid pro quo* relationship, inmates are expected to create a minimum of visible trouble for the correctional officers. In other words, the guard persuades convicts to behave by allowing them to deviate from rules in certain situations. This form of authority corruption stems from several factors. Correctional officers are not immune from general pressures to be "good guys." They probably find it difficult to associate with inmates on extremely distant and aloof terms, for they quickly discover that prisoners are quite ordinary humans and not monsters. More important, discretionary actions represent the easiest way for the guard to keep inmate disorder at a minimum. The officer without a club of some sort must persuade and cajole. Discretionary action represents the "carrot" by which he obtains a modicum of conformity to major rules and regulations.

In the public view, the job of correctional officer is fit for simpletons who need only follow explicit orders. In reality, it is probably one of the more difficult occupational tasks in American society. The job demands a high order of skill in manipulating and managing men. The officer must use discretion but at the same time must be alert to the dangers of being drawn into situations where he buys cooperation from prisoners at too great a price. He must avoid being lured into *sub rosa* relationships in which he takes contraband into or out of of the institution or performs other illicit services for inmates. The guard must use discretion up to a point but he risks being manipulated by convicts into discretionary actions beyond the tolerance point of his superiors. If he uses too much discretionary judgment, he may be fired or punished in some other way. To complicate his situation further, appropriate action

[19]Richard Korn and Lloyd W. McCorkle, "Resocialization Within Walls," *Annals of the American Academy of Political and Social Science,* no. 293 (May 1954), 91.

must be worked out by each officer, for the most part unguided by advice and instruction from anyone else. Cressey has suggested that in prisons of either custodial or therapeutic orientation, the guard faces a situation in which his superiors are not able to give him explicit directions as to precisely how he is to function in his discretionary role.[20]

For such reasons, prisons might be more accurately defined as partially disorganized rather than as model autocracies. They exhibit less than complete organizational consensus among employees and tend to show defective communication patterns. Orders are supposed to move down a chain of command to guards, where they are implemented, and information on which decisions are made moves up the command line. But distortions often occur in message flow, particularly in the feedback of explanations behind orders to such low ranking members as custodial officers. Consequently, prisons frequently show a degree of guard alienation from the institutional program.[21] Officers either do not understand the bases on which decisions and orders are formulated or disagree with these directives. This lack of internal consensus among employees regarding goals of the system is found in prisons of various kinds but is particularly severe in treatment-oriented prisons, where the guards are often more similar to the inmates than they are to the higher administrators. Because they tend to view therapy operations as a threat to sound custody, they are in accord, although for different reasons, with the prisoners' negative definitions of treatment programs.

"Treatment-Oriented" Prisons

The problems of prisons discussed to this point seem generic to treatment and custodial institutions alike. But some additional difficulties seem to be peculiar to therapy-oriented prisons.[22]

In our discussion of treatment in modern penitentiaries, we should note that the rehabilitative function has not been widely adopted or implemented in American prisons to date. As Alfred Schnur indicates, it does not make much sense to ask whether the "New Penology" oriented around rehabilitation is a success, for the "New Penology" still exists for the most part mainly in textbooks.[23] Schnur points out that, around 1958, about 27,000 persons were

[20]Cressey, "Contradictory Directives in Complex Organizations: The Case of the Prison," *Administrative Science Quarterly*, 4 (June 1959), pp. 1–19.

[21]Schrag, "Some Foundations for a Theory of Correction," pp. 336–38.

[22]Organizational differences between "punitive oriented" and "treatment oriented" prisons are discussed at length in Cressey, "Prison Organizations," pp. 1033–54; see also Johan Galtung, "The Social Functions of a Prison," *Social Problems*, 6 (Fall 1958), 127–40; Galtung, "Prison: The Organization of Dilemma," in Cressey, *The Prison*, pp. 107–45.

[23]Alfred C. Schnur, "The New Penology: Fact or Fiction?" *Journal of Criminal Law, Criminology and Police Science*, 49 (November–December 1958), 331–34; for some evidence suggesting that the "New Penology" has not been fully implemented in England either, see Terence Morris, "In the Nick," and Alan Little, "The Borstal Boys," *The Twentieth Century* (London), 170 (Winter 1962), 22–34, 35–42.

472   correctional social organization

employed in state and federal penal facilities to manage some 165,000 inmates —a ratio of one employee for every six prisoners. Only small numbers of these employees were assigned to treatment activities; most were custodial officers. Moreover, only a small proportion of the persons designated as treatment personnel were actually involved in therapy activities. According to Schnur, "more people, however, are employed to shuffle papers than to implement the new penology."[24] For example, only 23 psychiatrists were available full-time to treat 165,000 inmates, so the ratio of prisoners to psychiatrists was 7,026 to 1. If each convict received the same amount of psychiatric help, he would get eighty-two seconds of therapy per month.

In a similar study of 47 state correctional systems, Elmer Johnson[25] found that persons with master of social work degrees were employed in only fourteen states. Eighteen states indicated that no "social workers" were employed in their programs. Additionally, in those remaining states with social workers, this occupational category was defined so broadly as to include persons who did not have training in social work practice and techniques. The definition of social work was stretched to subsume a variety of institutional activities not conventionally thought of as social work.

Although the rehabilitative function is not yet widespread or fully developed, enough prisons have begun to move in this direction to provide some indication of the organizational difficulties that arise.

Addition of the treatment role has introduced views into the institution to the effect that a coercive, restrictive social climate is inimical to therapy. Prisoners need opportunities to ventilate hostility, work out new patterns of adjustment, and so on. Prisons have come to be regarded as serving ends similar to those presumed to characterize mental hospitals, with guards enjoined to be receptive, passive, and relaxed. Significantly, this new view is not usually shared by all members of the employee group. Such notions have frequently been brought into the institution by top administrators who attempt to impose them on the custodial force. However, a large segment of the guard group is made up of veterans of the "old order" who have served for many years under a straightforward custodial system. These officers are supported by the force of tradition in their belief that the "old ways" are better, and they tend to be unreceptive to rehabilitative declarations by recently arrived administrators. Nonetheless, correctional institutions attempting transformation into treatment-oriented systems do exhibit a more relaxed, less coercive social climate than the more traditional penal facilities. Although there are serious questions regarding the extent to which prisons can be converted into therapeutic communities, efforts to do so weaken the authoritarian order of the institution and disrupt relations among employees.

The most usual outcome of introduction of treatment into an institution

---

[24]Schnur, "The New Penology: Fact or Fiction?" 332.

[25]Elmer H. Johnson, "The Present Level of Social Work in Prisons," *Crime and Delinquency*, 9 (July 1963), pp. 290–96.

is an uneasy marriage of custodial and therapeutic activities, and security considerations often prevail in the operation of the organization.[26] In other cases, the rehabilitative goal pervades many facets of the prison in the face of resistance by some employee holdouts. The specific pattern that emerges probably depends mainly on how the treatment function is brought into the prison. If it is introduced by hiring middle level employees such as social case workers, but is not supported by the warden and his aides, the common consequence is that in practice it merely serves custodial ends. Psychiatrists are used in such institutions to "cool out" threatening inmates rather than to conduct therapy. In the same way, the treatment recommendations of other workers are subordinated to custodial decisions. The custodial force controls communication within the organization, so the therapists are kept ignorant of, and removed from, the important operations of the prison. They are reduced to a form of prison "window dressing."[27]

The outcome of the custody–treatment quarrel differs when the warden and other top level administrators introduce rehabilitation as an end or give allegiance to this goal. In this case, treatment workers are more influential in the operation of the institution and make important policy decisions. But again, the situation tends to be an uneasy one in which functional harmony is less than complete. No clear format for an effective therapy program operating within the limits of necessary security provisions has yet been devised. Treatment-oriented penitentiaries tend to lack unambiguous definitions of the specific manner in which rehabilitative agents are to operate. As a consequence, many of these employees come to see themselves as rescuers, helpers, and protectors of inmates rather than as rehabilitators. The worker who identifies his task as helping inmates sometimes comes to conceptualize his job as protecting convicts from the custodial force. He begins to see himself as a mediator between offenders and guards rather than as a coworker with the correctional officer. This kind of role performance probably exacerbates the treatment–custody conflict in prisons. It has been argued that the therapy agent who views his task as rescuing and helping inmates plays into the hands of the prisoners. He lends covert support to that group's attempts to "reject the rejectors" or deflect blame away from themselves and onto "society."[28]

The treatment-oriented prison creates special difficulties for the guard force. Not only are correctional officers told to maintain order without being given clear instructions as to how they are to accomplish this goal, they are also told to behave in ways that contribute to therapy. As Cressey notes:

It is clear that in treatment-oriented prisons, directions to guards regarding their relationships with inmates are likely to be confusing and contra-

[26]Donald R. Cressey, "Limitations on Organization of Treatment in the Modern Prison," in Cloward et al., *Theoretical Studies in Social Organization of the Prison*, pp. 78–110.
[27]Harvey Powelson and Reinhard Bendix, "Psychiatry in Prison," *Psychiatry*, 14 (February 1951), pp. 73–86.
[28]Korn and McCorkle, "Resocialization Within Walls," pp. 88–89.

dictory. There are to be no rules to enforce, but the guard is to enforce "understandings" to the extent necessary for the prison to achieve the minimum degree of orderliness it needs. There is to be no punishment, but guards are to report nonconformists to a central board for hearings, during the course of which punishments are ordered, in the name of justice. Guards are to "relax" but they are not to relax "too much."[29]

From Cressey's description, correctional officers in the treatment prison are pulled at from several different sides, so they are "damned if they do, and damned if they don't." Such a state of affairs could hardly add to the attractiveness of this kind of occupation.

As is evident from the discussion thus far, administrations of most prisons do not present a united front to the inmate group. Points of ambiguity exist within the organizations, conflicts between different administrative groups lie barely hidden and sometimes blossom into overt interorganizational conflict, and other difficulties characterize prisons. Little has been said so far about the inmate group. What is the nature of social life among prisoners in maximum security prisons?[30]

The Inmate Social System

One common but exaggerated view of convicts is that they are an aggregate of persons in opposition to the administrative regime. In the layman's view, inmates are assumed to be a collectivity of "wild beasts" from whom the guards have much to fear, continually engaged in attempts to escape and carrying on a variety of violent activities among themselves. Something of this same conception of the inmate group can be found in the sociological literature as well. Gresham Sykes and Sheldon Messinger have described an "inmate code" of normative prescriptions said to exist in all prisons.[31] By implication, allegiance to this code characterizes most convicts. The code consists of a collection of conduct definitions centering around directives to refrain from interfering with inmate interests, avoid quarrels and conflicts with other prisoners or go "no rap" with one's fellow convicts, and so on. The code defines the model convict, from the inmates' perspective, in terms that contrast markedly with the staff version of the good inmate. Prisoners are expected to cooperate with one another in overt and covert defiance of institutional expectations.

Several hypotheses have been advanced to account for this code. Sykes

[29]Cressey, "Prison Organizations," p. 1058.

[30]Public views on prison life tend to be stereotypical in the extreme. One common notion about prisons is that homosexuality is the major fact of prisoner life, with homosexual conduct being rampant in men's prisons. In fact, other prisoner values and interests tend to be more important than this one. For an analysis of prison homosexuality, see John H. Gagnon and William Simon, "The Social Meaning of Prison Homosexuality," *Federal Probation*, 32 (March 1968), pp. 23–29.

[31]Gresham M. Sykes and Sheldon L. Messinger, "The Inmate Social System," in Cloward et al., *Theoretical Studies in Social Organization of the Prison*, pp. 5–19.

and Messinger maintain that the most likely explanation is functional, in which the code is seen as serving to reduce the "pains of imprisonment" in custodial institutions.[32] These pains of incarceration include deprivations of liberty, goods and services, heterosexual relations, and autonomy, which offenders experience as psychologically painful. According to these authors, "as a population of prisoners moves in the direction of solidarity, as demanded by the inmate code, the pains of imprisonment become less severe."[33] McCorkle and Korn advance a compatible thesis. They hold that the code and prisoner solidarity in opposition to the authorities permit the inmate to "reject his rejectors" instead of himself.[34] That is, convicts are supported by their peers in a set of definitions and attitudes, which maintain that society is at fault for their criminality, so they are not forced to turn blame inward, to themselves. Cloward has advanced much the same argument.[35]

There is no question that an inmate code exists in prisons and that psychological pains accompany the experience of incarceration. But the existence of such a code does not necessarily mean that the code is solely the product of pressures of confinement.[36] It is conceivable that it exists in prisons in part because some prisoners bring it into the institution from the outside. Several pieces of evidence support a "diffusion" interpretation of inmate norms. Stanton Wheeler has shown that role conflict and discrepancies in role expectations between inmates and administrators are less than complete.[37] He found that prisoners had different expectations regarding the behavior of other inmates than did guards, but some offenders had similar views to those of correctional officers who approved of violations of inmate definitions. Wheeler also suggests that some of the conflict between prisoners and authorities is more apparent than real. His data show that prisoners judge other inmates to be more hostile to treatment and other institutional activities than they are in fact. This discrepancy between private sentiments and estimates of group views appears related to the greater visibility of the most antisocial persons in the prison. Individual prisoners gauge the degree of antiadministration sentiment among other offenders from observation of a biased sample of the total inmate group.

Wheeler has contributed a second kind of evidence supporting a diffusion interpretation of the inmate code. His findings from a number of Scandinavian prisons show that the pains of imprisonment are found in these places, but there is no clear parallel to the inmate code or prisoner solidarity observed

[32]*Ibid.*

[33]*Ibid.*, p. 16.

[34]Korn and McCorkle, "Resocialization Within Walls," pp. 88–89.

[35]Cloward, "Social Control in the Prison."

[36]For evidence in support of the functionalist thesis, see Charles R. Tittle and Drollene P. Tittle, "Social Organization of Prisoners: An Empirical Test," *Social Forces*, 43 (December 1964), 216-21. This investigation was conducted in the U.S. Public Health Service Hospital, which holds drug addicts.

[37]Stanton Wheeler, "Role Conflict in Correctional Communities," in Cressey, *The Prison*, pp. 229-59.

in American institutions.[38] Wheeler's interpretation of these results is that most prisoners in Scandinavian institutions enter from a society with a lower incidence of antiauthoritarian attitudes than the United States. Conversely, in American prisons, many offenders bring into the institution antisocial attitudes that are widespread among lower-class groups.[39]

Observations regarding social types or argot roles in prisons also lend support to diffusion hypotheses regarding the inmate code.[40] Schrag has shown that a pattern of four sets of inmate roles oriented around certain focal issues exist in the prison community. These role patterns are identified in the argot of inmates by such labels as "square John," "right guy," "outlaw," "ding," "rapo," and "politician," but Schrag uses more neutral terminology. Similarly, Sykes' report on the New Jersey state prison indicates that the inmates recognize the existence of different behavioral roles in their midst and employ argot labels such as "center man," "hipster," "gorilla," "real man," and "ball buster" to designate these inmate patterns. Apparently, a group of basic patterns of inmate adjustment arise in prison, so although the inmate terminology varies from one prison to another, the patterns are similar.

According to Schrag, prosocial inmates ("square Johns") consistently define role requirements in terms of the legitimate norms of the civilian community of law-abiding citizens, whereas antisocial inmates ("right guys") perceive role requirements in terms of the norms of prisoner society. The latter are loyal to other convicts and engage in minimal contact with prison officials. Pseudo-social prisoners ("politicians") shift their allegiance between legitimate norms and prisoner standards and engage in interaction with both inmates and administrators. Asocial inmates ("outlaws") are rebels against both legitimate norms and prescriptions and the the standards of inmate society.

Schrag summarizes a series of studies demonstrating that these role patterns are of primary importance in understanding inmate behavior within prisons. Among other observations, he notes that each role type is the product of a relatively distinct constellation of background experiences. Prosocial offenders are usually involved in crimes of violence or naïve property offenses. Their behavior appears to be the product of situational stress rather than long-term conditions of family instability or other kinds of disorganization. On the other hand, antisocial inmates are highly recidivistic, frequently involved in crime careers at an early age, and usually from urban, slum area backgrounds. They are gang delinquents "grown up." Pseudosocial inmates have engaged in so-

[38]Wheeler, "The Comparative Analysis of Prison Social Structure," paper read at meetings of the American Sociological Association, September 1962.

[39]See also Mathieson, *The Defenses of the Weak*. Mathieson reports that in the Norwegian prison he studied, "censoriousness" on the part of inmates replaced peer group solidarity. Censoriousness refers to complaining behavior, apparently not unlike the phenomenon of "bitching" in the military services in the United States.

[40]Schrag, "Some Foundations for a Theory of Correction," pp. 309–57; Schrag, "A Preliminary Criminal Typology," *Pacific Sociological Review*, 4 (Spring 1961), 11–16; Sykes, *The Society of Captives*, pp. 84–108.

phisticated and subtle property crimes involving manipulation of other persons rather than coercion and violence. They tend to develop out of relatively stable and comfortable economic backgrounds. Asocial prisoners have been involved in violent, bizarre forms of crime and closely resemble descriptions of "sociopaths." In most cases, such individuals seem to be the product of backgrounds of early and severe parental rejection.

In addition to differences in social background, Schrag notes other correlates of these role patterns. Social participation within the institution varies among these different types, as does the inmates' responses to such prison experiences as treatment programs or punishment. For example, prosocial inmates associate differentially with other prosocial prisoners and engage in frequent contacts with staff members. Prosocial convicts also make considerable use of the various treatment programs in the prison, in contrast to other types who shun such activities.[41]

The important point regarding social types, the inmate code, and the functional and diffusionist arguments is that many prisoners engage in some form of antiadministration, pro-inmate code activity, and these are usually called "right guys." Others cooperate with the authorities, uphold conventional norms, and reject the inmate code, and are termed "square Johns." Antisocial inmates are usually from lower-class backgrounds with long prior records and previous institutional commitments, whereas "square Johns" often show no prior criminal pattern or history of previous incarceration. If the pains of imprisonment lead to emergence of a prisoner code and allegiance to the code, how are prosocial "square Johns" to be explained? Certainly the situational first-offender criminal would be the most traumatized by prison, whereas the recidivism-prone, crime-wise, working-class prisoner would be less likely to experience a prison sentence as severe social rejection. The diffusionist view is that allegiance to an inmate code is the continuation, inside the walls, of a pattern of "rejection of the rejectors," which originated at a much earlier point in their careers. In many cases, the point of origin probably lies in early experiences with the police, juvenile courts, and so on. Elements of the inmate code represent institutional manifestations of hostility to the police and other attitudes widespread in lower-class society. The first offender experiences the pains of imprisonment and societal rejection, but his preprison experiences and involvement in prosocial reference groups outside the walls serve to insulate him from developing any serious loyalty to the inmate code. In addition, insofar as he is a novice in crime, the situational first offender

[41]One of the studies Schrag draws on in this discussion of role types is that by Garabedian in a maximum security prison in a western state. See Peter G. Garabedian, "Social Roles in a Correctional Community," *Journal of Criminal Law, Criminology and Police Science*, 55 (September 1964), 338–47; Garabedian, "Social Roles and Processes of Socialization in the Prison Community," *Social Problems*, 11 (Fall 1963), 139–52.

is likely to be rebuffed in any attempt to play the role of "real criminal" among the antisocial inmates in the prison.

A recent effort to unravel the threads of prison social life has been made by John Irwin and Cressey, who suggest that some elements of institutional culture are indigenous to penal facilities, whereas other facets of prison life are examples of "latent culture" brought in from outside the walls.[42] They suggest that the penitentiary is made up of three subcultures among inmates: a "prison culture," a "criminal subculture," and a "legitimate" or conventional system. Some prisoners, oriented toward "making out" *inside* the institution, often have spent most of their lives in custodial facilities. They participate in conniving and other antiadministration interaction, endeavor to obtain "bonaroos" (special clothing) and other material goods, and are members of a "convict" subculture. "Thieves" are the members of the "criminal" subculture oriented toward the society of lawbreakers *outside* the prison. They exhibit values centered about toughness, courage, and so on; these values are not indigenous to the institution but are widespread in general society. "Thieves" tend to remain aloof from participation in the conniving and machinations of convicts, for they prefer to "do their own time" and "go no rap" with other prisoners. The latter term refers to deliberate noninvolvement with criminal peers in the institution. Members of the legitimate subculture, "do-rights," are "square John" individuals who remain outside the groups of antisocial prisoners.

This analysis by Irwin and Cressey, as well as much of the other material previously discussed, stresses that the prison life that emerges among inmates is significantly influenced by characteristics these individuals import into the institution. This diffusionist view is favored in this book, and we shall see further evidence supporting this argument in the discussion of women's prisons.

Women's Prisons

Although a fairly large collection of works deals with various administrative aspects of women's prisons, few sociological investigations of these places have taken place.[43] One obvious reason for the lack of attention to women's institutions is that they are relatively few. In many states, no prison for females exists autonomous from the state prison because of the small number of female felons to be incarcerated.

[42]John Irwin and Donald R. Cressey, "Thieves, Convicts and the Inmate Culture," *Social Problems*, 10 (Fall 1962), 142-55; see also Julian Roebuck, "A Critique of 'Thieves, Convicts and the Inmate Culture,'" *Social Problems*, 11 (Fall 1963), 193-200.

[43]One early study is Ida Harper, "The Role of the 'Fringer' in a State Prison for Women," *Social Forces*, 31 (October 1952), 53-60.

Two studies of women's prisons have recently been reported, with findings quite similar for the two institutions. One investigation concerned the Federal Reformatory at Alderson, West Virginia,[44] and the other had to do with the state prison for women at Frontera, California.[45]

Rose Giallombardo's research in the federal facility turned up evidence that role problems and administrative conflicts similar to those noted for men's institutions are seen in women's prisons.[46] Many workers in the federal reformatory were hostile to the therapy program introduced a short time earlier. The correctional officers were held to ambiguous role requirements, for they were charged with the responsibility of carrying out counseling without the requisite knowledge for the task. Giallombardo indicates:

> In the new program, with its emphasis on freedom and understanding, the correctional officers were to counsel and to use friendliness and firmness to secure compliance from the inmates. This meant that they had to accept some expressions of aggressive behavior which might be distasteful to them. Their confusion was further intensified because they were expected to control some forms of aggression by suppression just as they had in the earlier program.[47]

Although therapeutic notions had gained entry into the institution and created problems for many workers, the rehabilitation program had not yet become the primary institutional activity. Maintenance and custodial concerns continued to be the primary determinants of organizational operations.[48]

Both studies of women's prisons provide information on the pains of imprisonment in such places.[49] Prisoners in both institutions felt loss of liberty and autonomy. Most inmates in Alderson were from places quite distant from the prison, so they rarely received visitors. The Frontera women were particularly troubled by the forced separation from their families, in that 68 percent were mothers and 59 percent had minor children.[50] Inmates in both places felt markedly deprived of various material goods that make life tolerable in free society, but this feeling was particularly true in the federal facility. In that reformatory, prisoners were dressed in shabby, ill-fitting prison clothing, including brown or white panties cut in the pattern of men's boxer shorts.[51] Although the women prisoners in these two places did not feel physically

[44]Rose Giallombardo, Society of Women (New York: John Wiley & Sons, 1966).
[45]David A. Ward and Gene G. Kassebaum, Women's Prison (Chicago: Aldine Publishing Co., 1965).
[46]Giallombardo, Society of Women, pp. 39–56.
[47]Ibid., pp. 47–48.
[48]Ibid., pp. 57–91.
[49]Ibid., pp. 92–104; Ward and Kassebaum, Women's Prison, pp. 1–29.
[50]Ward and Kassebaum, Women's Prison, pp. 14–16.
[51]Giallombardo, Society of Women, pp. 95–98.

threatened by other inmates, they did find life in a one-sex society quite disagreeable. At Alderson, the inmates complained of the "bitchiness" of other prisoners, contending that most of them were untrustworthy, predatory, and prone to "penitentiary darby," that is, involvement in malicious gossip. The women in Frontera seemed to have relatively little allegiance to an inmate code of loyalty among prisoners.[52]

One other pain of imprisonment in women's prisons is deprivation of heterosexual relations. These psychological problems of imprisonment influence the kind of social life that emerges among female felons, but the last seems particularly critical to an understanding of inmate life.

A large number of inmate social types were observed at Alderson, including "snitchers," "inmate cops," "squares," "jive bitches," and "homeys."[53] The first involves women who interfere with the lives of other prisoners, "squares" are prosocial inmates, "jive bitches" are troublemakers, and the last type consists of women from the same geographical area. "Connects" are inmate connivers, "boosters" are women who steal food and other goods, and "pinners" are lookouts who assist in illicit activities among other prisoners.

The most significant grouping of inmates in both prisons was centered about homosexual activities. David Ward and Gene Kassebaum estimate that about half the prisoners had been involved in at least one homosexual episode during their stay at Frontera.[54] In both places, "lesbians" or "true" homosexuals were distinguished from "penitentiary turnouts" ("jailhouse turnouts" in Frontera).[55] "True" homosexuals had been involved in homosexual activity prior to incarceration. Both studies suggest that patterns of sexual activity make up a variety of social-sexual roles, but the basic division is between "butches" or "stud broads" and "femmes." "Butches" are masculine-appearing women who are the active or aggressive partners in sexual activity, whereas "femmes" play a feminine, passive role in sexual episodes. More true homosexuals take the "stud broad" role than do the "jailhouse turnouts," but some of the latter engage in "butch" behavior.[56]

The evidence in both investigations indicates that prison homosexuality on the part of "jailhouse turnouts" is a transitory pattern of behavior representing an adjustment to prison life that is usually eschewed on release. The investigators contend that disruptions of conventional sex roles attendant on a prison commitment lead most women to involvement in a sexual-affectional dyadic relationship that buffers them against pains of prison life. However,

[52]Ward and Kassebaum, *Women's Prison*, pp. 30–55.

[53]Giallombardo, *Society of Women*, pp. 105–32; "snitchers" are also common in Frontera. See Ward and Kassebaum, *Women's Prison*, pp. 32–37.

[54]Ward and Kassebaum, *Women's Prison*, p. 92.

[55]*Ibid.*, pp. 95–98; Giallombardo, *Society of Women*, pp. 105–32.

[56]Ward and Kassebaum, *Women's Prison*, p. 104.

the difficulties of prison life for women arise out of the sex-role definition of women in American society; hence, Giallombardo avers:

> The deprivations of imprisonment may provide necessary conditions for the emergence of an inmate system, but our findings clearly indicate that the deprivations of imprisonment in themselves are not sufficient to account for the form that the inmate social structure assumes in the male and female prison communities. Rather, general features of American society with respect to the cultural definition and content of male and female roles are brought into the prison setting and function to determine the direction and focus of the inmate cultural systems.[57]

Prison Social Change

We have observed in a number of places in the last chapter and the present one that American prisons have gradually been modified from extremely repressive, punitive institutions to relatively humane places; some prisons have adopted treatment programs as well. In general, the changes wrought in prison life have been relatively crescive so that penitentiaries have drifted with the tide of broad trends in American life. These alterations have occurred over an extended time period, so reform leaders would be difficult to identify at any specific point in time. Much of the history of penal change has also been cyclical; humanitarian developments have been repudiated only to be followed by further humanitarian modifications. This ebb and flow of changes in prison systems has followed closely the shifting fortunes of state political parties.

However, it is possible to single out some instances of deliberate or planned correctional social change, the most prominent case being in California.[58] In that state, since 1943, an orderly and planned series of major improvements has been made in the penal system. These modifications have produced a correctional system generally acknowledged to be the most progressive, treatment-oriented in the United States.

Planned correctional social change, insofar as it occurs at all, tends to take place unobtrusively. In the past two decades, public attention has focused on prison riots and disturbances, which were particularly prominent in the early 1950s. These cases of prisoner insurgency have been viewed as attempts by the captives to obtain penal reforms. Although disturbances do not always produce modifications in correctional practices, they have had that result in at least some instances.

The wave of prison riots in this country began in 1952, with major uprisings

[57]Giallombardo, *Society of Women*, p. 187.

[58]For a history of correctional change in California, see Joseph W. Eaton, *Stone Walls Not a Prison Make* (Springfield, Ill.: Charles C Thomas, Publisher, 1962).

in the Southern Michigan Prison at Jackson and the New Jersey State Prison at Trenton,[59] followed by riots in Idaho, Illinois, Kentucky, Louisiana, Massachusetts, New Mexico, North Carolina, Utah, Ohio, California, Oregon, and Washington, among other states.

A kind of *morphology of prison riots* seemed to be common to these incidents—most of them followed the same general pattern. Prison revolts were preceded by extended periods of uneasiness and tension, often described by prisoners and employees in such expressions as "The joint is 'hot'; it's going to 'blow up.'" Some event, such as a rumor that the guards had beaten an inmate, sparked these tensions, which in turn touched off widespread destruction of property, seizure of hostages, and occasionally assaults on staff members and convicts. After some days of internal disorder in the prison, inmate leaders made demands for correctional reforms, including better food, improved medical care, segregation of sex offenders, and modifications in sentencing and parole practices. The offenders who stepped forward to act as leaders and spokesmen were frequently drawn from the "outlaw" group of violent and asocial persons, and the "right guys" remained in the background.[60] Moreover, many of the prisoners' grievances appeared to be invented after the riot rather than prior to its inception.[61] Negotiations between convicts and state officials usually resulted in promises of improvements in the penal program, at which point the inmates returned to their cells and the riot ended. On some occasions, the state eventually prosecuted the leaders, and the correctional authorities repudiated their agreements.

What was responsible for the unprecedented wave of rioting in prisons in the early 1950s? The American Prison Association produced a report on these disturbances, alleging that they were due to such evils as inadequate financial support for prison programs, inadequate and untrained staffs, widespread idleness, a shortage of well-trained leadership, overcrowding of prisoners in institutions of excessive size, and poor sentencing and parole practices.[62] These factors closely parallel the inmates' grievances. Certain prison uprisings, particularly those in the southern United States, do seem to fit this explanation. For example, a series of protest actions occurred at the Louisiana prison at Angola in 1951, culminating in the slashing of heel tendons by several dozen prisoners. A subsequent inquiry into conditions in that institution turned up

---

[59]For details of the Michigan riot, see John Bartlow Martin, *Break Down the Walls* (New York: Ballantine Books, 1954); for a popular treatment of the New Jersey disturbances, see Peg McGraw and Walter McGraw, *Assignment: Prison Riots* (New York: Holt, Rinehart and Winston, 1954).

[60]Maurice Floch and Frank E. Hartung, "A Social-Psychological Analysis of Prison Riots: An Hypothesis," *Journal of Criminal Law, Criminology and Police Science*, 47 (May–June 1956), 55.

[61]Lloyd E. Ohlin, *Sociology and the Field of Corrections* (New York: Russell Sage Foundation, 1956), pp. 23–24.

[62]Committee on Riots, *Prison Riots and Disturbances* (New York: American Prison Association, 1953).

evidence of severe abuses against inmates which closely fitted the aforementioned list. The public outcry following these disclosures resulted in construction of a new prison in that state.[63]

A number of authorities have criticized this "intolerable conditions" argument as an explanation of all riots. Ohlin has noted that conditions were generally worse in many states where riots had not taken place, whereas the prisons that had suffered disturbances had begun to move in the direction of improved penal practices.[64]

The alternative view of prison riots is a "disequilibrium" one, in which disturbances are said to stem from disruptions in the stability of inmate–administration relations in institutions. Maurice Floch and Frank Hartung offer this kind of explanation for "collective" riots, which they distinguish from uprisings due to brutal conditions.[65] They assert that protests and incidents grow out of the nature of the maximum security prison, with its overcrowding and other features along with the aggregation of a heterogeneous mixture of prisoners, and from the destruction of the semiofficial pattern of informal inmate self-government that occurs when a new reform administration takes over. When reform comes to the "con-run" institution, authorities endeavor to "tighten up" the organization by removing prisoners from positions of power and influence. These moves overlook the fact that the inmate leaders have been a stabilizing force in the prison, enforcing order among other prisoners in exchange for privileges from the administrators. As a result of their fall from power, the leaders turn their attention to subversive ends. They stir up dissatisfaction among other convicts, which smolders until finally triggered by some dramatic incident. These leaders then emerge during and after the riot as the champions of "mistreated prisoners," so they appear to be revolutionaries striving for a better way of life. But the leaders are really seeking a return to the older ways of life, rather than penological reforms.

Ohlin offers some similar hypotheses regarding prison unrest, but he also contends that these disturbances were most common in penitentiaries where reform efforts were only embryonic.[66] Prisons where progressive aims had been translated into programs of education and therapy experienced fewer incidents than places where tightening of security and removal of inmate leaders from influential positions represented the major reforms achieved. Ohlin also maintains that disturbances were fairly common in institutions characterized by decentralization of authority, for in these institutions, cooperation between

[63]Reed Cozart, "What Has Happened to 'America's Worst Prison'?" *Federal Probation*, 19 (December 1955), 32–38.

[64]Ohlin, *Sociology and the Field of Corrections*, p. 23.

[65]Floch and Hartung, "A Social-Psychological Analysis of Prison Riots," pp. 51–57.

[66]Ohlin, *Sociology and the Field of Corrections*, p. 24.

administrative units in the prison had broken down. These conditions produced disruptions in the established expectation system, which controlled relations between staff and inmates. Channels for airing grievances were closed off, leading to increased disciplinary incidents. Efforts on the part of the authorities to repress such incidents by increasing controls over prisoners then led to heightened tension among staff and inmates. The end product of this circular buildup of tension was often a prison riot. Such events seem to have touched off an insurrection in the Oahu Prison.[67]

Prison uprisings have continued, but less frequently than in the 1950s. However, in the past several years, prison riots, disturbances, and turmoil have sprung up again. During 1970 and 1971, dramatic prison incidents occurred in New York jails, Statesville–Joliet Prison in Illinois, and in several other places. One of the most well-publicized cases of prison violence involved an alleged escape attempt in San Quentin Prison in California, by George Jackson, a black prisoner and one of the "Soledad Brothers" charged with murdering a guard in another California prison. The single most violent instance of prison disorder took place in 1971 at Attica State Prison in New York, in which a large number of prisoners and guards were killed during police efforts to regain control of the institution following a prisoner strike and revolt.

What are the causes behind these recent instances of prison disorder? Can we expect more of these outbreaks in the 1970s? To begin with, these new episodes do not appear to be the same as the wave of prison riots that swept the United States during the 1950s. The latter involved large-scale protests and disorders, in which prisoners destroyed property, took hostages, and made various demands on state correctional authorities for prison reform. Most of these disturbances grew out of inmate discontent produced by prison reform efforts.

However, the recent cases of inmate protest and violence seem to stem from different causes. Although the sources of prison turmoil are multiple and complex, American racism is heavily implicated in them. The sense of injustice among black prisoners has increased markedly in the past decade. The writings of Eldridge Cleaver and other Black Panthers present forceful and highly articulate versions of the theme that American society is racist, that many blacks are virtually compelled to respond to the strains of American life by engaging in criminality, that the criminal justice machinery is grossly discriminatory and unfair in its handling of black offenders, that urban police embarked on policies of genocide, as witnessed by armed police attacks on Muslims and Black Panthers, and that blacks incarcerated in prisons are "political prisoners," held captive by their oppressors, not for being lawbreakers,

[67]Richard McCleery, "The Governmental Process and Informal Social Control," in Cressey, The Prison, pp. 149-98; see also Sykes, The Society of Captives, pp. 109-29.

but for being black.[68] Whether or not these views are accurate, a growing portion of the black population in penal institutions maintain these beliefs.

Discontent over perceived racial injustice appears to have been at the heart of protests that ultimately led to the Attica tragedy. Many black prisoners in California also regard parole policies as an instrument used to hold them in prison for excessive lengths of time.

We cannot dismiss these contentions about racial injustice simply as "revolutionary rhetoric" or as the sentiments of a few agitators. These beliefs are widespread among black offenders. Moreover, although some persons might quarrel with some of the assertions, without doubt these sentiments grow out of real injustice and discrimination against blacks, which are pervasive features of American life.

Prison order rests on the consent of the governed, just as it does in the outside society. Historically, most inmates served their time passively, without attempting to overthrow the prison administration or without trying to escape from the penitentiary. Most of them agreed in principle with the view that criminality is "bad" and that criminals deserve to be punished; hence, they believed they should suffer stoically while in prison.

Now, however, we witness American prisons being used to "warehouse" growing proportions of black offenders. As one case in point, about 85 percent of the Attica prisoners were blacks or Puerto Ricans; in addition, California institutions are heavily populated with black inmates, as are many other state penitentiaries. Many of these prisoners have begun to voice the "political prisoner" theme, refusing to acknowledge the moral right of their captors to hold them in custody.

The stage is now set for more violence and disorder in prisons, centering about the grievances of blacks and the efforts of the authorities to maintain order. Moreover, internal reforms of the institution are not likely to curtail these outbreaks. Nothing less than a massive attack on racism in the total society will make much of a dent on the feelings of disenchantment with American life black prisoners now express.

TRAINING-SCHOOL SOCIAL ORGANIZATION

Because this book is primarily concerned with adult lawbreaking, we have discussed only those patterns of juvenile delinquency that are career forerunners of criminality. For the same reason, our commentary on the social workings of correctional agencies centers on adult institutions and organizations. However, we should mention the social structure of training schools, if only

[68]Eldridge Cleaver, *Soul on Ice* (New York: McGraw-Hill Book Co., 1968).

because many adult lawbreakers begin their institutional experiences in these places. We shall briefly sketch the traditional form of social organization in state training schools and then examine some research evidence on these institutions.[69]

Most state training schools have smaller populations than do prisons. In many states, the boys' schools handle a few hundred boys or less, and the girls' schools are even smaller. The administrative staffs of juvenile facilities are also usually smaller than in adult institutions. Training schools normally show a physical structure quite different from that of prisons and reformatories. They are usually unwalled institutions made up of a number of dormitory buildings euphemistically called "cottages." Groups of several dozen or more juveniles, or "wards" as they are often called, inhabit these dormitories, and much of the social life of the institution goes on within these structures. Training schools also include an assortment of other buildings, and so on. Juvenile institutions more closely resemble residential academies or schools than prisons, although many of them appear more rundown and deteriorated. Escapes, or "rambles," as they are often called, are frequent from training schools, partly because of the ease of escape from such places.

The superintendent of the training school traditionally has been the product of the political "spoils system," such as an ex-county sheriff or similar person to whom a political debt is owed. He has often been a singularly unimpressive figure, ill-trained for the job of maintaining and managing a custodial institution. The rest of the staff tends to be divided into two general groups. The first includes work supervisors, teachers, and sometimes social case workers, who deal with the inmates during the day. Also included in this group are the kitchen personnel, clerks, and similar workers. The second general group of employees in the school is made up of cottage supervisors or cottage parents. They manage the wards at night and during those times of the day when the inmates are not involved in some formal program. The cottage workers have the greatest amount of interaction with the wards and the most difficult experiences with them. They are responsible for prevention of runaways and other disturbances of the institutional routine.

Training schools in the past have usually operated a minimal treatment program. Most inmates have been placed in a school program or some kind of vocational or other work experience. Occasionally, they receive individual therapy from a social case worker, but this tends to be a relatively infrequent event.

---

[69]Training schools for girls and detention facilities have gone relatively unstudied. For one excellent study of a private training school for girls, see Raymond J. Adamek and Edward Z. Dager, "Social Structure, Identification and Change in a Treatment-Oriented Institution," *American Sociological Review*, 33 (December 1968), 931–44. For a survey of detention facilities in California, see Helen Sumner, "Locking Them Up," *Crime and Delinquency*, 17 (April 1971), 168–79.

The overriding concern in juvenile institutions has revolved around prevention of escapes and large-scale disturbances. Staff members regard runaway behavior as serious, for even though most fugitives are quickly apprehended and normally do not create any incidents in the surrounding community, the community reacts negatively to escapes. Consequently, a juvenile institution that acquires a reputation for frequent escapes usually receives a good deal of hostile, highly vocal criticism. In turn, employees define runaways as extremely serious.

Juvenile facilities share certain structural shortcomings with their adult counterparts. In both places, uncooperative individuals must be restrained in some way, but a number of potentially effective control techniques are not available to the authorities. Although the training-school personnel can keep their charges "in line" by occasional beatings and other kinds of physical coercion, they must be circumspect in the use of force. Word may get out to the community if beatings become a regular part of the school's disciplinary program. Cottage parents who use physical aggression as a main technique of control are also in some danger of reprisals. The worker may be physically able to intimidate any individual ward but may not emerge the victor in a fight with a half-dozen or more inmates. This is not to say that corporal punishment is never used in juvenile institutions. Coercion beyond the official rules is employed, but it tends to be relatively mild and is used to supplement other control devices.[70]

The tactic commonly employed to deal with uncooperative boys parallels the arrangements in adult prisons. The institutional staff enters into tacit bargains with certain inmate leaders in the dormitories. These older, physically mature, sophisticated juveniles operate "kangaroo courts" in which they coerce other, weaker youths into docile behavior. In addition to keeping order and preventing "rambles," these toughs often use their power to force other inmates into homosexual practices, obtain money from them, and victimize them in other ways.

As these remarks suggest, a prisoner social system exists in juvenile institutions. A kind of inmate code characterizes most training schools. This is a juvenile parallel of that found in prisons, centering around the same kinds of antisocial norms as the adult counterpart, and antiadministration and antitreatment in content. It prescribes "playing it cool" as model behavior for wards, who are expected to do their time as pleasantly as possible without entering into meaningful relationships with staff members.

A pattern of role types also exists in juvenile institutions. The system tends to be relatively simple, based on differences in physical prowess and criminal sophistication. Two major role types emerge in training schools: "toughs" or

---

[70]Sethard Fisher, "Social Organization in a Correctional Residence," *Pacific Sociological Review,* 4 (Fall 1961), 88.

"dukes" and "punks." The former are juveniles who have been in the institution for a relatively long time, have extensive delinquency records, and are physically superior to other inmates. The second group is made up of boys who are physically immature and are often less sophisticated offenders.

The preceding comments are consistent with a body of impressions about state training schools presented some years ago by Albert Deutsch, who traveled around the United States looking at a large sample of these institutions.[71] At the end of his tour, Deutsch reported that ten "deadly sins" characterize most training schools: regimentation, institutional monotony (unvaried diets and the like), mass handling of inmates without regard to individual needs, partisan political domination, public penury, isolation, complacency, excessive physical and mental punishment, "Babelism," and enforced idleness. Babelism was his term for various semantic reforms that are common in corrections, in which "the hole" is renamed the "adjustment center" but the character of the punishment program not changed, the recreation program is retitled "mass treatment," or the name of the institution is changed from Boys' Industrial School to Brown Mountain School for Boys.

Lloyd Ohlin and William Lawrence discuss the treatment problems that arise in such places as training schools where interaction occurs among hostile "clients" and group norms define the model inmate as one who is "playing it cool," that is, refraining from significant involvement with therapeutic agents.[72] Their remarks parallel the earlier ones of Ruth Topping, who noted that treatment of "pseudosocial" delinquents (gang offenders) is complicated by the group interaction that develops among these offenders in institutions.[73] She reported that many delinquents exhibit a classical "crime–punishment" orientation in which they see themselves as serving time to pay their societal debt. Many of these same youngsters disavow any conception of themselves as having problems or in need of therapy. Both these investigations suggest procedures that might circumvent some of these difficulties, including development of treatment efforts centered within cottage units to make use of the inmate social organization in therapy.

Gordon Barker and W. Thomas Adams have described the social structure of a boys' training school in Colorado.[74] They report rigid interactional and communication barriers between inmates and staff members, along with a pervasive spirit of authoritarianism in which the offenders do not identify with the values and goals of the staff. The authors also note the existence of a

[71]Albert Deutsch, "A Journalist's Impressions of State Training Schools," Focus, 28 (March 1949), 33–40.

[72]Lloyd E. Ohlin and William C. Lawrence, "Social Interaction Among Clients As a Treatment Problem," Social Work, 4 (April 1959), 3–13.

[73]Ruth Topping, "Treatment of the Pseudo-Social Boy," American Journal of Orthopsychiatry, 8 (April 1943), 353–60.

[74]Gordon H. Barker and W. Thomas Adams, "The Social Structure of a Correctional Institution," Journal of Criminal Law, Criminology and Police Science, 49 (January–February 1959), 417-22.

status order among the inmates, heavily structured around displays of physical toughness and victimization of peers. They speculate that this system may be the result, at least in part, of widespread insecurities among delinquent boys regarding masculinity.[75]

Howard Polsky has provided a detailed description of the social structure among inmates through a study of the boys residing in a cottage within a private correctional institution.[76] He reports a diamond-shaped status system in which a few boys have high or low rank among their peers, with the largest group falling into a middle range. Polsky maintains that this system is independent of the particular youths who fill it in any particular period, for it persists relatively unaltered over time, even though cottage residents enter and leave the system. Departure of a leader, for example, produces competition, conflict, and jockeying among inmate aspirants for the position, followed by reestablishment of equilibrium. According to Polsky, the status types in the cottage include "toughs" and "con artists" at the apex of the order, "quiet types" in the middle range, and "bushboys" and "scapegoats" on the bottom of the system. The latter are subjected to unrelenting physical and psychological attacks by those higher in the order. Probably the most significant of Polsky's observations is that the institutional staff abets the inmate system. He notes:

> Thus, the theme of aggression with all its authoritarian overtones is structurally configured in the cottage. Under its roof the cottage parents join the older boys in scapegoating the defenseless low-status boys—the sneaks, punks, and the sick. The latter 'deserve' the beatings because of *their* provocativeness and 'unfitness.' The unwritten compact of cottage parents and toughs makes it unbearable for the 'deviants' because they are blamed for everything.[77]

A recent examination of a training school in California indicates that even in that state, where treatment goals have been emphasized in state institutions for several decades, training schools place primary emphasis on regimentation of youngsters in the interests of controlling them.[78] In this environment, therapeutic activities are subordinated to custodial ends. As part of this study, Fisher observed the social structure among inmates.[79] He found that both the wards and supervisors rank and victimize certain boys; moreover, the low-ranked boys in the eyes of officials are also the low-status inmates in the ward hierar-

[75]*Ibid.*

[76]Howard W. Polsky, "Changing Delinquent Subcultures: A Social-Psychological Approach," *Social Work*, 4 (October 1959), 3–15; Polsky, *Cottage Six* (New York: Russell Sage Foundation, 1962).

[77]Polsky, *Cottage Six*, p. 133.

[78]Carl F. Jesness, *The Fricot Ranch Study* (Sacramento: State of California, Department of the Youth Authority, 1965), pp. 8–17. A generous portion of this report appears in Don C. Gibbons, *Delinquent Behavior* (Englewood Cliffs, N.J.: Prentice-Hall, 1970), pp. 236–47; Peter G. Garabedian and Gibbons, eds., *Becoming Delinquent* (Chicago: Aldine Publishing Co., 1970), pp. 226–37.

[79]Fisher, "Social Organization in a Correctional Residence," pp. 87–93.

chy. Staff workers often interpret disruptive behavior by low-status boys as evidence of psychological maladjustment rather than as flowing out of the social structure and interactional patterns among offenders. Low-ranked, victimized inmates are defined as "mess-ups," implying that they willfully engage in disapproved behavior out of psychological tensions. Instead of attempting to undermine the inmate system, authorities react to boys in its terms, so institutional rewards are differentially accorded to boys with high status among their peers.

Some attention has been given to organizational problems that develop in training schools when rehabilitation is introduced as a major goal. One of the earliest warnings of the potential problems was sounded by R. L. Jenkins,[80] who indicated that treatment clinics are likely to become mere institutional "window dressing" if they are simply grafted on to a custodial program and unconnected to the rest of the institution. They become reduced to making diagnostic and treatment recommendations diverted to custodial ends or systematically ignored. To be effective, clinical operations must be heavily centered around the cottage groups and cottage personnel.

More recently, George Weber has identified a number of areas in which conflict arises between professional and nonprofessional personnel in institutions where treatment is introduced.[81] One major problem he identifies, and also noted by Ohlin,[82] centers around the role difficulties that develop for cottage workers. Their authority position is often reduced or undermined with the introduction of treatment goals. They are likely to feel that their prestige has been lowered with the entry of professional personnel into the program. Role redefinition also occurs, and the cottage worker is expected to run a quiet and well-disciplined dormitory and to contribute to therapy. But because he is not given clear instructions as to how he is to accomplish these ends, he experiences much the same role dilemma noted for prison guards. Weber and others suggest that a number of negative consequences develop from when "rehabilitation" is introduced into previously custodial institutions.[83] Staff cooperation is reduced and replaced by conflicts between professional and custodial personnel, defensive reactions develop among cottage workers, and other difficulties arise. Inmates manipulate these conflicts to their own ends by playing competing groups against each other.

[80]R. L. Jenkins, "Treatment in an Institution," *American Journal of Orthopsychiatry*, 11 (January 1941), 85–91.

[81]George H. Weber, "Conflicts Between Professional and Non-Professional Personnel in Institutional Delinquency Treatment," *Journal of Criminal Law, Criminology and Police Science*, 48 (May–June 1957), 26–43; see also Weber, "Emotional and Defensive Reactions of Cottage Parents," in Cressey, *The Prison*, pp. 189–228.

[82]Lloyd E. Ohlin, "The Reduction of Role-Conflict in Institutional Staff," *Children*, 5 (March–April 1958), 65–69.

[83]Weber, "Emotional and Defensive Reactions of Cottage Parents"; Mayer N. Zald, "Power Balance and Staff Conflict in Correctional Institutions," *Administrative Science Quarterly*, 7 (June 1962), 22–49.

The most ambitious research on training schools to date compares six juvenile institutions.[84] These training schools varied in size, several being small institutions and others having inmate populations of well over 100 boys. Some of the schools were private institutions; others were state schools. These facilities also varied in terms of program, ranging from institutions favoring obedience and strict conformity to treatment oriented, milieu operations. The researchers supposed that variations in size might influence the social structure of the institutions, as would the different auspices under which these places are operated. State schools should be under greater pressure from the general public. Finally, the investigators hypothesized that the treatment-oriented schools would be more conflict ridden than the strictly custodial plants.

In general, the findings supported these contentions. Among other things, the institutions varied in terms of the leadership "styles" of their executives. The staff members exhibited different perspectives on delinquents, the workers in custodial schools viewing boys as more willful than did employees in treatment institutions. Rather marked variations in the level of staff conflict existed from school to school, with greatest staff conflict in the rehabilitation-oriented institution in which a high degree of staff *interdependence* existed. That is, in the milieu treatment school, staff members representing different segments of the school program were in frequent communication with one another and were involved in much joint decision making.

PROBATION AND PAROLE ORGANIZATION

Parole and probation agencies can justifiably be discussed together, even though they differ in some important ways. The major dissimilarity is that parole involves more serious, criminalistic offenders than does probation; the former handles persons processed through institutions, whereas the latter does not. Penal commitment represents the harshest penalty outside of capital punishment, so it tends to be used with the most difficult and intractable law violators, whereas probation is a disposition commonly reserved for persons lacking in criminalistic orientation. Even though parole and probation differ in this respect, both deal with offenders in the community and have certain organizational features in common.

Our commentary on parole is mainly concerned with adult systems, in that juvenile parole programs are nonexistent or only slightly developed in many states. In particular, the notes on the general organization of parole should be read as a description of adult systems.[85]

[84]David Street, Robert D. Vinter, and Charles Perrow, *Organization for Treatment* (New York: The Free Press, 1966).

[85]For a study on juvenile parole, see William R. Arnold, *Juveniles on Parole* (New York: Random House, 1970).

The Structure of Parole and Probation

Parole programs in the United States have developed out of changes in criminal laws, which have established indeterminate sentences for offenses within the limits of minimum and maximum statutory penalties. Although criminal codes vary from one state to another, they have the same general structure. They allow for alternative penalties for convicted offenders, so that individuals can be placed on probation or committed to institutions. The maximum periods of incarceration are specified in statutes, but prisoners can be released at various points prior to expiration of their maximum sentences. Paroling authorities have been established to determine when inmates should be released from the penitentiary, to serve the remainder of their sentence under supervision in the community.

The paroling function is structured in different ways in the various states. In some, *ex officio* boards made up of government officials serve as the paroling agency; individuals who have major governmental responsibilities elsewhere make release decisions "on the side." The more common arrangement, particularly in the larger states, involves an agency called the "Board of Prison Terms and Paroles," "Adult Authority," or some similar label. The state governor appoints a group of persons, usually for fixed terms of office, and then gives the group the full-time task of deciding about release of prisoners to parole. Normally no qualifications are required for service on the board, but members are commonly drawn from corrections, law enforcement, legal, or academic backgrounds. In some states operating under this pattern, the board discharges two functions. It acts as a quasi-judicial board, setting release dates for prisoners, and it also administers the parole supervision organization. These boards establish policies for parole supervision and employ and supervise parole agents as well. However, recent correctional thinking has tended to define these functions as incompatible, so certain states, such as California, have removed the administrative task from the paroling agency and placed it within the correctional department.

In theory, decisions to release or not to release an inmate are based on such criteria as his behavioral change and favorable prognosis for success on parole.[86] In fact, the decisions tend not to be made in this fashion. For one thing, parole boards are often limited in the degree to which they can determine release dates by statutory minimum sentences, which require that persons convicted of certain crimes spend no less than some specific period in prison. The board frequently sets minimum sentences near the beginning of the prisoner's stay in the institution, so they are determined before a sufficient period of time has elapsed to estimate the person's response to therapy. In

---

[86]One of the few studies of parole board decision making is Don M. Gottfredson and Kelley B. Ballard, Jr., "Differences in Decisions Associated with Decision Makers," *Journal of Research in Crime and Delinquency*, 3 (July 1966), 112–19.

addition, parole boards are often made up of members ill-trained to estimate the rehabilitative prospects for inmates. Indeed, the knowledge on which such decisions must be based is not at hand, so no paroling authority, however assembled, could make accurate judgments. Finally, boards have to contend with factors other than the needs of the prisoners. In particular, they must be sensitive to public pressure, which demands that certain offenders be kept in prison for long periods of time. The decision to release a sex offender who will return to a small community from which he was convicted is frequently more contingent on estimates of the level of community tolerance than on the offender's needs. The prisoner is paroled if the board judges that such a decision will provoke only a slight amount of "heat."[87]

For such reasons, parole decisions are normally intuitive and tend to be based on a mixture of considerations: the type of offense, the offender's needs, and the general public's reactions. They are usually not as individualized as parole theory would lead one to suppose. Instead, paroling agencies develop informal precedents, and prison terms handed out for various offenses average out to a fairly specific figure, such as three years, with little variation around that average. Any marked departure from this standard becomes the focus of inmate grievances. Prison unrest and disturbances sometimes occur as inmates try to reestablish the former precedent in response to shifts in parole policies.

Variations are also seen in the structure of probation services. In some states, probation is an operation attached to parole services, and probation is sometimes shunted because of the heavy work demands of parole. As a consequence, few offenders are placed on probation. In a number of states, such as California, probation is county operated, with individual probation services in the various counties. Each of these is autonomous and managed by county supervisors or commissioners.

One variation between probation and parole, in addition to patterns of placement within governmental systems, has to do with involvement of probation officers in selection of offenders to be placed under their control. Parole agents receive their "clients" from the institution, without any option to select or reject in terms of some set of eligibility criteria. But in both adult and juvenile probation services, the workers play a major role in the selection process. In juvenile operations, they compile information about youths undergoing court hearings. This collection of data, called the "social investigation," is a principal source of evidence on which adjudication and disposition of

[87]For a harsh view of the California paroling agency, the Adult Authority, see Assembly Committee on Criminal Procedure, *Deterrent Effects of Criminal Sanctions* (Sacramento: California State Assembly, 1968). That study indicated that the paroling agency has been increasing the length of prison sentences over the years without any effect on recidivism rates. Parole decisions are made in terms of intuitive hunches. On occasion, allegations of crimes the parole candidate may have been involved in are considered, as well as other questionable kinds of information, in the decision to parole or not to parole the person. This committee called for drastic reforms in paroling policies in California.

cases is based. Similarly, in adult probation, convicted offenders are referred to probation agents for "presentence investigation." The presentence report prepared by the officer becomes, in turn, a major consideration in disposition of the case. This report normally includes the officer's sentence recommendations, which the judge customarily follows in his decision.

On Being a Probation or Parole Officer

Much of the literature on probation and parole implies that workers in these operations are highly-trained professionals who administer intensive and valuable therapy to correctional "clients." But several "time and motion" studies of probation officers indicate that they are harried by clerical tasks and huge case loads, which prevent them from rendering much professional help. For example, Lewis Diana investigated the kind and amount of assistance given to juvenile probationers in the Allegheny County (Pittsburgh), Pennsylvania, juvenile court.[88] He found that the average number of contacts between probationers and probation officers was about five within a sixteen-month period. Moreover, these meetings were for the most part quite superficial, only about 14 percent of the wards receiving any sort of casework treatment. Diana also found an inverse relationship between frequency of probation contacts and later criminality; offenders who had the least interaction with officers were less recidivistic than boys who had received more frequent assistance. These findings probably indicate that many juveniles placed on probation are not seriously delinquent, need little supervision from probation agents, and turn out to be "self-correctors." Accordingly, the officer tends to work with more serious offenders, ignoring the "low risk" cases in his case load.

Another study parallel to that of Diana turned up similar findings. Ralph England found that a group of adult probationers had a recidivism rate of only 17.7 percent but that this low rate was unrelated to treatment.[89] Most of the offenders received only routine surveillance and superficial help from the probation officers. England attributes the generally high success rates for probation as a form of disposition to most of the persons placed on probation being essentially "prosocial" and not in need of intensive resocialization.

Gertrude Hengerer's study of several juvenile probation departments suggests that most of what goes on in probation is something other than treatment.[90] The workers examined in that study spent most of their time writing

[88]Lewis Diana, "Is Casework in Probation Necessary?" *Focus*, 34 (January 1955), 1–8.

[89]Ralph W. England, Jr., "What is Responsible for Satisfactory Probation and Postprobation Outcome?", *Journal of Criminal Law, Criminology and Police Science*, 47 (March–April 1957), 667–76; see also England, "A Study of Postprobation Recidivism Among 500 Federal Offenders," *Federal Probation*, 19 (September 1955), 10–16. See also a more recent report that presents similar findings regarding federal probation work: Albert Wahl and Daniel Glaser, "Pilot Time Study of the Federal Probation Officer's Job," *Federal Probation*, 27 (September 1963), 20–25.

[90]Gertrude M. Hengerer, "Organizing Probation Services," *National Probation and Parole Association Yearbook, 1953*, pp. 45–59.

reports, driving from one place to another, and similar operations. They had large case loads and little time to provide therapy to their wards.

Lloyd Ohlin, Herman Piven, and Donnell Pappenfort[91] have closely examined the role dilemmas of probation and parole officers. These authors indicate that probation and parole services have traditionally been assigned a number of not entirely compatible functions. Probationers and parolees are supposed to be supervised, assisted, and treated, but at the same time officers are expected to collect fines, "protect society" in various ways, and perform other tasks having little to do with helping offenders. These agents must contend with persistent suspicion and hostility directed at them and their charges by the police and other groups in the community. Because of this antagonism, agencies often come to be as much concerned about shielding the organization from criticism as they are about protecting clients. Thus, officers spend some of their time giving speeches to citizen groups in which they argue for the merits of their services, agitate for greater financial support, and defend their agencies against charges of "softness," "coddling," and so on.

Several other specific consequences follow from the uneasy status of probation and parole in the public eye. First, the "public relations" orientations that develop frequently mean that occupational mobility in these agencies is more dependent on "public relations" talents than on technical competency. Organizational "con men" ascend to supervisory positions in the operation. Second, two main kinds of workers, "punitive" and "protective" agents, have developed. The former carry guns, regard themselves as law-enforcement officers rather than rehabilitative agents, are not trained in social service work, and define their responsibilities as principally those of protecting society. They attempt to coerce their charges into appropriate behavior, and punish noncooperative cases by revoking their parole or probation status. The "protective" agents sometimes have had training in corrections and regard themselves as responsible for treatment, but vacillate back and forth from protecting the public to helping clients.

Additional role problems have cropped up in parole–probation agencies in recent years following the recruitment of large numbers of "welfare workers" into these systems. The officer trained in social work enters these fields expecting to protect clients and to treat them as he would in other welfare settings. He comes prepared to apply "generic" principles in this setting. However, he soon discovers that his training has not covered the difficulties he encounters with treatment in corrections. Social work education is not much concerned with the special problems of dealing with captive, hostile persons. These subjects differ markedly from the conventional volunteer client

[91]Lloyd E. Ohlin, Herman Piven, and Donnell M. Pappenfort, "Major Dilemmas of the Social Worker in Probation and Parole," *NPPA Journal*, 2 (July 1956), 211–25.

who seeks help. The probation–parole social worker also finds that his training has not equipped him to deal with authority problems. He is not prepared to function within the special structure of corrections as both a representative of the punitive social control system and as a helper. In addition, the agent discovers that he lacks the knowledge to understand different client types or deal effectively with these types.

The agent trained in social work also discovers discrepancies between probation–parole settings and traditional images of the welfare agency. For one thing, the rules of client supervision, such as those forbidding probationers or parolees from using alcohol, differentiate correctional settings from noncorrectional ones. Other rules restrain the kinds of decisions workers can make, and the needs of the client must frequently be subordinated to these demands. The correctional social worker may experience considerable identity conflict because these agency rules and procedures force him to act in ways that depart from the conventional picture of his professional role.

According to Ohlin and his associates, the outcome of inadequate educational preparation and the discrepancies encountered between correctional and conventional welfare agencies is varied in form. Some workers solve these dilemmas by getting out of correctional work or out of social work entirely. Others stay in probation–parole, but with different "styles" of work adjustment. Those in relatively autonomous systems may be able to deport themselves in a fashion close enough to their notion of the welfare worker role to preserve a "social worker" identity. In most restrictive agencies, the agent may try to evade demands he regards as "unprofessional," such as collection of fines, and thereby retain a social worker role conception. But this arrangement is difficult to sustain over a long period of time and is also productive of marginal and ambivalent self-identification. Some workers become reconciled to the peculiarities of restrictive correctional settings and redefine their role as a special type social worker. They gradually lose interest in, or contact with, the general social welfare literature and social worker organizations.

Several studies lend support to this picture of the probation–parole agent and his occupational problems. In one of these studies, nearly 400 probation officers from various parts of the United States filled out a questionnaire on tasks they felt to be appropriate or inappropriate.[92] Most qualified as "professionals," in that 88 percent possessed bachelor's degrees, while 16 percent had completed master's degrees. Most of these officers agreed that various referral services and counseling activities are appropriate probation responsibilities. But these same agents demonstrated a good deal of disagreement and confusion about various law enforcement and supervisory actions. Some felt that the officer should assist the sheriff in arresting an absconding proba-

[92]Dale E. Van Laningham, Merlin Taber, and Rita Dimants, "How Adult Probation Officers View Their Job Responsibilities," Crime and Delinquency, 12 (April 1966), 97–108.

tioner; some thought he should make surprise home visits or contact the probationer's employer to check on work behavior, or engage in other surveillance activities. Some officers felt obliged to order probationers to pay their bills, refrain from hanging around pool rooms, or even go to church or marry their pregnant girl friends. At the same time, many of the workers regarded these as inappropriate responsibilities. Nonetheless, supervisory actions in which an offender is coerced into a line of conduct are often required of probation officers, even though they may regard these actions as alien to their "helping" role.

Seymour Gross inquired into the occupational activities of the eighty-four juvenile probation officers in Minnesota.[93] These workers are representative of the newer breed of "welfare worker," for 94 percent of them had some college training, 90 percent had bachelor's degrees, and 23 percent had master's degrees. Some indication of the extent to which these individuals had become dissociated from social welfare can be found in their reading habits. About half asserted they subscribed to *Federal Probation*, a correctional journal available without charge, but only a few subscribed to social work publications. In a similar vein, 83 percent said they read *Federal Probation*, while much smaller numbers read any other professional journal.

The officers in this study were also asked to indicate the factors they weighed most heavily in their recommendations about disposition of offenders. The agents contended that the juvenile's potential for more delinquent activity was the most important factor, and the need for psychotherapy and other considerations of that kind were less important.

More research on the decision-making behavior of probation and parole workers is surely in order, for few data are at hand on this question. In another investigation regarding juvenile probation officers, Francesca Alexander asked a group of agents who worked with female delinquents to choose girls they thought had a good or poor prognosis for nondelinquent behavior.[94] She endeavored to discover the bases on which they differentiated these two groups of delinquent girls. Alexander indicates that delinquents regarded as having a favorable prognosis tended to be of better economic status than the poor prognosis cases and were more commonly Caucasian girls, whereas the poor prognosis delinquents were more often Negroes. The good prognosis cases were thought to be the products of situational causation, whereas girls judged to be poor risks were seen as emotionally troubled. In short, the workers appeared to reach negative judgments about those girls who were from social backgrounds dissimilar to their own.

[93]Seymour Z. Gross, "Biographical Characteristics of Juvenile Probation Officers," *Crime and Delinquency*, 12 (April 1966), 109–16.

[94]Francesca Alexander, "A Preliminary Report on a Pilot Investigation of Some Social-Psychological Variables Influencing the Probation Officer," paper delivered at the Pacific Sociological Association meetings, 1964.

SUMMARY

This chapter has provided an overview of the social workings of correctional organizations. Much of the commentary has suggested a fairly dismal outlook for therapeutic endeavors in corrections, for agencies that press in this direction appear beset by all kinds of difficulties. Yet the prospects for treatment may not be entirely bleak. In any event, the matter of rehabilitation has only been addressed tangentially up to this point. In the next chapter, we shall consider a more direct and detailed study of "people-changing" activities that might be directed at lawbreakers.

20

TREATMENT
OF
OFFENDERS

We have observed at a number of points that the rehabilitative philosophy regarding handling of lawbreakers is a relatively recent development. Throughout most of history, offenders have been made to suffer so that society might extract retribution from them or potential law violators might be deterred from that course of action. The notion that punishment might also prevent recurrence of deviant behavior by the person being punished, because of his desire to avoid pain, has also been around for some time. But the view that the correctional processes should strive to reform, resocialize, modify, or remake the criminal so that he will refrain from further lawbreaking is of recent origin.

Since the therapeutic perspective is a late development, a number of indications of its immaturity can be found. These shortcomings can be seen in the correctional literature, such as *Federal Probation*, discussing rehabilitative hypotheses or ventures. For one thing, the treatment point of view is hardly more than a broad orientation to offenders, which stresses that something positive should be done to miscreants but does not spell out details. As we shall see in this chapter, programs designed to rehabilitate criminals or delinquents are frequently confused with activities directed at other goals. Contemporary correctional therapy programs are often based on vague assumptions about the etiology of lawbreaking or causal formulations that are empirically questionable. Finally, rehabilitation has been talked about a good deal more than it has been implemented in correctional practice. Accordingly, in this and the following chapter, we shall be hard pressed to discover much firm evidence about the effectiveness of any tactic of treatment.

The contemporary student of criminology might look back on earlier practices as "barbaric" or "senseless." But, at any point in time, the things done to offenders "make sense" because they are buttressed by images of man that rationalize the practices. In earlier times, when life was mean and harsh, early death from natural causes a common occurrence, and life expectancy short, societies had little hesitation in putting deviants to death. We have already noted that the classical views of punishment in the late 1700s were predicated on a conception of men as willful hedonists; hence, criminals were seen as individuals who had made deliberate decisions to be bad. Such persons could be deflected from criminality by judicious application of some kind of pain. The classical picture of the willful law violator has lingered, remaining the most fashionable orientation to offenders among both laymen and correctional workers. This image of the willful criminal lies behind endeavors to correct criminality by processing offenders through regimented programs involving work training or allied activities. Defenders of these programs maintain that when criminals are forced to conform to rules or are compelled to work regularly, they learn "good habits," and these experiences will carry over to their lives outside penal institutions.

Aside from the neoclassical ideas about criminality, two markedly different images of lawbreakers serve as the underpinnings of modern-day treatment proposals and practices. One holds that offenders are psychologically "sick" persons who need the services of a psychiatrist, whereas the other argues that law violators are no less "normal" than citizens generally. A number of tactics have been contrived around these two perspectives, and most of this chapter will be devoted to an examination of these different approaches.[1]

THE DEVELOPMENT OF TREATMENT

In Chapter Eighteen, we saw that humanitarian gestures made toward offenders during the past century have modified the conditions of punishment. Prisoners have been incarcerated under more relaxed and humane conditions than was once the case. In most modern prisons, inmates are well fed, their medical needs are served, they are allowed visitors, receive an unlimited number of letters, see movies and listen to radios in their cells, and so on. Youths in training schools are allowed to move about the institutional grounds quite freely, are usually protected from severe abuse by staff members or other wards, go into the community to engage in athletic events, are allowed home visits or leaves from the school, and so on. These developments, and many others as well, are examples of humanitarian reforms.

We are enthusiastically in favor of humanitarian moves. In our view, offenders are still dealt with in overly harsh ways, so humanitarianism could go still further. However, humanitarianism is often confused with treatment. Not infrequently, citizens and correctional workers assume that enlightened processing of lawbreakers must have therapeutic consequences. But the hope that good food and other forms of humane handling will cause deviants to mend their ways is naïve, for these actions are not directed at the factors that have drawn individuals into criminality. Treatment has to do with specific

---

[1]The discussion of treatment in this chapter is an abbreviated version of the analysis of treatment theory and therapeutic programs found in Don C. Gibbons, *Changing the Lawbreaker* (Englewood Cliffs, N.J.: Prentice-Hall, 1965).

efforts designed to modify social-psychological characteristics of persons, rather than with humane handling of them.

Korn and McCorkle have incisively stated the case for maintaining the distinction between humanitarianism and therapy. They point out:

It is the tragedy of modern correction that the impulse to help has become confused with treatment and seems to require defense as treatment. One of the more ironic difficulties with this position is that when one makes "rehabilitation" the main justification for humane handling of prisoners one has maneuvered oneself into a position potentially dangerous to the humanitarian viewpoint. What if humane treatment fails to rehabilitate—shall it then be abandoned? The isolated survivals of flogging and other "tough" techniques which still disgrace American penology remain to remind us that this is no mere academic question. The bleak fact is that just as the monstrous punishments of the eighteenth century failed to curb crime, so the more humane handling of the twentieth century has equally failed to do so.[2]

The confusion about what is and is not treatment extends to other programs, in addition to those developed to relieve the grimness of correctional experiences. Most modern institutions provide a variety of school activities and vocational training operations for inmates. These are sometimes pointed to as "treatment" in contrast to other operations identified as "custodial." However, these services, which have been created to implement the growing emphasis on rehabilitation as a correctional goal, represent *adjuncts* to treatment.

Endeavors such as education or vocational training are different from humanitarian acts, but they are not treatment programs. For example, the rationale behind inmate classification programs involves more than simply an interest in reducing the severity of serving time. The justification is that thorough investigation of the inmate's background is a prerequisite for effective treatment and custodial decisions. As a consequence, well-developed classification programs collect a mass of information about newly arrived prisoners, which is presented in a document called the "Admission Summary." This record becomes the basis for various institutional decisions made about these persons. But classification is only the starting point of treatment. Classification activities produce diagnoses and recommendations about what should be done with the prisoner, whereas implementation of the therapy recommendations constitutes treatment.

Other programs, such as vocational or educational training, religious activities, recreational participation, or prerelease planning, are examples of adjuncts to treatment because none deals directly with some therapy problem of the

[2]Richard Korn and Lloyd W. McCorkle, "Resocialization Within Walls," *Annals of The American Academy of Political and Social Science*, no. 293 (May 1954), 94–95.

prisoner. Vocational experiences may improve the rehabilitation potential of the offender subjected to such a program, to the extent that he acquires good work habits and vocational skills. But vocational training is likely to have some impact only when accompanied by some kind of direct resocialization experience in which the inmate comes to modify his negative attitudes toward work. Criminals engage in lawbreaking, not because they are unemployed or unemployable but because they embrace attitudes that devalue the importance of conventional work careers. If this is the case, offenders may be helped to a successful law-abiding adjustment by receiving some vocational aid, but only insofar as their perspectives on work are changed through involvement in therapy.

Let us now examine the theories of treatment that have grown up in corrections.[3] Rehabilitative theory has been heavily larded with psychogenic contentions picturing the offender as psychologically disturbed or "sick." In this view, the criminal is a parallel of the neurotic or psychotic individual, except his personality pathology is expressed in an illegal fashion. This perspective sees offenders as analogous to machines wired in a defective manner. The therapeutic corollary is that lawbreakers need to be "rewired" by a psychiatrist or some other psychiatric technician who can delve inside their psyches.

This approach to law violators, which divides the world into "bad guys" who are "sick," and "good guys" (correctional workers and other citizens) who are emotionally healthy, has been dominant in the rehabilitative theories with which correctional agents have operated.[4] The view remains vigorously alive, even though evidence examined in Chapter Seven and succeeding chapters runs counter to psychogenic arguments. Most findings uncovered by sociologists indicate that the large majority of law-violating deviants are relatively well socialized and "normal."

Some major improvements are in order in the operating principles on which treatment is based. Closer links must be forged between the etiological facts about criminality and the assumptions on which strategies of therapy are based. In other words, the treatment implications of the findings reported in Chapters Twelve through Seventeen need to be spelled out. If many lawbreakers are relatively normal individuals, but with group-supported antisocial attitudes and positive self-images of themselves as "thieves" and so on, rehabilitative theories will need to take these matters into account.

Existing versions of treatment theory are deficient in other ways, in addition to their inattention to sociogenic variables in deviant behavior. Much of this theory fails to acknowledge variations among types of lawbreakers. As Chapters Twelve through Seventeen have indicated, offenders constitute a

---

[3]Gibbons, *Changing the Lawbreaker*, pp. 6–12.

[4]See Stanton Wheeler, "The Social Sources of Criminology," *Sociological Inquiry*, 32 (Spring 1962), 139–59, for a discussion of some of the reasons why sociological theories have played an insignificant part in most correctional programs.

disparate collection of individuals. Although many criminals and delinquents are "normal," these persons are not all alike in attitudinal or self-image terms. Different tactics of therapy may be in order for these various patterns. Some persons fit the psychiatric picture of the abnormal offender, so psychotherapeutic activities may be called for in these cases. In summary, much of the treatment theory now in existence is based on overly simplified assumptions about law violators. If rehabilitation is to become a major goal of corrections, a more detailed form of treatment theory must be developed. We shall return to this matter in more detail later in this chapter.

SOME NEGATIVE VIEWS ON TREATMENT

Not everyone is sanguine about the prospects of rehabilitating offenders; but neither is the therapeutic orientation everywhere applauded. Many criminologists and sociologists question whether most offenders can be treated, however laudable that goal might be. Full-blown efforts at treatment will cost a great deal more money than has so far been invested in rehabilitation. Correctional skeptics see little justification for supposing that financial support for therapeutic programs will be forthcoming in the decades ahead. The pessimists on this issue also contend that law enforcement and correctional processes that single out offenders for attention inevitably stigmatize these persons, severely constricting their opportunities for law-abiding conduct. Once they are publicly identified as "bad" persons, this label stays with them and drives them into secondary deviance; they reorganize their lives around their status as "outsiders." Even if lawbreakers did not encounter these liabilities from being dealt with as criminals or delinquents, therapy would be difficult to accomplish because it requires offenders to take on negative views of themselves or to engage in self-rejection. The psychological price is too high for most law violators, who tend instead to reject their rejectors. Instead of blaming themselves for their predicament, they deflect blame onto "society." The offender who holds society responsible for his actions is hardly a likely candidate for therapy.

Another negative view of the prospects for treatment comes from those who stress the varied educational and training backgrounds from which correctional workers are drawn. Little progress has been made toward the standardization of training and knowledge of treatment workers. Great gaps continue in our knowledge of the basic correctional task, for we are still a long way from proven scientific generalizations regarding causation, which would provide the basis for a precise field of human engineering, correctional work. Because we do not often know what is "wrong" with the offender, we cannot be sure how to treat him. The consequence is that correctional therapy is a form of "tinkering" with individuals rather than an analog to medical practice or some allied professional activity involving relatively precise knowledge and skills.[5] Finally, many argue that the prospects for changing this correctional situation in the direction of greater precision and efficiency are dim at best.

Although many of these contentions about obstacles to rehabilitation are plausible, it is too early to tell whether such hypotheses are entirely accurate. Most of these arguments are speculative and conjectural rather than based on empirical research. But if they turn out to be correct, these hypotheses will probably apply most forcefully to treatment endeavors within penal institutions. Perhaps offenders can be resocialized, but less easily within walls than in other circumstances. The description of maximum security prisons in Chapter Nineteen suggested that to restructure these places in such a way as to carry on effective treatment within them is difficult at best. Because of security requirements, little time is available for activities other than counting, cell-searches, and so on. Prisoners must be regimented and ordered about if they are to be controlled. In addition, the inmate social system places the prisoner who shows signs of "reform" under great pressure. For these and other reasons, penal institutions strike many observers as most unlikely locations for therapeutic endeavors. There may be a good deal to recommend in a correctional program in which the offender's penal career would be divided into dissimilar episodes. The law violator might be placed in a prison for a time to satisfy demands that he be punished, and while there simply serve time under relatively humane conditions. The treatment might not be started until he is released from the institution. Such a program would reverse the current order of things, in which most therapy occurs within the prison.

THE NATURE OF TREATMENT[6]

Treatment consists of some explicit activity designed to alter or remove conditions operating on offenders, which are responsible for their behavior. What is the nature of these conditions to which therapy is directed? Our view is that criminal and delinquent activities are a function of *definitions of the situation*, which refer to individuals' self-concepts and attitudes toward criminality and other matters, that is, the belief systems and interpretive frameworks by which they "make sense" out of sensory perceptions and direct their behavior. If offenders are to be directed toward law-abiding behavior, certain aspects of their self-images, attitudes, and beliefs must be modified.

[5]The notion of "tinkering" and the "tinkering trades" comes from Erving Goffman, *Asylums* (Garden City, N.Y.: Doubleday and Co., 1961), pp. 321–86. Goffman's analysis deals with tinkering in mental hospitals, but many of the points he makes apply equally well to corrections.

[6]The matters discussed in this section are analyzed in greater detail in Gibbons, *Changing the Lawbreaker*, pp. 136–43.

Examples of definitions of the situation characteristic of lawbreakers are provided in abundance in Chapters Twelve through Seventeen. As one instance, we noted that Donald Cressey's research on financial trust violation indicates that individuals engage in embezzlement when they define themselves as having "nonshareable problems" and *after* they have managed to construct a set of justificatory arguments or rationalizations for trust violation.[7] The material on semiprofessional property offenders argues that these persons are involved in criminality, at least in part, because they think of themselves as having little opportunity to earn money in conventional ways and because they regard themselves as victims of a corrupt society. The analysis of joyriding auto thieves hypothesizes that they engage in this form of law violating out of personal concerns about masculinity.

Some further observations can be made about the definitions of the situation expressed by offenders. Although definitions are located inside individuals, some are widely shared whereas others are idiosyncratic. Earlier chapters have noted that some criminalistic definitions are common within certain social class groups, others are restricted to the members of such smaller collectivities as peer groups, and some are novel views held by isolated individuals.

Definitions of the situation also vary along a time dimension; some are acquired early in life from socialization experiences and remain with the individual throughout his lifetime, whereas others are of extremely short duration. Some interpretive beliefs arise out of specific interactional events and have an extremely short life span. Most homicides are examples of short-lived definitions and usually involve a quarreling husband and wife or other pairs of individuals in intense social interaction with each other. Homicide is often the culmination of a violent and drunken quarrel in which the killing of the victim was inadvertent. In these cases, conventional definitions prohibiting murder are suspended temporarily rather than replaced by new attitudes.

Because of temporal variations, some definitions of the situation are more difficult to modify than others. In extreme examples, certain definitions are so central a part of the personality configuration of the person as to be unamenable to modification. The beliefs of "overly aggressive" offenders that other persons are basically mean and untrustworthy represent major anchorage points of their personalities and are extremely difficult to alter. At the other extreme, some definitions are of recent origin, tenuously held, and as a consequence rather easily modified. "One-time losers" are individuals with transitory definitions favorable to criminality.

Offenders are characterized by various patterns of definitions rather than a uniform set of attitudes and beliefs, which separates them from noncriminals or nondelinquents. The typological descriptions in Chapters Twelve through Seventeen elaborated on the different views lawbreakers exhibit. Because

[7]Donald R. Cressey, *Other People's Money* (Belmont, Calif.: Wadsworth Publishing Co., 1971).

definitions vary, as do the experiences producing them, no single kind of therapy activity can be expected to accomplish the rehabilitative task.

VARIATIONS IN TREATMENT TACTICS[8]

The various treatment procedures for dealing with law violators can be lumped into two major categories: psychotherapies and environmental therapies. The first group of strategies proceed from psychogenic assumptions that because offenders are emotionally troubled to some degree, their psyches must be altered. Psychotherapeutic programs endeavor to reveal the inner workings of the person so his problems can be dissolved. In general, psychotherapeutic approaches center about the individual, with less concern for his group affiliations or social circumstances.

Environmental treatment activities operate from a different perspective on offenders. They assume that lawbreakers are relatively normal individuals who exhibit antisocial conduct definitions related to their interactional experiences and social relations. Consequently, environmental tactics are directed at groups of deviants rather than at individuals.

These major categories of treatment involve a number of subtypes. Let us take a glance at some of these variations.

Psychotherapies

"Depth" psychotherapy has often been advocated as an appropriate strategy for treatment of criminals. In this view, law violators are regarded as persons whose behavior is a function of cognitive elements buried deep within the "inner layers of personality." These deep-seated tensions are dimly perceived by the individual, or may be unperceived by him, but can be made apparent by a skilled psychiatrist. Once the actor becomes cognizant of the bases of his behavior, the way is opened for him to change himself. This intensive individual therapy has widely been urged for mentally disordered individuals. It has been portrayed in countless movies and television plays.

Group psychotherapy is another kind of treatment closely parallel to individual "depth" psychotherapy. The major difference between the two is that in group psychotherapy, a therapist endeavors to bring about "insight" and "catharsis" on the part of a number of patients who meet together, whereas "depth" psychotherapy goes on in dyads made up of a patient and a therapist.

[8]Variations in treatment procedures are discussed at greater length in Gibbons, *Changing the Lawbreaker*, pp. 142–88. For another explication of the elements of different forms of intervention, see LaMar T. Empey and Steven G. Lubeck, *The Silverlake Experiment* (Chicago: Aldine Publishing Co., 1971), pp. 74–98.

Although individual and group forms of "depth" psychotherapy have frequently been suggested as ideal tactics for use in correctional treatment, they are rarely used in fact, primarily because of the great shortage of trained psychotherapists in correction.

"Client-centered therapy" is another pattern of psychotherapy used quite regularly with offenders.[9] This kind of counseling is predicated on a picture of clients as persons who have problems of social adjustment. However, they are seen as normal individuals who can be aided toward working out their social difficulties in a relatively short time without intensive probing psychotherapy. As a general set of procedures for dealing with persons in trouble, probation officers and other correctional employees use client-centered therapy with their clients. This kind of treatment is quite similar to "reality therapy," which psychiatrist William Glasser advocates.[10] These procedures are used in correctional practice when probation officers strive to get check forgers to adopt nondeviant solutions to their problems or try to persuade individual predatory delinquents to adopt new perspectives on work, the police, and so on.

Environmental Programs: Group Therapy

One of the most prominent trends in the mental health field and corrections since World War II has been the rise of group forms of treatment. For a variety of reasons, dissatisfaction has developed with individual therapy as the sole tactic for dealing with offenders or mental patients. The suggestion has been voiced from a number of quarters that group treatment offers more promise in rehabilitation of deviants. Much of the commentary on group endeavors implies that this is a single form of therapy, even though it is variously labeled "group psychotherapy," "group therapy," "guided group interaction," or "group counseling."

Two distinct kinds of therapy involve the "group" label. *The first, group psychotherapy, is essentially individual therapy in a group setting, whereas the second is "group" therapy in the true sense and is designed to change groups, not individuals.* The aims of these two programs differ, the role of the therapist differs, the group activities differ, and still other contrasts can be identified.[11]

[9]Carl R. Rogers, *Client-Centered Therapy* (Boston: Houghton Mifflin Co., 1951).

[10]William Glasser, *Reality Therapy* (New York: Harper & Row, Publishers, 1965).

[11]Donald R. Cressey, "Contradictory Theories in Correctional Group Therapy Programs," *Federal Probation*, 18 (June 1954), 20-26. See also Dogan K. Akman, Andre Normandeau, and Marvin E. Wolfgang, "The Group Treatment Literature in Correctional Institutions: An International Bibliography, 1945-1969," *Journal of Criminal Law, Criminology and Police Science*, 59 (March 1968), 41-56.

The outlines of true group therapy have been sketched in the following terms:

> This treatment stratagem focuses upon groups as the "patient." It assumes that specific persons exhibit unfavorable attitudes, self-images, and the like because of the associational network in which they are involved. Because the person's interactional associates are extremely meaningful to him, any attempt to change the person without altering those groups with which he associates is likely to fail. Accordingly, group therapy proceeds on the premise that entire groups of persons must be recruited into therapy groups and changed. In addition, it is argued that treatment in which an individual's close associates are participants is likely to have more impact upon a specific person than some other form of treatment. Group therapy encourages the participants to put pressure on each other for behavioral change and to get the group to define new conduct norms. In a real sense, individual participants in group therapy are at the same time patients and therapists. The person who is formally designated as a therapist frequently comes to play a secondary role in the therapeutic process as it develops over time. In summary, group therapy represents a kind of primary group relationship in which behavioral change is attempted through the same mechanisms by which attitude formation and behavioral change take place in conventional primary groups.[12]

The individuals to whom group therapy is directed are viewed as aberrant persons who need to gain insight into their peculiarities. Group therapy (group counseling, guided group interaction) proceeds out of different premises, for the therapy subjects are viewed as normal individuals who can be changed through manipulation of group relations. Cressey has lucidly identified the principles underlying group therapy in the following terms:

1. If criminals are to be changed, they must be assimilated into groups which emphasize values conducive to law-abiding behavior and, concurrently, alienated from groups emphasizing values conducive to criminality. . . .

2. The more relevant the common purpose of the group to the reformation of criminals, the greater will be its influence on the criminal members' attitudes and values. . . .

3. The more cohesive the group, the greater the members' readiness to influence others and the more relevant the problem of conformity to group norms. . . .

4. Both reformers and those to be reformed must achieve status within the group by exhibition of "pro-reform" or anticriminal values and behavior patterns. . . .

[12]Gibbons, *Changing the Lawbreaker*, p. 151.

5. The most effective mechanism for exerting group pressure on members will be found in groups so organized that criminals are induced to join with noncriminals for the purposes of changing other criminals. . . .

6. When an entire group is the target of change, as in a prison or among delinquent gangs, strong pressure for change can be achieved by convincing the members of the need for change, thus making the group itself the source of pressure for change.[13]

The principles of group therapy operate in a number of ongoing correctional programs and allied structures. For example, Alcoholics Anonymous is a voluntary, nongovernmental organization devoted to rehabilitation of alcoholics, which operates in ways parallel to those outlined by Cressey. Alcoholic individuals join groups of ex-alcoholics as a way of refraining from drinking. These groups strive to get new members to take on new norms against drinking, both by exerting group pressure and by rewarding them with group approval. As he continues in this interaction, the ex-alcoholic is eventually expected to lend his support to new recruits in their efforts to stay sober. As he succeeds in these efforts, his self-image as a reformed drunk is strengthened and reinforced.

Detached worker programs, or street worker programs as they are also called, are a second illustration of group relations principles in action. These operations have centered on delinquent gangs in urban neighborhoods. Street workers are employed who are usually fairly young persons with social backgrounds similar to those of the gang youths with whom they work. The worker tries to become an associate of a particular fighting gang, with an eye toward drawing the members into nondelinquent recreational activities, community services, or other nondeviant patterns of behavior. The detached worker also attempts to woo the boys over to more positive work attitudes and other prosocial sentiments. Part of his role involves assisting delinquent youths, such as helping them obtain jobs or aiding them in getting readmitted to school.[14]

Group therapy programs have also been tried in a number of institutional settings. In some of these institutions, the professional treatment agents have conducted group treatment sessions with inmates, oriented along group relations lines. A variant of group treatment called "group counseling" has been

---

[13]Donald R. Cressey, "Changing Criminals: The Application of the Theory of Differential Association," *American Journal of Sociology*, 61 (September 1955), 118-19; see also Cartwright's more general statement on which Cressey's model is based: Dorwin Cartwright, "Achieving Change in People: Some Applications of Group Dynamics Theory," *Human Relations*, 4, no. 4 (1951), 381-92.

[14]As illustrative of this approach, see James R. Dumpson, "An Approach to Anti-Social Street Gangs," *Federal Probation*, 13 (December 1949), 22-29; P. L. Crawford, D. I. Malamud, and J. R. Dumpson, *Working with Teen-Age Gangs* (New York: Welfare Council of New York City, 1950); Walter Bernstein, "The Cherubs are Rumbling," *New Yorker*, 33 (September 21, 1957), 129-59; John M. Gandy, "Preventive Work With Street Corner Groups: Hyde Park Youth Project, Chicago," *Annals of The American Academy of Political and Social Science*, no. 322 (March 1959), 107-16; Stacy V. Jones, "The Cougars, Life With a Brooklyn Gang," *Harper's*, 209 (November 1954), 35-43.

suggested as a useful way of mobilizing resources of the institution in the rehabilitative task by using lay persons, such as guards, as therapists.[15]

Doubtless the task of treating prisoners effectively through group methods within the confines of a custodial institution is fraught with problems. Inmates often attempt to make a sham performance in therapy groups by pretending that they have acquired new perspectives and attitudes from the group interaction. Many employees have antagonistic feelings toward these rehabilitative ventures, for they fear that the freedom allowed prisoners will undermine the security of the institution. Finally, the correctional administrator has a difficult time finding meaningful rewards he can bestow on individuals who seem to have truly changed in their orientations toward criminality. The warden cannot release inmates when he regards their prognosis as favorable to law-abiding adjustment; the prisoners must wait for the decisions of a parole board. For such reasons, group treatment programs subjected to research evaluation have not achieved dramatic results.

Environmental Programs: Milieu Management

Milieu management is a form of treatment not too different from group therapy; indeed, the latter is often included as part of the former. Milieu programs usually go on in institutions where efforts are made to coordinate all parts of the operation to the goal of rehabilitation. The developers of milieu programs try to construct "therapeutic communities" that provide opportunities for inmates to experiment with law-abiding social living. Similarly, milieu treatment institutions try to ensure that all events which occur to the prisoners will be therapeutic. In a conventional prison, such an operation might take the form of group therapy augmented with regularized work experiences. The guards would also be dissuaded from expressing views that psychiatrists are "head shrinkers" or "bug doctors" and the caseworkers immature "college boys," and from other acts that might have a negative effect on treatment.

The Highfields Project in New Jersey is a clear example of milieu management.[16] The delinquent subjects were placed in a small institution of two dozen boys, where they were subjected to a treatment diet of "guided group interaction" in the evenings. In addition, these youths were given opportunities to work for pay during the daytime at a nearby mental institution. They were not compelled to work and could be fired if they did not perform adequately. The developers of this system regarded delinquent boys as normal

---

[15]Norman Fenton, *An Introduction to Group Counseling in State Correctional Service* (New York: The American Correctional Association, 1958); Fenton, ed., *Explorations in the Use of Group Counseling in the County Correctional Program* (Palo Alto, Calif.: Pacific Books, 1962).

[16]Lloyd W. McCorkle, Albert Elias, and F. Lovell Bixby, *The Highfields Story* (New York: Holt, Rinehart and Winston, 1958).

youngsters with antisocial attitudes and delinquent self-images. The boys tended to denigrate the importance of conventional work careers and regard other conforming behavior patterns scornfully. The entire program of guided group interaction, along with the related work experiences and peer interaction, was directed toward pressuring the delinquents toward new perspectives and improved work skills.

The private organization called Synanon, which deals with drug addicts, is a second illustration of milieu management.[17] In that program, newly admitted persons are subjected to a harsh form of group therapy so that they come to reject their former selves as addicts. At the same time, they are given a good deal of psychological comfort by ex-addict peers with whom they live at Synanon. Residents work at maintenance tasks in the residence facility or at a Synanon industry, such as a service station. The residential program as a whole is calculated to prepare the ex-addict for eventual return to free society, completely cured. To date, however, the majority of Synanon members have either remained within one of the Synanon institutions or become employed as executives of a new Synanon facility.

The supporters of Synanon contend that this kind of treatment represents the model for the future, and Synanon members have been particularly immodest in praise of this program. Synanon has managed to keep a good many persons "clean" (free from drug use) for extended periods of time.[18] But we ought to be cautious in looking for a correctional panacea in this operation. Those not so optimistic about general applicability of this model to corrections have raised a number of questions.[19] Synanon is a private operation rather than governmental, and voluntary rather than coercive. Thus, the question arises as to the ease with which this format might be imposed on such places as prisons, with their collections of hostile and noncooperative inmates. However, the most important limitation on the Synanon structure as a general guide for corrections has to do with the aims of official correctional devices, which are designed to achieve "rehabilitation" of lawbreakers so that they will eventually reenter free society as conventional citizens. Regardless of whether this goal is achieved, it is different from the one Synanon seems to pursue. As David Sternberg has pointed out, Synanon appears to offer *protection* of addicts rather than reintegration into society.[20] There are serious doubts about the extent to which official corrections can or will be remade in the direction of long-term protection of offenders.

[17]Lewis Yablonsky, *The Tunnel Back: Synanon* (New York: The Macmillan Co., 1965); Yablonsky, "The Anticriminal Society: Synanon," *Federal Probation*, 26 (September 1962), 50–67; Daniel Casriel, *So Fair a House: The Story of Synanon* (Englewood Cliffs, N.J.: Prentice-Hall, 1963).

[18]Rita Volkman and Donald R. Cressey, "Differential Association and the Rehabilitation of Drug Addicts," *American Journal of Sociology*, 69 (September 1963), 129–42.

[19]David Sternberg, "Synanon House—A Consideration of Its Implications for American Correction," *Journal of Criminal Law, Criminology and Police Science*, 54 (December 1963), 447–55.

[20]*Ibid.*

Korn and McCorkle have developed another version of milieu management as a prescription for converting conventional penal institutions into treatment milieus.[21] Their program involves systematic frustration of the inmate in his attempts to "beat the system" by manipulating officials. The offender is prevented from developing exploitive techniques by which he can do "easy time." The program aims at bringing prisoners to the ultimate realization that they have much to gain by living within conventional rules, first in the prison and later in the free community.

A final case of milieu therapy can be seen in an experimental treatment program at Fricot Ranch, a training school for boys in California.[22] One of the cottages in this institution was singled out as the target of an intensive milieu effort. A series of coordinated experiences running throughout the day was established to obtain behavioral change on the part of the wards.

As the importance of a coherent, positive institutional climate for achievement of treatment ends becomes generally acknowledged, other milieu efforts similar to those described here are likely to be created in prisons and training schools.

Environmental Programs: Environmental Change

This last form of treatment attempts to change various features of natural social environments, such as urban community areas. Environmental modification strives to bring about such results as an improvement in community social organization, so it is not as individual-centered as other therapeutic endeavors. Environmental operations are frequently pointed at social agencies and noncriminals as well as offenders. Yet their ultimate aim is to modify the antisocial sentiments of citizens and thereby reduce rates of criminality.

Most environmental change efforts to date have been oriented toward prevention, geared toward curtailing budding delinquent careers before they get under way, so that rehabilitation of persons already known to be law violators is a secondary goal of these efforts. Most cases of environmental change have had to do with delinquency rather than with adult criminality.[23]

Consider some examples of environmental change. One of the earliest was the Chicago Area Project.[24] The goals and assumptions of that project, which

[21]Richard R. Korn and Lloyd W. McCorkle, *Criminology and Penology* (New York: Holt, Rinehart and Winston, 1959), pp. 540-52.

[22]Carl F. Jesness, *The Fricot Ranch Study* (Sacramento: State of California, Department of the Youth Authority, 1965).

[23]For a summary of many of these, see Helen L. Witmer and Edith Tufts, *The Effectiveness of Delinquency Prevention Programs*, U.S. Children's Bureau Publication, no. 350 (Washington, D.C.: U.S. Government Printing Office, 1954).

[24]Witmer and Tufts, *The Effectiveness of Delinquency Prevention Programs*, pp. 11-17; Solomon Kobrin, "The Chicago Area Project—A 25-Year Assessment," *Annals of The American Academy of Political and Social Science*, no. 322 (March 1959), 19-29.

operates in certain Chicago working-class, high delinquency neighborhoods, are as follows:

> The Chicago Area Project operates on the assumption that much of the delinquency in slum areas is to be attributed to lack of neighborhood cohesiveness and to the consequent lack of concern on the part of many residents about the welfare of children. The Project strives to counteract this situation through encouraging local self-help enterprises through which a sense of neighborliness and mutual responsibility will develop. It is expected that delinquency will decline as youngsters become better integrated into community life and thereby influenced by the values of conventional society rather than by those of the underworld.[25]

The kind of delinquency on which this project operates contends that delinquency and criminality in working-class neighborhoods flow out of the unavailability of conventional routes to American success goals and are thus a response to economic and social frustration. The area project also presumes that lower-income areas are to a degree "disorganized," in that they are characterized by value conflicts and lack of social cohesion. Criminal persons exist side by side with law-abiding citizens, and many social ties unite the deviants with the conformists. The area project attempts to bring about cohesiveness in the neighborhood through establishment of a neighborhood center, staffed principally by indigenous leaders. Thus, the Chicago Area Project tries to develop an "antidelinquency society" in slum neighborhoods to reduce pressures toward delinquency and criminality.

The "Midcity Project" in Boston is a more recent example of environmental change, also directed principally at reduction of delinquency.[26] This multifaceted program was designed to improve the degree of coordination and cooperation between existing social agencies in the community. "Chronic-problem" families in the area were provided different kinds of assistance so as to make them less dependent on social agencies. Detached workers were also employed to work with delinquent gangs.

The Midcity Project was a demonstration effort, designed to illustrate the usefulness of a "total community" approach to delinquency. Unfortunately, the project did not achieve a significant reduction in misbehavior, although it did accomplish some other important ends. Community social organization was improved, so the project might have a delayed effect on delinquency in the long run.

The most ambitious program of environmental change to date has been the multimillion dollar "Mobilization for Youth" operation in a lower east

---

[25]Witmer and Tufts, *The Effectiveness of Delinquency Prevention Programs*, p. 11.

[26]Walter B. Miller, "The Impact of a 'Total Community' Delinquency Control Project," *Social Problems*, 10 (Fall 1962), 168–91.

side neighborhood in New York City.[27] The basis for the undertaking was Cloward and Ohlin's "opportunity structures" theory, which we examined in Chapter Twelve. Those investigators contended that working-class, subcultural delinquency is the product of disjunction between the goals of lower-class youths and their opportunities to achieve these goals through legitimate or conventional pursuits. Mobilization for Youth involves thirty separate "action" programs in the four major areas of work, education, community, and group services. All these devices and structures are pointed at the task of opening up or increasing the law-abiding opportunities for success and achievement in slum neighborhoods. For example, an "Urban Youth Service Corps" provides employment for unemployed, out-of-school youths, and a "Youth Jobs Center" serves as an employment office and tries to find permanent jobs for young-sters. Several devices have been conjured up as techniques for improving school performance of the youths, while efforts have also been made to strengthen the existing community social agencies.

Research evaluation of this program has not yet been undertaken, so its results are unknown. Moreover, given the many components included in this operation, it would be exceedingly difficult to untangle the specific contribu-tion, if any, that each part has made to an end result, such as reduced rates of deviant behavior. At least one critic of Mobilization for Youth has suggested that such undertakings will produce only slight results unless major changes are made in the general employment structure of American society. In other words, these programs are involved in preparing persons for conventional jobs, which are either relatively unrewarding or, in many cases, nonexistent.[28] This point holds for other federally funded efforts to create employment and other kinds of legitimate opportunities carried on in a number of other cities in the United States, following the model of Mobilization for Youth.

TYPES OF TREATMENT AND TYPES OF OFFENDERS

Most literature on treatment contains singular treatment prescriptions. Group therapy or some other form of handling is recommended for all offenders as though they all exhibit much the same problem for rehabilitative action. Although different types of law violators require different kinds of attention, the implications of this view have not been spelled out in detail until recently.

The most detailed theoretical attempt to match diagnostic types of offend-

[27]A Proposal for the Prevention and Control of Delinquency by Expanding Opportunities (New York: Mobilization for Youth, 1961); see also A Report on Juvenile Delinquency (Washington, D.C.: Hearings of the Subcommittee on Appropriations, 1960), pp. 113–16.

[28]Robert Arnold, "Mobilization for Youth: Patchwork or Solution?" Dissent, 11 (Summer 1964), 347–54. For another pessimistic report on this kind of program, see James C. Hackler, "Boys, Blisters, and Behavior: The Impact of a Work Program in an Urban Central Area," Journal of Research in Crime and Delinquency, 3 (July 1966), 155–64.

ers to varied forms of therapy has been made by the author.[29] This is not the place to review this argument in detail, but a few comments about it are in order. It endeavored to show that the population of lawbreakers is made up of individuals who run the entire gamut of human variations. Many criminal or delinquent persons are quite normal and well socialized but have acquired subcultural standards that emphasize hostility toward the police or other antisocial perspectives. Other criminal individuals, such as naïve check forgers or joyriders, are relatively stable and unconventional and not members of deviant subcultures but have adopted illegal problem-solving techniques. Finally, several different kinds of offenders, such as violent sex offenders or psychopathic assaultists, are relatively aberrant individuals. The data regarding offender careers presented in Chapters Twelve through Seventeen indicated the nature of these variations in detail.

The several forms of treatment identified previously are not equally applicable to the twenty-one offender patterns discussed in this book. Group therapy is a more likely tactic for some role careers than for others, and, in the same way, psychotherapeutic approaches make sense for some of these patterns and not others. Accordingly, the author has developed some fairly detailed programmatic recommendations about the therapy forms which should be fitted to different criminal role patterns. For example, the suggestions regarding naïve check forgers center about use of client-centered therapy, either in probation or in prison settings. The hypothesis is advanced that check forgers might respond to a kind of "shock therapy" early in their correctional careers, in which they might be placed in jail for a short sentence of a few weeks or a month. Following this sentence, they might be released on probation, where they would receive intensive counseling. This initial jail term would serve as a dramatic warning about the consequences of such acts. Currently, check forgers are repeatedly placed on probation. They often violate the conditions of probation, apparently in part because they regard writing "bad checks" as innocuous behavior without much risk. But eventually these persons exhaust the patience of the courts and the probation officials, and they find themselves in prison.

The treatment hypotheses advanced by the author are based on role-career variations among lawbreakers. Group therapy or milieu forms of therapy are suggested for semiprofessional property offenders, drug addicts, joyriders, aggressive rapists, and certain other types. Intensive psychiatric treatment is indicated for nonviolent sex offenders, incest cases, male homosexuals, violent sex offenders, and psychopathic assaultists. A program of minimal treatment is recommended for statutory rapists and for "one-time loser" property or personal offenders.

These program guidelines represent a collection of speculative judgments about therapy strategies which appear to bear some relationship to the dif-

---

[29]Gibbons, *Changing the Lawbreaker*, pp. 228–82.

ferent characteristics of offender role types. At this point in the development of correctional treatment, evidence on the effectiveness of particular tactics with specific criminal or delinquent groups is not available. Actual treatment ventures of this sort are exceedingly scarce.

The typological formulation and treatment proposals of the author have been used on a limited scale in several cases of correctional intervention. One of these was conducted at the Stonewall Jackson Training School in Concord, North Carolina, and dealt with delinquent offenders.[30] A second project involves a community-based probation treatment program for semiprofessional property offenders, carried on in Utah under the joint auspices of Thiokol Chemical Corporation and the state correctional agency.[31] Finally, another attempt to employ a diagnostic typology in a probation setting was conducted in San Mateo County in California.[32]

The most ambitious attempt in the direction of typologically-oriented treatment is presently under way in California, where the Community Treatment Project is studying the use of community-based treatment as an alternative to incarceration of relatively serious delinquents in institutions.[33] The research subjects have been sorted into nine diagnostic types, classified in terms of levels of interpersonal maturity. The youngsters have been designated as asocial aggressives, asocial passives, immature conformists, cultural conformists, manipulators, acting-out neurotics, anxious neurotics, cultural identifiers, or as exhibiting situational emotional reactions. Different techniques for therapeutic management of each of these nine patterns are outlined.[34]

Doubtless a good deal will eventually be learned about treatment and types of offenders from this and other research now under way in California and other states. If therapeutic goals are to become truly significant in corrections, many studies of this sort will be needed. The evidence now at hand concerning the results of treatment is fragmentary and incomplete, revealing little about the effects of therapy and almost nothing about the merits of specific tactics for particular kinds of lawbreakers. We turn to an examination of this data in Chapter Twenty-one.

[30]Stonewall Jackson School, *Project Report: An Empirical Evaluation of Delinquency Typologies* (Raleigh: North Carolina Department of Corrections, 1970).

[31]Utah State Division of Corrections, *Quarterly Narrative Report: Utah Community Based Treatment Program* (Salt Lake City: Utah State Division of Corrections, March 1971).

[32]Clayton A. Hartjen and Don C. Gibbons, "An Empirical Investigation of a Criminal Typology," *Sociology and Social Research*, 54 (October 1969), 56–62.

[33]Marguerite Q. Warren and Theodore B. Palmer, *Community Treatment Project: An Evaluation of Community Treatment for Delinquents, Fourth Progress Report* (Sacramento: State of California, Department of the Youth Authority, 1965).

[34]John E. Riggs, William Underwood, and Marguerite Q. Warren, *Interpersonal Maturity Level Classification: Juvenile* (Sacramento: State of California, Department of the Youth Authority, 1964). For critical comments on this material, see Don C. Gibbons, "Differential Treatment of Delinquents and Interpersonal Maturity Levels Theory: A Critique," *Social Service Review*, 44 (March 1970), 22–33; Paul Lerman, "Evaluative Studies of Institutions for Delinquents: Implications for Research and Social Policy," *Social Work*, 13 (July 1968), 55–64.

LEGAL AND ETHICAL FRONTIERS IN
CORRECTIONS[35]

What are the legal and ethical boundaries beyond which we should not go in our efforts to punish and treat lawbreakers? Who deserves to be punished? How much punishment do they deserve? We shall examine complex and thorny issues in this concluding section. Recently a physician who served in an informal advisory role to President Nixon proposed a program of massive intervention toward preventing delinquency. In this program, six-year-olds would be subjected to psychiatric screening; those children thought to be potential lawbreakers would be carted off for some kind of preventive therapy. However, the behavioral knowledge this proposal implies does not exist, so predelinquents cannot be picked out from among potential nondelinquents with any degree of accuracy.[36] But what if it did exist? What if social engineering were so well developed that potential deviants could be identified at an early age? Does it follow automatically that in a democratic society we are warranted in doing something to them to deflect them from deviance? Quite obviously, many persons would recoil from this proposal and would raise violent objections to it.

The example of prediction and treatment of potential delinquents at age six is an outrageous proposal, sufficiently so that nearly every rational man would reject it. However, most legal and ethical issues in correctional treatment are a good deal more subtle than this one and a good deal more difficult to address. In general, these ethical or legal problems fall into the following groupings: those involving the extent to which the penal sanction should be used at all, the limits to the degree of punishment to be dealt out to the lawbreaker, and the restrictions to be imposed on coercive application of treatment to offenders. Additionally, the question of due process for law-breakers after they have been convicted of crimes is an important one, as is the matter of how far we are permitted to go in using human subjects against their will in correctional experiments. Finally, some prickly problems develop around such things as electronic surveillance procedures that might be used to gain therapeutic or deterrent effects.

First, let us take the question of the limits of the penal sanction. To what kinds of misconduct should criminal penalties be applied? The superficial answer is that they should be handed out to individuals who engage in "antisocial" acts. But that answer will not do, for few people agree on what is or is not antisocial behavior. Is an act of homosexuality carried on in private

---

[35]This discussion is an abridged version of material appearing in Abraham S. Blumberg, ed., *Introduction to Criminology* (New York: Alfred A. Knopf, forthcoming).

[36]See Jackson Toby, "Early Identification and Intensive Treatment of Predelinquents: A Negative View," *Social Work*, 6 (July 1961), 3-13.

by two consenting adults antisocial? Is a poker game among friends, or an act of prostitution, a criminal, antisocial act?

Herbert Packer has provided a set of criteria for the imposition of the criminal sanction:

1. The conduct is prominent in most people's view of socially threatening behavior, and is not condoned by any significant segment of society.
2. Subjecting it to the criminal sanction is not inconsistent with the goals of punishment.
3. Suppressing it will not inhibit socially desirable conduct.
4. It may be dealt with through even-handed and nondiscriminatory enforcement.
5. Controlling it through the criminal process will not expose that process to severe qualitative or quantitative strains.
6. There are no reasonable alternatives to the criminal sanction for dealing with it.[37]

Let us assume that some agreement exists on the forms of misconduct that are dangerous and antisocial and therefore should be controlled by criminal legislation and punishment. At that point, we must face the question of how much punishment or suffering we may legitimately inflict on offenders. This question is *not* principally one of efficiency, that is, of how much punishment is required for specific deterrence. Instead, the initial and fundamental issue is one of *justice* and *humanity*: what degree of punishment does the offender *deserve*? For example, suppose hard evidence were available, showing that most conventional property offenders will refrain from further lawbreaking if they are made to undergo a prison experience of social isolation for one year, but they do not respond well to alternative forms of punishment. If so, shall we then support isolation on pragmatic grounds that it "gets the job done"? Perhaps, but many people would contend that a year of social isolation goes beyond the limits of just punishment, that it subjects the offender to pain out of proportion to the gravity of his crime. That this question is an ethical rather than an empirical one in no way reduces the need of criminologists as well as citizens to consider it. Adopting a stance of ethical neutrality would put sociologists in the position of tacitly supporting the status quo and whatever ethical stance happens to be fashionable among the general public.

Unrestrained advocacy of questionable treatment measures often crops up in the writings of psychiatrists, as they urge preventive detention of some

[37]Herbert L. Packer, *The Limits of the Criminal Sanction* (Stanford, Calif.: Stanford University Press, 1968), p. 296.

lawbreakers, psychiatric therapy for others, early identification of potential offenders, and other, related tactics. Karl Menninger tends to put unwarranted faith in the effectiveness of psychiatric counseling, along with a willingness to intervene drastically in the lives of offenders under the guise of treatment and without much in the way of due process safeguards.[38] Menninger's recommendations stand in marked contrast to the writings of Thomas Szasz, who warns us of the potential tyranny of psychiatrists as they go about depriving persons of their liberty, subjecting them to therapy, and tinkering with them in other ways in the guise of mental health treatment.[39] More specifically, Sternberg offers a number of cautionary observations about prison group psychotherapy, contending that the involuntary assignment of prisoners to this kind of treatment raises some prickly ethical questions about justice and equitable punishment.[40] In brief, how far are we permitted to go in probing about in the psyches of convicts, particularly in view of the fact that the outcome of this tinkering activity is pretty much a mystery?

The concern for procedural safeguards which the Supreme Court has shown in the areas of police work and court operations appears to be extending to correctional decision making. Fred Cohen has warned correctional administrators that the time may rapidly be approaching when they will have to show greater concern for standards of due process in matters of probation revocation, punishment for disciplinary infractions in prison, parole granting and revocation, and other crucial decisions.[41] Correctional decision makers may be compelled to provide specific grounds for the actions they take against offenders; provision for legal advice and appeal may be demanded, and other due process strictures may grow in number and importance. It will probably also become more difficult for correctional agents to play fast-and-loose with the criminal client in the area of treatment decisions as well.

Along somewhat similar lines, Gilbert Geis has devoted careful attention to the ethical and legal issues in experimental programs. He argues that restrictions must be imposed against wholesale experimentation with involuntary clients in correction and that beyond certain boundaries the search for correctional answers is not permissible.[42]

[38]Karl Menninger, *The Crime of Punishment* (New York: The Viking Press, 1968).

[39]Thomas S. Szasz, *Ideology and Insanity* (Garden City, N.Y.: Doubleday and Co., 1970); Szasz, *Law, Liberty, and Psychiatry* (New York: The Macmillan Co., 1963); Szasz, *The Myth of Mental Illness* (New York: Hoeber-Harper, 1961).

[40]David Sternberg, "Legal Frontiers in Prison Group Psychotherapy," *Journal of Criminal Law, Criminology and Police Science*, 56 (December 1966), 446–69.

[41]Fred Cohen, *The Legal Challenge to Corrections: Implications for Manpower and Training* (Washington, D.C.: Joint Commission on Correctional Manpower and Training, 1969).

[42]Gilbert Geis, "Ethical and Legal Issues in Experimentation with Offender Populations," in Joint Commission on Correctional Manpower and Training, *Research in Correctional Rehabilitation* (Washington, D.C.: Joint Commission on Correctional Manpower and Training, 1967), pp. 34–41.

Let us close this brief examination of ethical questions with a look at electronic rehabilitation and surveillance measures, which have recently been suggested. Ralph Schwitzgebel is the most prominent advocate of the use of modern electronic technology in corrections.[43] He indicates that devices are now available through which the activities of parolees and other correctional wards could be electronically monitored so that offenders under treatment could be kept under continuous surveillance. Schwitzgebel tells us that we might use these gadgets in a variety of ways: "Thus, for example, if a parolee who had previously been very inconsistent in his work patterns was at work on time he might be sent a signal from the parole officer that meant: 'You're doing well,' or that he would receive a bonus. On the other hand, if it appeared that the parolee was in a high crime rate area at two o'clock in the morning, he might be sent a signal reminding him to return home."[44]

Doubtless the use of mechanical and electronic gadgetry could do more to curtail some forms of criminality than is currently possible through conventional means of rehabilitation. Markedly increasing the illumination intensity of street lights in urban areas might do more to curb strong-armed robbery than nearly any other strategy available to us. Much more attention should be given to the development of improved automobile locks to deter car theft, television monitoring systems to deter shoplifting, and a host of other mechanical deterrents of this kind. Electronic surveillance of parolees through sensors and similar devices clearly falls into this general category of technological measures to alleviate the crime problem.

However, there is a difference between the question: "Can it be done?" and the query: "Should it be done?" Schwitzgebel is *not* a Dr. Strangelove, conjuring up some kind of Orwellian "Big Brother" system for totally removing the individual citizen's privacy so that no one would be safe from the eyes or ears of the electronic monitor. Quite the contrary, he is aware that although some things are technologically possible, they should not be used because of the potential harm that might result. The danger is not that Schwitzgebel will engage in unconscionable excursions into the privacy of offenders; rather that less restrained individuals may seize on the electronic parole officer as a panacea, unleashing all manner of excesses in their haste to cure the crime problem. From much past history in corrections, we have learned that many people who have used treatment recommendations have not always shown the restraint and ethical sensitivity demonstrated by the originators of the ideas.

[43]Ralph K. Schwitzgebel, "Issues in the Use of an Electronic Rehabilitation System with Chronic Recidivists," *Law and Society Review*, 3 (May 1969), 597–611; see also Bernard Beck, "Commentary," 611–14.

[44]Schwitzgebel, "Issues in the Use of an Electronic Rehabilitation System," p. 603.

This section has been a brief and inadequate discussion of the legal and ethical problems ushered in by the rising urge to treat criminals. However, enough mention has been made of the variety of issues to warrant restraint from enthusiastically embracing any proposal that offers the prospect of reducing crime rates, without first coming to grips with questions of justice and equity.

21

THE
RESULTS
OF
TREATMENT

What happens to individuals after they are placed on probation? Do they continue to engage in criminality? What are the effects of a penal commitment? Do offenders refrain from further lawbreaking after they have been given some kind of attention in an institution? This chapter addresses such questions.[1]

Unfortunately, the answers that appear here will have to be tentative and partial, given the paucity of good evidence on the effects of correctional practices. Correctional agencies have rarely been involved in systematic gathering of statistics on the posttreatment careers of persons whom they process. Data dealing with the effects of specific kinds of correctional intervention are even more uncommon. Controlled experiments on the effectiveness of treatment tactics can be conducted; indeed, some have already been carried out. But to date, few of these experimental studies of correctional actions have been undertaken.

The correctional agencies of the state of California have produced the majority of detailed, sophisticated studies of correctional efforts. Both the California Youth Authority and the Department of Corrections have operated research departments for a number of years, so more is known about the workings of California corrections than of any other state system. Accordingly, we shall make heavy use of California studies in the following pages.[2]

There are a variety of reasons for the scarcity of empirical studies of the effects of correctional actions, not the least of which is lack of financial support, which prevents funding of research on a sustained basis. In view of the lack of therapeutic activities in the past, concern for evidence about programs has been premature until relatively recently. Evaluative research is not always en-

---

[1] For a useful analysis of the problems of correctional evaluation research, see Leslie T. Wilkins, *The Evaluation of Penal Measures* (New York: Random House, 1969).

[2] For a summary of studies in progress in the California Youth Authority, see Department of the Youth Authority, *The Status of Current Research in the California Youth Authority* (Sacramento: State of California, 1969).

525

thusiastically supported, so even supporters of treatment sometimes have ambivalent feelings about this kind of investigation. The problem with careful and objective research is that it sometimes turns up unpalatable findings! As an illustration, consider the case of a Catholic-operated training school for girls with which the author is affiliated. The prominent citizens who donate money to that institution frequently volunteer remarks to the staff of the following kind: "You are doing wonderful work here." A careful research study of this training school might produce dysfunctional results if it showed that the institution is achieving only modest rather than complete success with the delinquent wards it processes. Perhaps the affluent sponsors would be less willing to contribute to the program if they had a more accurate perspective on the workings of the place.

THE OUTCOME OF CORRECTIONS

Probation

In Chapter Nineteen, we observed that adult probation departments generally show results of the kind in which three-fourths or more of the probationers are "successes," in that they apparently refrain from further criminality. At the same time, studies of probation departments indicate that little or no counseling occurs, so the high success rates must be explained some other way.[3] The explanation appears to be that probation departments select out prosocial, "square John" kinds of offenders for placement at the same time that they divert more troublesome lawbreakers toward prisons. These prosocial individuals are "self-correctors" who deter themselves from repeated criminality.

Probation success rates vary somewhat from one jurisdiction to another, depending on the variations in proportions of offenders sent to penal institutions. In California, where probation is granted to relatively large numbers of more serious criminals, failure rates are higher than in many other states.[4] The greater use of probation accounts for the seemingly anomalous situation in which probation violation rates are quite high in a state with well-developed probation services.

---

[3]See Ralph W. England, Jr., "What is Responsible for Satisfactory Probation and Post-Probation Outcome?" *Journal of Criminal Law, Criminology and Police Science*, 47 (March–April 1957), 667–76; England, "A Study of Postprobation Recidivism Among 500 Federal Offenders," *Federal Probation*, 19 (September 1955), 10–16.

[4]State of California, *Delinquency and Probation in California*, 1965 (Sacramento: State of California, Bureau of Criminal Statistics, 1966), passim.

Juvenile Institutions[5]

The efficiency of training schools in arresting progress of deviant careers is largely conjectural, in that careful follow-up studies of these places are hard to find. However, one study has been carried out in California, which has a juvenile correctional system widely acknowledged to be the most advanced in the United States.[6] The results of that investigation are not encouraging and surely do not lead to much confidence in the operations of training schools in other states. In this research, 4,000 delinquent wards discharged from the Youth Authority in 1953 and 1958 were examined. Less than 20 percent of the female wards acquired any sort of criminal record in the five year follow-up period after discharge, so the girls most commonly become "successes." The boys followed quite different paths. About 22 percent of the male wards had been discharged from Youth Authority custody as a result of being sent to prison. Another 22 percent were sentenced to prison within five years after discharge, and another 26 percent received one or more nonprison sentences (fines, jail, and/or probation). Thus, only 30 percent of the boys managed to remain free from detected criminality.

State training schools in California vary in a number of ways. Some hold young, relatively prosocial youngsters, whereas others work with older, more sophisticated delinquents. These institutions have different treatment programs as well. Not surprisingly, the different schools show somewhat varied results. One recent follow-up investigation tabulated parole violations by boys from different facilities in the first fifteen months after release.[7] Parolees from the two reception centers showed a violation rate of 40 percent, whereas the rate for Fricot Ranch releases was 43 percent and for Fred C. Nelles School boys it was 60 percent. Boys from Paso Robles School had a violation rate of 57 percent, and those from camps showed a rate of 36 percent. Parolees from Preston School of Industry behaved differently from parolees from Youth Training School, Deuel Vocational Institution, or Soledad Prison. Robert Beverly and Evelyn Guttmann assert that these different outcomes are the consequence of selection factors that influence commitment policies, and variations in institutional treatment influences.[8]

What is the meaning of these statistics showing that most wards released

---

[5]For a more detailed discussion of the impact of training schools, see Don C. Gibbons, *Delinquent Behavior* (Englewood Cliffs, N.J.: Prentice-Hall, 1970), pp. 247–54.

[6]Carolyn B. Jamison, Bertram M. Johnson, and Evelyn S. Guttmann, *An Analysis of Post-Discharge Criminal Behavior* (Sacramento: State of California, Department of the Youth Authority, 1966).

[7]Robert F. Beverly and Evelyn S. Guttmann, *An Analysis of Parole Performance by Institution of Release, 1956-1960* (Sacramento: State of California, Department of the Youth Authority, 1962).

[8]Some other California data indicate that even higher proportions of offenders become reinvolved in criminality within five years of release from the training school. See Gibbons, *Delinquent Behavior*, pp. 250–51.

from training schools become reinvolved in misconduct? Are these institutions directly responsible for recidivism? Not necessarily, for the juveniles who are paroled from training schools might have continued in criminality even if they had been dealt with in some form of community treatment. In other words, parole failures may be attributable mainly to the characteristics and experiences wards bring with them to the training school rather than to the effects of the institution itself.[9]

The Community Treatment Project in California presents data bearing on this issue.[10] In that experimental effort, youths who would normally be sent to training schools are instead being dealt with in the community. Two kinds of intervention are involved; in one, differential treatment units consisting of a supervisor, treatment agents, and a work supervisor counsel wards who have been sorted into diagnostic types. In the second kind of intervention, guided group interaction units are administering group treatment to offenders. Youths in the community treatment experimental groups have been matched with institutionalized control group subjects. Wards have been randomly assigned either to community treatment or to the training school.

The findings on this project seem to indicate that community treatment is more effective than institutionalization, in that the experimental subjects had a lower parole violation rate than the control subjects. However, we should not be too quick to accept these results as an indictment of training schools. Paul Lerman points out that the parole violation figures are misleading. The community-treated youths actually committed more violations in the parole period than did the control cases. Although the parole agents observed more lawbreaking on the part of the community-treated parolees, the agents took action more frequently against the control subjects. The percentages of offenders who had their paroles revoked for offenses of low or medium seriousness were considerably higher for the control cases than for the experimentals. From these data, Lerman concludes that the behavior of the parole agents of the two groups differed, producing the different parole violation figures.[11]

[9]Most of the available evidence suggests that training schools have a benign influence on delinquents, as far as attitude change is concerned. Juvenile wards do not adopt more positive attitudes while in the institution, and they do not acquire markedly more antisocial sentiments. This evidence is reviewed in *ibid.*, pp. 251–54.

[10]Department of the Youth Authority, *The Status of Current Research in the California Youth Authority* (Sacramento: State of California, 1966), pp. 22–27.

[11]Paul Lerman, "Evaluative Studies of Institutions for Delinquents: Implications for Research and Social Policy," *Social Work*, 13 (July 1968), 55–64. For another well-known community treatment project, see LaMar T. Empey and Jerome Rabow, "The Provo Experiment in Delinquency Rehabilitation," *American Sociological Review*, 26 (October 1961), 679–95; the recidivism rates for youths in this program appear to be significantly lower than for comparable boys who were committed to training schools. See The President's Commission on Law Enforcement and Administration of Justice, *Task Force Report: Corrections* (Washington, D. C.: U.S. Government Printing Office, 1967), p. 39.

Prisons

Most studies of populations of offenders in adult institutions show that large numbers of these persons have previously been in trouble with the authorities. Furthermore, these surveys note that incarcerated offenders often show prior records of institutionalization. These figures fail to indicate the proportion of prison inmates who succeed on parole. That prisoners have often been in custody before does not necessarily mean that most inmates fail on parole. Instead, many of them may succeed on release at the same time that a group of chronic failures flow into, out of, and back into the penitentiary.

One indication of postrelease adjustments made by inmates can be obtained from the California statistics in Table 17, which shows the percentages of parolees returned to prison as parole violators.[12] These violations are divided into returns resulting from new commitments due to crimes committed on parole and returns resulting from technical violations of parole rules. As Table 17 shows, changes in policies regarding technical violations have largely produced the increase in parole violations since 1954.

Daniel Glaser's survey of the federal prison system indicates that prisoners frequently make adequate parole adjustments.[13] Glaser noted that the notion is frequently expressed that two-thirds of those who are imprisoned subsequently recidivate. However, one study of federal prison parolees in 1943 and 1944 showed that only about 25 percent were returned to prison within five

Table 17 CALIFORNIA PAROLE VIOLATORS RETURNED TO PRISON, 1954-65

	New Commitments	Technical Returns	Total Violations
1954	10.8	9.7	20.5
1955	7.6	8.7	16.3
1956	8.5	7.4	15.9
1957	9.4	8.7	18.1
1958	11.0	13.1	24.0
1959	10.0	11.2	21.2
1960	11.9	12.8	24.7
1961	10.9	16.9	27.8
1962	11.0	17.1	28.1
1963	10.4	21.6	32.0
1964	8.4	21.2	29.6
1965	8.9	22.4	31.3

[12]State of California, *Crime and Delinquency in California, 1965* (Sacramento: State of California, Bureau of Criminal Statistics, 1966), p. 136.

[13]Daniel Glaser, *The Effectiveness of a Prison and Parole System* (Indianapolis: Bobbs-Merrill Co., 1964), pp. 13-35.

years. Glaser also reviewed a collection of surveys indicating that only about one-third of the parolees from state insitutions are returned to penitentiaries within five years after release.

Glaser identified some major variables associated with parole success or failure. Younger prisoners more often violate parole. Parolees who had been confined in juvenile institutions, left home at an early age, or had records of repeated property crime most commonly failed on parole.[14]

Glaser's investigation of the federal prison system provides a rich source of materials on the workings of penitentiaries. This study shows that inmates did not violently dislike treatment personnel in institutions but also did not accord them much respect or positive feelings. Thus, the therapeutic impact of treatment on convicts may be negligible.[15] Glaser also suggests that training in vocational skills is less important as an influence on parole behavior than habituation of inmates to regularity in employment. Personal attention directed by supervisors to prisoners is an important contributor to rehabilitation.[16] Glaser presents ninety-one conclusions from his research.

Glaser's work suggests that positive effects of prisons do not necessarily produce good behavior by offenders on parole. Rather, the most successful releasee is able to assume a conventional social role outside the prison, *despite* having been imprisoned. Thus, Glaser remarks:

> This half-century's most promising correctional development for alleviating post-release problems of prisoners consists of the counseling centers in metropolitan areas to which prisoners scheduled for release are transferred some months before their release date, and from which they regularly go forth to enter the job market and to develop correctionally acceptable post-prison social relationships, before they are released on a regular parole or any other type of release from prison.[17]

The rehabilitative potential of prison is pessimistic in the light of Walter Bailey's review of 100 studies of correctional outcome published between 1940 and 1960.[18] Bailey notes that about two-thirds of the programs were based on a "sick" model of the offender, who was in need of psychotherapeutic handling. From these studies, Bailey concluded:

> Since positive results were indicated in roughly one-half of the total sample of 100 reports analyzed, the problem of interpretation is not unrelated to that of determining "whether the cup is half empty or half full." But, when

---

[14]*Ibid.*, pp. 36–53.

[15]*Ibid.*, pp. 134–39.

[16]*Ibid.*, pp. 504–13.

[17]*Ibid.*, p. 511.

[18]Walter C. Bailey, "An Evaluation of 100 Studies of Correctional Outcome," *Journal of Criminal Law, Criminology and Police Science*, 57 (June 1966), 153–60.

one recalls that these results, in terms of success or failure of the treatment used, are based upon the conclusions of the authors of the reports, themselves, then the implications of these findings regarding the effectiveness of correctional treatment become rather discouraging. A critical evaluation of the actual design and the specific research procedures described in each instance would substantially decrease the relative frequency of successful outcomes based upon reliably valid evidence. *Therefore, it seems quite clear that, on the basis of the sample of outcome reports with all of its limitations, evidence supporting the efficacy of correctional treatment is slight, inconsistent, and of questionable reliability* (emphasis added).[19]

In an incisive analysis of the effects of prisons on offenders, Stanton Wheeler asserts that little or no resocialization of prisoners occurs in these places.[20] According to Wheeler:

1. Persons do not enter prison motivated to seek a basically new and different vision of themselves.

2. To the extent that they do change, the change is produced as much by the reaction to being confined and separated from the free community as it is by the dynamics of life within the institution.

3. The values and attitudes expressed by prison inmates are shaped in important ways by the circumstances to which inmates have been exposed prior to their period of incarceration.

4. In addition to its impact on the values held by entering inmates, the external world influences the kind of culture and social organization that is formed within the prison, and which serves as the social context within which adaptation to imprisonment takes place.

5. As a result of these conditions, whatever impact the experience of imprisonment itself might have on inmates, either positive or negative, is sharply attenuated. *It is the social definition of the prison in society, rather than the social status of the inmate within the prison, that appears to be most relevant for the future life and career of prison inmates* (emphasis in the original).

6. It follows from all of the above that a full understanding of processes of socialization and resocialization within the prison requires much greater attention than has heretofore been given to the relationship of both the prison and the prisoner to the external world.

    It is clear from all these studies that different patterns of formal organization and structure may produce differences in inmate organization and in attitudes toward the prison experience. But these studies have not gone on to demonstrate the relationship between participation in inmate society and future behavior. Thus, as much as these studies

[19]*Ibid.*, p. 738.

[20]Stanton Wheeler, "Socialization in Correctional Institutions," in *Handbook of Socialization Theory and Research*, ed. David A. Goslin (Chicago: Rand McNally and Co., 1969), pp. 1005-23.

tell us about the different patterns of organization within the prison and potentially different socialization processes, they have not yet shown whether changes occur that are deep and long lasting enough to produce real differences in rates of recidivism.

A number of other studies have examined the rates of recidivism for men housed in different types of institutions. This has been part of a long-term series of studies supported by the California Correctional System. And if there is one conclusion that appears to be safely drawn from these studies, it is that differences in prison organization themselves apparently produce relatively little difference in recidivism rates. Once one takes account of the nature of the inmate population in the different prisons, the institutional differences in recidivism rates tend to disappear. Relatively small effects may be shown for one or another aspect of prison programs, but the overall sense one gets from such studies is that the differences attributable to institutions are small relative to the differences attributable to the prior backgrounds of individual inmates.[21]

Throughout his analysis, Wheeler maintains that prisons may deflect some persons from continuation in criminality. But this effect has to do more with the kinds of persons who come into different penal institutions than with variations in the correctional programs and social organization. Finally, the penitentiary apparently operates punitively in terms of specific deterrence by instilling abhorrence of imprisonment in offenders rather than by winning them over to prosocial sentiments.

Along this line, John Irwin contends that many convicts come to entertain negative views of prisons and resolve to stay out of these places.[22] But for most of his stay in prison, the inmate is primarily concerned with avoiding trouble *within* the walls. Once released from prison, the parolee often has a difficult time striving to stay out of trouble. According to Irwin, parole agents often enforce a set of rigid Puritanical norms, exacerbating the parolee's difficulties of readjustment.[23] The parolee faces other problems that sometimes push him in the direction of recidivism. Irwin claims that:

> . . . from the standpoint of the felon a successful postprison life is more than merely staying out of prison. From the criminal ex-convict perspective it must contain other attributes, mainly it must be dignified. This is not generally understood by correctional people whose ideas on success are dominated by narrow and unrealistic conceptions of nonrecidivism and reformation. Importantly, because of their failure to recognize the felon's

[21]*Ibid.*, pp. 1019-20.
[22]John Irwin, *The Felon* (Englewood Cliffs, N.J.: Prentice-Hall, 1970), *passim*.
[23]*Ibid.*, pp. 152-73.

viewpoint, his aspirations, his conceptions of respect and dignity, or his foibles, they leave him to travel the difficult route away from the prison without guidance or assistance; in fact, with considerable hindrance, and with few avenues out of criminal life acceptable both to him and his former keepers.[24]

PSYCHIATRIC TREATMENT

We have noted at other points that the psychiatric orientation turns up in a variety of places in criminology. Psychogenic formulations are exceedingly popular as causal explanations. The treatment corollary of these views, which contends that most offenders need psychiatric aid, has enjoyed widespread popularity. Whatever the reasons for allegiance to these notions, they are not supported by much evidence. Instead, most research data at hand run counter to psychiatric claims. Lawbreakers who have been subjected to psychotherapy rarely seem to respond favorably to this experience.

One investigation that casts doubt on psychiatric treatment has been carried out by LaMay Adamson and H. Warren Dunham,[25] who examined the history of the Wayne County (Detroit) Clinic for Child Study. From 1924 to 1948, the clinic staff was heavily augmented with additional psychiatric professionals, so its effects on wards should have become more prominent if psychotherapy is effective. But follow-up study of boys who had been in court in 1930, 1935, 1940, and 1948 showed almost no reduction in the proportions of treated youths who got into further trouble. In 1930, 45 percent of the boys were later arrested by the police, as contrasted to 39 percent of those who had been in the clinic in 1948. Decreased recidivism did not accompany the markedly increased costs of clinic operation. From these results Adamson and Dunham concluded that psychiatric therapy is inappropriate for the hard-core, working-class delinquents at which it was directed.

A second study of psychotherapy took place in California with the Intensive Treatment program at San Quentin and Chino prisons.[26] That operation was an experimental undertaking involving treatment groups that received intensive individual and group psychotherapy, along with control groups processed through the regular institutional program. The theory was that most violators are psychologically troubled and hence needed psychotherapy. Results of the program showed no important differences in parole adjustment between the treated and untreated prisoners. Here again, psychiatric treatment appears inappropriate for many prison inmates.

[24]*Ibid.*, p. 204.

[25]LaMay Adamson and H. Warren Dunham, "Clinical Treatment of Male Delinquents: A Case Study in Effort and Result," *American Sociological Review*, 21 (June 1956), 312–20.

[26]California Department of Corrections, *Second Annual Report, Intensive Treatment Program* (Sacramento: State of California, Department of Corrections, 1958).

A third case of psychotherapy is the PICO (Pilot Intensive Counseling Organization) project, which concerned treatment and control groups of prisoners at Deuel Vocational Institution in California.[27] California Youth Authority wards between seventeen and twenty-three years of age were the subjects of the program. The treated subjects were given intensive, individual interview therapy similar to "depth" psychotherapy several times a week, along with some group therapy. The control group wards received institutional attention and therefore much less counseling. The individuals in the project were also sorted into "amenable" and "nonamenable" categories before they were introduced into the research experiment. Cases judged to be amenable to treatment were characterized by a level of anxiety that would make them likely to respond to therapy, whereas the nonamenables were assessed as lacking this prerequisite for treatment. The experimental and control groups both involved a mixture of amenable and nonamenable offenders.

The therapists in this experiment were trained in clinical psychiatry or psychiatric social work. They administered therapy to their assigned subjects for a period averaging about nine months per ward. Each treatment worker worked with a case load of about twenty-five inmates.

The impact of this program was measured in several ways, but the major criterion of failure was "return to custody" or parole violation. The treated amenables showed the best postrelease performance, followed by the control group amenable prisoners. Surprisingly, the treated nonamenable inmates made the poorest postrelease records. They apparently got worse rather than better as a result of treatment. The researchers concluded that the treated amenables acquired adjustment skills from the program, and the treated nonamenables may have been given the wrong kind of therapy.

Another California program, reported by Guttmann, had to do with the effects of short-term psychiatric treatment on youths in two training schools.[28] Treatment and control groups of boys were established at Fred C. Nelles School and the Preston School of Industry. In both places, the treatment wards were processed through a Psychiatric Treatment Unit, staffed by psychologists, psychiatric social workers, and a psychiatrist, where the boys were given individual interview therapy. Youths at the two schools were not identical, for the Preston inmates were generally older than the Nelles wards. Other differences concerning personality characteristics were reported by workers at the institutions.

The evidence indicates that the Nelles parolees subjected to intensive treatment had lower violation rates than did control group boys from the same

[27]Stuart Adams, "The PICO Project," in The Sociology of Punishment and Correction, eds. Norman Johnston, Leonard Savitz, and Marvin E. Wolfgang, 2nd ed. (New York: John Wiley & Sons, 1970), pp. 548-61.

[28]Evelyn S. Guttmann, Effects of Short-Term Psychiatric Treatment on Boys in Two California Youth Authority Institutions (Sacramento: State of California, Department of the Youth Authority, 1963).

school, but at Preston the controls showed less recidivism than did the treated boys. Guttmann suggests that the discrepant results may stem from differences in the organizational climate of the two facilities. At Nelles School, the Psychiatric Treatment Unit was new, and a kind of therapeutic milieu with high staff morale and other positive features existed. The Psychiatric Treatment Unit at Preston was the focus of considerable hostility from staff members. Consequently, boys in the special treatment program received invidious handling from staff members and other inmates. Thus, certain features of the general training school structure probably worked against psychiatric intervention at Preston.

Supporters of psychiatric treatment for lawbreakers can derive little comfort from most of these results. Still, clinical observations based on small samples occasionally suggest that psychotherapy is effective with some offenders. For example, J. H. Conn has presented some observations indicating that individual therapy can aid nonviolent sex offenders toward law-abiding conduct.[29] As we have noted, psychiatric intervention did seem to have some impact on certain subjects in these experiments. This observation might indicate that psychiatric therapy is useful when employed with a restricted sample of offenders. If so, future applications of psychiatric strategies will need to pay more attention to the selection of cases to receive such aid.

In all likelihood, lawbreakers amenable to psychiatric tactics are similar to law-abiding citizens who respond to these experiences. Amenable patients tend to be relatively middle-class individuals who are voluble and introspective, able to engage in psychiatric interaction. Such individuals are likely to be most frequently encountered among "square Johns" rather than in groups of hostile, defiant "right guys." The latter have slight appreciation of notions about psychological distress and do not apply these kinds of hypotheses to themselves. They are loath to define themselves as "crazy" and to enter into relationships in which they pour out their inner thoughts to a psychiatrist. Many of them would probably have difficulty in articulating their feelings about themselves even if they were motivated to do so.

ENVIRONMENTAL TREATMENT

The Highfields Project

Chapter Twenty described the experimental program at Highfields in New Jersey, involving a milieu form of treatment and guided group interaction. Two different efforts have been made to measure the impact of this experience

---

[29]J. H. Conn, "The Psychiatric Treatment of Certain Chronic Offenders," *Journal of Criminal Law and Criminology*, 32 (March–April 1942), 631–35.

on the boys processed through the institution.[30] In the first, Highfields boys were compared with a group of youths in Annandale Reformatory, where they were given conventional institutional handling. Although they had been incarcerated before the Highfields institution had opened, the Annandale inmates were judged to be similar to individuals at Highfields, so they were felt to be a good control or comparison group. Recidivism comparisons for the Highfields and Annandale boys showed that 18 percent of the former violated parole in the first year after release, as contrasted to 33 percent of the Annandale boys who failed on parole. Highfields youths performed better over extended periods of parole, so fewer of them were violators within two, three, or five years after release.[31]

The second evaluation of Highfields, carried out by H. Ashley Weeks, also compared Highfields wards with similar boys sent to Annandale Reformatory. Weeks found that 63 percent of the Highfields boys completed treatment and remained in the community for at least a year, contrasted to 47 percent of the Annandale boys who succeeded on parole.[32] He observed little difference between white boys from Annandale and Highfields, but the black wards from these two places behaved quite differently on release. Nearly 60 percent of the blacks from Highfields were successful on release, but only 33 percent of the Annandale boys stayed out of further trouble.[33]

In one assessment of the Highfields program, Richard Jenkins contends that the guided group interaction experience pressures "adaptive" delinquents to reexamine their self-attitudes, gets them concerned about their delinquency, and makes them anxious about their prospects for law-abiding conduct. On release from the program, many of them try to stay out of trouble. However, the Annandale experience turns out boys who have resolved only to avoid getting caught in the future. According to Jenkins, the program at Highfields has added effects on black boys, in that they encounter social acceptance in that setting instead of the social rejection they find outside the institution.[34]

These results from the Highfields program indicate why this experiment has attracted widespread attention and been emulated in other correctional innovations. But excessive optimism about Highfields as a model for correctional reform should be tempered by McCorkle, Elias, and Bixby's observation that the institution achieved its most noticeable results when it remained

---

[30]H. Ashley Weeks, *Youthful Offenders at Highfields* (Ann Arbor: University of Michigan Press, 1963); Lloyd W. McCorkle, Albert Elias, and F. Lovell Bixby, *The Highfields Story* (New York: Holt, Rinehart and Winston, 1958).

[31]McCorkle et al., *The Highfields Story*, p. 143.

[32]Weeks, *Youthful Offenders at Highfields*, p. 42.

[33]*Ibid.*

[34]Richard L. Jenkins, "Treatment Considerations with Delinquents," in Weeks, *Youthful Offenders at Highfields*, pp. 149–56.

small. These authors reported that when the facility had more than about eighteen or twenty boys, aggressive and hostile interpersonal incidents became noticeable.[35] Perhaps conventional institutions made up of large dormitories filled with fifty or more wards cannot easily be converted into duplicates of Highfields.[36]

The C-Unit Experiment

One detailed indication of the sizable obstacles treatment innovations in institutional settings must overcome is provided by the C-Unit experiment of Elliot Studt and others, carried on in Deuel Vocational Institution in California.[37] This program attempted to develop a social community among inmates and staff, in which a common moral code would develop to regularize social interaction among members. During the first year of this experiment, a strong inmate system pursuing collective goals and controlling the behavior of members, along with joint problem solving, did begin to emerge.[38] However, the administration of the reformatory frustrated this development by refusing to allow the C-Unit staff to discard distinctions between "honor" and "non-honor" prisoners, locked and unlocked cells, and other conventional features of custodial arrangements.[39] In addition, the developers of C-Unit were never permitted to design unit procedures for controlling deviance according to the unit value system.[40] According to Studt, Messinger, and Wilson, their project did indicate that modification of inmate–staff social interaction and institutional social life in prisons is possible in theory. But the C-Unit report chronicles an experiment that failed because of the unwillingness, inability, or both, of the prison staff and the statewide correctional organization to engage in the reciprocal change required for innovation to succeed.

[35]McCorkle et al., *The Highfields Story*, pp. 166-67.

[36]Lerman has recently reanalyzed Weeks' data, showing them to be less convincing as a demonstration of the effectiveness of Highfields. Lerman indicates that 18 percent of the Highfields subjects did not complete treatment, having been returned to court as unsuitable for the program. Few Annandale subjects failed to complete a stay there. When the Highfields boys who did not complete the program were included as program failures, the success rates for the two institutions turned out to be quite similar. The luxury of being able to reject potential wards for treatment is mainly enjoyed by private agencies, so caution is in order in evaluating claims they might advance about their rehabilitative effectiveness. See Lerman, "Evaluative Studies of Institutions for Delinquents," pp. 58-60. A more recent, sophisticated and detailed experiment modeled in a number of ways after the Highfields plan is LaMar T. Empey and Steven G. Lubeck, *The Silverlake Experiment* (Chicago: Aldine Publishing Co., 1971). These investigators report only modest success for their milieu program, when compared to a conventional training school program.

[37]Elliott Studt, Sheldon L. Messinger, and Thomas P. Wilson, *C-Unit: Search for Community in Prison* (New York: Russell Sage Foundation, 1968). See also Peter G. Garabedian, "The Natural History of an Inmate Community in a Maximum Security Prison," *Journal of Criminal Law, Criminology and Police Science*, 61 (March 1970), 78-85, for a parallel experiment in Washington State.

[38]*Ibid.*, pp. 192-228.

[39]*Ibid.*, pp. 90-124.

[40]*Ibid.*, p. 126.

Group Counseling, California

California has been quick to respond to such treatment innovations as High-fields. One case has to do with experimental group counseling programs established in several Youth Authority institutions.[41] At Paso Robles School, where the wards live in fifty-boy living units, one of the dormitories was organized to provide small group counseling once a week, involving groups of six to eight boys. Another dormitory held community meetings four times per week in an attempt to develop a therapeutic milieu within the unit, and a third dormitory provided a program combining small group counseling and community meetings. One living unit served as a control in which a conventional pattern of surveillance and discipline was maintained.

In the second institution, Youth Training School, the four living units holding fifty boys each were divided so that two units held small group counseling sessions once a week and the other two served as controls, with regular institutional programs.

The findings from this experiment are much less impressive than those from Highfields. The parole violation rates for groups released from these different dormitories at Paso Robles ranged from 68 to 79 percent within the thirty-month period of supervision on parole, whereas violation rates ranged from 50 to 63 percent for groups released from Youth Training School. In both cases, wards in the experimental program did no better on parole than the untreated boys. The major result of the experimental undertaking was to improve the institutional climate in those living units where counseling or group meetings were held; assaults were reduced and staff–ward communication patterns improved.

The failure of group counseling in these two facilities can be explained by the social structure of training schools. Apparently, treatment activities did not sufficiently alter the custodial orientation of the institutions, which places a premium on orderly behavior by wards and also encourages them to "play it cool." More substantial alterations are probably required in institutional living before inmates can be drawn into meaningful treatment experiences.

Another effort at intensive group treatment is currently under way in California in the Intensive Treatment Program at Chino.[42] An experimental group isolated from the rest of the correctional facility has been structured in the form of a therapeutic milieu. Staff members are involved in unconventional

---

[41]Joachim P. Seckel, *Experiments in Group Counseling at Two Youth Authority Institutions* (Sacramento: State of California, Department of the Youth Authority, 1965).

[42]Dennie L. Briggs, "Convicted Felons as Social Therapists," *Corrective Psychiatry and Journal of Social Therapy*, 9 (3rd Quarter 1963), 122-27; Briggs and John M. Dowling, "The Correctional Officer as a Consultant: An Emerging Role in Penology," *American Journal of Correction*, 26 (May–June 1964), 28-31.

role patterns, in that they wear no uniforms and perform both treatment and custodial assignments. The therapy subjects participate in daily community meetings of prisoners and staff and in social therapy groups of a dozen or so men five times each week.

One novel feature of this Intensive Treatment Program is that some of the inmates have been given the role of "social therapists." The inmate therapists are prisoners who have been in the program for some time and have shown evidence of behavioral change. As social therapists, they engage in the same activities as the civilian treatment workers.

To date, evidence on the Intensive Treatment Program is positive.[43] Inmates who have gone through the milieu program show better parole adjustment than do prisoners in the regular institutional program. However, the contrast is most marked for offenders who have gone through the intensive program in the later stages, when inmates have been serving as therapists and the control subjects.[44]

The Fremont Experiment[45]

Another milieu venture in California, the Fremont Program, was a short-term residential treatment project carried on at the Southern Reception Center Clinic of the Youth Authority. The experiment dealt with sixteen- to nineteen-year-old males, committed from Southern California, who were eligible for a work-therapy program. After diagnostic processing at the clinic, the eligible offenders were placed either in the Fremont Program or in a regular institutional program through random assignment. The Fremont wards stayed a fixed period of five months in the program, whereas the control boys were incarcerated for nine months on the average.

The Fremont boys were subjected to a treatment diet of small group therapy, large group forums, half-day work assignments at the clinic, school classes, home visits, and field trips to various places of interest in the community—a rather rich and varied therapeutic program in contrast to the more usual institutional experience.

[43]James Robison and Marinette Kevorkian, *Intensive Treatment Project, Phase II, Parole Outcome: Interim Report* (Sacramento: State of California, Department of Corrections, 1967).

[44]One quasi-experiment in the California system centers about the California Rehabilitation Center, where drug addicts are subjected to an intensive group treatment program. According to Duster, the program fails to have much positive impact on the drug users who proceed through it. He contends: "However, the very existence of CRC as a separate institution for addicts, and the very notion of a group session of addicts, reinforce the idea of the addict as a separate kind of person, thereby creating unanticipated and very undesirable side effects. To a lesser extent, this occurs with every prisoner, addict or not, but it is greatly exacerbated by two practices current with addicts." See Troy Duster, *The Legislation of Morality* (New York: The Free Press, 1970), p. 149.

[45]Joachim P. Seckel, *The Fremont Experiment: Assessment of Residential Treatment at a Youth Authority Reception Center* (Sacramento: State of California, Department of the Youth Authority 1967).

Unfortunately, the experimental outcome was not similarly impressive when contrasted to regular institutional handling. The experimental and control group youths showed no statistically significant differences in recidivism after two years of follow-up exposure to parole. In addition, no differences were discovered in the seriousness of postrelease offenses in which they engaged, so the experimental cases showed no improvement in that respect either.

One bright feature in the report is that parole adjustment was better for boys who had gone through the program at a time near its inception than for those who had proceeded through it at a later point. No differences of this sort emerged in the control group. The researcher speculated that this result may have been a reflection of high staff turnover in the Fremont operation in its later stages. If this speculation is true, the results may be more indicative of effective treatment tactics than first appearances suggest, in that a stable and continuous program might turn out improved youngsters.

The Fricot Ranch Study

One of the most elaborate ventures into milieu treatment within a state correctional system took place in 1965 at Fricot Ranch, a California Youth Authority institution.[46] Fricot Ranch is a training school for boys from eight to fourteen years of age.

Carl Jesness indicates the conventional form of training school life, which the Fricot Ranch project was designed to circumvent:

> When admitted to an institution for delinquents, boys bring with them delinquent values, a hostile attitude toward authority, and a rejection of conventional goals. The normal tendency of young boys in institutions is to cluster into informal groups, erect subtle barriers toward administrative efforts to reach them, and to maintain value systems at odds with the rehabilitative aims of the school. New boys coming into the school program participate in these natural groupings and are apt to undergo an experience which tends to reinforce their delinquent value system. While they may conform outwardly to the school program, no basic modification of delinquent attitudinal patterns takes place. When released, they once again seek associations and engage in behavior congenial to their delinquent character and values.[47]

On the administrative side of traditional training-school organization, obsessive concern for maintenance of custody and security results in a situation in which the wards are rewarded for "playing it cool." The authorities endeav-

[46]Carl F. Jesness, *The Fricot Ranch Study* (Sacramento: State of California, Department of the Youth Authority, 1965).
[47]*Ibid.*, p. 4.

or to get boys to show outward signs of conformity, with little attention directed at the boys' attitudes. Staff members overlook victimization patterns among wards as long as the older, domineering youths keep order among their peers. In this kind of situation, little or no treatment takes place.

The design of the Fricot Ranch project involved a twenty-boy experimental lodge and a regular, fifty-boy living unit. The experimental unit was planned to provide intensified contacts between group supervisors and wards and to offer other therapeutic experiences. Boys were randomly assigned to the treatment and control units.

Results of the Fricot Ranch project are at the same time encouraging and discouraging.[48] Wards who had been in the experimental unit and were exposed to parole for twelve months showed a violation rate of 32 percent, as against the failure rate of 48 percent for the control subjects. These differences continued for wards from the two units who had been exposed to parole for fifteen months. But the failure rates for wards who had been released and exposed to parole for longer periods were the same for both experimental and control boys. In other words, participation in the intensified program at Fricot Ranch had a retarding effect on recidivism; treated wards stayed out of further trouble for longer periods than did the control subjects. But about 80 percent of both the treated and control boys failed on parole sometime within a three-year follow-up period.

The boys who went through the Fricot Ranch experience were subjected to various examinations in addition to the parole follow-up observations. Jesness indicates that anxious, neurotic boys and immature, aggressive youths gained most from the Fricot program, but more mature delinquents were less affected by it.

The Fricot Ranch study has provided the model for another experiment of this kind currently in progress at Preston School of Industry. However, no data are yet available on the results of that project.

PAROLE PROGRAMS

Theories of parole usually suggest that parolees ought to receive a good deal of attention and guidance. But in fact most parole agencies are understaffed and have case loads so large that almost no positive assistance is rendered to parolees. When these excessive case loads are made the subject of discussion, the companion claim is frequently made that parole violations could be markedly reduced if staffs were increased and case loads reduced.

One effort to test this hypothesis was made in California in the SIPU (Special

[48]*Ibid.*, pp. 85–90.

Intensive Parole Unit) Project.[49] Small case loads in which parolees received intensive counseling were contrasted with regular, large case loads in which releasees got minimal assistance. The result of this experiment was that parolees who experienced the intensive care did no better on parole than those who had been in regular case loads.

Another suggestion centers about the use of halfway houses so that parolees would not have to undergo an abrupt change from incarceration to freedom.[50] One research investigation of halfway houses has been made in the case of a facility for narcotic addicts in Los Angeles.[51] The results do not provide much support for enthusiastic views of halfway houses, in that about the same proportion of halfway house subjects and control group cases completed a year on parole without using drugs.[52]

According to Geis, the halfway house was a failure for several reasons. The residents were assigned to the place and were not voluntary subjects. They received no rewards for participation in the program and were compelled to conform to restrictions not enforced with the control subjects. Finally, the period of stay in the halfway house was apparently too short.[53]

THE FUTURE OF TREATMENT

What major conclusions shall we draw from Chapters Twenty and Twenty-one, regarding the prospects for correctional treatment? The author has offered some relatively pessimistic and cautious observations in another essay, which argues:

> The preceding paragraphs should not be read as a recommendation for the abandonment of the rehabilitative goal. But recognition should be given to the prospect that therapeutic intervention will continue to involve a heavy measure of experimentation and tinkering, rather than the application of verified principles of applied science. Enough is now known about correctional institutions to indicate that these places will probably continue to have at best only benign effects upon the persons who are warehoused in them. If so, Glaser and others are probably correct in advocating halfway

---

[49]Walter T. Stone, "Administrative Aspects of the Special Intensive Parole Program," pp. 126-31; Bernard Forman, "Report on the Special Intensive Parole Unit-Research Investigation by the Division of Adult Paroles, Adult Authority, State of California," pp. 132-39, in *Proceedings of the American Correctional Association, 1956*; Ernest Reimer and Martin Warren, "SIPU: Relationship Between Violation Rate and Initially Small Caseload," *NPPA Journal* (July 1957), pp. 222-29.

[50]For example, see Robert F. Kennedy, "Halfway Houses Pay Off," *Crime and Delinquency*, 10 (January 1964), 1-7.

[51]Gilbert Geis, *The East Los Angeles Halfway House for Narcotic Addicts* (Sacramento: Institute for the Study of Crime and Delinquency, 1966).

[52]*Ibid.*, pp. 138-86.

[53]*Ibid.*, pp. 245-54.

house and work-release forms of transitional facilities through which prisoners can be introduced back into civilian society. But more than that, the trend toward retaining persons in the community without sending them to penal institutions in the first place should be encouraged. There is a considerable financial saving to be effected through community treatment, as well as the net gain of keeping individuals out of the stigmatizing situation of incarceration, which may increase their difficulties in withdrawing from criminality. Additionally, an open and inquiring frame of mind is in order concerning rehabilitation tactics, so that the potentialities of using ex-offenders as treatment agents, the use of volunteers, and other innovations of that sort ought to be given continued attention. Finally, a spirit of caution and humility ought to be entertained. We ought to acknowledge that our halting efforts toward rehabilitation may be harmful rather than helpful, so that we might extend our services in a cautious fashion only to those lawbreakers who appear to be markedly in need of assistance.[54]

[54]Don C. Gibbons, "Punishment, Treatment, and Rehabilitation: Problems and Prospects," in *Introduction to Criminology*, ed. Abraham S. Blumberg (New York: Alfred A. Knopf, forthcoming).

THE
CHALLENGE
OF
CRIME

22

The concluding chapter of the first edition of this book presented a brief discussion of the prospects for eventual reduction or eradication of crime in American society. The commentary centered about the recommendations of The President's Commission on Law Enforcement and Administration of Justice.[1] The commission report represents the most comprehensive and searching study of crime in American society ever undertaken by the federal government. The list of over 200 commission recommendations for control and prevention of crime constitutes a detailed and ambitious program of wider scope than any other set of guidelines offered.

In a great many ways, the contents of this book parallel the contents of the commission report, which portrayed crime as a complex problem made up of many different kinds of lawbreaking. The report implied that crime is a reflection of some central features of American society; a social system that frustrates the legitimate yearnings of many of its citizens must expect many of them to direct their frustration at that society. Accordingly, lawbreaking will be markedly reduced only when the root sources of antisocial sentiments are reduced or removed.

The President's Commission report warned against facile proposals for the cure of crime, which aim to come down hard on various groups in society. Crime control demands more than token gestures, offering a few severely punished offenders as proof that "crime does not pay." The report eschewed those palliatives and proposed solutions that would not escalate the hostility between society and its criminals. The report pointed to major renovations in American social structure rather than at some minor tinkering.

The first edition of this book asked whether the challenge of crime prevention and the commission recommendations will be met. Now, some years later, we ask about the extent to which these recommendations have already

[1]The President's Commission on Law Enforcement and Administration of Justice, *The Challenge of Crime in a Free Society* (Washington, D.C.: U.S. Government Printing Office, 1967).

been realized. But first, let us examine an abridged version of the summary statement from the commission report. Let us see what steps were urged in that report.

SUMMARY OF THE PRESIDENT'S COMMISSION REPORT[2]

This report is about crime in America—about those who commit it, about those who are its victims, and about what can be done to reduce it. . . .

The report makes more than 200 specific recommendations—concrete steps the Commission believes can lead to a safer and more just society. These recommendations call for a greatly increased effort on the part of the Federal Government, the States, the counties, the cities, civic organizations, religious institutions, business groups, and individual citizens. They call for basic changes in the operations of police, schools, prosecutors, employment agencies, defenders, social workers, prisons, housing authorities, and probation and parole officers.

But the recommendations are more than just a list of new procedures, new tactics, and new techniques. They are a call for a revolution in the way America thinks about crime.

Many Americans take comfort in the view that crime is the vice of a handful of people. This view is inaccurate . . . [m]any Americans also think of crime as a very narrow range of behavior. It is not. An enormous variety of acts make up the "crime problem" . . . [m]any Americans think controlling crime is solely the task of the police, the courts, and correction agencies. In fact, as the Commission's report makes clear, crime cannot be controlled without the interest and participation of schools, businesses, social agencies, private groups, and individual citizens. . . .

Under any circumstances, developing an effective response to the problem of crime in America is exceedingly difficult. And because of the changes expected in the population in the next decade, in years to come it will be more difficult. Young people commit a disproportionate share of crime and the number of young people in our society is growing at a much faster rate than the total population. Although the 15- to 17-year-old age group represents only 5.4 percent of the population, it accounts for 12.8 percent of all arrests. Fifteen- and sixteen-year-olds have the highest arrest rate in the United States. The problem in the years ahead is dramatically foretold by the fact that 23 percent of the population is 10 or under.

Despite the seriousness of the problem today and the increasing challenge

[2]*Ibid.*, pp. v–xi.

in the years ahead, the central conclusion of the Commission is that a significant reduction in crime is possible if the following are vigorously pursued:

First, society must seek to prevent crime before it happens by assuring all Americans a stake in the benefits and responsibilities of American life, by strengthening law enforcement, and by reducing criminal opportunities.

Second, society's aim of reducing crime would be better served if the system of criminal justice developed a far broader range of techniques with which to deal with individual offenders.

Third, the system of criminal justice must eliminate existing injustices if it is to achieve its ideals and win the respect and cooperation of all citizens.

Fourth, the system of criminal justice must attract more people and better people—police, prosecutors, judges, defense attorneys, probation and parole officers, and corrections officials with more knowledge, expertise, initiative, and integrity.

Fifth, there must be much more operational and basic research into the problems of crime and criminal administration, by those both within and without the system of criminal justice.

Sixth, the police, courts, and correctional agencies must be given substantially greater amounts of money if they are to improve their ability to control crime.

Seventh, individual citizens, civic and business organizations, religious institutions, and all levels of government must take responsibility for planning and implementing the changes that must be made in the criminal justice system if crime is to be reduced.

In terms of specific recommendations, what do these seven objectives mean?

1. Preventing Crime

The prevention of crime covers a wide range of activities: Eliminating social conditions closely associated with crime; improving the ability of the criminal justice system to detect, apprehend, judge, and reintegrate into their communities those who commit crimes; and reducing the situations in which crimes are most likely to be committed.

Every effort must be made to strengthen the family, now often shattered by the grinding pressures of urban slums.

Slum schools must be given enough resources to make them as good as schools elsewhere and to enable them to compensate for the various handicaps suffered by the slum child—to rescue him from his environment.

Present efforts to combat school segregation, and the housing segregation that underlies it, must be continued and expanded.

Employment opportunities must be enlarged and young people provided with more effective vocational training and individual job counseling. Programs to create new kinds of jobs—such as probation aides, medical assistants, and teacher helpers—seem particularly promising and should be expanded.[3]

2. New Ways of Dealing with Offenders

The Commission's second objective—the development of a far broader range of alternatives for dealing with offenders—is based on the belief that, while there are some who must be completely segregated from society, there are many instances in which segregation does more harm than good. Furthermore, by concentrating the resources of the police, the courts, and correctional agencies on the smaller number of offenders who really need them, it should be possible to give all offenders more effective treatment.

A specific and important example of this principle is the Commission's recommendation that every community consider establishing a Youth Services Bureau, a community-based center to which juveniles could be referred by the police, the courts, parents, schools, and social agencies for counseling, education, work, or recreation programs and job placement. . . .

To make community-based treatment possible for both adults and juveniles, the Commission recommends the development of an entirely new kind of correctional institution: located close to population centers; maintaining close relations with schools, employers, and universities; housing as few as 50 inmates; serving as a classification center, as the center for various kinds of community programs and as a port of reentry to the community for those difficult and dangerous offenders who have required treatment in facilities with tighter custody.

Such institutions would be useful in the operation of programs—strongly recommended by the Commission—that permit selected inmates to work or study in the community during the day and return to control at night, and programs that permit long-term inmates to become adjusted to society gradually rather than being discharged directly from maximum security institutions to the streets.

Another aspect of the Commission's conviction that different offenders with different problems should be treated in different ways, is its recommendation about the handling of public drunkenness, which, in 1965, accounted for one out of every three arrests in America. The great number of these arrests—some 2 million—burdens the police, clogs the lower courts and crowds the penal institutions. The Commission therefore recommends that communities develop civil detoxification units and comprehensive aftercare programs, and that

---

[3]A number of important comments regarding technological devices and improvements that could be used in the fight against crime, such as improvements in police call boxes and mechanical safeguards against auto theft, have been omitted from the original commission recommendations.

with the development of such programs, drunkenness, not accompanied by other unlawful conduct, should not be a criminal offense.

Similarly, the Commission recommends the expanded use of civil commitment for drug addicts.

3. Eliminating Unfairness

The third objective is to eliminate injustices so that the system of criminal justice can win the respect and cooperation of all citizens. Our society must give the police, the courts, and correctional agencies the resources and the mandate to provide fair and dignified treatment for all.

The Commission found overwhelming evidence of institutional short-coming in almost every part of the United States.

A survey of the lower court operations in a number of large American cities found cramped and noisy courtrooms, undignified and perfunctory procedures, badly trained personnel overwhelmed by enormous caseloads. In short, the Commission found assembly line justice.

The Commission found that in at least three States, justices of the peace are paid only if they convict and collect a fee from the defendant, a practice held unconstitutional by the Supreme Court 40 years ago.

The Commission found that approximately one-fourth of the 400,000 children detained in 1965—for a variety of causes but including truancy, smoking, and running away from home—were held in adult jails and lockups, often with hardened criminals.

In addition to the creation of new kinds of institutions—such as the Youth Services Bureau and the small, community-based correctional centers—the Commission recommends several important procedural changes. It recommends counsel at various points in the criminal process.

For juveniles, the Commission recommends providing counsel whenever coercive action is a possibility.

For adults, the Commission recommends providing counsel to any criminal defendant who faces a significant penalty—excluding traffic and similar petty charges—if he cannot afford to provide counsel for himself.

In connection with this recommendation, the Commission asks each State to finance regular, statewide assigned counsel and defender systems for the indigent.

Counsel also should be provided in parole and probation revocation hearings.

Another kind of broad procedural change that the Commission recommends is that every State, county, and local jurisdiction provide judicial officers with sufficient information about individual defendants to permit the release without money bail of those who can be safely released.

In addition to eliminating the injustice of holding persons charged with a crime merely because they cannot afford bail, this recommendation also would save a good deal of money. New York City alone, for example, spends approximately $10 million a year holding persons who have not yet been found guilty of any crime.

Besides institutional injustices, the Commission found that while the great majority of criminal justice and law enforcement personnel perform their duties with fairness and understanding, even under the most trying circumstances, some take advantage of their official positions and act in a callous, corrupt, or brutal manner.

Injustice will not yield to simple solutions. Overcoming it requires a wide variety of remedies including improved methods of selecting personnel, the massive infusion of additional funds, the revamping of existing procedures and the adoption of more effective internal and external controls.

The relations between the police and urban poor deserve special mention. Here the Commission recommends that every large department—especially in communities with substantial minority populations—should have community-relations machinery consisting of a headquarters planning and supervising unit and precinct units to carry out recommended programs. Effective citizen advisory committees should be established in minority group neighborhoods. All departments with substantial minority populations should make special efforts to recruit minority group officers and to deploy and promote them fairly. They should have rigorous internal investigation units to examine complaints of misconduct. The Commission believes it is of the utmost importance to insure that complaints of unfair treatment are fairly dealt with.

Fair treatment of every individual—fair in fact and also perceived to be fair by those affected—is an essential element of justice and a principal objective of the American criminal justice system.

4. Personnel

The fourth objective is that higher levels of knowledge, expertise, initiative, and integrity be achieved by police, judges, prosecutors, defense attorneys, and correctional authorities so that the system of criminal justice can improve its ability to control crime. . . .

In many jurisdictions there is a critical need for additional police personnel. Studies by the Commission indicate a recruiting need of 50,000 policemen in 1967 just to fill positions already authorized. In order to increase police effectiveness, additional staff specialists will be required, and when the community service officers are added manpower needs will be even greater.

The Commission also recommends that every State establish a commission on police standards to set minimum recruiting and training standards and to provide financial and technical assistance for local police departments.

In order to improve the quality of judges, prosecutors, and defense attorneys, the Commission recommends a variety of steps: Taking the selection of judges out of partisan politics; the more regular use of seminars, conferences, and institutes to train sitting judges; the establishment of judicial commissions to excuse physically or mentally incapacitated judges from their duties without public humiliation; the general abolition of part-time district attorneys and assistant district attorneys; and a broad range of measures to develop a greatly enlarged and better trained pool of defense attorneys.

In the correctional system there is a critical shortage of probation and parole officers, teachers, caseworkers, vocational instructors, and group workers. . . .

To meet the requirements of both the correctional agencies and the courts, the Commission has found an immediate need to double the Nation's pool of juvenile probation officers, triple the number of probation officers working with adult felons, and increase sevenfold the number of officers working with misdemeanants.

Another area with a critical need for large numbers of expert criminal justice officers is the complex one of controlling organized crime. Here, the Commission recommends that prosecutors and police in every State and city where organized crime is known to, or may, exist develop special organized crime units.

5. Research

The fifth objective is that every segment of the system of criminal justice devote a significant part of its resources for research to insure the development of new and effective methods of controlling crime.

The Commission found that little research is being conducted into such matters as the economic impact of crime; the effects on crime of increasing or decreasing criminal sanctions; possible methods for improving the effectiveness of various procedures of the police, courts, and correctional agencies.

Organized crime is another area in which almost no research has been conducted. The Commission found that the only group with any significant knowledge about this problem was law enforcement officials. Those in other disciplines—social scientists, economists and lawyers, for example—have not until recently considered the possibility of research projects on organized crime.

A small fraction of 1 percent of the criminal justice system's total budget is spent on research. This figure could be multiplied many times without approaching the 3 percent industry spends on research, much less the 15 percent the Defense Department spends. The Commission believes it should be multiplied many times. . . .

6. Money

Sixth, the police, the courts, and correctional agencies will require substantially more money if they are to control crime better.

Almost all of the specific recommendations made by the Commission will involve increased budgets. Substantially higher salaries must be offered to attract topflight condidates to the system of criminal justice. . . .

The Commission also recommends new kinds of programs that will require additional funds: Youth Services Bureaus, greatly enlarged misdemeanant probation services and increased levels of research, for example.

The Commission believes some of the additional resources—especially those devoted to innovative programs and to training, education, and research— should be contributed by the Federal Government.

The Federal Government already is conducting a broad range of programs —aid to elementary and secondary schools, the Neighborhood Youth Corps, Project Head Start, and others—designed to attack directly the social problems often associated with crime.

Through such agencies as the Federal Bureau of Investigation, the Office of Law Enforcement Assistance, the Bureau of Prisons, and the Office of Manpower Development and Training, the Federal Government also offers comparatively limited financial and technical assistance to the police, the courts, and correctional authorities.

While the Commission is convinced State and local governments must continue to carry the major burden of criminal administration, it recommends a vastly enlarged program of Federal assistance to strengthen law enforcement, crime prevention, and the administration of justice.

The program of Federal support recommended by the Commission would be directed to eight major needs:

(1) State and local planning.

(2) Education and training of criminal justice personnel.

(3) Surveys and advisory services concerning the organization and operation of police departments, courts, prosecuting offices, and corrections agencies.

(4) Development of a coordinated national information system for operational and research purposes.

(5) Funding of limited numbers of demonstration programs in agencies of justice.

(6) Scientific and technological research and development.

(7) Development of national and regional research centers.

(8) Grants-in-aid for operational innovations.

The Commission is not in a position to recommend the exact amount of money that will be needed to carry out its proposed program. It believes, however, that a Federal program totaling hundreds of millions of dollars a year during the next decade could be effectively utilized. The Commission also believes the major responsibility for administering this program should lie within the Department of Justice.

The States, the cities, and the counties also will have to make substantial increases in their contributions to the system of criminal justice.

7. Responsibility for Change

Seventh, individual citizens, social-service agencies, universities, religious institutions, civic and business groups, and all kinds of governmental agencies at all levels must become involved in planning and executing changes in the criminal justice system.

The Commission is convinced that the financial and technical assistance program it proposes can and should be only a small part of the national effort to develop a more effective and fair response to crime. . . .

The Commission recommends that in every State and city there should be an agency, or one or more officials, with specific responsibility for planning improvements in criminal administration and encouraging their implementation. . . .

While this report has concentrated on recommendations for action by governments, the Commission is convinced that governmental actions will not be enough. Crime is a social problem that is interwoven with almost every aspect of American life. Controlling it involves improving the quality of family life, the way schools are run, the way cities are planned, the way workers are hired. Controlling crime is the business of every American institution. Controlling crime is the business of every American. . . .

The responsibility of the individual citizen runs far deeper than cooperating with the police or accepting jury duty or insuring the safety of his family by installing adequate locks—important as they are. He must respect the law, refuse to cut corners, reject the cynical argument that "anything goes as long as you don't get caught."

Most important of all, he must, on his own and through the organizations he belongs to, interest himself in the problems of crime and criminal justice, seek information, express his views, use his vote wisely, get involved.

In sum, the Commission is sure that the Nation can control crime if it will.

Many of these observations and recommendations parallel those in this book. The commission report and this book both stress the heterogeneity of crime and criminals. Both suggest that crime is common in American society, although only a fraction of it becomes officially known. Both identify the manifold difficulties under which law enforcement, judicial, and correctional agencies labor. The commission report recommends a number of correctional programs, noted in Chapters Twenty and Twenty-one, and stresses that a variety of tactics will be needed because of the variations among lawbreakers. The commission report has been more direct and outspoken in its recommendation that millions of dollars be expended in a war on crime.

The war on crime would be waged on many fronts. Programs to eradicate poverty would be teamed with efforts to employ science in the service of law enforcement. Sizable sums of money would be pumped into correctional endeavors.

During the past fifteen years, the existence of an "other America" of urban ghettos populated by blacks, American Indians, and other disadvantaged groups has been widely acknowledged.[4] Social critics such as Michael Harrington and James Baldwin[5] have directed attention at the poverty and social injustice in American life and at their consequences, one of which is believed to be widespread criminality and other forms of social disorganization. Jackson Toby has argued that the prospects for reducing delinquency rates in industrial societies are not favorable, unless massive changes are wrought in modern life.[6] He avers that delinquency will continue to be a major problem for some time, in part because the sociocultural gulf between adolescents and adult citizens appears to be widening and because traditional agencies of socialization and social control have become less effective. Toby also contends that the sting of economic deprivation has increased so that residents of the "other America" have become resentful of their place in life.

These allegations about poverty and its consequences have led to the establishment of a number of programs directed at eradication of poverty.[7] The federal government has invested relatively modest sums of money in a variety of endeavors that provide employment and other kinds of assistance to lower-class citizens. As we noted in Chapter Twenty, the privately funded Mobilization for Youth project in New York City was the prototype of federal efforts directed at delinquents in a number of American cities.

But to date, this war on poverty has been more a token skirmish than a

[4]Michael Harrington, The Other America (New York: The Macmillan Co., 1962).

[5]James Baldwin, The Fire Next Time (New York: Dial Press, 1963).

[6]Jackson Toby, "The Prospects for Reducing Delinquency Rates in Industrial Societies," Federal Probation, 27 (December 1963), 23–25.

[7]See the issue, "Antipoverty Programs," of Law and Contemporary Problems, 31 (Winter 1966).

full-scale campaign. Most of these activities have provided help for only a limited number of youths, and in many cases the employment assistance has only been temporary. As Robert Arnold notes with respect to Mobilization for Youth, disadvantaged youths need to be trained for new careers, but efforts must also be made to generate permanent, rewarding jobs for them.[8]

The kind of crime prevention implied in the President's Commission report calls for nothing less than massive changes in the economic system of the United States. Poverty cannot be removed by minor tampering in the way of temporary or low-paying jobs.

That little has been accomplished in the war on economic deprivation can be seen in the fact that unemployment rates in the United States are currently at high levels, particularly for black Americans and other disadvantaged groups. On this point, Thomas Cook reports that income differentials between white and black citizens in the United States, observed in 1959, have persisted to 1968, with little closure of the gap between the two groups.[9] For example, the average income of whites with only elementary education was $4,349 in 1968, but was only $3,438 for blacks. White college graduates earned $13,094 in 1968, but black college graduates had an average salary of only $11,388.[10] For such reasons, the question about meeting the crime challenge must be regarded as moot. The wealth of the United States is being spent on the war in Southeast Asia, military hardware, and "defense" rather than on a war on poverty, pollution, environmental deterioration, or other attempts to halt the deterioration of life in American society.

The reforms and improvements the commission report calls for in law enforcement, correctional systems, and research will all require great sums of money.[11] Judging from past experiences in which state or federal commissions have reported on the shortcomings of correctional or enforcement agencies, dramatic identification of such problems has not always brought about a prompt and positive response. For example, the history of American prisons is generally a dismal one in which gross scandals have often failed to produce any sustained pressure for change.

The federal government has responded to the challenge of the President's Commission report mainly by the passage of the Omnibus Crime Control and Safe Streets Act of 1968, along with amendments to the act in subsequent sessions of the Congress. This crime control bill was not designed to bring about basic reforms in the criminal justice system; rather, it was a response

[8]Robert Arnold, "Mobilization for Youth: Patchwork or Solution?", *Dissent*, 11 (Summer 1964), 347–54.

[9]Thomas J. Cook, "Benign Neglect: Minimum Feasible Understanding," *Social Problems*, 17 (Fall 1970), 145–52.

[10]*Ibid.*, p. 148.

[11]For a recent statement on the need for correctional research, see Robert H. Fosen and Jay Campbell, Jr., "Common Sense and Correctional Science," *Journal of Research in Crime and Delinquency*, 3 (July 1966), 73–81.

to current fears of crime, agitation regarding urban riots in ghetto areas, and hatred of the Supreme Court for allegedly tying the hands of the police through such decisions as *Mallory* and *Miranda*.[12] The Omnibus Crime Control bill overturned the *Miranda* ruling, by allowing all "voluntary" confessions to be accepted as evidence in federal courts. It also provided for admission of all police lineup identifications in federal cases, regardless of whether the accused person was represented by an attorney at the lineup. The measure also allowed for delay between arrest and charge, reversing *Mallory*.

The crime control bill also provides financial assistance to state and local criminal justice operations. However, the initial funding of the measure was meager, with most of the money providing weaponry and other technological aids to the police and only modest amounts provided to courts, correctional agencies, or for research.[13] The funding of the crime control measure in subsequent years has been increased substantially. The Law Enforcement Assistance Administration budget for 1971 was nearly a half billion dollars, of which $120,000,000 was earmarked for prison reform programs.

Doubtless, some positive consequences will derive from this relatively modest investment of federal funds in law enforcement, criminal justice operations, and corrections. Yet we should not be too sanguine about the prospects. For example, Frank Furstenberg has complained that political interference and pressures have frustrated the research opportunities for the study of the criminal justice system, which this crime control legislation was to provide.[14] On a somewhat different note, one report is at hand concerning youth service bureaus, funded with federal money.[15] The youth service bureau, which the President's Commission report envisions, would be an agency for youths who have been *diverted out* of the official juvenile court machinery by the police and other agencies. The youth service bureau was designed to reduce the number of referrals to juvenile courts. But in the nine experimental youth service bureaus in California, only about one-third of the referrals were from the police and probation agencies. No reduction in juvenile court case loads was accomplished. In short, it appears that creation of the youth service bureau has worked to entangle more youngsters in the juvenile justice system than to divert them out of it. The lesson from that experiment is that these endeavors in crime and delinquency control may not always turn out the way their designers had planned.

[12]Richard Harris, *The Fear of Crime* (New York: Frederick A. Praeger, Publishers, 1968).

[13]Richard W. Velde, "A Shot in the Arm for Corrections," *Federal Probation*, 33 (September 1969).

[14]Frank F. Furstenberg, Jr., "Political Intrusion and Governmental Confusion: The Case of the National Institute of Law Enforcement and Criminal Justice," *The American Sociologist*, 6 (June 1971), 59–62.

[15]Elaine B. Duxbury, *Youth Service Bureaus in California: A Progress Report* (Sacramento: Department of the Youth Authority, 1971).

The first edition of this book closed with the conclusion: "Perhaps the 1970s will be the decade in which the United States began to win a war against crime." Hopefully, it will also be the decade in which other rents and tears in the social fabric will begin to be mended. At the same time, there is good reason to suppose that the crime problem will persist in scope and seriousness for a long time. Subsequent revisions of this book will probably be written. Let us hope that the next version can report some progress in the war on crime.

NAME INDEX

Only those authors whose works are actually discussed in the text are included in this index.